Photoshop 6:
The Complete Reference

Adele Droblas Greenberg
Seth Greenberg

Osborne/**McGraw-Hill**

New York   Chicago   San Francisco
Lisbon   London   Madrid   Mexico City
Milan   New Delhi   San Juan
Seoul   Singapore   Sydney   Toronto

Osborne/**McGraw-Hill**
2600 Tenth Street
Berkeley, California 94710
U.S.A.

To arrange bulk purchase discounts for sales promotions, premiums, or fund-raisers, please contact Osborne/**McGraw-Hill** at the above address. For information on translations or book distributors outside the U.S.A., please see the International Contact Information page immediately following the index of this book.

Photoshop 6: The Complete Reference

234567890 CUS CUS 01987654321

Book p/n 0-07-213165-9 and CD p/n 0-07-213166-7
parts of
ISBN 0-07-213167-5

Publisher
Brandon A. Nordin
Vice President & Associate Publisher
Scott Rogers
Acquisitions Editor
Megg Bonar
Project Editor
Lisa Theobald
Acquisitions Coordinator
Alissa Larson
Technical Editor
Pam Trickey
Copy Editors
Marilyn Smith, Andy Carroll

Proofreaders
Paul Medoff, Lisa Theobald
Indexer
James Minkin
Computer Designers
Lauren McCarthy, Tara Davis,
Kelly Stanton-Scott
Illustrators
Lyssa Sieben-Wald, Beth E. Young
Series Design
Peter F. Hancik

This book was composed with Corel VENTURA™ Publisher.

To our family, Angelique and Laurence

About the Authors

Adele Droblas Greenberg is an artist and computer consultant who specializes in digital video. She has worked in the computer industry for many years. She has taught at Pratt Institute and Columbia University. Adele has also served as the training director at a New York City Prepress house.

Seth Greenberg is a computer consultant, database/multimedia/Web programmer, and writer. He has also worked as a television producer and scriptwriter, and he has written articles for several computer magazines.

Contents

Part I

Photoshop Basics

Part II

Image Editing Fundamentals

Part III

Applying Effects to Your Images

Part IV
Appendixes

Acknowledgments

A book as extensive as *Photoshop 6: The Complete Reference* could not have been written without the help of numerous people. Above all we'd like to thank the editorial, production, marketing, and sales staff at Osborne/McGraw-Hill, particularly Publisher Brandon Nordin, Associate Publisher Scott Rogers, and Acquisitions Editor Megg Bonar. Thanks to Megg for her help and enthusiasm during the writing, editing, and production stages of the book. We'd also like to thank Megg for her work in securing the tryouts and permission for this book's CD-ROM.

We also owe a special debt of gratitude to Lisa Theobald, project editor, for help and guidance and the many hours she spent overseeing this complex book through to production. We'd also like to also express our gratitude to acquisitions coordinator Alissa Larsen, who tracked chapter delivery and made sure all text and graphics were in their proper place. Thanks are also due to copy editors Marilyn Smith and Andy Carroll. Marilyn not only provided superior copy editing, but contributed additional help in the technical review of the book.

Thanks to Lyssa Sieben-Wald for her illustration additions to the color theory chapter on the CD, and for overseeing and laying out the book's gorgeous color insert. We'd also like to thank Peter Hancik, who prepared the CD-ROM contents for manufacturing.

Our thanks to proofreader Paul Medoff and to indexer James Minkin. We'd also like to thank Pam Trickey for her technical reviews. Thanks also to the entire talented staff of the Osborne Production Department for all their hard work—including Lauren McCarthy, Roberta Steele, Tara Davis, Melinda Lytle, Kelly Stanton-Scott, Dick Schwartz, and Jim Kussow.

Thanks to everyone at Adobe Systems, especially Christie Evans and Theresa Bruno, who helped us out during the Adobe Photoshop 6.0 Beta cycle. Thanks as well to the Photoshop programmers who have created and developed such an outstanding product. Their accomplishments make our work look like magic.

We'd like to thank the many corporations who have graciously provided assistance. Finally, we'd like to thank the Photoshop artists who contributed their excellent artwork to this book's color insert.

Thanks to everyone who has touched our lives in so many ways. Especially those who have been friends and practice love, peace, and happiness for everyone on earth. The following words came to us from Buenos Aires, Argentina. The words in the letter touched our lives. Here are some excerpts that you may wish to think about when you find yourself spending too much time in front your computer. (If you wish to read the full version of the letter in English and in Spanish, go to www.bonitavida.com.)

Everyday that you live is a special day...life should be filled with experiences to enjoy, not just to live by.... Tomorrow we all take for granted.... Everyday hour, every minute is special.... Don't be too lazy or too busy to take a few moments to touch someone's life, or to talk to a friend, or to tell a loved one you love them or too busy to do something special to help this world be a brighter, happier, kinder place.... If you think to yourself, I'll do it one of these days, then one of these days may be become so far away that one of these days may never happen.

Introduction

Photoshop's Beginnings

In the late 1980s Thomas Knoll, a University of Michigan graduate student, created a computer program whose primary purpose was to open and display different graphics files on a Macintosh Plus. This was the humble beginning of the program that was eventually to become Photoshop.

Thankfully for Photoshop users, Tom found that working on a computer program proved to be much more fun than writing a thesis paper. With the encouragement of his brother John Knoll, a special effects supervisor at George Lucas's Industrial Light and Magic Company, Tom began adding image-editing capabilities to his program.

Adobe took Tom's creation under its wing. Soon Tom's brother John was creating filters for the program, and through the collaborative efforts of the Knoll brothers with Adobe's programmers, Photoshop evolved into a software package that began revolutionizing the color publishing world.

As Photoshop grew in power and popularity, its users sought help. As consultants, trainers, and Photoshop users, we were encouraged to write an easy-to-understand book that would thoroughly cover Photoshop features and yet go well beyond the basics. The result is *Photoshop 6: The Complete Reference.*

About This Book...

Whether you are new to Photoshop or an experienced user, we're sure you'll find *Photoshop 6: The Complete Reference* to be unique, both as an instruction book and a reference manual. We not only cover virtually every command and dialog box in the program, but we also have you try them out. The book is filled with instructions, hints, tips, step-by-step tutorials, and full-fledged Photoshop projects. You can re-create these projects with the images included on the CD-ROM at the back of the book. If you have any questions or comments for the authors, you can e-mail them at adele@addesigngraphics.com and seth@addesigngraphics.com.

How the Book Is Organized

This book progresses through three stages: Chapters 1 through 5 are introductory chapters that guide you through the fundamental tools and basic features of the program. Chapters 6 through 10 focus on image editing to bring you to an intermediate level, and Chapters 11 through 19 provide more advanced techniques.

- Chapter 1 introduces you into the world of Photoshop with a tour of the program's menus, palettes, options, and tools. This chapter also discusses how to separate and "dock" palettes to customize your workspace.

- Chapter 2 provides a guide to Photoshop 6's Color Management System. Follow along in this important section to set up Photoshop's Color Settings dialog box. This chapter helps ensure that your monitor is properly calibrated, and that when you start your Photoshop work, the colors on your screen are displayed as accurately as possible.

- Chapter 3 introduces you to the type capabilities of Photoshop 6. This chapter not only provides a detailed look at Photoshop's numerous type options but includes several tutorial exercises for creating type effects. The chapter also includes a look at Photoshop 6's new Type Warp command.

- Chapter 4 gives you an overview of the selection tools. You may be surprised to see that even with the program's basic selection tools, you can create attractive montages, collages, and vignettes.

- Chapter 5 covers Photoshop's painting tools. Here you'll find out how to create custom brushes and how to get the most out of Photoshop's different blending modes.

- Chapter 6 offers an introductory look at image-editing techniques. In this chapter you'll learn how to use the Blur/Sharpen, Dodge/Burn/Sponge, and Clone Stamp tools. You'll also get a chance to try out Photoshop 6's History palette and History brush.

■ Chapter 7 covers the steps involved in digitizing images and understanding how to use Photoshop's Image Size dialog box. The chapter features an in-depth discussion of how choose the correct resolution when creating and digitizing images.

■ Chapter 8 discusses how to transform images. It includes a discussion on cropping and rotating images. We round out this chapter by explaining the Image > Rotate Canvas and Edit > Transform commands.

■ Chapter 9 provides an introduction to Web file formats, such as GIF, JPEG, and PNG. The focus here is on preparing high-quality images for the Web, using both Photoshop and ImageReady.

■ Chapter 10 focuses on the special effects you can create for the Web with ImageReady. Topics here include creating Web animation and learning to use rollovers, image maps, and image slices.

■ Chapter 11 shows you how to use Photoshop's Actions and History palettes. The Actions palette lets you record and play back Photoshop commands. The History palette gives you virtually unlimited ability to undo your edits. This chapter also explains how to use the Photoshop 6 Batch command to apply actions to multiple files.

■ Chapter 12 covers the fascinating filters available in Photoshop: Unsharp Mask, Gaussian Blur, Motion Blur, Lighting Effects, Emboss, and Spherize. If you like special effects, you'll especially enjoy this chapter.

■ Chapter 13 provides an in-depth discussion of switching modes—in particular, converting an RGB file to CMYK and converting from RGB mode to Grayscale mode. This chapter also leads you, step by step, through the processes of creating duotone and mezzotint images.

■ Chapter 14 introduces you to Photoshop's powerful Pen tool. Here you can try your hand at creating paths and Bézier curves. You'll also learn how to use Photoshop Magnetic Pen and Freeform Pen tools. This chapter concludes with step-by-step instructions for creating clipping paths, which allow you to silhouette images for use in other programs.

■ Chapter 15 details the processes of creating masks and using channels and introduces Photoshop's versatile Quick Mask feature. Here you'll learn how to save and load selections. The chapter concludes with step-by-step instructions for creating spot colors with Photoshop's Spot Color channels.

■ Chapter 16 provides a thorough look at Photoshop's powerful layering features and explains how to use the Layers palette. The techniques presented here include creating, viewing, hiding, moving, linking, blending, merging, and flattening layers.

■ Chapter 17 leads you through the more advanced features of layers, including creating shapes in layers and clipping groups. This chapter features a detailed discussion of Photoshop's powerful layer masks, which allow you to blend layers seamlessly. Also covered here are Photoshop's adjustment layers, which let you undo and redo your color corrections as often as needed.

■ Chapter 18 shows you how to create special effects with the Layer Style commands. Tutorials also show you how to create special effects using filters and layers.

■ Chapter 19 leads you through the processes of retouching and color correction. The exercises in this chapter show you how to correct old and damaged photographs. You'll also learn how to use the Curves and Levels dialog boxes and the Color Sampler tools. Photoshop's Channel Mixer is also covered here.

■ As an added bonus, we've included a chapter on color theory on the CD. Understanding color theory is one of the prerequisites to successfully using Photoshop for color publishing. This chapter takes a thorough look at the difference between the RGB (red/green/blue) and CMYK (cyan/magenta/yellow/black) color models. Also discussed are the HSB (hue/saturation/brightness) and Lab color models.

■ Appendix A provides a look at how to import files into Photoshop and how to save files in different formats for use in other programs.

■ Appendix B covers printing and calibration. This appendix provides a detailed look at the options in the Print and Page Setup dialog boxes. It also includes a section on how to print using Photoshop 6's Color Management options.

■ Appendix C lists the contents of the book CD-ROM. As you'll soon see, the CD-ROM features tutorial images from the book. Use these images to re-create the step-by-step tutorials featured throughout the book. The CD also includes a tryout version of Photoshop 6 for those readers who haven't yet upgraded or purchased Photoshop 6.

The Complete Reference

Part I

Photoshop Basics

The
Complete
Reference

Photoshop 6

Chapter 1

Getting Started in Photoshop

P hotoshop is truly magical. It can pluck a pyramid from the sands of Egypt and gently drop it down on the Champs Elysées, making it look so real that even a Parisian might not think anything is out of place. Photoshop can make the wrinkles of age vanish magically or create them where they haven't yet appeared. It can transform a scan of a torn and discolored photograph so that it looks like a flawless image taken by a master photographer. And Photoshop can turn your blank computer screen into an artistic masterpiece—a blend of photorealistic images, fantastic designs, patterns, and colors.

Although you undoubtedly are eager to jump right in and start turning your artistic visions into reality, your best approach is to gain some insight into how Photoshop works. Then ensure that Photoshop is installed correctly, and tour the program to obtain a basic understanding of its tools and layout. In this chapter, you'll do just that.

Understanding the Photoshop Design Process

As you'll see in the many professional art and design samples throughout this book, especially in the color insert, the Photoshop design process can take many forms and can lead in a multitude of directions. Photoshop is an electronic passport to high-end color desktop publishing, as well as prepress, multimedia, animation, digital photography, and painting.

Photoshop transports you to these ports of call in many different ways. Once an image is input into Photoshop from a scanner, digital or video camera, video recorder, or Photo CD image, it can be retouched, painted, color-corrected, sharpened, rippled, or distorted. An image can be cut apart, juxtaposed, or blended into another image. It can then be output to the Web, to a slide recorder, a videotape recorder, a black-and-white or color printer, or an imagesetter to create the final film, which is used to make plates for a printing press. Figure 1-1 illustrates the various input and output devices that cooperate in the Photoshop design and production processes.

What's behind the scenes in Photoshop? Every Photoshop (and ImageReady) image is composed of a grid of tiny squares called *pixels*. When you paint, retouch, cut, paste, or alter an image in Photoshop, you are changing pixels.

A pixel is the smallest picture element in every square inch of the image (in a 72-pixel-per-inch image, there are 72 pixels per row in an inch × 72 pixels per column in an inch = 5,184 pixels). Photoshop can perform image-editing tricks because it can alter any pixel or every pixel on the screen when it executes a painting or special-effects command.

When you work with pixel-based program, often called a *raster program*, you should think like a painter. When you paint with Photoshop, you are filling in pixels on your screen, painting on an electronic canvas. As you create, the paint "dries" on the canvas, almost as if it were embedded on the screen. If you wish to move the image area, you'll need to use the proper tool, which essentially cuts the object out of its background so it can be lifted and moved to replace other pixels. To delete the image area, you may need to paint over it.

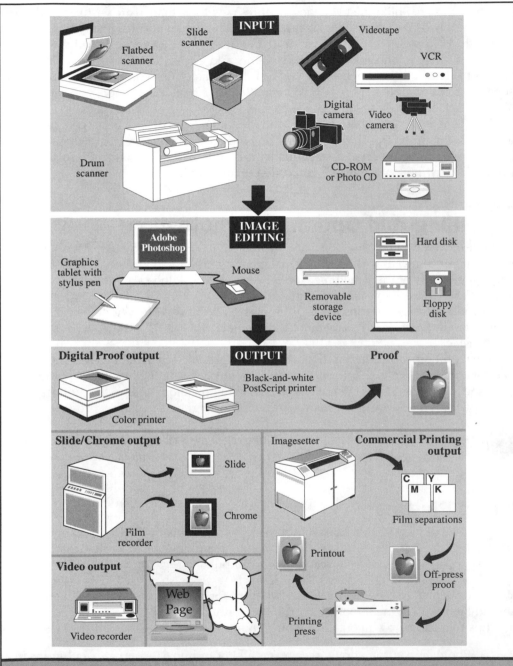

Figure 1-1.   *The Photoshop design and production process*

Photoshop 6, unlike past versions, features new tools that create vector-based shapes and text. Vector-based images are based on mathematical algorithms rather than a grid of pixels. These tools are similar to those found in vector-based drawing programs, such as Adobe Illustrator, Freehand, and CorelDRAW, which use lines and curves to create shapes. Each shape you draw and each letter you type is an object, separate from other objects. When you want to move or resize a shape, you can often simply click on it and drag it with the mouse.

Photoshop 6's vector-based shapes and text can be exported to other programs as vector text and vector shapes. When Photoshop vector-based text and shapes are output on a PostScript printer, their quality is determined by the output resolution, rather than by the Photoshop file resolution (pixels per inch).

Installing and Optimizing Photoshop

If you are running Photoshop on a Mac, you must use System 8.5 or later with a minimum of 64 MB of RAM (with virtual memory on). If you wish to run Photoshop and ImageReady at the same time, you'll need 128 MB. Adobe also recommends at least 125 MB of available hard disk space.

On a PC, Photoshop runs under Windows 98, Windows Me, Windows NT (4.0 or later), or Windows 2000. The memory requirements for the PC are the same as those for the Mac.

We won't repeat the installation instructions provided by Adobe in the Photoshop package. Installation is simple and involves merely running the installation program from the installation CD. If you haven't installed Photoshop, refer to the guide included with the software for instructions on running the installation process.

Before running Photoshop for the first time, open the Read Me file that is installed along with the program. This file explains any changes to the program that are not included in the Photoshop manual.

Installing Plug-ins

After you've installed Photoshop, your next step is to install any Photoshop plug-ins created by third-party software vendors. *Plug-ins* are programs that work within Photoshop, often created to run scanners or to output images to printers more efficiently.

On both Mac and PC systems, all plug-ins that you wish to use in Photoshop should be copied to the Plug-ins folder. Plug-ins for scanners and digital cameras should be placed in the Import/Export folder within the Plug-ins folder. Here are a few tips that can help you organize your plug-ins:

■ Photoshop automatically recognizes all Photoshop 6.0-compatible plug-ins in the Plug-ins folder or in a folder within the Plug-ins folder.

■ Photoshop 6 allows you to choose a second folder for plug-in installation. To specify another plug-in folder, choose Edit > Preferences > Plug-ins & Scratch Disks. In the Plug-ins & Scratch Disks dialog box, click on the Additional Plug-ins directory checkbox and then click on the Choose button to specify the folder that you wish to use.

■ On the Mac, you can "hide" plug-in subfolders so that Photoshop won't load their plug-ins. To hide a subfolder in the Plug-ins folder, type ¬ (by pressing OPTION-L) in front of the subfolder's name.

Allocating Memory

As you probably know, image files can be huge. You'll want to make sure that Photoshop uses available memory for running the program and for your scratch disk.

Allocating Memory for Photoshop on the Mac

Mac users should be aware that Photoshop won't access all free memory in your computer unless you allocate it to Photoshop. Just because 100 MB of RAM is available on your Mac doesn't mean that Photoshop will grab extra memory when you're working on a large color image. You need to allocate the amount of memory you want to reserve for Photoshop. On the Mac, allocating memory is handled from the Finder.

To allocate memory to Photoshop, first make sure that Photoshop is not running; otherwise, you will not be able to edit its memory size options. Next, click once on the Photoshop program icon, which is in the Adobe Photoshop folder. When you select Photoshop, the program's icon will turn darker. Then choose File > Get Info. Choose Memory in the Show pop-up menu at the top of the window.

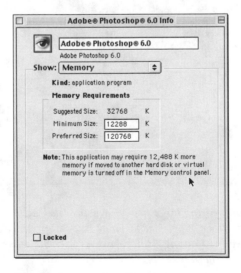

As you can see in the Adobe Photoshop 6.0 Info window, the suggested size for the program on a Power Macintosh system is about 33 MB. Notice that there are two editable fields: Minimum Size and Preferred Size. You should allocate as much memory as you can afford in the Preferred Size field (but leave some memory left over for system operations). When Photoshop loads, it checks to see if you have enough memory free to use your Preferred Memory setting. If your system does not have this much memory available, Photoshop will use at least the amount of memory set in the Minimum Size field (provided your computer has enough memory available).

After you've set the memory allocation, close the Adobe Photoshop Info window. The next time you use Photoshop, it will open into the memory partition size that you designated.

Allocating Memory for Photoshop on the PC

For Windows users, memory allocation is handled automatically within Photoshop. Thus, to change or view memory allocation, you will need to load Photoshop. To load Photoshop, double-click on the Adobe Photoshop icon.

When Photoshop first loads, it automatically grabs a percentage of free memory. If you wish to increase the percentage, choose Edit > Preferences > Memory & Image Cache and change the value in the Used by Photoshop field.

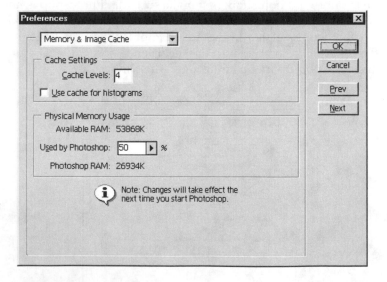

If you are editing or creating large images, raising the Cache Levels setting in the Edit > Preferences & Memory & Image Cache dialog box can produce speed improvements, particularly in screen redrawing. However, a large cache setting causes Photoshop to use more RAM and hard disk space.

Resetting the Scratch Disk

Your last installation step is to check the memory allocated to your scratch disk. In order to do this, you'll need to load Photoshop. To start Photoshop, double-click on the Adobe Photoshop icon in the Adobe Photoshop folder (most Windows users will probably start Photoshop from the Start menu). After the program loads, you may want to reset the scratch disk that Photoshop uses for virtual memory.

As mentioned earlier in this chapter, when Photoshop needs more memory than it can find in RAM, it will start using your hard disk as virtual memory. By default, Photoshop designates your startup drive as the first scratch disk. (You can designate up to four different scratch disks.) If your computer has another hard disk that is faster or has more space available, you may want to set it as the first scratch disk.

If you wish to reset the scratch disk, choose Edit > Preferences > Plug-ins & Scratch Disks. In the Preferences dialog box, click on the First, Second, Third, and/or Fourth pop-up menus and choose the desired drive. Your first scratch disk should be the fastest and emptiest hard drive connected to your system.

If you wish to boost the performance of Photoshop, be sure that the free space on your hard disk is as contiguous as possible. If you've been accessing your hard disk frequently during your computer sessions, available free space may be spread over many different sectors. Windows systems include a disk defragmenter utility that you can use to organize your disk's hard space more efficiently. Mac users can purchase this type of software. For example, the Norton Utilities package includes optimization programs that will reallocate the files on your hard disk so that the free space is as contiguous as possible.

Touring Photoshop

Adobe® Photoshop® 6.0

When you are ready to begin your tour of Photoshop, launch the program by double-clicking on the Photoshop icon. After Photoshop is loaded, its menu bar, Toolbox, and four palette groups appear on the screen. Figure 1-2 shows the screen as it appears on a Mac, and Figure 1-3 shows the Photoshop screen on a Windows system.

Unlike many programs, Photoshop does not automatically open a new document for you to work in. So, before you explore the features of the Photoshop screen, you'll learn how to create a new file.

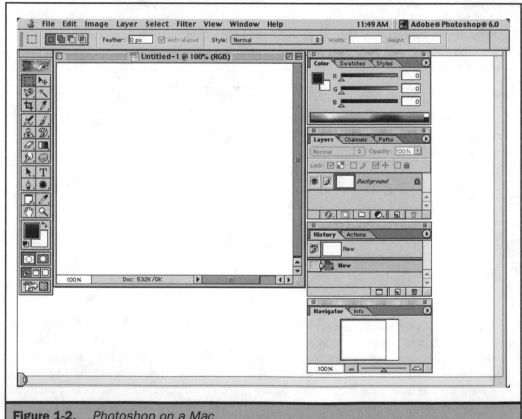

Figure 1-2.   *Photoshop on a Mac*

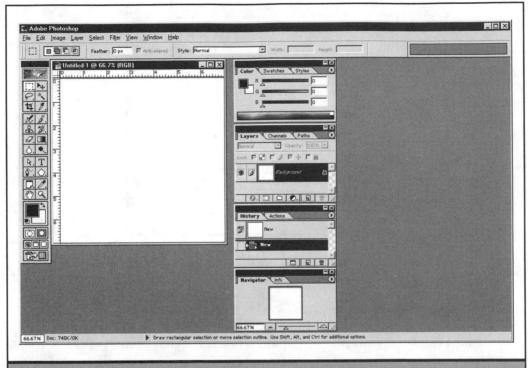

Figure 1-3.   *Photoshop on a Windows computer*

A New File

Without a document on screen, you won't be able to use Photoshop's palettes or any of its tools. To begin, you'll create a document that is 7 inches wide and 5 inches high, which will provide a comfortable working area on most monitors. Follow these steps to create your new document:

1. Select File > New. The New dialog box appears. The settings in the New dialog box will be Photoshop's default settings or the settings that were last used. As you work in Photoshop, you'll find that the program often retains the dialog box settings that were last used.

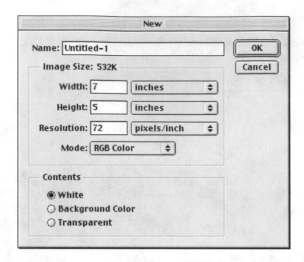

Note *If you copy or cut a selection, the dimensions of the selection appear in the New dialog box. If you wish, you can override this by pressing* OPTION *(*ALT*) when choosing File > New.*

2. In the Name field, you can enter a title for your document. Naming your document when you first create it can be helpful when you have more than one unsaved document open. At this point, leave your document untitled.

3. If the Width and Height measurement units are not set to inches, change them by selecting Inches in the pop-up menus to the right of the Width and Height fields. A pop-up menu is represented by a box containing a down-pointing arrowhead and is outlined with a drop shadow. To access a pop-up menu, Mac users can click anywhere on the pop-up menu. Windows users must click on the down arrow in the pop-up menu.

4. If Width is not set to 7 and Height is not set to 5, enter these values now. Click on the Width field to select it, and type **7**. Press TAB to move to the Height field and type **5**. You can move among the fields in a dialog box by either clicking on the field or by pressing the TAB key to move the cursor from one field to the next. If you make a mistake, press DELETE (*BACKSPACE* in Windows), and then retype your entry.

5. If another setting has not been used last, the Resolution field will be set to 72 pixels/inch (ppi). Photoshop uses 72 ppi as the default resolution because many monitors display 72 pixels for every inch of screen area. In other words, you are setting the resolution of your document to be about the same as the resolution of your monitor. If necessary, change the Resolution setting to **72**.

Tip *If you make the Resolution, Height, or Width setting larger, the size of your file will also grow. Try to avoid large images when practicing; they're cumbersome to work with and they slow down your computer.*

6. The Mode option should be set to RGB Color (red/green/blue). Photoshop uses RGB Color as the default display mode because RGB is the standard color model used by video monitors to display colors. In RGB mode, colors are created from red, green, and blue values. When the Mode is set to RGB Color, all of Photoshop's painting and editing features are available. If necessary, set the Mode option to RGB Color by clicking on the Mode pop-up menu and choosing RGB Color. (The other Mode options are described in Chapter 13.)

7. To ensure that the background of your new document is white, click on the White radio button in the Contents group. If you choose the Background Color option instead, the background color that was last used in Photoshop will be used for your new document. If you choose Transparent, you'll be working in a layer with a background that is clear, without any color values.

Note *If you're confused about the difference between a white background and a transparent background, imagine that you have created a black, doughnut-shaped object on a transparent background. If you copy the doughnut with the transparent background into a document that has a colored background, the color will show through the doughnut hole. Had you created the same doughnut with a white background, you would see white in the doughnut hole, even after copying it into a colored document.*

8. Click on OK to close the New dialog box. A new document window appears on your screen. In the window's title bar are the document's file name (Untitled), the current display mode, and the magnification percentage.

You can scroll, resize, and close the Photoshop window as you would in most Windows or Mac applications. You can move the window by clicking and dragging in the title bar.

If you wish to magnify the screen, select View > Zoom In or press COMMAND-+ (CTRL-+), To zoom out, select View > Zoom Out or press COMMAND - - (CTRL- –). You can press the + (plus) and – (minus) keys on either the keyboard or the numeric keypad with NUM LOCK on. (Mac users can press SHIFT-CLEAR/NUM LOCK on the numeric keypad to activate the numeric keypad.)

Tip *If you are viewing a high-resolution image and wish to see the image at its actual printing size, choose View > Print Size.*

The Photoshop Menus

Photoshop's menu bar includes nine pull-down menus. The more familiar you are with how Photoshop divides its power—how the menus are organized—the more likely you are to take the right path when you begin to work with the program. The following sections provide a brief summary of the commands found on Photoshop's menus.

Image Resolution Settings

Most IBM PC-compatible monitors display 96 ppi; many Macintosh monitors display 72 ppi. Monitors that display 640 × 480 pixels output at 72 pixels per inch.

If you create a file with a pixel-per-inch setting higher than your monitor's 72 (or 96) pixels per inch, Photoshop displays the image larger than actual size, because it needs the extra screen area to display the extra pixels. For example, on a 72 ppi monitor, Photoshop displays a 300 ppi file approximately four times larger than its actual size, because there are about four times as many pixels on the 300 ppi grid as on a 72 ppi grid. In other words, because your monitor can only display 72 dots per inch, Photoshop stretches the image across a wider screen area in order to display it.

If you are creating an image that will eventually be output to the Web or to a multimedia program, the image resolution need not be greater than the resolution of a computer screen (usually 72 ppi). Setting the resolution higher does not result in better quality; it only results in files that consume more memory. Furthermore, high-resolution images are enlarged on the screen.

You should raise the Resolution setting only when necessary. For instance, when creating a file that will be printed on a commercial printing press, resolution should generally be 1.5 to 2 times the screen frequency measured in lines per inch (lpi). For more information about resolution, see Chapter 7.

If you get tired of always dragging your mouse to the top of the screen to access commands from the menu bar, you can use Photoshop's "context-sensitive" menus instead. Context-sensitive menus pop up whenever Mac users click the mouse while pressing the CONTROL key and whenever Windows users click the right mouse button. The contents of the menus change depending on which tool is activated and where you click on the screen. The menus even change when you click on a palette.

The File Menu

Most of the commands in the File menu are for storing, loading, and printing files. The New, Open, Save, Save As, Page Setup, Print, and Quit (Exit on Windows systems) commands work very much as they do in other Macintosh and Windows applications.

The Save As and Save a Copy commands allow you to save your file in different formats so that it can be output to service bureaus, the Web, and multimedia programs. The Save for Web command allows you to save your file for output on the World Wide Web. Using Save for Web, you can not only choose a Web file format such as GIF or JPEG, but you can also help ensure that your image is saved with Web-safe colors. Using Save for Web is covered in detail in Chapter 9.

The File > Import command allows you to digitize images from scanners, digital cameras, and video-capture boards directly into Photoshop. The Export command allows you to export a file in GIF format (for Web images) and to export Photoshop paths to Illustrator.

The Automate commands allow you to run Photoshop commands automatically on a group or "batch" of files. For instance, using the Automate commands you can automatically convert a folder full of files to GIF or JPEG format for use on the Web. The Automate commands are discussed in Chapter 11.

The Jump To command allows you to immediately jump to other programs, such as Adobe ImageReady or Adobe Illustrator.

The Edit Menu

The Edit menu is generally used for duplicating or moving parts of images to other areas of a document or to other files. It also features an Undo command, which allows you to void the action of your last command. Mac and Windows users will recognize standard Edit menu commands: Undo, Cut, Copy, and Paste. Photoshop's Edit menu also allows you to paste an image into a selection.

The Define Pattern command allows you to designate a selected area as the basis of a pattern that you can paint (with the Pattern Stamp tool) or fill. Creating patterns is discussed in Chapter 6. The Fill and Stroke commands are used to fill and outline images or selections, as discussed in Chapter 4. Free Transform and Transform allow you to scale, rotate, and distort selections, as explained in Chapter 8.

The Color Settings commands allow you to set up Photoshop to provide consistent and accurate color output. The commands also provide the settings for converting a file from RGB (red/green/blue), the standard computer color monitor display mode, to CMYK (cyan/magenta/yellow/black), the mode used for four-color process printing. The Color Settings commands are discussed in Chapter 2.

The Preferences commands display dialog boxes with choices for changing Photoshop's default setup. Preferences are discussed in the "Using Preferences to Change the Defaults" section at the end of this chapter.

The Image Menu

The Image menu allows you to convert a file from RGB to CMYK or to convert an image to Index Color mode, a step you might take as you prepare an image for the Web or for a multimedia program. The Image menu also allows you to change a color image to grayscale, and then from grayscale to black-and-white. Changing modes is covered in Chapter 13.

Using the other commands on the Image menu, you can manipulate the sizes of files and canvases and analyze and correct colors in an image. For example, you can adjust its color balance, brightness, contrast, highlights, midtones, and shadows. Image manipulation is discussed in Chapters 7 and 8. The Duplicate, Apply Image, and Calculations commands can be used for creating special effects, as you'll learn in the exercises in upcoming chapters. The Extract command allows you to isolate or "mask" image areas. After the image area is isolated, it can be edited or copied and pasted into another file.

The Layer Menu

The Layer menu features commands that allow you to create and manipulate layers. A *layer* is somewhat similar to a sheet of clear plastic in an invisible plane above your image. Some of the commands in the Layer menu are also found in the Layers palette— New Layer, Duplicate Layer, Delete Layer, and Layer Options. You'll learn all about layers and how to apply these commands throughout this book, and Chapters 16 and 17 are devoted to layers.

The Select Menu

The Select menu allows you to modify a selection or select an entire image. In Photoshop, before you can change any part of an image, you often need to isolate or select it. The Deselect command deselects an image on screen. The Reselect command reselects the previous selection on screen. Grow expands a selection, and Inverse reverses a selection so that everything that isn't selected will be selected.

The Modify submenu commands allow you to turn a selection into one that borders the previous selection, smooth a selection, or expand or contract a selection. The Feather command blurs the edges of a selection. The Transform Selection command allows you to scale, rotate, or skew a selection by clicking and dragging the mouse. Photoshop also allows you to save and reload a selection using the Save Selection and Load Selection commands. The Select commands are covered in Chapter 4.

The Filter Menu

The Filter menu offers a variety of filters, which create effects similar to those of a photographer's filter that is placed in front of a camera lens to produce a special effect. By applying a Photoshop filter available on one of the Filter submenus, you can sharpen, blur, distort, stylize, and add lighting effects and noise to an image or part of an image. Photoshop features more than 50 different filters, which are covered in Chapter 12.

The View Menu

The View menu allows you to change the view of your document (zoom in or out, or fit your view on screen). You can also create a new window to view the same image simultaneously at different magnifications; when an image is edited, both windows are updated. With the View menu, you can show or hide Photoshop's rulers, guides, and grid. The View menu also allows you to hide the edges of a selection or a path outline temporarily. The View menu's Preview command is a powerful feature that provides a preview of how your document will look when in CMYK mode. The Gamut Warning command alerts you if you have chosen any colors that are beyond the printable spectrum of colors.

The Window Menu

The Window menu allows you to move from one open document to another and to open and close Photoshop's various palettes.

The Help Menu

The Help menu provides quick access to information about Photoshop features and commands. In many respects, the Help screens are like having the Photoshop user manual a few mouse clicks away. Simply choose Help > Help Contents see the Help choices.

Photoshop 6's Help menu includes two "wizards" that walk you step by step through different production process. The Resize Image Wizard leads you through the steps of properly resizing an image. The Export Transparent Wizard leads you through the steps of saving an image against a transparent background for the Web or for printed output. (Windows users can also access Photoshop's Help contents by pressing F1.)

The Magnification, File, and Memory Indicators

At the lower-left corner of the document window, you will find the document's magnification percentage. You can change the magnification percentage by simply editing this number, then pressing RETURN (*ENTER* in Windows). For instance, if you click and drag over the number, type **200,** and press RETURN (*ENTER*), the setting changes to 200%—twice its normal viewing size.

To the right of the magnification percentage indicator is the file size indicator by default; however, you can change this indicator to show other information. When you click on the arrow to the right of the two numbers, a pop-up menu appears.

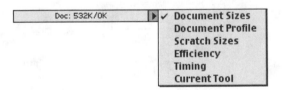

When Document Sizes (the default) is selected, the left number indicates the document size without any layers. You can also think of this number as the size of the image when all layers are flattened, or when the document is output to a printer. The number on the right indicates the file size when all layers, alpha channels, and data are included. (This number originally reads 0 when you begin with a blank canvas or solid-colored background canvas.) The number is often larger than the amount of space actually consumed on your hard disk, because Photoshop can compress information when it saves the file to disk.

Another useful display is Scratch Sizes. When this option is selected, the first number indicates how much memory all open documents are consuming (as well as any memory being used by the Clipboard). The second number reveals the amount of RAM available to create and edit your images. More specifically, this number is the available memory minus the memory Photoshop needs to work. When the first number is larger than the second number, Photoshop needs to rely on your scratch disk rather than RAM, because additional memory is needed. When the scratch disk is used instead of RAM, Photoshop performance slows.

The other options display different types of information:

- The Document Profile option displays the document's ICC color profile (see Chapter 2 for information about ICC color profiles).

- When Efficiency is selected, the number on the screen represents the percentage of work handled in RAM (as opposed to the scratch disk). If the number is 100%, Photoshop is not using the scratch disk.

- When Timing is selected, the number indicates the amount of time it took to complete the last action.

- The Current Tool option displays the name of the current tool.

Photoshop's Rulers, Guides, and Grids

No matter what magnification ratio you are working in, it's generally a good idea to display Photoshop's horizontal and vertical rulers on screen. That way, you won't lose sight of how large or small your file's dimensions and images are. To make the rulers visible if they're not already on your screen, choose View > Show Rulers.

The rulers continually indicate your position in the window with a mark that glides along each ruler as you move the mouse. If you haven't noticed the marks, keep an eye on either the horizontal or the vertical ruler and move the mouse diagonally across the screen until you see them.

If you are moving images or lining up objects on screen, you can drag nonprinting guides out of Photoshop's horizontal or vertical rulers. The guides can be moved using the Move tool or locked using the View > Lock Guides command. To create a guide, simply position the mouse a little above the horizontal ruler or a little to the left of the vertical ruler. Press and hold down the mouse button and begin to drag the mouse. You'll see the mouse pointer change to a two-arrow icon. As you drag, a guide will appear. Drag the guide to where you want to position it on screen. If you want the guides to disappear temporarily, choose View > Show > Guides. Choose View > Show > Guides again to make the guides reappear.

Here are a few tips about using guides:

- If you wish to reposition a guide after you create it, activate the Move tool and then click and drag on the guide.

- Double-click on a guide to open the Preferences dialog box for Guides & Grids.

- By default, the View menu's Snap to Guide command is set on (indicated by a checkmark next to the menu command). When this option is on, selections and image areas that you move on screen jump to the nearest guide when you move the object to within a few pixels of the guide. To turn this feature off, choose View > Snap to Guide. The checkmark will disappear when the option is off.

- To change the color of grid lines or make them dashed, choose Edit > Preferences > Guides & Grids.

- To line up a guide on a ruler tick mark, press and hold down SHIFT when dragging a guide.

- To convert a vertical guide to a horizontal one (or vice versa), press OPTION (*ALT* in Windows) when dragging a guide.

- To remove all guides from the screen, choose View > Clear Guides.

- If you resize an image or resize or rotate the work canvas, Photoshop guides maintain their relative positions in the image, if the guides are not locked.

Photoshop's Grid option can also be a handy aid in lining up objects on screen, as well as a balancing aid when composing an image. To see the grid on screen, choose View > Show > Grid (to hide the Grid, choose View > Show > Grid again). By default, the grid is set to a matrix of 1 × 1-inch squares, with 16 smaller squares within each larger square. If you wish to change the size of the grid squares or their subdivision of smaller squares, choose Edit > Preferences > Guides & Grids.

Like Photoshop's guides, Photoshop grid lines attract objects that you drag near them. This feature of snapping to the grid can be helpful when you want to align objects on grid lines. To turn this feature off, choose View > Snap to > Guides. This removes the checkmark next to the menu command.

The Photoshop Toolbox

Along the left side of the window is Photoshop's Toolbox. The Toolbox contains the essential tools for painting, selecting, and editing graphics. Each tool is depicted by an icon. Understanding the purpose and power of each tool is the key to learning Photoshop. Just as an artisan must know the right tool to use for each job, so must the Photoshop user.

There are more than 40 tools in the Photoshop Toolbox, as shown in Figure 1-4. Each tool provides a specific utility to aid you when you're creating, editing, and

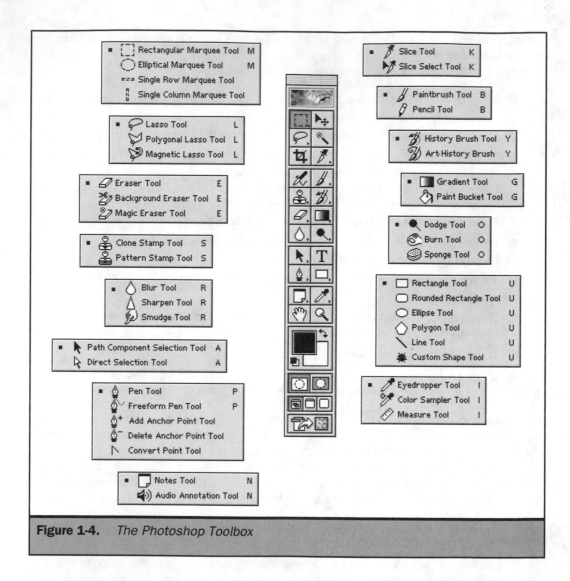

Figure 1-4.   *The Photoshop Toolbox*

color-correcting images. The following sections describe how to select tools from the Toolbox and provide an introduction to each of the tools, as well as the other icons in the Toolbox.

Selecting Tools from the Toolbox

Notice the tiny arrow that appears at the lower right of several Toolbox locations. When you see the arrow, it means that several tools share one location, as illustrated in Figure 1-4. To see all of the occupants of a Toolbox location, move the mouse pointer over the Toolbox location and press and hold down the mouse button. To select one of the tools, move the mouse over the tool and click on the tool to select it. When you release the mouse, the tool is selected and it appears in the Toolbox.

If you keep the mouse pointer over a tool for a few seconds, a yellow bar appears over that tool, displaying its name and the letter to press on your keyboard to select it. (If you wish to turn these tool tips off, choose Edit > Preferences > General and turn off the Show Tool Tips option.) You can press the shortcut key to select the tool that appears in the Toolbox. To select a tool that shares its Toolbox location with other tools, press SHIFT and the keyboard shortcut for that tool. For instance, pressing SHIFT-M allows you to select different selection tools. Pressing SHIFT-P allows you to select different pen tools.

> **Note** *Most of the tools found in ImageReady's Toolbox function similarly to those found in Photoshop. Web-specific tools (such as ImageReady's Slice tool) are covered in Chapters 9 and 10. In ImageReady, tool groups can be dragged away from the Toolbox to serve as their own floating palettes. For instance, you can click and drag the Slice tools and easily switch between the Slice and Slice Select tools from the Slice palette.*

The first time you load Photoshop after it is installed, the Marquee is the selected tool. Thereafter, when you load Photoshop or create a new file, the last tool used remains selected. When a tool is selected, its Toolbox location turns gray. When you select a tool, the choices available in the Options bar (described later in this chapter) change to options specific to the selected tool.

The Selection Tools

The first tool on the top row and the two tools in the second row of the Toolbox are the selection tools. If you wish to make changes to an object, you'll usually need to select it with one of these tools first.

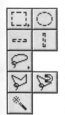

At the upper-left Toolbox location are the Marquee tools, which allow you to create different shaped selections. If you position the mouse pointer over the Marquee's Toolbox location, and then press and hold down the mouse button, the list of Marquee tools appears. These tools allow you to create rectangular or elliptical selections, or vertical or horizontal selections just 1 pixel wide. If you want to switch Marquee tool options, keep the mouse button pressed and simply drag the mouse pointer over to the tool icon. You can also press M to select the Marquee tools.

If you choose the Elliptical Marquee, the icon in the Toolbox changes to a circle. If you choose the Single Row or Single Column Marquee, the icon in the Toolbox changes to a thin horizontal or vertical rectangle. If you wish to quickly switch from the Rectangular to the Elliptical Marquee tool, press OPTION (*ALT* in Windows) and click on the Marquee in the Toolbox.

Below the Marquee tool is the Lasso tool, which can be used as a freehand tool; you use it to outline irregularly shaped selections. Two other Lasso tools share the standard Lasso tool's Toolbox location: the Polygon Lasso tool and the Magnetic Lasso tool. The Polygon Lasso tool allows you to create straight-edged polygon selections by clicking on different points on screen. Each time you click, Photoshop adds to the selection, creating a blinking selection line from one mouse click location to the next. The Magnetic Lasso automatically snaps to high-contrast edges as you drag the tool over an image. To end the selection when using either the Magnetic Lasso or Polygon Lasso tool, click again at the point you first clicked on or double-click anywhere in the image window. If you wish to toggle between the Lasso tools, press OPTION (ALT in Windows) and click on the Lasso in the Toolbox. You can also press L to activate the Lasso tools.

The Magic Wand selects according to similarity of colors. It can be helpful when you wish to select an area that has a different color than other areas in your image. Click on the tool's icon or press W to select the Magic Wand.

Several of the selection tools also allow you to fill them with color to create shapes. You will learn how to use the selection tools in Chapter 4.

The Crop Tool

The Crop tool is used to cut out a portion of an image and remove the rest. You can also activate the Crop tool by pressing C. The Crop tool is covered in Chapter 8.

The Move Tool

The Move tool is used to move selections or layers. If you're working in a layer, you can click and drag with the Move tool to move the entire layer. You can activate the Move tool by pressing V on your keyboard. You can also activate the Move tool when using most other tools by pressing COMMAND (CTRL). However, this doesn't work when you are using the Hand or Pen tool.

The Eyedropper, Color Sampler, and Measure Tools

The Eyedropper, Color Sampler, and Measure tools share their Toolbox location. You can use the mouse or press I to select these tools.

The Eyedropper picks up colors from your image and changes the foreground or background color to the color you click on with the Eyedropper. Press OPTION (ALT) to change to the background color. You can also use the Eyedropper to take color readings as you color-correct an image.

Using the Color Sampler tool, you can click on four different points in your image and view their color values in the Info palette. You can also move the four points on screen to analyze the colors of other image areas.

The Measure tool allows you to click and drag over an image area to measure the distance between two points. As you click and drag, a nonprinting line appears in your image. The distance, angle, and X and Y position of the nonprinting line appear in the Info palette. Using the Measure tool, you can even drag the nonprinting line to compare measurements of different image areas.

The Painting Tools

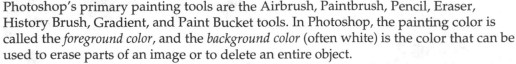

Photoshop's primary painting tools are the Airbrush, Paintbrush, Pencil, Eraser, History Brush, Gradient, and Paint Bucket tools. In Photoshop, the painting color is called the *foreground color*, and the *background color* (often white) is the color that can be used to erase parts of an image or to delete an entire object.

The Paint Bucket, Paintbrush, and Airbrush tools paint with the foreground color. The Paint Bucket (shortcut key G) fills areas with the foreground color or a pattern. The Paintbrush (shortcut key B) and Airbrush (shortcut key J) tools are electronic versions of these artist's tools. The Pencil tool (shortcut key B) shares its Toolbox location with the Paintbrush tool, and simulates drawing with a pencil, in either the foreground or background color.

The Gradient tool (shortcut key G) shares its Toolbox location with the Paint Bucket. It can create blends with the foreground or background color, or from a transparent background to the foreground color and vice versa. You can also click in the Gradient Options bar and choose to create Linear, Radial, Angled, Reflected, or Diamond gradients.

The Eraser paints with the background color and can erase parts of an image so that a transparent background can show through the image. The Magic Eraser and Background Eraser tools allow you to remove unwanted parts of your image quickly. For instance, when using the Magic Eraser, you can set the tool to erase according to color similarity. When using the Background Eraser, you can specify that you only want to erase image edges; this prevents the eraser from erasing image areas that include the foreground color. The shortcut key for the Eraser tools is E.

All of the painting tools are covered in Chapter 5.

The Shape-Creation Tools

The shape-creation tools include the Rectangle, Rounded Rectangle, Ellipse, Polygon, Line, and Custom Shape tools (all with the shortcut key U). They allow you to create shapes in three different modes:

■ Shapes that appear on layers as separate objects that can be freely resized and moved

■ Shapes that are closed paths

■ Shapes that are filled, as if painted

Shapes that are created as separate filled objects in a layer are the most versatile. These shapes are vector-based, and they can be output as sharp, high-quality objects. Furthermore, after you create a shape in a layer, you can change its opacity or apply a layer style to it by clicking on a style in the Styles palette or by choosing Layer > Layer Style, then picking a style such as Bevel and Emboss in the Layer Style pop-up menu. To learn more about shapes, see Chapter 14.

The Editing Tools

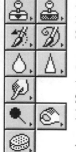

Although often classified as painting tools, the following tools are often used to edit images: Clone Stamp, Pattern Stamp, History Brush, Art History Brush, Blur, Sharpen, Smudge, Dodge, Burn, and Sponge.

The Clone Stamp is a cloning tool. You can use it to sample an area and clone (copy) it elsewhere, pixel by pixel, by clicking and dragging the mouse. You may use this tool frequently when retouching images or creating special effects. The Pattern Stamp tool shares a Toolbox spot with the Clone Stamp tool (both have the shortcut key S). You can use this tool to add patterns to images by clicking and dragging.

Perhaps the most unusual tool is the History Brush, which is used in conjunction with the History palette. Using the History Brush, you can paint over your image to return it to a previous History state. The Art History Brush allows you to create painterly effects from a previous version of your image. The History Brush and Art History Brush share a Toolbox location (with the shortcut key Y).

The Blur, Sharpen, and Smudge tools appear in one Toolbox location (with the shortcut key R). Blur softens hard edges, and Sharpen brings out more detail. The Smudge tool allows you to create a watercolor effect. It smudges a color to make it look as if water has been applied to it. You can toggle between the Blur and Sharpen tools by pressing OPTION (*ALT*) and clicking on the Toolbox location, or by pressing SHIFT-R.

The Dodge, Burn, and Sponge tools change the color and/or gray tones in an image. Like Blur and Sharpen, Dodge, Burn, and Sponge share a Toolbox location (with the shortcut key O). Dodge and Burn, traditional darkroom tools, are used to correct an exposure by lightening and darkening specific areas. Sponge allows you to saturate or desaturate (intensify or reduce intensity of) the color in an image. You can toggle between these three tools by pressing OPTION (*ALT*) and clicking on their Toolbox location.

All of the editing tools are covered in Chapter 6.

The Path Tools

The Pen tool (shortcut key P) allows you to create paths. Sharing the Pen tool's Toolbox location are other tools that allow you to create and edit paths: the Freeform Pen, Add Point, Delete Point, and Convert Point tools.

Although Pen paths can be used to create outlines for filling and stroking, paths are commonly used to create shapes for masks. A mask can be used to create an electronic stencil that protects image areas from being changed while you edit in an unprotected area. To use the Pen path as a mask, you can convert the path to a selection. Photoshop also allows you to turn a path into a *clipping path*, so that the mask can be used to create a transparent background when the image is placed into Illustrator, PageMaker, or QuarkXPress.

The Freeform Pen tool (shortcut key P) allows you to create a path by clicking and dragging as if you were sketching over an image. The Add Point and Delete Point tools add and subtract points from paths. The Convert Point tool can change a soft curve into a sharp corner or vice versa. If you wish to switch from the Pen tool to a path-editing tool, press OPTION (*ALT*) and click on the tool in the Pen tool's Toolbox location.

In Photoshop 6, the Magnetic Pen tool can be accessed from the Pen tool's Options bar when the Freeform Pen tool is selected in the Toolbox. The Magnetic Pen tool helps create masks by snapping to image edges as you drag the tool over an image. The Magnetic Pen tool bases its image-embracing decisions on image contrast.

The Pen tool and the path-editing tools work virtually identically to the pen and path-editing tools in Adobe Illustrator.

The Direct Selection and Path Component Selection tools (shortcut key A) allow you to select paths. Use the Direct Selection tool to select individual anchor points or segments. After clicking an anchor point or a segment, you can edit the path by clicking and dragging. The Path Component Selection tool selects entire paths with one click of the mouse.

You'll learn all about making and editing paths in Chapter 14.

The Type Tool

Photoshop 6's Type tool (shortcut key T) allows you to type text directly in your document. By switching modes in the Type tool's Options bar, you can create type in a layer or in a selection.

The Type tool works in conjunction with the Character and Paragraph palettes. The Character palette provides controls for formatting individual characters and type color. The Paragraph palette provides options for formatting paragraphs, as well commands that allow you to set justification and hyphenation. Type can also be converted to shapes (Layer > Type > Convert to Shape) or paths (Layer > Type > Create Work Path).

The Type tool is covered in Chapter 3 and in exercises throughout this book.

When layer-based type is output to PostScript printers or saved in DCS format, it can retain its vector information and thus can appear with sharp, crisp edges. Images with type saved in Photoshop EPS or DCS 1.0 or 2.0 format can retain vector information only when imported into other programs. If you import an EPS or DCS file into Photoshop, the vector information is rasterized (converted to a pixel-based image).

The Hand Tool

The Hand tool (shortcut key H) allows you to scroll through a document to view areas that don't fit in the Photoshop window. It allows more control than the window's scroll bars because you can click on the document and scroll in any direction. When any tool is activated, you can temporarily access the Hand tool by pressing and holding down the SPACEBAR on your keyboard.

The Zoom Tool

The Zoom tool (shortcut key Z) increases or decreases the magnification of an image. Dragging with the Zoom tool zooms in on the area that you click and drag over. If you press OPTION (ALT in Windows) with the Zoom tool selected, you can zoom out. If you have any tool selected, you can temporarily access the Zoom tool, as follows:

- To zoom in, press COMMAND (CTRL in Windows) and hold down the SPACEBAR while you click on your document.

- To zoom out, press OPTION (ALT) and hold down the SPACEBAR while you click on your document.

After zooming, you may need to use the Hand tool to reposition the area you zoomed in to. You will use the Hand and Zoom tools in the next chapter and throughout the book.

The Slicing Tools

The Slice tool (shortcut key K) allows you to slice up an image for Web output. When the sliced image is saved to disk, Photoshop or ImageReady divides the image into the separate slices and generates the HTML code to load the slices on a Web page. The separate images often load faster than a single image. Slices also can be used as rollovers on Web pages. Sharing the Slice tool's Toolbox location is the Slice Select tool, which allows you to select different sliced areas on your screen. Slices are discussed in Chapter 10.

The Annotation Tools

The Notes and Audio Annotation tools (shortcut key N), which share a Toolbox location, allow you to add annotations to documents. Notes can be used to provide comments about color-correcting or special effects.

The Notes tool creates textual notes on your screen in a floating layer above your images. When you print your document, the notes are not output.

The Audio Annotation tool is probably Photoshop's most unusual tool because it's the only one that can talk to you. Use it to provide audio notes about images. To create an audio annotation, you must have a microphone connected to your computer. First, activate the tool and then click in your image. In the dialog box that appears, click on the Start button to begin recording and then speak into the microphone attached to your computer. Click on the Stop button to end the recording session. (Mac users can click on Pause while recording and should click on Save when finished.)

An icon with a picture of a speaker represents the audio notation in the document. You can move it on your screen with the Move tool. If you wish to change the color of the audio notation icon, click in the color swatch in the Audio Annotation tool's Option bar. To clear all audio notations, click on the Clear All button in the tool's Options bar. To play back the audio notation, double-click on the audio notation icon.

The Color-Control Icons

 Just below the Hand and Zoom tools in the Toolbox are several color-control icons that allow you to view and switch colors:

- The Foreground Color and Background Color icons (the larger rectangular swatches) display the current foreground and background colors. If you click on either icon, Photoshop's Color Picker dialog box appears, allowing you to change either the foreground or background color. The Color Picker is explored in the chapter on the CD.

- Clicking on the Switch Colors icon (↰) changes the foreground color to the background color and vice versa. You can also press X on the keyboard to switch between the foreground and background colors.

- The Default Colors icon (▤) restores the default colors for the foreground color (black) and the background color (white). Pressing D on the keyboard also restores the default colors.

The Mode Icons

 Beneath the control-control icons in the Toolbox are the mode icons. The icon on the right represents the Quick Mask mode, which allows you to create, view, and edit a *mask* easily. This lets you view your work through a tinted overlay and edit areas in a cutout (similar to a *rubylith*—a red film that is used to shield objects in print production). The area outside the cutout is normally protected; the area inside is unprotected. Clicking on the Quick Mask mode icon (or pressing Q) turns on the masking function. Once you enter the Quick Mask mode, you can create a mask and edit its shape with the selection tools and painting tools.

 If you're unfamiliar with the concept of a mask, think of a painter laying down masking tape around an area so that he or she can paint there without harming surrounding areas. In Photoshop, working in the cutout allows you to refine your work without affecting areas beyond the cutout.

The icon on the left is the Standard mode icon. Clicking on this icon takes you out of the Quick Mask mode. Creating masks is discussed in Chapter 15.

The Screen-Display Icons

 The three screen-display icons beneath the mode icons at the bottom of the Toolbox change the window-display mode. The icon on the left represents the standard window. Clicking on the middle icon zooms the window out to occupy the full screen. Clicking on the icon on the right also zooms out to full-screen size, and it hides the menus as well. The keyboard shortcut for switching from one screen display to another is F.

The Graphics Editor Icon

 The Graphics Editor icon at the very bottom of the Toolbox allows you to jump to the default graphics editor application. This is usually Adobe ImageReady.

Photoshop's Floating Palettes

Now that you're familiar with the Toolbox, take a quick look at Photoshop's other floating palettes. Unlike other windows, palettes always float above your active window. This means that they are always accessible and never drop behind any open document windows. (Windows that are not palettes can drop behind other windows; when more than one document is open, clicking on a Photoshop window causes it to jump in front of all other document windows on the screen.)

 Previous versions of Photoshop included an Options palette and Brushes palette. The Options palette has been replaced by the Options bar, which provides options for tools. The Brushes palette now appears as the Brush pop-up menu in painting tools' Option bars.

Photoshop's palettes are accessed by clicking on the Window menu and then choosing Show Tools, Show Options, Show Brushes, Show Color, Show Swatches, Show Styles, Show Layers, Show Channels, Show Paths, Show Info, Show Navigator, Show History, or Show Actions. (If a palette is already open on screen, the menu choice for that palette switches from Show to Hide; for instance, Show Info changes to Hide Info.) The design of Photoshop's palettes and their ability to lock together into specific groups provide quick and easy access to commands and options that are frequently used. The following sections describe how to work with palettes and provide an introduction to each of the palettes.

 The Actions, Channels, Layers, Navigator, History, and Paths palettes can be resized. To resize a palette, click and drag on the resize box in the lower-right corner of the palette (click and drag on the palette's border in Windows).

Working with Palettes

By default, many Photoshop palettes are organized into palette groups. A palette group is essentially one window with several palettes in it. For instance, the Navigator and Info palettes open together in one palette group; the Color, Swatches, and Styles palettes in another. The individual palettes in each group are easily distinguished by a palette tab with the palette's name on it. To bring a palette to the front of a palette group, simply click on its tab.

> **Tip** *You can hide all palettes by pressing* TAB. *Press* TAB *again to view the palettes. Pressing* SHIFT-TAB *hides all palettes except for the Toolbox.*

You can also click and drag on a palette tab to move the palette from one group to another or to pull it out of a group to use it alone. Custom palette groups can also be created. For instance, if you wish to use the Info and Actions palettes together in a palette group, you can drag the Info palette out of its palette group and then drag the Actions palette out of its group. Next, drag the Info palette into the Actions palette. After the palettes are joined together, they remain as one palette group. The next time you choose Show Actions or Show Info from the Palettes submenu, your new palette group will open (with both palettes in it).

In Photoshop 6, you can not only join palettes but you can also "dock" one palette beneath group, as shown in Figures 1-5 and 1-6. You can also attach a palette to the Options bar, as described in the next section.

Certain features are common to all the palettes:

- The title bar, which you click and drag on to move the palette
- The close box in the upper-left corner (the X in the upper-right corner in Windows 98, Windows NT and Windows 2000) of the title bar, which closes the palette

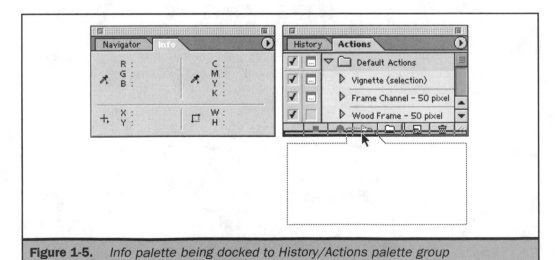

Figure 1-5.   *Info palette being docked to History/Actions palette group*

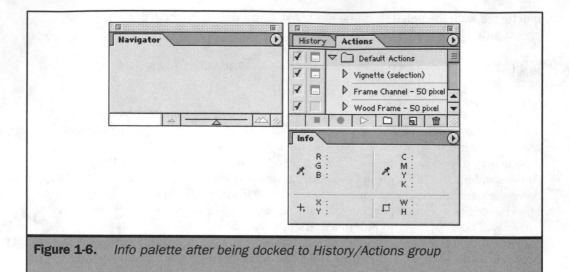

Figure 1-6. *Info palette after being docked to History/Actions group*

■ The expand/collapse box, which allows you to shrink a palette so that it occupies less room on your screen (so you can view more of your image), as shown here:

■ The palette's pop-up menu arrow below the expand/collapse box, which displays a menu of options, as shown here:

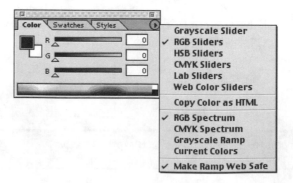

To shrink the palette to its smallest size, press OPTION *(*ALT*) and click on the expand/ collapse box or double-click on the palette's tab. After a palette shrinks, you can expand it again by clicking once on the expand/collapse box or by double-clicking on the palette's tab.*

The Options Bar

The Options bar is a palette that provides options for Photoshop's different tools. For instance, the Options bar for the Type tool, shown next, allows you to choose whether to create type in a layer or in a selection, as well as the font family, font style, font size, alignment, and other text settings.

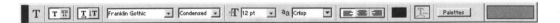

The Options bar is not only shaped differently than Photoshop's other palettes, but it also functions quite differently. It can be opened by double-clicking on a tool, as well as by choosing Window > Show Options. There is no close box on the Options bar.

To attach a palette to the Options bar, separate it from its palette group, and then drag it to the dark rectangular area at the far right of the bar. The palette locks into the Options bar, where it can be accessed by clicking on it, as shown here:

The Color Palette

In the Color palette, you can change the foreground or background color by using sliders based on Web colors or color models such as RGB and CMYK or by clicking on the color spectrum bar at the bottom of the palette. The Color palette pop-up menu can be used to switch to sliders based on different color models and to change the color spectrum bar to show only Web-safe colors. Using the Color palette is discussed in the color theory chapter on the CD.

The Swatches Palette

The Swatches palette is used for quickly picking a foreground or background color by clicking on a swatch. The Swatches palette pop-up menu allows swatches to be added to the palette, saved on disk, and reloaded. You can even load a palette of Web-safe color swatches from the Color Swatches folder. Using the Swatches palette is discussed in the color theory chapter on the CD.

The Styles Palette

The Styles palette is filled with predefined layer styles. Many of the styles provide three-dimensional bevels and unusual color or pattern effects. The Photoshop package includes several styles that can be loaded into the palette, such as text effects, glass buttons, and image effects. To apply a style, simply create or select a layer in the Layers palette and click on the style in the Style palette.

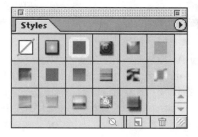

The Layers Palette

As mentioned earlier in the chapter, a layer is like a clear plastic overlay that can be placed over the background electronic canvas. Objects in one layer can be easily moved independently of objects in another layer. This provides an extremely efficient means of compositing images together and previewing their effects.

The Layers palette allows you to create new layers, move from layer to layer, rearrange layers, and group and merge layers. The Opacity pop-up slider in the Layers palette provides a simple means of blending one layer with another. The palette's blending mode pop-up menu (to the left of the Opacity setting) provides special effects for blending layers together. For instance, using the Darken mode, you can replace lighter image areas in one layer with darker image areas from another layer (blending modes are described in Chapter 5). Layers are covered in exercises throughout this book and are discussed in detail in Chapters 16 and 17.

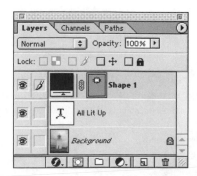

In the Layers palette, the word Background *appears as your base layer if you create a new file with the Contents radio button set to White or Background Color. If you choose the Transparent Contents radio button instead, Layer 1 appears as the first layer. In all layers other than the Background, areas without color are transparent.*

The Info Palette

If you move the mouse pointer over colored or gray areas, the Info palette functions as a *densitometer* (an instrument used by printers to measure color density), displaying color values as you move over them. By default, the Info palette displays the RGB (Red, Green, and Blue) and CMYK (Cyan, Magenta, Yellow, and Black) color components. For instance, a dark red might be displayed as R: 141, G: 55, B: 57 in the RGB section of the palette; in the CMYK section of the palette, it might be displayed as C: 13%, M: 88%, Y: 72%, K: 18%.

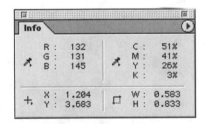

You can change the display of the color components by clicking on either of the two eyedropper icons. After you click on the eyedropper, you can choose to display color components according to RGB, CMYK, HSB, Lab, and Web color modes or Grayscale. You can also display total ink coverage and layer opacity. Color modes are discussed in the chapter on the CD.

The Info palette also displays the X coordinate (horizontal) and Y coordinate (vertical) of the mouse pointer. Move the mouse pointer across the screen, and you'll see the X and Y values in the palette change. If you wish to change the measurement units for the mouse coordinates displayed in the Info palette, access the Info palette's pop-up menu or click on the tiny + in the palette. The mouse coordinates can be displayed in inches, points, pixels, centimeters, or percentages.

 When you use the Color Sampler tool, the Info palette displays the color values of the sampled areas.

The Paths Palette

The Paths palette allows you to edit and control paths created with the Pen tool. The Paths palette's pop-up menu can be used to outline or fill paths with colors and to change paths into selections. You can also assign names to paths and duplicate and delete paths using different palette options. The Pen tool and Paths palette are covered in Chapter 14.

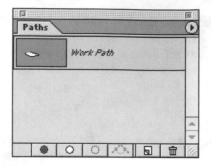

The Channels Palette

A *channel* is similar to a plate in commercial printing. The Channels palette allows you to easily view a channel or edit an image in a channel.

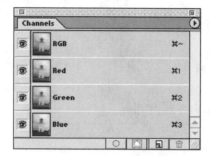

The Channels palette displays different channels, depending on the current file's image mode. If you are working in an RGB color file, the Channels palette displays the separate channels for each of the Red, Green, and Blue color components of the image, along with the RGB composite. If you are viewing a CMYK color file, the Channels palette displays the separate channels for Cyan, Magenta, Yellow, and Black, along with the CMYK composite. For example, if you wanted to alter only the Yellow component of a CMYK image, you could click on Yellow in the Channels palette and then make your changes.

The Channels palette pop-up menu allows you to create and name alpha channels to use as masks. See Chapter 15 for an in-depth discussion of using channels and masks.

The Navigator Palette

The Navigator palette allows you to zoom in and out quickly to specific image areas. The palette features a miniature version of your image and a view box that shows the area of your document that appears on the screen. As you drag the view box, the image on the screen changes to display only the area within the view box. To zoom out while dragging the view box, press COMMAND (*CTRL* in Windows).

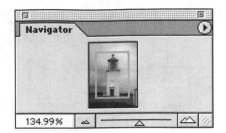

To change the zoom percentage, you can click and drag on the sliders in the palette, click on a mountain icon at either end of the slider, or enter a specific zoom percentage by editing the number in the lower-left corner of the palette. Using the palette, you can zoom from 19% to 1600%.

The Actions Palette

The Actions palette allows you to record Photoshop actions and play them back. Using the palette, you can create a sequence of actions that can be played back and applied to different images. Actions can be edited by dragging an action up or down in a palette. You can even assign actions to function keys. The Actions palette is discussed in detail in Chapter 11.

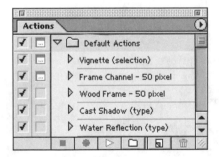

The History Palette

The History palette is Photoshop's answer to user requests for multiple "undos." As you work with Photoshop, the History palette lists all of the changes you've made to an image while working on it. (The number of steps is limited by the amount of scratch disk space available and the maximum history states setting in the History Options dialog box.) If you wish to revert to a previous stage, you simply click on the step in the History palette. At crucial image-editing stages, you can also use the palette to take a *snapshot* of your image. You can then quickly return to the snapshot version of the image by clicking on the snapshot in the palette.

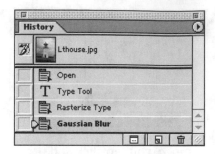

The History palette further encourages experimentation when used with the History Brush. After you click on the History Brush column alongside a historical step in the palette, you can paint effects with the History Brush using different blending modes. Chapters 6 and 11 discuss the History palette and History Brush.

Storing and Retrieving Files

Although Photoshop requires you to think like a painter, it doesn't allow you to work exactly like one. When your work is done, you can't just turn out the lights in the studio and go home for the day. If you wish to return to your Photoshop work for another session, you need to save your file.

Saving a File

Saving a file in Photoshop is quite similar to saving a file in any other Mac or Windows program. Here are the steps for saving your work after you've made changes to a file:

1. Select File > Save. The Save As dialog box appears the first time you save your file.

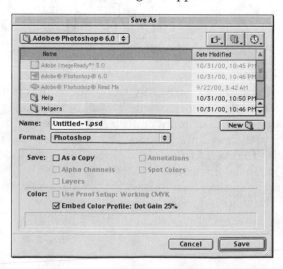

2. In the Name text box, you'll see Untitled-1 (unless you named your new file when you created it). Type a name for your file. (When Untitled-1 is highlighted, you can replace it with the name of your file when you type.)

3. Notice that the Format box (the Save As box in Windows) displays Photoshop, which is the default file format. You can change to another file format or back to Photoshop (if necessary), by clicking on this pop-up menu.

4. Look at the folder icons in the dialog box to see where you're saving your file. Make sure that you are saving it to a location that you will remember.

5. When you're ready to save the file, click on the Save button. After Photoshop saves your file, its name appears in the title bar of your document window.

As you work on any Photoshop file, you can save as often as you like by choosing File > Save or by pressing COMMAND-S. (*CTRL-S*). Be aware, though, that the Save command always replaces the previous version of your file. If you wish to make a copy of your file, you should use the Save As command.

 System crashes, however rare, do occur. To avoid losing hours of your hard work in the electronic void, save your work frequently.

Using Save As

The Save As command opens the Save As dialog box so that you can save your file under a new name or in a different location. This lets you create different versions of a file or save it to another hard drive or storage device as a backup version.

To save another version of your file, choose File > Save As. The Save As dialog box appears, in which you'll see the original file name waiting to be renamed. Enter a new name or choose a new location for your file and then click on the Save button (the OK button in Windows).

 Mac users who are working with PC files may wish to save their files with PC file extensions. To add file extensions, choose Edit > Preferences > Saving Files. In the Append File Extension pop-up menu, choose either Always or Ask When Saving. You can also add an extension by pressing OPTION *when clicking in the Format pop-up menu.*

As you work on new versions of your practice file, you can continue to use Save As to rename your file so that you can always return to any previous version of your file.

Using the Revert Command

Photoshop also offers you the option to revert to a previous version of a file. If you would like to do this, choose File > Revert. The Revert alert box appears, and in a few seconds, the document on your screen is replaced with the previously saved version.

 The Revert command is irreversible. Once you revert to a previous version, you can't return to the version you were working on when you selected the command.

Once you've saved your file and determined that the image on your screen is exactly the way you want it, you'll probably want to output it to your printer. The next section covers printing and Photoshop's page preview feature.

Previewing and Printing Pages

Before you print a document, it's often a good idea to preview your output, particularly because graphic images take a long time to be processed by most printers. Although Photoshop does not provide a print preview of your image, it does let you preview page orientation and other specific printing options, such as crop and registration marks.

Previewing Your File

To preview your file, click on the file size number in the lower-left corner of the Photoshop window. A preview of your page's orientation—landscape or portrait—pops up in the lower-left corner of the window.

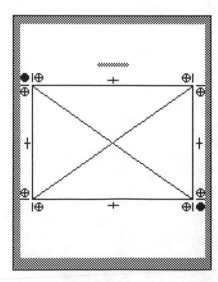

The preview can also show labels, crop marks, registration marks, calibration bars, negatives, and emulsion type. These are all options that can be selected (after a file is saved) in the Page Setup dialog box, accessed through the File menu.

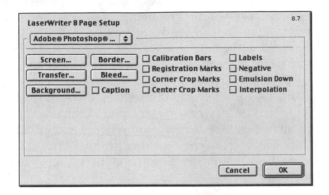

If you click on the file size number while pressing the OPTION (*ALT* in Windows) key, Photoshop will display information about your file's size, resolution, and number of channels.

```
    Width: 504 pixels (7 inches)
   Height: 360 pixels (5 inches)
 Channels:   3 (RGB Color)
Resolution:  72 pixels/inch
```

Printing Your File

To print your document, select File > Print. The Print dialog box that appears contains standard Mac or Windows print options.

The Selection option in the Print area section allows you to print only an area that is selected on screen. If no area is selected, this option will be dimmed. The Source Space and Print Space sections of the dialog box allow you to print using Photoshop 6's color management features. Using these options is discussed in Appendix B. Photoshop's color management features are discussed in Chapter 2.

Using Preferences to Change the Defaults

Changing the Photoshop default settings lets you customize your Photoshop environment to make it more comfortable for you to use and possibly save you some time. The settings that you can change are in the Preferences dialog box.

Although most Preferences settings are simple in concept, some might be confusing until you've had a chance to work with Photoshop.

Most of Photoshop's Preferences options are found by choosing Edit > Preferences > General. These general preferences cover a wide variety of settings, from how the screen displays imported images to whether your computer beeps when it has completed a task. For example, if you would like all palettes and dialog boxes to return to the positions you left them in, choose Edit > Preferences > General and select the Save Palette Locations option in the Preferences dialog box.

Many other Preferences settings are available in various categories, which you can select from the pop-up menu at the top of the Preferences dialog box or directly from the Edit menu. For example, to change the Photoshop ruler's measuring units, select Edit > Preferences > Units & Rulers. In the Preferences dialog box, you can change the measuring units to pixels, inches, centimeters, points, picas, or percentages. The Column Size settings allow you to specify a column width and gutter as a measuring unit. If you are using points, you can choose either the PostScript (72 points/inch) or Traditional (72.27 points/inch) setting by clicking on the appropriate radio button in the Preferences dialog box.

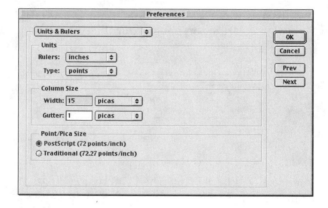

Note *In the New, Image Size, Canvas Size, and Crop Tool dialog boxes, the columns measurement unit can be used in place of inches, points, pixels, or centimeters. This can be helpful when you're working with images that will be placed in columns in page layout programs such as QuarkXPress and Adobe PageMaker.*

Another example of a Preferences setting is the appearance of the transparent background. By default, a checkerboard grid pattern represents the clear area. If you would like to switch to a different representation, choose Edit > Preferences > Transparency & Gamut and change the Transparency settings.

Chapter 2

Using Photoshop's Color Management System

One of the most frustrating aspects about digital imaging is the unpredictability of color. Countless Photoshop users have created design projects, only to find that printed colors or colors viewed on a Web page don't match what they saw on their screen during image editing. To ensure that the colors you see on screen match printed colors and colors displayed on other monitors, it's important to understand how Photoshop manages colors. Photoshop 6.0's color management system provides a major update over previous Photoshop versions.

Photoshop 6.0 embeds industry standard International Color Consortium (ICC) color profiles in images. The profiles are designed to help provide consistent colors no matter what scanner or monitor is used. Working with devices such as scanners and monitors that use profiles helps provide a workflow that results in consistent color.

To help provide better color workflow, Photoshop 6.0 (unlike Photoshop 4 and earlier versions) does not use your monitor's color space as the image-editing color space. Instead, Photoshop 6.0 allows you to choose an image-editing RGB color space that is separate from your monitor's RGB color space. This helps ensure that the colors in your Photoshop file remain consistent when loaded on another system, computer platform, or application, regardless of what monitor is being used.

This chapter describes how to set up Photoshop's color management options. You may wish to start using Photoshop immediately and delve into the subject of color management at a later time; however, we recommend that you return to this chapter before you begin sharing files with other Photoshop users or working on projects that will be output on a printing press.

Getting a Quick Start to Color Management

If you're in a hurry to get started, here are the important steps you need to take to set up your system. Each of the steps is discussed in detail later in the chapter.

1. Calibrate your monitor using Photoshop's Adobe Gamma utility. (Macintosh users updating from version 4.0 or earlier should not use the old Gamma control panel.)

2. Open the Color Settings dialog box by choosing Edit > Color Settings.

3. In the Settings pop-up menu, choose a setting that describes the type of work you will be doing. Most U.S. Photoshop users will pick either U.S. Prepress Defaults or Web Graphics Defaults. After you choose a setting, the other options in the dialog box change to correspond with your choice.

4. Click on OK.

If you follow the steps listed above, you'll be off to a consistently colorful future when using Photoshop. For a more detailed description of Photoshop's color management system and the options in the Color Settings dialog box, read on; otherwise, you may wish to skip ahead to Chapter 3.

Understanding ICC Profiles

As mentioned at the beginning of this chapter, the colors that you view on screen may not match printed colors or colors other Photoshop users view on their screens. To address this issue, software and hardware manufacturers formed the ICC. The ICC created a series of specifications for creating *profiles* to describe colors. It also created specifications for embedding *tags* in files with profile information in them. For instance, software included with a scanner may be able to embed a scanned file with a profile that describes the scanner's color properties (and possibly its idiosyncrasies). If the scanner's software tags the file with an ICC profile, Photoshop can read the ICC color tag.

When you save files, Photoshop can embed the file with a color tag. One aspect of the tag describes the *color space* you are working in, so that other Photoshop users can load the file and view colors that match those in the file, no matter what type of monitor they are using.

When you follow the steps for calibrating your monitor and choosing color spaces, Photoshop can properly tag the files you create. Your first step to ensure color consistency is to calibrate your monitor.

Calibrating Your Monitor

In order for the colors you see on screen to match those on the printed page as closely as possible, your monitor needs to be properly calibrated. You can calibrate your monitor by using the Adobe Gamma utility that comes with Photoshop or a third-party calibration package.

 Manufacturers such as Kodak and Radius create hardware and software calibration devices. Many users may get better results calibrating their monitors with third-party calibration hardware and software than with Adobe's Gamma utility. If you use a third-party utility, you may need to specify your monitor in Apple's ColorSync control panel.

Preparing for the Calibration Process

Before you begin to calibrate your monitor, take these steps:

1. Make sure your computer's screen display has been turned on for half an hour or more. This stabilizes your monitor.

2. Adjust the room lighting, if necessary, so it is at the level you will maintain while working on the computer. Remember that if you are working near a

window, colors may appear different, depending on the amount of sunlight entering your room.

3. Adjust your monitor's brightness and contrast to the desired levels using its controls. Once the brightness and contrast are set, you may wish to put tape across the monitor's knobs so they can't be changed.

4. Set your monitor's background color to gray. This will prevent background colors from altering your color perception while you are calibrating and while working in Photoshop. (For instance, if the background color on your screen is blue, yellows might appear to have a greenish shade around them.) Mac users with System 9 should open the Desktop Pictures control panel, click on the Pattern button, click on the right arrow to reach the gray pattern, and then click on the Set Desktop button. Windows users should choose Start > Settings > Control Panel, double-click on the Display icon, click on the Appearance tab, choose Desktop from the Item pop-up menu, and change the color to gray.

When a document is open on your screen, you can click on the middle icon at the bottom of the Photoshop toolbox (full-screen mode) to see images against a neutral background.

Now you're ready to use the calibration program. The next section describes how to run the Adobe Gamma utility. If you're using a third-party calibration system, follow the instructions that came with it.

The Adobe Gamma utility does not work with LCD monitor displays.

Running the Adobe Gamma Utility

After you've followed the preparatory steps outlined in the previous section, you can follow these steps to begin the actual calibration process using the Adobe Gamma utility:

1. Start the Gamma utility. Mac users should click on the Apple menu in the upper-left corner of your screen, choose the control panels menu, and select Adobe Gamma. Windows users should choose Start > Settings > Control Panel and double-click on the Adobe Gamma icon. Alternatively, Windows users can run the program by following this path: Program Files\Common Files\Adobe\ Calibration\Adobe Gamma.

2. In the Adobe Gamma dialog box, click on Step by Step Assistant, if it is not already selected. To continue, click on the Next button.

3. Load a monitor profile. Both Mac and Windows users can click on the Load button and load a profile if they wish to choose one that is different from what already appears in the dialog box. Next, enter a new name for the profile in the Description field. To continue, click on the Next button.

Note *Mac users who have designated a monitor in their ColorSync control panel will see the name of their monitor profile in the Adobe Gamma Assistant dialog box. Windows 98 users who have already set a default ICC monitor profile should see that profile in the dialog box.*

4. In the next dialog box, follow the instructions to set brightness and contrast settings. Click on Next to continue.

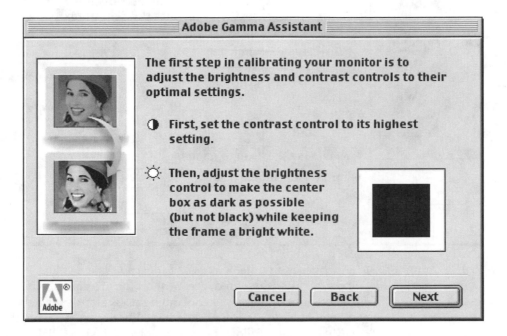

5. The Adobe Gamma Assistant now attempts to display the phosphors your monitor uses to create colors. Many Apple, SuperMac, and Radius monitors manufactured by Sony use Trinitron as their Phosphors setting. If your monitor is not on the list, try to obtain the proper red, green, and blue chromacity coordinates from your monitor's manufacturer. To enter these, choose Custom from the Phosphors pop-up menu. Click on Next to continue.

6. In the next dialog box, adjust the slider to establish the current gamma, as described in the on-screen instructions. If you prefer, you can turn off the single gamma settings and make the adjustments to red, green, and blue gamma settings. The Gamma pop-up menu should automatically show the

system, and the box beside it should show 1.8 for Mac users and 2.2 for Windows users. (The Gamma pop-up menu does not appear on all Windows systems.) Click on Next to continue.

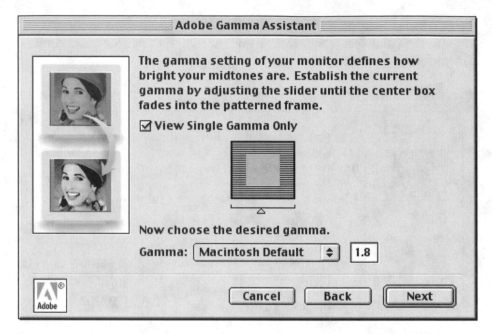

7. The Gamma Assistant chooses a white point. The *white point* is the color measure of white when the intensity of red, green, and blue are equal. For instance, 6500°K is the color temperature of cool daylight. (K stands for Kelvin, a temperature measurement scale.) If you wish to have Photoshop measure the white point, click on Measure and follow the instructions in the next dialog box. Once the white point is selected, click on Next. Most users should leave the Adjusted White Point to the Same as Hardware setting. Click on Next to go to the final dialog box.

8. Gamma Assistant gives your monitor's ICC profile a name. Click on Finish to save the profile on disk.

 Most monitors change over time. For best results, you should check your monitor's calibration periodically.

After you've calibrated your monitor, your next steps are to choose color settings that tag your Photoshop image with a profile and determine how RGB images are converted to CMYK Color and Grayscale modes. You perform these tasks through Photoshop's Color Settings dialog box.

Choosing Color Settings

Once you've calibrated your monitor, you can proceed to entering specific settings in Photoshop's Color Settings dialog box, shown in Figure 2-1. These settings help ensure that you are using the correct profiles for different Photoshop color modes: RGB, CMYK, and Grayscale. To open the Color Settings dialog box, choose Edit > Color Settings.

To avoid frustration, you should take a few minutes to explore Photoshop's Color Settings dialog box. This dialog box not only determines how colors appear on your screen, but also provides a means of managing colors of files that will pass from one Photoshop user to another. By properly setting your color working space, you can help ensure consistent color as an image passes from scanner to a Photoshop user on one computer platform, to another Photoshop user on a different computer platform, to the printed page or the Web.

Your best starting point is to choose a preset color management option, which allows you to pick a workflow, such as outputting to an offset printing press or outputting to the

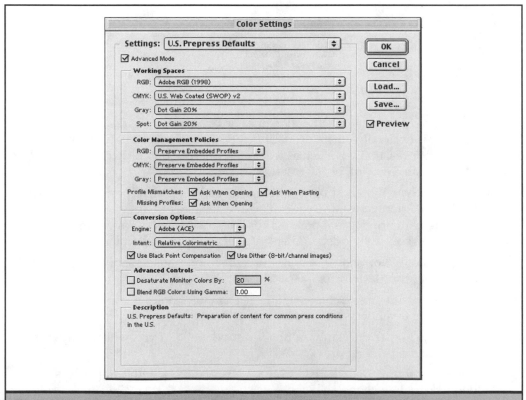

Figure 2-1. *The Color Settings dialog box, with U.S. Prepress Defaults settings*

Web. Once you choose a workflow, the profiles for an RGB work space, as well as settings that determine how RGB images are previewed and converted to CMYK and Grayscale modes, are chosen for you. You can use these as a beginning point before customizing the color settings for your own specific needs.

 To see a description of a choice in the Color Settings dialog box, move the mouse pointer over it as you work. The description appears at the bottom of the dialog box.

Choosing a Preset Color Management Option

Select a preset color management from the Settings pop-up menu at the top of the Color Settings dialog box.

You have the following choices:

- The Color Management Off option does not save color profiles with documents. Select this option if you are primarily working with applications that create on-screen presentations, such as Adobe Premiere, Adobe AfterEffects, Macromedia Director, or Microsoft PowerPoint.

- The ColorSync Workflow option (Mac only) uses ColorSync profiles specified in the Mac's ColorSync control panel. You may wish to use this system if you are working with printing and prepress applications created by other software vendors as well as by Adobe. (Users must be working with ColorSync 3.0 or later.)

- The Emulate Photoshop 4 option simulates color management of Photoshop 4 and earlier for Macintosh.

- The Europe Prepress Defaults option is a suitable choice if you will be outputting to a European printing press.

- The Japan Prepress Defaults option is a good choice if you will be outputting to a Japanese printing press.

- The Photoshop 5 Default Spaces option lets you work with color spaces as defined in Photoshop 5.

- The U.S. Prepress Defaults option is the one you should select if you will be outputting to an offset printing press in the U.S.

■ The Web Graphics Defaults option is the one you should pick if you will primarily be creating Web graphics.

After you select an option from the Settings pop-up menu, the other options in the dialog box are filled in automatically.

Choosing Color Working Spaces

Perhaps the most important settings in the Color Settings dialog box are the Working Spaces options. The profiles assigned to an image in the Working Spaces section determine several aspects of your colors:

■ The relationship between the colors on your screen and their numeric values

■ How colors appear in new documents and documents that are not tagged with profiles

■ Which profile will be embedded in an image when you save it

Even though the working spaces are automatically set when you choose a workflow in the Settings pop-up menu (as described in the previous section), you might wish to change a working space setting. For instance, even though you choose the U.S. Prepress Defaults setting, you may wish to change the CMYK working space setting from coated to noncoated paper.

Setting the RGB Working Space

Your monitor creates colors by combining red, green, and blue (RGB) color values. A computer monitor cannot actually display every single RGB color. The phosphors, white point, and internal dynamics of your computer monitor determine exactly which colors in the RGB color gamut (range of colors) you can see.

Various manufacturers and professional organizations have established standards for different types of digital and video color work. The standards use the monitor's phosphor settings and white point to define an RGB color space. For instance, the color space of broadcast television in the U.S. is different from the color space of European television. The color space for High Definition Television is different from both the American and European broadcast standards.

If you are creating images for video as opposed to print, you'll want your monitor to display colors specifically geared toward your final output. Furthermore, since different monitors can display different RGB color spaces, it makes sense to attempt to work in a specific color space rather than the color space provided by your monitor manufacturer.

Visually, the RGB workspace appears like a triangle. You might find it easier to conceptualize RGB color space as the colors that fit within a triangular shape. The larger the color space, the larger the triangle.

Thus, the key to successful color work in Photoshop 6.0 is to use an RGB work space that encompasses the colors you need to use. This is particularly important for those Photoshop users who will be outputting images for print. The colors you see on your screen are determined by the RGB color space you choose. The colors created during a conversion to CMYK Color mode from RGB Color mode are influenced by the RGB color space. For instance, the color gamut of Adobe RGB is greater than the default sRGB workspace. If you convert from RGB to CMYK, Adobe RGB provides better results than sRGB. Therefore, if you will be working on projects that will be output for print, you will probably want to use Adobe RGB.

| Note | *In early versions of Photoshop, there was no option to select an RGB working space. You edited your images in the RGB space provided by your monitor. This presented problems with color consistency. Photoshop 6.0's RGB working space settings help to keep colors consistent on different monitors.* |

Here are a few important points to remember about choosing an RGB color space:

- It's best to choose one RGB color space and not change the settings. If you change RGB color space and load an image you've saved in another color space, the color values may change when you load the image and resave it. If you wish to have Photoshop alert you when one color space is being loaded into another, see the "Setting Color Management Policies" section later in this chapter.

- If you change the settings of the RGB color space while an image is open, the colors may change on screen, but the actual image data in the file will not change. When Photoshop saves the file, it will still save the image with the original profile. If you wish to change the color profile of an image on screen and the embedded color tag, see the "Converting Color Spaces of Open Images" section later in this chapter.

- Once you have chosen an RGB color workspace, you can have everyone in your work group choose it as his or her common color space for work.

The following RGB workspace choices are commonly used by Photoshop users. Note that some of these choices are available only if the Advanced Mode checkbox above the Working Spaces section is selected.

sRGB   Standard RGB (sRBG) is Photoshop's default setting. It is also the choice designated if you choose Web Graphics Defaults in the Settings pop-up menu. sRGB was chosen as the default because a variety of hardware and software manufacturers, most notably Microsoft and Hewlett-Packard, endorse it. Some digital-imaging industry experts expect it to be the default color space of desktop scanners and low- to mid-range printers.

Since the sRGB color space is supposed to represent the standard PC monitor, it's probably a good choice for those Photoshop users who primarily create graphics for the Web. Photoshop artists who will be working with images that will be printed should choose an RGB color space that provides a wider gamut of colors. For instance, high percentages of printable cyan cannot be represented in the sRGB color space.

Adobe RGB 1998   Formerly SMPTE-240M in Photoshop 5.0, Adobe RGB 1998 is the preset RGB working space if you choose U.S. Prepress Defaults in the Settings pop-up menu. It is the recommended choice for Photoshop users who are creating graphics for printed output. The color used by Adobe RGB gamut is wider than sRGB. The downside of Adobe RGB is that this color space includes more colors that are beyond the CMYK printing gamut than sRGB or ColorMatch RGB.

Apple RGB   Apple RGB was the color space for the previous version of Photoshop. The color space is based on Apple's 13-inch monitor with Trinitron phosphors. The color gamut is not larger than that of sRGB, but it can be useful for creating images for Mac intranets, multimedia, or Web sites particularly devoted to Mac users.

CIE RGB   CIE RGB is the color space specified by the Commission Internationale d'Eclairage. This option provides a large color gamut, but high values of cyan are not displayed. If you choose this option, you'll find that many images are not displayed properly, because Photoshop cannot handle images with such a wide color gamut.

ColorMatch RGB   ColorMatch RGB is the color space based on Radius PressView monitors. If you are working with PressView-based equipment, ColorMatch should provide a wide enough gamut to handle your prepress needs. ColorMatch RGB is also a suitable color space for prepress work.

NTSC (1953)   NTSC (1953) is the color space for the original NTSC television standard. It generally is not used because it has been replaced by the SMPTE-C standard.

PAL/SECAM   PAL/SECAM is the color space used for European broadcast television. If your work will be output to video for European broadcast television, you probably should choose PAL/SECAM.

SMPTE-C   SMPTE-C is the color space used for U.S. broadcast television. If your work will be output to video for U.S. broadcast television, you should consider using SMPTE-C.

Wide Gamut RGB   Wide Gamut RGB provides a very broad range of colors. This color space is probably too broad for most Photoshop users, because the color space encompasses many colors that cannot be printed, as well as colors that cannot be displayed properly on computer monitors.

Monitor RGB   Monitor RGB uses the same color space defined by your monitor as the image-editing workspace. This color space is not recommended, because colors will appear differently on different monitors.

Custom   The Custom choice allows you to create your own RGB color space. This can be handy if you know your scanner's RGB color space and wish to re-create that color space in Photoshop. You may also see postings at different Web sites for custom RGB color spaces that attempt to improve on the prebuilt color spaces in Photoshop. When you select Custom, you can choose a gamma, a white point, and primaries for your color space.

Setting the CMYK Working Space

Just as the RGB working space choice sets an RGB color space, your CMYK working space choice sets a CMYK color space for images that will be printed. In CMYK images, colors are created from different combinations of cyan, magenta, yellow, and black (the same colors used by printing presses to create color using the four-color process). If you are not going to be creating CMYK color images or converting RGB color images to CMYK color, you do not need to change the CMYK working space setting in the Color Settings dialog box.

The default CMYK working space choice designated if you choose either U.S. Prepress Defaults or Web Graphics Defaults from the Settings pop-up menu is U.S. Web Coated (SWOP) v2. This choice assumes 300 percent total ink coverage, with coated stock, and provides a good conversion from RGB to CMYK for offset printing on coated stock. However, if you are outputting to a Kodak proofing or another printing system for proofs, you may wish to choose another CMYK working space.

Note	*The word Web in U.S. Web Coated designates web offset printing. It refers to a roll of paper on a press, rather than individual sheets. It has nothing to do with the World Wide Web.*

The CMYK pop-up menu in the Working Spaces section of the Color Settings dialog box offers the other CMYK working space choices.

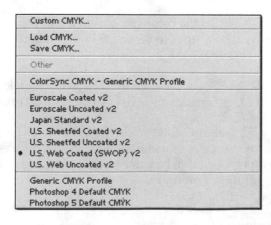

These choices are straightforward—pick the one that is appropriate for the printing system you plan to use. For example, if your images will be printed using the Kodak SWOP proofer on uncoated paper, choose Kodak SWOP Proofer CMYK-Coated Stocks.

If you wish to create your own working space, choose Custom CMYK from the CMYK pop-up menu. It's also useful to take a look at the options for a custom CMYK working space if you wish to understand how color settings determine CMYK colors. When you select Custom CMYK, the Custom CMYK dialog box appears, as shown in Figure 2-2.

The default settings are for the SWOP (Coated) CMYK working space. You can rename the working space in the Name text box and then choose other settings.

 You should not change any values in the Custom CMYK dialog box without first consulting your print shop. For now, you can explore the available settings discussed here, but when you're finished, be sure to click on Cancel in the dialog box to exit it without changing any settings.

Ink Colors   Click on the Ink Colors pop-up menu (shown on the following page) to view the other ink choices available.

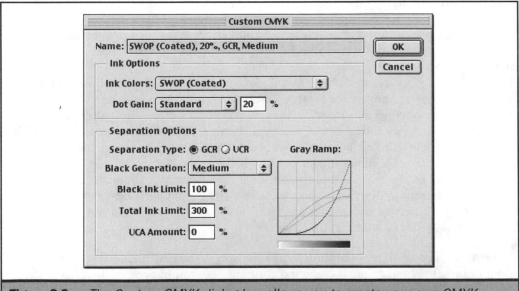

Figure 2-2.   *The Custom CMYK dialog box allows you to create your own CMYK working space*

```
Custom...
Other
AD-LITHO (Newsprint)
Dainippon Ink
Eurostandard (Coated)
Eurostandard (Newsprint)
Eurostandard (Uncoated)
✓ SWOP (Coated)
SWOP (Newsprint)
SWOP (Uncoated)
Toyo Inks (Coated Web Offset)
Toyo Inks (Coated)
Toyo Inks (Dull Coated)
Toyo Inks (Uncoated)
```

Choosing one of the SWOP settings means you are choosing inks and papers according to these specifications. If none of the colors suit your needs, you can select Custom and enter custom ink color settings in the Ink Colors dialog box.

Dot Gain   After you make a choice in the Ink Colors pop-up menu, the value in the Dot Gain field is updated automatically. The Dot Gain field indicates the percentage of dot gain expected on a printing press. As long as you know the printing process you will be using, you generally won't need to change the value in the Dot Gain field.

Dot gain is the *bleed*, or spreading, of the ink that occurs on paper when an image is printed on a printing press. Dot gain is caused by halftone dots that print larger or smaller than their actual size on film or on the printing plate. This unavoidable phenomenon is most noticeable in midtones and shadow areas of printed images, where the halftone dots are the largest. The degree of dot gain is determined primarily by the printing paper.

When Photoshop converts to CMYK Color, it adjusts CMYK percentages in the converted image to compensate for dot gain. The percentage is measured in terms of the ink increase beyond the size of midtone halftone dots in the film output from the image setter. Photoshop then takes the dot gain value and creates a "power" curve that it uses to calculate dot gain in other areas besides midtones. In general, higher dot gain percentages result in a lighter final separated image.

If you wish to see a visual representation of how much dot gain compensation is applied to different image areas, choose Curves in the Dot Gain pop-up menu in the Custom CMYK dialog box. Editing this curve is described in the "Setting the Grayscale Working Space" section later in this chapter.

Separation Type   The Separation Type selection in the Custom CMYK dialog box controls how the black plate is created during the separation process. In most cases, the default setting should provide good results.

Cyan, magenta, and yellow can theoretically produce all of the colors needed for commercial printing. Unfortunately, however, when the three colors overprint, ink impurities produce a muddy brown color instead of pure black. To remedy this, a black plate is added to increase contrast and produce blacker blacks. When black is added, levels of cyan, magenta, and yellow can be reduced to enhance printing quality. The two primary techniques used to substitute black for process colors are UCR (Under Color Removal) and GCR (Gray Component Replacement).

The decision to use either GCR or UCR in Photoshop is often determined by paper stock and printing requirements. GCR is generally used for coated stock, and UCR is typically used for uncoated stock.

In UCR separation, levels of cyan, magenta, and yellow are subtracted from gray and shadow areas and replaced with an appropriate amount of black. In GCR separation (Photoshop's default), levels of cyan, magenta, and yellow are subtracted from both gray and colored areas. To compensate for the removal of one or all three of the colors when GCR is chosen, an appropriate amount of black is added.

The basic theory underlying the GCR system is that one of the three process inks (cyan, magenta, or yellow) often is the gray component of a color. The gray component is the ink that lightens or darkens; the other two inks provide most of the color. When GCR is applied, the gray component ink is reduced and black is added. For instance, consider a digitized image of green grass that is primarily composed of cyan and yellow, with a small percentage of magenta darkening the image. During the separation process, if the GCR option is selected, a portion of the magenta is reduced and replaced with black. Theoretically, GCR can result in better gray balance and better reproduction of saturated colors; however, it may also remove some details from darker areas.

Gray Ramp and Black Generation   The Gray Ramp grid in the Custom CMYK dialog box (Figure 2-2) provides a visual representation of how the process inks produce neutral or gray colors based on the settings in the dialog box. The x-axis charts the color value, from 0 to 100 percent. The gray bar depicts the actual shade of gray, from white to black. The y-axis charts the ink that will be used to produce the gray value.

The best way to understand how the Gray Ramp grid works is to see what happens when you turn off the black plate while the GCR option is enabled. To turn off the black plate, select None in the Black Generation pop-up menu. This menu controls the amount of black substituted in the image when the GCR option is used.

As soon as you click on None, the Gray Ramp grid changes, showing you that the grays will be produced with approximately equal amounts of cyan, magenta, and yellow, but no black. If you use None as the setting and convert from RGB to CMYK, no black plate is generated.

Now click on Medium in the Black Generation pop-up menu. The Gray Ramp grid shows that cyan, magenta, and yellow levels are reduced, with black used to help produce grays starting in areas just lighter than the image's midtones. Switch among the choices in the Black Generation menu, and you'll see that as more black is added, the more the color inks are reduced. If you choose Maximum and convert from RGB to CMYK, black and grays are created from the black plate. This setting is commonly used when outputting images that contain large amounts of black.

To see how the UCR option affects the Gray Ramp grid, click on the UCR radio button for Separation Type. Notice that the black ink is barely used in midtone areas, and the appropriate process colors are increased in these areas.

The Custom option in the Black Generation pop-up menu lets you manually control the generation of the black plate. When you choose Custom, the Black Generation dialog box appears, in which you can customize black generation by clicking and dragging on a curve. After you adjust the curve and click on OK, the cyan, magenta, and yellow levels are changed according to the black curve.

Before continuing, if you have changed the Black Generation menu selection, return it now to the default setting, Medium. In most situations, Medium provides good results when you convert from RGB to CMYK.

Ink Limits   The Black Ink Limit field in the Custom CMYK dialog box (Figure 2-2) allows you to tell Photoshop the maximum ink density that your commercial printer's press can support. The default value is 100%, which means that the darkest black (K) value in your converted CMYK color image can be 100 percent.

The default setting for the Total Ink Limit field is 300%. This means that the total percentage of your CMY inks together will not be over 200 percent (300 percent – 100 percent = 200 percent, 100 percent being the Black Ink Limit). If you lower the values in these fields, you'll see that the maximum values for the CMYK inks drop in the Gray Ramp grid.

To view the total percentage of CMYK inks in the Info palette, set one of the Eyedropper readouts to Total Ink.

UCA Amount   When you choose the GCR separation option, the UCA (Under Color Addition) Amount field at the bottom of the Custom CMYK dialog box allows you to add cyan, magenta, and yellow back into the areas that contain the highest percentage of black in an image. When you add cyan, magenta, and yellow, black is not subtracted. This results in more intense blacks, which can help prevent shadow areas from appearing too flat.

Values between 0 and 100% are accepted in the UCA Amount field. Once again, if you change the setting, you will see the results in the Gray Ramp grid.

Remember   *Any value entered in the UCA Amount or other fields in the Custom CYMK dialog box should be approved by your commercial printer or prepress house.*

Setting the Grayscale Working Space

The Grayscale working space choice in the Color Settings dialog box defines how Photoshop displays grayscale images on your screen and how it converts from RGB Color to Grayscale mode. The default setting when you choose U.S. Prepress Defaults in the Settings pop-up menu is Dot Gain 20%. The Gray pop-up menu in the Working

Spaces section of the Color Settings dialog box offers Dot Gain and Gamma choices; Mac users can also select ColorSync Gray.

```
Custom Dot Gain...
Custom Gamma...

Load Gray...
Save Gray...

Other

ColorSync Gray - Generic Gray Profile

  Dot Gain 10%
  Dot Gain 15%
• Dot Gain 20%
  Dot Gain 25%
  Dot Gain 30%
  Gray Gamma 1.8
  Gray Gamma 2.2

Generic Gray Profile
```

If you are working on images that will be displayed on the screen or the Web, you will want Photoshop to use a monitor gamma level to display grayscale images, rather than dot gain. If you are producing images for printed output, choose a Dot Gain setting.

The default Windows gamma setting is Gray Gamma 2.2. The default Macintosh monitor setting is Gray Gamma 1.8, which is lighter than the Windows default. If you are working on presentations that will be displayed on Macs only, choose the 1.8 option. For Web work, use the 2.2 option, which is the gamma setting if you choose Web Graphics Defaults in the Settings pop-up menu.

The settings for dot gain and gamma are particularly important if you are converting RGB or CMYK images to grayscale. If you choose a higher dot gain setting, the converted grayscale image will be lighter than an image converted with a lower dot gain setting. Photoshop makes the image lighter to compensate for the spreading of ink, which darkens the image on press.

If the Advanced Mode checkbox is selected in the Color Settings dialog box, you can create a custom dot gain curve. To create a custom dot gain curve, choose Custom Dot Gain in the Gray pop-up menu. This opens the Custom Dot Gain dialog box, shown in Figure 2-3.

 You should not create a custom dot gain curve without first consulting your prepress house or print shop.

Before you edit the curve, Adobe recommends that you print a proof with calibration bars, and then use a densitometer to take readings (a *densitometer* is used by prepress houses to measure the density of printing dots). After you've taken a reading, you can enter the adjustments in the text boxes or click and drag on the curve to make adjustments. For instance, if the densitometer indicates that a 40 percent dot is printing at 45 percent, enter **45** into the text box adjacent to 40. After you've changed the curve, enter a name for the custom setting in the Name text box, and then click on OK.

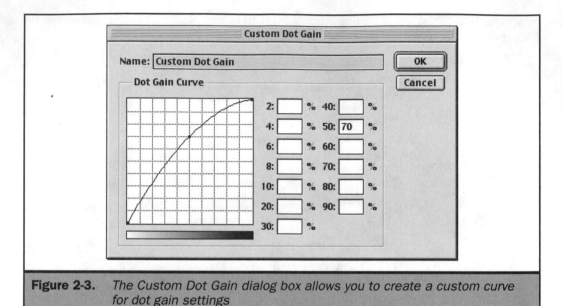

Figure 2-3. *The Custom Dot Gain dialog box allows you to create a custom curve for dot gain settings*

Setting the Spot Color Working Space

The Spot Color working space is designed for images that will be processed through spot-color printing. The choices on the Spot pop-up menu in the Working Spaces section of the Color Settings dialog box allow you to adjust dot gain settings. The choices are same as the dot gain settings for the Grayscale working space, as described in the previous section. See Chapter 15 for details on using spot colors in Photoshop.

Setting Color Management Policies

If another Photoshop user loads an image that you created, Photoshop may automatically convert the image into a different color space. This can cause a shift of colors on the screen. For instance, if you create an image using the Adobe RGB color space, and another Photoshop user loads it into the sRGB color space, he or she may not see the colors on screen as you intended them to be viewed. Photoshop's Color Management policies help avoid this problem by providing guidelines for loading images with no profile or with profiles that are different from the working space on the screen.

In the Color Management Policies section of the Color Settings dialog box, shown next, you can specify whether or not images should be converted to the color spaces you specified in the Working Spaces section.

Choosing RGB, CMYK, and Gray Policies

The Color Management policies are available for RGB, CMYK, and Grayscale images. The RGB, CMYK, and Gray pop-up menus in the Color Management Policies section each offer the following choices.

Off   The Off setting turns off Color Management policies for new documents and when opening documents whose embedded profiles do not match the current working space. Thus, be aware that documents that do not match the current working space will be untagged. This setting is automatically selected if you pick Web Graphics Defaults in the Settings pop-up menu.

Preserve Embedded Profiles   When you select this option, if a profile is embedded in the document, Photoshop does not change the embedded profile to the working CMYK, RGB, or Grayscale working space setting. Instead, it leaves the profile intact. If the document is untagged, Photoshop uses the current working space during editing but does not tag the document with the working space.

    This setting is automatically selected if you pick U.S. Prepress Defaults in the Settings pop-up menu. To maintain a consistent color workflow, most Photoshop users will want to leave the Preserve Embedded Profiles setting selected.

Convert to Working RGB, CMYK, or Grayscale   This option converts the file to the current working space if the profile of the document being loaded does not match the current working space. When you choose this setting, untagged documents loaded into a working space use the current working space, but they are not tagged when you save them (unless the Ask When Opening checkbox is selected in the Missing Profiles section). However, tagged documents that do not match the working space are converted to the current working space and tagged.

Dealing with Profile Mismatches and Missing Profiles

The checkboxes at the bottom of the Color Management Policies section determine whether or not an alert appears when you load documents that do not match the profile of the working space in the Color Settings dialog box or documents that are missing profiles.

Profile Mismatches   If you choose the Ask When Opening or Ask When Pasting checkbox in the Profile Mismatch section, the Embedded Profile Mismatch dialog box appears when you load an image that has a profile that does not match the current working profile.

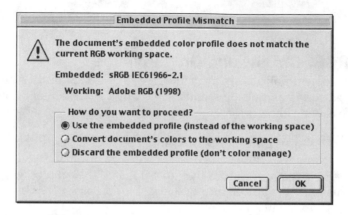

The Embedded Profile Mismatch dialog box provides three choices:

- You can use the embedded profile instead of the working space. If you choose this option, colors may shift on screen, but the numeric values of the colors do not change. (You may wish to use this setting to prevent changing color values of images with Web-safe colors.)

- You can assign the working space profile to the file, which changes the numeric values of the colors.

- You can remove the embedded profile altogether.

Missing Profiles   If you choose the Ask When Opening checkbox in the Missing Profiles section, the Missing Profile dialog box appears when you load an image that does not have a profile.

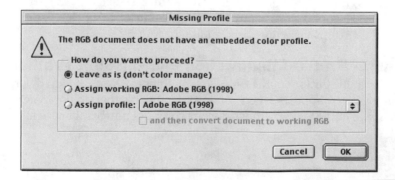

The Missing Profile Mismatch dialog box provides three choices:

- You can choose not to assign the document a profile.
- You can assign the working space profile to the document.
- You can assign a profile from the Assign Profile pop-up menu.

If you choose the Assign Profile option and select the "and then convert the document to working RGB (CMYK or Grayscale)" checkbox, the working profile will be assigned when you save the document.

Choosing Conversion Options

The Conversion Options section in the Color Settings dialog box focuses on how colors change when you change color modes. Most Photoshop users should leave these options at their default settings.

```
┌─ Conversion Options ──────────────────────────┐
│  Engine:  [ Adobe (ACE)           ▼]           │
│                                                │
│  Intent:  [ Relative Colorimetric ▼]           │
│                                                │
│  ☑ Use Black Point Compensation  ☑ Use Dither (8-bit/channel images) │
└────────────────────────────────────────────────┘
```

Choosing an Engine

The option you choose from the Engine pop-up menu determines which company's Color Management system you wish to use. For the best results with Adobe applications, choose Adobe (ACE).

Selecting an Intent

The choices in the Intent pop-up menu determine how Photoshop converts colors from one color space to another. Intents are provided primarily for color professionals and advanced Photoshop users.

When Photoshop converts from RGB to CMYK, it first converts the RGB colors to Lab mode, and then from Lab mode to CMYK. Most of the choices on the Intents menu specify the conversion algorithm or mathematical formulas used to map colors from RGB to Lab and Lab to CMYK. (See Chapter CD-1 for information about the CMYK and Lab Color modes.) For instance, suppose that you are working in an RGB image that must be converted to CMYK, and one color is 20 percent brighter than another. When Photoshop shifts the colors, should it attempt to maintain the 20 percent in brightness, even if the color changes? The following options on the Intent pop-up menu answer that question.

Perceptual   Choose Perceptual to maintain color relationships among the colors, even if the colors fall out of gamut. In general, it produces attractive color.

Saturation   Choose Saturation to maintain the saturation relationship among the colors. This is generally a good choice if you are printing color charts and graphs.

Relative Colorimetric   Relative Colorimetric is the default choice for color conversions. It provides the best conversion option when the source colors are not out of the destination gamut. As Photoshop converts from RGB to Lab, then from Lab to CMYK, this choice attempts to map color coordinates from one color space to other. During the process, it also remaps the white points from the source to the destination color space.

Absolute Colorimetric   Absolute Colorimetric is generally not recommended for color conversion. This method attempts an exact match between destination and source Lab coordinates.

Compensating for Black Points

When you select the Use Black Point Compensation, Photoshop analyzes source and destination black points and adjusts colors to provide the fullest dynamic range of colors when converting.

Using Dither

Selecting the Use Dither checkbox in the Conversion Options section helps control banding that might occur in 8-bit-per-channel images. Dithering creates a mixture of colors to simulate missing colors in the destination working space. Photoshop creates a pattern of colors to eliminate banding. However, choosing this option can increase the image file size.

Selecting Advanced Controls

The Advanced Controls section of the Color Settings dialog box should be changed only by color professionals and Photoshop experts. If you tamper with these controls, screen colors will not match printed output.

```
┌─ Advanced Controls ──────────────────────────┐
│  ☐ Desaturate Monitor Colors By:   [20    ]  % │
│  ☐ Blend RGB Colors Using Gamma:   [1.00  ]    │
└───────────────────────────────────────────────┘
```

To understand the Desaturate Monitor Colors option, it's important to be able to conceptualize the difference between the actual color gamut of a working space and a computer monitor's color space. The gamut of the working space can exceed the actual gamut of colors displayed on a computer display. The Desaturate Monitor Colors By option lowers the intensity of colors on screen. Adobe provides this control to allow advanced users to visualize colors that are in the color space gamut yet cannot be displayed on the monitor.

The other option in the Advanced Controls section is Blend RGB Colors Using Gamma. If this option is turned on, Photoshop uses the gamma setting in the text box to blend RGB colors, rather than blending the colors in the current working space.

Converting Color Spaces of Open Images

If an image is already open on screen, Photoshop's Assign Profile and Convert to Profile commands provide a means of converting the image to a new or different color space. You may wish to use one of these commands to convert the color space of an image that wasn't converted when you opened it. You may also need to change profiles because you want to change the output settings. Both Assign Profile and Convert to Profile should be executed only by advanced users.

Assigning Color Profiles

The Assign Profile command can remove a color tag or assign a color tag to an open document. You can also change color tags without changing the actual numerical color values in an image.

The Assign Profile command can cause color shifts on screen due to the shift in color profiles.

To use the Assign Profile command, open the image in Photoshop and choose Image > Mode > Assign Profile. Photoshop displays the Assign Profile dialog box, as shown here:

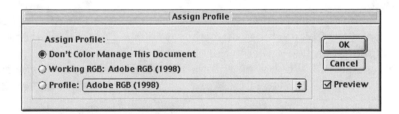

In the Assign Profile dialog box, you can choose from three options:

■ The Don't Color Manage This Document option removes a profile from a document that has been tagged.

- The Working RGB (or CMK or Grayscale) option assigns the profile of the current working space (the one designated in the Color Settings dialog box) to the document.

- The Profile option assigns a profile other than the current working profile to the document. With this option, the display of colors on screen may shift dramatically. However, Photoshop does not change the actual color values in the file. The colors change occurs because Photoshop remaps the screen display of colors to the new profile.

Click on OK to complete the profile assignment. When you save the document, Photoshop assigns the new profile to it.

Converting from One Profile to Another

You can use the Convert to Profile command to convert colors in a tagged document to another profile. This command switches image profiles and remaps color values to the working space as well. When making the conversion, Photoshop attempts to prevent screen colors from changing. However, this often results in a change in the actual color values of the image. Essentially, Photoshop must adjust the color values as it adjusts the color profile, in an attempt to keep the colors from changing.

 You can use the Color Sampler tool to specify points on screen whose color settings you wish to monitor. Then open the Info palette. As you change colors in the Convert to Profile dialog box, the Info palette shows the change in colors.

To use the Convert to Profile command, choose Image > Mode > Convert to Profile. Photoshop displays the Convert to Profile dialog box, shown in Figure 2-4.

In the Destination Space section, select the color profile that you wish to convert to. The document will be converted to profile and tagged with it when you save that document.

The Conversion Options section offers the same options as those in the Conversion Options section of the Color Settings dialog box, which are described in the "Choosing Conversion Options" section earlier in this chapter.

After you click on OK, Photoshop will convert the file to the profile you specified.

Saving Color Tags

Unlike previous versions, Photoshop 6.0 clearly displays a document's profile when you save it. You can find this information in the Save dialog box, at the bottom left with the Color settings, as shown next. Tags are saved with the Photoshop (PSD), DCS, EPS, Photoshop PDF, PICT, TIFF, and JPEG formats.

Save: ☐ As a Copy   ☐ Annotations
        ☐ Alpha Channels   ☐ Spot Colors
        ☐ Layers

Color: ☐ Use Proof Setup: Working CMYK
        ☑ Embed Color Profile: Adobe RGB (1998)

Here are a few document tagging rules:

- New documents are automatically saved with the working color tag.
- Documents that are assigned a profile are saved with the assigned file tags.
- Despite the working color space, if you load an untagged document and don't assign it a profile, the document will not be saved with a tag.

In most cases, you will save the document with its color tag. However, you can deselect the tagging option if you do not want the document to include an embedded profile. If the document does not have a profile, you can tag it with the working color profile by selecting the ICC profile checkbox.

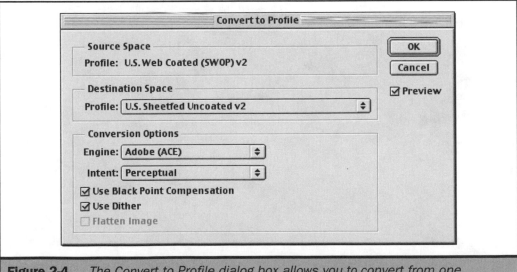

Figure 2-4.   *The Convert to Profile dialog box allows you to convert from one profile to another*

Changing a Document Profile to the Proof Profile

Advanced users may wish to change an image's profile to its soft proof profile (proof profiles are discussed in Chapter 13). For instance, you might want to print a proof using a profile other than the working CMYK profile.

To switch the document profile to a custom proof profile, follow these steps:

1. Choose a custom proof setup by selecting View > Proof Setup > Custom.

2. In the Custom dialog box, click on the pop-up menu and choose the proof profile for the proof that you wish to use.

3. Choose File > Save As. Save the file in one of the following formats: PDF, EPS, DCS 1.0, or DCS 2.0.

4. Select the Use Proof Setup checkbox. After you select the checkbox, the ICC profile changes to the proof's profile.

5. Name the file and save it.

Note   *Color Profiles can also be used to soft proof images on screen. They can also be set as the Source profile when printing. For more information about soft proofs, see Chapter 13. For more information about choosing profiles when printing, see Appendix B.*

The
Complete
Reference

Photoshop

Chapter 3

Using Type in Photoshop and ImageReady

Undoubtedly you've heard the expression "a picture is worth a thousand words." When it comes to graphic design, words (although you probably won't need a thousand) can also add some worth to a picture. Words can add interest and convey a message. They can reinforce a point or put the punch in the punch line of a humorous image.

In Photoshop and ImageReady, you add words to your images by using the Type tool. Once you master the Type tool, you'll not only be able to add text to your images, you'll soon be able to create amazing type effects as well. For instance, you can place images in type, create drop shadows from type, and create three-dimensional bevel effects. Using Photoshop's new Text Warp command, you can even bend and stretch type.

This chapter describes how to use the Type tool and its options to add and format text. It also presents many examples that illustrate the diversity of effects possible with type in Photoshop and ImageReady.

Setting Type Tool Options

Creating type in Photoshop and ImageReady is quite easy: You select the Type tool, click in the document, and start typing. However, the Type tool offers different modes and settings for how you enter type and how your text appears, so you should become familiar with these choices before adding text. The Type tool's Options bar becomes active when you select the Type tool in the Toolbox.

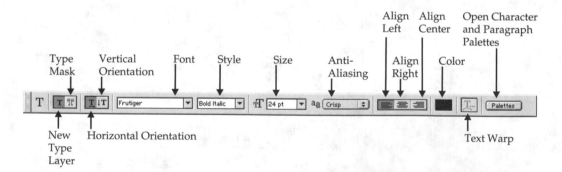

When you click on the screen to begin entering or editing type, the Options bar switches to edit mode. In edit mode in Photoshop, the OK (☑) and Cancel buttons (☒) appear in the Options bar.

The Type tool's Options bar settings work as follows:

■ **New Type Layer**   Click on this button to create type in a new layer. The type is filled with the foreground color or the color chosen in the Type tool's Options bar. This setting is covered in the following section.

- **Type Mask**   Click on this button to create type surrounded by selection border, or a *type mask*. You can fill or paint the masked text area. This setting is discussed in the "Using the Type Mask Option" section in this chapter.

- **Horizontal Orientation**   Click on this button to create type horizontally in a new layer.

- **Vertical Orientation**   Click on this button to create type vertically in a new layer.

- **Font**   To change typefaces, click on the Font pop-up menu and choose a font.

- **Style**   To change the type style (such as italic or bold), click on the Style pop-up menu to the right of the Font pop-up menu. The choices on the Style pop-up menu depend on the typeface in use.

- **Size**   To change type size, pick a size from the Size pop-up menu or enter a number in the Size field.

- **Anti-Aliasing**   Anti-aliasing smoothes the edges of type. From the Anti-Aliasing pop-up menu, choose Smooth to create the smoothest edges for type, Crisp to make the type stand out more, or Strong to make the text appear fatter. If you don't wish to apply any anti-aliasing, choose None.

- **Alignment**   To align text flush left, centered, or flush right from the point in the document where you click to the end, click on the appropriate alignment icon.

- **Color**   To change the color of text created in a type layer, click on the color swatch. This opens Photoshop's Color Picker.

- **Text Warp**   To bend or reshape text in a type layer, click on this button, which opens Photoshop's Text Warp dialog box. This feature is covered in the "Warping Text" section in this chapter.

- **Palettes**   Click on the Palette button to open the Character and Paragraph palettes. Using these palettes is covered in the "Formatting with the Character and Paragraph Palettes" section in this chapter.

Creating Type in a New Layer

If you click on the New Type Layer button, and then click on your screen and begin typing, Photoshop automatically creates a new layer and places the type in the layer. (Layers are covered in detail in Chapter 16). When you create type in a layer, you can output the type as vector graphics, or you can choose to rasterize the type if you wish to paint over it or apply filters to it.

As you enter type, the text appears on your screen filled with the current foreground color or the color chosen in the Type tool's Options bar. You can easily edit the type by using the BACKSPACE key or by clicking and dragging over letters. You can easily move text by clicking and dragging it around on screen. You can even click between letters and edit text as you would in a word processing program.

Creating type in a layer provides you with the most versatility. Once the type is created in a layer you can manipulate it in many ways:

- Apply layer styles, such as bevel and emboss effects, by selecting Layer > Layer Style.

- Transform the type, such as rotating or scaling, by selecting Edit > Transform.

- Move the text or transform it with the Move tool.

- Convert the type to a shape, which can be moved separately from the background layer, by selecting Layer > Type > Convert to Shape. After type is converted to a shape, you can overlap, intersect, and add shapes together using the options in the Shape tool's Options bar.

- Convert the type to a path that can be edited with the path editing tools by selecting Layer > Type > Create Work Path.

- Rasterize the text by selecting Layer > Type > Rasterize. If you wish to paint over layer type or apply filters to it, you must rasterize it first.

You'll see how you can use these techniques to create effects with text later in this chapter.

Vector-Based Type vs. Rasterized Type

Photoshop creates vector-based type when you create type in a layer. Vector type is resolution-independent. This means that the quality of the type does not depend on the resolution of the image; the quality depends on the device that outputs it, in particular the number of dots per inch (dpi) that the output device creates; the higher the dots per inch, the better the quality of the type. If you output vector type at a high resolution, the type will appear crisp and sharp. For instance, when outputting to an imagesetter, you can specify that you want the image output at settings such as 1,200 or 2,540 dpi.

If you are exporting a Photoshop file to other applications and wish to preserve the vector-based type, save the file in Photoshop EPS or Photoshop DCS format by choosing File > Save As. In the EPS or DCS dialog box, select Include Vector Data. Note that this option is specifically for importing Photoshop files into other applications. If you load an EPS or DCS file into Photoshop, the type will be rasterized, whether or not Include Vector Data was selected. When printing to a PostScript printer, the vector data is also preserved, thus ensuring crisp, high-quality type.

When you fill type created with the Type Mask option, you create raster graphics that "dry" on the background canvas. You can also choose to rasterize layer type, so that you can fill it or apply filters to it. Rasterized type is resolution-dependent. This means that quality is based on the resolution of the image. Thus, if you tried to output text created at 72 dpi for the Web on an imagesetter, the quality would not greatly improve. If you're designing for the Web or multimedia, this presents little or no problem. Most Web images and multimedia productions are created at 72 ppi. When your audience views the images on a computer monitor with a resolution of 72 ppi, the text looks fine. It looks pretty much the way you viewed it when you created it.

When you create type in Photoshop and ImageReady for the Web, you must save it in one of the Web graphics formats: GIF, JPEG, or PNG, which are raster file formats. They do not support vector type. Since type effects used as graphics on Web pages take longer to download than text, most Web designers do not use Photoshop to create many lines of text. Use Photoshop and ImageReady to create type that will be used for logos, buttons, single words, and/or phrases.

Using the Type Mask Option

If you click on the Type Mask button in the Type Options bar and then click on the screen to begin to type, Photoshop begins by creating a red overlay mask with the type cut out in the mask. While the mask is on the screen, you can move the type by clicking and dragging the on it with the Type tool. To turn the mask into a blinking selection, click on the OK button.

Once the mask is on your screen, you can fill it or paint over it. You can also use the Move tool to scale or transform it. When you fill or paint the type, the text selection functions like a stencil, or mask, so that only the masked text area is filled or painted. After you create type with the Type Mask option, you can copy and paste it into another Photoshop file or copy it to a layer.

When you deselect the type, it is locked into place on the background pixels of the layer that you are working in. Once the text is locked down, it cannot be moved easily.

Typing with the Type Tool

Photoshop provides two modes for using the Type tool:

- Point mode is used to enter one line of text or text on separate lines that do not need paragraph formation.
- Paragraph mode is used to enter larger blocks of text and use paragraph formatting options.

Tip *You can convert point text to paragraph text by choosing Layer > Type > Convert to Paragraph Text. To convert paragraph text to point text, select Layer > Type > Convert to Point Text.*

The following sections provide step-by-step instructions for creating type with Photoshop's Type tool in point or paragraph mode.

Entering Separate Text Lines in Point Mode

When using the Type tool, you can enter text line by line by pressing the RETURN (ENTER) key. To enter type in this mode, called the *point mode*, follow these steps:

1. Select the Type tool.

2. In the Type tool's Options bar, select the New Type Layer button. Set any other options you desire for the text.

3. Move the mouse pointer to the area on the screen where you wish to enter type and click.

4. Type your text. If you need to create a new line, press RETURN (ENTER).

5. To exit text editing mode, click on the OK button (the checkmark) in the Options bar or press ENTER (on the numeric keypad) or COMMAND-RETURN (CTRL-ENTER). If you wish to cancel and remove the type from the screen, click on the Cancel button (the X) in the Options bar or press ESC.

Entering Blocks of Text in Paragraph Mode

If you are creating large blocks of type and wish to use Photoshop's paragraph formatting options, you must enter type in paragraph mode. You enter paragraph mode by clicking and dragging on the screen to create a boundary box before you type. When you type, the words wrap from line to line as you reach the end of right end of the boundary box. To enter type in this mode, follow these steps:

1. Select the Type tool.

2. In the Type tool's Option bar, select the New Type Layer button. Set any other options that you desire for the text.

3. Click and drag diagonally on the screen to create a box to fit the text that you wish to enter. After you release the mouse, the bounding box appears.

If you press OPTION (ALT) while clicking and dragging, the Paragraph Text Size dialog box opens, into which you can enter specific values for the width and height of the bounding box.

4. Type your text. As you type, the text that reaches the borders of the boundary box wraps to the next line, as shown here:

text entered into
a box wraps at
the end of the

5. To exit text editing mode, click on the OK button (checkmark) in the Options bar or press ENTER (on the numeric keypad) or COMMAND-RETURN (*CTRL-ENTER*). If you wish to cancel and remove the type from the screen, click on the Cancel button (the X) in the Options bar or press ESC.

Formatting with the Character and Paragraph Palettes

If you want more control over the formatting of your text, you can use the Character and Paragraph palettes. You do not need to select text or have the Type tool selected to change options in the Character or Paragraph palettes.

Using the Character Palette

The Character palette and the Character palette's pop-up menu provide options primarily related to formatting individual characters. To open the Character palette, click on the Palettes button in the Type tool's Options bar or select Window > Show Character.

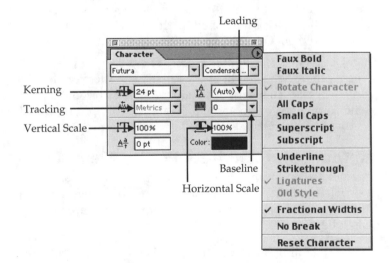

Setting Character Palette Options

Like the Type tool's Options bar, the Character palette allows you to choose a font, a size, and a style color. The other options work as follows:

- **Kerning**   To change kerning (space between two letters) manually, first click between two letters and then enter a value in the Kerning field. Positive values increase the space between letters; negative values decrease the space. (The

Metrics choice in Photoshop's Kerning pop-up menu indicates that the font's default or automatic kerning is turned on. ImageReady's choice is Auto in its Kerning pop-up menu.)

- **Leading** Leading controls the space between individual lines of text. If you leave Leading set to Auto, the typeface's default leading is used. To change the leading, click on the Leading pop-up menu and choose a leading point size from the list. In Photoshop, leading is measured from baseline to baseline.

- **Tracking** To change tracking (space between more than two letters of text), select the letters that you want to change and enter a value in points in the Tracking field. Higher numbers increases the distance; negative values decrease the distance.

Note *Kerning and tracking are measured in units that are 1/1,000 of an em space. An em space is a typographical unit of measure roughly equal to the size of the letter M in the currently selected typeface. It can also be thought of as the distance that is equal to the height of the type.*

- **Baseline** To raise or lower the text above or below other letters, enter a value in the Baseline field; to shift the baseline lower, enter a negative number. The baseline of the type is established by the dash on the I-beam cursor when you click on the screen with the Type tool.

- **Vertical Scale and Horizontal Scale** These two commands designate the ratio between a character's height and width. If you increase the vertical percentage, the type increases in height. If you increase the horizontal percentage, the type stretches out. Since width and height are related, you may wish to increase both the vertical and horizontal scale to keep the text proportional.

Using the Character Palette's Pop-up Menu

The Character palette's pop-up menu provides more style features for text. You can choose styles such as All Caps, Superscript, or Underline before you enter the text or later select the text and choose a style. The commands that are not straightforward styles work as follows:

- The Faux Bold and Faux Italic commands allow you to add bold and italic effects to typefaces that don't include these styles.

- The Rotate Character command allows you to rotate vertical type. (This option is available only when you are creating vertical type.)

- When Fractional Widths is selected, Photoshop adjusts the spacing in fractions of pixels between letters to produce the best typography. However, when creating text at small type sizes for the Web and multimedia, you may wish to deselect Fractional Widths, which can cause small text to be too tightly spaced, and thus unreadable.

- The Ligatures and Old Style options should be selected if you wish to use Ligatures and Old Style numerals (if supported by the selected type face). Ligatures combine two letters, such as fi or fl, into one letter. Old style numerals are not as tall as standard numbers and can descend below the baseline.

- The No Break option allows you to prevent words from breaking at the end of a line. For instance, you may want *New York* to not be broken over two lines. To prevent a word or group of words from breaking, select them with the Type tool and choose No Break.

- The Reset Character option returns the Character palette fields to the default settings for the type.

Using the Paragraph Palette

Photoshop's Paragraph palette features options that allow you to format and control large blocks of text. To open the Paragraph palette, click on the Palettes button in the Type tool's Options bar or select Window > Show Paragraph.

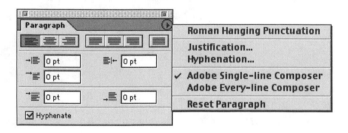

Most of the paragraph options can be accessed only when you've created type using Photoshop's paragraph mode. Many of the commands are similar to those that you might find in a page layout program such as Adobe InDesign, Adobe PageMaker, and QuarkXPress

Setting Paragraph Palette Options

The icons across the top of the Paragraph palette control the text alignment in the paragraph. The first three icons (from left to right) are for left-aligned, centered (line by line), and right-aligned type. The next four icons are for justified type. Click on the appropriate one to left-align the last line, center align the last line, right align the last line, or justify all lines (including the last one).

If you choose the Vertical Orientation button in the Type tool's Options bar, the icons in the Paragraph palette change when you are in edit mode.

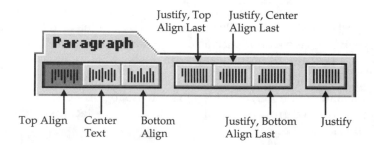

The Paragraph palette fields control indentation and spacing around the paragraph, as follows:

- The Indent Left Margin field changes the left indent of the text.

- The Indent Right Margin field changes the right indent of text.

- The Indent First Line field changes the indent of only the first line of each paragraph, relative to the setting in the Indent Left Margin field.

- The Add Space Before Paragraph field adds additional space before each paragraph.

- The Add Space After Paragraph field adds additional space after each selected paragraph.

 *Although the default measurement unit in the Paragraph palette's fields is points, you can change the measurement unit to inches by entering a value and then typing **in**.*

When the Hyphenate checkbox is selected, Photoshop automatically hyphenates words according to the line space settings in the Hyphenation dialog box, discussed in the "Using the Hyphenation Dialog Box" section coming up shortly.

Using the Paragraph Palette's Pop-up Menu

The Roman Hanging Punctuation option on the Paragraph palette's pop-up menu allows type and punctuation to hang or appear outside the margin. When this option is selected, a checkmark appears to its left.

The Justification and Hyphenation options each open a dialog box for controlling those aspects of your paragraph. The settings in the Justification and Hyphenation dialog boxes are discussed in the next sections.

The two Adobe Composer options evaluate possible breaks and choose the one that best supports the hyphenation and justification options you've specified for a given paragraph. The Adobe Single-line Composer option evaluates each line as a single entity. As it evaluates, it applies rules for each line. The Single-line Composer expands or compresses words before it hyphenates, yet it will hyphenate before its expands or compresses. When spacing needs to be altered, it compresses before it expands. The Adobe Every-line Composer option analyzes the paragraph as one entity and statistically attempts to provide an even spacing with few hyphens.

The Reset Paragraph option resets the paragraph to its default settings.

Using the Justification Dialog Box

To control justification for paragraph mode text, choose Justification from the Paragraph palette's pop-up menu. This opens the Justification dialog box, which controls spacing for an entire paragraph of text. These settings are most valuable when applied to justified text, but they also can work with unjustified text.

Justification				
	Minimum	Desired	Maximum	OK
Word Spacing:	80%	100%	133%	Cancel
Letter Spacing:	0%	0%	0%	
Glyph Scaling:	100%	100%	100%	☐ Preview
Auto Leading:	120%			

The dialog box is divided into three sections:

■ The Word Spacing settings control spacing between words.

■ The Letter Spacing settings control spacing between letters (this also affects kerning and tracking).

■ The Glyph Scaling settings control the character width.

The entry fields allow you to specify minimum, desired, and maximum spacing percentages. At 100%, no additional spacing is added. Thus, values greater than 100 increase spacing; values less than 100 decrease spacing.

Using the Hyphenation Dialog Box

To control hyphenation in text created in paragraph mode, choose Hyphenation from the Paragraph palette's pop-up menu to open the Hyphenation dialog box, shown in Figure 3-1.

The Hyphenation dialog box includes the following settings:

■ Words less than the value (number of letters) entered in the Words Longer Than field will not be hyphenated. This is the minimum character value for hyphenation.

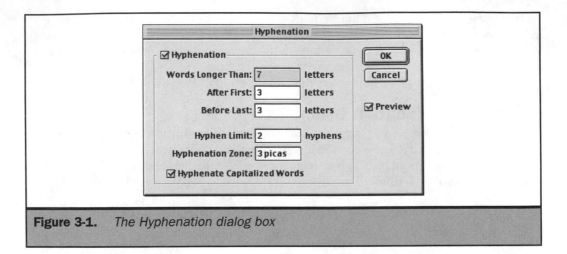

Figure 3-1.   *The Hyphenation dialog box*

- The After First field allows you to enter the minimum number of characters before hyphenation can occur. Thus, no hyphenation can occur before the number of characters specified in this option. At the default setting of 3, no hyphenation can occur before the first letters.

- The Before Last field works like the After First field, but it applies to the minimum number of characters at the end of a word in which hyphenation can occur. No hyphenation can occur after the number of characters specified.

- The Hyphen Limit field allows you to limit the number of hyphens that can occur in consecutive lines of text. If you enter **0**, no restriction is placed on the number of hyphens.

- When the Adobe Single-line Composer option (on the Paragraph palette's pop-up menu) is activated for unjustified type, the value in the Hyphenation Zone field sets the distance at the end of lines that will make a word break.

- The Hyphenate Capitalized checkbox allows words that begin with an uppercase letter to be hyphenated. Deselect this if you do not want capitalized words to be hyphenated.

Working with Rasterized Type

As explained earlier, the Type tool's Type Mask option creates a type mask on your screen. Filling the type with a color creates rasterized type, which "dries" on the electronic canvas. To acquaint you with how you can work with rasterized type, you will create some and then examine the letters on the screen.

Adding the Text

To begin, you'll use the Type tool's Type Mask option to add some text to a new document:

1. Select File > New and create a 7-by-5-inch, RGB color file. Set Resolution to 72 ppi and Contents to White.

2. Check to see that black is the foreground color icon and white is the background color icon in the Toolbox. If black is not the foreground color and white is not the background color, click on the Default Colors icon or press D on your keyboard. (This will ensure that your text is black and the Eraser tool erases with white.)

3. Select the Type tool in the Toolbox.

4. In the Type tool's Options bar, select the Type Mask button. Click on the Font pop-up menu and choose Times or any other font. In the Size pop-up menu, choose a large size such as 72 or 100. In the Anti-Aliasing pop-up menu, choose Crisp.

5. Move the mouse pointer toward the document window. When the pointer appears over the document window, it changes to a cursor called the I-beam. To enter text in the upper-left corner of the window, move the I-beam to this part of the screen. Click the mouse where you want the text to appear.

6. A red overlay appears on screen with a blinking cursor at the point where you clicked. Type **ben** (or your own name, in lowercase letters) in the text box. As you type, Photoshop creates a white stencil on the screen, showing where the type will be appear.

7. Check to make sure you haven't made any typos. If you made a mistake, this is your chance to fix it. The simplest way to replace a character is to position the cursor to the right of the character you want to change, press DELETE (*BACKSPACE*), and then type the correct character. At this point, you also can reposition the text by simply moving the mouse pointer above or below the text, or to the right or left of the text, and then clicking and dragging it.

8. When you're finished, click on the OK (checkmark) button in the Type tool's Options bar. A marquee selection of your text appears on screen.

The marquee indicates that the text is a *mask,* meaning that it works like a stencil. When you paint with a painting tool or execute Photoshop's fill command (Edit > Fill), only the area with the selection is filled.

If you create type with the Type tool in a layer and then create type with the Type Mask button, you will not be able to fill the type created with the Type Mask tool until you rasterize the type layer.

Moving the Text-Selection Marquee

If you wish to move a text selection marquee, you must first select a selection tool, such as the Rectangular Marquee. After you switch tools, you can click and drag to move the selection marquee. You can also move the text selection by pressing the directional arrow keys on the keyboard. Try it. Each time you press an arrow key, the text selection moves up, down, left, or right 1 pixel.

At this point, you may be tempted to fill the text with color immediately. If you fill the text with color or paint over the text, the paint "dries" onto the background canvas. This is fine if you don't want to move your text after you've filled it with color. If you do try to move the selection after you fill the text with color, Photoshop moves only the selection and leaves a copy of the filled letters in the background. How do you avoid this situation? You can make the text "float" above the image background by copying the selection on screen (before filling it) and then moving the selection. Alternatively, you can copy the text into a new layer before filling the selection.

Here are a few points that you should be aware of when moving and filling text created with the Type Mask option:

- If you try to move a filled text selection by clicking and dragging in the selection with a selection tool, only the selection moves. The original filled text is left behind.

- If you move a filled text selection with the Move tool, the filled type and the selection marquee move. However, Photoshop leaves behind a copy of the text filled with the background color. This will not happen if you are in a transparent layer. Clicking and dragging with the COMMAND (*CTRL*) key pressed temporarily activates the Move tool when the Type Mask option is selected.

- If you copy a text selection on your screen before you fill it with color, Photoshop won't leave a painted copy of the text behind when you move it with the Move tool. To copy the text (before you fill it with color), press and hold down OPTION-COMMAND (*ALT-CTRL*) and click and drag on the text to move it. After you've executed these steps, you can fill the text and move it.

- You can copy a filled text selection and move it by pressing OPTION-COMMAND (*ALT-CTRL*) and clicking and dragging your text selection.

- If you want to isolate your text selection so you can move it at any time, you can copy the selection to a layer by choosing Layer > New > Layer via Copy. After you copy the text to a new layer, you can fill the text using the Edit > Fill command (make sure the Lock Transparency checkbox is selected), or you can paint over the text with a painting tool. (Make sure the Lock Transparency option is selected in the Layers palette.) For more information about working with layers, see Chapters 16 and 17.

■ If you know beforehand that you are going to move the text after filling it with color, you may want to use the Type tool without the Type Mask option selected.

Filling the Text

Now that you have your text on the screen, positioned as you want it, you can fill it. Choose Edit > Fill. In the Fill dialog box, choose Foreground Color in the Use pop-up menu. Make sure that the Mode pop-up menu is set to Normal. Change the Opacity percentage, if desired. Then click on OK.

After you apply the Fill command, notice that the color only fills inside the letters. The masking effect of the type prevents the color from splashing anywhere else. (To see the masking effects, you can also fill the text by painting over it or even paste a photograph into the selection.)

To deselect the type, choose Select > Deselect or press COMMAND-D (*CTRL-D*). This deselects the text and removes the marquee selection from the screen.

To return the last selection you created, choose Select > Reselect. You can also save and reload selections using alpha channels. See Chapter 4 for more information about selections. See Chapter 15 for details on using alpha channels.

Zooming in on the Type

Examining type is a helpful if you wish to understand how raster or bitmapped images are created. There are several ways to zoom in to magnify text so that you can see the matrix of pixels that combine to make the letters you typed. The traditional way is to use the Zoom tool. The most efficient way to zoom, however, is to use Photoshop's Navigator palette.

Using the Zoom Tool

The Zoom tool lets you point to any area in the document window and magnify it by clicking. Each time you click with the Zoom tool, the magnification grows. You can zoom in to a specific area on screen by clicking and dragging over that area with the Zoom tool. You can quickly access the Zoom tool from another tool by pressing COMMAND-SPACEBAR (*CTRL-SPACEBAR*) and clicking the mouse. To zoom out, press COMMAND-OPTION-SPACEBAR (*CTRL-ALT-SPACEBAR*) and click.

After you zoom, you can use the Hand tool if you need to scroll the document in any direction. To use the Hand tool, simply click and drag on screen. Be aware that the Hand tool does not move objects on the screen; it only provides a fast way of scrolling.

Zooming with the Navigator Palette

The fastest and most versatile way to zoom in and out is to use the Navigator palette. Unlike the Zoom tool, the Navigator palette allows you to zoom in or out to any percentage between 0.19% and 1600%. To open the Navigator palette, choose Window > Show Navigator.

In the Navigator palette, you'll see a tiny version of your document window. You can zoom in or out by clicking and dragging the slider at the bottom of the screen. Drag to the right to increase the zoom. As you drag, Photoshop zooms in. In the Navigator palette, you'll see a rectangle indicating the visible area on screen. You can click and drag to move this rectangle over the area that you want to zoom to. Try dragging the slider to the right; then drag the rectangle in the Navigator palette over text in the palette. Drag all the way to the right until the percentage indicator reaches 1600%.

When using the Navigator palette, you can zoom in and out by typing a number in the lower-left corner of the palette and pressing ENTER. Alternatively, you can click on the tiny mountain icon in the lower-left corner of the palette to zoom out and click on the larger mountain icon in the lower-right corner of the palette to zoom in. If you want to make the preview area larger on screen, enlarge the size of the palette.

Examining Pixels

Once you zoom in on your text, you can begin to see how Photoshop creates images. Notice that your zoomed text looks jagged. This is because the letters are made of pixels. The jaggies are the pixel edges. Notice how different combinations of pixels form the various letters.

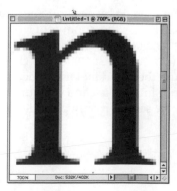

All images in Photoshop are basically created the same way—from pixels. You might notice that some of the hard edges in the zoomed text are blurred or partially filled in. Photoshop tries to eliminate the jaggies as much as possible by using this blurring effect, which is called *anti-aliasing*.

Note   *If you create your file at a resolution of 72 ppi, each linear inch of your image is composed of 72 pixels. At this resolution, there are more than 5,000 pixels in every square inch of your image (72 × 72).*

Editing Pixels with the Eraser Tool

Since the letters in rasterized text (created with the Type Mask option or the Layer > Type > Rasterize command) are not individual objects but are locked together on a grid of pixels, there's no way of slipping a cursor between them to delete or edit them. To delete and edit rasterized text in Photoshop, you need to paint over the pixels of any letter you wish to remove with the background color (in this case, white) and then make your changes.

Note   *If you create type with the Type tool (as opposed to the Type Mask tool) and don't rasterize it (by selecting Layer > Rasterize > Type, you can edit letters after typing them.*

The following steps demonstrate how to use the Eraser tool to "white-out" the lowercase *b* from the word *ben* and replace it with an uppercase *B*. (You can do the same with the first letter of whatever text you've typed for this chapter's exercise.) To follow along with the exercise, you need to have a word created with lowercase letters. If you used the Type tool instead of the Type Mask tool, make sure you render it by choosing Layer > Rasterize > Type.

1. Click on the Eraser tool in the Toolbox. The mouse pointer changes to a small eraser, and the Options bar displays Eraser options. (If the Options bar isn't open, open it by choosing Window > Show Options so that you can see the Eraser tool's options.)

2. By default, the Eraser tool's Options bar is set to erase by painting with a paintbrush stroke. In order to see the Eraser's pixel-by-pixel erasing effects more clearly, switch tool types by clicking on the pop-up menu and choosing Block. With this setting, you will erase blocks of pixels with 100 percent of the background color (in this case, white).

3. Position the Eraser over any part of the *b* in *ben* (or the first letter of your text) and click. Photoshop replaces the black in that pixel with white.

4. Click over different parts of the letter to create a speckled effect. At first glance, it seems like the Eraser is merely removing black from each individual pixel. You are, however, actually painting with the default background color of white. This may seem like a slow way of deleting, but it's actually one of the strengths of Photoshop: You can edit any object at the smallest possible level, the pixel. In most other programs, you can edit text, but not pieces of type.

5. Continue whiting-out the letter until you have deleted it. To work a little faster with the Eraser tool, keep the mouse button pressed as you move the Eraser back and forth over the letter, much as you would use a rubber eraser on paper.

 If you accidentally erase part of another letter in your text, choose Edit > Undo. This will cancel your last action.

6. To enter the capital *B*, click on the Type Mask button and then click below the letters on your screen. Type **B** and click on the OK button in the Type tool's Options bar.

7. When you're satisfied with the position of your new capital letter, fill the letter with the foreground color by choosing Edit > Fill.

8. Deselect the text by choosing Select > Deselect or pressing COMMAND-D (*CTRL-D*). The letter locks down on the screen.

Selecting Letters in Text

Occasionally, you may wish to move individual letters in your text. Here are a few tips for selecting letters (selecting is covered in detail in Chapter 4):

- To add a type selection to the selection on your screen, press and hold down the SHIFT key before you click on the screen to create type with the Type Mask button activated.

- To delete a character in a text selection that already exists, press and hold down OPTION (*ALT*) and click and drag around the letter with the Lasso tool. The character will disappear from the screen.

- Text selections can be converted to paths and then edited. After editing, the path can be turned back into a selection, filled, and stroked. You'll see how to convert text to a path in the "Creating Paths Out of Text" section later in this chapter.

Creating Type Effects

Throughout this book, you'll find numerous examples of creating special effects with type. We've included a few here to give you an idea of how you can use the Type tool's options, along with layer styles, to add interest to your text.

 You'll see examples of the use of layer styles in the rest of this chapter and in the following chapters. For a full discussion of layer styles, see Chapter 18.

Duplicating Layers to Create Text Drop Shadows

After you've created a layer with text in it, you can duplicate that layer to create a drop shadow. Figure 3-2 shows an image with text and a drop shadow created by duplicating a layer.

Here are the steps for creating a drop shadow for text:

1. Open an image or create a new file.

2. Choose a foreground color.

3. Select the Type tool.

4. In the Type tool's Options bar, click on the New Type Layer button. Set the other options as you wish.

5. Enter some type in your document. If you wish, type **Shadow**.

| Tip |

Before creating the shadow, you may want to alter your text using one of the Edit > Free Transform commands. You can apply these commands to type before it is rendered. For more information about using these commands, see Chapter 8.

Figure 3-2.   *Text and drop shadow created with layers*

6. Duplicate the layer by choosing Layer > Duplicate Layer. In the As field of the Duplicate Layer dialog box, you can enter a name for your layer. Type **Text**. Don't change the Destination option.

7. Notice that the Text layer is selected and the paintbrush icon and eye icon are activated in the palette. In the other layer, Shadow, there is no paintbrush icon, but the eye icon is activated. This means that you can view this layer, but not edit it. (You can edit only one layer at a time.)

8. Click on the Shadow layer in the Layers palette to activate it. Then select the Move tool in the Toolbox. With the Move tool activated, click and drag the text a little to the right and down to offset the layer for the shadow effect. As you click and drag, you'll be moving the text in the Shadow layer.

Caution *Normally, clicking and dragging with the Move tool in a layer moves only the currently selected layer. However, if the Auto Select Layer option is activated in the Move tool's Options bar, clicking and dragging in a transparent area of the active layer may actually move another layer. This option activates any layer that has nontransparent areas if you click and drag over them.*

9. Your next step is to fill the shadow text with black. However, you can't fill the text unless it is rendered. To render the text, choose Layer > Rasterize > Type. Next choose Edit > Fill. In the Use pop-up menu, choose Black. Make sure the Preserve Transparency option is selected, and then click on OK.

Note *If the Preserve Transparency option is dimmed in the Fill dialog box, it means that the Preserve Transparency option is selected in the Layers palette. When the Preserve Transparency option is selected, it means that Photoshop fills only the areas of your layer that aren't transparent.*

If you want your shadow to be soft-edged rather than hard-edged, you can blur the edges of the shadow layer. First, turn off the Lock Transparency option in the Layers palette. (This allows the transparent area bordering the text to be changed.) Then render the type (by selecting Layer > Rasterize > Type). Next, choose Filter > Blur > Gaussian Blur. In the Gaussian Blur dialog box, the more you move the slider to the right, the softer the shadow will become. When you're happy with the preview, click on OK.

Tip *The steps in this section demonstrated how to create a drop shadow by hand. You also can easily create a drop shadow using Photoshop's layer styles. To apply a drop shadow, simply choose Layer > Layer Styles > Drop Shadow. Click on OK to apply the default settings.*

Creating Vertical Type

The Type tool's Vertical Orientation option creates type vertically in a new layer. We used this option and Photoshop's layer styles to create the image in Figure 3-3. We

Figure 3-3.   *Type created with vertical orientation*

used filters to create the background and then used a layer mask to blend the photo onto the image.

To create the text effects in Figure 3-3, we loaded the picture of the people and selected the Type tool. In the Type tool's Options bar, we clicked on the New Type Layer button and selected the Vertical Orientation option. Then we typed *Ecuador*. To add interest to the type, we applied several Layer > Layer Style commands.

We created a new layer by choosing Layer > New > Layer, and then used the Paintbrush tool to draw a shape around the word *Vacations* (in the layer below). We then applied the Layer > Layer Style > Bevel and Emboss command to give the shape a three-dimensional look.

Since the photograph of the two people was in black and white, we used the Paintbrush with the Color mode selected in the Paintbrush tool's Options bar to colorize the image. For more information about using the Paintbrush tool and different color modes, see Chapter 5.

Creating Paths from Text

Photoshop 6 allows you to convert your layer text into paths with a single command. After you've turned text into a path, you can use Photoshop's pen and path-selection tools to alter the type to create interesting effects. (The pen and path-selection tools, as well as the Paths palette, are discussed in detail in Chapter 14.)

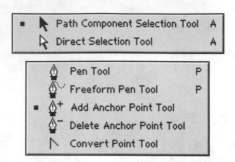

Since paths are vector information, the edited type can be output crisply at a high resolution, as shown in Figure 3-4. Figure 3-5 shows the transition of the word *kick* from layer type to a path to an edited path. To create the final version, we transformed the text, stretched parts of the letter *k*, and added anchor points to the *k* to add a bend effect. We also selected individual letters and raised them.

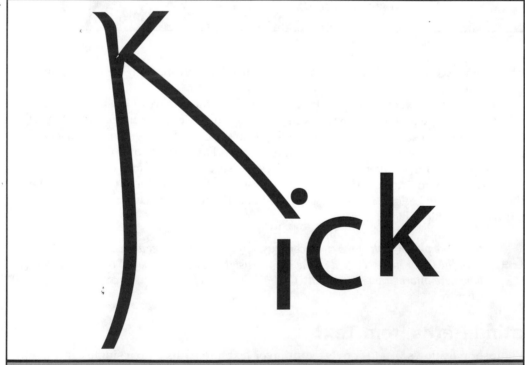

Figure 3-4.   *Photoshop text turned into a path and edited with the path editing tools*

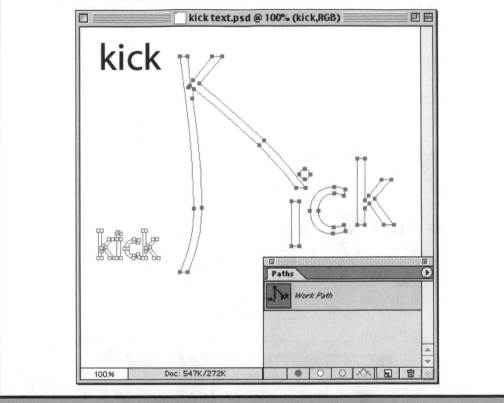

Figure 3-5.   *The transition from layer text to path to edited path*

Here are the steps for converting text to a path and editing it:

1. Select the Type tool in Toolbox.

2. Click on the New Type Layer button in the Type tool's Options bar. Set any other options you like for the text. We used the Myriad typeface set at 48 points and chose Crisp from the Anti-Aliasing pop-up menu.

3. Click on the screen at the point where you wish to have the text appear and type a word (**kick** in this example).

4. Click on the OK (checkmark) button in the Options bar to exit editing mode.

5. To transform the text into a path, choose Layer > Type > Create Work Path.

6. To distort the text, click and drag on an anchor point with Direct Selection tool.

7. To select an entire letter, click on it with the Direct Selection tool. After selecting a letter, you can move it.

8. To transform the type, select the letter or letters that you wish to transform and choose Edit > Transform Path or Edit > Free Transform Path.

9. To create more effects, you can add anchor points using the Add Anchor Point tool, remove anchor points using the Delete Anchor Point tool, or change the path shape by using the Convert Point tool.

10. To flatten the image so that you can fill the path, choose Layer > Flatten Image. (Alternatively, you can rasterize the layer or text before filling the path: Layer > Rasterize.)

11. When you are finished editing, click on the Work Path icon in the Paths palette. (Select Window > Show Paths to open the Paths palette.)

12. Fill the path by choosing Fill Path from the Paths palette's pop-up menu.

Raising Type Out of an Image

Creating text directly out of a digital image can often prove to be a compelling and attractive effect. For instance, Figure 3-6 shows text created out of the background flower image. The text is in a separate layer and can be freely moved around on the screen or even dragged into another document.

Figure 3-6.   *A raised-type effect created using the Type Mask option and layer styles*

Here's how to create a raised-type effect using the Type Mask option to create type and then converting it into a layer:

1. Select the Type tool in Toolbox.

2. Click on the Type Mask button in the Type tool's Options bar. Choose any other text style and formatting options you want to use. We used the Frutiger typeface set at 48 points.

3. Click where you wish to position the text and type the word (**Flower** in Figure 3-7).

4. To create a blinking selection border out of the type, as shown in Figure 3-8, click on the OK button in the Type tool's Options bar.

5. Create a layer from the type selection by choosing Layer > New Layer via Copy.

6. Create a bevel effect by choosing Layer > Layer Style > Bevel and Emboss. Use the settings in the Layer Style dialog box to fine-tune the effect. Click on OK to complete the effect.

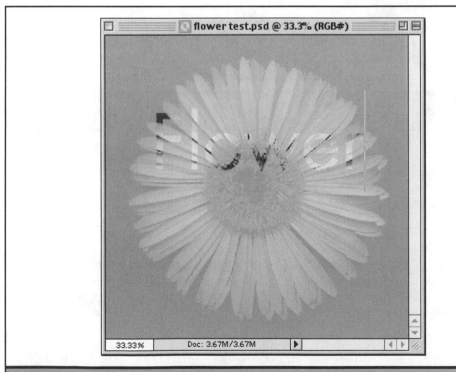

Figure 3-7.   *The word* Flower *appears over the image*

Figure 3-8. *The type shows as a blinking selection border*

Now that the type is in a text layer, you can move the layer by clicking and dragging on it. If you want to use the type in another document, you can click and drag the layer from the Layers palette directly into it.

Warping Text

The Warp Text option of the Type tool's Options bar allows you to create unusual effects with your type. Selecting this option brings up the Warp Text dialog box, which offers a variety of warping styles and controls for bending and distorting your text. Figure 3-9 shows an example of text being warped, with the Warp Text dialog box on the screen. The Layers palette shows that Drop Shadow and Bevel and Emboss layer styles were added to the text before warping it.

To warp text, select the Type tool and choose the New Text Layer button in the Type tool's Options bar. Add your text and apply any layer styles that you desire. Then

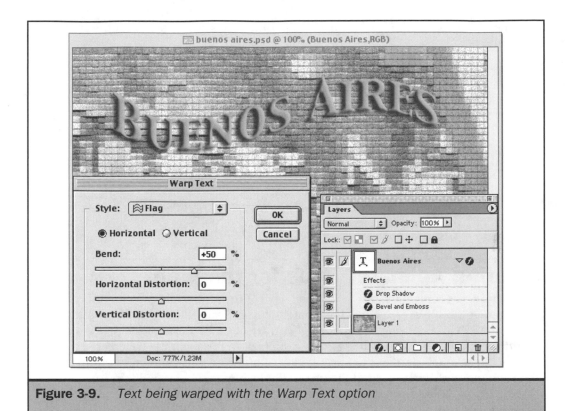

Figure 3-9.   *Text being warped with the Warp Text option*

click on the Warp Text button in the Options bar or choose Layer > Type > Warp Text. In the Warp Text dialog box, click on the Style pop-up menu and choose a style.

Then set the other options for the style. For the Flag style, you can set the following options:

- Click and drag the Bend slider to add or subtract the bend effect to the text.
- Click and drag on the Horizontal Distortion slider to add or subtract horizontal perspective.
- Click and drag on the Vertical Distortion slider to add or subtract vertical perspective

When you're finished, click on OK to apply the warped-text effect.

 If you wish to warp text that has already been created, select the text layer with the text in the Layers palette and open the Warp Text dialog box.

Creating Animated Type for the Web

Animating text is one of the most effective ways of communicating information and attracting viewers to a Web page. Fortunately, ImageReady makes text animation a simple affair. The following exercise leads you step by step through the process of creating a simple animated GIF file of flashing text. In this example we created a flashing "Welcome" sign for the form section of our Web page, shown in Figure 3-10. Although we could have created the text in Photoshop and animated it in ImageReady, we used ImageReady from start to finish to give you an idea of how to create and edit text in ImageReady.

Adding Text to an ImageReady File

First, you need to open a file in ImageReady and add some text to it.

1. Create a new file in ImageReady by choosing File > New. In the New dialog box, choose the size for your animated file. We chose 350-by-50 pixels on a transparent background. We made the width large so that the text would fit above the width of the form on our page. After you click on OK, ImageReady creates a new file.

2. Activate the Type tool. Click in your document and start to type the word that you want to animate. We typed **WELCOME!** at 60 points. If you wish to reposition the text, click and drag on it with ImageReady's Move tool.

3. ImageReady indicates that the type is selected by placing an underline beneath the text. If the text isn't selected, you can click and drag over it with the Move tool.

Figure 3-10.   *A Web page displaying animated type created in ImageReady*

4. Use the pop-up menus in the Type Options bar to pick a font and a style. We chose Charlemagne Bold. We set the Anti-Alias pop-up menu to Crisp in order to produce the non-jagged type. If desired, you can change the kerning (the spacing between two letters) or tracking (the spacing between more than two letters).

Note   *For Web type, you may wish to use type with no anti-aliasing because anti-aliasing adds to the number of colors in an image. If you later reduce the colors in your image when optimizing it for the Web, the type may appear ragged. Also note that you may obtain smoother-looking animated text by creating text in a layer above a background that is the same color as your Web page. See Chapter 9 for more information about using Web images that have transparent backgrounds.*

5. One of the fastest ways to change colors for your text is to use a layer style. Choose Layer > Layer Style > Color Overlay. In the Color Overlay dialog box, click on the Color pop-up menu. To pick a Web-safe color, click on Other to open ImageReady's Color Picker.

Animating the Text

ImageReady's Animation palette provides an easy way to animate images and text.

1. Open ImageReady's Animation palette by choosing Window > Show Animation. In the Animation palette, you'll see a thumbnail frame representing the image on your screen.

2. Open the Animation palette menu by clicking the arrow in the upper-right corner. Note whether the Add Layer to New Frames option is selected. If it is, click on it to turn it off. Otherwise, a new layer will be created each time you create a new frame.

3. To create another frame, click on the New button in the palette or choose New Frame from the Animation palette's menu.

4. Change the overlay color by using the technique described in step 5 of the previous section. To reopen the Color Overlay dialog box, click on the effects button in the Layers palette and choose Color Overlay.

5. Continue adding four or five more frames, filling each with a different color. As you work, you can set the duration of each frame by clicking on the Frame Delay pop-up menu directly below the frame. We set our animation to 2 seconds.

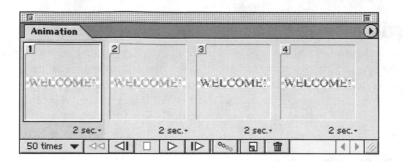

Tip   *To set all frames to the same speed, click on the first frame, hold down the* SHIFT *key, and click on the last frame. This selects all of the frames. Now choose a duration for any frame, and all of them will be set to the same duration.*

6. If you wish to have your animation play a specific number of times, click on the Looping Options pop-up menu directly below the first frame. Change the default setting from Forever to a specific amount.

7. Before saving your work, preview it by clicking on the right arrow icon below the frames. Stop the preview by clicking on the square icon to the left of the right arrow.

8. Save your work by choosing File > Save. This saves the file in Photoshop format.

9. At this point, you are ready to optimize the file using the Optimize palette (as described in Chapter 9). Then you can choose File > Save Optimized to save it in GIF format. If you wish ImageReady to create the HTML that loads the movie onto a Web page, select the HTML and Images option in the Format pop-up menu in the Save Optimized As dialog box.

10. To preview the file in your Web browser, choose File > Preview in, and then choose your browser from the pop-up menu.

11. If you use a Web page layout program (such as Adobe GoLive, Adobe PageMill, or Macromedia Dreamweaver), you can simply load the image onto the page, and the HTML will be written for you automatically. Otherwise, the following simple line of HTML code does the trick (we named our file flashing).

```
<img height="50" width="350"  src="flashing.gif">
```

Importing Type from Adobe Illustrator

Despite the versatility of Photoshop, you might find that you can create and control type more efficiently in a drawing program like Adobe Illustrator. For instance, in Illustrator you can quickly create type on a curve or within objects and edit the text you create. Figure 3-11 shows text on a curve created in Illustrator and imported into Photoshop.

Here are the steps for creating curved text in Illustrator and importing it into Photoshop:

1. Begin by loading Illustrator and creating some text.

2. To create type on a curve in Illustrator, you first need to create a curve. You do this by creating an oval with Illustrator's Oval tool. Next, activate the Path Type tool. (You may need to click and keep the mouse button pressed, and then click and drag to activate the Path Type tool.) With the Path Type tool selected, click on the edge of the curve and begin typing. If you wish, you can change the alignment to center, which will center the text on the curve.

Figure 3-11. *Text created in Adobe Illustrator and imported into Photoshop*

3. Now you need to save your file. You can save your Illustrator file in either Illustrator format or EPS format. After you save your file, you may want to quit Illustrator, depending on how much RAM your computer has (the more RAM, the more programs you can keep open at one time).

4. Load Photoshop, if it is not already loaded.

5. You can import text from Illustrator into Photoshop in one of four ways:

   ■ If you want to import your Illustrator text into a new Photoshop file, use File > Open. When you use the File > Open command, a dialog box appears asking you to determine the width, height, resolution, and so on, in order to rasterize your text. After the Illustrator text is rasterized, it is opened in a new Photoshop file, in a layer with a transparent background (unless you created a background in Illustrator).

   ■ If you are going to place your Illustrator text over a photograph in Photoshop, you'll want to use the File > Place command, because the text is placed in a new layer in the currently open document. When the text is placed on the screen, you can scale it if you wish. You also need to activate the text by double-clicking on it.

   ■ If you wish to drag and drop your text from Illustrator into Photoshop, both Illustrator and Photoshop should be opened on your screen. Select the text in Illustrator with the Selection tool, and then click and drag it over to the Photoshop window.

   ■ If you wish to copy and paste text from Illustrator into Photoshop, select the text in Illustrator with the Selection tool and choose Edit > Copy. Open or activate Photoshop. In Photoshop, choose Edit > Paste. A dialog box will open, allowing you to choose whether to paste the file as pixels, a path, or a shape layer.

Once you've brought your text into Photoshop, you can manipulate it with Photoshop's tools, as described earlier in this chapter.

Chapter 4

Working with Selections

It is virtually impossible to complete any Photoshop or ImageReady project without using at least one of the selection tools. The selection tools, which can be found at the top of both Photoshop's and ImageReady's Toolbox, are used primarily for outlining and isolating specific areas in images. After you've selected a portion of an image, you can modify, move, or copy it.

In this chapter, you'll be introduced to the concept of selections and discover why they're so important in Photoshop and ImageReady. Along the way, you'll learn how to use each of the selection tools, fill and stroke (outline or frame) a shape with the foreground and background colors, and modify selections.

Understanding Selections

It doesn't matter what shape a selection is, because Photoshop treats them all the same. Once you select an area on the screen, Photoshop directs its attention to the selection. You can execute virtually any image-editing command, and only the selected area will be affected.

When you make selections in Photoshop, it's important to remember that you are using a pixel-based (sometimes called *raster*) program, not an object-oriented (sometimes called *vector*) drawing program. In object-oriented drawing programs, you can select an object with the mouse and delete it. In Photoshop, your electronic canvas is filled with either colored or "transparent" pixels. To delete a selected area (that isn't a shape or path) on a white or colored background, you need to paint over it with the background color, in much the same way you use a liquid white-out product to correct typing mistakes. If, however, you are working on a layer (other than the Background), selecting an object and deleting it causes the transparent background or the layer beneath it to show through the hole you have created in your electronic canvas. (For a complete discussion of layers, see Chapters 16 and 17.)

Because Photoshop is pixel-based, you need to take special care when selecting and moving objects. If you don't understand the fundamentals of these actions, you may get some surprising and unwanted results. But once you've learned the basics of how to create and use selections, you'll be on your way to creating successful Photoshop design projects.

If you follow the exercises in this chapter, you'll be able to create selections and shapes—the stepping stones to image creation and editing. The exercises will also help you understand what a selection is.

ImageReady's selection tools and Select menu are very similar to Photoshop's. Although the exercises in this chapter focus on Photoshop, most of them are also applicable to ImageReady.

Creating, Filling, and Moving Selections

As a starting point for learning about selections, you will first create a selection and then make it come to life by filling it with a color (in the foreground or background). Then you will explore how to move selections and change their opacity.

Before beginning to work with the selection tools, create a new document to use for the following exercises. Also, it's a good idea to add Photoshop's rulers and Info palette to the window before you start working with selections. These features help you judge the size of the selections that you create.

1. Select File > New. In the New dialog box, check to see that the Width and Height measurement units are set to inches. If they aren't, click on the pop-up menu for each field and change the units to inches.

2. In the Width field, type **5**. In the Height field, type **4**. Resolution should be set to 72 pixels per inch. If it isn't, press TAB to move to the Resolution field and enter **72**.

3. If Mode is not set to RGB Color, click on the pop-up menu and change the setting.

4. In the Contents section, select the White radio button.

Remember *When you create a new file with the Contents radio button set to White, Photoshop creates a base layer called Background. Working in the Background is like painting on a white canvas. See Chapter 2 for information about the Background Color and Transparent options.*

5. Click on OK to create the new document.

6. To make the rulers visible, select View > Show Rulers.

7. To open the Info palette, select Window > Show Info.

Creating a Selection with the Rectangular Marquee Tool

Let's start with the Rectangular Marquee tool, which allows you to create and select squares and rectangles. When the Rectangular Marquee tool is selected, the default Style setting is Normal, which creates rectangular selections of any size. For this exercise, you'll use this and the other default settings on the tool's Options bar. The other options for the Marquee tools will be covered later in this chapter.

1. If the Rectangular Marquee tool does not appear in the Toolbox, click in the Marquee Toolbox location and hold down the mouse button. When the Marquee pop-up menu appears, select Rectangular Marquee Tool.

2. In the Marquee Options bar, check to see that Normal is selected in the Style pop-up menu. If it isn't, select it. If the Feather value in the palette is not set to 0, change it to 0 now.

 The Option bar settings for all of the tools in Photoshop retain the last settings used. They do not automatically return to their default settings. To reset a tool to use its default settings, click on its icon in the tool's options bar and choose Reset Tool. To reset all tools to their default settings, choose Reset All Tools from the pop-up menu.

3. Move the mouse pointer to the document window. Notice that when the pointer moves over the document area, it changes to a crosshair ($+$). Now you can start using the Rectangular Marquee tool to create a selection.

4. Position the crosshair at the 1-inch mark both vertically (Y-axis) and horizontally (X-axis). To make sure you are positioned at 1 inch both vertically and horizontally, refer to the Info palette. As you move the mouse, the X and Y readings next to the crosshair icon show your horizontal (X) and vertical (Y) positions. The X and Y readings next to the anchor icon indicate your original X and Y positions.

Note   *You can change the measurement units in the Info palette by choosing Palette Options from the palette menu. In the Info Options dialog box, click on the Ruler Units pop-up menu and choose Inches. As a shortcut, you can click on the small crosshair in the lower-left side of the palette and choose Inches from the pop-up menu.*

5. When the Info palette shows both X and Y reading 1, click and drag diagonally down from left to right to make a rectangular selection of about 2 × 2 inches. When your selection looks like Figure 4-1, release the mouse. Refer to the width (W) and height (H) readings of the selection in the Info palette to size the selection.

6. Your selection is represented on the screen by a blinking marquee, which appears as a series of dashed lines. The selection is now an isolated area that you can work with as an independent object, separate from the rest of the screen.

7. Click again anywhere in your document outside your rectangular selection. This signals to Photoshop that you're finished working with the selection. It deselects your original selection, and the marquee disappears.

The next sections introduce you to techniques for editing the selection marquee and creating shapes by filling selections with colors.

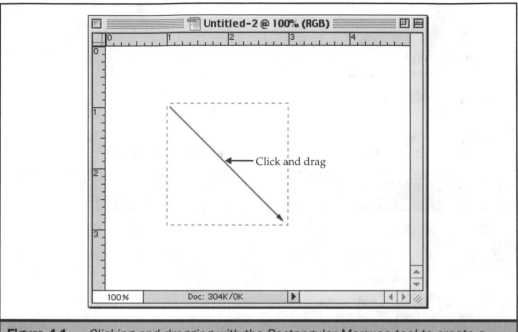

Figure 4-1. *Clicking and dragging with the Rectangular Marquee tool to create a selection*

  The selections you create with the Rectangular Marquee tool share the same characteristics as all other types of selections. Photoshop treats selections the same, no matter which selection tool created them.

Filling a Selection with the Foreground or Background Color

To fill a selection, you can use the Edit > Fill command. Photoshop also provides shortcuts for filling with the foreground and background colors, as listed in Table 4-1.

Action	Keystroke
Fill a selection with the foreground color.	OPTION-DELETE (*ALT-BACKSPACE*)
Fill a selection with the background color.	DELETE (*BACKSPACE*)

Table 4-1. *Keyboard Shortcuts for Filling Areas*

Action	Keystroke
Fill a selection in a layer (other than the Background) with the background color.	COMMAND-DELETE (*CTRL-BACKSPACE*)
Fill the nontransparent areas of a layer with the foreground color.	OPTION-SHIFT-DELETE (*ALT-SHIFT-BACKSPACE*)
Fill the nontransparent areas of a layer with the background color.	COMMAND-SHIFT-DELETE (*CTRL-SHIFT-DELETE*)

Table 4-1.   *Keyboard Shortcuts for Filling Areas* (continued)

Note   *If you have a selection on screen, when you press the keys to fill nontransparent areas of a layer, the selection will be filled instead.*

To make it easier to follow the instructions in this exercise, start with the foreground and background colors at their default settings (black foreground and white background). Check the Foreground Color and Background Color swatches in the Toolbox. If the foreground color is not black and the background color is not white, click on the Default Colors icon to reset the colors to their defaults. (You can also press D on the keyboard.)

Note   *If you have a layer on screen and the Preserve Transparency option is selected in the Layers palette, the Edit > Fill command fills the nontransparent areas of the layer.*

Start by creating a rectangular selection and filling it with the foreground color; then fill it with the background color.

1. Notice that the Rectangular Marquee tool is still selected—it's the last tool you used, and Photoshop keeps it active. To create the rectangular selection, click approximately 1 inch from the upper-left corner of the screen and drag down diagonally approximately 2 or 3 inches. Release the mouse button.

2. To fill the selection with the foreground color, press and hold down the OPTION (*ALT*) key, and press DELETE (*BACKSPACE*). Your rectangular selection immediately turns black. Notice that the selection marquee still surrounds your rectangle.

3. To fill with the background color, press DELETE (*BACKSPACE*).

   The rectangle disappears but the selection remains. This often gives new Photoshop users the mistaken impression that the DELETE (*BACKSPACE*) key deletes objects. Actually, this keystroke fills with the background color, and therefore can be considered a painting tool. You have just painted your black rectangle white. If you're still skeptical about this concept, you'll be convinced when you press DELETE (*BACKSPACE*) with a background color other than white.

Note *If you are in a layer other than the Background, pressing DELETE (BACKSPACE) cuts a hole in the layer, allowing either the layer below or the transparent background to show through the deleted area.*

Changing the Foreground and Background Colors

Photoshop provides a variety of ways to choose colors for the foreground and background. The simplest method of picking colors is from the color bar spectrum at the bottom of the Color palette. In the exercise in this section, you will change colors and then create an object and fill it with the new background and foreground colors. (You can find out more about the Color palette in Chapter CD-1.)

1. To display the Color palette, select Window > Show Color. Notice the two squares in the upper-left corner of the Color palette. The top square is the Foreground selection box and represents the foreground color. It overlaps a second square, the Background selection box, which represents the background color. A white band surrounding the selection box indicates that that color is active and ready to be changed.

2. Click on the Foreground selection box so that you can change the foreground color.

3. To change the foreground color to red, position the mouse pointer over a red area in the color bar. The mouse pointer changes to an eyedropper. Click on the red area. The Foreground selection box and the Foreground Color icon in the Toolbox both change to red.

Note *If you don't see a spectrum of colors at the bottom of the Color palette, click on the Color palette's pop-up menu arrow and choose Color Bar. When the Color Bar dialog box opens, choose RGB Spectrum or CMYK Spectrum in the Style pop-up menu. Then click on OK.*

4. Click on the Background selection box, which is currently white. The white band jumps to and surrounds this box.

5. Point to the color bar and click on a blue area. Again, notice the change in both the Background selection box in the Color palette and the Background Color icon in the Toolbox.

Tip *If the Foreground selection box is activated, pressing OPTION (ALT) and clicking in the color bar changes the background color. If the Background selection box is activated, pressing OPTION (ALT) and clicking in the color bar changes the foreground color.*

6. Using the Rectangular Marquee tool, create a rectangular selection.

7. To apply the background color, press DELETE (*BACKSPACE*). The rectangle fills with blue. If you are in a layer, press COMMAND-DELETE (*CTRL-BACKSPACE*).

8. To apply the foreground color, press OPTION-DELETE (*ALT-BACKSPACE*). The rectangle changes to red.

9. To remove the marquee from the selection, position the crosshair anywhere inside the document window and click. Alternatively, to deselect, choose Select > Deselect.

The marquee disappears, indicating that the rectangle is no longer selected. Clicking away from a selection causes it to be deselected. If you wish to continue experimenting with the colored rectangle on screen, you can reselect it by choosing Select > Reselect.

Transforming a Selection

Once you create a selection on screen, you may wish to edit it—make the selection marquee larger or smaller, rotate or move it, or even change its shape to distort it. Fortunately, Photoshop 6 and ImageReady allow you to transform a selection without altering the image area within the selection. After selecting, you can use the Select > Transform Selection command to modify your selection marquee.

As a simple experiment, try the following steps to transform a selection on your screen.

1. To select the rectangle from the previous section, position the Rectangular Marquee crosshair so that it touches the top-left corner of the object, as shown below.

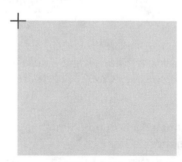

2. Click and drag diagonally down to the bottom-right corner, and release the mouse button.

3. To transform a selection marquee, choose Select > Transform Selection. Handles (tiny squares) appear around the selection. Figure 4-2 shows how the selection handles look when transforming a selection around a digital image. (If you would like to practice with this image, the Crab&Shell file can be found in the Chapter 4 folder on the book CD.)

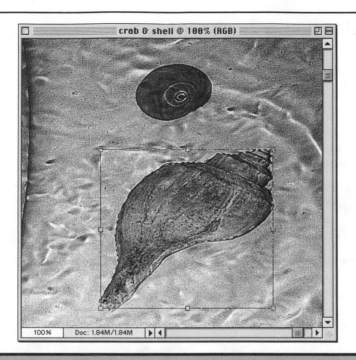

Figure 4-2. *Selection handles appear around the selection*

4. To resize the marquee, click and drag on any of the handles on the edge of the transformation box. To constrain the aspect ratio, press SHIFT while you click and drag on a corner handle.

5. To rotate the selection marquee, click on or near the edge of the transformation box and drag, but don't click on a handle. If you wish to change the center point for the rotation, click and drag on the center point icon and then rotate the selection.

6. To distort the selection, press COMMAND (*CTRL*) and click and drag on a handle.

7. To move the selection marquee, simply click in the middle of the bounding box and drag.

8. To complete the transformation, press ENTER.

9. If you wish to undo the transformation, choose Edit > Undo, or click above the Free Transform Selection state in the History palette.

Note   *Don't confuse the Select > Transform Selection command with Photoshop's Edit > Transform commands. The Edit > Transform commands transform image areas, not the selection marquee. See Chapters 8 and 16 for more details about Edit > Transform.*

Moving a Selection with the Mouse

Once you have created a selection, you may want to move it to the perfect location on your screen. In this exercise, you'll move a selection using the mouse.

1. Make sure you have a rectangle selected on the screen and the Rectangular Marquee tool activated.

2. To move the rectangle with the mouse, start by positioning the crosshair over the middle of the rectangle. The crosshair changes to an arrow pointer with a small rectangle at the end of it.

3. Once the arrow pointer appears on screen, click and drag it to move the rectangle about 1 inch to the right and about 0.5 inch down. Notice that just the selection moved—not the filled rectangle.

4. Click on Undo, or reselect the rectangle with the Rectangular Marquee tool.

5. To move both the selection and the filled rectangle inside it, press and hold the COMMAND (*CTRL*) key while you click inside the selected rectangle. A small scissors icon replaces the small rectangle icon at the bottom of the arrow pointer.

Note   *You can also use the Move tool to move both the selection and the filled rectangle inside it.*

6. Drag the selection and rectangle into position. As you move the object, you will see that Photoshop leaves a duplicate of the rectangular selection in its original position, filled with the background color, as shown in Figure 4-3. (Note that if the background color in the Toolbox and the document color are both white, you will not see a change.)

Tip   *As you create a rectangular selection in Photoshop or ImageReady, you can move it without releasing the mouse: after you create the selection, keep the mouse button down, press the SPACEBAR, and continue to drag the selection to move it.*

You may find it annoying that Photoshop leaves the background color on the portion of the screen from which an object was moved. (If you are working in a layer other than the Background, moving a selection causes the transparent background or the layer beneath it to show through.) Figure 4-4 shows the effects of moving a rectangular selection (with the Move tool) in a scanned image. Here, too, Photoshop has cut a hole in the image. (The Mountain file shown in Figure 4-4 is included on this book's CD-ROM.)

Most of the time, when you move an object, you won't want a hole left behind filled with the current background color. A simple way to avoid this is to copy the selected area before you fill it with a color. You'll use this technique in the "Duplicating and Moving a Selection" section, coming up after you learn how to clear the screen.

However, before proceeding, note that you can now freely move the selection on screen by clicking and dragging it. You can also using the arrow keys on the keyboard

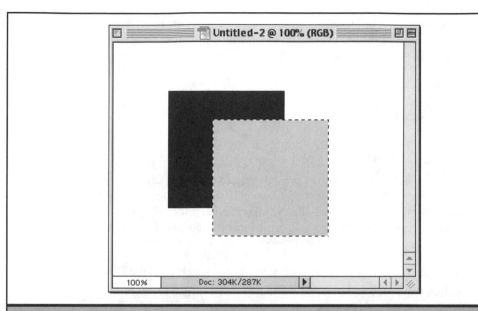

Figure 4-3.   *Photoshop leaves a duplicate of the selection in its original position*

Figure 4-4.   *Cutting and moving a portion of an image leaves the background color behind*

to move a selection. Press any directional arrow key three or four times. With each keypress, the object will move 1 pixel up, down, left, or right. This time, Photoshop does not rip a hole out of the background.

 When you move a selection for the first time with the Move tool, Photoshop creates a "hole" in your image. To restore your original image, click in the History palette and then choose Edit > Undo File > Revert.

Clearing the Screen

To give yourself more room to work, try deleting everything on your screen. In Photoshop, one method of clearing the screen is to execute the Select > All command, which selects the entire screen. Once the entire screen is selected, it can then be "erased" by filling it with white. The Select > All command is also helpful when you wish to apply a Photoshop command to everything on your screen.

1. Change the background color back to white by clicking on the Default Colors icon.

2. To select the entire screen, choose Select > All or press COMMAND-A (*CTRL-A*).

3. Press DELETE (*BACKSPACE*). The entire screen fills with the background color, white.

4. Notice the marquee surrounding your screen, indicating that the entire screen is still selected. To deselect it, choose Select > None or press COMMAND-D (*CTRL-D*).

 If you "erase" the screen in a layer other than the Background, the layer will be cleared and images in the underlying layers will then be visible.

Duplicating and Moving a Selection

In this exercise, you'll create a rectangular selection and then duplicate it so you can move it, fill it with a color, or delete it without affecting the underlying pixels. This is called "floating" a selection.

1. Start by resetting the foreground color to red and the background color to blue. If you don't change the background color, you won't see the effects of floating a selection.

2. If the Rectangular Marquee tool is not selected, select it now.

3. Click on the upper-left corner of your window and drag diagonally 2 or 3 inches to the right to create a rectangular selection. Do not deselect.

4. To duplicate and move the selected area, hold down the OPTION-COMMAND (*ALT-CTRL*) keys while you click and drag inside the rectangular selection on screen.

You can also activate the Move tool, and then press OPTION (ALT) while clicking and dragging.

5. Fill the object with the foreground color by pressing OPTION-DELETE (*ALT-BACKSPACE*).

6. Position the pointer in the middle of the rectangle and drag about 1 inch down and to the right. Do not deselect. This time, when you moved the selection, the background did not change.

7. Once the selected area has been moved, you can delete it by pressing DELETE. Do this now.

   Notice that the selected area was deleted, and Photoshop didn't fill the deleted area with the background color. Once you move a selected object, it's almost as if the object were floating above the background pixels. Thus, pressing DELETE affects only the selected floating area.

Changing Selection Opacity

If you move a selection on screen, you may wish to create a blend between the selection you move and the pixels beneath it. In Photoshop, you can change the opacity of a selection that you moved by using the Fade command.

After moving the selection with the Move tool or by pressing OPTION (*ALT*) while dragging, simply choose Edit > Fade. In the Fade dialog box, lower the opacity by dragging the Opacity slider to the left. You can also choose a blending mode from the Mode pop-up menu. The blending modes create special effects by blending the pixels in the moved selection with pixels in the underlying area. (Blending modes are discussed in Chapters 5 and 16.)

> **Tip** *You can also access the Edit > Fade command after painting with a painting tool, filling a selection using the Edit > Fill command, color correcting with an Image > Adjust command, or applying one of Photoshop's Edit > Transform commands to a selection.*

Working with Copy and Paste

The selection tools are integral to the creation of photomontages (multiple photographs from different images) and collages (various images and graphics blended together). These tools also allow you to quickly turn scanned images into line art and to create special effects such as vignettes (pictures that gradually fade off into the surroundings). For these types of projects, you will often use the Edit > Copy and Edit > Paste commands to copy and paste a selection from one file into another. When you copy or cut a selection and paste it into another file, Photoshop automatically creates a new layer with the selection in it.

For example, to create the image in Figure 4-5, we scanned a photograph of a dock and a photograph of a telephone booth, shown in Figure 4-6, at the same resolution. (Both images are included on this book's CD-ROM.) Next, we selected the telephone

Figure 4-5.   *The telephone booth pasted into the dock image*

Figure 4-6.   *The images used to create the collage*

booth with the Rectangular Marquee tool, as shown in Figure 4-7, copied it, and pasted it into the dock document. Photoshop automatically placed the telephone image into a new layer in the dock document after the Paste command was executed.

 You can drag a selection border from one Photoshop document to another or from one ImageReady document to another.

When the telephone booth was in the dock document, we scaled it using the Edit > Transform > Scale command. Once the telephone booth was scaled, we moved it into position using the Move tool. For the final touch, we used the Eraser tool to erase the extra areas around the telephone booth from the original file that we did not want included in the collage, shown in Figure 4-8.

 While you are learning how to work with selections, you can practice working with the sample images on this book's CD-ROM before you move onto more complicated, real-life jobs. You'll find all of the images shown in the examples in this chapter on the CD-ROM.

Storing and Purging the Contents of the Clipboard

Before you begin to experiment with Photoshop's or ImageReady's Cut, Copy, and Paste commands, you need to understand how both programs handle memory when you cut or copy the material you want to paste. When Edit > Cut and Edit > Copy

Figure 4-7. *Selecting the telephone booth with the Rectangular Marquee tool*

Figure 4-8. *Erasing the unwanted areas*

commands are executed, Photoshop and ImageReady automatically copy the contents of a selection in the active layer to an area of the computer's memory called the Clipboard. The Clipboard is a temporary storage area for copied or cut items.

Every time a selection is copied into the Clipboard, that selection replaces any existing Clipboard contents; only one item at a time can be stored in the Clipboard. When the Paste command is executed, the contents of the Clipboard are copied into the active document and placed in a new layer.

Note   *If you wish to copy an image from Photoshop's Clipboard to another Mac or Windows application, you must first select the Export Clipboard option in the General Preferences dialog box (Edit > Preferences > General). Mac users should note that Photoshop places a 4MB limit on PICT images that can be exported from the Clipboard. You can disable this limitation by installing the Unlimited Clipboard Size plug-in, which is located in the Optional Plug-ins folder in the Goodies folder on the Adobe Photoshop CD-ROM.*

It is important to realize that when the contents of a large selection are being held in the Clipboard, there is less memory available to use. In this situation, you might receive an out-of-memory message. To prevent this from happening, make sure that you allocate as much RAM as possible to Photoshop and/or ImageReady and that your scratch disk's storage capacity is as large as possible. Ideally, of course, the best solution is to purchase more RAM or a larger hard disk.

If you think the contents of the Clipboard are consuming too much memory (and you no longer need to store that information) in Photoshop, you can remove the memory used by the Clipboard by choosing Edit > Purge > Clipboard.

Handling Different Resolutions During Paste Operations

When you paste a selected area from one Photoshop file into another file with a different resolution, you may be surprised at the consequences. The contents of the selection you paste will take on the resolution of the file into which you paste it. Thus, if the selection's resolution is higher than that of the target file, the selection will enlarge when pasted. If you paste a selected area with a low resolution into a higher-resolution file, the selection will shrink when pasted.

To understand this phenomenon, remember that there are more pixels per square inch in a high-resolution file than in a low-resolution file. For example, if you select an area of 72 pixels × 72 pixels in a file set to a resolution of 72 pixels per inch (ppi), the selection is 1 inch. But if you paste the selection into a file with a resolution of 300 ppi, the selection shrinks to about one-quarter of an inch in the new file. The selection is still composed of 72 pixels × 72 pixels, but the pixels must diminish in size when they are placed in an image where a square inch comprises 300 pixels × 300 pixels.

If a selection's size increases or decreases after pasting, you can resize the pasted area by using the Edit > Transform > Scale command (discussed in Chapter 8). However, be aware that this command adds or subtracts pixels in the image, which can degrade image quality.

Creating Fill and Stroke Selections in a Layer

You've seen how the Rectangular Marquee tool creates rectangular selections. But what if you need to select a perfectly square area? That's the purpose of the Constrained Aspect Ratio option on the tool's Options bar. This option allows you to constrain your selections to specified ratios. When you use this option with the Elliptical Marquee tool, it creates perfect circles.

In the following exercises, you will work with the Rectangular and Elliptical Marquee tools to make selections, and then fill and stroke them. You'll do this in a layer that has a transparent background, which means that any layers beneath the layer in which you are working can be seen through areas in your file that are not filled with color.

Before beginning the next exercises, close any other documents you might have open on screen. This will keep memory usage to a minimum. Then create a new document as follows:

1. Select File > New. In the New dialog box, check to see that the Width and Height measurement units are set to inches.

2. In the Width field, type **7**. In the Height field, type **5**. (This size will give you sufficient room to practice.)

3. If Mode is not set to RGB Color, click on the pop-up menu and change the setting.

4. In the Contents section, select the Transparent radio button.

5. Click on OK to create the new document. Notice that the screen is filled with a checkerboard-like pattern. This indicates that the background of your file is transparent. Notice also that the title bar of your document window includes the words "Layer 1."

6. If the Layers palette is not open, open it now by choosing Window > Show Layers. The words "Layer 1" appear in the Layers palette instead of the word "Background," because you chose the Transparent radio button in the New dialog box.

7. If the rulers and Info palette are not already on your screen, display them now (View > Show Rulers and Window > Show Info).

8. Use black as the foreground color and white as the background color. Check to see that these are your current settings. If they aren't, click on the Default Colors icon in the Toolbox.

You can modify the grid that indicates you are working in a layer with a transparent background. In the Preferences Transparency & Gamut dialog box (Edit > Preferences > Transparency & Gamut), choose a size from the Grid Size pop-up menu and/or choose colors from the Grid Colors pop-up menu. (In ImageReady, choose Edit > Preferences > Transparency.)

Constraining Rectangular Selections

We'll start by exploring the Constrained Aspect Ratio option, which creates selections according to proportions specified in the tool's Options bar. Although the Constrained Aspect Ratio option is often used to create squares, you can use it to create rectangles at other proportions.

1. Select the Rectangular Marquee tool in the Toolbox.

2. In the tool's Options bar, click on the Style pop-up menu and choose Constrained Aspect Ratio. Leave both the Width and Height fields set at 1, the defaults. These settings will constrain the mouse selection so that the width and height are always drawn at a 1:1 ratio—the width and height of the rectangular selection will always be equal to each other.

3. Move the crosshair to the upper-left corner of your document, and then click and drag down diagonally from left to right. As you drag, notice that your selection is a square. Release the mouse.

4. Now try creating another rectangular selection. No matter how hard you try, you will not be able to create anything other than a square selection. The selection can be any size, but it will always be a square, because the width to height proportion has been constrained to a 1:1 ratio.

5. In the Rectangular Marquee tool's Options bar, change Height to **2**.

6. Click and drag to create a selection. Because you constrained the selection to a 1:2 ratio, no matter how large your selection, the height will always be double the width.

7. In the Rectangular Marquee tool's Options bar, change Width **2** and Height to **1**.

8. Click and drag to create a selection. Because you constrained the selection to a 2:1 ratio, the width will always be double the height.

The other Style option available for the Rectangular Marquee tool is Fixed Size. When you select this option, the tool will create rectangles that are always the same size.

Using the Elliptical Marquee Tool

The Elliptical Marquee tool functions similarly to the Rectangular Marquee, except that it creates round rather than rectangular shapes. In the Elliptical Marquee Options bar's Style pop-up menu, the Normal, Constrained Aspect Ratio, and Fixed Size options work exactly as they do with the Rectangular Marquee tool. Drawing an ellipse with the mouse is not too different from drawing a rectangle, primarily because you can click and drag diagonally to create the shape. The perimeter of the ellipse starts where you click, and the shape grows according to the size of the angle and distance you drag.

1. Select the Elliptical Marquee tool by clicking in the Marquee Toolbox location and holding down the mouse button until you see the list of Marquee tools. Move the mouse over Elliptical Marquee Tool, and then click to select it. Alternatively, you can OPTION-click (*ALT-click*) on the Rectangular Marquee icon in the Toolbox.

2. Check to see that Normal is selected in the Style pop-up menu in the tool's Options bar. If it is not, select it now.

3. To draw an ellipse, click on the upper-left corner of your screen and slowly drag diagonally toward the lower-right corner. When you have an elliptical selection on the screen, release the mouse button.

4. To practice a bit more, try drawing another ellipse. This time, drag only about one-half inch down and then drag across to the right, almost to the edge of the screen. This produces a cigar-shaped ellipse.

5. To see how the Constrained Aspect Ratio works with the Elliptical Marquee tool, select that option from the Style pop-up menu in the Options bar. If Width and Height are not set to 1, type **1** in both the Width and Height fields.

6. Click and drag diagonally down from the upper-left corner of your screen toward the bottom-right corner. Your selection will be a perfect circle.

7. Change Height to **2** and create another selection. The ellipse selection has a 1:2 ratio.

8. Change Width to **2** and Height to **1**. Drag out a selection, which will have a 2:1 ratio.

If the Constrained Aspect Ratio option is not activated, you can still create a perfect square or perfect circle by pressing SHIFT after you start dragging the mouse.

As a practical example, the clock collage shown in Figure 4-9 was created using the Elliptical Marquee tool. We started by scanning a photograph of clouds and a clock with the signs of the zodiac, shown in Figure 4-10, at the same resolution. (Both images are included on this book's CD-ROM.)

Figure 4-9.   *The clock pasted into the clouds image, and the two images used to create the collage*

Use CNTL + R↲

Figure 4-10.   *Selecting the clock image with the Elliptical Marquee tool*

Next, we selected the clock with the Elliptical Marquee tool (Figure 4-10), copied it, and pasted it into the cloud image. When we pasted the oval selection, Photoshop automatically placed the zodiac sign clock image into a new layer in the clouds document. Finally, we moved the clock into position using the Move tool.

Note   *Instead of copying and pasting, we could have dragged the clock image with the Move tool and dropped it into the clouds document.*

Using the Fill and Stroke Commands

The Edit > Fill command allows you to fill a selection with the background color, foreground color, black, white, 50 percent gray, a pattern, or the currently set History state in the History palette. The Fill dialog box also provides settings for blending modes and changing opacity. Here, we will cover plain fills. The Pattern and History options are covered in Chapter 6, and changing Opacity and using the blending modes are covered in Chapter 5.

Tip   *As soon as you create a shape with one of Photoshop's or ImageReady's Shape tools (with the New Shape Layer icon selected in the Options bar), it creates the shape in a new layer and fills it with the foreground color. You can change the fill color of text and shapes in a layer by choosing Layer > Layer Style > Color Overlay. In the Layer Style dialog box, click on the color swatch to open the Color Picker to change colors. You can also stroke a shape by choosing Stroke in the Layer Style dialog box.*

The Edit > Stroke command allows you to put a border or outline around a selection, using the current foreground color (you cannot stroke with the background color). You set the stroke width in pixels, ranging from 1 to 16 pixels. You can designate whether you wish the stroke to be along the outside of the selection marquee, inside it, or in the middle. You can also create a stroke with a tint (a percentage of the foreground color) and apply a blending mode. Working with tints is discussed in Chapter 5.

Continuing with your practice document, you will fill a circular selection with white using the Edit > Fill command. Then you will use Edit > Stroke to stroke the selection. Before closing this file, you will also take a look at some aspects of working in a layer.

1. Before you fill or stroke an object, you need to create a selection on screen. Select the Elliptical Marquee tool, and then click and drag to create a circle about 2 inches in diameter.

2. If the foreground and background colors are not set to black and white, click on the Default Colors icon to change them.

3. To fill the selection with white, open the Fill dialog box by choosing Edit > Fill. You can also press and hold SHIFT, then press the DELETE (*BACKSPACE*) key to open the Fill dialog box.

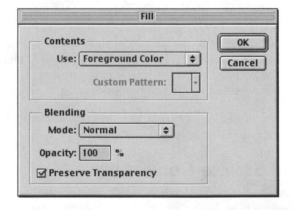

4. In the Use pop-up menu, choose either Background Color or White. Leave Opacity set to 100% and Mode set to Normal. Do not select the Preserve Transparency checkbox; otherwise, the transparent area in the selection (in this case, the entire selection) will not be affected. Click on OK.

5. To stroke the selection, open the Stroke dialog box by choosing Edit > Stroke.

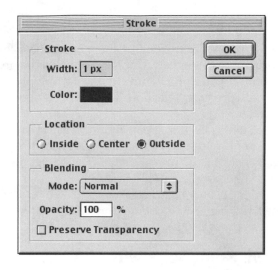

6. To set the size of the stroke, type **5** in the Width field. Set Location to Center, Opacity to 100%, and Mode to Normal. Then click on OK. The circle appears, with a 5-pixel outline. In the middle of the circle's 5-pixel stroke, you'll see the selection marquee still blinking. The stroke was created in the center of the selection.

7. Click away to deselect and see the stroke.

8. Select the Move tool, and then click and drag on the circle. The circle moves, even though you did not select it first.

9. Close this practice file.

In this exercise, you saw that you can move all of a layer's contents by clicking and dragging with the Move tool. This does not mean that you don't need the selection tools anymore. If you had two circles in the same layer and wanted to move them independently of one another, you would need to select the one you wanted to move first.

Selecting with the Lasso and Magic Wand Tools

Four other selection tools that you will find useful are the three kinds of Lasso tools and the Magic Wand tool. The Lasso tools—Lasso, Polygon Lasso, and Magnetic Lasso—are frequently used to create selections by tracing over image areas. The Magic Wand tool is normally used to select areas according to similarity of color.

Using the Lasso Tools

Although they are not as precise as the Pen tool, the Lasso tools can often create intricate selections. Using one of the Lasso tools, you click to begin a selection and drag to complete the selection. If you don't return to the starting point of your selection, each of the tools always closes your selection. They will not allow you to leave an open curve or angle on screen.

In general, the Lasso tool is used to create freeform selections. The Magnetic Lasso tool, the newest member of Photoshop's Lasso family, is used to create precise selections, because it automatically snaps to an image's edge. The Polygon Lasso tool is used to create selections shaped like polygons.

The Lasso, Polygon Lasso, and Magnetic Lasso tools all reside in the same Toolbox location. To select the Lasso Toolbox location, press L on your keyboard. To switch from tool to tool, you can press SHIFT-L.

Creating Freeform Selections with the Lasso

In this section, you'll try your hand with the Lasso tool by creating a freeform, kidney-shaped selection.

1. Create a new file, 7 × 5 inches, to give you sufficient room to practice with these tools. You can set the background Contents to either White or Transparent.

2. Select the Lasso tool from the Toolbox. Take a look at this tool's Options bar.

3. The Feather option provides a means of softening the inside and outside edges of a selection. The value that you type here determines the width in pixels of the feathered edge. You will learn how to use the Feather option in the "Feathering the Edges of Selections" section later in this chapter. For now, if this value is not currently set to 0, type **0** in the field now.

4. The Anti-aliased option softens the hard edges of pixels by partially selecting them. This will cause selection edges to appear less jagged when filled with a color. If the Anti-aliased checkbox is not selected by default, select it now.

5. With the Lasso tool active, move the pointer into the middle of the document window. As you move the mouse, the pointer changes to a Lasso icon. Position the Lasso in the upper-left corner of the screen.

If you press the CAPS LOCK key, the mouse pointer will turn into a crosshair. The crosshair is provided as an alternative to the Lasso pointer, because it allows you to select more precisely. You can also set the crosshair to appear by choosing Edit > Preferences > Display & Cursors and setting Other Cursors to Precise.

PHOTOSHOP BASICS

6. To create the kidney shape, click and drag as shown below. As you drag the mouse, be careful not to release the mouse button. If you do, the Lasso tool will finalize the selection by connecting the starting and ending points. If this happens, click outside the selection to deselect it and start over again.

7. When you've completed the kidney shape, release the mouse button.

Tracing with the Magnetic Lasso Tool

The Magnetic Lasso tool is a true time-saver. It helps you create intricate selections by automatically snapping to image edges that you trace over. Before you try out the tool, load an image that includes an area that you wish to select. Then activate the Magnetic Lasso tool in Photoshop's Toolbox. (ImageReady does not offer the Magnetic Lasso tool.)

As you can see from the choices in the tool's Options bar, the Magnetic Lasso tool is the most sophisticated of the Lasso tools.

Along with the same Feather and Anti-aliased options that are available for the Lasso and Polygon Lasso tools, the Magnetic Lasso tool has three more settings:

■ The Width setting controls image edge detection. The Magnetic Lasso tool uses this value to determine how far from the point to look for image edges. When the value is set to 10 pixels (the default setting), the Magnetic Lasso tool detects image edges up to 10 pixels away. If you are trying to trace over an image that includes twists and turns, you'll probably want to lower the value. Acceptable values are between 1 and 40 pixels.

Stylus users should click the Stylus Pressure option in the dialog box. Adding pressure to the stylus decreases the pen's width.

■ The Frequency setting controls how fast the Magnetic Lasso tool adds fastening points. Higher values drop fastening points faster. Enter values between 1 and 100.

■ The Edge Contrast setting controls how the Magnetic Lasso tool reacts to different contrast values along image edges. Enter higher values to have the Magnetic Lasso tool recognize edges that contain more contrast. Enter lower percentage values to detect lower contrast.

When selecting high-contrast images, set high Width and Edge Contrast values. For images that don't display much contrast along image edges, set lower Width and Contrast values.

To trace an image with the Magnetic Lasso tool, start by clicking to establish a magnetic point, and then move the Magnetic Lasso along the edge of the object (you don't need to keep the mouse button depressed). The Magnetic Lasso starts creating a selection based on the image's edge contrast and the tool's settings in its Options bar. If the selection jumps off the edge you are tracing, simply click to establish another fastening point segment, and then continue to move the mouse along the object. If you wish to delete the previous segment, press DELETE.

To end the selection created with the Magnetic Lasso tool, double-click or press RETURN (ENTER), If you wish to close the selection with a straight segment, press and hold down the OPTION (ALT) key while you double-click.

To temporarily activate the Lasso tool while using the Magnetic Lasso tool, press OPTION (ALT) while you click and drag. To temporarily activate the Polygon Lasso tool while using the Magnetic Lasso tool, press OPTION (ALT) and click.

Figure 4-11 shows an image created with the Magnetic Lasso tool. We selected the cow from a scanned photo, as shown in Figure 4-12, and placed it into another background (both images are included on this book's CD-ROM). We used the Lasso tool to create the balloon, and then stroked it with white and filled with 50-percent white. We also stroked the balloon with black at a 90 percent opacity with the mode set to Color Dodge. To give the balloon caption depth, we applied the Layer > Effects > Drop Shadow command and Effects > Outer Glow command. Next, we used the Type tool to add text and applied the Layer > Effects > Drop Shadow command to the text.

Constraining the Lasso Selection

The Polygon Lasso tool allows you to create polygons by clicking at different points on the screen. As you click, the Lasso connects the points with selection lines. The Polygon Lasso tool has the same options as the Lasso tool.

Try out the Lasso's constraining option by creating a simple triangle.

1. Activate the Polygon Lasso tool.

2. When working with the Polygon Lasso tool, it's often a good idea to use the crosshair pointer to make more accurate selections. Press CAPS LOCK to activate the crosshair pointer.

Figure 4-11.   *The cow placed in a new background, with a balloon caption*

Figure 4-12.   *Selecting the cow with the Magnetic Lasso tool*

3. Move the crosshair down to about 1 inch from the top side of your file and 4 inches to the right of the left edge, and click.

4. Move the pointer diagonally, about 2 inches to the right and about 3 inches down. Click again. You now have a straight line connecting your first and second mouse clicks.

5. Move the mouse horizontally to the left about 4 inches and click.

6. Return to your original starting point. When you see a small circle appear next to the Polygon Lasso tool icon, your ending and starting points have met. Click to close the selection. Your shape will look like the one shown below. Don't deselect yet, because you'll need to use this triangular selection in the next exercise, in which you'll start working with the Magic Wand.

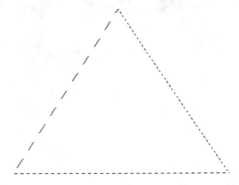

If you wish to end a selection created with the Polygon Lasso tool without returning to the selection's starting point, double-click or COMMAND-click (*CTRL-click*). To delete a segment created with the Polygon Lasso tool, press DELETE.

 Instead of using the Polygon Lasso tool, you can make the Lasso tool work in this mode. Press OPTION (ALT) to constrain your selection and keep it pressed as you create the triangle.

As an example, to create the image in Figure 4-13, we scanned the photograph of two gondolas shown in Figure 4-14 (the Gondola file is included on this book's CD-ROM). Next, we selected the gondolas with the Polygon Lasso tool, as shown in Figure 4-14. Then we copied and pasted them into a new document (after filling the new document with yellow and applying the Noise filter to it to give the background some texture). To complete the flyer, we used the Type tool to add text.

Using the Magic Wand

 Of all Photoshop's selection tools, the Magic Wand is usually considered the most unusual, because it can create selections that would be nearly impossible to reproduce by hand. This tool works by selecting a color range with one click of the mouse.

Figure 4-13.   *The Gondola Rides flyer*

Figure 4-14.   *Selecting the gondolas with the Polygon Lasso tool*

Before you begin to use the Magic Wand, select it and take a look at its Options bar.

You'll see the following options for the Magic Wand tool:

- The Tolerance option controls the color range that the Magic Wand will select; the greater the Tolerance setting, the broader the color range. You can enter a value from 0 to 255. The default value is 32.

- The Anti-aliased option functions exactly as it does in the Type and Lasso Options bars.

- The Contiguous option controls whether the selected colors will be adjacent. When it isn't chosen, the Magic Wand selects all colors that fall within the tolerance range, jumping over colors that don't fall within the color range

- The Use All Layers option tells the Magic Wand tool to analyze not only the pixels you click on, but also the pixels in all visible layers.

To see the Magic Wand's color-selecting capabilities in action, you'll need to fill a triangular selection (the one you just created in the preceding section) with a color. (If you don't have a triangular selection on your screen, use the Polygon Lasso tool to create one.) You'll also create a circle in the center of the triangle and fill it, so that you will have two shapes and two colors with which to test the Magic Wand tool's powers.

1. If the Color palette is not on your screen, open it by choosing Window > Show Color. Change the foreground color to orange by clicking on an orange area in the color bar in the Color palette.

2. Fill the selection (the triangle) by pressing OPTION-DELETE (*ALT-DELETE*). Click away from the object to deselect, and release CAPS LOCK.

3. Use the Elliptical Marquee tool to create a circle in the middle of the triangle. Set the style to Normal in the Options bar, if necessary.

4. Change the foreground color to yellow, and fill the circle with yellow.

5. Select the Magic Wand tool in the Toolbox. Change the Tolerance setting in the Options bar to **0**.

6. Point to the yellow circle you just created. Notice that the mouse pointer changes to a wand icon when you move it over the document area. (If the mouse pointer is a crosshair and not a wand icon, CAPS LOCK is still on.)

7. Click on the circle. The Magic Wand selects only the circle.

8. Click on the triangle. The Magic Wand selects only the orange area of the triangle. Since the Tolerance value is set to 0, in both cases, the Magic Wand selects only one color.

9. Change the Tolerance setting in the Magic Wand tool's Options bar to **255**.

10. Click again on the yellow circle. This time, the Magic Wand selects both the circle and triangle because the high Tolerance setting allowed more colors to slip into the selection.

In this exercise, you saw that if the Magic Wand's Tolerance is set to 0, and the Contiguous checkbox is selected (the default), the Magic Wand selects an area of contiguous pixels that are only the same color as the pixel that you click. If you increase the Tolerance setting, the Magic Wand expands the selection to include a greater range of color, using the color you clicked on as its starting point. A very high Tolerance setting creates a selection over a color range that can vary greatly from the color originally selected.

You also saw that even with this less-than-intricate selection, the Magic Wand still proves to be a time-saver. If you used the Lasso tool to reselect the triangular selection, you would need to click precisely over your original mouse clicks.

The Select menu's Color Range command provides another means of creating a selection based on color. This command is covered in Chapter 15.

The collage shown in Figure 4-15 was assembled primarily by using the Magic Wand tool. We scanned in a photograph of a statue of some kids and another one of a building with a fancy window, shown in Figure 4-16, at the same resolution. (Both images are included on this book's CD-ROM.) Next, we selected the kids with the Magic Wand tool, as shown in Figure 4-17. After creating the selection, we copied the kids and pasted them into the selection of the window (created with the Magic Wand tool) in the building document.

Note that to get both kids selected, we needed to adjust the Tolerance value in the Magic Wand Options bar a few times until we got the right value. We also needed to add to and subtract from the selection to obtain the selection we desired. Adding and subtracting from selections is discussed in the next section.

Modifying Selections

Even though you've learned to use all of Photoshop's selection tools, your selection knowledge won't be complete until you know how to change your selections by adding to them, subtracting from them, and intersecting them. You'll also find some useful commands for modifying selections on the Select menu and the Layer > Matting submenu.

Figure 4-15. *The kids in a window collage*

Figure 4-16. *The images used to create the collage*

Figure 4-17.   *Selecting the kids with the Magic Wand*

Adding to and Subtracting from Selections

If you've used other Mac or Windows programs, you can probably guess that you can add to a selection by SHIFT-clicking. Just hold down the SHIFT key when you make a new selection, and Photoshop or ImageReady adds to a previous selection. However, unlike many Mac and Windows programs, you cannot subtract from a selection by pressing SHIFT and clicking on a selection.

Suppose you want to remove part of a selection but leave other areas selected. To subtract from a selection, press and hold down the OPTION (*ALT*) key while you click and drag over or within the selection.

Try removing a corner from a rectangular selection using the Lasso tool. First, create a rectangular selection on your screen. Then activate the Lasso tool. While holding down OPTION (*ALT*), click and drag to create a curved selection over any corner of the rectangle on screen. When you release the mouse, the corner is subtracted from the selection.

You can also create a selection that is the intersection of two selections. To try this, press both OPTION (*ALT*) and SHIFT, and then click and drag to make a selection that overlaps the rectangular selection. Fill with the foreground color, and you'll see that Photoshop paints the *intersection*—only the common areas of the two selections.

If you already have selections on the screen, you can add, subtract, or create an intersection out of the selections by simply clicking on the appropriate button in the currently activated selection tool's Options bar.

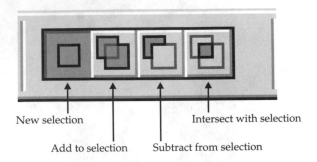

New selection   Intersect with selection

Add to selection   Subtract from selection

Changing Magic Wand Selections

The Select menu includes two commands that can help when you are selecting with the Magic Wand:

- Select > Grow expands the selection on the screen as if you had doubled the Tolerance range in the Magic Wand's dialog box.

- Select > Similar makes the selection jump over areas beyond the Magic Wand's tolerance to select areas that fit within its tolerance. For instance, suppose that you have an image that contains a black bridge over a river, which prevents the Magic Wand from selecting the entire river. You could choose Select > Similar, and the selection will jump over the bridge and select the rest of the water.

 ImageReady includes a Select > Similar command, but not Select > Grow.

Expanding and Contracting Selections

The Select > Modify > Expand and Select > Modify > Contract commands allow you to make a selection grow or shrink by a specified number of pixels. As with Select > Grow and Select > Similar, these commands are used after a selection is created. For instance, if you have selected an area and wish to expand it by 1 pixel, choose Select > Modify > Expand, enter **1** in the Pixel field of the Expand Selection dialog box, and click on OK. The selection will grow 1 pixel outward. Select > Modify > Contract works in the same way to decrease selections inward by the number of pixels you specify.

The Expand and Contract commands can be especially helpful when you're removing extraneous pixels that get selected or including pixels that aren't selected because of anti-aliasing. For instance, you might use Select > Modify > Contract to remove extra pixels when selecting with the Magic Wand tool. Select > Modify > Expand can be useful to slightly expand a selection created by COMMAND-clicking (CTRL-*clicking*) in a layer in the Layers palette to select the nontransparent areas of the layer.

The Select > Modify > Smooth command also alters selections by adding to or deleting from the original selection. Like Expand and Contract, Smooth allows you to type in a pixel value to control the effect. The Smooth command, however, uses the pixel value as a radius. For instance, when you type in a pixel value of 8, Photoshop radiates out from a central location, evaluating 8 pixels in each direction. Thus, the actual distance examined for smoothing is 16 pixels.

The Smooth command evaluates whether most of the pixels in the radius area are selected; if they are, it selects the unselected pixels. If most of the pixels in the radius area are not selected, it deselects the selected pixels.

The Smooth command can be helpful when you are trying to combine selections, blend a selection into its surroundings, or smooth the sharp edges of a selection.

To try out the Smooth command, create a star-shaped selection with the Lasso tool or the Polygon Lasso tool. Connect the points of the star by clicking and moving the mouse. Once you've created the star, execute Select > Modify > Smooth. Enter **5** pixels in the dialog box and click on OK. The edges of your star will be smoothed.

For a more dramatic look at the Smooth command, create a rectangular selection. Press SHIFT and create two other rectangular selections directly above the first, about a quarter-inch apart. Execute the Smooth command with a high pixel value. The Smooth command will join all three selections into one selection.

Replacing a Selection with a Border

The Border command is another Select > Modify menu option that changes a selection. Select > Modify > Border replaces a selection with a border surrounding the area of the original selection. The size of the border is specified in the Border dialog box.

If you wish to see the Border command in action, create any selection, and then choose Select > Modify > Border. In the Border dialog box, enter a pixel width for the border, and then click on OK. Fill the new selection with a color. You'll see that the border around the selection is filled, not the original selection.

Using the Matting Commands

When you select an area with the Magic Wand, the Lasso, or the Elliptical Marquee tool, you might encounter a mysterious halo of color that seems to tag along with your image. Photoshop may include extra colored pixels along the edges of the selection, which can become noticeable when a selection is pasted or moved. This effect is especially apparent when a light image is moved onto a dark background or a dark image is moved onto a light background.

The extra colored pixels are often the result of Photoshop's Anti-Aliasing feature, which partially blurs fringe pixels. In that process, extra pixels around the perimeter are added to the selection. Photoshop's Layer > Matting command allows you to remove the unwanted pixels.

Defringing a Pasted Image

With the Layer > Matting > Defringe command, you can remove the unwanted color from fringe pixels. The Defringe command replaces the colors on the fringes of a selection with a color that is closest to the fringe from within the selection. In order for the Defringe command to be accessible, the area you want to defringe should be in a selection that you've moved or in a layer with a transparent background. When you select Defringe, a dialog box appears, allowing you to specify the pixel width of the fringe area to be colored.

If you wish to try out the Defringe command, open any file. Activate the Magic Wand tool and set the Tolerance in the Options bar. Make sure the Anti-aliased checkbox is selected. Click on an object in your file to select it. Now copy and paste the object into a new file with a white background. Zoom in, and you'll most likely see a thin border of darker or lighter pixels lining the image edges. To remove these pixels, choose Layer > Matting > Defringe. In the Defringe dialog box, enter **3** as the Pixel Width. After you click on OK, the colored fringe will be gone.

 The Select > Modify > Contract command can also be useful when trying to remove fringe pixels from a selection.

Using a Black-and-White Matte

If you select an image in a black background, choose Layer > Matting > Remove Black Matte to remove extraneous black fringe pixels. Use Remove Black Matte after copying or moving a light image that is on a dark background and placing it on another light background. Remove Black Matte removes some of the dark pixels that tag along with the image. Figure 4-18 shows an example of an image on a dark background and how it looks after being copied and pasted with the Remove Black Matte command applied.

Figure 4-18.   *Using the Remove Black Matte command to remove fringe pixels; the image at left is the original, and the image at right is the pasted image with Remove Black Matte applied*

If you select an image in a white background, choose Remove White Matte from the Layer > Matting submenu to remove the extraneous white fringe pixels.

Feathering the Edges of Selections

As mentioned earlier in this chapter, the Feather option allows you to soften the edges of a selection. The Feather option is on the Options bar for the Marquee and Lasso tools. It's also available on the Select menu for other selections.

The number that you type in the Feather field determines the width of the feather edge. The maximum value allowed is 250. Since the feather edge extends both inside and outside the selection, the actual feather will be twice the pixel value.

Feathering Rectangular Selections

To take a look at how the Feather option works, try this exercise with the Rectangular Marquee tool:

1. Create a new file, 5 × 5 inches, to use as a practice document.
2. Click on the Default Colors icon to reset the foreground and background colors.
3. Select the Rectangular Marquee tool in the Toolbox.
4. In the Feather field in the Options bar, type **15**. This value will give you a feather edge of 30 pixels.
5. Click and drag to make a rectangle.
6. Press OPTION-DELETE (*ALT-BACKSPACE*) to fill the rectangle with the foreground color. The feathered rectangle will look like this:

Notice what has happened: The edges in the object have been softened across 30 pixels. The feathering begins 15 pixels within the selection and extends 15 pixels beyond the selection. The outer edges of the black rectangle have a gradient effect—they start out black and then turn gray, until they blend into the white background. This effect, called a *vignette*, is also sometimes called a *halo* or *glow*.

Feathering Oval Selections

The Feather option for the Elliptical Marquee tool was used to create the vignette shown in Figure 4-19. If you want to try creating this type of special effect, start by opening an image on your screen. If you wish, you can use the Grandparents file in Figure 4-19, on this book's CD-ROM.

1. With a image on your screen, select the Elliptical Marquee tool in the Toolbox.

2. In the Options bar, set the Feather value to **10**. (Leave the Style set to Normal.)

> **Note** *Depending on the resolution and dimensions of your image, you may wish to experiment with different Feather values.*

3. Click and drag to create an ellipse surrounding the area where you want to add the vignette effect. (The vignette will not appear until after you copy and paste the selection.)

4. Choose Edit > Copy.

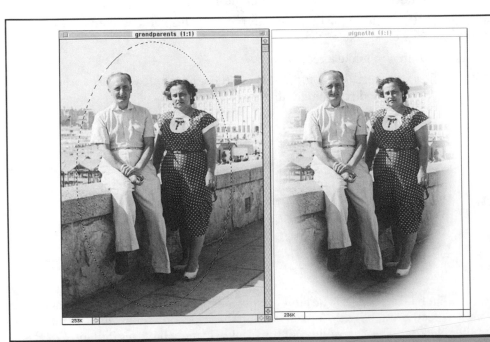

Figure 4-19. *A vignette created with the Elliptical Marquee tool*

5. Create a new file in which you will paste your selection. Choose File > New, and change the Width and Height settings to make them larger, if desired. Click on OK.

6. Choose Edit > Paste. The image is pasted into a new layer with the feathering effect that creates the vignette.

The vignette exercise is the last of the selection tool design projects in this chapter. However, we've included one more simple exercise that illustrates how selections can be used to create special effects.

Creating Glowing Text

In this Photoshop exercise, you'll create a glowing, or backlit, effect for text by copying, pasting, and using the Select menu's Modify > Border and Feather commands. The Border and Feather commands control the width and intensity of the glow. The Select > Feather command works just like the Feather option in the Lasso and Marquee tools' Options bars.

Tip *Although this example creates a glowing background for text, you can produce the same effect on any kind of selection.*

You're going to create yellow text with a red glow, and you'll create the text first. Here are the steps:

1. Create a new file in Photoshop, 6 × 4 inches, in RGB Color mode, and at 72 ppi. Set the background Contents to either Transparent or White.

2. Change the foreground color to yellow and the background color to white.

3. Activate the Type tool. In the Type tool's Option bar, click on the Type mask icon, and then set the font to Helvetica (Windows users should use Arial). Enter **120** in the Size field. In the Style pop-up menu, choose Bold. Set the Anti-Alias pop-up menu to Smooth.

4. Click on the center of your document and type the word **Glow**. When you're done typing, click on the checkmark in the Type tool option bar to see the type selection on screen.

5. Once the text appears on screen, activate any Marquee selection tool. Use this tool to move the text selection to the center of the document by clicking inside the text selection and dragging it. Do not deselect.

6. Fill the text selection with the foreground color by pressing OPTION-DELETE (*ALT-BACKSPACE*).

7. Choose Edit > Copy, and keep the text selected. This places the text into the Clipboard, so that it can be copied back into the image after you have bordered, feathered, and filled it.

8. Place a border selection around each letter of the text. Choose Select > Modify > Border, type **20** in the Width field, and click on OK.

9. To soften the edges of the newly created border, choose Select > Feather. Type **6** and click on OK. The 20-pixel border now has a 6-pixel feather beyond its edges. (The Feather command feathers 6 pixels within the selection and 6 pixels beyond the selection.)

10. Fill the selection on screen with the foreground color (red) to start creating the glow effect. Change the foreground color to red, and then choose Edit > Fill. In the Fill dialog box, make sure Foreground Color is set in the Use pop-up menu, the Opacity is 100%, and Mode is Normal. Click on OK. You will see the soft edges of the feathered border.

11. To make the text sharper and more readable, paste the text from the Clipboard back onto the soft-edged glow by selecting Edit > Paste. When you paste, the yellow text in the Clipboard returns to the screen. Notice that a new layer was created when you executed the Paste command. You now have glowing text.

For a more dramatic effect, you can use one or more of Photoshop's filters. Here, we applied the Spherize filter after flattening the file. (For more information about filters, see Chapter 12.)

Note   *The Layer > Effects submenu includes commands for creating Inner and Outer Glow effects. Layer > Effects commands are covered in Chapter 18.*

The Complete Reference

Photoshop 6

Chapter 5

Using the Painting and Eraser Tools

E ven if you're not an artist, the scope, power, and rich diversity of Photoshop's painting capabilities are certain to inspire the creativity within you. You'll marvel at the realistic and electronic effects within your grasp. At times, you might even expect to see paint dripping down your screen from your electronic brushes! In this chapter, you'll try your hand at painting, using electronic versions of a paintbrush, pencil, eraser, paint bucket, and airbrush. These tools, along with the Line, Gradient, and Eyedropper tools, will open a world of infinite artistic possibilities for you.

 ImageReady also features Paintbrush, Pencil, Eraser, Paint Bucket, Airbrush, and Line tools, which function nearly identically to their Photoshop counterparts.

Photoshop's Eraser tools are not only valuable for their obvious correction capabilities, but also for Web and multimedia design work. Using these tools, you can erase colors to reveal layer transparency. Once you've replaced color with transparency, you can load images on a Web page and see the Web page background through the transparent areas. This chapter also explains how to use the Eraser tools.

Setting Painting Tool Options

Before you start experimenting with any of the painting tools, take a look at the options that available for these tools. (If the Options bar is not visible on your screen, choose Window > Show Options to display it.) In the Toolbox, click on a painting tool, such as the Pencil or Paintbrush, to select it. Once a painting tool is selected, its Options bar switches to show the painting tool's settings. Most painting tools' Options bars include the Brush, Mode, and Brush Dynamics pop-up menus and an Opacity or Pressure slider.

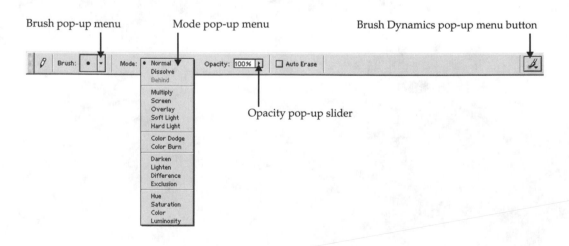

Photoshop's Fade command is accessible after you paint with any of the painting tools. After using any painting tool you can lower the opacity of your last stroke by choosing Edit > Fade. In the Fade dialog box, drag the Opacity slider to the left to fade the stroke. In the dialog box, you can also choose a blending mode.

Choosing a Brush

Most painting tools have a Brush setting, which shows the currently selected painting brush. To choose a different brush, click on the down arrow to open the Brush pop-up menu. Then move the mouse over the brush that you wish to paint with and click on it. You can add your own custom brushes to the menu, as described in the "Creating and Using Custom Brushes" section later in this chapter.

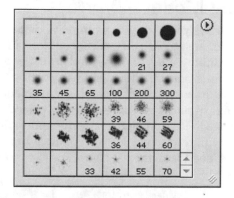

 Brushes that are too large to be depicted by icons in the Brush menu are represented by a brush with a number below it, indicating the pixel width of the brush's diameter.

The effect of the brush you use changes depending on your image's resolution, because the brushes in the Brush menu are calculated based on pixels per inch. This means that a medium-sized brush will be fat when painting in an image with a resolution of 72 ppi but thin when painting in an image at 300 ppi.

You may wish to switch Photoshop's Preference settings so that the painting tool pointer is the same size as the brush with which you are painting. This can help give you a preview before painting of how a brush stroke will affect an image. To set the painting tool pointer to reflect your brush size, choose Edit > Preferences > Display & Cursors. In the Preferences dialog box, click on the Brush Size radio button in the Painting Cursors group. If you choose the Precise option, the tool pointer appears as a crosshair, which allows more precise alignment while working with the painting tools or other tools. The Standard option keeps the painting tool pointer set to the default settings.

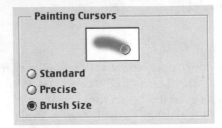

Selecting a Blending Mode

The Mode pop-up menu allows you choose a painting mode to create different painting effects. In the Options bar of most tools, you can choose from a wide range of blending modes, sometimes called painting modes. These modes are generally used to change colors and create special effects when painting or when pasting or blending previously colored areas. How those areas are affected depends on the blending mode, the color being applied, and the range of pixels that are painted or pasted over. For instance, if you apply a red color to an image in Darken mode, only the underlying pixels that are lighter than red will be darkened with the red color. If you paint in Lighten mode, only pixels darker than red will be lightened with the red color. The expanded menu is shown here:

In addition to appearing in the Options bar, blending modes can also be set in the Layers palette and in several dialog boxes such as those for Fill, Stroke, Fill Path, Apply Image, Calculations, and New Layer.

This section describes the fundamental purpose of each mode. For most of this chapter, you will be working in Normal mode, which is the default setting. For some of the Gradient tool exercises, you will experiment with several different modes. As you work through this book, you'll gain experience with the other modes and see how they can produce effects ranging from simple to startling.

 You can cycle forward and backward through the blending modes of a tool by pressing SHIFT-– *(minus) and* SHIFT-+.

Normal Mode

Normal mode modifies every underlying pixel with the color being applied. In Normal mode, with Opacity set to 100%, underlying pixels will be completely replaced with the color being applied. If Opacity is less than 100%, the color of underlying pixels will show through the color being applied.

 Normal mode changes to Threshold when you are editing a Bitmap or Indexed Color file.

Dissolve Mode

When colors are applied in Dissolve mode, the painting color randomly replaces underlying pixels. The resulting color is a mixture of the painting color and the color of the original underlying pixels. Results depend on the opacity of the painting color and the opacity of the underlying colors. This can produce anything from a speckled paint to a sandpaper effect. For more dramatic results, use Dissolve mode with a large brush and experiment with different opacities.

Behind Mode

Behind mode is available only when you are working in a layer other than the Background (see Chapters 16 and 17 for more information about layers). Behind mode simulates the effect of painting behind an image on the screen, like painting on the back of a clear plastic acetate rather than on a painter's canvas. Painting over nontransparent (colored) areas has no effect, but the paint applied appears over the transparent areas.

Clear Mode

Clear mode is also available only when you are working in a layer other than the Background. It appears in the Line and Paint Bucket Options bars' Mode pop-up menu, in the Edit > Fill Mode pop-up menu, and in the Mode pop-up menu of the Fill Path or Fill Subpath dialog box. Editing in this mode is similar to using the Eraser tool while working in the layer. Clear mode wipes away color, making pixels transparent.

Multiply Mode

Multiply mode multiplies color values, causing underlying pixels to darken. Each time a color is applied, pixels receive more of the painting color's values. Painting with black in Multiply mode produces black. Painting with white has no effect. Painting in Multiply mode can be similar to applying colored markers over an image.

Screen Mode

Screen mode whitens underlying pixels, leaving them in a tint of the color being applied. If you repeatedly apply color in Screen mode, pixels grow lighter and lighter. The Screen mode is the opposite of the Multiply mode. Thus, painting with white in Screen mode produces white; painting with black has no effect.

Overlay Mode

When painting in Overlay mode, underlying pixels are either screened or multiplied to blend with the painting color. When you paint, darker underlying colors cause the painting color to be multiplied; lighter underlying colors cause the painting color to be screened. When painting over images, highlights and shadows are maintained. Overlay produces no effect when painting over white or black pixels.

Soft Light Mode

Soft Light mode produces the effect of pointing a soft spotlight on an image. If your painting color is lighter than underlying pixels, the image is lightened. If your painting color is darker than underlying pixels, the image is darkened. The effect is one of diffuse, not harsh, light being applied.

Hard Light Mode

Hard Light mode produces the effect of pointing a harsh spotlight on an image. If your painting color is lighter than underlying pixels, the image is lightened. If your painting color is darker than underlying pixels, the image is darkened. Painting with black in Hard Light mode produces black; painting with white produces white.

To see the difference between Soft and Hard Light modes, open an image on screen. Set the foreground color to yellow or yellow orange. Select the entire screen by choosing Select > All. Use the Edit > Fill command to fill using Soft Light mode and then undo and use the Edit > Fill command to fill in Hard Light mode.

Color Dodge Mode

Color Dodge mode lightens image areas, functioning similarly to the Dodge tool. If you are using this mode with a painting tool or in the Layers palette, you can control the effect by adjusting the Opacity slider. Painting with Color Dodge has no effect if the painting color is black.

Color Burn Mode

Color Burn mode darkens image areas, functioning similarly to the Burn tool. If you are using this mode with a painting tool or in the Layers palette, you can control the effect by adjusting the Opacity slider. Painting with Color Burn has no effect if the painting color is white.

Darken Mode

Darken mode affects only colors lighter than the color you are applying, causing them to be darkened by the painting color. When you use Darken, Photoshop compares the color values of the painting color with the color value of the underlying color and then creates a blend color using the darkest pixel values. For example, if R100, G50, B25 is painted over R25, G100, B75 in Darken mode, the resulting color will be R25, G50, B25.

Lighten Mode

Lighten mode is the opposite of Darken mode. Only pixels darker than the color you are applying are modified. The darker colors are lightened by the painting color. When you use Lighten, Photoshop compares the color values of the painting color with the color value of the underlying color and then creates a blend color using the lightest pixel values. For example, if R100, G50, B25 is painted over R25, G100, B75 in Lighten mode, the resulting color will be R100, G100, B75.

Difference Mode

Difference mode subtracts the color values of the painting color from the color values of the underlying pixels. For instance, if R100, G50, B25 is painted over R25, G100, B75 in Difference mode, the resulting color will be R75, G50, B50.

When you're using Difference mode, it's helpful to remember that the pixel value of black is 0 and the brightness value of white is 255. Painting with black in Difference mode has no effect on underlying pixels. Painting over black in Difference mode produces the color you are painting with (because you are subtracting a color value from 0). Thus, if you had a black stripe against a green background and filled the entire image using Difference mode with green, the result would be a green stripe with a black background. Painting over white in Difference mode produces the inverse of the color you are painting with. Painting with white produces the inverse of the color you are painting over.

Exclusion Mode

Exclusion mode is very similar to Difference, except the resulting color is softer than one obtained with Difference. However, painting with white or black produces the same effect as Difference. Painting with black produces no effect. Painting over white in Difference mode produces the inverse of the color you are painting with. Painting with white produces the inverse of the color you are painting over.

Hue Mode

When you paint or edit in Hue mode, you paint with only the hue of the painting color. Thus, only the Hue value of the affected pixels—not their Saturation or Luminosity value—is modified by the painting color. Applying colors to black or white pixels in Hue mode has no effect.

 The Hue, Saturation, Color, and Luminosity blending modes are based on a Hue/ Saturation/Luminosity (HSL) color model, which is slightly different from the Hue/ Saturation/Brightness (HSB) color model. Thus, if you try to evaluate the effects of painting in these modes using the HSB readouts in the Info palette, it may seem that the modes do not work exactly as specified. For instance, when you paint over a color using Hue mode, the HSB readout in the Info palette may show that the color's saturation, as well as its hue, has changed.

Saturation Mode

When you edit or apply color in Saturation mode, you paint with the Saturation value of the painting color. Thus, only the Saturation values of underlying pixels will change. Applying colors to black or white pixels in Saturation mode will have no effect.

Color Mode

In Color mode, you paint with the Hue and Saturation of a painting color. Thus, the Hue and Saturation values of underlying pixels change, but not their Luminosity value. Color mode is often used to colorize gray or monochrome images, because underlying shadows and contours will show through the color that is being applied. The effect is similar to colorizing old black-and-white movies.

 If you wish to colorize a Grayscale file, you must convert the file to a Color mode, such as RGB Color, using the Image > Mode command. For more information about colorizing and changing modes, see Chapter 13.

Luminosity Mode

Luminosity measures a color's brightness. When you paint in Luminosity mode, you paint with only the luminance value of a color. In Luminosity mode, the lightness and darkness values of an underlying color's pixels will change, but the color values will not. Luminosity mode is the opposite of the Color mode.

Photoshop's internal formula for computing a pixel's luminosity is approximately

30% of *Red value* + 59% of *Green value* + 11% of *Blue value*

This formula always produces a number between 0 and 255. The closer a number is to 255, the closer the luminosity is to white; the lower the number, the closer the luminosity is to black. When you apply color in Luminosity mode over black or white, all RGB color values will switch to the luminosity value produced by the formula, which will apply a gray shade to your image.

Threshold Mode

Threshold mode appears only when you are working in Bitmap mode files. It indicates that you will be painting with black if the foreground color is set to 50% black or greater; otherwise, you will be painting with white.

Setting Opacity or Pressure

The tool you are using determines which element is controlled by the pop-up slider in the Options bar. When you are using the Line, Pencil, Paint Bucket, Paintbrush, Gradient, and Rubber Stamp tools, the slider sets opacity. For the Airbrush, Smudge, and Blur/Sharpen tools, the slider sets pressure. For the Dodge/Burn/Sponge tool, the slider sets exposure. (You will be introduced to the Clone Stamp/Pattern Stamp, Blur/Sharpen/Smudge, and Dodge/Burn/Sponge tools in Chapter 6.)

If Opacity is set to less than 100%, you will not be painting with an opaque color but rather with a tint—a transparent version of a color. Painting with a tint can create a transparent effect and different shades of colors. When you lower the Opacity percentage, you make a color more translucent; when you raise it, you make the color more opaque. To change opacity, click the right-pointing arrow next to the current Opacity setting to display the slider and drag the Opacity slider control, or press any number from 0 to 10 on your keyboard (0 represents 100% opacity).

 After you set the opacity and blending mode of a tool, they stay set for that tool until you change them.

Adjusting Brush Dynamics

The Paintbrush, Airbrush, Pencil and Eraser tools allow you to choose additional options from the Brush Dynamics menu. These settings allow you to fade out stroke size, opacity, and color according to the number of steps you specify.

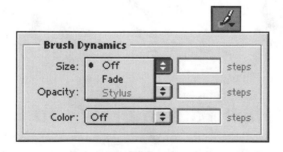

If you choose the Fade option in the Stroke, Size, or Opacity fields, you can gradually fade out the Stroke, Size, and Opacity according to a specified number of steps. In the Steps field, you enter how many pixels (1 to 9999) the tool will paint before the fade begins. The larger the value, the longer the brush stroke will be before fading.

The Stylus Options

The three pop-up menus in the brush dynamics palette allow you to choose a stylus option that lets you control the size, color, and opacity of your painting by applying different amounts of pressure to the stylus. If you do have a stylus, these options are invaluable Following are brief explanations of the Stylus Pressure options available for the Pencil, Paintbrush, and Airbrush tools.

 The Stylus options can only be activated if you have a stylus and graphics tablet connected to your computer.

Size   When this checkbox is selected, you can control the size of your brush strokes by applying different pressure with the stylus. Light pressure creates a small brush stroke; heavy pressure creates a large brush stroke. (The Stylus Pressure options for the Airbrush tool do not include size.)

Color   When this checkbox is selected, you can apply the foreground color, the background color, or an intermediate color—a blend of the foreground and background colors. Use heavy pressure to apply the foreground color, light pressure to apply the background color, and a medium amount of pressure to apply an intermediate color.

Opacity   When this checkbox is selected, you can use stylus pressure to control how opaque or transparent your brush strokes will be. The heavier the pressure, the more opaque the color; the lighter the pressure, the more translucent the color.

The figures in the following illustration, which show the various Stylus Pressure options, were created with a Wacom stylus with the Pencil tool activated.

Using the Pencil Tool to Draw and Erase

 Photoshop's electronic Pencil tool is unlike any pencil you've ever used before. It not only emulates a real pencil, but it can also draw lines between mouse clicks, and it can erase by painting with the background color.

You may be surprised to learn that the Pencil tool's "lead," or *stroke,* is controlled by a brush chosen in the Brush pop-up menu. This gives the Pencil tool tremendous versatility. When you use the Pencil tool, the stroke can be thick or thin, round or square. The tool's smallest stroke is 1 pixel wide, which is handy for retouching images 1 pixel at a time.

Apart from retouching individual pixels, the Pencil tool can be used for freehand sketching. When you click and drag with the Pencil tool, it paints with the foreground color, using a Brush, Mode, and Opacity settings in its Options bar. No matter what the brush size or shape, the Pencil tool will always paint with a hard edge, unlike the Paintbrush and Airbrush tools, which can paint with soft edges. The Auto Erase option in the Pencil tool's Options bar allows the Pencil tool to work as an eraser. Turning on the Auto Erase option triggers the Pencil tool to switch to the background color automatically when you paint over the foreground color. You'll experiment with this option in the next exercise.

To activate the Pencil tool, click on it in the Toolbox. If the Pencil is not visible in the Toolbox, click on the Paintbrush tool and hold down the mouse. When the Pencil tool appears, move the mouse pointer over it and then click to select it. Once the Pencil tool is activated, you can create a pencil stroke by clicking and dragging on your screen. The stroke is created with the foreground color and the width of the currently active brush (set in the Brush menu).

The Pencil tool also allows you to create lines by connecting one stroke after another. To use this technique, you simply click on the screen with the Pencil tool and then release the mouse. Next, move the mouse to another area, press and hold down SHIFT, and click again. The Pencil tool connects your mouse clicks.

Note	*If you click and drag the Pencil tool with* SHIFT *pressed, the Pencil paints in 90-degree increments.*

Creating an Image with the Pencil Tool's Auto Erase Option

In the following exercise, you will create a file with a transparent background in which you will paint the word *ART* using the Pencil tool's Auto Erase option. Because the word will be created on a transparent background, you'll be able to drag and drop it into another file without needing to select the letters. Also, when the word is dropped into another file, the ART file's transparent background will allow color from the destination file to show around the letters.

1. Select File > New to create a new file. In the New dialog box, set both the Width and Height to 5 inches, Resolution to 72 ppi, and Mode to RGB Color. To make the background transparent, click on the Transparent radio button in the Contents group. Click OK to create a new, untitled document.

2. When the new document appears, notice that the document title bar displays "Layer 1." If the Layers palette is not open, choose Window > Show Layers. In the Layers palette, you'll also see Layer 1 listed. When you create a new file with Contents set to Transparent, Photoshop automatically creates a new layer,

with a transparent background as the base layer. (For more information about working with layers, see Chapters 16 and 17.)

3. Select a vivid color for the foreground color and its complement for the background color from the Color palette. For instance, try blue as the foreground color and yellow as the background color. If the Foreground selection box is not active in the Color palette, click on it. To choose a blue foreground color, click on the first blue swatch in the first row of the Swatches palette. Then click on the Background selection box in the Color palette. To choose a yellow color, click on the yellow swatch in the first row of the Swatches palette.

4. Select the Pencil tool. In its Options bar, click on the Brush pop-up menu and click on the largest brush in the first row of the menu (start with a large brush size so that the Pencil tool's stroke will be dramatic). Click on the Auto Erase checkbox to turn on this option. Before proceeding, make sure that Normal appears in the blending mode menu in the Options bar and Opacity is set to 100%.

5. Click and drag to start creating the left, slanted side of the capital letter *A*. As you drag, the Pencil tool paints with the foreground color. When you finish the stroke, release the mouse button.

6. To begin creating the right side of the letter *A*, position the mouse at the top of the stroke you just produced, and then click and drag diagonally to the right. (Notice that as soon as the mouse detects the foreground color, the Auto Erase option causes the Pencil tool to paint with the background color.)

7. Connect the two slanted lines by drawing the crossbar of the *A*. If you start the bar by touching the left side, your bar will be yellow. If you start painting by touching the right side, the crossbar will be blue.

Tip   *If you wish, you can choose View > Show Grid to display the grid and make it easier to follow a straight line. To change the gridline increments, choose Edit > Preferences > Guides & Grid.*

8. When you have completed the letter *A*, start drawing the letter *R*. Immediately, the Pencil tool returns to the foreground color. As you draw the *R*, the Auto Erase feature causes the Pencil tool to switch to the background color whenever a stroke begins on the foreground color.

9. To create the letter *T*, try a different painting technique as a special effect: Instead of dragging with the mouse, create the *T* with mouse clicks. Begin by clicking once to create a foreground-colored spot, and then move the mouse halfway into the colored spot and click again. This creates a background-colored spot. Keep using overlapping mouse clicks to gradually create the letter. When you have finished, the letter will be created from Pencil marks that alternate between the foreground and background colors.

10. For an added effect, add a drop shadow to your letters by choosing Layer > Layer Style > Drop Shadow.

 If you are using a tablet, make sure that the Size, Color, and Opacity tablet settings are off; otherwise, you will not obtain the results just described.

Dragging and Dropping a Layer into Another File

After you have finished creating the word *ART* (in the exercise in the previous section), you are ready to drag and drop the image into another file. One of the most efficient ways of dragging and dropping one file into another is to click and drag a layer from one file to another.

1. Open a file in which you wish to place the word *ART*. Place the two image windows side by side or position them so that they overlap.

2. Activate the Move tool and position the mouse pointer over the Art layer in the Layers palette.

3. Click and hold down the mouse button, and then drag *ART* over the image you just opened. As you drag, you'll see a tiny grabbing hand icon appear. After you've dragged the layer to the other file, release the mouse. The word will drop onto the file. Because *ART* was created in a file with a transparent background, you can see through the holes in the letters *R* and *A*, as if they had been created on a clear acetate over the background file.

4. In the Layers palette, notice that Photoshop automatically created a new layer for the ART image. The two eye icons in the Layers palette next to the Background and Layer 1 layers indicate that both layers are being viewed. The paintbrush icon and the highlight color surrounding Layer 1 indicate that you are currently working in this layer.

5. Try using the Move tool to move *ART* into another position on screen. Because you are working in a layer, you can reposition the entire layer without needing to use a selection tool to select it, and you can move it without affecting the Background.

6. If you wish to save the file with its new layer, use the File > Save As command and save your file in Photoshop format.

Most page layout programs cannot read Photoshop files. Before you export a file to a program like QuarkXPress, you will need to flatten layers and save it in a file format such as TIFF, EPS, or DCS. Appendix A includes information about saving Photoshop files in other formats.

Using the Paintbrush Tool

 The Paintbrush tool is Photoshop's electronic version of an artist's paintbrush. The Paintbrush tool paints with the foreground color, using your choice of brush sizes. Using the Brush Dynamics Fade option, you can also create colors that fade, or dissolve, as you paint.

Like the Pencil tool, the Paintbrush tool allows you to connect painted brush strokes by pressing SHIFT while clicking the mouse. Unlike the Pencil tool, the Paintbrush tool offers soft brush strokes that simulate paint applied with a paintbrush. (The Brush pop-up menu includes a row of soft-edged brushes that are not available when you are using the Pencil tool.)

The Paintbrush tool shares its Toolbox location with the Pencil tool. If the Paintbrush isn't visible in the Toolbox, click on the Pencil, keep the mouse button pressed until the Paintbrush appears, and then select it with the mouse. If the Paintbrush Options bar is not displayed, double-click on the Paintbrush tool to open its Options bar.

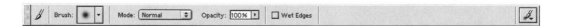

You'll notice that the Paintbrush's options are almost identical to those of the Pencil tool, except that the Paintbrush does not have the Auto Erase option and includes the Wet Edges option. The Wet Edges option produces the effect of painting with watercolors or markers rather than acrylic or oil paint. The colors created have a fully saturated appearance at stroke edges but not in the center of the stroke. If you paint an image using Wet Edges in a layer, underlying layers show through the brush strokes. You'll experiment with Wet Edges in the next section.

Creating an Image with the Paintbrush's Wet Edges Option

In this section, you will use the Paintbrush's Wet Edges option to create a flower like the one shown in Figure 5-1. In order to help you create the flower, you will add a new layer over an existing flower image and then use the underlying flower image as a kind of tracing guide. Before beginning this exercise, make sure that the Layers palette is open. If it isn't, choose Window > Show Layers.

    1. Open the flower file found in the Chapter 5 folder of the *Photoshop Complete Reference* CD-ROM.

Figure 5-1.   *A flower created with the Wet Edges option*

2. To use the flower as a tracing guide, you'll need to create a new layer to use like an acetate cover. To create the layer, choose Layer > New. In the New pop-up menu, choose Layer. Make sure that the layer's Opacity is set to 100%, Mode is set to Normal, and Group With Previous Layer is not selected. In the Name field, type **Painted Flower**. Then click on OK to create the layer. (Creating and working with layers are covered in Chapters 16 and 17.)

3. Notice that the name of the layer you just created now appears in both the title bar and the Layers palette. The paintbrush icon and highlight color surrounding the layer name indicate that it is the layer in which you will be painting.

4. Activate the Paintbrush tool. In the Options bar, select a brush size and choose the Wet Edges option. Optionally, select a Fade option in the Brush Dynamics pop-up menu. Choose a foreground color.

5. Click and drag to paint with the Paintbrush tool. Notice that as you paint, the colors look as if they were slightly diluted with water, with the edges less diluted. Try painting one color over another. If you release the mouse and then reapply paint over areas you've already colored, the paint grows darker.

6. Try painting with different brushes, both soft and hard, at different opacities.

7. Finish the flower by adding a stem and a few leaves around the stem.

8. After you have finished painting, open a file in which you wish to place the flower you just painted. Place the two files side by side or so that they overlap.

9. Use the Move tool to drag the Painted Flower layer into the newly opened file. Because you created the flower in a layer, you can drag and drop or copy and paste the flower into another file without needing to use the selection tools to select it. When the Painted Flower layer is in the newly opened file, you'll see that there is a new layer called Painted Flower in the Layers palette. Also notice that you can see through the translucent areas of the flower.

10. Move the flower into position using the Move tool. Because you are working in a layer, the flower moves above the Background layer.

11. If you wish to save your file with the Painted Flower layer, use the File > Save As command and save your file in Photoshop format.

Creating a Painter's Palette with Brush Dynamics Options

For more practice with the Paintbrush, try creating the Painter's palette shown in Figure 5-2. For parts of this palette, you'll use the Fade options in the Brush Dynamics pop-up menu.

1. Select File > New and create a 5-by-5-inch, RGB color file. Set Contents to White.

2. Set the foreground color to a dark gray or any dark color.

3. Select the Paintbrush tool. In the Options bar, choose a medium-sized brush from the first row of brushes in the Brush pop-up menu. Click and drag the Opacity pop-up slider control to 100% or press 0 on your keyboard. In the Brush Dynamics pop-up menu, check to see that none of the settings in the Brush Dynamics menu is set to Fade. If Fade is set in any of the fields, change the setting to Off.

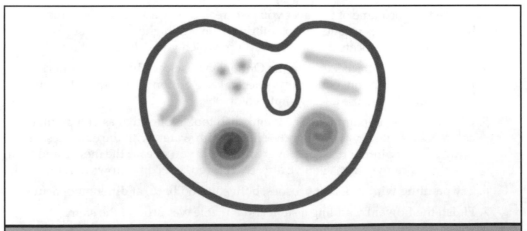

Figure 5-2.   *A painter's palette created with the Paintbrush tool*

4. Position the Paintbrush tool about 0.5 inch from the top of your screen and click and drag to create a kidney shape, representing the palette (refer to Figure 5-2 as a guide). To paint the handle hole in the middle of the palette, click and drag again in an elliptical motion with the Paintbrush.

> **Tip**   *You can use the Pen tool to create a path of the painter's palette. Then select the path, fill it with white, and stroke it.*

5. Double-click on the Paintbrush to activate the tool's Options bar. Click the Brush Dynamics pop-up menu. Set the Color field to Fade, then enter **75** in the corresponding Steps field. These settings will cause the painting color to fade out over 75 pixels.

6. Create a couple of circular paint dabs in the painter's palette. Pick a foreground color and choose a medium-sized, soft-edged brush in the Brush pop-up menu. Again using Figure 5-2 as your guide, click and drag with the Paintbrush tool in a circular motion in the palette. As you click and drag, the paint will gradually fade out. Do this one more time with another color to create another paint dab.

7. In the Options bar, click on the Brush Dynamics pop-up menu. Set the Color field to Fade and type **35** in the corresponding steps field. Set the foreground color and then click and drag to create the two wavy lines in the upper-left part of the palette. You'll notice that the fade-out occurs as you draw these lines.

8. Click three times to apply three soft-edged dots adjacent to the handle hole. To finish up, draw two more short, straight lines at the top-right side of the palette. Your painter's palette should look similar to the one shown in Figure 5-2.

Suppose that you want to add a few more artistic touches to the palette, with the same colors that you used to paint the lines and circles. For this, you need to use the Eyedropper tool, as described in the next section.

Using the Eyedropper and Color Sampler Tools

The Eyedropper tool doesn't paint, but it is an invaluable tool in the painting process. It is used to sample, or read, an image's color so that it can be used as the foreground or background color. For example, it would be a lot of work to mix colors in the Color palette to obtain a particular flesh tone that appears in a scanned image. With the Eyedropper tool, on the other hand, you need only click that colored portion of the image, and Photoshop's foreground color instantly changes to the flesh tone you need. This technique is a tremendous time-saver when you are color-correcting and retouching scanned color images.

Using the Eyedropper's Sampling Options

Before trying out the Eyedropper tool, first select it in the Toolbox. If you see the Color Sampler tool in the Toolbox instead of the Eyedropper, click on the Color Sampler tool and hold down the mouse. When you see the Eyedropper appear, select it. Next, take a look at the Eyedropper Options bar. (If the Options bar isn't open, press ENTER.)

All of the Eyedropper tool's options reside in the Sample Size pop-up menu. The default Sample Size setting is Point Sample, which narrows the Eyedropper's sample to the color value of the pixel on which you click. The 3 by 3 Average option reads the average color value of a 3-pixel × 3-pixel area, and the 5 by 5 Average option operates similarly.

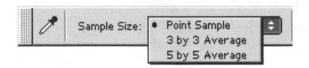

When you're using the Eyedropper tool, the Info palette displays the color values of the pixels underlying the tool, using various color models. You can display one or two color model values at a time. If you will be sending your file to a printing press, it can be helpful to view CMYK colors at the same time that RGB or HSB colors are displayed. When CMYK colors are displayed in the Info palette, an exclamation point appears next to CMYK percentages that are out of gamut. If you are color-correcting, it's very helpful to have both RGB and CMYK colors on your screen, because you will have a readout of the primary colors and their complements.

You can change to RGB, CMYK, HSB, Lab, or Grayscale colors by clicking on either of the eyedropper icons in the Info palette. This opens a pop-up menu that allows you to choose another color model or to display opacity or the percentage of ink coverage when working with CMYK or Duotone images. (Ink coverage is discussed in Chapter 13.)

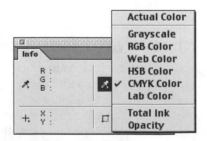

From time to time, you may wish to use the Eyedropper tool to change the background color when the Foreground selection box is activated in the Color palette, or to change the foreground color when the Background selection box is activated. To switch, simply press OPTION (ALT) while clicking on a color in the image with the Eyedropper tool.

PHOTOSHOP BASICS

 If you press OPTION *(ALT) while using the Pencil, Line, Paintbrush, Paint Bucket, Airbrush, or Gradient tool, that tool will change to the Eyedropper tool.*

If you have the painter's palette that you created in the previous section open, you can try out the Eyedropper's color sampling powers (If you didn't create the painter's palette, you can try out the Eyedropper with any color image on screen.)

1. Select the Eyedropper tool. In its Options bar, make sure that Point Sample is selected for Sample Size.

2. With the Eyedropper tool pointer positioned over the first paint dab that you created, click the mouse. Notice that the foreground color immediately changes to match the color you've clicked.

3. Move the Eyedropper tool to the outer edge of the paint dab circle (or over a light color in the digitized image you have on screen) and click the mouse. The foreground color changes to a lighter shade, reflecting the color created by the Fade option you used with the Paintbrush tool to make the paint dab.

 You can also click and drag over colors with the Eyedropper tool activated. As you drag, watch the foreground color change from color to color; stop when you see the color you need.

4. Change the background color by pressing OPTION (ALT) and clicking with the Eyedropper tool on any colored element in the painter's palette.

Sampling with the Color Sampler Tool

 Sharing the Toolbox with the Eyedropper is the Color Sampler tool, which samples up to four different colors on the screen and provides readouts in the Info palette. When you click with the Color Sampler tool, Photoshop leaves a marker on screen at the area you've clicked on. In the Info palette, the color values of the sample appear.

The Color Sampler tool is most useful when you are adjusting or correcting colors. For instance, you can place sampler marks at the lightest, darkest, and midtone areas of your image. As you make adjustments to the image, the Info palette shows you how the adjustments affect different areas on screen. If you wish to move the samples on the screen, you can click on one of the samples and drag it to another area. To delete a sample, press and hold down the OPTION (ALT) key while you click on the sample you want to remove. The Color Sampler tool is discussed in more detail in Chapter 19.

Painting with the Airbrush Tool

 The Airbrush tool is an electronic version of the mechanical airbrush that artists use to create three-dimensional shading effects. The tool is also used to soften images with a hint of color. In retouching and painting work, the Airbrush tool is often the best tool for adding highlights and shadows.

The Airbrush tool paints in much the same manner as the Paintbrush tool, except that the Airbrush colors with a softer edge. Like the Pencil and Paintbrush, the Airbrush allows you to choose from a variety of brushes from the Brush pop-up menu. Unlike the other tools, however, the Airbrush tool's Options bar does not have an Opacity setting; instead, it has a Pressure setting. The greater the Pressure setting, the more paint is sprayed when you click and hold down the mouse button.

Try out the Airbrush tool now.

1. Click on the Airbrush tool to activate it.

2. For the foreground color, choose any color swatch in the Swatches palette or create a color using the slider controls in the Color palette.

3. In the Airbrush tool's Options bar, pick a large, soft-edged brush from the Brush pop-up menu. If Pressure is not set to 100%, click on the arrow to display the slider and drag it all the way to the right. Make sure Mode is set to Normal.

4. Move the mouse pointer toward the document area. As you move, the pointer changes to an airbrush. (If CAPS LOCK is on or if the Painting Cursors group is set to Precise or Brush Size, your pointer will be a crosshair, but the tool will still work as the Airbrush.)

5. Move the Airbrush pointer anywhere in the document. Click the mouse and keep it pressed for a second or two. Notice that paint keeps spilling out. Now click and drag slowly for a few inches to see the soft, diffused spray created by the tool.

6. To observe the effects of painting with a lower pressure, click and drag the Pressure slider in the Options bar to 50%. Move the Airbrush pointer back into the document and click and hold down the mouse button. This time, less paint is sprayed by the brush.

7. Continue experimenting with the Airbrush tool, choosing various brush sizes and Pressure settings. Also try experimenting with the Fade options in the Brush Dynamics pop-up menu.

Using the Line Tool in Painting Mode

Photoshop's Line tool creates three different types of lines: shapes, paths, and painted lines that immediately dry on the background canvas. To use the Line tool to create painted lines, you must select the Create Filled Region icon in the Line tool's Options bar. (Chapter 17 covers using the Line tool to create shapes. Paths are covered in Chapter 14.)

Create Work Path

Create Shape Layer   Create Filled Region (painting mode)

Here's how to use the Line tool in painting mode:

1. Since the Line tool paints with the foreground color, start by choosing a color in the Color palette or Color Picker.

2. Click on the Line tool in the Toolbox.

3. In the Line tool's Option bar, make sure that the Create Filled Region icon is selected. Set the line thickness in the Weight field. If you wish to enter values in pixels, type a number followed by **px**. To specify a number in inches, enter a value followed by **in**. If you want to create semitransparent lines, lower the Opacity setting. Leave the Anti-Aliased checkbox selected to produce lines with soft edges.

4. To draw a line, click and drag on the screen. To draw a straight line or a line at 45-degree increments, press SHIFT as you click and drag.

Using the Paint Bucket Tool to Paint and Fill

The Paint Bucket tool lets you quickly fill areas of an image with the foreground color or a pattern. The area painted by the tool is determined by how similar in color the adjacent pixels are to the pixel that you click on.

The Magic Wand (covered in Chapter 4) and the Paint Bucket work in a similar way, by first analyzing the color of the pixel that is clicked on and then using the Tolerance settings in the tool's Options bar to determine the range of pixels affected. With the Paint Bucket, as with the Magic Wand, the greater the Tolerance, the larger the pixel range affected; the lower the Tolerance, the smaller the pixel range affected.

There is a clear difference between the two tools, however, that you need to understand: The Magic Wand selects according to the Tolerance setting, but the Paint Bucket paints over image areas according to that setting. You might use the Paint Bucket tool primarily to paint over areas that have been outlined with either the Paintbrush or Pencil tool or that have been previously painted.

Setting Paint Bucket Options

The Paint Bucket tool's Options bar contains the same Mode and Opacity settings as the other painting tools discussed in this chapter. You can alter the way the Paint Bucket tool paints by choosing a blending mode other than Normal. For instance, if you are working in a layer, you can work with the Paint Bucket tool in Clear mode, which erases image areas rather than painting them.

The Fill pop-up menu lets you paint with either the foreground color or a pattern. (You will be creating and using patterns in Chapter 6.) The Anti-Aliased option ensures that the paint applied with the Paint Bucket tool appears smooth, without jagged edges.

The Paint Bucket's Tolerance range is 0 to 255. If you type a low number in the Tolerance field, Photoshop applies the foreground color to contiguous areas that are very similar in color to the pixel you click on. If you enter a large number in the Tolerance field, Photoshop applies the foreground color over contiguous areas that vary greatly from the pixel you click on.

The Contiguous checkbox allows you to specify whether you wish the Paintbucket to paint contiguous pixels. If you turn off Contiguous, the Paint Bucket skips over colors that don't fall within the Tolerance range, and paints all colors that fall within the Tolerance range. For instance, suppose that you have a series of red stripes on screen and the foreground color is blue. If you click on one red stripe with the Paint Bucket set to Contiguous, only the stripe you clicked on will turn blue. If you turn off the Contiguous option, all of the stripes will turn blue.

The Use All Layers option applies the Tolerance setting to the layer you are in, based on a sample of the colors in all visible layers. This option has no effect if you are not working in a file with layers.

When changing colors in an image, you may wish to use Photoshop's Image > Adjust > Replace Color command. This command, covered in Chapter 19, is somewhat like using both the Magic Wand and Paint Bucket tools together.

Painting with the Paint Bucket Tool

If you would like to try out the Paint Bucket tool, you'll need an image to click on. Try creating several crossing red and yellow lines with different opacities with the Line tool and then follow these steps:

1. Select the Paint Bucket tool from the Toolbox. The Paint Bucket shares a Toolbox location with the Gradient tool. If the Gradient tool appears in the Toolbox, click and hold down the mouse on it. When the Paint Bucket appears, move the mouse over it and click.

2. In the Paint Bucket's Options bar, change Tolerance to **0**.

3. In order to see the Paint Bucket tool in action, you'll need to change the foreground color. Do this by picking a swatch from the Swatches palette or by dragging the color sliders in the Color palette. Try picking a bright blue color.

4. Move the mouse pointer to the first red, horizontal line. As you move into the document window, the mouse pointer changes to a paint bucket. Position the tip of the paint bucket directly over any part of the line and click. With a 0 Tolerance setting, the Paint Bucket tool fills only the opaque lines.

Note *If you want to use a crosshair instead of the paint bucket, either turn on* CAPS LOCK *before you use the Paint Bucket tool or choose Precise in the Cursors group in the Preferences dialog box. To access the dialog box, choose Edit > Preferences > Display & Cursors.*

5. To force the Paint Bucket tool to spread its paint over all the red lines—opaque *and* non-opaque—you will need to increase the Tolerance setting. Before testing this, choose Edit > Undo to reset the line's color back to red. Then change Tolerance to **200** in the Paint Bucket's Options bar.

6. Once again, move the paint bucket (or crosshair) over the horizontal opaque line and click. This time, the Paint Bucket tool paints all of the adjoining lines. The higher Tolerance level causes the Paint Bucket tool to paint over pixels that have a color range broader than just opaque red.

Note *The Paint Bucket tool can also be used to fill a selection. When a selected area exists on screen, the Paint Bucket tool, like all painting tools, paints only within the selection.*

As a more practical example, Figure 5-3 shows an image for which we used the Paint Bucket tool to change the color of the T-shirt (the background) and the hands and feet on the T-shirt. (The T-Shirt image file is included in the Chapter 5 folder of this

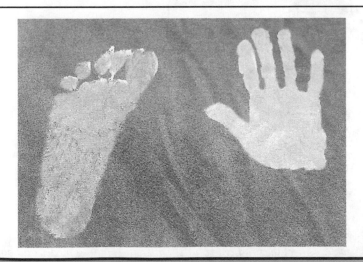

Figure 5-3. *The Paint Bucket tool was used to change colors in this T-shirt image*

book's CD-ROM.) To change the colors but retain the luminosity, we set the blending mode in the Paint Bucket's Options bar to Hue. This preserved the T-shirt texture, but changed the colors in the different areas where we applied the Paintbrush.

 Tip *You can use the Paint Bucket to change the area surrounding the work canvas to the foreground color. Press SHIFT while you click with the Paint Bucket tool on that area.*

Creating Gradients

The Gradient tool allows you to fill an image or a selection with a blend that gradually changes from one color to another or from a color to transparency. Gradients are often used to produce shading and lighting effects, as well as to create visually pleasing backgrounds quickly. By changing Opacity and/or Mode settings, you can create interesting effects by applying gradients over images and over other gradients.

Setting Gradient Options

The Gradient tool's Options bar includes options for creating and editing gradients. (If the Options bar is not open, double-click on the Gradient tool icon in the Toolbox.)

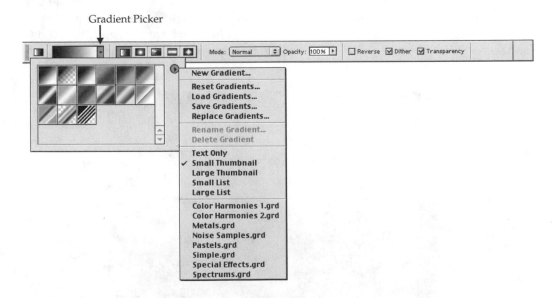

Gradient Picker

 Note *Various factors affect the gradient results. Different blending modes and opacities change the gradient's appearance, as you'll see in the "Using Blending Modes with Gradients" section of this chapter. The blend's printed output will depend on the colors you use, the length of the blend, the file mode you are in, and the resolution at which you are printing.*

Picking a Gradient

The first setting in the Options bar is the Gradient Picker. Clicking on the Gradient Picker's down arrow opens a gallery of preset gradients, including these:

- A gradient from the current foreground color to the current background color
- A gradient from the current foreground color to a transparent background
- A gradient from black to white

The rest of the choices in the Gradient Picker are preset colors that can be edited or added to by choosing options in the Gradient Picker's menu. The Gradient Picker menu allows you to manage gradients, as well as to change the appearance of the gradients that appear in the Gradient Picker:

- The New Gradient choice allows you to create and name a new gradient from the current foreground and background colors.
- The next commands allow you to reset, load, save, and replace the contents of the Gradient Picker gallery.
- If you wish to rename or delete a gradient, select the gradient in the palette first; then choose the corresponding command from the menu.
- The fourth section of the menu contains commands that change how the gradients appear in the Gradient Picker.
- The bottom menu options allow you to load preset gradients into the palette by name. When you pick a named gradient, Photoshop will ask if you want to replace the current gradients or append to them.

Choosing a Gradient Style

Next to the Gradient Picker in the Options bar are icons for five gradient styles. To access any of the different styles, simply click on its icon. The tiny thumbnails provide a miniature picture of how each gradient style appears. Here's a brief description of each style, from left to right in the Options bar:

- Linear creates a gradient along a straight line. This style is often used to create background patterns.
- Radial creates a gradient out from the center of a circular shape. For example, this style is suitable for creating glowing planet effects.
- Angle creates a gradient around a starting point. The angular gradient colors change around the circumference (as opposed to the radial gradient, where the colors radiate out from the middle).
- Reflected creates a gradient on both sides of the starting point. A short click and drag can create a soft, pipe-like effect.

■ Diamond creates a gradient in a diamond shape. The diamond is created outward from the starting point where you click and drag. The point where you release the mouse button defines one tip of the diamond.

Choosing Other Gradient Settings

The Mode and Opacity settings in the Gradient tool's Options bar work in the same way that they do for the other painting tools. If you wish to reverse the color placement of the gradient, choose the Reverse checkbox.

When the Dither checkbox is selected, Photoshop smoothes the foreground and background using a process called *dithering*. This should help prevent banding when outputting a blend. When banding occurs, steps or breaks are seen in the blend.

Another technique for eliminating banding is to add a bit of noise with Photoshop's Add Noise filter, although this can affect white areas. See Chapter 12 for details on using Photoshop filters.

When the Transparency option is selected, areas of the gradient can be made transparent, allowing image areas below the gradient to show through. The opacity of the transparency can be controlled using options in the Gradient Editor dialog box, as described in the "Editing Gradients" section later in this chapter. If Transparency is not selected, color is used instead of transparency.

You can apply a gradient, and then modify it if you wish. Alternatively, you can edit a gradient before applying it.

Applying a Gradient

When you apply a gradient, you can specify where you want the blend to occur by selecting an area beforehand with one of the selection tools. You can even apply a gradient inside text by clicking and dragging with the Gradient tool over a text selection created with the Type Mask option.

If you use the Type tool to create text, type is created in a layer. After you render the layer (Layer > Rasterize > Type), make sure the Lock Transparency checkbox in the Layers palette is selected before you apply a gradient to the text. If it is not, the whole layer is filled with the gradient, not just the text.

To apply a gradient blend to your document, select the Gradient tool and then adjust the settings in the Gradient tool's Options bar. Next, click and drag in the direction you want the blend to "move" toward. You can also adjust how the blend is applied by how far you drag with the Gradient tool.

Applying a Linear Gradient

The Linear style creates a blend along a straight line. The blend is created from the point where you click and start dragging, and ends where you release the mouse. Try applying a blend that simulates a change in lighting:

1. Create a new RGB Color file (select File > New). Set Contents to White.

2. To produce a blend for a lighting effect, you want to pick colors that do not contrast too much. Choose a yellow foreground color (the first yellow color swatch in the Swatches palette). For the background color, choose an orange color.

3. You'll create the blend in a rectangular selection, so activate the Rectangular Marquee tool and click and drag to create a rectangle about 2.5 inches wide and 2 inches high.

4. Select the Gradient tool in the Toolbox. The Gradient tool shares its Toolbox location with the Paint Bucket. If the Gradient tool is not visible in the Toolbox, click the mouse button and hold it down. When the Gradient tool appears, select it with the mouse. You can also press OPTION (*ALT*) as you click on the Paint Bucket tool in the Toolbox.

5. In the Gradient tool's Options bar, make sure that the foreground to background gradient is chosen in the Gradient Picker and that the Linear style is selected.

6. Position the crosshair pointer about 0.5 inch inside the left edge of the selection. Click and drag to the right—the direction in which you want the blend to go. As you drag, Photoshop will create a line on the screen, indicating where the blend will be created. To produce the blend, release the mouse about 0.5 inch away from the right side of the selection.

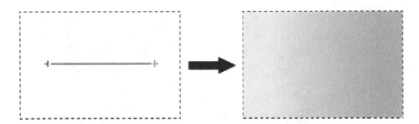

7. Notice that the gradient appears between the two endpoints of your mouse selection. Photoshop fills the area directly before the blend with the solid foreground color and the area after the blend with the solid background color. To get a sense of how Photoshop fills in the intermediate colors, open the Info palette (if it isn't already open), slowly move the mouse pointer over the blend from left to right without clicking, and watch the color values in the Info palette gradually change.

If you would like to experiment with a few more linear blends, clear your screen first. Then try creating some angled blends by clicking and dragging at an angle with the Gradient tool. You can even hold down the SHIFT key to create blends at a 45-degree angle.

You can choose View > Hide Edges to hide a selection marquee temporarily. The area will remain selected, but you will not see the marquee on the screen.

Applying a Radial Gradient

In the next exercise, you'll see the effects of creating a radial blend in a circular selection. This time, you'll use the foreground-to-transparency blend style and then move the blended image into another file.

1. Create a new 3-by-3-inch, RGB color file. Set Contents to Transparent.

2. Set the foreground color to yellow.

3. To create the circular selection, click and drag with the Elliptical Marquee tool.

4. Select the Gradient tool. In the Options bar, click on the Gradient Picker and select the choice showing the foreground color blending to transparency (second choice). Then select the Radial style.

5. To create the blend, position the mouse in the center of your elliptical selection. Click and drag in any direction toward the edge of the elliptical selection. This time, Photoshop creates the blend radiating out from the center, instead of in a straight line. Notice that you can see through the lightest area of the blend. This is because you used the foreground-to-transparent gradient.

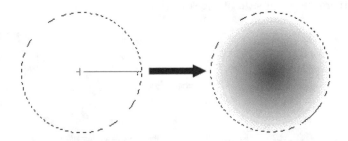

6. Deselect the area by choosing Select > Deselect.

7. Open any other image. Activate the Move tool and drag the gradient over that image window. You'll see that the image shows through the transparent part of the blend. The same effect could also have been produced by creating a new layer and then creating the transparent-to-foreground blend in it.

At this point, you'll probably want to do some experimenting with radial blends. If you wish, you can undo your gradient and redo it. This time, when you create your gradient, click and drag in a different direction and drag for either a shorter or longer length. The distance you drag controls the distance from the start of the blend, where the foreground color is displayed as a solid color, to the end of the blend.

If you create a gradient with an opacity of less than 100 percent over an image, the underlying object will appear through the translucent blend.

Using Blending Modes with Gradients

In the next exercises, you will try using different blending modes with the Gradient tool to see how these modes completely change how a blend is applied.

Using Darken and Lighten Modes

First, you'll create a radial blend behind some text; then you'll create a linear blend within the letters of the text.

1. Create a new 5-by-5-inch, RGB color file. Set Resolution to 72 ppi and Contents to White.

2. Select the Type tool. In the Type tool's Options bar, click on the Type Mask icon, Set the Size to **72**. Set the Anti-Alias pop-up menu to Smooth. Click in the document and type **BLEND**. Then click on the OK icon (checkmark) in the Type Options bar.

3. Choose Edit > Fill. In the Fill dialog box, set the Use pop-up menu to Black and click on OK. Then deselect the text by choosing Select > Deselect.

4. Select the Gradient tool in the Toolbox. In the Gradient tool's Options bar, select the Spectrums gradient (first choice in the third row) from the Gradient Picker's pop-up menu and then click the Radial Gradient icon. Click on the Mode pop-up menu in the Options bar and choose the Darken mode. Set Opacity to 100%.

5. Click and drag diagonally from the upper-left corner of your document to the lower-right corner. The blend appears with the text over it. Because you used the Darken mode, only the areas lighter than the painting color were affected, not the darker areas. Thus, even though you created the blend over the entire document, only the white pixels are affected, not the black text.

6. Select Edit > Undo to remove the effects of the blend that was created in Darken mode.

7. In the Gradient tool's Options bar, select the Linear style. Make sure the Gradient Picker's menu is set to Spectrums. Click on the Mode pop-up menu and change the mode to Lighten.

8. To create the blend, position the mouse to the left of the word *BLEND* and click and drag to the far-right side of the screen. When you release the mouse, you'll see that the blend is created inside the text, without affecting the white background. (The background is white because you chose Edit > Undo in step 6.)

The Lighten mode only lightens areas darker than the painting color. Thus, the black text was lightened by the blend, and the background white area was not affected. By switching to Lighten mode, you were able to change the text without first selecting it.

Using Behind Mode

Next, try an exercise that demonstrates how the Behind mode simulates painting behind your image:

1. Create a new 5-by-5-inch, RGB color file. Set Resolution to 72 ppi and Contents to Transparent.

2. Set the foreground color to purple.

3. Select the Type tool. In the Type Options bar, select the Text Layer icon, pick a font, and set the size to **100**. Choose Smooth in the Anti-Alias pop-up menu. Click in the document and type **Paint**. Click on the OK icon (checkmark) in the Options bar.

4. Render the type by choosing Layer > Rasterize > Type.

5. Select the Gradient tool in the Toolbox. In the Options bar, open the Gradient Picker's pop-up menu and choose either Copper or Chrome (the last two gradients in the second row). Then click on the Linear Gradient style icon and set Mode to Behind.

6. Use the Gradient tool to click and drag from left to right over the entire image.

The resulting image will appear as if you had painted behind the word on screen. The transparent background is filled with the gradient; the word is not affected.

Using Hue Mode

Next, try Hue mode with a linear gradient.

1. Create a new 5-by-5-inch, RGB color file. Set Resolution to 72 ppi and Contents to White.

2. Set the foreground color to purple.

3. Select the Type tool. In the Options bar, select the Type Mask icon, pick a font, and set the size to **100**. Choose Smooth in the Anti-Alias pop-up menu. Click in the document and type **Paint**. Then click on the OK checkmark in the Options bar.

4. Choose Edit > Fill. In the Fill dialog box, set the Use pop-up menu to the Foreground Color option. Then click on OK.

5. Deselect the selection by choosing Select > Deselect.

6. Select the Gradient tool in the Toolbox. In the Options bar, set the Gradient Picker's pop-up menu either to the Red, Green option or the Violet, Green, Orange option. Click on the Linear style button and set Mode to Hue.

7. Use the Gradient tool to click and drag from left to right over the entire image.

When you use the Hue blending mode, the color of the gradient is applied to the text and not to the white area of the document. The Hue mode replaces one color with another.

You have just seen several examples of how powerful Photoshop's blending modes are. You now have new options at your disposal to edit pixels, not according to whether they are selected, but according to their color values.

Editing Gradients

Photoshop allows you to edit preexisting gradients or create your own custom gradients and save them. To edit, create, or save a gradient, you need to use the Gradient Editor dialog box. To access the Gradient Editor dialog box, click on the current gradient that appears in the Gradient tool's Options bar.

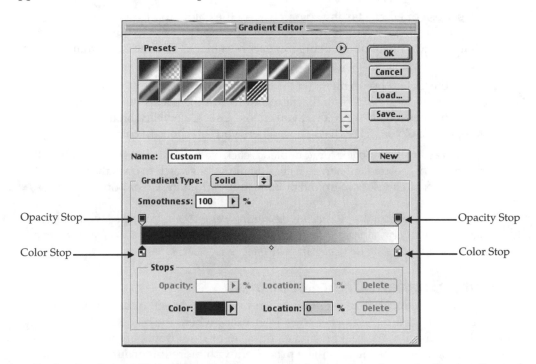

In the Gradient Editor dialog box, you can pick a gradient from the Presets list and then edit it. When you edit the gradient, you are changing the original. The safest approach is to pick a gradient, click on the New button, and then rename the gradient in the Name field. This way, you won't lose the original gradient. After you've finished editing a gradient, as described here, click on OK to save your changes.

The Load and Save buttons allow you to save and load different libraries of gradients as you need them. That way, you don't have a huge scrolling Presets list.

The Gradient Type pop-up menu offers the choices Solid and Noise. The Solid choice provides a smooth transition of colors. The Noise option produces a gradient from random colors within the colors designated in the Gradient Editor dialog box. If you choose Noise, the dialog box changes to allow you to pick a color model (RGB, Lab, or HSB) to specify the range of colors.

The Smoothness value determines the number of transitions in the gradient; higher values produce smoother gradients. You can drag the slider or enter a value in the Smoothness field.

Defining Gradient Colors

Here's how to specify starting and ending colors in a custom gradient:

1. To choose or edit a starting color, click on the color stop icon (the small pentagon shape) beneath the left side of the gradient bar in the Gradient Editor dialog box. The tip of the pentagon becomes black. This indicates that you can now choose a color for the starting point.

2. From the Color pop-up menu (at the bottom of the dialog box), choose Foreground to add the foreground color, Background to add the background color, or User Color to specify another color. If you choose User Color, click on the color swatch to open the Color Picker dialog box, where you can choose a color.

3. To choose an ending color for your blend, click on the pentagon shape on the bottom right side of the gradient bar; then click on the color swatch to open the Color Picker dialog box or choose Foreground or Background from the Color pop-up menu.

You can also pick a color by clicking the eyedropper over any color in your document or the foreground or background color swatch in the Toolbox. To pick a color from your image, simply click on that color in your image.

Changing Gradient Color Locations

You can change the location of the starting, ending, or midpoint of the blend. The midpoint slider beneath the gradient bar determines where the blend begins to change from the foreground to the background color, or to or from transparency. If you move the slider to the right, the blend will be produced with more foreground color than background color. Move the slider to the left, and the blend will be created with less foreground color and more background color.

To change locations, click on the starting, ending, or midpoint icon and drag it onto the gradient bar. You can also adjust the color by entering a value in the Location field. Higher values move the color to the right; lower values move the color to the left.

To edit the gradient further, you can create intermediate points on the gradient bar. If you wish to create an intermediate point, click below the gradient bar where you want the intermediate point to appear. This creates a new pentagon icon. Then choose a color as described in the previous section. To remove an intermediate color, click on the pentagon icon and drag it down.

Changing Gradient Transparency

One of the most intriguing features provided by the Gradient Editor is its ability to create transparent blending effects. You can create blends that start at one color and blend to 100 percent transparency or create effects that blend from one percentage of transparency to another.

To change or create a transparency, click on one of the pentagon icons above the gradient bar and enter a percentage in the Opacity field. You'll see a preview of the transparency effect. To add more stops to control transparency, click on the top of the bar.

Editing Color Stops

If you wish to edit any of the color stops, click on a stop to select it. Then you can change its opacity or color or remove it, as follows:

- To change opacity, click on one of the stops on the top of the gradient bar. Use the Opacity field to change the opacity percentage. To change the location (length) of the opacity effect, either click and drag the stop on the gradient bar or change the value in the opacity Location field.

- To change colors, choose Foreground, Background, or User Color in the Color pop-up menu, as described earlier in the "Defining Gradient Colors" section. To change the location of the color, either click and drag on the stop or change the percentage value in the color Location field.

- To delete a color stop, select it and click on the Delete button.

If you wish to reset the Gradient Editor dialog box, press OPTION *(ALT). This changes the Cancel button to a Reset button. Click on the Reset button.*

Using Photoshop's Eraser Tools

As you work with Photoshop's painting tools, you may want to erase part of your work, or you may wish to erase areas to add special effects. You also may wish to erase background areas in an image before placing it on a Web page. On a Web page, you can make the background color of the Web page show through the transparent areas in the image that you've erased.

For those users of Premiere and AfterEffects, you place an image with a transparent background in one video track, and see background tracks in the transparent areas.

Photoshop features three Eraser tools, which share a Toolbox location:

- **Eraser** Erases using different brushes: Paintbrush, Airbrush, Pencil, and Block. If you paint on the Background layer, the Eraser tool simulates erasing by simply painting with the current background color. When you erase in a layer, the Eraser tool washes away the painted area, leaving transparency "holes" that allow you to see the layer beneath. The Eraser tool also allows you to erase an image back to an earlier state in the History palette.

 If the Preserve Transparency option is selected in the Layers palette, the Eraser tool paints with the background color when erasing in a layer.

- **Background Eraser** Erases areas in layers with options that allow you to control transparency and the sharpness of image edges. Using the Background Eraser, you can mask intricate images. (*Masking* separates an image from its background.)

- **Magic Eraser** Erases similar colored or contiguous pixels, without the need to drag the tool. One click of the mouse can erase pixels in many parts of your image. The Magic Eraser also allows you to erase data in different layers and control transparency as you erase.

To switch from one Eraser tool to another quickly, press OPTION (*ALT*) while clicking on the Eraser tool in the Toolbox or press SHIFT-E on the keyboard.

Using the Eraser Tool

 The simplest way to erase a portion of your image is to use the Eraser tool. To use it, select it in the Toolbox.

Setting Eraser Options

The Eraser tool's Options bar includes the Brush pop-up menu, which allows you to pick a brush to control the size of the erased stroke.

The Mode pop-up menu controls how the Eraser tool erases. It offers the choices Paintbrush, Airbrush, Pencil, and Block. By selecting one of the first three, you can erase as if you were using the Paintbrush, Airbrush, or Pencil tool. The Block option erases pixels as if the tool were an electronic version of a rubber eraser. When using the Pencil, Paintbrush, or Airbrush option, you can change the opacity and chose a Fade or Stylus option from the Brush Dynamics pop-up menu. In Paintbrush mode, the Wet Edges option is also available. The Erase to History option allows you to click and drag to return a portion of your image to a specific state in the History palette.

To try out the Eraser tool, open a digitized photograph or create a new file and paint in it. Select the Eraser tool in the Toolbox and then click and drag in your image. As you click and drag, the Eraser erases. If you are erasing on the image's Background, the Eraser paints with the background color. If you are erasing in a layer, the Eraser tool erases to transparency. Try setting the Eraser tool's mode to Block and erasing several areas of the image.

 If you are working on an image that does not have a transparent background, the Eraser tool paints with the background color. When working in a layer other than the Background, the Eraser tool clears pixels as if wiping colors off a clear acetate, leaving a transparent background.

After you've erased, you can return your image to its original state by clicking on the snapshot of the image in the History palette or by clicking on a previous state in the History palette. You can also paint back a state set in the History palette by choosing the Erase to History option, as described in the next section.

Using the Erase to History Option

Even if you're not familiar with the History palette (covered in Chapters 6 and 11), the Erase to History option is easy to use and understand. To see how it works, you'll create a gradient over an image and then use the Erase to History option to return a portion of the image to its original state.

1. Open the Red Car image file from the Chapter 5 folder of this book's CD-ROM (or you can use any RGB or CMYK image file).

2. Create a gradient over the image by selecting the Gradient tool in the Toolbox. Then click and drag over your image. This replaces the image with a gradient.

3. Open the History palette by choosing Window > Show History. Notice that a thumbnail version of the image appears in the palette with a paintbrush icon adjacent to it. The paintbrush icon indicates that painting with the Erase to History option paints the original version of the image back on the screen.

4. Select the Eraser tool in the Toolbox. In the Eraser tool's Options bar, click on the Erase to History checkbox. In the Mode pop-up menu, choose the Block option.

5. Click and drag with the Eraser tool. As you click and drag, you paint back the original version of your file.

 You can activate the Erase to History option by pressing OPTION *(*ALT*) while clicking and dragging over previously saved image areas with the Eraser tool.*

Masking an Image with the Background Eraser Tool

 The Background Eraser allows you to separate an image from its background precisely, based on color. You can erase colors that match the background color, for instance, or a color you've clicked on. You can also have the Background Eraser erase colors, but specifically avoid erasing the foreground color.

The Background Eraser tool is especially handy for removing white or a flat background color from an image. Once the background is removed, you can place another layer beneath the image or place the masked image on a Web page (after saving it in the correct file format). As mentioned earlier, the transparent area allows the Web page background to show through. If you place the edited image on another layer, the other layers show through the transparent area.

You can use the Background Eraser tool to help mask an image that you've outlined with the Pen tool. After creating and selecting the path, choose Stroke Subpath from the Path palette's pop-up menu. In the Stroke Path dialog box, choose Background Eraser in the Tools field.

Setting Background Eraser Options

The Background Eraser tool's Options bar includes settings for the brush size and choosing colors.

The Limits pop-up menu offers choices that determine how the Background Eraser spreads over an image area:

- Contiguous allows the Background Eraser to erase adjacent pixels.
- Discontiguous allows the Background Eraser to erase pixels that are not adjacent to each other.
- Find Edges erases contiguous colors but also attempts to maintain image edges.

The Tolerance setting determines the translucency of the erasure, from 1% to 100%; setting the Tolerance to 100% erases 100 percent. Selecting the Protect Foreground Color checkbox prevents the Background Eraser from erasing the foreground color.

The Sampling choices determine colors that should be erased:

- Continuous tells Photoshop to erase the color that you click and drag over.
- Background Swatch erases only Photoshop's background color, no matter what color you click and drag over.
- Once samples the color you click. Use this to erase *only* the color you click.

Erasing and Replacing a Background

As an example, you'll use the Background Eraser to erase just the dark background of an image and then add a pattern to the transparent background, as shown in Figure 5-4.

Figure 5-4.   *An image (left) before erasing the background and (right) after adding a pattern as the background*

1. Load the Smiley image file from the Chapter 5 folder of this book's CD-ROM.

2. Select the Eyedropper tool in the Toolbox and position it over the color that you wish to erase. To set the Toolbox background color to this color, press OPTION (*ALT*) and click in the image. As soon as you click, the background color changes.

3. Select the Background Eraser tool in the Toolbox. In the Background Eraser's Options bar, set the Limits pop-up menu to Contiguous. Start with a Tolerance setting of 10%. Set the Sampling pop-up menu to Background Swatch. This tells the Background Eraser tool to erase only the color that matches Photoshop's background color.

4. Click and drag in the background section of your image. As you erase, you'll see the background gradually becomes transparent. However, since the pixels in the background do not all match the background color, you won't erase every pixel.

5. To increase the color range for erasing, change the Tolerance setting to 25%. Now click and drag. As you drag, the background becomes transparent, but the other colors in the image are not erased. (If you erase too much of your image, either choose Edit > Undo or File > Revert or use the History palette to undo the changes.)

6. After you have completely erased the dark background, you are ready to create a new background. In the Layers palette, convert the background to a new layer by double-clicking on it.

7. Create a new layer by selecting Layer > New > Layer. In the Layers palette, drag the new layer below the first layer.

8. Use the Rectangular Marquee tool to select a small smiley face from the foot of one of the balloons.

9. Define this small smiley face as a pattern by choosing Edit > Define Pattern. Then name the pattern in the Pattern Name dialog box. Next, deselect by choosing Select > Deselect.

10. Apply the new pattern to the new layer by choosing Edit > Fill. In the Fill dialog box, choose Pattern in the Use pop-up menu. Then pick your pattern in the Custom Pattern pop-up menu. Make sure the Preserve Transparency option is not selected. Click on OK to apply the pattern. Now you should have a small smiley face pattern in the background.

11. Since there is too much empty space at the top, copy one of the smiley balloons and paste it at the top. Select the Lasso tool from the Toolbox. Use it to select the bottom-middle balloon. Copy it into a new layer by choosing Layer > New Layer > Layer Via Copy. Next, rotate the balloon so the smiley face is facing you.

12. Apply a drop shadow to the smiley balloons by choosing the Layer > Layer Style > Drop Shadow.

Erasing Colors with the Magic Eraser Tool

The Magic Eraser tool works in a manner similar to the Magic Wand. However, instead of *selecting* areas based on similarity in color, the Magic Eraser *erases* based on color similarity.

Setting Magic Eraser Options

The Magic Eraser tool's Options bar contains settings for controlling how the tool erases colors.

When you click with the Magic Eraser tool, Photoshop samples the color you click. The Tolerance setting determines the extent of the colors that are erased. A low Tolerance setting tells the Magic Eraser to erase only colors similar to the color you've clicked on. A high Tolerance setting allows a greater range of colors to be erased.

The Opacity setting determines the transparency level of the Magic Eraser. Low opacity leaves more of the image intact. High opacity creates a more transparent effect.

The three checkboxes control the Magic Eraser as follows:

■ Selecting Anti-Aliased creates smooth edges in the erased area.

■ If you select Contiguous, the Magic Eraser erases one continuous area. If you deselect Contiguous, the Magic Eraser erases in different parts of your image, jumping over areas that are not within the Tolerance settings.

■ When Use All Layers is selected, the Magic Eraser samples colors from all of the layers in the image (but does not erase in all layers).

Creating a Collage with the Magic Eraser Tool

The Magic Eraser can be used to erase parts of images so that you can easily blend images together. We used the Magic Eraser to create the collage shown in Figure 5-5. To create the collage, we used the three files shown in Figure 5-6 (these files are included on this book's CD-ROM).

First, we loaded the windows image and used the Magic Eraser to erase the dark wall area of the image. Then we opened the sky image and used the Move tool to drag and drop the sky into the window image. Next, we dragged the sky layer to the bottom of the Layers palette, so that we could see the sky through the archway and doorway.

Note   *If you are trying out this example, you may need to use the Eraser tool to erase more of the edges around the window and doorway so that the sky file shows through. Remember that you can press SHIFT as you click with the Eraser tool to erase at a 90-degree angle.*

Figure 5-5.   *A collage created with the Magic Eraser tool*

Figure 5-6. *The images used in the collage*

We also used the Magic Eraser to delete everything from the sailboat image except for some of the algae and the boat. Using the Move tool, we dragged the plants and boat image and dropped it into the window and doorway image to create the final collage (Figure 5-6). Again, to clean up the final collage, we used the Eraser tool to erase unwanted areas.

Creating and Using Custom Brushes

Thus far in this chapter, you have been using the default brushes that appear automatically in Photoshop's Brush pop-up menu. It's likely, however, that you will want to create your own custom brushes (by specifying their size, shape, and other characteristics) to add more variety and style to your work.

Choosing Custom Brush Settings

As an example of creating a custom brush, you'll base a new brush on one of the brushes already in the Brush pop-up menu. You will use a large brush as the model because its diameter, hardness, and roundness attributes will be more noticeable than those of a smaller one. Click on the largest hard-edged brush in the first row of the Brush menu to begin.

Your next step in creating a new brush is to choose the New Brush command in the Brush submenu. Click on the small triangle at the upper-right side of the Brush pop-up menu to display this submenu, and then click on New Brush. The New Brush dialog box (Figure 5-7) appears, displaying the settings for the brush that was selected. In this dialog box, you'll see sliders for controlling Diameter, Hardness, and Spacing and boxes for entering Angle degrees and Roundness percentages.

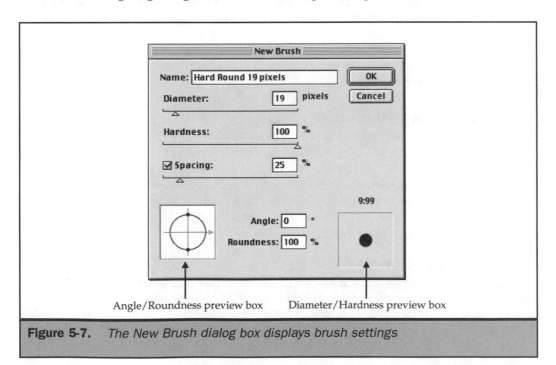

Figure 5-7.   *The New Brush dialog box displays brush settings*

For this example, we will use the following settings in the New Brush dialog box:

- Diameter: 27 pixels
- Hardness: 0%
- Spacing: 300%
- Angle: 45°
- Roundness: 40%

The following sections describe each of the settings in more detail. When you're finished with the New Brush dialog box, click on OK to accept the settings.

Setting the Brush Diameter

Start by exploring the Diameter setting, which determines the size of the brush. To change this, click and drag on the slider control or type a value (in pixels) into the Diameter field.

Try clicking and dragging the slider control to the right. As you drag, watch the preview box in the lower-right corner of the dialog box. It may take a moment or two, but eventually a preview of the new brush size will appear. As you drag the slider to the right, the brush's diameter grows. Change the diameter to 27. If you make the brush any larger than 27 pixels, the brush is represented by a small oval icon with the size below it.

 File resolution affects the stroke of a brush. A brush that paints thickly at 72 ppi produces a thinner stroke at 300 ppi.

Adjusting Brush Hardness

Now test the Hardness slider, which controls whether the brush paints with a soft or hard edge. This value is a percentage of the center of the brush. The best way to visualize this is to gradually drag the Hardness slider to the left and stop at every 25 percent interval to check the changes in the preview box. As you drag, you'll see a light shade surrounding the brush gradually grow. This shading indicates the soft area of the brush. In the Hardness field, 0% produces the softest brush, and 100% the hardest. For this example, drag all the way to 0% for the softest setting.

Setting Brush Spacing

The Spacing option controls the distance that the brush paints as you make a stroke. The Spacing option is turned off or on with a checkbox. When the Spacing option is on, the distance you set with the slider (or type in the Spacing field) is a percentage of the brush's diameter. Thus, when Spacing is set to 100%, the brush will leave dabs of paint spaced the same distance apart as the brush's diameter. The largest value you can enter is 999%.

When the Spacing option is off, the brush's stroke is controlled by your mouse or stylus dragging speed. Drag slowly and more pixels on screen "absorb" paint; drag quickly and the brush skips over pixels.

For this example, select the Spacing checkbox and set the value to 300%. This will produce a change that will be easily seen when you start painting with your custom brush.

Specifying Brush Angle and Roundness

The next two options in the New Brush dialog box, Angle and Roundness, work together. The Angle setting changes the brush shape only if Roundness is not set to 100%. (A Roundness setting of 100% produces a circular brush.) Therefore, start by changing the brush shape from a circle to an ellipse.

You can change the roundness by either typing a value in the Roundness field or by clicking and dragging either of the two dots in the preview box in the lower-left corner of the dialog box. So, to create an elliptical brush, click and drag one of the two dots toward the other one. As you drag, you will decrease the percentage of roundness; the lower the percentage of roundness, the more elliptical your brush will be.

Once you have created the elliptical brush, you can change the Angle setting. You can either type in a value between –180° and 180° or click and drag on the arrowed axis line in the preview box. For this example, you will change the Angle value to create a brush that will be dramatically different from the original one.

Set the Angle to 45° and the Roundness to 40%. Notice that both preview boxes reflect the changes.

 **Angle:** 45 °   **Roundness:** 40 %

Using a Custom Brush

Experiment with your custom brush using the Paintbrush tool.

 1. Select the Paintbrush tool. In the Options bar, select your custom brush in the Brush pop-up menu. Your new brush will appear in the bottom row of the Brush pop-up menu.

2. Click and drag in a document to test it. You'll see that the brush paints a stroke at an angle of 45 degrees and creates a dotted effect, because of the Spacing setting in the New Brush dialog box.

3. To return to your new brush's settings, click on the brush you just created in the Brush pop-up menu.

4. In the New Brush dialog box, change Spacing to 25% and set Hardness to 100%.

5. To see the change, try painting once again with your custom brush. As you paint, you'll see the brush now has a hard-edged stroke, and the white spaces between the brush strokes have disappeared.

If you wish to continue experimenting, try turning off the Spacing option by deselecting the Spacing checkbox in the Brush dialog box. Try a few quick brush strokes and then a very slow brush stroke. You'll see that when you paint slowly, more paint is "absorbed" by the pixels on screen. When you paint faster, fewer pixels are filled in.

Saving and Loading Custom Brushes

If you like the custom brushes you have created and wish to use them again, you can save the entire Brush menu to disk. When you need it again, you can load the brushes from the disk.

To save brushes, including all the custom brushes you have designed, select Save Brushes from the Brush submenu. To keep all of your custom brushes together, it might be a good idea to save them in the Brushes folder. When you install Photoshop, the Brushes folder is automatically installed. Once you have located the folder, name your brush palette **MyBrush** and click on Save.

Note   *If you wish to add custom brushes that already exist in a saved brushes file to the Brush pop-up menu currently active on your screen, choose Load Brushes from the Brush submenu. After you load the brushes from your hard disk, they will be appended to the current set of brushes. If you wish to replace the brushes in the pop-up menu with a set of brushes saved on disk, choose the Replace Brushes command from the menu.*

You may have noticed that within Photoshop's Brushes folder are three different brush files: Assorted Brushes, Drop Shadow Brushes, and Square Brushes. If you wish to load any of these or other custom brushes, just select Append or Replace Brushes from the Brush submenu. For example, if you choose Assorted Brushes and replace the current brushes, your Brush pop-up menu will look like the one shown below.

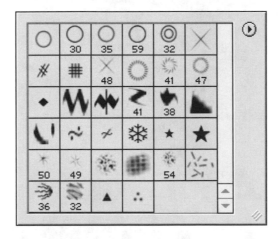

To return to the original set of brushes, choose Reset Brushes from the brush palette's menu. After the Confirm dialog box appears, click on OK.

The
Complete
Reference

Part II

Image Editing Fundamentals

The
Complete
Reference

Photoshop 6

Chapter 6

Introduction to
Image Editing

In image editing, the magic of Photoshop truly comes alive. With Photoshop's and ImageReady's image-editing tools at your command, objects once hidden in darkness will suddenly emerge from the shadows. Images almost lost in the distance will gradually sharpen into focus. Images that are bland, barren, or unbalanced can be populated with just the right objects in precisely the right places. In short, Photoshop's image-editing tools allow you to make your images appear exactly the way that you want them to look.

The goal of this chapter, though, is not to concentrate on the fantastic and amazing, but rather to provide you with an introduction to the basics of image editing. We'll begin by performing a little image-editing magic with the Blur/Sharpen/Smudge and Dodge/Burn/Sponge tools, and then we'll experiment with the Clone Stamp, History Brush, Art History Brush, and Pattern Stamp tools.

> **Note**   *ImageReady's Blur/Sharpen/Smudge, Dodge/Burn/Sponge, and Clone Stamp tools function almost identically to Photoshop's tools of the same name. ImageReady does not include a History Brush, Art History Brush, or Pattern Stamp tool, however.*

Improving an Image with the Image-Editing Tools

In many of the exercises in this chapter, you will be working on a digitized image of an oriental fan. The fan image can be found in the Chapter 6 folder of the *Photoshop Complete Reference* CD-ROM.

Figure 6-1 shows the original scanned image of the oriental fan with its imperfections. You can see that light areas need to be darkened and shadowed areas need to be lightened. You'll use the Dodge and Burn tools to lighten overexposed and darken underexposed areas. The flowers need to be sharpened and their colors intensified so that they will stand out. You'll use the Sponge tool to saturate (intensify) and desaturate (weaken) the colors in your image. The edges of the fan also need to be softened so that the fan will blend into a background photograph. (The background image, Table.jpg, also can be found in the Chapter 6 folder of the CD ROM that accompanies this book.) Once you've improved the image's exposure levels, you'll use the Blur and Sharpen tools to soften and clarify certain areas. With the Smudge tool, you'll blend small parts of the image to create watercolor and finger-painting effects.

Figure 6-2 shows the corrected fan as part of a completed project. Notice that the fan now has more flowers than in the original image—these flowers were cloned, or copied, to make the fan look more interesting. You'll use the powerful Clone Stamp tool to clone areas of the image.

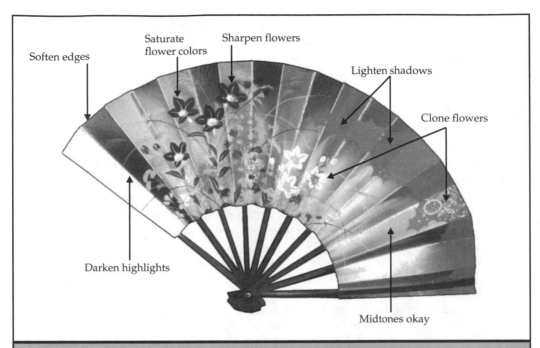

Figure 6-1. *Corrections needed for the oriental fan image*

Figure 6-2. *Oriental fan added to background image*

We achieved the translucent effect of the type in Figure 6-2 by using the Type tool to add the text and setting Opacity to 50% in the Layers palette. See Chapter 3 for details on using the Type tool.

Working with the Dodge and Burn Tools

Photographers can often improve even their best work by using dodging and burning darkroom techniques to block out light from or add light to a negative to enhance image definition. In photography, dodging is usually employed to lighten shadowed areas (the darkest portions of an image), and burning is employed to darken highlights (the brightest parts of an image). Both techniques increase the detail in a photograph. The Dodge and Burn tools have begun enticing photographers out of the darkroom and into the Photoshop studio, because these tools produce the same effects in a digitized image.

The Dodge, Burn, and Sponge tools share one location in the Toolbox; only one tool's icon is visible at a time. (Dodge is the default tool.) You can switch among the Dodge, Burn, and Sponge tools by pressing SHIFT-O (That's the letter O, not a zero!). To see a pop-up menu displaying all the tools, simply click and hold down the mouse button on the Dodge/Burn/Sponge tool location.

Setting Dodge and Burn Options

When either Dodge or Burn is activated, the Options bar includes Brush, Range, and Exposure settings. The width of the area you edit is determined by the size of the brush you pick in the Brush pop-up menu and whether it is hard-edged or soft-edged.

  As you work, don't forget that the effects of a brush differ according to image resolution. A 10-pixel diameter brush has a greater effect on a 72-ppi image than it does on a 300-ppi image, for example.

The Options bar also includes an exposure setting. In photography, an overexposed image is one that is too light, and an underexposed image is too dark. Clicking on the Exposure pop-up menu opens an Exposure slider control that you can use to set the exposure level from 1% to 100%. By typing a number from your keyboard, you can step through exposure settings in intervals of 10%. Increasing the exposure while you're using the Dodge tool intensifies the tool's lightening effect. Increasing the exposure while you're using the Burn tool intensifies the tool's darkening effect. You can change exposures by typing in a number when the Dodge or Burn tool is selected. For example, typing **1** sets the exposure to 10%, typing **2** sets the exposure to 20%, and typing **25** sets the exposure to 25%. Typing **0** (zero) sets the exposure to 100%.

Note *Changing settings in the Brush Dynamics pop-up menu in the Options bar provides even more control when editing images with the Dodge/Burn/Sponge tool. The Brush Dynamics pop-up menu allows you to fade brush size and pressure based on the number of steps entered in the Steps field. If you set the Brush Dynamics settings to Stylus, you can change Pressure and Brush size by applying more or less pressure to the stylus pen.*

When you use the Dodge or Burn tool, the Range pop-up menu in the Options bar displays three options:

- Shadows, which are the darkest components of an image
- Midtones, which are halfway between highlights and shadows
- Highlights, which are the brightest components of an image

By selecting one of these options, you can apply the Dodge or Burn tool to correct shadows, midtones, or highlights. For instance, if you select Highlights, only highlighted areas will be affected. The following illustration shows the Range options as well as the Exposure set to 50%.

By allowing you to choose a brush size, an exposure level, and an image's highlights, midtones, or shadows, Photoshop provides tremendous control over brightness and darkness levels. Using a soft-edged brush with a low exposure creates a subtle effect; using a hard-edged brush with a high exposure produces a more dramatic effect.

Note *The display of the mouse pointer (often called cursor) when using these tools depends on your Preferences settings (select Edit > Preferences > General > Display & Cursors). See Chapter 5 for details.*

Open the fan image (Figure 6-1) from the CD-ROM. Before you make any changes, choose File > Save As and save the file under a new name so that you don't alter the original image.

Caution *Use the Dodge and Burn tools carefully. Heavy dodging and burning can create destructive effects. Always keep a backup of your original, or make sure that you have a snapshot of the original in the History palette. Snapshots are discussed later in this chapter and in Chapter 11. The History palette is also discussed in Chapter 11.*

As you can see, the light areas on the left side of the fan are too light—almost white. The dark areas on the top of the fan are almost the same color as the flowers, causing the flowers to fade into the background. In the image, look for areas that are too bright or too dark. Focus on these areas when you use the Dodge and Burn tools.

 You can apply Dodge and Burn effects using the Color Dodge and Color Burn modes in the Layers palette pop-up menu or the Mode pop-up menu in the Edit > Fill dialog box.

Using the Dodge Tool to Lighten Image Areas

 Now you will use the Dodge tool to lighten shadows so that more detail is visible in the dark areas of the image.

1. If the Dodge tool is not shown as the active tool in the Toolbox, click and hold the mouse over the tool in the Dodge tool's Toolbox location and select the Dodge tool from the pop-up menu. Then click to select the Dodge tool.

2. In the Brush pop-up menu in the Options bar, pick a soft-edged brush to make subtle changes, set Exposure to 20%, and select Shadows from the Range pop-up menu.

3. Move the mouse pointer over a dark area of your image. (The mouse pointer changes to the Dodge tool when it enters the document window, unless CAPS LOCK is depressed or Precise or Brush Size is selected in the Display & Cursors Preferences dialog box.)

4. Click and drag with a few short mouse movements. As you do, you'll see that the darkest areas that you are dragging over become lighter. In Figure 6-3, you can see that the Dodge tool has lightened shadows to add tonal balance to the fan.

5. Continue using the Dodge tool to lighten all of the dark areas in your image. As you work, try clicking and dragging in a circular motion to create a more natural look. You might need to change the Brush, Exposure, and Range settings to produce the desired effect.

Using the Burn Tool to Darken Image Areas

Next, you will use the Burn tool to darken some of the highlights in the image.

 1. To switch to the Burn tool, press SHIFT-O.

2. In the Options bar, choose a small, soft-edged brush to create a subtle darkening effect, set Exposure to 10%, and choose Highlights in the Range pop-up menu.

 The effect produced may depend on image resolution. A 10% exposure creates more burn in a low-resolution image than it does in a high-resolution image. A 10-pixel brush size produces a larger stroke in a low-resolution image than it does in a high-resolution image.

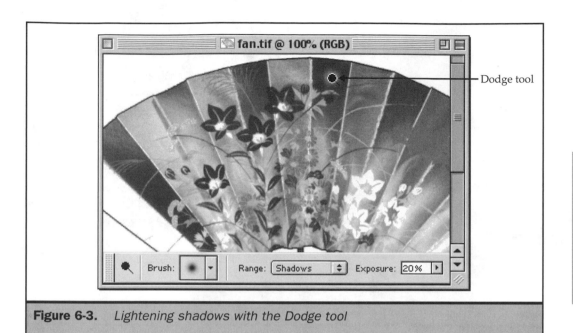

Figure 6-3.   *Lightening shadows with the Dodge tool*

3. In your image, look for a bright portion and position the pointer over this area.

Tip   *To zoom in quickly on an area of an image, hold down COMMAND-SPACEBAR (CTRL-SPACEBAR) and click over the area that you wish to zoom in. To zoom out, click the mouse while pressing OPTION-SPACEBAR (ALT-SPACEBAR).*

4. When you are ready to begin, click and drag several times over the area using short strokes. As you drag, the lightest part of the image turns slightly darker. Now you can see how the rate of the darkening reflects the brush size and exposure setting you use. Because the exposure setting is low and you are using a soft-edged brush, the burn progresses slowly.
   Figure 6-4 shows the Burn tool adding tone to an overexposed area of the fan.

Tip   *If an image area requires that you lighten or darken in a straight line (90-degree increments)—for example, if you're lightening or darkening the edges or corners of a book—press SHIFT while clicking and dragging with either the Dodge or Burn tool activated.*

5. If you wish to darken shadow or midtone areas that are too light, continue editing by changing the Range selection to Shadows or Midtones and using various brush sizes and exposure percentages.

IMAGE EDITING
FUNDAMENTALS

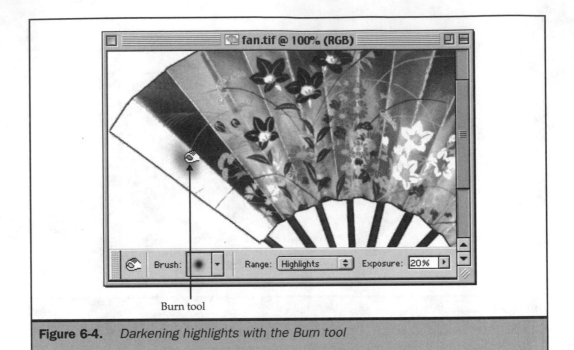

Burn tool

Figure 6-4.   *Darkening highlights with the Burn tool*

Now that you've had some practice using the Dodge and Burn tools, you're ready to try some of the other image-editing tools on your practice document. Next, we'll experiment with the Sponge tool, which increases or decreases color intensity.

Using the Sponge Tool to Saturate and Desaturate Image Areas

The Sponge tool is used to increase or decrease the saturation or intensity of a color. When saturation is added to a color, the gray level of a color diminishes, so it becomes less neutral. When you choose the Sponge tool, the Options bar displays Pressure rather than Exposure, and you can choose either Desaturate or Saturate from the pop-up menu.

The Sponge tool's Desaturate option can be quite useful when an RGB color image displays CMYK out-of-gamut colors. By dragging the Sponge tool over these out-of-gamut colors, you can gradually dilute them so that they drop into the CMYK spectrum of printable colors. You can also get help to prevent you from oversaturating the colors. If you make your colors too intense, the Info palette's CMYK out-of-gamut alarm (an exclamation mark) appears.

Note

As explained in Chapter CD-1 (located on this book's CD-ROM), gamut refers to the visible color range of a color model. For more information about using the Sponge tool to correct out-of-gamut colors, see Chapter 13

Now you will use the Sponge tool to intensify colors in your image. First, you will use the Info palette to alert you if you are oversaturating.

1. Open the Info palette by choosing Window > Palettes > Show Info. The out-of-gamut alarm appears only when the CMYK readouts are displayed in the Info palette. If you don't see the CMYK readouts in the Info palette, click on one of the eyedroppers in the palette and choose CMYK Color.

2. As mentioned earlier, the Sponge tool shares a Toolbox location with the Dodge and Burn tools. To switch to the Sponge tool, select it from the Toolbox's pop-up menu or press SHIFT-O.

3. Move the Sponge tool to an area of your image where the colors look dull. Before you begin to saturate the area, notice the CMYK Color readouts in the Info palette.

4. In the Options bar, select a medium-sized, soft-edged brush from the Brush pop-up menu; select Saturate from the pop-up menu; and set the Pressure to 30%. This will produce a slow and gradual saturation. If you set the Pressure to 100%, the colors would saturate very quickly.

5. Start saturating by clicking and dragging the Sponge tool over the dull-colored areas in your image.

Tip

You could also use the Color Sampler tool to sample four different areas in the image, and then observe how using the Sponge tool changes the color values of the four different areas. See Chapter 5 for details on using the Color Sampler tool.

6. After you've saturated the colors in an image area, look at the CMYK Color readouts in the Info palette. If you see an exclamation point after the CMYK Color readouts, you've overstepped the CMYK color gamut, which means that the colors on screen cannot be printed on a commercial printing press. If you are outputting to slides or videotape, you do not have to worry about out-of-gamut CMYK colors.

Note

RGB colors may fall beyond the range of acceptable colors for video. You can use Photoshop's NTSC Color filter (choose Filter > Video > NTSC Color) to adjust out-of-gamut colors so they fall into the NTSC (National Television System Committee, the U.S. television standard) color range.

IMAGE EDITING
FUNDAMENTALS

7. If you've oversaturated and want to desaturate, choose Desaturate from the pop-up menu in the Options bar. Use the Sponge tool to lower the intensity of the colors so that they are not out of gamut. Don't desaturate too much; if you do, your colors will turn gray.

Note   *If you wish to desaturate an image or selection completely, use Photoshop's Image > Adjust > Desaturate command. This will change all colors to shades of gray.*

This should give you an idea of what you can do with the Sponge tool. Next, you'll work on your practice document with the Blur and Sharpen image-editing tools.

Working with the Blur and Sharpen Tools

The Blur tool softens parts of an image by, as you probably guessed, blurring them. Its counterpart, the Sharpen tool, makes image areas sharper and more distinct. Photoshop's Blur tool works by decreasing the contrast among the pixels you drag over; the Sharpen tool works by heightening contrast in neighboring pixels.

Like the Dodge and Burn tool combination, Blur and Sharpen are often used to enhance the quality of digitized images. You may wonder why anyone would want to make an image blurry. Here are some reasons:

- Scanners sometimes accentuate edges too much, causing images to look too harsh. These edges can be softened with the Blur tool.

- The Blur tool can help soften the jagged edges of an image that is pasted into a document, so that it blends more smoothly into its surroundings.

- The Blur tool can be used to create subtle shadow effects.

The Blur and Sharpen tools share a location in the Toolbox with the Smudge tool. By default, when Photoshop or ImageReady is first loaded, only the Blur tool appears in the Toolbox. As with Dodge/Burn/Sponge, you can switch among the Blur, Sharpen, and Smudge tools by clicking and dragging the mouse in the Toolbox. You can also press the OPTION key (*ALT*) and click on the active tool in the Toolbox, or press SHIFT-R to toggle among tools.

Setting Blur and Sharpen Options

Let's take a look at the Blur/Sharpen Options bar. If the Options bar is already open, click once on the Blur/Sharpen tool. If the bar isn't open, double-click on the tool to display it. Click on the Mode pop-up menu to view the different modes, which include Normal, Darken, Lighten, Hue, Saturation, Color, and Luminosity. (See Chapter 5 for a discussion of the different blending modes.) By switching modes, you can control which image areas will be affected; for instance, if you choose Darken, only lighter pixels will be changed. As with the Sponge tool, the Options bar includes a Pressure setting.

The Pressure slider (which appears when you click the Pressure pop-up menu) controls the amount of sharpening and blurring that these tools produce. The higher the Pressure percentage, the greater the effect of the sharpening or blurring. As usual, the size of the area that changes is determined by the brush size you are using. Smaller brushes affect smaller areas; larger brushes affect larger areas.

 If you use a stylus and digitizing tablet, you can also take advantage of the two Stylus Pressure options for the Blur and Sharpen tools: Size and Pressure. These two options can be found in the Brush Dynamics pop-up menu.

When the Blur/Sharpen, Clone Stamp, or Smudge tool is active, the Use All Layers checkbox option is available. When this option is not selected, Photoshop analyzes pixel values only in the layer in which you are currently working. If this option is selected, Photoshop samples and edits using pixel values from all visible layers when the tool is used. Since you are working in only one layer, selecting the Use All Layers checkbox will have no effect on your image editing. (See Chapters 16 and 17 for more information about layers.)

Using the Sharpen Tool to Increase Contrast

 Because it's easier to recognize the need for sharpening image areas than the need for blurring them, you'll start by experimenting with the Sharpen tool.

1. If the Sharpen tool is not active, switch to it.

2. Pick a brush size and a Pressure value in the Options bar. Leave the Mode set to Normal. If you use a medium-sized, soft-edged brush and a low Pressure value, the sharpening effect will be barely noticeable. A large, hard-edged brush with a high Pressure value will produce a more intense effect.

3. Now decide which area you want to work on, move the Sharpen tool over that area, and click and drag the mouse to begin increasing contrast. Try moving to other areas in the image to see the results of sharpening with different Pressure settings.

Beware of sharpening too much. If you overdo it, the colors break up and become pixelated, as shown in Figure 6-5. Here, the Sharpen tool is being used to heighten the contrast in the fan's flowers. To avoid oversharpening, use the Zoom tool to zoom in and keep a close eye on the pixels being affected.

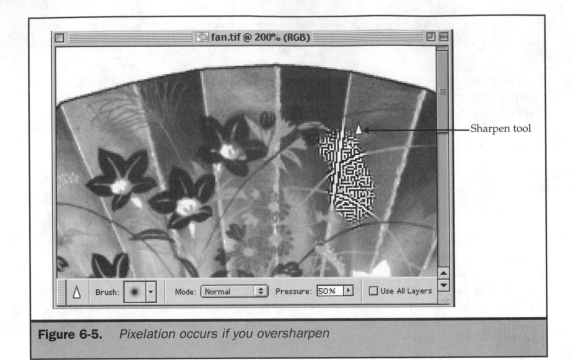

Sharpen tool

Figure 6-5. *Pixelation occurs if you oversharpen*

Using the Blur Tool to Soften Hard Edges

You can use the Blur tool to soften hard edges produced when digitizing oversharpens an image. You can also use the Blur tool to soften overly bright highlights or reflections that appear digitized.

To switch to the Blur tool, press and hold OPTION (*ALT*) while clicking on the Sharpen tool. You can also press and hold down the mouse button while you select the Blur tool, or press SHIFT-R. Look for areas in your image that are too sharp or that have hard edges that need to be softened. Work these edges first with a low Pressure setting in the Options bar, so that you don't blur your image too much.

You can bring an oversharpened or overblurred image back to a previous state by clicking on a previous step in the History palette. Blurring an oversharpened area does not bring a digital image back to its previous state. The History palette is discussed in Chapter 11.

Figure 6-6 shows the Blur tool being used to help soften the pixelation that occurred when the fan's flowers were being sharpened (in Figure 6-5). The Blur tool was also used to soften all of the hard edges of the fan, including the ridged perimeter after it was pasted into the final photograph.

Note   *In addition to using the Blur and Sharpen tools, you can apply filters to make entire images more or less distinct. (Filters are discussed in Chapter 12.)*

If you wish, continue to experiment with the Blur and Sharpen tools. When you're finished, save your work and close the practice file. Then proceed to the next section to try your hand at more image-editing techniques.

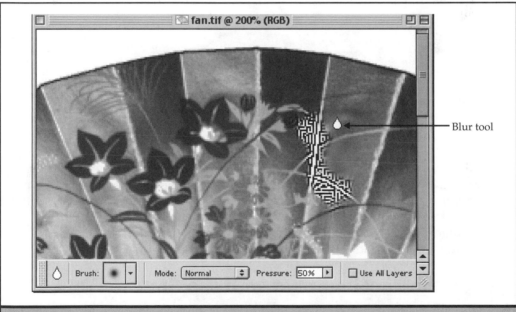

Figure 6-6.   *Using the Blur tool to soften an image*

Working with the Smudge Tool

The Smudge tool lets you blend colors as if you had smudged them together with your finger. When you use the Smudge tool, Photoshop starts with the color you click on and mixes it with the colors you drag over. Besides blending colors and mixing paint, the Smudge tool can be used to produce a watercolor-pastel, crayon-like effect in your image.

 The Smudge tool cannot be used on Indexed Color or bitmap images.

Setting Smudge Options

The Smudge tool's Options bar includes Brush, Mode, and Pressure settings. The brush controls how the colors are smudged together. If you use a large brush with a high Pressure value, you will create a large smudge that will completely distort your image. A lower Pressure value with a small- or medium-sized brush will decrease the size of the smudge and create a less dramatic effect.

The Mode pop-up menu displays the standard blending mode choices (as discussed in Chapter 5). These can provide further control of your smudge. For example, if you use the Hue mode, only the hue values will be smudged (not the saturation or the luminosity values). Similarly, use Saturation mode to change only the saturation values and Luminosity mode to smudge only the luminosity values.

If you have more than one layer on your screen, you can also choose to smudge using sampled pixel values from all visible layers. To do this, click on the Use All Layers checkbox.

The Finger Painting checkbox allows you add colors to an image. You will experiment with this option after seeing how the Smudge tool works without it.

Creating a Watercolor Effect with the Smudge Tool

Now you will have a chance to experiment with the Smudge tool by transforming a digitized image into one resembling a watercolor painting.

1. Before proceeding, open any scanned image file, or reopen the file you started with at the beginning of this chapter. Use Save As to create another copy of your file. Name your file **Water Painting**. By using Save As, you will keep your original file from being affected by the changes you are going to make in the following exercises.

Note

Creating different snapshot versions of your file enables you to experiment with various designs and return to them as you are working on a project. (Snapshots are discussed later in this chapter and in Chapter 11.) You might also choose to duplicate a file by selecting Image > Duplicate.

2. Activate the Smudge tool by clicking on the Blur/Sharpen/Smudge Toolbox location and selecting the Smudge tool.

3. If the Smudge tool's Options bar isn't open, press RETURN (*ENTER*) or double-click on the Smudge tool.

4. In the Options bar, pick a medium-sized, soft-edged brush; set the Mode Normal; and set the Pressure to 50%. You'll begin by using the Smudge tool without the Finger Painting option. If necessary, deselect this option by clicking on the checkbox.

5. Move the Smudge pointer anywhere in your document, and click and drag the mouse in one direction. You'll see that a small smudge of colors appears on screen.

6. Zoom in to see a close-up view of the smudge.

7. Create a few more smudges, and your image will start looking more like a watercolor painting, as in Figure 6-7.

8. Experiment with various brush sizes. Also, try switching modes a few times before smudging different parts of your image.

Tip

The Smudge tool can be used to soften unwanted wrinkles and blemishes in flesh tones.

Using the Smudge Tool's Finger Painting Option

You have created a watercolor effect by smudging the colors of your image together. What if you want to create a watercolor effect and add new color to your image at the same time? You can do this by activating the Smudge tool's Finger Painting option, which smudges using the foreground color at the beginning of each click and drag of the mouse. Try it out.

1. For this exercise, set the foreground color to a bright color so you can easily view the Finger Painting effects.

2. Double-click on the Smudge tool. In the Options bar, select the Finger Painting checkbox and leave the other settings as they are (continue to use a medium-sized, soft-edged brush and leave the Pressure set to 50%).

Tip

To automatically activate the Smudge tool's Finger Painting option, press and hold OPTION (ALT) as you work with the tool.

Smudge tool

Figure 6-7. *Creating a watercolor effect using the Smudge tool*

3. Click and drag over an area on your document. Notice how the Smudge tool smudges with the selected foreground color each time you click and drag.

4. Continue to experiment using other foreground colors. When you're finished, close the file and save it, if you wish.

In the next section, you'll learn about one of Photoshop's most versatile tools—the Clone Stamp.

Cloning with the Clone Stamp Tool

The Clone Stamp is a cloning tool. *Cloning* allows you to choose different parts of an image and duplicate them to areas in the same file or in another file. This is quite different from copying and pasting. During the cloning procedure, Photoshop or ImageReady *samples*, or reads, a source area and clones it to a target area. As you click and drag in the target area in the file, a clone of the sampled area gradually appears. This process can produce an undetectable blend of old and new pixels. When executed properly, the cloning effect is often seamless and—even to the experienced Photoshop user—frequently amazing.

The Clone Stamp tool always clones based on how the image appeared before the last stroke with the Clone Stamp tool. This prevents you from recloning the area that you just cloned.

Setting Clone Stamp Options

The Clone Stamp tool's Options bar includes Brush, Mode, and Opacity settings. The Opacity setting can be from 0% (transparent) to 100% (opaque). You can create some fascinating blends between image areas by cloning one image area over another at a low opacity.

 When the Clone Stamp tool is activated, the Brush Dynamics pop-up menu provides two Stylus Pressure options—Size and Opacity.

The Aligned checkbox allows you to clone different parts of an image to different areas of the same file or another file. When you clone using the Aligned option, Photoshop retains the same distance and angular relationship between the source area that you are sampling and the target area where the clone appears. For instance, you may wish to clone an image 2 inches directly above the original sample. After you finish cloning, if you move the mouse to another area of the file and then click and drag, Photoshop or ImageReady will clone whatever is located 2 inches directly above the mouse pointer.

If the Aligned option is turned off, the Clone Stamp tool automatically keeps sampling the original source area, so you can clone the same sample in many places after you release the mouse. For the completed fan image in Figure 6-2 (shown at the beginning of the chapter), the Clone Stamp tool's Aligned option was used to duplicate different flowers in various areas of the fan. Had the designer wanted to clone the same flower in many parts of the fan, she would have cloned with the Aligned option off.

If you are cloning in a file that has layers, you may wish to select the Use All Layers checkbox in the Clone Stamp's Options bar. This allows you to clone from all visible layers, rather than just the layer in which you are working.

Using the Clone Options to Duplicate Image Areas

Cloning can be tremendously helpful when you edit an image or retouch a photo. For example, one of the authors of this book once retouched a cover for a proposed *Reader's Digest* travel guide. The picture that the book's art director wished to use was a photograph of a small New England town. Everything in the photo was beautiful—except for the telephone wires crisscrossing through the scene. With the Clone Stamp tool, parts of the trees that surrounded the wires were easily cloned over the wires to make them disappear. (You'll see this example in Chapter 19, where advanced retouching techniques are introduced.)

In the next exercise, you will work with the oriental fan image to learn the basics of using the Clone Stamp tool.

1. Open the fan file you used in the previous exercises, or load any digitized image.

2. Select the Clone Stamp tool in the Toolbox.

3. If the Clone Stamp tool's Options bar isn't open, press RETURN (*ENTER*) or double-click on the Clone Stamp tool in the Toolbox.

4. In the Options bar, pick a large brush and set a high Opacity setting. With a large brush and a high Opacity setting, the cloning will happen faster and its effect will be more obvious. Leave the Mode set to Normal. Select the Aligned checkbox.

5. To clone part of your image, move the Clone Stamp pointer so that it's over the area you wish to duplicate. Press and hold the OPTION (*ALT*) key, and then click the mouse to sample the area. Notice that the small black triangle at the base of the Clone Stamp (🖫) turns white and moves up a pixel. This indicates that an area has been sampled. Once you've sampled an area, release the OPTION (*ALT*) key and move the Clone Stamp pointer to the area where you wish the clone to appear.

6. To begin cloning, click and drag the mouse, moving the Clone Stamp pointer over the target area. As you move the mouse, the clone will begin to appear in that area. Notice that a crosshair in the source area follows the movements of your Clone Stamp pointer in the target area. The crosshair always remains the same distance and the same angle from the Clone Stamp pointer, as shown in Figure 6-8.

Note *As you click and drag, the Clone Stamp tool always clones from the original source; it will not clone an area that was already cloned. This prevents a "hall of mirrors" effect—cloning the cloned area of a clone area.*

7. Continue clicking and dragging the mouse. The greater the area that you click and drag over, the greater the area that is cloned.

8. When you use the Aligned option, it's important to remember that the distance and the angle between the sampled area and the area where the clone is placed are always the same. To verify this, release the mouse button and then move the Clone Stamp pointer to another area on the screen. Click and drag—Photoshop (and ImageReady) resamples and starts cloning again.

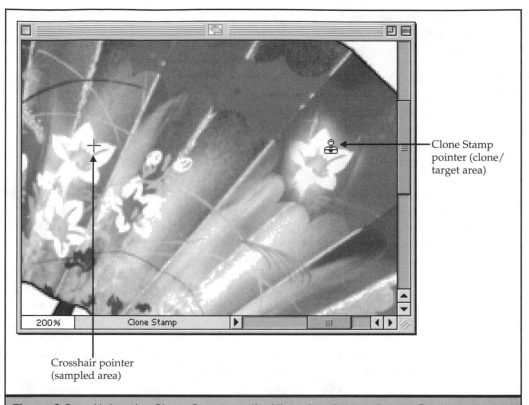

Clone Stamp
pointer (clone/
target area)

Crosshair pointer
(sampled area)

Figure 6-8.   *Using the Clone Stamp tool's Aligned option to clone a flower*

IMAGE EDITING
FUNDAMENTALS

Note

Notice that when you clone the new area, the distance and angle between the crosshair and the Clone Stamp pointer are the same as in the previous sample/clone pair. If you want to reset the distance between the source area and the target area, move the Clone Stamp pointer to another area that you wish to sample, press OPTION (ALT), and click the mouse. Now you can move the Clone Stamp tool to the area where you wish to clone the new sample. Subsequent sample/clone pairs will then be separated by this new distance and angle. The cloning will begin as soon as you click and drag.

9. If you wish to clone the same sample to different areas in your image, deselect the Aligned option. Try this now. After you deselect the Aligned checkbox, once again press OPTION (*ALT*) and click the mouse to sample.

10. Move the Clone Stamp tool to the area where you want to apply the clone, and then click and drag. After you've created the clone of the image, release the mouse button.

11. Move to another area of the screen where you wish to duplicate the sample, and click and drag again. As you click and drag, another clone of the first sampled area will be created.

Tip *You can press the CAPS LOCK key to turn the Clone Stamp pointer into a crosshair. It's easier to use the middle of the crosshair than the Clone Stamp pointer as a guide to judge the specific area that you are cloning. When you use this technique, you'll have two crosshairs on screen: one indicating the sample area and the other indicating the target area where the clone appears. You can distinguish between the two crosshairs because the one indicating the sample target area has a dot in it.*

12. As you work, you'll want to make the cloned image look as natural as possible. You don't want the clone to stand out from its surroundings. To make your clone blend in, experiment using the Clone Stamp tool with different brushes, opacities, and modes. In the fan example, a soft-edged brush was used. This helped blend the new flower at the top of the fan to look as though it had always been there.

Tip *You can also clone an image from one file to another. To do this, open the two files side by side on your screen. Press OPTION (ALT), click over the area you wish to sample, and then activate the target file. Position the Clone Stamp pointer over the area where you wish to place the clone and click and drag. If you are working with layers, you can sample in one layer and create the clone in another layer.*

A Clone Stamp Design Project

If you would like more practice using the Clone Stamp tool, you can re-create the Tropical Getaways image shown here. For this project, we used the Clone Stamp tool because we could clone from multiple files and create a painterly effect within the circular area as we cloned.

To create the logo, we used five files: waterfall (the background image of the logo), bluebird, swan, red flower, and green plant. If you want to re-create the Tropical Getaways logo, you can copy these files from the Tropical folder in the Chapter 6 folder on this book's CD-ROM. All of the images in the logo project were originally video files transferred into Adobe Premiere from a Sony digital camcorder. In Premiere, the individual frames were exported to disk and then opened in Photoshop.

Here are the basic steps we used to create the logo file:

1. Create a circular selection on screen.

2. Clone each image into a new layer within the circular selection.

3. Stroke the circular selection.

4. Use a layer style (such as Layer > Layer Style > Bevel and Emboss) to produce a three-dimension effect for the circle outline.

5. Add text above and below the circle.

6. Use a layer style to bevel the text.

After completing your work, you could reduce the image using the Image Size command, and use it on a Web page. You also could use techniques described in Chapter 10 to turn it into a rollover, so that when you moved the mouse over it, the image changes to another one.

Using the History Brush and Art History Brush

The History Brush and Art History Brush miraculously bring the digital past into the present. Both tools allow you to paint a previous version of your image into the current file on screen. Both also allow you to create digital effects as you work. The History Brush allows you to change blending modes and opacity as you paint. The Art History Brush provides special options for changing the brush strokes to turn an image into a digital "painting."

The History Brush and Art History Brush share one Toolbox location. Press Y to select the History Brush and Art History Brush Toolbox location. Press SHIFT-Y to toggle between the History Brush and Art History Brush.

Bringing the Past into the Present with the History Brush

One of the most unnerving aspects of image editing is the prospect of making too many changes that cannot be undone. Fortunately, Photoshop's History Brush allows you to paint back a previous version of your work. Thus, in many respects, the History

IMAGE EDITING
FUNDAMENTALS

Brush is a cloning brush. It clones a previous version of the image into an image. When you paint with the History Brush, you paint in a previous version of your image. When an image is first loaded, the History Brush is automatically set to paint in the original version of the file.

The History Brush's Options bar includes the Brush pop-up menu, Opacity, and Mode settings. These options—for example, using a soft-edged brush or lowering the opacity—can prove valuable for blending the reverted part of a file into the image on screen.

Note   *The History Brush and History palette are discussed in detail in Chapter 11.*

Returning a File to Its Original State with the History Brush

In the following exercise, you will alter a file by coloring the entire screen with the background color. Then you'll use the History Brush to return part of the file to its original state. (In the next section, you will use the History Brush to paint in a *snapshot* version of the file.)

1. Open any digitized image; then change the background color to any color other than white.

2. If the History palette isn't opened, open it by choosing Window > Show History. Notice that an icon representing the History Brush appears next to a thumbnail of the original image in the palette. This indicates that painting with the History Brush will return your image to its original state.

3. Choose Select > All. Then press DELETE (*BACKSPACE*) to fill the screen with the background color.

4. Double-click on the History Brush tool. In the Options bar, pick a large brush, set Opacity to 100%, and leave the Mode setting as Normal. When you start using the History Brush, these settings will return your file to its original form using a large brush stroke and its original opacity.

5. Move the History Brush pointer to an area that you want to revert, and then click and drag over the area. As you move the brush, you'll see parts of your image being restored; they will match the size and shape of your brush.

6. Before you finish, change Opacity to 50% and then click and drag in the document window. Now the image is being restored with a 50% opacity. Keep this technique in mind. It might come in handy when you wish to create special effects.

Tip   *Using the History Brush with an Opacity setting lower than 100% can produce a ghostlike effect.*

7. Continue experimenting. Keep Opacity set to 50% and the large, soft-edged brush selected, but switch modes from Normal to Dissolve. Dissolve randomly dissolves the pixels in the image. The results of this effect will vary according to the image's original color. When you're finished, keep your file open and proceed to the next section.

Blending Using a Snapshot and the History Brush

As you're working on an image-editing project, it's reassuring to be able to return to different versions of your file. If you take a snapshot of your image as you work, you can use the History Brush to paint back in the snapshot version of your work.

To explore how snapshots work, you'll blend two images together using a snapshot. In order to see the two options in action, you'll need to open two images: a source and a target image. You'll drag the source image over the target image to create a new layer, and then blend the two images together. Figure 6-9 shows the effects of blending Figure 6-10 with Figure 6-11.

Note   *In Chapters 16 and 17, you'll use layers and layer masks to combine images.*

Figure 6-9.   *The doll and fan images blended together by the History brush*

Figure 6-10. *The doll image before being blended with the fan*

Figure 6-11. *The fan image before being blended with the doll*

1. Open two images on your screen and place them either side by side or so that they overlap. In this exercise, we will use a doll image as the source image (Figure 6-10) and the fan image as the target image (Figure 6-11). The Doll and Fan files are both in the Chapter 6 folder of the book's CD-ROM.

2. Activate the source file (the doll image) so that you can select it, and then place it over the target file (the fan image).

3. Select the Rectangular Marquee tool to select part of the source file. In the Marquee's Options bar, set the Style pop-up menu to Normal and type **5** in the Feather field. Using the Marquee tool, click and drag over the area you want to select in the source file.

Note

Using the Feather option softens the edges of the source file when it is moved to the target file and helps blend the two images together. See Chapter 4 for more information about feathering.

4. Once the source image is selected, activate the Move tool. Place the Move tool in the center of the selected image, and then drag and drop it over the target file. This creates a new layer in the target file.

5. Using the Move tool, position one image over the other, as desired.

6. When the source image is in position, take a snapshot of your image so that you can recall this version of your file if you need to. To take a snapshot of your image on screen, choose New Snapshot from the History Palette menu. In the New Snapshot dialog box, name the Snapshot **Combined**. To ensure that all layers are captured in the snapshot, make sure that the From pop-up menu is set to Full Document. After you click on OK, a thumbnail of the current state of the image appears in the History palette.

7. Now you can start blending the two images together. You'll use the original snapshot so that it blends into the target file and looks like it was always there. Activate the History Brush. In the History Brush's Options bar, set Opacity to 75%, and leave the Mode set to Normal. In the Brushes pop-up menu, pick a medium-sized, soft-edged brush. Now you're ready to revert your image to 75% of the snapshot version.

8. Position the History Brush over the edges of the source image, and then click and drag. As you move the mouse, you'll see the History Brush return the image to the original snapshot of the file.

9. If you take away too much of the source image and want to bring it back, you can reset the History Brush to revert to using the Combined snapshot. To set the History Brush to use the Combined snapshot, click in the gray square next to the snapshot that you named Combined. After you click, a History Brush icon appears.

10. If you wish, change the opacity and the blending mode in the History Brush Options palette and the brush size in the Brush pop-up menu. Next, position the History Brush pointer over the area where you want to bring back the source image, and then click and drag. As you move the mouse, you'll see that the History Brush gradually returns your image to the Combined snapshot version of the file

11. You have now seen how Photoshop gives you the ability to blend two files together using snapshots. If you wish, continue experimenting using different opacities, modes, and brushes. When you're finished, select File > Save As to save your file, and then close the file.

Using Edit > Fill, you can revert an image or selection to a step or snapshot designated by the History Brush in the History palette. To revert to a History version, first click on a snapshot or History stage in the History palette, and then choose Edit > Fill. In the Fill dialog box, choose History from the Use pop-up menu.

Turning Photos into Paintings Using the Art History Brush

 The Art History Brush transforms a digitized photograph into a digitized painting. Like the History Brush, the Art History Brush works its magic by painting back the currently selected history or snapshot state selected in the History palette. Unlike the History Brush, the Art History Brush provides several choices for producing painterly effects.

Art History Brush Options

Along with the standard Brush, Mode, and Opacity settings, the Art History Brush's Options bar offers Style, Fidelity, Area, and Spacing settings.

The additional Art History Brush options work as follows:

- The Style choices allow you to control the brush stroke. The options allow you to paint with dabs, tight strokes, or loose strokes.

- The Fidelity percentage controls how much the painting color differs from the color in the source History state or selected snapshot. Higher percentages produce colors that closely match the original; lower values produce greater color changes.

- The Area option controls how much of the area is affected by the paint. Higher values mean that more area is affected.

- The Spacing percentage allows you to limit image areas that are painted based on color. Enter a high percentage to limit painting to image areas that are different in color than the original history state. Enter a low percentage to paint anywhere in your image.

- The Brush Dynamics pop-up menu (the last box on the Options bar) includes controls for fading Brush size and Opacity. To create a fade out, choose Fade in the Size or Opacity pop-up menu. Then enter the distance in pixels for the fade out in the Steps field. If you choose the Stylus options in the palette, you can change brush pressure and opacity by applying more pressure.

Painting over a Transparent Background with the Art History Brush

One of the best approaches for using the Art History Brush is to paint back an image over a transparent background. This technique works well because the Art History Brush leaves gaps. After you paint, you can then place any other image behind the Art History Brush painting's transparent areas to achieve attractive transparency effects. We created the painterly composite in Figure 6-12 by combining the sails from Figure 6-13 and the lifeguard chair scene from Figure 6-14.

The following steps illustrate this technique:

1. Open an image on screen. If you'd like, use either the Sails (Figure 6-13) or Lifeguard files (Figure 6-14) found in the Chapter 6 folder of the CD-ROM. With your file on screen, notice that a Background layer appears in the Layers palette. (By default, most scanned images are called the Background layer in the Layers palette). In order to create the collage effect in Figure 6-12, you'll need to delete the image in the Background layer so that you can see another image underneath it.

2. To paint back over a transparent background, you must change the Background layer of your image to a transparent layer. The fastest way to do this is to double-click on the Background layer in the Layers palette. This opens the Make Layer dialog box, which automatically renames the background Layer to Layer 0. After you click on OK, your image will have a transparent background (which you won't see until the next step).

Figure 6-12. *A painterly collage created with the Art History Brush*

Figure 6-13. *Sails used to create the painterly collage*

Figure 6-14.   *Lifeguard chair scene used to create the painterly collage*

3. Delete the image on screen from Layer 0. Do this by selecting Layer 0 in the Layers palette, if it is not already selected. Then choose Select > All and press DELETE (*ALT-BACKSPACE*). The image in Layer 1 disappears and is replaced by Photoshop's checkerboard pattern, indicating a transparent background. Make sure that to deselect, you choose Select > Deselect.

Note *A checkerboard pattern is the default setting for a transparent background. To change the setting, choose Edit > Preferences > Transparency & Gamut.*

4. If the History palette isn't on screen, open it by choosing Window > Show History. Note that a small Paintbrush icon appears adjacent to the original version of your image in the Snapshot section of the History palette. This means that the Art History Brush will paint using this version of the image.

Caution *You cannot use the Art History Brush if the current canvas or image size does not match that of the History state. This means that if you rotate the canvas or change its size, Photoshop will not allow you to paint with the Art History Brush.*

5. Double-click on the Art History Brush to select it and open the Art History Brush's Options bar.

6. Start painting in an area of your image using the Dab paint style (select Dab from the Style pop-up menu). As you paint, tiny blotches of paint spread over the transparent background, and you gradually see a painted version of your image come into view.

7. Try experimenting with the other paint styles, such as Loose Curl. This distorts the image into thin curling strokes. Try also using the Tight Short option and some of the other options, such as Opacity. Continue painting and experimenting until you've turned a section of your image into a painting. You may also want to change the size of your brush.

8. To create a collage (as in Figure 6-12), you need to open another image, repeat steps 2 through 4, and then start painting. Paint until the image reappears and you have the desired effect.

9. When you've completed painting, create the painterly collage by copying and pasting. If both images are on screen, you can drag one over the other using the Move tool. Then use the Move tool to move the layers into position. If you like, you can offset them as we did in Figure 6-12. You can also use the Edit > Free Transform command to scale the images in the separate layers.

10. Use the Type tool to create text at the top of the collage.

11. Add more color to your collage by creating another layer and placing it under the two layers. Then use the Gradient tool to add color to that layer.

 For some interesting effects, you can try changing the Mode and Opacity in the Layers palette.

 # Using the Pattern Stamp Tool

 The Pattern Stamp tool shares a location in the Toolbox with the Clone Stamp tool. This tool allows you to paint with a pattern. Patterns can be used to create special effects, background textures, and fabric or wallpaper designs.

You can apply patterns that come with Photoshop, or you can create and define your own patterns.

Using Photoshop's Patterns

When you install Photoshop, a Patterns folder is saved to your hard disk. This folder contains PostScript patterns that were created in Adobe Illustrator for you to use in Photoshop. You can open a file and define any image or part of an image as a pattern. (In this example, you'll select the entire image.) As you work, you might decide that the pattern would look better with a little color. One easy way of doing this is to paint the entire screen with a color, and then use a blending mode to help paint the pattern back into the picture. You'll try out this technique in the following exercise.

1. To access one of Adobe's patterns, choose File > Open. In the Open dialog box, locate and open the Postscript Patterns folder (inside the Presets folder).

2. You will see a long list of files. Select the Mali Primitive file (Windows users: mali.ai) and open it. In a few moments, Photoshop's Rasterize Generic EPS Format dialog box will appear. Since the pattern was created in Illustrator, which is a vector program, Photoshop needs to convert it to Photoshop's native format, bitmap. You do not need to change any of the dialog box settings if you have the default settings activated (Width: 1.25 inches; Height: 0.625 inches; Resolution: 72; Mode: CMYK Color; and Anti-aliased and Constrain Proportions selected). Just click on OK.

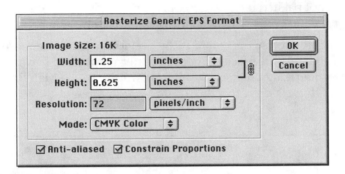

3. Choose Select > All. To define the pattern, choose Edit > Define Pattern. The pattern has now been defined, and you can proceed to use the Clone Stamp or Paint Bucket tool or the Edit > Fill command to apply it to your file.

4. With the pattern defined and in memory, you no longer need the pattern file (Mali Primitive) open, so close it without saving.

5. Create a new RGB file, 5 by 5 inches, which you'll use to see the effects of painting with a pattern using the Pattern Stamp tool.

6. When you have a new file on screen, select the Pattern Stamp tool. If the Pattern Stamp's Options bar isn't open, press RETURN (*ENTER*).

7. In the Options bar, choose a large brush size. Select the Aligned option, set Opacity to 100%, and set the Mode to Normal. The Aligned option allows you to apply a continuous pattern, no matter how many times you stop and start. If you deselect the Aligned option, the pattern restarts every time you release the mouse button and click and drag again in your image.

8. Your pattern now appears in the Pattern pop-up menu. Choose your pattern, and then click and drag with the Pattern Stamp tool to start painting. As you paint, the Pattern Stamp tool applies the selected pattern. If you wish, try other brush sizes and Opacity settings.

9. Change the background color to green or any color that you want to add to your pattern (other than black or white). Choose Edit > Fill. In the Fill dialog box, choose Background color from the Use pop-up menu, and then click on OK.

10. Once the background color appears over your image, activate the Pattern Stamp tool. Set Opacity to 100% and pick a large brush.

11. Establish a reference point on screen by painting a few brush strokes with the Mode set to Normal, and then switch to the Lighten mode. This will lighten only areas that are darker than the pattern with which you are painting. Thus, when you paint the pattern with the Pattern Stamp tool in Lighten mode, the white part of the pattern will paint over the green colors on the screen. The black part of the pattern is not painted over because it is darker than the green color on screen. Try painting several brush strokes on the screen to see the effect.

12. If you wish to reverse the colors in the previous example, choose the Darken mode. Now, only the black part of the pattern is applied because black is darker than the underlying green color. Figure 6-15 shows the Mali Primitive pattern applied with the Normal, Lighten, and Darken modes.

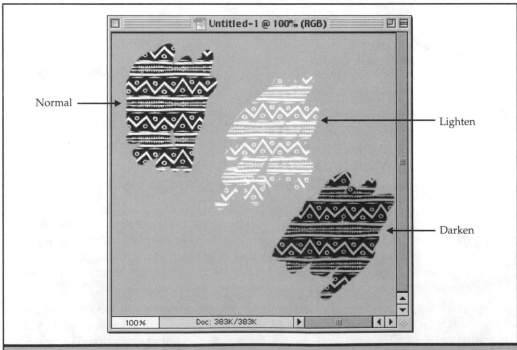

Figure 6-15. *Applying a pattern with the Pattern Stamp tool in Normal, Lighten, and Darken modes*

You can add colors to one of Photoshop's pattern files. Choose RGB or CMYK from the Mode pop-up menu when you open the file. Alternatively, open the file and then choose RGB Color or CMYK Color from the Image > Mode menu.

Creating, Defining, and Applying Custom Patterns

Now that you know how to apply one of Photoshop's patterns, you're ready to learn how to create one of your own. Although you can create a pattern in any file, it's probably best to make one in a new file. If you create each pattern in a separate file that you name and save, you'll have an easier time accessing your patterns when you wish to use them again. Since these files will be used solely to hold the design of your pattern, they don't need to be very large.

To create a pattern, follow these steps:

1. Open a new file, 2 inches by 2 inches. If you will be applying your pattern over an image, you may wish to choose Transparent from the contents group in the New dialog box. This will allow you to see the underlying image through the noncolored areas of your pattern.

2. Use any of Photoshop's tools to create a pattern.

 You can also select a portion of a digitized image to use as a pattern.

3. Use the Rectangular Marquee tool to select the area you wish to include in your pattern file, as shown here. If the background of your pattern file is white and you select any white background area with your pattern, that white area will be included when you paint with the pattern.

4. While the pattern is selected, choose Edit > Define Pattern.

5. Save your file and close it.

6. To apply your pattern, create a new file, 5 inches by 5 inches, or open a file to which you wish to apply the pattern.

7. When the file appears, you can use the Pattern Stamp tool, the Paint Bucket tool, or the Edit > Fill command to apply the pattern. For this exercise, use the Pattern Stamp tool. Double-click on the Pattern Stamp tool. From the Pattern Stamp's Options bar, select the Aligned option.

8. Click and drag in the document to paint with the pattern using the Pattern Stamp tool.

To make your pattern more interesting, you may wish to create a custom brush and apply it to different areas in the image. The music notes shown in this illustration were created with a custom brush from the Sonata typeface. (See Chapter 5 for more details on creating a custom brush.)

Renovating a Kitchen

Here's a tip for architects, interior designers, or anyone who might be involved in a renovation project. This project demonstrates how to take a scanned image of an old, dusty kitchen and transform it into a clean, modern one.

Certainly, one of the major advantages of a computer is that you can experiment with various interior and scenic designs without paying anyone to lift a hammer or a paintbrush. If you wish to use Photoshop for this type of project, you will need to scan (or have a service bureau scan) photographs of the rooms that you wish to renovate. If you are thinking of using different wallpaper or colors, take photographs that include the wallpaper samples. This way, you can easily create a pattern in Photoshop from the wallpaper, and it will be at the proper proportions. Of course, you can also create your own patterns for wallpaper and floor tile designs.

Once you have digitized an image of a room, with its wallpaper and floor patterns, load your file. The illustration shown next is a digitized image of a photograph of a kitchen before image editing in Photoshop (this kitchen image is included in the Chapter 6 folder on the CD-ROM that accompanies this book). Notice the wallpaper samples hanging on the wall.

The next illustration shows the same digitized image after the electronic renovation. In this example, the Clone Stamp tool's cloning powers were used to remove unwanted items such as the dishes, bottles, old-fashioned light fixture, paper towel holder, and pots and pans. The Edit > Fill command was used to fill a pattern created from a wallpaper sample taped to the wall. The Burn tool dissipated the highlights, and the Sharpen tool made certain areas of the image more distinct.

The
Complete
Reference

Photoshop 6

Chapter 7

Digitizing and Changing Image Size

Digitized images are at the core of most Photoshop and ImageReady design projects. When you *digitize* a visual image, you translate it into digital signals so that it can be broken down into pixels and loaded into the computer. Ensuring that images are digitized correctly is crucial to the success of your work. If you don't digitize an image properly, image quality will likely be unacceptable and colors may be flawed. Images that are digitized at a low a resolution may look jagged or blurred; too high a resolution may cause the file size to grow too large. Furthermore, high-resolution images on Web pages usually appear too large and take a long time to download to a browser. Picking the correct resolution is one of the focal points of this chapter.

There are various ways to digitize images. If your images are on photographic film, you can have them digitized through Kodak's Photo CD process and load the images into Photoshop or ImageReady from your CD-ROM drive. If you don't already have photographs or slides to work with, you may want to use a digital or video camera to digitize your images at the time you are shooting them. You can also digitize a still frame from videotape by using a video capture card (in your computer) connected to a video recorder. For digitizing flat art, slides, or photographic prints, you will undoubtedly use a scanner.

 When working with digitized images, make sure you secure all reproduction rights before using them.

This chapter begins with a discussion of how to use the different types of digitizing equipment. Then you will learn how to use Photoshop's and ImageReady's image-sizing features.

Using a Scanner

The most important point to consider when choosing a scanner is that different models provide different output quality; just as some cameras produce high-quality photographs and some don't.

Using a low-end scanner is much like shooting a picture with an inexpensive camera. A low-end desktop scanner may suit your needs for images intended for the Web or low-resolution printing. You might also place low-end desktop scanned images in documents to test layout and design concepts; this is often called *FPO* (for position only). After the design has been finalized, the FPO image is replaced with a high-end scanned image, before the project starts its journey to the printing press.

High-end digitizing is the domain of the service bureau. A service bureau can scan your image on expensive prepress equipment, such as Scitex's flatbed scanner, or a rotary drum scanner manufactured by DuPont Crosfield, Linotype-Hell, or Optronics. All of these scanners employ sophisticated optical and color-correcting systems to make your images sharp. Most will also digitize an image directly as a CMYK Color file.

Be aware that any image editing you do in Photoshop to FPO images cannot automatically be converted to a high-resolution scan. The work will need to be re-created on the higher quality image. Most service bureaus and prepress houses will do this work for you if your own computer system cannot handle the file size of the high-resolution scans.

You may be able to avoid the expense of high-end equipment by using a midrange scanner. Such scanners produce highly acceptable images, because they can process more color information than low-end scanners and they are more sensitive to the color range of an image.

Choosing a Scanning Resolution

Before you begin scanning, you should know the dimensions of your final image and calculate the correct scanning resolution. Like monitor resolution, scanning resolution is measured in pixels per inch (ppi). More pixels in an image means that it contains more information. Thus, in general, the more pixels you can pack into an image, the sharper it will be. If you scan at too low a resolution, your image may be blurry, or you may see the individual jagged pixel elements in the image.

Considering the Output Format and File Size

Notwithstanding the value of high-resolution images, it is generally unnecessary to scan at the highest possible resolution, because eventually you reach a point of diminishing returns. Printing presses can produce images at a limited number of lines per inch, so the extra resolution will be wasted and may even result in images that look flat. The same holds true if your scans will be output on the Web. Since most users are viewing images on monitors that output at a minimum resolution of 640 by 480 pixels (72 ppi), it is usually unnecessary to scan images at any resolution greater than 72 ppi. If you are outputting to video, you shouldn't need to scan images at higher resolutions, since the American television standard closely translates to a 640-by-480-pixel image. (The pixel dimensions for video digitized with a DV camcorder are 720 by 480.)

Why not scan everything at a high resolution, just to be safe? Consider that file size is directly related to an image's resolution. Images that are scanned at higher resolution produce larger file sizes than images scanned at lower resolution. For instance, if you scan an image at 72 ppi, scan it again at 144 ppi, and then rescan it at twice that resolution, the new file will be approximately four times as large as that of the 72-ppi image. Furthermore, if you replace a 72-ppi image on a Web page with one digitized at 300 ppi, the high-resolution image will appear about four times larger than the low-resolution image.

Some users of low-end scanners find that they get better results by scanning at high resolution and then reducing the resolution. For instance, you may find that scanning text for the Web at 300 ppi and then reducing the size to 72 ppi provides better results than simply scanning at 72 ppi.

IMAGE EDITING FUNDAMENTALS

Calculating Resolution for Printed Images

If you are producing output for a printing press, calculate the image's resolution based on the printing resolution. The resolution of a printing press is measured in lines per inch (lpi), often called *line screen, halftone screen*, or *screen frequency*. Your scanning resolution (measured in ppi) is directly related to the screen frequency.

In the electronic printing process, screen frequency is determined by rows of cells composed of halftones. These halftones are built from the tiniest dots that can be produced by printers—from lasers to imagesetters. (Imagesetter dots are sometimes called *rels*, or *raster elements*; laser printer dots are frequently called *pixels*.) Figure 7-1 shows how a halftone is built from a grid of pixels. Different-sized halftones combine to produce the illusion of continuous tones of grays and colors in photographs. (Halftones are discussed in greater detail in Appendix B.)

When scanning, use this as a general rule: 1.5 to 2 image pixels are needed for each halftone to produce high-quality output for images that will be printed on a printing press. Thus, the process of calculating the correct scanning resolution can often be reduced to the simple formula of multiplying the screen frequency times 1.5 (scanning resolution = 1.5 × screen frequency, or lpi) of 2 (scanning resolution = 2 × lpi). For instance, if your commercial printer requires 133 lpi, you can scan images at 266 ppi.

> **Note**   *When an image is printed, a file scanned at two times the line frequency actually has four times as much information than the same file scanned at the line frequency. The number of pixels is quadrupled because pixels are added for each horizontal and vertical line screen.*

If you don't know what screen frequency will be used to print your work, ask your printer. When discussing printing resolution with your printer, you should also know what type of paper will be used. Generally, newspapers are printed at 85 lpi. Most magazines are printed on an offset press using 133 or 150 lpi. Some art books printed on coated paper use 200 lpi. Once you know what lpi you'll be using, you can calculate the resolution, or how many pixels per inch (ppi), you will need when you scan.

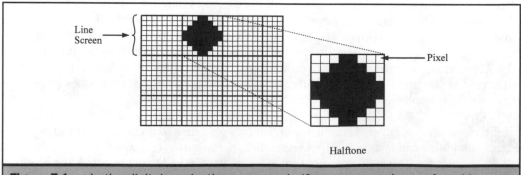

Figure 7-1.   *In the digital production process, halftones are made up of a grid of pixels*

Calculating Resolution for Images You Are Enlarging   If you are going to enlarge the scanned image dimensions (if you are scanning slides, for instance), you'll need to increase the scanning resolution before you scan. Increasing the number of pixels in the image ensures that the quality is maintained when the image is enlarged. If you don't boost the resolution, image clarity will suffer and the image may become pixelated. (The individual pixels in the image become evident when the image dimensions are enlarged.)

To calculate the correct scanning resolution for an image that will be enlarged for printing, use the following formula:

$$\text{Scanning resolution} \approx \frac{\text{largest size in final image}}{} \div \frac{\text{largest size in original image}}{} \times 2 \times \text{screen frequency}$$

Thus, if you are enlarging a 2-inch-by-3-inch image to 4 inches by 6 inches, and the printing screen frequency is 150, the calculation is:

$6 \div 3 \times 2 \times 150 = 600$ ppi (scanning resolution)

Here's a more complex formula that produces the same result. We supply it because it better explains the relationship between pixels and screen frequency:

$$\text{Scanning resolution} \approx \frac{\text{longest dimension of final image}}{} \times \frac{\text{screen frequency (lpi)}}{} \times \frac{\text{pixel-to-line screen ratio}}{} \div \frac{\text{longest dimension of original image}}{}$$

Here's a step-by-step explanation of how to apply the more complex formula to scan an image of 2 inches by 3 inches that you want to enlarge to 4 inches by 6 inches (and your screen frequency is 150 lpi):

1. Multiply the longest dimension (height or width) of the final image by the screen frequency (lpi). This produces the minimum number of pixels necessary to produce the longest dimension of the image. In our example, the calculation is $6 \times 150 = 900$ pixels.

2. Since 2 pixels are needed for every line-screen inch (or every halftone dot), 2 is the pixel-to-line screen ratio. In our example, the calculation is $2 \times 900 = 1800$, the minimum number of pixels necessary to produce the longest dimension of the image.

3. To obtain the scanning resolution, divide the minimum number of pixels needed to produce the longest dimension by the longest dimension of the original image. In our example, the calculation is $1800 \div 3 = 600$ ppi, the final scanning resolution.

After you've calculated the correct resolution and scanned your image at that resolution, you can then use Photoshop's Image Size dialog box to enlarge the image, as described in the "Enlarging an Image for Printing" section later in this chapter.

IMAGE EDITING FUNDAMENTALS

> **Note**   *If you are uncertain about what screen frequency or pixel-to-line screen ratio you should use, check with your service bureau or commercial printer.*

The resolution calculation is extremely important when you are scanning slides. For example, let's say that you are enlarging the longest dimension of a slide to 5 inches. Since the longest dimension of a 35mm slide is 1.375 inches, you would use the following calculation (if your screen frequency is 150):

$$5 \times 150 \times 2 \div 1.375$$

This calculation results in a scanning resolution that would be a little less than 1,100 ppi.

Choosing a Resolution for Black-and-White Line Art

Black-and-white images, such as line art, logos, and text, are sometimes referred to as *bitmap* images. If you are scanning bitmap images, you may be surprised to learn that the resolution must sometimes be set higher than it is when you're working with color. In color and grayscale images, gradations of colors and grays can hide edges and make an image blend into its background. In black-and-white images, the stark contrast between black and white draws the eye's attention to outlines.

Many printing professionals suggest scanning at a resolution as high as that of your output device. If you are producing output for an imagesetter with a resolution of 1,200 dpi, you should scan at 1,200 ppi. If you are printing to a laser printer that outputs 300 dpi, you may as well scan at 300 ppi. Even if you scan at 1,000 ppi, your 300-dpi printer cannot add any more resolution to the image (although many printers can smooth raster images when they output them).

Calculating Resolution for Web and Multimedia Images

If you are scanning an image that will be output to the Web or to a multimedia program, the general rule is to digitize images at 72 ppi (the monitor's resolution). If you will be enlarging the image, calculate the scanning resolution by multiplying the scaling factor by the monitor's resolution. You can use the following formula:

$$\text{Scanning resolution} \approx \left(\frac{\text{longest dimension of final image}}{\div} \frac{\text{longest dimension of original image}} \right) \times \text{monitor resolution}$$

Thus, if you are scanning an image that is 1 inch long and need to enlarge it to 3 inches, you should scan at 216 ppi:

$$(3 \div 1) \times 72 = 216$$

You can then set the size of your image (either to enlarge it or make it smaller) using the settings in Photoshop's Image Size dialog box, as explained in the "Setting the Size of a Web Image" section later in this chapter.

Scanning Images into Photoshop or ImageReady

After you've decided which scanner to use and have calculated your scanning resolution, you are ready to start scanning. In order to scan, you will need to install the plug-in (driver) that is provided by your scanner's manufacturer, which allows you to operate the scanner from within Photoshop or ImageReady. To install the plug-in, copy it into the Import-Export folder within the Plug-ins folder. If you install the plug-in while you have Photoshop open, you'll need to Quit and restart Photoshop before you continue.

Note *If your scanner did not come with a Photoshop plug-in, you may need to scan using the software packaged with your scanner.*

Once your scanner plug-in is installed, and before you begin digitizing an image, read the instructions that came with your scanner. In particular, find out whether your scanner allows you to set the white point (sometimes called the *highlight point*) and the black point (sometimes called the *shadow point*). From these two endpoints, your software may be able to create a tone curve to ensure that the scanner captures the widest density range, or dynamic range. A scanner's *dynamic range* is the range of colors it can identify, from the brightest to the darkest.

Note *The explanations in this section are based on the Agfa Arcus II scanner, a midrange scanner available for both Mac and Windows users, using the Agfa FotoLook PS 3.03 plug-in. The Arcus II scanner scans reflective objects, such as photographs and line art, as well as transparencies, such as slides. The steps described here are similar to those you'll perform for most desktop scanners.*

When you're ready, turn on the scanner (if it isn't already on) and follow these steps:

1. Place the image face down on the scanner's glass plate. Try to place the image as straight as possible; otherwise, the scanned image will appear crooked or

possibly cropped when it appears in Photoshop or ImageReady. If you are using a slide scanner, place the slide in the slide holder.

Caution   *If you rotate an image to correct crooked placement in a scanner, Photoshop or ImageReady needs to resample the image, which impairs image quality.*

2. To begin the scanning process within Photoshop or ImageReady, select File > Import. If your scanner has a plug-in, you will see it in the Import submenu. Select your scanner driver from the Import submenu.

III 7-1

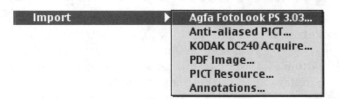

3. To preview the image, click on the Preview button. In a minute or so, the preview will appear in your scanner's dialog box, as shown in Figure 7-2. (This tells you right away if you've put the image in the scanner upside down.)

4. Choose a specific area of the image to scan. If you don't do this, the final image will be as large as the scanner's entire scanning area, and you will wind up with a very large file size. Most scanner selection controls work similarly; typically, you need to click and drag over the specific part of the previewed image that you wish to scan. Notice that the Agfa FotoLook scanner dialog box produces a handy readout of image size.

Note   *Don't worry about selecting too precisely. Once the image has been scanned, you can crop out extraneous portions in Photoshop.*

5. Click on the Mode pop-up menu and choose Color, RGB, Gray-Scale, or Lineart (sometimes called Bitmap) for your scanning mode.

6. Choose a resolution. In this example, the Input pop-up menu was used to change the resolution to 150 lpi.

7. Before scanning, examine the controls in your own scanning dialog box. For example, many scanners allow you to change exposure settings before you scan. If you wish, you can experiment with these settings now, or you can make adjustments to your image later in Photoshop. If you don't know the purpose of each option, consult your scanner's manual. Some of the Agfa FotoLook settings are described after these steps.

8. When you're ready to scan the image, click on the Scan button. In a few minutes, the scan will be completed, and the image will appear in a Photoshop window.

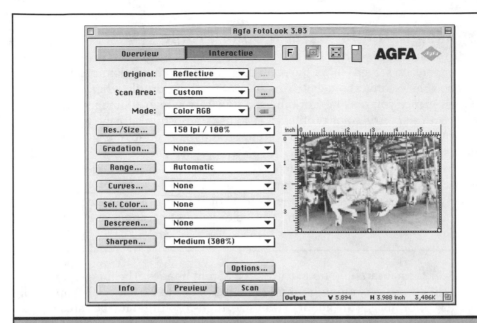

Figure 7-2.   *The Agfa FotoLook scanner plug-in previews an image and its file size and provides options for correcting images*

The Agfa FotoLook scanning dialog box (see Figure 7-2) includes some useful settings for controlling how your image is scanned:

- When the Range setting is set to Automatic, the scanner will prescan the image to measure the brightest highlight and the darkest shadow. This helps the scanner capture the broadest dynamic range possible.

- To eliminate color casts (shifts in color toward red, green, or blue), you can choose Color from the Preferences pop-up menu. This opens the Color Preferences dialog box, where you can adjust the sliders for red, green, and blue values.

- The Sharpen setting can be used to enhance image edges.

- The Descreen option can help eliminate moiré patterns when you are scanning images that have been printed using screens.

Using Photo CD Images

If you need to have your images photographed first before digitizing them, you might be able to avoid scanning altogether. Eastman Kodak's Photo CD process transforms a roll of film into a CD-ROM filled with digitized images. Each disc stored in Kodak's

Using Assign Profile to Set a Color Profile

If you scan an image directly into Photoshop, you can assign a color profile after the image opens on screen—after the scan. (Depending upon your color settings, you may be able to convert images to the current working profile when you select File > Open.) Since you may be working on a project in which all images need to be tagged with a specific color profile, you can use Photoshop's Image > Mode > Assign Profile or Image > Mode > Convert to Profile to tag an image with no color space to a specific profile.

If you use the Assign Profile command to assign a profile, screen colors may change as Photoshop reinterprets the image's color values based upon the new profile. If you choose Convert to Profile, Photoshop attempts to prevent screen colors from changing, yet it may change the color values to accommodate the new profile.

standard Master format can hold up to a hundred 35mm images. The images are stored at five different sizes, ranging from 128 by 192 pixels to 2,048 by 3,072 pixels. Low-resolution color images are about 72K in size; high-resolution images are around 18MB. Table 7-1 shows the Photo CD image dimensions in pixels and file sizes.

When you load the file using the File > Open command, you can choose not only which image to load, but also which version of the image you wish to load.

Dimensions in Pixels	Dimensions in Inches (at 72 ppi)	File Size
126 x 192	1.75 x 2.0	72K
256 x 384	3.5 x 5.33	288K
512 x 268	7.1 x 10.6	1.12K
1,024 x 1,536	14.2 x 21.3	4.5K
2.048 x 3,072	28.4 x 42.7	18MB
4,096 x 61,444	56.9 x 85.3	72MB

Table 7-1. *Kodak Photo CD Image Sizes*

Note   *You may find that the quality of Photo CD images differs, depending on the service bureau that outputs your images.*

Setting Photo CD resolution is discussed later in this chapter, in the "Choosing Resolution for Photos CD Images" section.

Using Digital and Still-Video Cameras

Digital and still-video cameras provide even more versatile alternatives to scanning. With these cameras, you don't need to purchase film, wait for it to be developed, and then scan or convert to Photo CD. If you are digitizing with a still-video or digital camera, you can quickly see the results by shooting in a studio with the camera connected to a computer. If the image doesn't please you, you can usually change your lighting setup and reshoot.

Still-video cameras are video cameras primarily used for taking still pictures. Many cameras require that a video-capture board be installed in the computer so that images can be stored on a hard drive. Digital cameras immediately digitize an image, which can usually be downloaded directly as a digital file to the computer through a serial, USB, or SCSI connection.

Many digital cameras provide Photoshop plug-ins, so you can use the File > Import command to load the image directly into Photoshop. Figure 7-3 shows the Photoshop plug-in transfer dialog box for Kodak's DCS-240 digital camera, which connects through either the serial or USB port.

Many digital cameras feature on-board disks, memory cards, or hard disks. The DCS-240 is packaged with a removable 8MB memory card, which can be removed and replaced while shooting.

For many photographers, the easiest way to begin evaluating the features of a digital camera is to study the camera's optical system. Since some digital cameras are really converted still cameras, you can start by shopping for a digital camera as you would for a still camera. Nonetheless, you should be familiar with digital terms, such as bit depth and resolution.

A digital camera's dynamic range—the range of tones captured from lightest to darkest elements—is primarily determined by *bit depth*. As with scanners, the higher the bit depth, the better the image quality. Low-cost cameras, such as Kodak's DC 120, capture 24 bits of color (8 bits for each RGB color). Higher-end cameras, such as Kodak's DCS 460, capture 36 bits, resulting in a more detailed picture with less noise. High-end studio equipment, like the Leaf Digital back, can capture 14 bits per RGB color.

The resolution of a digital camera is based on the total number of pixels the camera can produce in an image. If you study the specifications for digital cameras, you'll quickly notice that the high-priced cameras provide better image resolution than low-priced ones. For instance, Kodak's DCS 460 features a resolution of 3,060 by 2,060 pixels. The DCS 240 outputs at 1,280 by 600 pixels. Low-cost models capture

IMAGE EDITING FUNDAMENTALS

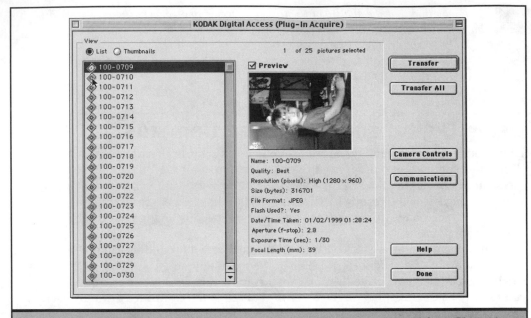

Figure 7-3.   *The DCS-240 digital camera transfer dialog box viewed from Photoshop*

at least 640 by 480 pixels. Understanding how these resolution figures translate to image quality is extremely important, particularly if your image will eventually be printed by a commercial printer. See the "Computing Resolution for Digital Camera Images" section for details on digital camera image resolution.

Once you understand how a digital camera's bit depth and resolution affect image quality, you'll be better able to judge whether one will suit your needs. Before you invest in one, however, be aware that not all models produce perfect color fidelity. Also, note that the lenses in many low-end cameras are not designed to shoot flat art—use a scanner instead. Even if you are using an expensive digital camera, you will probably need to do some tweaking in Photoshop. Depending on the lighting conditions, you may need to sharpen your image. (See Chapter 12 to learn how to use Photoshop's sharpening filters.) You may also need to correct colors (as covered in Chapter 18).

Tip

You can use Photoshop's Convert to Profile command to convert the color space of an image taken with a digital camera after it loads into Photoshop. See the discussion of Convert to Profile earlier in this chapter, and refer to Chapter 2 for more details.

Digitizing Video Images

If you need to place a frame from a videotape production into Photoshop or ImageReady, you'll need to have the video digitized.

Most new camcorders digitize video directly onto video tape. The digitized video can then be transferred directly to a computer that has a FireWire (IEEE-1394 port). Most new Macs and Sony PCs come with IEEE-1394 ports preinstalled. (You can install an IEEE 1394 board on most newer computers.) Using the software that comes with these computers, you can transfer the digitized video directly from your camcorder into your computer. Once the digital video is loaded on your computer, you can view frames from the clip in ImageReady.

Digitizing with a Capture Board

If you need to capture a video frame that is on video tape or that has been recorded with an analog video camera, you will need a capture board in your computer to digitize it and save it to your hard disk. Often, you'll need to purchase cables to make the connection from your camcorder or tape machine to the capture board. Many older camcorders are sold with cables for *composite* video. These cables plug into the video-out ports of the camcorder and the video-in ports of the capture board on the computer. (Most newer camcorders and capture boards can transfer video using S-video cables, which provide better quality than composite video.)

After you've connected the video device to your computer, you capture the video using software that comes with the capture board. Many boards use compressors that can be read by Adobe's digital video editing and production program, Premiere. Using Premiere, you can capture the video in the program's Movie Capture dialog box, shown in Figure 7-4, and then immediately start using it in a video project, as described in the next section.

Note

The standard video frame size of video digitized by a DV (Digital Video) camcorder in the United States is 720 by 480. Since DV video utilizes non-square pixels and your computer uses square pixels, create full-screen graphics that will be output at 720 by 480 (NTSC-US TV) at 720 by 540. (PAL-European TV 720 by 540.) When you load the image into Adobe Premiere, the program will rescale the image without distorting it.

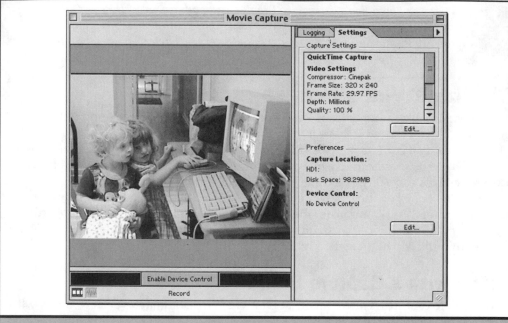

Figure 7-4.   *Capturing video in Adobe Premiere*

Opening Digital Video in ImageReady

Once your video has been digitized, you can import one frame from a video clip or a range of clips directly into ImageReady, as follows:

1. To import digital video into ImageReady, choose File > Open.

2. In the Open dialog box, select the video clip; then click on Open.

3. In the Open Movie dialog box, shown in Figure 7-5, choose the range of clips that you wish to import.

   ■ To import the entire clip, choose Select From Beginning to End.

   ■ To import a specific range, choose Selected Range Only (as shown in Figure 7-5). Then drag the slider in the video preview area to find the first frame you wish to import. To specify the range you wish to import, press SHIFT while clicking and dragging.

   ■ To skip over frames while importing, Select the Limit to Every option and enter a value in the Frame field.

4. Click on OK to import the frames into the Animation and Layers palette.

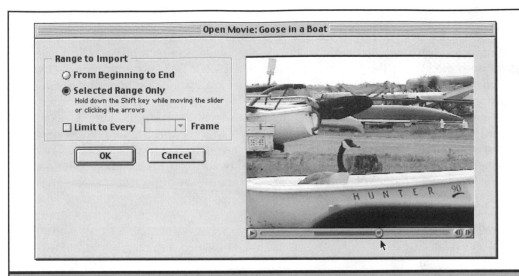

Figure 7-5.   *Use ImageReady's Open Movie dialog box to specify a range of video frames to import*

When the frames load, they appear as separate frames in the Animation palette and as separate layers in the Layers palette.

Setting Image Size and Resolution in Photoshop

Photoshop provides many options for controlling the size and resolution of your images. However, if you prefer, Photoshop can calculate the scanning resolution for you automatically. When Photoshop calculates the resolution, it also determines the file size of the image that you will be scanning.

File size is directly related to an image's resolution—the higher the resolution, the larger the file size.

Where to Get Digitized Stock Photos

Numerous sources of stock digital images are available. Stock photo collections for both the PC and the Mac are now sold on CD-ROMs. Many collections allow unlimited usage, and some contain images that are scanned on high-end drum scanners in 24-bit color.

Before purchasing stock photos, check to see that the resolution and size of the images meet your needs. Also, find out whether the images are compressed, and if they are, whether a lossy or lossless compression method was used. *Lossless compression* means that no loss of picture quality occurs during compression.

Here are the names of some companies that provide digitized images:

- Adobe
- ColorBytes
- American Databankers Corp.
- COREL
- PhotoDisc
- Gazelle Technologies
- Image Club Publishing
- Aztech New Media Corp.
- Dana Publishing
- Digital Stock

These companies provide digitized backgrounds:

- Pixar (One Twenty Eight)
- Xaos (Artist Residence)
- ArtBeats (Marble & Granite, Marbled Paper Textures, and Wood and Paper)
- 'D'Pix

Many digital stock suppliers allow you to preview images on their Web sites and download both high- and low-resolution versions as well. Here are a few Web addresses to check out:

- www.imageclub.com
- www.photodisc.com
- www.digitalstock.com
- www.vividdetails.com

Letting Photoshop Calculate Image Size and Resolution

In this section, you'll learn how to have Photoshop calculate both the file size and the resolution for a grayscale or color image.

1. Create a new file by choosing File > New.

2. In the New dialog box, enter the dimensions of the image you will be scanning. For the example here, use 3.5 inches for the Width and 5 inches for the Height. For now, leave the resolution set to 72 ppi. (Eventually, Photoshop will change this value.) If you are scanning a color image, leave the mode set to RGB Color (because most desktop scanners produce colors from red, green, and blue values). If you are scanning a grayscale image, switch to Grayscale mode.

Note   *If you are scanning in Grayscale mode, your file size will be smaller than in RGB Color mode because Photoshop will not need to store as much information. Most scanners use a minimum of 24 bits per pixel of information to create colors, and a minimum 8 bits per pixel for grayscale. Photoshop, however, can load 16-bit-per-pixel grayscale images and 48-bit-per-pixel RGB color images.*

3. Notice that Photoshop has already calculated a file size. At 3.5 by 5 inches and with Mode set to RGB Color, the dialog box displays 266K as the file size. Before continuing, make sure that the Contents radio button is set to White, and then click on OK.

4. After the new file appears, select Image > Image Size. Notice that the Image Size dialog box, shown in Figure 7-6, contains all of the information you entered in the New dialog box: Width and Height are set to the size of your image, Resolution is set to 72 ppi, and the file size is the same as it was in the New dialog box. You'll also see the Constrain Proportions and Resample Image checkboxes, which are discussed in the next section.

5. To have Photoshop calculate your scanning resolution, click on the Auto button to display the Auto Resolution dialog box.

III 7-2

IMAGE EDITING FUNDAMENTALS

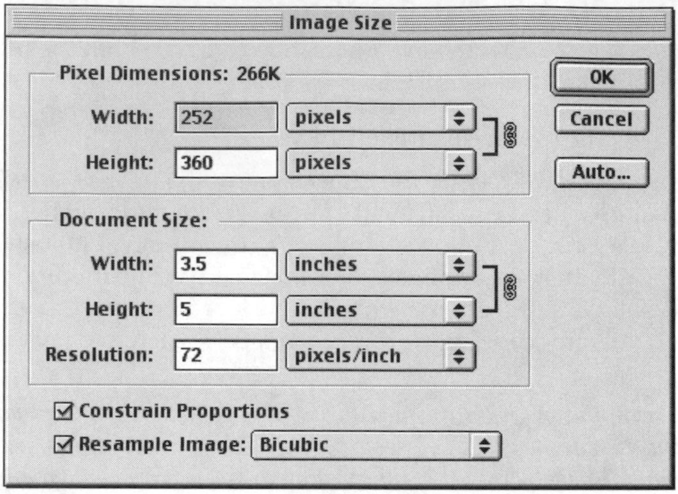

Figure 7-6. The Image Size dialog box allows you to change dimensions and resolution

6. In the Screen field, type the screen frequency that you'll be using. For this example, enter **133**.

7. Click on one of the three Quality radio buttons to designate how you want Photoshop to calculate image resolution. If you click Best, Photoshop multiplies the screen frequency by 2 to compute the resolution. For Good quality, Photoshop multiplies the screen frequency by 1.5. If you pick Draft and your screen frequency is not less than 72, Photoshop uses 72 as the scanning resolution. If you enter a screen frequency less than 72 in the Screen field, Photoshop uses that number as your scanning resolution.

8. Click on OK. Photoshop will calculate your resolution and return you to the Image Size dialog box.

When the Image Size dialog box reappears, notice that the New Size and Resolution values have changed. Resolution now displays the desired resolution, according to your screen frequency. New Size displays the size of the file you will be working with.

Setting Image Size Options

When you're working on project for print or the Web, you'll often need to change the dimensions of your digitized production files. Photoshop's Image Size dialog box is well equipped to handle all of your production needs. Whether you are outputting to a printing press or the Web, it's important to ensure that you resize images at the proper resolution. To make the best choices, you need to understand how the options in the Image Size dialog box affect your images.

The Image Size dialog box, shown in Figure 7-7, is divided into two main sections. By default, the Pixel Dimensions section shows the image size in pixels and the Document Size section displays the size in inches. The Document Size section also displays how many pixels per inch compose your image. Why does Photoshop provide these two sections for width and height?

Conceptually, this setup provides a better representation of image size and resolution. For instance, a 300-pixel-by-300-pixel image is one square inch if the Resolution field is set to 300 pixels per inch. However, if the Resolution field is set to 72 pixels per inch, the image is now approximately 4 inches by 4 inches. Thus, the number of pixels in two images can be identical, but their widths, heights, and pixels per inch can be different.

As a further illustration, consider a 1200-by-1200-pixel image digitized by a digital camera and loaded into Photoshop. When the image loads, the number of pixels per inch in the Resolution field reads 72, as shown in Figure 7-7.

Many Photoshop users consider 72 ppi to be low resolution and 300 ppi as high resolution. Is this 1200-by-1200 pixel image high or low resolution? If you reduce the image width and height to 4 inches, the resolution changes to 300 ppi, as shown in Figure 7-8. At this size, the image can certainly be printed in color and produce high-quality results. Thus, knowing pixel dimensions—width, height, and pixels per inch—provides a full understanding of the digital image's resolution and quality.

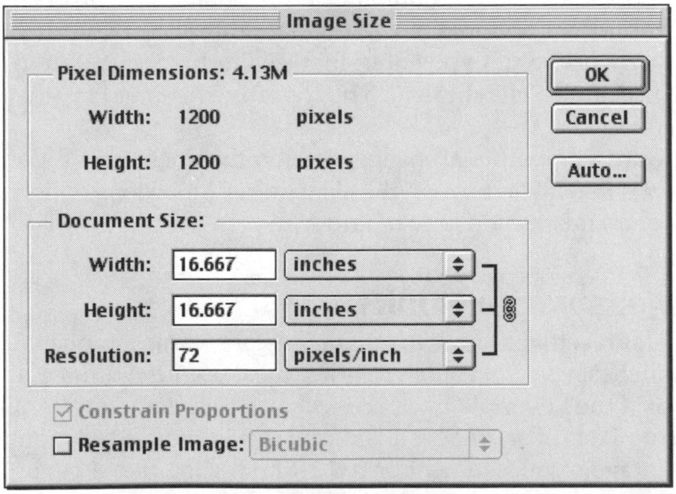

Figure 7-7. *A 1200-by-1200 pixel image at 72 ppi*

IMAGE EDITING
FUNDAMENTALS

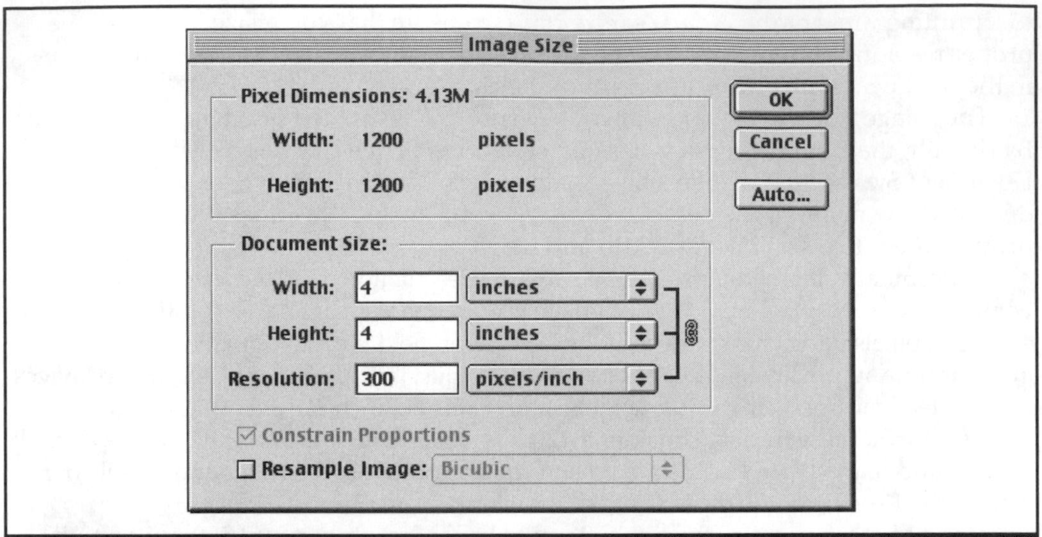

Figure 7-8. *A 1200-by-1200-pixel image at 300 ppi*

Constraining Proportions

In the Image Size dialog box, note the chain-link icon next to the Document Size fields. This icon appears when the Constrain Proportions checkbox is selected. With the Constrain Proportions option, the width-to-height ratio of your image remains constant no matter what values you enter; that is, altering the Width field causes a proportional change in the Height field. The chain-link icon next to the fields indicates that the values are linked.

If you don't want a proportional change, deselect the Constrain Proportions checkbox. Be aware, however, that if you turn off the Constrain Proportions option and then change the dimensions of an image, you may distort it.

Changing Measurement Units

Although the default settings show Pixel Dimensions values in pixels and Document Size settings in inches, you can switch to other measurement units in the Image Size dialog box if the Resample Image checkbox is selected. (Resampling changes the number of pixels in an image; it is discussed in the next section.) If you know the percentage of enlargement or reduction for the file to be digitized, you can change the measurement unit in the Pixel Dimensions section to percent. You can also change the Width and Height field measurements in the Document Size section from inches to percent, centimeters, points, picas, or columns. Click on the pop-up menu arrow next to the field and choose the measurement unit you prefer.

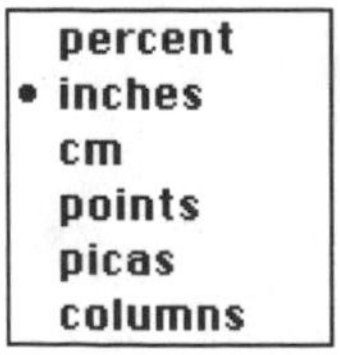

```
  percent
• inches
  cm
  points
  picas
  columns
```

IMAGE EDITING
FUNDAMENTALS

> **Note**
>
> *The columns measurement unit available for the Width and Height field in the Image Size dialog box is useful if you will be exporting your file into a desktop publishing program that has multicolumn page-layout capability. The columns measurement uses the column size specified in the Unit & Rulers Preferences dialog box (Edit > Preferences > Units & Rulers).*

Resampling Images

When you increase or decrease an image's width or height, Photoshop can add or subtract pixels in your image. Adding or subtracting pixels is called *resampling*. By default, the Resample Image checkbox in the Image Size dialog box is selected. If you turn off resampling, Photoshop does not add or subtract pixels.

It's important to realize that when you resample, Photoshop must make some sacrifices in image quality. If you decrease the dimensions of your image size, Photoshop must subtract pixels; if you increase your image size, Photoshop must add pixels. When Photoshop adds pixels, it interpolates. During *interpolation*, Photoshop attempts to smooth the difference between the original pixels and the ones it adds. This can result in a somewhat blurred image.

By default, Photoshop uses the best possible method of resampling. This method is called *Bicubic.* To see the other choices, click on the pop-up menu to the right of the Resample Image checkbox. Nearest Neighbor is the fastest but least exact interpolation method. If you use this method, your image will probably look jagged after rotating or using other manipulation commands. With Bicubic, Photoshop attempts to improve contrast while interpolating. Although it's the best, it's also the slowest. Bilinear is the middle ground between Nearest Neighbor and Bicubic.

> **Caution**
>
> *If you resample down (that is, decrease file size) and then later resample back up, the final image will not be as sharp as the original. This is because Photoshop must remove pixels, and when you resample back up Photoshop interpolates and cannot add the original pixels that were subtracted earlier.*

With the Resampling Image checkbox selected, type a smaller number into the Width or Height field in the Document Size section. Notice that the file size value decreases, and the Width and Height values in pixels (in the Pixels Dimensions section) decrease. Although the number of pixels in the image changes, the number of pixels per inch remains the same.

Here are a few important notes to remember about changing values in the Image Size dialog box when the Resample Image option is selected:

- If you decrease the Width or Height setting in the Document Size section, the image file size decreases. The number of pixels in the image decreases. The Resolution setting (pixels per inch) does not change.

- If you increase the Width or Height setting in the Document Size section, the file size grows. The number of pixels in the image increases. The Resolution setting does not change.

- If you decrease the Resolution setting, the file size decreases. The Width and Height settings in the Document Size section do not change, but the number of pixels in the image decreases.

- If you increase the Resolution setting, the file size grows. The Width and Height settings in the Document Size section do not change, but the number of pixels in the image increases.

Changing Image Dimensions Without Resampling

When you deselect the Resample Image checkbox, Photoshop will not change the file size of your image when you modify its dimensions or resolution. In order to keep the file size constant, Photoshop must compensate by changing the image resolution (the number of pixels per inch) when you change the document size dimensions, or by changing the document size dimensions when you change the resolution. To avoid adding or subtracting pixels, Photoshop decreases the resolution if you increase the document size dimensions of your image. If you decrease the document size dimensions of your image, Photoshop increases the resolution.

Take a moment and try this out—it's important to understand how file size, image dimension, and resolution are related because they all affect your work.

1. If the Resample Image checkbox is selected, deselect it. If the Constrain Proportions option is selected, notice that the chain-link icon now shows that the image dimensions and resolution are linked.

2. In the Document Size section, enter a larger value in either the Width or Height field. You'll see that the Resolution setting drops. This makes sense: If you want to make an image larger but you don't add any information to it, the resolution (number of pixels per inch) decreases.

Note
If you resize without resampling, the size of your image on the screen will not change, because you have not added or subtracted pixels. If Photoshop's rulers are displayed, they will indicate any change in image dimensions.

3. Enter a higher value into the Resolution field, and watch the file's dimensions drop. If you want more pixels per inch and you don't want the file size to change, the image's dimensions must decrease. If you decrease the Resolution setting, Photoshop will increase the image dimensions.

Remember
Photoshop displays your image at your monitor's screen resolution (72 ppi or 96 ppi, in most cases). The image quality on the screen does not change if you raise the resolution of the image beyond your screen's resolution. You'll see a difference only when the image is printed.

If this concept seems confusing, here's an analogy: Assume that you have a balloon with a painted image on it, consisting of many tiny dots of paint. If you stretch the balloon out to make the image size greater, the space between each dot grows, and you have fewer dots per square inch. This is the same as decreasing resolution when file dimensions are increased. Let air out of the balloon to make the image smaller, and the dots get closer together. Similarly, an image's resolution increases when the file dimensions are decreased. In both cases, whether you stretched or shrank the balloon, the actual mass of rubber or the number of dots did not change.

The following chart summarizes how the Resample Image option affects your image.

	Increase Document Size	**Decrease Document Size**	**Increase Resolution**	**Decrease Resolution**
Resample Image checkbox selected	Increases file size; resolution doesn't change	Decreases file size; resolution doesn't change	Increases file size; print size doesn't change	Decreases file size; print size doesn't change
Resample Image checkbox not selected	Decreases resolution; file size is unchanged	Increases resolution; file size is unchanged	Decreases print size; file size is unchanged	Increases print size; file size is unchanged

At this point, you should have a good idea about how you can control Photoshop image dimensions, file sizes, and resolution.

Tip   *If you wish to reset the Image Size dialog box options to their original settings, press and hold* OPTION (ALT). *This causes the Cancel button to change to a Reset button.*

Setting the Size of a Web Image

Now that you understand how the options in the Image Size dialog box work, you can try them out for a practical applications. Suppose that you have an image scanned at 100 ppi that you want to make 50 percent smaller for use on the Web. Since the image is for the Web, you don't need the resolution to be higher than 72 ppi. When you reduce the image size with the Resample Image checkbox selected, the resolution will not change.

1. Load the Web_Image file from the Chapter 7 folder of the *Photoshop Complete Reference* CD-ROM.
2. Open the Image Size dialog box by choosing Image > Image Size. In the dialog box, make sure that the Constrain Proportions and Resample Image checkboxes are selected.
3. In the Document Size section, change the pixels measurement field to percent. You'll see the width and height of the document change to 100%.
4. In the Width field in the Document Size section, change the percent to **50**.

5. When you change the percentages, the Document Size of your image is reduced by 50 percent. Also note that the file size shown at the top of the screen is reduced, but the number of pixels per inch did not change.

6. Change the Resolution value to **72** pixels per inch. Notice that the file size of the image is further reduced.

7. Click on OK to have Photoshop reduce the image size.

If you wanted to enlarge an image for the Web, after scanning it in at the correct resolution (see the "Calculating Resolution for Web and Multimedia Images" section earlier in this chapter), you would deselect the Resample Image checkbox. Then when you changed the size, the Resolution value would drop.

Enlarging an Image for Printing

If want to enlarge an image before you print it, you need to prevent Photoshop from adding pixels to the image, which would reduce the image's quality. To do this, you need to deselect the Resample Image checkbox. For example, suppose that you want to enlarge the dimensions of a high-resolution, 1-inch-square image to 4 inches.

1. Load the Print_Image file in the Chapter 7 folder of the *Photoshop Complete Reference* CD-ROM.

2. Open the Image Size dialog box by choosing Image > Image Size. Notice that the resolution of the image is 1200 ppi.

3. In the dialog box, make sure that Constrain Proportions is selected. Deselect the Resample Image checkbox.

4. In the Document Size section, change the Width setting from 1 to **4**. When you change the Width field, the Height changes proportionally. Equally important, notice that the Resolution field changed to 300 (which is more than enough for most printed images). Photoshop needed to reduce the number of pixels per inch to compensate for the change in image dimensions.

5. Click on OK to have Photoshop enlarge the image.

6. To see your image as it will appear when printed, choose View > Print Size.

Choosing Resolution for Photo CD images

When you load a Photo CD image into Photoshop, the Resolution field is automatically set to 72 ppi. How do you choose which Photo CD resolution is the right one for your project? How do you determine if the number of pixels in the image is adequate for your outputting requirements? First, you must know the size of the image you need and the number of pixels per inch required for output. Assume you need to place a 3-inch image on your Web page. Since Web graphics do not need to be larger than the resolution of a standard monitor, your image resolution should be 72 ppi. If you look at Table 7-1, shown earlier in this chapter, you'll see your best bet is probably going to be 256 x 384. We created that table by simply typing the different pixel dimensions of Photo CD images into Photoshop's dialog box with the Resample Image checkbox selected.

Now assume that you need to print a 4-inch-wide image in a publication requiring 225-ppi resolution. Since you want the pixels per inch setting to increase when you reduce the image, you need to deselect the Resample Image checkbox. Next, you enter the **225** into the Resolution field. Immediately, the Width and Height fields will tell you the maximum image size you can use at 225 ppi.

Computing Resolution for Digital Camera Images

As discussed earlier, to achieve the best quality for print output, the image resolution in Photoshop should be approximately twice the screen frequency used for printing. Assume that you are using Kodak's DCS 460 camera and need to send a 6-by-6-inch, 300-ppi image to a magazine. How can you determine whether the camera can produce an image at the quality you need? Simple—let Photoshop do it for you. Here's how:

1. Start by creating a new file in Photoshop (File > New).

2. In the New dialog box, set the measurement units to pixels. Enter the pixel dimension used by your digital camera into the Width and Height fields. For the Kodak DCS 460, you would enter **3020** and **2020**. If you were using a lower-priced camera, you might enter 640 and 480. Set the Resolution value to 72 ppi. Click on OK to create the new image.

3. Choose Image > Image Size.

4. In the Image Size dialog box, deselect the Resample Image checkbox. This turns on the link between image dimensions and resolution.

5. Change the Resolution field to the resolution needed to output your image— in this case, 300 ppi.

6. Change the measurement units for the Document Size section Width and Height fields to inches.

Immediately, the Width and Height fields change to display the largest image you can create at 300 ppi. For the DCS 460, the largest image size is 10 by 6.7 inches. For the resolution of a lower-priced 640-by-480 camera, you would find that the largest image size for an image at 300 ppi is only 2 by 1.6 inches. Obviously, this camera wouldn't provide the quality you need to output a 6-by-6 image at 300 ppi.

Tip *If your computer isn't handy, you can calculate the maximum image size for a specific resolution by dividing the camera's horizontal and vertical dimensions (in pixels) by the pixels per inch you need for an image. For instance, 3,000 ÷ 300 = 10 and 2,000 ÷ 300 = 6.7.*

Changing Image Size in ImageReady

To change Image Size in ImageReady, choose Image > Image Size. ImageReady's Image Size dialog box, shown in Figure 7-9, is designed specifically for online images. Each time you change the image's size, ImageReady resamples the image, changing the number of pixels in the image. You cannot turn resampling off.

When you change image size, the Constrain Proportions option helps ensure that changing the width automatically changes the height, or changing the height automatically changes the width. This prevents your image from being distorted when you change image size.

ImageReady's Image Size dialog box also includes an Action Options section. Clicking Action Options opens options related to batch processing images with actions and droplets. You should use these features only when you are recording an action. (To learn more about batch processing, see Chapter 11.) The Fit Image By pop-up menu allows you to constrain batched images to the new size in the Image Size dialog box according to Width or Height, Width & Height, or Percent. If you select the Do Not Enlarge option, images that are smaller than the specified new output size (designated when recording the action) will not be enlarged when the different images are processed.

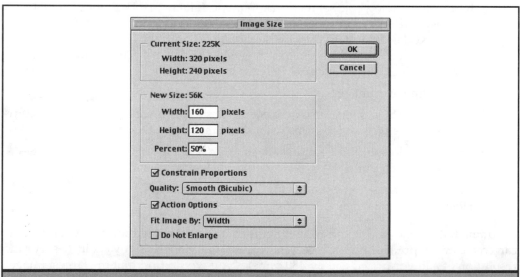

Figure 7-9.   *ImageReady's Image Size dialog box is designed for sizing online images*

Using the Resize Image Assistant

If you find the calculation and procedures for correct sizing a bit overwhelming, you can turn to Photoshop's Resize Image Assistant for help. The Resize Image Assistant automatically calculates resolution, and then resizes a copy of your image. It also warns you if your image needs to be rescanned at a higher resolution.

To try out the Image Assistant, load a sample image, and then choose Help > Resize Image. This opens the Resize Image Assistant, as shown in Figure 7-10. All you need to do is complete the information on screen, and then click on the Next button. The Image Assistant asks you to enter the final size of the image that you will be creating, the halftone screen frequency, the quality you desire, and whether you want the image sharpened. If you don't like math, using the Image Assistant is the best way to ensure that the images you resize maintain their quality.

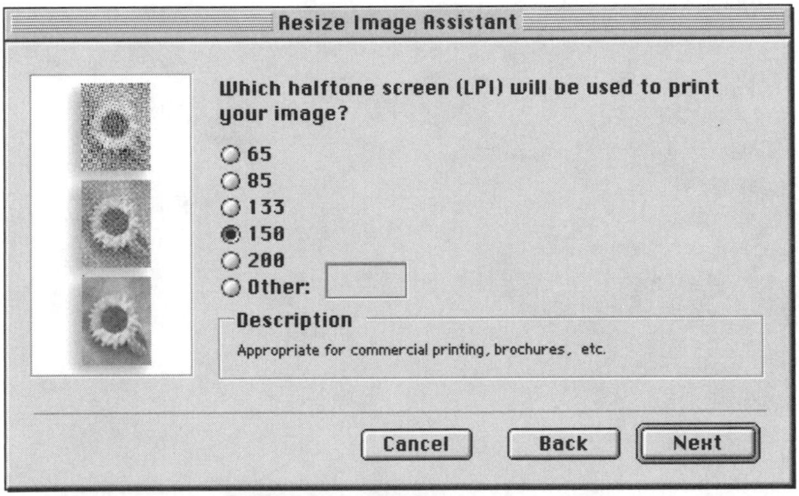

IMAGE EDITING
FUNDAMENTALS

Figure 7-10.   *The Resize Image Assistant leads you step by step through the process of resizing an image*

Chapter 8

Cropping, Transforming, and Adjusting Images

O nce you've digitized the images that you want to use in Photoshop or ImageReady, your next step is to fit them into your design project. Often, this means cropping or trimming images and sometimes rotating or even flipping them. Later, you may need to scale or distort them to create special effects or adjust their tone or color.

When dealing with commands that transform images, Photoshop distinguishes between those that affect the entire work area and those that affect only selected areas or layers. For example, if you want to rotate the entire image and all layers, use the Image > Canvas commands. When you want to rotate, scale, or distort selections or layers, use the Edit > Transform commands.

This chapter covers the tools and commands you'll need to transform images, as well as the commands that adjust the tone or color of images. You can use these commands to improve your images or create special effects.

Cropping Images

Cropping is similar to using a pair of scissors to cut around a rectangular area of an image. In Photoshop and ImageReady, you'll often need to crop an image to remove unwanted areas after it has been digitized.

Using the Crop Tool

In both Photoshop and ImageReady, you typically crop an image using the Crop tool. To begin, select the Crop tool in the Toolbox. If the Crop tool Options bar isn't displayed, double-click on the Crop tool to display it.

Before you click and drag with the Crop tool, you can change the width, height, and resolution of your image by changing the values in the corresponding fields in the Options bar. To clear the Settings, click on Clear. To make the settings reappear, click on Front Image.

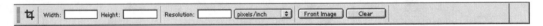

 When cropping in ImageReady, click on the Fixed Size option to enter values in the Width and Height fields. Click on the Front Image button to have the dimensions displayed in the Width and Height fields.

If you enter values in the Width and Height fields in the Options bar, you can execute the crop immediately by clicking on the checkmark button. If you don't set any values in the Crop tool's Options bar, you can crop freely by clicking and dragging the mouse over the image area that you wish to retain. When you click and drag and release the mouse, the options in the Options bar change, as shown next.

The settings for the active Crop tool work as follows:

- The Shield Cropped Area option hides the area that is being cropped away while you click and drag.

- If you selected Shield Cropped Area, you can click in the color swatch to pick a color for the screen area that is being cropped away.

- If you selected Shield Cropped Area, you can change the Opacity setting for the area being cropped away. This allows you to dim out the area being cropped away so that you can see the area that you are discarding, as well as the area that you are retaining, as shown in the next illustration.

- If you wish to transform the image (skew it, rotate it, or create perspective), click on Perspective. You can than click and drag to edit the handle positions in the image. To rotate, click and drag right or left above or below the image.

- The Delete option deletes the cropped area from the image. This option is dimmed if your image has only a Background layer.

- The Hide option hides the cropped area. This option is available only for images that are on layers. If you hide image areas when cropping, you can reveal them by using the Move tool. This option can be handy when creating animation in ImageReady.

After you click and drag over the area that you wish to retain, handles will surround the selected area: one handle at each corner and a handle in the middle of each side. If you need to make any adjustments to the crop, click and drag on any of the handles to resize the selected area. To move the entire selection marquee, click and drag in the middle of the selection area.

To execute the crop, click on the checkmark button in the Options bar or press the RETURN (*ENTER*) key. If you want to cancel the crop, click on the X button in the Options bar.

 You can also crop an image by selecting it with the Rectangular Marquee tool and choosing Image > Crop.

Trimming Images with the Trim Command

Both Photoshop and ImageReady include a Trim command, which provides a handy way to crop an image based on color or transparency. The Trim command is an effective way to crop images that appear on a transparent or one-colored background. For instance, using the Trim command, you can instantly trim a white or black border surrounding an image. The Trim command trims away the background color or transparency, without cropping the main focus of the image.

To use the Trim command, choose Image > Trim. In the Trim dialog box, choose whether you wish to trim the image based on transparent pixels, the top-left pixel color, or the bottom-right pixel color. Then specify whether you wish to trim the top, bottom, left, and/or right border of the image. If you leave all of the Trim Away checkboxes selected, the Trim command trims the image from all sides. Click on the OK button to execute the trim.

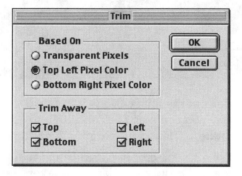

Transforming the Canvas

The Canvas commands on the Image menu allow you to rotate or flip the entire image and all layers or to expand the entire work area. These are the commands you will most likely need to use after you digitize images.

 When you want to rotate, scale, or distort selections or layers, use the Edit > Transform commands. These commands are discussed in the "Transforming Selections and Layers" section later in this chapter.

Rotating the Canvas

When your scanned image appears in Photoshop or ImageReady, you may see that, despite your best efforts, the image is tilted or upside down. You may have scanned an image sideways, so that it would fit on the scanner flatbed, or inadvertently scanned an image upside down. Both Photoshop and ImageReady feature a Rotate Canvas command that can help you fix these problems.

  Rotate Canvas rotates the entire image, regardless of whether there is a selection on screen. If you need to rotate a selection path or layer, use the Edit > Transform command, discussed later in this chapter.

To rotate the entire canvas, choose Image > Rotate Canvas. The Rotate Canvas submenu provides several choices.

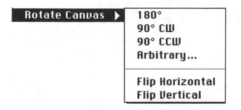

Each option rotates your image according to the angle indicated. (CW means clockwise, and CCW means counterclockwise.) The Arbitrary option allows you to specify a particular degree of rotation. When you select Arbitrary, the Rotate Canvas dialog box appears. Here, you can enter the degrees of rotation that you wish to use in the Angle field, ranging from –359.99 to 359.99 degrees. Click on the CW or CCW radio button to specify clockwise or counterclockwise rotation, respectively.

As an example, select Image > Rotate Canvas > Arbitrary, enter **45**, click on the CW radio button (to rotate clockwise), and click on OK. You'll see that the entire screen image rotates 45 degrees clockwise. To return the canvas to its original position, rotate the image again, this time 45 degrees counterclockwise.

  If you rotate your image by any angle other than 90 or 180 degrees, Photoshop must interpolate to complete the rotation, possibly degrading image quality.

How Crooked Is It?

It's possible that you will need to rotate an image but have no idea exactly what angle is required. How do you measure an angle on screen? Use Photoshop's Measure tool, as follows:

1. If the Info palette isn't open, choose Window > Show Info to display it.
2. Select the Measure tool, which shares its Toolbox location with the Eyedropper tool.
3. Position the Measure tool at the base of the image area that is tilted.
4. Click and drag from the base of the image area along its edge.
5. Check the distance and angle in the Info palette.

As a shortcut, you may be able to check whether an image is crooked by aligning its edges with a guide or with the edges of a palette.

Flipping the Canvas

The Flip commands in the Rotate Canvas submenu let you flip an image so that it faces in a different direction. These commands apply to the entire electronic canvas.

 If you wish to flip a selection, or layer, or path, choose Edit > Transform > Flip Horizontal or Edit > Transform > Flip Vertical.

To flip your image horizontally, choose Image > Rotate Canvas > Flip Horizontal. Your image will flip along a vertical plane and face in a new direction. Return to the Rotate Canvas submenu and choose Flip Vertical to see the image flip along a horizontal plane, turning it upside down. Flip your image again to make it right-side up.

 ImageReady also includes an Image > Flip Canvas command, similar to Photoshop's Image Rotate > Rotate Canvas > Flip commands.

Changing the Canvas Size

As you work on a Web, multimedia, or print project, you may wish to increase the dimensions of your work area on screen. You can do this by changing the canvas size of your image. When you increase the canvas size, you extend the perimeter of your document. This puts a usable border around the image or on any side of the image. (In the "Scaling, Rotating, Skewing, and Distorting Selections" section later in this chapter, you'll see how you can use this border as an area for adding text and extra images to a document.)

When a border is added to an image that is not on a layer, Photoshop uses the current background color as the canvas color. If your image is on a transparent background, the extended canvas area is transparent.

> **Tip**   *If you want the canvas color to match one of the colors in your image, you can quickly switch background colors (as long as the Foreground selection box is activated in the Color palette). Activate the Eyedropper by clicking on it, press OPTION (ALT), move the Eyedropper pointer over the color you wish to use as your background color, and click.*

To change the canvas size, choose Image > Canvas Size to display the Canvas Size dialog box. In the dialog box, your image's current dimensions appear in the Width and Height fields. At this point, they are the same as those for the canvas. To expand the canvas size, increase the values in the Width and Height fields in the New Size section of the dialog box.

> **Note**   *ImageReady's Image > Canvas Size command adds to the work area on screen. It does not add the background color. If you click on the Relative checkbox in ImageReady's Canvas Size dialog box, you can enter how many border pixels you wish to add to the width and height of the image.*

The Canvas Size dialog box also allows you to indicate the placement of your image in the canvas. The Anchor setting at the bottom of the dialog box is a grid of nine boxes. By clicking on a box, you specify the position of your image in relation to the canvas. If you select the center box, Photoshop centers your image in the canvas. If you click on the lower-middle box, Photoshop drops your image to the lower-middle part of the canvas.

In the example shown in Figure 8-1, 1 inch is added to both the Width and the Height of the canvas, and the Anchor is set to the lower-middle box. The result is a 0.5-inch border on the left and right sides of the image, and a 1-inch canvas area on top.

> **Tip**   *You can move images so that they extend beyond the canvas. However, the Select > All command selects only to the borders of the canvas.*

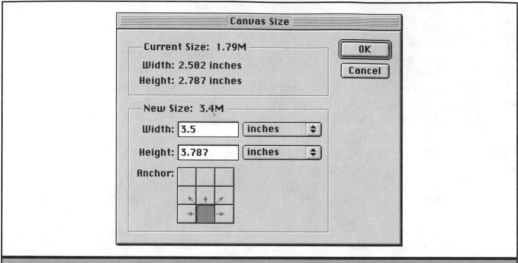

Figure 8-1.   *The Canvas Size dialog box allows you to change the canvas size and specify image placement on the canvas*

Transforming Selections and Layers

The commands available on Photoshop's Image > Rotate Canvas submenu allow you to manipulate the canvas. Often, you'll need to manipulate a selection or layer instead. The commands that allow you to perform these transform operations can be reached by choosing Edit > Transform.

Scaling, Rotating, Skewing, and Distorting Selections

To transform a selection, first create a selection on the screen and then choose Edit > Transform. The Transform submenu offers commands for scaling, rotating, skewing, distorting, adding perspective, and flipping selections.

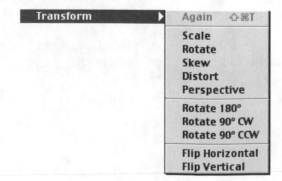

The Edit > Transform commands work as follows:

- **Scale**   This command allows you to resize a selection or nontransparent area of a layer. To scale in proportion, press the SHIFT key while using the Scale command; then click and drag on a corner handle.

- **Rotate and Flip**   These commands work exactly the same as the Rotate and Flip commands on the Image > Rotate Canvas submenu, except that they allow you to rotate and flip a selection, a layer, or a group of layers.

- **Skew**   Use this command to slant an image. When you skew a selection, click and drag on any handle. All handles always move along a horizontal or vertical plane as the object is slanted.

- **Distort**   Use this command to stretch an image in different directions. You can distort a selection by clicking and dragging on any handle in any direction. With the Distort command, you can create effects that look like those created with Perspective and Skew, except that you have more control over the selected area.

- **Perspective**   Use this command to create the appearance of depth in an image. When you use the Perspective command, try dragging one handle up and the opposite one down or diagonally in and out. As you drag one handle, another one will move in the opposite direction to create a depth effect. Figure 8-2 illustrates the effect of applying the Perspective command to text. Note that before applying the Perspective command (or Distort) to text in a layer, you must choose Layer > Rasterize > Type.

Figure 8-2.   *When using Edit > Transform > Perspective command, dragging a handle distorts the image and creates depth*

IMAGE EDITING
FUNDAMENTALS

To try a Transform command, first create a selection and then choose Scale, Skew, Perspective, Rotate, Flip, or Distort from the Edit > Transform submenu. After you choose an Edit > Transform command, Photoshop creates a bounding box around the area that will be affected by the transformation. With the mouse, click and drag on the handles to preview the effect. When you want to apply the effect to your image, press the RETURN (ENTER) key. To cancel before pressing ENTER, press COMMAND-. (ESC).

Be aware that when you use many of the commands in the Edit > Transform submenu, Photoshop must interpolate. Image quality depends on the interpolation method set in the Preferences dialog box (Edit > Preferences > General) and on how many times the image is transformed.

Take a few minutes to try out each Edit > Transform command. If you don't wish to apply the commands to your current image, open a new file and create some text that you can experiment with. Remember that these commands can be applied only to selections or nontransparent image areas in layers, paths, and masks in Quick Mask mode. After you've finished experimenting, you may want to use the Revert command to retrieve the last saved version of your file before you continue. Alternatively, you can click on the first snapshot in the History palette to return to the original version of your file.

As an example of a practical application of image transformation techniques, the following exercise creates the design project shown in Figure 8-3.

1. Load the Bangkok image from this book's CD (or any digitized image) and choose a background color.

2. Select the Image > Canvas Size command. In the Canvas Size dialog box, enter values in the Width and Height fields in the New Size section to add 1 inch to both the width and the height of your image. For the Anchor setting, click on the lower-middle box to select it (see Figure 8-1, shown earlier in the chapter).

3. To fill the half-inch border on the right and left sides with a duplicated portion of your image (see Figure 8-3 as an example), use the Rectangular Marquee tool to create a rectangular selection. It doesn't matter whether the selection is bigger than the half-inch canvas border, because you can scale it to fit.

4. With the image area selected, duplicate it by pressing COMMAND-OPTION (CTRL-ALT) while you click and drag the selection toward the upper-left canvas border area. *Don't deselect.*

5. Choose Edit > Transform > Scale. Scale the image by clicking on one of the four corners. If you wish, press SHIFT to constrain the dimensions proportionally.

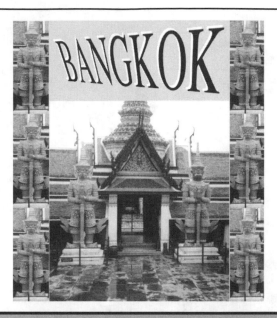

Figure 8-3.   *A design project created using the Edit > Transform commands*

6. When you are satisfied with the scaling, press ENTER. You can see the effects of the scaling in Figure 8-4.

7. Keep the scaled image selected so that you can reproduce it several times in order to cover the entire left and right borders. While pressing OPTION (*ALT*), click and drag with the Move tool to duplicate the image. Do this as many times as necessary to cover the borders.

8. Once you've assembled the border, you are ready to start creating the distorted text. Before you begin, make sure that the foreground color is set to the color you wish to use for the text. (We used white.)

9. Select the Type tool and click on the upper canvas area. When the Type tool's Options bar appears, pick an appropriate font and size in the pop-up menus.

10. Type the heading you want to appear in your image. In our example, we used *BANGKOK*. Then click on the OK button (checkmark) in the Type Options bar.

Figure 8-4. *Using the Edit > Transform > Scale command to shrink a selection that was created by duplicating part of the image*

11. Your next step is to distort the type, which is not possible unless the type is rasterized. Choose Layer > Rasterize > Type. Then choose Edit > Transform > Distort. (If you prefer, you can create a different effect by choosing Perspective or Skew.) When the handles appear, click and drag on them to create the look you want. In this example, all four handles were dragged to create the distortion, as shown in Figure 8-5.

12. Move the distorted text into position. If you'd like to enhance the effect, duplicate the text, fill it with another color (we used black), and offset it. This effect can be seen in the final version of the design project (Figure 8-3).

13. If you wish to execute any more image effects, feel free to experiment. Save your work by choosing File > Save.

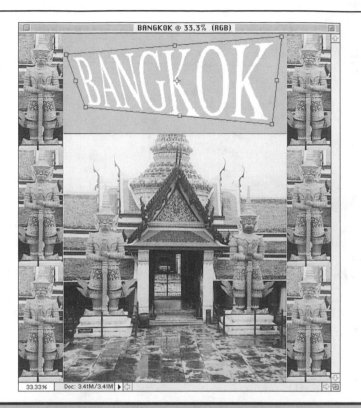

Figure 8-5.   *Using the Edit > Transform > Distort command to distort the type*

Using Numeric Transform in ImageReady

If you need to make precise transformations, you may not wish to create them by clicking and dragging the mouse. Instead, you can use ImageReady's Numeric Transform dialog box, shown in Figure 8-6. To open the dialog box, choose Numeric Transform from the Edit > Transform submenu.

In the dialog box, you can choose which type of transformation you wish to execute by clicking on the appropriate checkbox: Position, Scale, Skew, or Rotate. Then enter the value you wish to move or scale by, or the number of degrees you wish to rotate. If you wish to move a selection consisting of the nontransparent portion of a layer relative to its last position, keep the Relative checkbox selected. Otherwise, the movement will take place based on a zero point in the upper-left corner of your image. If you click on the Constrain Proportions checkbox in the Scale section, changing either the Width or Height field produces a proportional change in the other field.

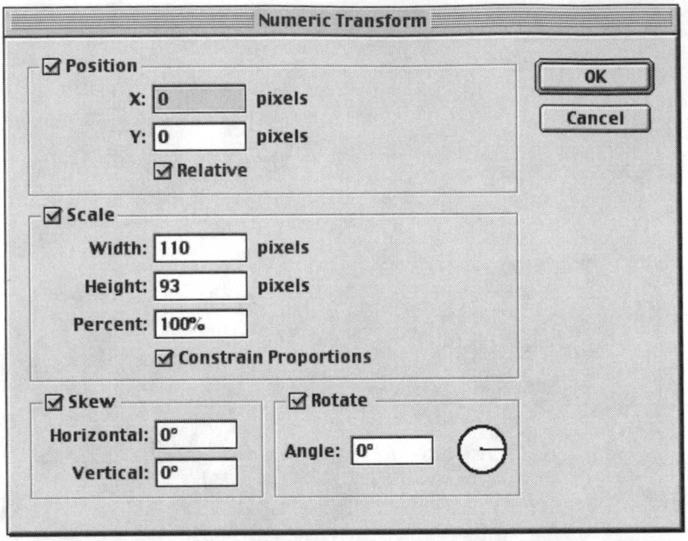

Figure 8-6. *For precise transformation, use ImageReady's Numeric Transform dialog box*

Using Free Transform

If you wish to apply several effects at once, you can use Free Transform. Using this command, you can move, scale, rotate, or skew a selection or create perspective using keyboard commands and clicking and dragging the mouse.

First, use a selection tool to select an area that you wish to transform. If you want to transform an entire layer, you do not need to select anything as long you are in any layer other than the Background. Then choose Edit > Free Transform. A bounding box appears, indicating the area that will be transformed. If necessary, move the bounding box into position by clicking and dragging within it. If you are not working with a selection, you can use the Move tool to move the entire layer. Then you can transform the selection or layer as follows:

■ To scale the image, click and drag on a handle. To scale proportionally, press SHIFT as you click and drag a corner handle. As you drag, keep an eye on the Info palette, which displays the percentage change in width and height, as well as the size in width and height.

■ To rotate, move the mouse pointer just beyond the bounding box area. When you see a curved double arrow, click and drag in the direction in which you wish to rotate the image. Pressing SHIFT while rotating constrains the rotation to 15-degree increments.

- To distort, press COMMAND (*CTRL*) while you click and drag on a handle. To distort symmetrically, press OPTION (*ALT*) instead of COMMAND.

- To skew, press COMMAND-SHIFT (*CTRL-SHIFT*) while clicking and dragging over a side (not corner) handle. The pointer turns into a white arrow with double arrows nearby.

- To create perspective, press COMMAND-OPTION-SHIFT (*CTRL-ALT-SHIFT*) while clicking and dragging over a corner handle. When you see a gray arrow, click and drag on the handle.

- To apply the transformation, press RETURN or ENTER (*ENTER* for Windows users). If you wish to cancel, press COMMAND-. or ESC (*ESC* for Windows users).

When you choose Edit > Free Transform in Photoshop, the Options bar allows you to click on a reference point and enter values in the Options bar to transform the image. The entry fields allow you to move, scale, rotate, and skew. The functionality is similar to ImageReady's Edit > Transform > Numeric command and the Numeric Transform command found in previous versions of Photoshop.

IMAGE EDITING
FUNDAMENTALS

Adjusting Images

The Invert, Equalize, Threshold, Posterize, and Brightness/Contrast commands on the Image > Adjust submenu are used to remap, or reassign, pixel values in a selection or in an entire image. These commands let you alter your digitized images to distribute tone and color evenly, or they can be used to create special effects that drastically change brightness values. For instance, you can transform a color or grayscale image into a high-contrast black-and-white image or invert all of the color values in an image to produce a negative of the original.

The Invert, Threshold, Posterize, and Brightness/Contrast commands can be applied in an adjustment layer. Adjustment layers allow you to see editing changes through a layer mask without changing the actual pixels of the image. Adjustment layers also allow you to paint to add and subtract these effects. Adjustment layers are discussed in detail in Chapter 17.

Creating a Negative Using Invert

The Image > Adjust > Invert command (available in both Photoshop and ImageReady) reverses your image, turning it into a negative of the original: All black values become white, all white values turn black, and all colors are converted to their complements. Pixel values are inverted on a scale from 0 to 255. A pixel with a value of 0 will be inverted to 255, a pixel with the value of 10 will change to 245, and so on. You may invert a selection or an entire image; if no area is selected, the entire image is inverted.

Figure 8-7. *Using the Image > Adjust > Invert command to create a reverse (negative) effect*

To create the example shown in Figure 8-7, we created black text and selected the bottom half using the Rectangular Marquee tool. Then we applied the Image > Adjust > Invert command to the rectangular selection. The black text within the selection turned white, and the white area between the letters turned black.

You can use the Filter > Fade command to fade the effects of the Invert, Equalize, and Posterize commands.

Expanding Tonal Range with Equalize

The Image > Adjust > Equalize command distributes light and dark values evenly. It is useful for adjusting dark scans to make them lighter. When the Equalize command is executed, Photoshop remaps light and dark values over the full tonal range from black to white. The darkest areas in the images are darkened as much as possible, and the lightest are lightened as much as possible. All other values are distributed according to the new tonal range. Images will often look brighter, exhibiting more balance and contrast, as you can see in the example shown in Figure 8-8.

If an image area is selected and you execute Image > Adjust > Equalize, the Equalize dialog box will appear. Choose the Equalize Selected Area Only radio button to equalize only the selection. If you choose Equalize Entire Image Based On Selected Area, Photoshop equalizes the entire image based on the lightness and darkness values of the selected area.

<table>
<tr><td colspan="2" align="center">Equalize</td></tr>
<tr><td>Options
○ Equalize selected area only
● Equalize entire image based on selected area</td><td>OK
Cancel</td></tr>
</table>

Figure 8-8.   *A scanned image before (top) and after (bottom) applying the Image > Adjust > Equalize command*

Converting an Image to Black and White with Threshold

The Image > Adjust > Threshold command converts a color or grayscale image into a high-contrast black-and-white image. The Threshold dialog box allows you to pick a Threshold Level—a dividing line between black and white pixels. All pixels lighter than or equal to the Threshold Level value become white; all pixels darker than the Threshold Level are converted to black.

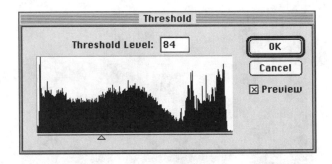

In the dialog box, you see a *histogram*, which graphically presents the brightness, or luminance, values of the pixels in the current image or selection. The histogram plots the number of pixels at each tonal level of the image. Darker values are plotted on the left side of the histogram, lighter values on the right side. (You'll read more about using histograms in Chapter 19.)

You can click and drag on the slider control below the histogram to change the Threshold Level (dragging right raises the value; dragging left lowers it), or you can enter a value between 1 and 255 in the Threshold Level field (the default is 128). If the Threshold command is executed at the default settings, all of the pixels with values greater than or equal to 128 will turn white, and all of the pixels with values less than 128 will turn black. If the Preview checkbox is selected, Photoshop will show you the results of the Threshold command. Figure 8-9 shows the results of applying the Threshold command to the image in Figure 8-8.

The following exercise shows how you can create an interesting artistic effect by decreasing the number of colors in an image.

1. Open any color image. If you don't have one to use, load a file from this book's CD.

2. Select the entire image by pressing COMMAND-A (*CTRL-A*), and then choose Edit > Copy. (Choose Copy Merged to copy all visible layers.)

3. Paste the image over itself by choosing Edit > Paste. As soon as you paste, Photoshop automatically creates a new layer with the pasted image in it. If the Layers palette isn't on your screen, choose Window > Show Layers to view the layer.

Figure 8-9.   *Applying the Image > Adjust > Threshold command to the image in Figure 8-8*

4. To convert the new layer to black and white, choose Image > Adjust > Threshold. In the Threshold dialog box, make sure the Preview checkbox is selected, and then drag the slider control to choose a level that creates an attractive black-and-white image. When you like what you see, click on OK. Don't deselect.

5. To create the decreased colors effect, you'll need to blend the pixels of the image in the layer with the underlying background. To add the image's original color back into the dark areas of the image, choose Lighten from the mode pop-up menu in the Layers palette.

The result will be a composite image with color in what was once the darker areas and white in the lighter areas.

If you wish, continue to experiment with different opacities and modes, such as Screen and Overlay. When you are ready to continue to the next section, save your file, if desired, and close it.

Reducing Tonal Levels Using Posterize

You can reduce the tonal levels in an image by using the Image > Adjust > Posterize command. This command can create some unusual special effects, because the contours in an image disappear and are replaced by large flat-color or gray areas.

The Posterize dialog box includes the Levels field, in which you enter the number of tonal levels you wish to appear in the image or selected area. Acceptable values range from 2 to 255; the lower the number, the fewer the tonal levels. When the Preview checkbox is selected, Photoshop will preview the results of the Posterize command.

For a dramatic effect, enter **4** in the Levels field. Then raise the number of levels a few increments at a time to see the different effects. Figure 8-10 shows a scanned image before and after applying the Posterize command with Levels set to 4. Four tonal levels yields 12 colors: 4 levels for red, 4 levels for green, and 4 levels for blue.

Adjusting Brightness and Contrast

Contrast is the difference between the lightest and darkest parts of an image. *Brightness* is the degree of light that is reflected from an image or transmitted through it.

Some scanners have a tendency to darken images, causing them to lose contrast. Images frame-grabbed from videotape also have a tendency to darken when loaded into Photoshop. When you need to make simple adjustments to the brightness and contrast levels of your image, you'll find that the Brightness/Contrast command in the Image > Adjust submenu (of both Photoshop and ImageReady) may solve the problem. (If your image needs more extensive color-correction and retouching, refer to Chapter 19.)

To use the Brightness/Contrast controls, first select an area to be adjusted. If you don't make a selection, the adjustment will be applied to the entire image. Then choose Image > Adjust > Brightness/Contrast. The Brightness/Contrast dialog box contains a Preview checkbox and sliders for adjusting Brightness and Contrast.

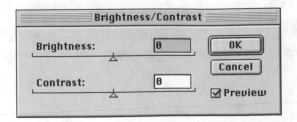

IMAGE EDITING
FUNDAMENTALS

Figure 8-10.   *A scanned image before (top) and after (bottom) applying
Image > Adjust > Posterize with Levels set to 4*

First, make sure the Preview checkbox is selected so you can watch the results
of your adjustments, and then begin by testing the Brightness slider. Drag the slider
control to the right to brighten your image or to the left to darken your image. Take a
few moments now to adjust brightness to the best level for your image. Be careful not
to overexpose or underexpose the image.

When you are satisfied with the brightness level, try adjusting the contrast. Moving
the slider control to the right adds more detail, because it increases the difference

between the lightest and darkest portions of the image. If you drag the slider control to the left, the lightness and darkness levels will begin to merge.

If the image doesn't look as good as it did when you started, you can either drag both sliders back to their zero points or click on Cancel. You can also press OPTION (*ALT*) to make the Cancel button change to a Reset button. Once you are satisfied with the new brightness and contrast levels, click on OK.

Chapter 9

Preparing Images
for the Web with
Photoshop and
ImageReady

W hy has the popularity of the World Wide Web skyrocketed? The Web's graphics capability is certainly one reason. Graphics and creative design are the keys to an attractive and successful Web site. How many people would be using the Web if there were no graphics—if all Web sites were purely text? And who is creating much of the graphics on the Web? Photoshop artists are the main source.

Photoshop's power as both a creative tool and a production tool has made it virtually essential to any artist interested in outputting sophisticated images to the Web. Unfortunately, preparing graphics for the Web is not always a simple affair. As you're probably aware, Web graphics often seem to download at a glacial pace. Compressing image file size and reducing colors can lead to faster downloading times, but often result in sickly looking colors and ragged image edges.

This chapter provides a detailed look at how to output images to the World Wide Web using both Photoshop and ImageReady. Use the information presented here as a guide to achieving the best compromise between fast download speeds and image quality.

Understanding Web Page Basics

If you will be creating or outputting graphics for the Web, you should have an idea of exactly how a Web browser such as Netscape Communicator or Microsoft Internet Explorer actually displays an image on a page. Understanding the basic concepts of how Web pages work will help you plan your workflow and understand how to set up your own Web site. Thus, before embarking on a hands-on tour of the intricacies of Web graphics, spend a few moments reviewing some Web browser basics.

Note   *If you're connected to the Internet, you can access information from Adobe's Web site (www.adobe.com) directly from Photoshop or ImageReady: Simply click on the eye icon at the top of the Toolbox palette (or choose File > Adobe Online). When the Adobe Online dialog box appears, click on Configure to set up your browser. You can also choose whether you wish to update the Adobe Online dialog box automatically and how often you want it updated. To manually update the dialog box, click on Update.*

Loading Images into Web Pages

Even if you won't be designing Web pages, it's helpful to understand how an image is actually loaded into a Web page. The process is quite different from that used with desktop publishing software, where images are loaded directly on a page, and then printed from the graphics files on disk.

Images viewed in a Web browser such as Netscape Communicator or Internet Explorer are sent to the browser from a computer with Web server software. The instructions to load the graphics to the Web page are written in Hypertext Markup Language (HTML). After you enter a request in your browser to find a Web site, such as www.adobe.com, the browser usually loads a home page from the computer server hosting the Web site. Typically, the home page is a text file named index.htm.

Embedded in the index.htm file are HTML tags to format text and to load graphics. Even though the tag-based HTML text file instructs the browser to load the graphics at specific locations on the page, the graphics are not actually in the page.

Note   *If you are writing or editing HTML, be aware that many Web servers are case-sensitive; so, for example, Index.htm is not the same thing as index.htm.*

Typically, a tag is a letter, word, or group of letters surrounded by less-than and greater-than brackets (< >). Tags are simply instructions that the browser can understand. For instance, <B> is the tag for boldface type. To tell the browser to send text in bold, you would enter the <B> tag, type the text that should appear in bold, and follow that text with the ending tag </B>. The slash symbol within the tag indicates that the tagged block is complete. For example, in the middle of the HTML describing a Web page, you might see something like the following:

```
<B>The words between the two tags shown here will appear in
boldface text</B>
```

The first tag on a Web page is <HTML>; it simply tells the browser that the HTML language will be used. A <TITLE> tag indicates text that will appear in the title bar of the browser window when the Web page is accessed. The <HEAD> tag tells the browser how to interpret the page. Information about scripting languages and typographical character sets typically appear here. The <TITLE> tag indicating the page window title also appears within the title section. The <BODY> tag starts the section that delivers most of the actual contents of the page—text, link code, and code to load graphics appear here. For example, the following snippet of text places the words "My Home Page" in the browser's title bar, and places the words "Welcome to my home page!" in bold in a large font size. (H1 stands for Header 1, a large font size.)

```
<HTML>
    <HEAD>
        <TITLE>My Home Page</TITLE>
    </HEAD>
    <BODY>
        <H1><B>Welcome to my home page!</B></H1>
    </BODY>
</HTML>
```

Tip   *You can experiment with HTML by typing the preceding example into a word processor and saving it as a text file with the filename index.htm. Then open the file in your browser, and the page will be displayed as it would be on the Web.*

Of course, most Web users would consider this page quite dull. We can spice it up with a graphic by adding the <IMG> tag. The <IMG> tag sends a message from the browser instructing the Web server to load a specific image from the Web server's hard disk. The following HTML snippet tells the Web server to load a file named boy.gif.

```
<IMG HEIGHT=251 WIDTH=286 SRC="boy.gif">
```

The preceding lines are included in the following example. Here you see the completed code for an entire Web page.

```
<HTML>
    <HEAD>
        <TITLE>Toys on the Web</TITLE>
    </HEAD>
    <BODY bgcolor="#ccccff" link="#ccccff">
        <ENTER>
            <H1>Welcome To</H1>
                <IMG HEIGHT="251" WIDTH="286" SRC="boy.gif">
            <H1>Toys on the Web!
                <A HREF="bears_page.htm">
                    <IMG HEIGHT="94" WIDTH="72" SRC="bear.gif"></A>

</H1>
    </BODY>
</HTML>
```

Notice that we've added a tag for the page's background color (bgcolor="#ccccff"), a light blue. We've also added a link. The following code instructs the browser to load the bears_page.htm page when the bear.gif image is clicked.

```
<A HREF="bears_page.htm">
    <IMG HEIGHT="94" WIDTH="72" IMG SRC="BEAR.GIF"></A>
```

Figure 9-1 shows our actual sample Web page, as previewed in Netscape Communicator.

Outputting Your Page to the Web

If you've never worked with Web graphics, you may be wondering how the actual HTML files and graphics are sent to the Web server and how you can start setting up your own Web site. Your first step is to contact an Internet Service Provider (ISP), such

Figure 9-1.   *A sample Web page, created with HTML*

as Earthlink or Mindspring, and arrange for the ISP to host your Web site. Your ISP will charge you for the initial setup of your site (and for an e-mail account). Typically, you'll pay about $20 a month for e-mail, and another $20 for the Web site.

Next you'll need to choose your domain name. The *domain name* is the part of the URL (universal resource locator) that users type to have their browsers access a site. Adobe's domain name, for example, is www.adobe.com. Apple's is www.apple.com. Microsoft's is www.microsoft.com. Ours is www.addesigngraphics.com, and our publisher's is www.osborne.com. You'll also need to register your domain name. Usually, your ISP will help you with this. Typically, you'll pay $70 for the first two years of domain registration and then a yearly fee after that.

Note   *No two domain names can be the same, so you may not be able to register your first choice. If someone else has already registered the name you want, you'll need to come up with another name for your Web site.*

After you've taken care of the practical arrangements, you can create your Web site. To get yourself up and running without spending hours and hours typing and correcting HTML tags, you might wish to purchase a program that will write the HTML for you. Programs that can do this include Adobe PageMill, Claris Home Page, Microsoft FrontPage, Symantec Visual Page, and many others. If you want to build a very sophisticated site, you should invest in a more powerful program, such as Adobe GoLive, Macromedia Dreamweaver, or NetObjects Fusion.

Once you've finished making your page, it's time to send the files you've created to your ISP. Your ISP will assign you a password that will grant you access to your site's directories on the ISP's Web server. Adobe GoLive and Macromedia Dreamweaver not only allow you to set up Web pages, but they also make it easy to send your entire site to the Web server from your computer. Otherwise, you may wish to obtain FTP (File Transfer Protocol) software created solely for the purpose of connecting to your site, allowing you to send new files and to delete any files that you no longer wish to include.

Among Macintosh users, the most popular FTP program is Fetch. If you're using a PC, try FTP Pro. You can find these and other FTP programs on the Web at www.shareware.com.

Considering Image Colors, Resolution, and Size

Once you've become comfortable with the basics of designing and building your Web site, your next concern is creating the best-looking site possible. In Web design, three important aspects are the colors, image resolution, and image size.

Choosing Web Colors

When you are working with images for the Web or multimedia, you'll undoubtedly want the colors you see on screen to match the colors your audience sees on their own computer monitors. Unfortunately, as discussed in Chapter 1, different monitors and different computer systems display colors differently. As a first step in attempting to minimize the differences between systems, Web servers and multimedia producers should calibrate their monitors.

If you haven't already done so, run Adobe's Gamma utility, and then choose an RGB color space. (See Chapter 2 for details.) If you are creating images for the Web and most multimedia programs, you'll probably want to stick with sRGB (Standard RGB). sRGB is Photoshop's default RGB color space and represents how most computer monitors display colors. If most of the design work you do is for the Web, you can set the options in Photoshop's Color Settings dialog box for Web graphic work. To do this, choose Edit > Color Settings. In the Color Settings dialog box, shown in Figure 9-2, choose Web Graphics Defaults in the Settings pop-up menu.

Choosing Image Resolution for the Web and Multimedia

If you are outputting for either the Web or multimedia, one of your first concerns should be to ensure that you are creating your graphics at the correct resolution. If image resolution is too high, viewing your Web site or multimedia production could

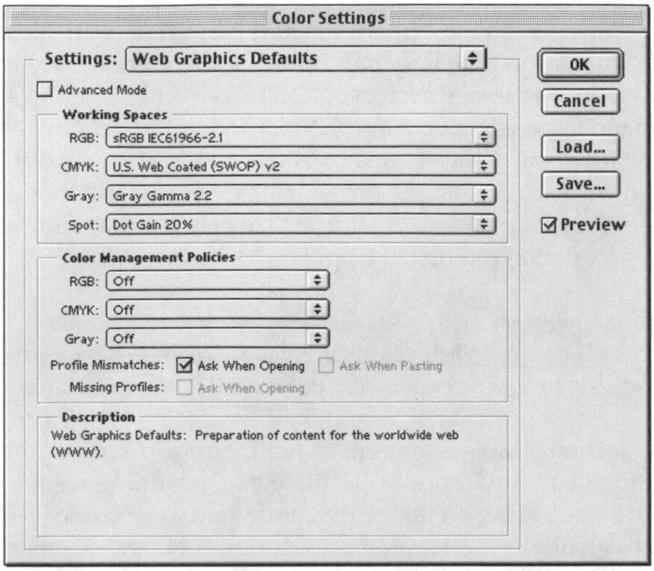

Figure 9-2.   *To quickly set your system up for Web work, choose Web Graphics Defaults in the Color Settings dialog box*

prove to be a frustrating experience for even the most patient viewer. When resolution is too high, an image's file size increases, which means it takes longer to download to a Web browser and longer to redraw on the screen.

If you are creating images for the Web or for a multimedia program, the resolution of your images need only be as high as the resolution of a computer display (usually 640 × 480 pixels, 72 ppi). When viewed on screen, high-resolution images do not look any better than 72 ppi images. As explained in Chapter 7, high-resolution images appear larger on the screen than low-resolution images do.

The monitor you use may be set to a higher resolution than 72 ppi. However, since virtually all computer monitors can display images at 72 ppi, most Web designers create images at 72 ppi. This ensures that all Mac and Windows users can view images properly. If someone is viewing an image created at 72 ppi on a monitor set to a higher resolution, the image will appear smaller than its creation size. Nevertheless, it should still be sharp.

Resizing Web Graphics

As you begin to create images for the Web or multimedia, it's important to remember that most users viewing your Web images will be downloading them from modems and may be viewing your work on systems not as powerful as yours. (You should also remember that some Web browsers don't even show any graphics on screen.) To help ensure that your viewers won't get frustrated and surf off to other locations, keep your graphics small in dimension. The larger an image is, the more slowly it downloads.

If you need to reduce an image's size, you can use either Photoshop's or ImageReady's Image Size command (choose Image > Image Size). In Photoshop's Image Size dialog box, make sure that the Resample Image checkbox is selected. Enter the new dimensions for your image. When you click on OK, the image will be resized, and the 72-ppi resolution will be maintained. (You can also use the Image Size dialog box to simply reduce a high-resolution image's resolution setting to 72 ppi.)

> **Tip** *When optimizing images, you can reduce the dimensions of an image in Photoshop's Save for Web dialog box. When you reduce image size in this dialog box, Photoshop subtracts pixels from an image and does not increase image resolution.*

If you will be scanning images and enlarging them, you should multiply your enlargement scaling factor by 72 ppi to calculate your scanning resolution. For instance, if you will be enlarging an image that you want to be twice its original size, multiply 2 × 72 to calculate your scanning resolution, 144 ppi. To enlarge your image, open Photoshop's Image Size dialog box, deselect the Resample Image checkbox (to avoid adding pixels), and then enter the new dimensions for your image. Immediately, the resolution drops to 72 ppi. Click on OK to complete the adjustment.

For more information about choosing image resolution and resizing images, see Chapter 7.

Choosing Web File Formats

To help ensure that Web graphics download as fast as possible, the original creators of the Web chose graphics file formats that allowed for color and image compression. The two most common Web graphics formats are GIF (usually pronounced "giff" by Webmasters) and JPEG (pronounced "jaypeg"). Recently, PNG (usually pronounced "ping") was created as a third alternative. PNG comes in two flavors: PNG 24 and PNG 8.

As you create graphics for the Web, it's important to understand the advantages and limitations of each file format. For instance, if you are showcasing your own artwork on your own Web site, you might wish to save all of your files in JPEG format. However, if you are displaying a logo originally created in Adobe Illustrator, you may wish to output it in GIF format. Table 9-1 summarizes the differences between saving in JPEG, GIF, and PNG formats, and the following sections describe these Web file formats in more detail.

Using JPEG File Format

JPEG (Joint Photographic Experts Group) is a file format commonly used to output scanned images to the Web. It is primarily used when images need to display transitional colors, often when images must display thousands or millions of colors. JPEG is used

File Format	Advantages	Disadvantages
GIF	Yields small file size	May not produce good results from scanned images with many colors
	Good for flat color	Must reduce color palette to 256 or fewer colors
	Allows transparency control by means of layer transparency (from an RGB file) Allows interlacing Allows animated GIF	
JPEG	Allows control of image quality	Does not provide automatic control of transparency
	Displays millions of colors	Images viewed on 256-color systems may not look correct
	Good for continuous-tone scanned images Allows progressive scans in which images gradually become sharper	
PNG 24	Displays millions of colors	Older browsers may not recognize this file format
	Allows transparency Provides lossless compression Multilevel transparency up to 256 levels reduces jagged edges	
PNG 8	Reduces colors to 256 or fewer	Older browsers may not support file format
	Yields file size that is often smaller than GIF files Compresses without losing data Allows transparency control	

Table 9-1. *Advantages and Disadvantages of JPEG, GIF, and PNG File Formats*

IMAGE EDITING
FUNDAMENTALS

for Web images because it can reduce file size by compressing images. It does this by subtracting image data from files, which means that image quality may be degraded.

When you output your file as a JPEG image, you can specify whether you need a high-, medium-, or low-quality image. The higher the quality, the larger the file's size; the lower the quality, the smaller the file's size.

If you decide to save your files in JPEG format, remember that users with 8-bit color boards can view only 256 colors on screen at a time. If you save a 24-bit color file in JPEG format, it may look ragged and the color quality may appear poor to viewers using 8-bit systems. To preview your image in 8-bit color depth, change your color display to view 256 colors. Users of Mac, Windows 95/98, and Windows NT systems can easily do this by changing settings accessed through their operating system's Control Panel settings. Previewing images in a Web browser is discussed in the "Previewing Browser Dither" section later in this chapter.

Using GIF File Format

The most common file format for outputting images to the Web is GIF (Graphic Interchange Format). GIF file format requires that the number of colors in an image be reduced to 256 or fewer. This is a major factor in reducing file size. An image using 256 colors will generally require about one-third the storage space needed by the same image saved in millions of colors.

Since the maximum number of colors in an image can be only 256, GIF is commonly used for flat images that don't display many color transitions. Figure 9-3 compares the type of image you might wish to convert to GIF format with another that you would probably save in JPEG format. The GIF image was created using Adobe Illustrator.

Buttons, logos, and other Web art are commonly saved in GIF file format and optimized with a Web-safe palette of 256 colors. (For more details about this palette, see the "Shifting to Web-Safe Colors" section later in this chapter.)

GIF also allows you to maintain image transparency. For instance, suppose that you want to place a logo from Photoshop text on your Web page, and you want the background color of the Web browser to show through the letters. You could first

GIF format   JPEG format

Figure 9-3. *An image saved in GIF format displays fewer color transitions than a similar image saved in JPEG format*

create the text on a layer with a transparent background, and then optimize the image in Photoshop or ImageReady using either of the programs' transparency settings (described in the sections about optimizing specific file formats and the "Handling Web Transparency" section later in this chapter).

Using PNG File Format

PNG (*portable network graphics*) file format was created as a replacement for GIF. Photoshop and ImageReady can work with PNG 8 and PNG 24 files.

Although PNG has advantages over both JPEG and GIF, it is not supported by older browsers. Furthermore, not all digital imaging software can save in PNG format. Thus, despite its advantages over JPEG and GIF, PNG format is not as widely used.

Like JPEG, PNG 24 compresses images and allows you to maintain millions of colors. However, unlike JPEG, PNG 24 uses *lossless compression*, which means that image quality is not sacrificed when the image is compressed. One of PNG 24's chief advantages over JPEG is its support of *alpha transparency*. Photoshop uses alpha transparency to smooth image edges, providing 256 levels of transparency. This feature helps eliminate jagged edges when images are created with a transparent background or when a portion of the image is transparent.

Note *If you save an image in PNG 24 format with an alpha channel used to create a transparency effect, Macromedia Director (version 7 and later) displays the effect.*

Like GIF, PNG 8 supports up to 256 colors. Thus, PNG 8 should be used for logos, buttons, and images in which colors are constant and don't gradually change. PNG's sophisticated compression algorithm produces better compression than GIF. PNG also supports Photoshop layer transparency. This means you can set up PNG images so that transparent image areas show the background color of the Web page. Unlike PNG 24, PNG 8 does not support alpha transparency.

Optimizing Images for the Web

To ensure that Web images are as appealing as possible, yet don't clog up Web users' phone and cable lines, you'll want to optimize them. Optimization reduces file size in an attempt to make the download times of graphics files bearable to Web users. The optimization process starts when you convert an image from one graphic file format to a Web graphic format such as GIF, JPEG, or PNG. Fortunately for today's Photoshop user, the optimization process is fairly straightforward and logical. In the early days of Web design, image optimization was usually a time-consuming, trial-and-error affair, often fraught with frustration.

Current versions of both Photoshop and ImageReady allow you to preview different settings, as well as compare the original to the optimized version. As you work, you can preview the image in a Web browser and save your optimization settings so that they can be applied to other images. As a bonus, both programs can generate HTML code snippets that let you easily integrate your images into Web pages.

Previewing Options

Photoshop's Save for Web dialog box and ImageReady's document window are your launching pads for image optimization. Before you get started, you should become familiar with the key features of each program's optimization windows.

In Photoshop, begin by choosing File > Save for Web. All of the optimization commands are quickly accessible in the Save for Web dialog box, shown in Figure 9-4.

In ImageReady, the document window is already set up for immediately viewing optimized images. Optimization options are handled through ImageReady's Optimize palette, shown in Figure 9-5. The features you see here are nearly identical to those in Photoshop.

Viewing Multiple Versions of Optimized Images

Both Photoshop and ImageReady provide multiple views of optimized images. For instance, in one window you can view the original; in another, a JPEG image; in another, a GIF with 256 colors; and in another, a GIF with 128 colors. In Photoshop's Save for Web dialog box, each tab provides a different optimized view: Original shows the original image with no optimization, Optimized shows the image using the current optimization settings, 2-Up displays a two-image version of your original, and 4-Up shows a four-image version of your original.

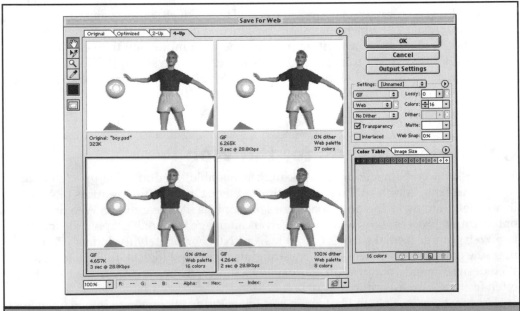

Figure 9-4.   *Photoshop's Save for Web dialog box*

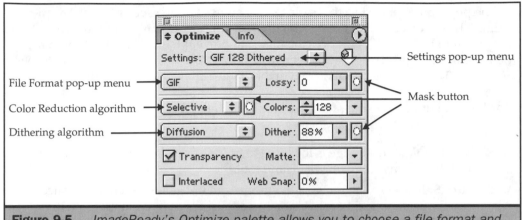

Figure 9-5.   *ImageReady's Optimize palette allows you to choose a file format and reduce the number of colors in an image*

In ImageReady, viewing multiple versions of an optimized image is simply a matter of clicking the tab at the top of ImageReady's document window, and changing settings in the Optimize palette. The tabs at the top of ImageReady's document window are similar to those in Photoshop's Save for Web dialog box. Each provides a different optimized view.

Reviewing Save for Web Dialog Box Features

Before you begin optimizing your images, take a few moments to familiarize yourself with some key landmarks in the Save for Web dialog box. Notice the three pop-up menu icons located in circle buttons in the upper-right area of the dialog box. Clicking the pop-up menu in the upper-right corner of the dialog box (in an area called the *document panel*) displays this menu:

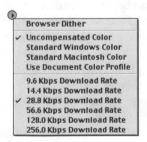

Undoubtedly, the most valuable item in the menu is the Browser Dither option. Choosing this item displays the selected image on screen as it would appear in a Web browser. Mac users might wish to sample the Standard Windows Color Preview option occasionally to view how the image would appear on Windows systems (usually darker than on Macs). The Download Rate choices in the menu change the display to show how fast the optimized image downloads at the selected modem speeds.

The pop-up menu next to the Settings area allows you to save your optimization settings. This is discussed in the next section. The pop-up menu next to the Color Table allows you to lock specific colors in the image to prevent them from changing when you optimize images. The pop-up menu also allows you to shift specific colors to Web-safe colors. These options are discussed in the "Fine-Tuning Web Image Quality" section later in the chapter.

Along the upper-left side of the Save for Web dialog box are six tools that prove handy as you are optimizing an image:

- **Hand tool**   If the image is too large to fit in the display windows, you can click and drag to move it using the Hand tool.

- **Slice Select tool**   If you wish to optimize an image within an image slice, select it with the Slice Select tool. (Using image slices is covered in Chapter 10.)

- **Zoom tool**   If you wish to enlarge the image, select the Zoom tool and click and drag in your image. To reduce magnifications, press OPTION (*ALT*) and click with the Zoom tool.

- **Eyedropper tool**   You may need to sample colors when locking colors and shifting to Web-safe colors. You can use the Eyedropper for color sampling. (See the "Shifting to Web-Safe Colors" section later in this chapter for details.)

- **Color swatch**   Clicking on the color swatch icon opens the Color Picker, where you can choose a color to add. (See the "Locking and Editing Colors in a Color Table" section later in this chapter for details.)

- **Show slices**   Clicking on the Show Slices icon turns on and off the display of slices.

Choosing Optimization Settings

Both Photoshop and ImageReady provide extremely easy and efficient means of optimizing images for the Web. You can choose from preset settings in the Settings pop-up menu. You can also save your own custom settings by choosing Save Settings from the pop-up menu in the dialog box. In ImageReady, choose from the pop-up menu in the Optimize palette.

 If you wish to change an optimized image back to the original version, click on the optimized image and choose Original from the Settings pop-up menu.

Your next step is to pick a file format and begin choosing optimization settings. The Save for Web dialog box changes depending on the file format you select. The optimization settings for each file format are covered later in this chapter.

Before you begin optimizing for specific file formats, here are a few optimization tips that work with all file formats:

■ If you need to output your image at a specific file size, you can choose Optimize to File Size from the pop-up menu next to the Settings area. In ImageReady, choose this feature from the Optimize palette's pop-up menu. In the Optimize to File dialog box, enter a file size and click on OK.

■ When viewing the 4-Up preview mode, choose Repopulate Views from the pop-up menu next to the Settings area. Each new image display is more optimized than the previous one.

■ Each time you change settings, both Photoshop and ImageReady automatically regenerate optimized images on screen. You can toggle automatic regeneration off or on in ImageReady by deselecting or selecting the Auto Regenerate option in the Optimize palette's pop-up menu. When Auto Regenerate is off, you can edit images without waiting for the optimization each time you change the image. Then you can regenerate an optimized preview by choosing Regenerate from the Optimize palette's pop-up menu.

■ In ImageReady, you can change optimization window preferences by choosing File > Edit > Preferences > Optimization.

Using Alpha Channels for Weighted Optimization

Both Photoshop and ImageReady allow you to create a range of optimization settings in different parts of your image, based on alpha channel masks. For example, suppose that you wish to optimize a flower image with the focal point at the center of the image. You want the best optimization at the center of the image; optimization at the exterior of the image isn't important. By using different levels of optimization, you ensure high quality where you need it with good download times. You can set up different optimization levels by creating an alpha channel in your image. When you optimize the image, Photoshop creates different optimization settings in your image based on the mask in the alpha channel.

An *alpha channel* is an extra layer in your image that contains masking information. You can create alpha channels by saving selections or by clicking on the New Channel button in the Channels palette. In the alpha channel, a mask is represented by as a shape with up to 256 levels of gray. When using alpha channels, Photoshop reads the white and light parts of the mask to determine which areas to apply the most optimization. Figure 9-6 shows an image with an alpha channel with a mask of a polar bear. Using weighted optimization for JPEG images, you could apply high-quality compression to the image areas corresponding to white and low-quality compression to dark areas.

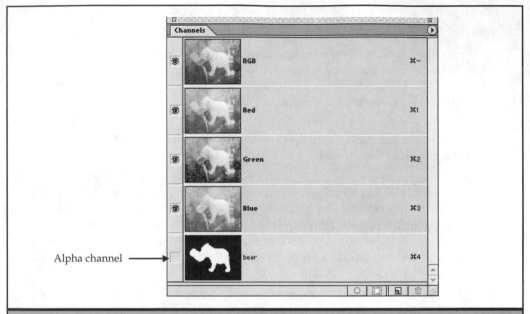

Alpha channel

Figure 9-6. *Weighted optimization allows you to control optimization based on gray values in an alpha channel*

Creating Alpha Channels

Creating and using alpha channels is covered in detail in Chapter 15, but you may wish to create an alpha channel for use in this chapter. Since only Photoshop allows you to edit alpha channels and view them in its Channels palette, it's probably best to work with channels in Photoshop. Here's how to create an alpha channel:

1. Open an image in Photoshop. You can use the Flower file provided in the Chapter 9 folder of this book's CD-ROM.

2. Create a selection on screen (using any of Photoshop's selection tools, such as the Lasso tool).

3. Choose Select > Save Selection. In the New Channel dialog box, you can provide a name for the channel.

If you wish to edit the channel, select it in the Channels palette. To view both your image and the alpha channel on screen, and edit the channel in a red overlay, make sure the channel is selected in the Channels palette, and then click on the eye icon next to the RGB channel in the Channels palette. Painting with black, white, and shades of gray edit the mask, not your image.

Optimizing GIF and PNG 8 Images

The optimization settings for GIF and PNG 8 are nearly identical. Settings for both formats allow you to reduce the number of colors in your image. However GIF, unlike PNG, also allows you to compress the file size by using a lossy file compression. This means that pixels are subtracted from the image during the compression process, which often results in a quality loss in the image. Small reductions usually do not greatly affect the image quality.

 Certain optimization options change the colors in your image. Both Photoshop and ImageReady let you lock your colors so that they do not shift during optimization.

When you optimize GIF and PNG 8 files, you are presented with a number of choices for the color-reduction algorithm, dithering technique, and transparency. We'll look at the options available for these optimizations and then go through the steps for optimization.

Selecting a Color-Reduction Algorithm

The color-reduction algorithm determines how individual colors actually appear in the final optimized images. The pop-up menu (under the file type setting) includes the following color choices:

- **Perceptual** Attempts to choose colors to which human vision is most sensitive.
- **Selective** Usually produces good results because it employs the concepts used to create the perceptual table, but it also tries to maintain Web colors and areas of color similarity.
- **Adaptive** Creates a color table from the most common colors in your image.
- **Web** Uses the standard Web-safe palette. This table is composed of 216 colors using different combinations of six evenly spaced color values. The color values of the six colors are 0, 51, 102, 153, 204, and 255. Using the palette ensures that a browser will not dither colors when displaying images.

Caution *Using the Web palette can result in larger file sizes than needed.*

- **Custom** Prevents the color palette from changing when the image is edited. Use Custom when you do not want to change the palette of an image that includes a perceptual, selective, or adaptive color palette.

- **Black & White** Converts images to black and white.

- **Grayscale** Converts to image with up to 256 levels of gray.

- **Mac OS** Uses the standard 256-color Mac palette.

- **Windows** Uses the standard 256-color Windows palette.

Selecting a Dithering Technique

Dithering is a digital technique that combines colored pixels in such a way that the eye is fooled into thinking that more colors exist in an image than actually do. The dither pop-up menu (under the color-reduction setting) includes the following options:

- **No Dither** No dither is applied.

- **Pattern** Uses square patterns resembling halftones to mimic colors that don't exist in the chosen color table.

- **Diffusion** Applies a random pattern to simulate colors. This usually provides the best results. The technique is called *diffusion* because the colors are "diffused" over neighboring pixels.

- **Noise** Like Diffusion, Noise applies a random pattern. The colors are not diffused, however, so results usually aren't as good as they are with Diffusion.

 The dither pop-up menu controls the dithering that appears in ImageReady and Photoshop (referred to as application dither). Don't confuse this with browser dither. Browsers dither on 8-bit computer systems (256 colors) when the browser attempts to display colors that are not part of its color palette. You can prevent browser dither by choosing only Web-safe colors. For more information, see the "Fine-Tuning Web Image Quality" section later in this chapter.

Setting Transparency

You can choose a transparency option by selecting the Transparency checkbox or by using the Matte pop-up menu. If you select the Transparency checkbox, Photoshop and ImageReady will not make semi-transparent pixels transparent. (Semi-transparent pixels allow soft image edges.) The Transparency option affects only image areas that are 100 percent transparent.

If you wish to fill transparent and semi-transparent pixels with a particular color, do not select Transparency. Choose a matte color by clicking in the Matte pop-up menu. Choose Black or White to fill transparent areas with black or white, or choose Other to select a color from the Color Picker. If you wish to use a color in the image as the matte color, click on the image with the Eyedropper tool, and then choose Eyedropper in the Matte pop-up menu.

If you wish to make 100 percent transparent pixels transparent and semi-transparent pixels match a background Web color, choose the Transparency option and the Matte option. This often produces the smoothest results for images whose original background is different from the background Web page color. See the "Handling Web Transparency" section later in this chapter for more information about using the Transparency and Matte settings.

Setting Optimizations for GIF and PNG 8 Images

Here are the steps for optimizing GIF or PNG images using the Save for Web dialog box:

1. Choose GIF or PNG in the file format pop-up menu, at the top-left side of the Settings section.

2. If desired, choose a preset setting in the Settings pop-up menu.

3. To compress the image by reducing pixels, enter a value in the Lossy field or click the arrow and drag the slider. Adobe suggests that values of between 5 and 10 can usually be applied without visually harming the image.

Note   *If your image contains an alpha channel, the mask icons next to the Lossy, color reduction algorithm, and color field settings appear darkened. Using this feature to create weighted optimization is explained in the next section.*

4. Select a Color Reduction algorithm option (see the "Selecting a Color-Reduction Algorithm" section). After you make a color table choice, the change is displayed in the Color Table area of Photoshop's Save for Web dialog box. In ImageReady, the color table is displayed in the Color Table palette.

5. Choose the number of colors in your image. Enter a value in the Colors field, or click on the up or down arrow to change colors. Images with fewer colors are smaller and download faster. After you make a change, the Color Table area changes.

Note   *Your image may actually contain fewer colors than the numbers specified in the Colors field.*

6. If you wish to have a low-resolution version of your image gradually displayed on screen while the image is downloading, choose Interlaced. If you are using ImageReady, access the Interlaced option by clicking on the up or down arrow next to the word "Optimize" in the Optimize palette. Alternatively, select Show Options from the Optimize palette's menu.

7. Choose a Dither option (see the "Selecting a Dithering Technique" section).

8. Choose the amount of dither by entering a percentage into the Dither field or by dragging the slider.

Note   *If no dither is selected, you cannot change the Dither value. If your image contains an alpha channel and you choose Diffusion, you can choose the Dither value using weighted optimization. This feature is described in the next section.*

9. Choose a transparency option from the Transparency checkbox or the Matte pop-up menu (see the "Setting Transparency" section).

10. To snap or shift colors to Web-safe colors, enter a number or click and drag on the Web Snap slider. Higher percentages result in more colors shifting to Web-safe colors, thereby reducing browser dithering.

Photoshop's GIF and JPEG options allow weighted optimization based on alpha channels in an image. Weighted optimization is available for color reduction, lossiness, and dithering settings, as explained in the next sections.

Using Alpha Channels with Color Reduction

To change color-reduction settings using an alpha channel, follow these steps:

1. In the Color Reduction Algorithm (Color Palette) pop-up menu, choose a setting.

2. In the Colors field, choose the number of colors that you wish to have in your image.

3. Click on the mask button (shown in Figure 9-5) to the right of the Color Reduction Algorithm pop-up menu.

4. In the Modify Color Reduction dialog box, click on the Channel pop-up menu and choose the channel that you wish to use to control optimization.

5. If the Preview checkbox is selected in the Modify Color Reduction dialog box, you'll see the effects of the color reduction previewed on your screen.

6. Click OK to close the dialog box.

Using Alpha Channels with Lossiness or Dither Settings

If you are using an alpha channel to change lossiness or dither settings, follow these steps:

1. Click on the mask button to the right of the Lossy or Dither field.

2. In the Modify Lossiness Setting dialog box or Modify Dither Setting dialog box, choose an alpha channel from the Channel pop-up menu.

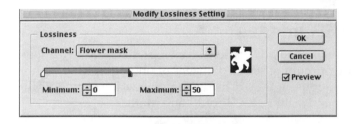

3. Click and drag on the maximum and minimum sliders to set the minimum and maximum quality. For lossiness, the left slider controls high quality, and the right slider controls lower quality. For dithering, the left slider provides less dithering, and the right slider provides more. For both options, white and lighter areas receive maximum values, and black and darker areas receive minimum. If the Preview checkbox is selected, the effect is previewed as you click and drag on the slider.

4. Click on OK to choose the settings and execute the changes.

Optimizing PNG 24 Images

When you're working with PNG 24 images, Photoshop and ImageReady provide three options: Interlaced, Transparency, and Matte.

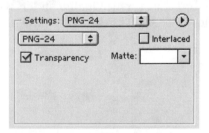

These options work similarly to their corresponding PNG 8 and GIF 8 settings. There is no color table affiliated with this file format, because PNG 24 supports millions of colors. PNG 24 can produce high-quality images, particularly those that include transparent areas. If you select the Transparency option and select None from the Matte pop-up menu, your images will probably not appear jagged, since PNG supports "alpha transparency," which allows up to 256 levels of transparent pixels.

Optimizing JPEG Images

JPEG optimization is generally chosen for images that need to display more than 256 colors. If you are outputting scanned images of photographs or high-quality artwork, you should consider using JPEG. The JPEG optimization settings include Quality, Optimized, Progressive, Blur, ICC Profile, and Matte.

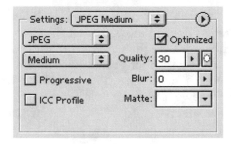

Setting Optimizations for JPEG Images

Choose a setting from the Quality pop-up menu. The choices include Low, Medium, High, or Maximum. As you can probably guess, higher-quality images are larger in file size and thus download slower. To further fine-tune quality, you can enter a percentage in the Quality field or click and drag on the Quality slider, which appears after you click on the right arrow below the Quality field. Pop-up menu equivalents are as follows:

- Low: 10%
- Medium: 30%
- High: 60%
- Maximum: 80%

If your image includes an alpha channel, you can choose Quality based on gray levels in the alpha channel mask, as described in the next section.

For the best file optimization, select the Optimized checkbox. Note, however, that older browsers do not support JPEG optimization.

If you select the Progressive option, you can choose to have the JPEG image gradually appear on screen. Essentially, a low-resolution image appears while the high-resolution image downloads. Once again, note that not all browsers support this feature.

Choose a Blur setting, if desired. This option reduces file size and applies a blur to the image, similar to the Gaussian blur available in Photoshop or ImageReady. Blurring may eliminate artifacts (odd-colored pixels that sometimes appear as random specks on an image); however, as you might expect, blurring softens images and makes them less sharp. Adobe recommends a Blur setting between 0.1 and 0.5.

Select whether to use the image's ICC Profile. Newer browsers may be able to color-correct images using a Photoshop image's ICC profile (the image must be created in Photoshop). If you don't see this feature in ImageReady, expand the palette by clicking on the up or down arrow to the left of the word "Optimize" in the Optimize palette; alternatively, choose Show Options from the Optimize palette's menu.

Use the Matte pop-up menu to set a matte color for transparent image areas. This option is typically used to set transparent image areas to the background color of your Web page. If an image contains transparent areas, you can set transparent areas to specific colors by choosing from the Matte pop-up menu. In the Matte pop-up menu, select Black or White to fill transparent areas with black or white. Choose Other to select a color from the Color Picker. If you wish to use a color in the image as the matte color, click on the image with the Eyedropper tool, and then choose Eyedropper in the Matte pop-up menu. See the "Handling Web Transparency" section later in this chapter for more information about using the Transparency and Matte settings.

Using Alpha Channels with JPEG Optimization

Photoshop's JPEG optimization settings allow weighted optimization based on alpha channels in an image. If your image includes an alpha channel and you wish to pick quality based on the gray levels in the alpha channel mask, follow these steps:

1. Click on the mask icon to the right of the Quality field. This opens the Modify Quality dialog box.

2. In the Modify Quality dialog box, click on the Channel pop-up menu and choose the channel that you wish to use to control optimization.

3. Click and drag on the maximum and minimum sliders to set the minimum and maximum quality percentage. White and lighter areas receive high optimization values, and black and darker areas receive lower optimization settings. If the Preview checkbox is selected, the effect is previewed as you click and drag on the slider controls.

4. Click on OK to close the dialog box and apply the optimization.

Fine-Tuning Web Image Quality

As you begin to optimize images and output them to the Web, you may find that the optimization process often results in images that download quickly but are poor in quality. Or you might also find that when you finally view your images on the Web, they're ringed by halos or appear very jagged. To help you prevent these problems, Photoshop and ImageReady provide a variety of features that help you better evaluate and control Web images. Both programs allow you to preview your images in Web browsers and lock in colors so they won't change when reducing or changing color palettes. Using either Photoshop or ImageReady, you can control different transparency options and choose which image colors to shift to the nearest Web-safe color. These features are covered in the following sections.

Previewing Browser Dither

When a browser used on an 8-bit computer system (256 colors) displays a GIF or PNG 8 image that does not use Web-safe colors, the browser dithers the colors to try to simulate missing colors. Browser dither is different from application dither, which is the dither you see when using Photoshop or ImageReady's dither controls. It's important to understand that application dither does not necessarily show you how the image will look in a browser.

Fortunately, you can open your browser and preview images directly from Photoshop or ImageReady. Photoshop provides two options for previewing browser dither: in the Save for Web dialog box or directly in your browser.

Previewing Browser Dither in Photoshop

To preview browser dither directly in the Save for Web dialog box, simply click on the optimized image that you wish to preview and then choose Browser Dither from the document panel pop-up menu. (This menu was discussed in the "Reviewing Save for Web Dialog Box Features" section earlier in this chapter.)

If you wish to preview your image directly in a Web browser such as Netscape Communicator or Microsoft Internet Explorer, click on the Browser pop-up menu in the lower-right corner of your screen. Choose your browser in the menu (or choose Other, navigate to your browser, and select it). After you pick your browser, your image will open in the browser (Photoshop still remains open) with the HTML code already written, as shown in Figure 9-7.

 You can also preview your image in a browser by clicking on the browser's icon in the bottom-right corner of the Save for Web dialog box.

Previewing Browser Dither in ImageReady

To preview browser dither in ImageReady, select the optimized image on screen, and then choose View > Preview > Browser Dither. This places a checkmark next to the Browser Dither command. To end browser dithering, select View > Preview > Browser Dither to remove the checkmark.

You can also instruct ImageReady to open the on-screen image in a browser by choosing File > Preview In. When the pop-up menu appears, click on the name of your browser.

Shifting to Web-Safe Colors

The effects of browser dither can ruin an otherwise satisfactory Web image. You can eliminate the effects of browser dither in GIF and PNG 8 images by changing your

IMAGE EDITING FUNDAMENTALS

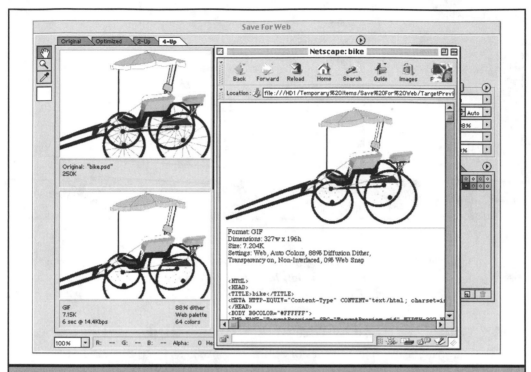

Figure 9-7.   *A Photoshop image previewed in a Web browser*

image's color table to a Web-safe palette, or you can selectively shift specific colors to Web-safe colors.

The steps for shifting a specific color to its closest Web color are quite easy. In Photoshop, you start by selecting the Eyedropper tool in the Save for Web dialog box. In ImageReady, you edit the image's color table. The Color Table palette in ImageReady is shown in Figure 9-8.

The Color Table palette's pop-up menu includes an option that allows you to select all non-Web-safe colors automatically in an image. After you select them, you can shift them to Web-safe colors.

To shift colors to Web-safe colors selectively, select the Eyedropper tool. Click in the image area that contains the color that the browser dithers, and then click on the Web Shift icon. Alternatively, you can select a color in the color table, and then click on the Web Shift icon. You can also choose Web Shift/Unshift Selected Colors in the Color Table palette's pop-up menu. After the color is shifted, a tiny box appears in the color table location.

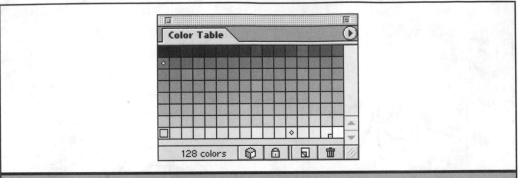

Figure 9-8. *ImageReady's Color Table can be used to shift, lock, and add colors*

 If you wish to shift a Web-safe color back to its original color, click on the color in the color table and click on the Web Shift Icon. Alternatively, you can select the color and then choose Web Shift/Unshift Selected Colors in the Color Table palette's pop-up menu.

Locking and Editing Colors in a Color Table

One of the most common techniques of optimizing images is to reduce the number of colors in an image. Once you convert an image to GIF or PNG 8, both ImageReady and Photoshop display the image's color table on screen. The color table is essentially all the colors used in the image. If you wish to reduce the number of colors in an image, you may find that Photoshop removes colors that are an integral part of the image. If this happens, you can return to the original or a less-optimized version of the GIF or PNG 8 image and lock colors that you don't want to shift.

To lock a color, click on it in the color table and then click on the lock icon. Alternatively, you can click on a color in your image with the Eyedropper tool to select the color in the color table and then click on the lock icon. Optimize the image once again and reduce the colors. The color that you locked remains in the image.

Here are a few tips for working with color tables:

■ To select a range of colors in a color table, start by clicking on the first color that you wish to select. Press SHIFT and click on the last color you wish to select.

■ To group similar colors together, choose Sort by Hue in the Color Table palette's pop-up menu.

■ To change a color in the color table, double-click on it. This opens the Color Picker, where you can choose another color. After you change colors, the image is updated to reflect the new color.

- To change a group of colors in the color table, click on the first color that you wish to select. Then move the mouse pointer over the last color that you wish to select. Press and hold SHIFT while you click on the last color that you wish to select.

- To add a color to the color table, deselect all colors in the color table by clicking in the gray area below all the colors in the table. Next select the original image. (To add a color that isn't in the original image, click on the color swatch in Photoshop's Save for Web dialog box, which opens the Color Picker dialog box.) Click on a color with the Eyedropper tool. Finally, choose a new color from the Color Table pop-up menu. Alternatively, you can click on the New Color button in the Color Table palette

- If you would like to select colors in a color table that correspond to different image areas, select the image area with any selection tool. In the Color Table palette's menu, choose Select All from Selection. After you choose this command, the colors corresponding to the selected colors in the image are selected in the color table.

Handling Web Transparency

Often, when you place images on a Web page, you'll want the background color of the page to appear as if the image were cut out and pasted directly on the Web page. You may also want to create a logo of text in Photoshop and have the background color of the Web page appear through the letters. To create these effects, you need to place your text or image on a transparent layer. You can also use Photoshop's masking and eraser tools to create transparency effects.

Once the background is transparent, you can set the transparency options when you optimize your image. If you know the exact color of the Web page, you can fill the transparent areas in Photoshop with that color using Photoshop's and ImageReady's Matte options. If you wish for any background to be seen through transparent areas, you can choose the Transparency option. The following sections describe techniques for using the Transparency and Matte options to reduce halos and jagged edges.

Creating Transparency Effects in GIF and PNG 8 Images

If you don't know the background color of your Web page, you can create transparency effects by clicking on the Transparency option in the Save for Web dialog box or Optimize palette. Choosing Transparency affects all pixels that are 100 percent transparent. It does not affect semi-transparent pixels, which help smooth image edges. Thus, the Transparency option is best used for images with sharp edges. If you choose this option for Photoshop text or images with smooth edges, you're likely to end up with an image with jagged edges.

If you wish to fill all transparent and semi-transparent pixels with the background color of your Web page, you can use the Matte option for your GIF, PNG 8, PNG 24, or JPEG images. In fact, using a matte color is the only way to simulate transparency in JPEG images, since the file format doesn't allow transparency. See the sections about setting optimizations for each file type for more information about the Matte option.

Smoothing Jagged Edges in GIF and PNG 8 Images

To prevent jagged edges in PNG and GIF images, use a combination of the Transparency and Matte options. Selecting the Transparency checkbox makes all 100 percent transparent pixels transparent on your Web page, but it does not affect pixels that are semi-transparent. If you know the color of your Web page background, set the Matte color to the Web page color. Matting changes the semi-transparent pixels to the color of your Web page. The combination of Transparency and Matte removes halos and jagged edges from images. Figure 9-9 compares a GIF image without matting to the same image with matting. As you can see, the image that is not matted is more jagged, and parts of the thin wheel spokes have completely disappeared.

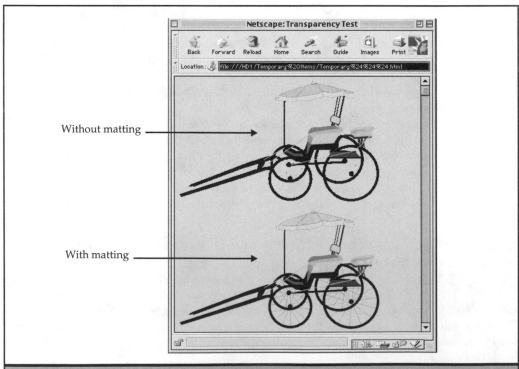

Figure 9-9. *Photoshop's Matte option can produce a smoother image that shows finer detail*

PNG 24 supports 256 levels of transparency. If you are using PNG 24, select the Transparency checkbox and leave the Matte option set to None. For transparency to work, the browser must support PNG 24 format images.

Saving Your Optimized Images

Once you've finished optimizing your image, your next step is to save it in GIF, PNG, or JPEG format. The options for saving are different in Photoshop and ImageReady.

Saving Optimized Images in Photoshop

When you are finished optimizing an image in Photoshop, you can save it in GIF, PNG, or JPEG format by simply clicking on the OK button in the Save for Web dialog box. In the Save Optimized dialog box that appears, name your image. If you want Photoshop to generate a separate text file with HTML code that can be used to load your image on a page, select the HTML and Image option in the Format pop-up menu (the Save As type pop-up menu in Windows systems). The HTML code provides instructions for the browser to load the file onto a Web page. To save the image without the HTML code, choose Images Only in the pop-up menu.

Saving Optimized Images in ImageReady

After you've optimized your image using ImageReady's Optimize palette, save it by choosing File > Save Optimized or File > Save Optimized As. If you wish ImageReady to generate a separate text file with HTML code that can be used to load your image on a page, select the HTML and Image option in the Format pop-up menu (the Save As Type pop-up menu in Windows systems). To save the image without the HTML code, choose Images Only in the pop-up menu.

 The output setting defaults in both Photoshop and ImageReady primarily relate to slices and rollovers. See Chapter 10 for details on the output settings.

Using the DitherBox Filter to Create Custom Dither Patterns

If you don't like the dither patterns created by Adobe's dithering options or you would like to create your own customized artistic dithers, you can use the DitherBox filter. DitherBox not only allows you to create a custom dither pattern, but it also applies that pattern to a selected area of your image.

When creating dithers with the DitherBox filter, you can start by choosing a color from your image, or you can choose a color later from the Color Picker. To create the dither pattern, you decide how many colors you want in your pattern and click in a color table to choose the colors.

Here are the steps for creating your own custom dither pattern. In this example, we start with a color taken from an image.

1. Open an image that contains an area that you wish to dither.

2. Pick a starting color by clicking on the area you wish to dither with the Eyedropper tool. The color you click on will become your new foreground color.

3. Select the area that you wish to fill with the dither pattern. Use one of Photoshop's selection tools to select this area. (For instance, if you are dithering a multimedia button, you can select that button.)

4. Select Filter > Other > DitherBox to open the DitherBox dialog box.

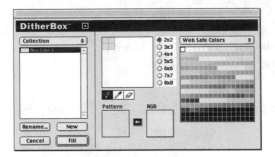

5. Here you'll see the RGB color swatch filled with the foreground color. If you wish to change this color, click on the swatch. This opens the Color Picker. In the Color Picker, choose a color.

6. Choose a color palette from the pop-up menu above the color table—most likely you'll choose Web-Safe Colors. However, if you are using the DitherBox filter for multimedia purposes, you may wish to choose the Load Color Table option (in the pop-up menu), which allows you to load another color table.

7. Pick a matrix size for the dither pattern by clicking in the list of numbers. 2×2 indicates 2 pixels by 2 pixels (a total of 4 colors), 8×8 indicates 8 pixels by 8 pixels (64 colors), and so on.

8. Add colors to the pattern by selecting a color in the color palette. Activate the DitherBox's Pencil tool and click on one of the colors in the color table. To add this color to the dither pattern, click on one of the small matrix squares. After you click, the color appears in the square. As you add colors, the Pattern swatch previews your dither pattern.

9. If you want to delete a color from the pattern matrix area, select the DitherBox's Eraser tool, and then click on the color in the pattern matrix area at the top middle of the dialog box.

10. Give your pattern a name by clicking on the Rename button and then entering a name. The name is added to the currently selected collection. (Creating your own collection is described in the next section.)

11. When you've completed the work on the pattern, click on the Fill button to fill the selected area with the pattern.

Using Dither Collections

The DitherBox filter allows you to collect your custom dither patterns into groups called *collections*. Collections can be handy because they allow you to find and organize your patterns quickly and efficiently.

To create a new collection, before creating your pattern, click on New in the Collection pop-up menu. Provide a name for your collection by entering it into the Name field. Each pattern you create is added to the collection. Click on the New button to add patterns to the currently selected collection.

After you place patterns into a collection, you can easily apply the pattern. Just open the DitherBox dialog box, select your collection from the Collection pop-up menu, select the dither pattern from the Collection list, and click on the Fill button.

To rename a collection, select Rename Collection from the Collection pop-up menu.

 You can copy and paste patterns from one collection to another using Photoshop's and ImageReady's standard Edit > Copy and Edit > Paste commands.

Creating a Master Palette in ImageReady

Many of ImageReady's Web color table commands provide excellent results when you're preparing images for multimedia. Multimedia producers often must keep file sizes small and work with systems that display 256 or fewer colors. When assembling graphics for a multimedia page, all of the images must use the same color palette to prevent dithering. ImageReady features a *master palette* option (sometimes called a *superpalette*) that combines the colors of many images into one palette.

Here are the steps for creating a master palette:

1. You may need to clear the master palette to ensure that images that were previously displayed will not contribute to the master palette. Start by choosing Image > Master Palette > Clear Master Palette. (This command may be grayed out if you haven't yet created a master palette.)

2. Open an image that contains colors that you wish to add to your master palette.

3. Choose Image > Master Palette > Add to Master Palette.

4. Open other images that you wish to add to the master palette. After you open the images, choose Image > Master Palette > Add to Master Palette.

5. At this point, you can choose to change the palette or reduce the number of colors using the Optimize palette.

6. Create the final master by choosing Image > Master Palette > Build Master Palette.

7. Save the master palette by choosing Image > Master Palette > Save Master Palette. To make the master palette available with the default color tables, save the master palette in the Optimized Color folder inside the Adobe Photoshop Presets folder.

If you've saved your master palette in the Optimized Color folder you can access the palette from ImageReady's Color palette menu. In Photoshop, the palette appears in the Save for Web dialog box in the Color Table panel. Multimedia producers may also wish to access the color when converting to Indexed Color in Photoshop. Choose Image > Mode > Indexed Color. In the Palette pop-up menu, choose Custom, and click the Load button. Navigate to your custom table, and then click on the Load button in the Open dialog box.

The Complete Reference

Photoshop 6

Chapter 10

Creating Web Effects with Slices, Animation, and Rollovers

Not too long ago, having a Web site meant that you or your company were on the cutting edge of technology. In today's world, where the corner dry cleaner, pizzeria, and even newborn babies have their own home pages, it's important to distinguish your own site from the thousands of new sites springing up every day. That might mean adding a touch of sparkle to your site with a bit of flashing animation, including some sophisticated interactivity with rollovers (graphics or words that change on screen when the mouse rolls over them), or using tabs with links created from image maps or image slices.

Fortunately, ImageReady and Photoshop can help you quickly and easily enhance your Web site. Using ImageReady and/or Photoshop, you can quickly turn an image with multiple layers into an animated GIF movie. You can also use ImageReady to create image slices to enhance interactivity with rollover effects and image maps. This chapter will show you how to create Web effects, ranging from simple background images to sophisticated enhancements.

Creating Background Images for Web Pages

Displaying a pattern or background image for a Web page can make it more attractive and add an interesting backdrop to your work. To place graphics and text over your background and to ensure fast download times, the best technique is to create one small graphic tile and have ImageReady turn it into a background image for the page. For instance, here is a small textured graphic that we used for the background of one of our Web pages:

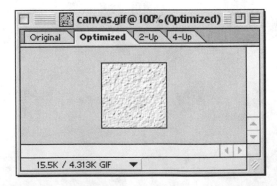

Figure 10-1 shows the Web page with the background graphic repeated to fill the entire page. The small file helped ensure that the page downloaded quickly.

If you wish to create a background pattern for a Web page, you can prepare the graphic in either Photoshop or ImageReady. However, only ImageReady includes a Background command that creates an HTML file specifically for your graphic.

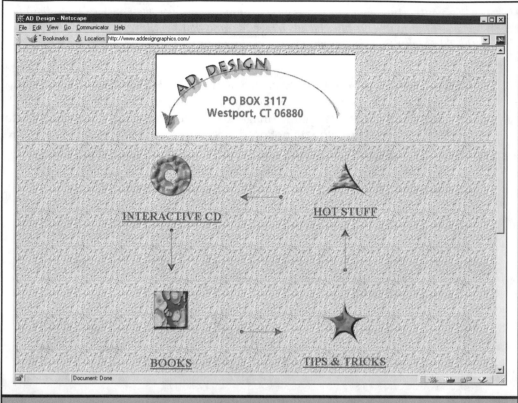

Figure 10-1.   *Web page with a graphic tiled as a background image*

 You don't need an Internet connection to try out the examples in this chapter. ImageReady's File > Preview In command allows you to preview effects in a Web browser, even if you are not connected to the Web.

Using ImageReady's Background Command

Here are the steps for creating a background graphic in ImageReady:

1. Load a small image or create a pattern in ImageReady that you wish to use as the background for your Web page. If you don't have a graphic to use, load the Canvas or Twirl files from the Chapter 10 folder of the CD-ROM that accompanies this book.

Before outputting your graphic as a background image, you may wish to apply the Tile Maker filter to it. This filter blends image edges so that the tiles appear smoother. Using the Tile Maker filter is described in the next section.

2. Choose File > Output Settings > Background. In the HTML Background dialog box, set the View As option to Background. When you choose the Background option instead of the File option, ImageReady uses the image on your screen for the background. Thus, you do not need to specify a file name in the dialog box.

3. If you wish to have a color appear through transparent areas of your image, or if you would like a color to appear while your Web page background is downloaded, choose a color from the Color pop-up menu.

4. Save the file by choosing File > Optimized As. In the Save As pop-up menu, choose the HTML & Images option.

5. Click on OK. ImageReady saves the image and creates an HTML file that instructs a Web browser to load the file as a background file. (ImageReady gives the HTML file the same name as your image, but with an .html file extension.)

6. Preview the file in your Web browser by choosing File > Preview In. Then choose your Browser in the submenu. You'll see your image tiled as a Web background page, as in Figure 10-2. The HTML code that creates the background looks something like this:

```
<BODY BGCOLOR=#FFFFFF BACKGROUND="twirl.gif">
```

 To create an interesting effect, try creating a small animated GIF file and using it as a Web page background image. The entire page will come alive. See the "Creating Animated GIF Files" section later in this chapter for details.

Using ImageReady's Tile Maker Filter

The Tile Maker filter can smooth the image edges of a background graphic to help blend it into a Web page. If you don't use the Tile Maker filter, you may find that distinct border edges appear around each tile when it appears in a browser.

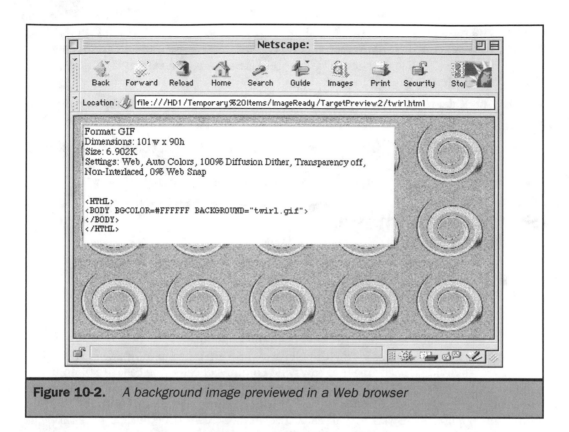

Figure 10-2. *A background image previewed in a Web browser*

To use Tile Maker, first load an image in ImageReady. If you wish to have a portion of the image tiled, select this area with the Rectangular Marquee tool. Open the Tile Maker dialog box by choosing Filter > Other > Tile Maker.

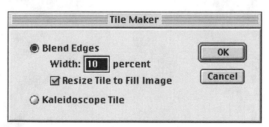

Here are descriptions of the options available:

- The Blend Edges option creates a blend between tiles. In the Width box, enter a value of up to 20 percent to control the edge blur; the greater the percentage, the greater the blur will be between image edges.

- The Resize Tile to Fill Image option blurs and resizes your image to fill the selected area. If you do not select this option, the filter creates a tile smaller than the original selection. The selection is bordered by a transparent area that is determined by the blend percentage.

- The Kaleidoscope Tile option creates an abstract kaleidoscope effect by flipping and duplicating the selection horizontally and vertically.

After you click on OK, the Tile Maker filter alters your image. If you created a selection on the screen before running the filter, you'll probably want to crop the image using the selection as the image border. To crop the selection, choose Image > Crop.

Slicing Web Images

Photoshop and ImageReady's Slice tool allows you to carve an image into individual rectangular pieces. Once an image is sliced, the pieces can be used as rollover areas or as different optimized sections of a Web page. For instance, if you wish to create a series of tabs at the top of your Web page, you can create slices around the tabs and then add rollover effects or links when the user clicks on the tab. Slicing also allows you to optimize different slices of an image with different settings. You can even create one slice as a GIF and another as a JPEG from the same image.

To understand how slices work, it's helpful to have an understanding of HTML tables. HTML tables divide a page area into rows and columns of cells. The cells are often used to place data in columns or create forms in a column. When you create image slices and save the file, ImageReady divides the image into multiple files. It also outputs HTML code, which tells the browser to load each slice on the screen. Together, the slices appear as if they are one image. This tab layout shows the different image slices on screen:

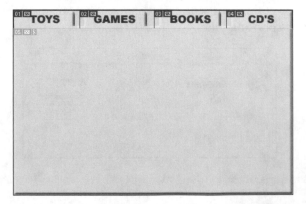

When we saved the file in ImageReady, it created five different images from the slices. By dividing the image into slices, we could easily create rollovers for the tabs, with the added benefit of faster downloading times. The HTML code generated by ImageReady is shown in Figure 10-3.

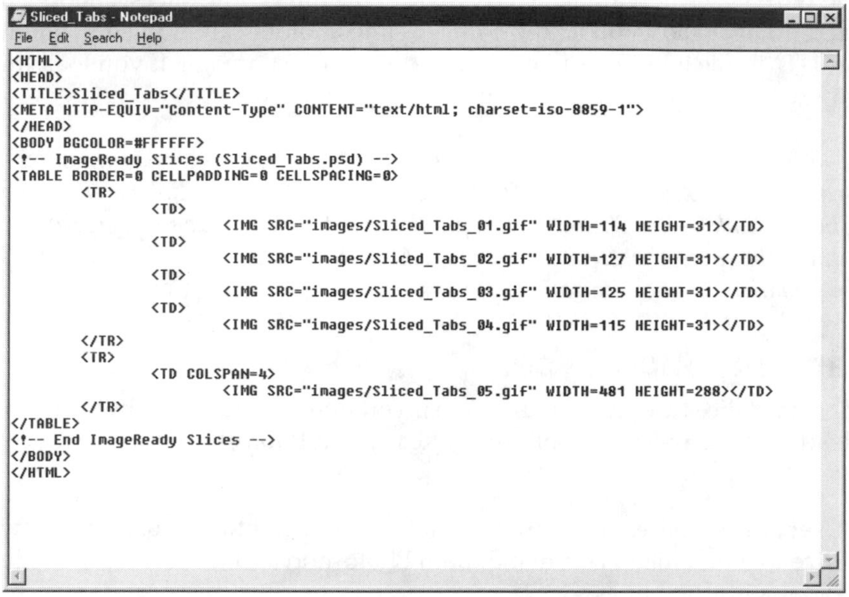

Figure 10-3. *HTML code for slices generated by ImageReady*

IMAGE EDITING
FUNDAMENTALS

Getting a Quick Start with Slices

The best way to get started using slices is to practice slicing an image. Then you can learn all of the details about creating, selecting, and managing slices in the following sections.

In this example, you will create two slices and then optimize each one with different settings:

1. In ImageReady, open one of the Chapter 10 images from the CD-ROM.

2. Select the Slice tool in ImageReady's Toolbox. Once you select the Slice tool, you'll notice a colored outline around the image and the number 01. This is the image's default slice.

3. Divide this slice into two pieces by moving the Slice tool to the left-middle area of the screen and clicking and dragging down diagonally to the bottom-right area. A new slice is created.

4. Select the Slice Select tool in ImageReady's Toolbox and click on one of your slices.

5. Open the Optimize palette by choosing Window > Show Optimize. Set this slice to the JPEG file format.

6. With the Slice Select tool, select the other slice. Set this slice to be a GIF slice in the Optimize palette.

If you wish to see how ImageReady divides the image into slices, choose File > Save Optimized. ImageReady will load the images into a folder called Images, and it will create an HTML file with the same name as your original image. If you load this into your browser, you'll see that the two images appear as one.

 You can optimize a group of slices by first selecting and then linking the slices. To select multiple slices, press SHIFT and click the different slices. To link the slices, choose Slices > Link Slices. Then use the Optimize palette to optimize the image areas. To unlink the slices, choose Slices > Unlink All or Unlink Set. See Chapter 9 for more information about optimization.

Understanding Slice Types

You'll find that slices are easier to manage if you understand how Photoshop and ImageReady categorize slices. Both ImageReady and Photoshop provide four types of slices:

- **User slices**   Slices that you, the Photoshop/ImageReady user, create with the Slice tool or a menu command. Both Photoshop and ImageReady border user slices with solid lines.

- **Auto slices**   Slices created by Photoshop/ImageReady from the remaining portion of the image when you create a user slice in an image. For example, if you create one slice in the middle of a screen, Photoshop/ImageReady divides the rest of the area into sliced rectangles as well. Auto slices are automatically numbered and are bordered by dotted lines. As you move or edit a user slice, Photoshop/ImageReady automatically adjusts the auto slices.

- **Layer-based slices**   Slices created from the entire nontransparent image areas of layers. Layer-based slices are an efficient way to create one slice out of text or shapes (which are automatically created in new layers).

- **Subslices**   Slices that are automatically created when you overlap slices, and automatically edited when you change the overlapping (stacking order of slices). Subslices cannot be edited by the user.

Figure 10-4 shows an example of a graphic with a user slice in the middle of the screen and the auto slices created by Photoshop.

Note   *By default, each ImageReady document is created as one auto slice.*

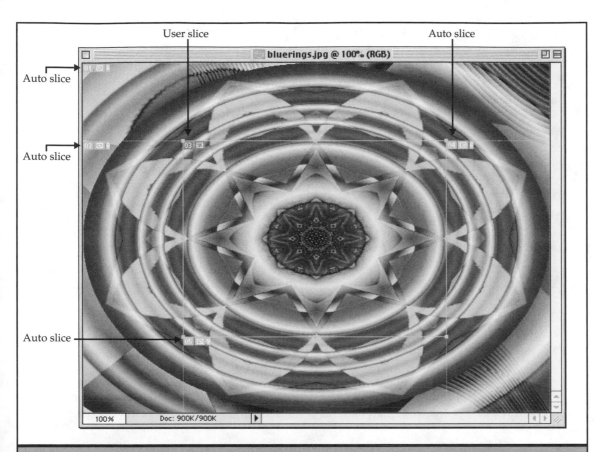

Figure 10-4.   *User slice bordered by auto slices*

Creating Slices

Photoshop allows you to create slices by clicking and dragging with its Slice tool. Photoshop will also create a slice out of the non-transparent areas of a layer. ImageReady provides four different methods for slicing images. As in Photoshop, you can create slices using ImageReady's Slice tool. You can also create slices out of layers, selections, or guides. Additionally, ImageReady provides more utilities for saving and editing slices than you'll find in Photoshop. For instance, in ImageReady you can divide and combine slices.

Creating Slices with the Slice Tool

One of the easiest ways to create a slice in Photoshop and ImageReady is to use the Slice tool. The Slice tool shares it Toolbox location with the Slice Select Tool. If the Slice tool is not visible, click and hold down the mouse button on the Slice Select tool. In the pop-up menu that appears, select the Slice tool.

After you select the Slice tool, the Slice tool's Options bar provides a variety of options for creating slices.

The Style pop-up menu offers a choice of three slice types:

- The Normal style allows you to click and drag to create a rectangular slice of any size.

- The Constrained Aspect Ratio style locks in a horizontal-to-vertical ratio. For example, if you select this style and enter **1** in both the Width and Height fields of the Options bar, you will create slices that are perfect squares. Enter **4** for Width and **3** for Height to create slices that match the aspect ratio of a video screen.

- The Fixed Size style creates a slice of a specific size. If you select this style, enter the slice dimensions (in pixels) in the Width and Height fields in the Options bar.

The Show Slice Number checkbox controls whether or not slice numbers appear on your screen when you create slides. The Line Color pop-up menu lets you select the color for your slices.

 You can also change the slice color by choosing Edit > Preferences > Slices.

If you choose the Normal or Constrained Aspect Ratio style, click and drag diagonally on your screen to create the slice. If you choose the Fixed Size style, just click on the area to create the slice.

Here are two keyboard tips for creating slices:

- To create a square slice, press SHIFT while clicking and dragging with the Slice tool.

- To create a slice from the center out, press OPTION (*ALT*) and click and drag.

As the slice is created, Photoshop/ImageReady creates rectangular user slices and divides the rest of the screen into auto slices.

Creating Layer-Based Slices

Layer-based slices are slices created from the nontransparent areas of layers. To creating a layer-based slice, simply select the layer that you wish to use as a layer-based slice, or create a shape or text in your document, and then choose Layer > New Layer Based Slice.

Creating Slices from Guides and Selections

ImageReady not only provides a Slice tool for creating slices, but it also provides menu commands for quickly creating several slices in your images:

- To create slices from a guides, create guides in a document, and then choose Slices > Create Slices from Guides. Note that all user slices are deleted as soon as you create guide slices.

- To create slices from a selection, first create a rectangular selection on screen, and then choose Slices > Create Slice from Selection.

Photoshop guides (covered in Chapter 1) automatically appear when a Photoshop file is loaded into ImageReady. You can create guides in ImageReady by dragging from the ruler area or by choosing View > Create Guides.

Selecting Slices with the Slice Select Tool

Once you create a slice, you may wish to change its dimensions or move it. You might also need to select a slice so that you can optimize its contents, animate its contents, or create a rollover from its contents.

You select a slice with the Slice Select tool. The Slice Select tool shares its Toolbox location with the Slice tool. If the Slice Select tool is not visible, click and hold down the mouse button on the Slice tool. In the pop-up menu that appears, select the Slice Select tool.

With the Slice Select tool active, you can work with slices as follows:

- To select a slice, click on it or on one of its edges.

- To move a user slice, click and drag on it with the Slice Select tool. As you move the slice, auto slices are moved or resized accordingly.

- To resize a user slice, click and drag on its edge with the Slice Select tool, or click and drag diagonally on a corner handle. As you resize a slice, the auto slices are automatically resized.

If you select an auto slice, you can convert it to a user slice by clicking on the Promote to User Slice button in the Slice Select Options bar or by choosing Slices > Promote to User-slices in ImageReady.

If you will be creating several slices in a file, you can use ImageReady's Slice Select tool's options to align, distribute, and stack them. In order to use these options, more than one slice must be selected on the screen.

In ImageReady only, to select several slices at one time, click and drag over them with the Slice Select tool. If the slices are not next to one another, you can select more than one slice by pressing SHIFT while clicking in the middle or edge of a slice.

You can line up slices along their top, bottom, left, or right edges, or along their horizontal or vertical centers. To align the selected slices, click on the appropriate button in the Slice Select Options bar.

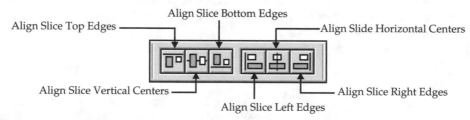

 To snap a slice to a guide or another slice, choose View > Snap to Slices. If you drag within 4 pixels of the guide or slice, the slices snap together.

If you have more than two slices selected, you can use the distribution buttons on the Slice Selection tool's Options bar to distribute the space between the selected slices.

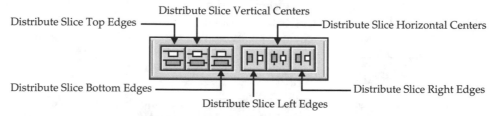

If you have slices stacked on different layers, you can use the stacking order buttons on the Slice Select tool's Options bar. Click on the appropriate button to send a slice to the front or back of the stack, or simply one level forward or one level back.

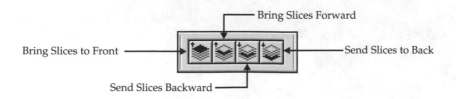

Using ImageReady's Slices Menu

Once you start using slices, you'll want to take advantage of ImageReady's slicing aids. Most of these tools are found in ImageReady's Slices menu.

Here's a review of some handy Slices menu commands:

- To save selected slices, choose Save Slice Selection. In the Save Slice Selection dialog box, name your slice and click on OK. Note that this command saves the selection; it does not save the slices.

- To load a saved slice selection, choose Load Slice Selection. Then choose the saved slice selection form the pop-up menu.

- To delete a saved slice selection, choose Delete Slice Selection. Then choose the saved slice selection from the pop-up menu.

- To duplicate a slice, choose Duplicate Slices.

- To turn a default slice into a user slice, choose Promote to User-slice.

- To automatically divide a slice into multiple slices, choose Divide Slices.

Using ImageReady's Slice Palette

ImageReady's Slice palette provides an efficient means for managing navigational controls for slices. To open the Slice palette, load an image in ImageReady and choose Window > Show Slice. To see the expanded version of the palette, as shown in Figure 10-5, choose Show Options from the Slice palette's menu.

Now use the Slice tool to create some slices on screen. As you create slices, they appear in the Slice palette. To view other slices in the Slice palette, select the Slice Select tool and click on a slice.

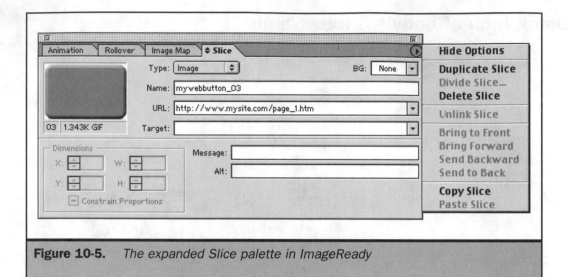

Figure 10-5. *The expanded Slice palette in ImageReady*

Note *If you wish to load an image that already has slices in it, you can use the file you created in the "Getting a Quick Start with Slices" section earlier in the chapter, or load the Tabs file from this book's CD-ROM.*

Apart from previewing the selected slice, the Slice palette allows you to create navigational controls for image areas or to place text in table areas that correspond to image slices, depending on which mode you selected in the Type pop-up menu: Image or No Image mode. Working in these modes is described in the following sections. The following Slice palette settings apply to both modes:

■ The BG pop-up menu allows you to choose a background color for your slices. The background color fills transparent areas in slices.

■ The Message text field allows you to enter text to appear in the status area of the browser. Typically, the URL from the URL field appears in the status area of the browser. If you enter a message here, it replaces the URL in the status area.

■ The Alt text field allows you to enter text to appear in place of slices in browsers that cannot display graphics. You can also use this feature to display a message in browsers that do display graphics. The message will appear on the screen before the image downloads.

Working in Image Mode

When Image is selected in the Slice palette's Type pop-up menu, the Slice palette allows you to enter a custom name for your slice area, a URL, and a Target frame. If you enter a name in the Name field, ImageReady uses that name when it creates the HTML code for the table.

If you wish to create a link for the slice image area, enter the URL in the URL field. When you enter the URL, include the http:// prefix, as in http://www.mysite.com/page_1.htm. After you enter a URL, you can enter a frame name for it.

Frames allow you to load different HTML pages into one page in a browser, which gives the appearance of dividing the Web page into different sections. If you enter a frame name in the Target field, it must match a frame name used in your page's HTML file. If you don't enter a name, you can choose from the following:

- **Blank**   Opens the linked page in a new window, leaving the original open on screen.
- **Self**   Opens the linked page in the same frame as the frameset. It opens the page in the same window if the original page was not in a frameset.
- **Parent**   Opens the linked page in the parent frameset.
- **Top**   Removes all frames. The linked file appears in place of the sliced file.

> **Note**   *Frames require advanced HTML knowledge. Fortunately, HTML layout programs such as Adobe GoLive can automatically create and manage frames.*

Working in No Image Mode

When you select No Image from the Slice palette's Type pop-up menu, a text box appears. Here, you can enter text that will appear in the slice when viewed on a Web page.

If you wish to place a background color on screen for your text (or even without text), click on the BG color swatch to choose a color form the Color Picker, or click on the pop-up menu to choose a color from the current color table.

Saving Sliced Files

When you save a file with slices, Photoshop and ImageReady divide the image into separate files and save them on disk. Along with the files, Photoshop and ImageReady save the HTML code that instructs the browser to reassemble the slices in a Web browser.

By default, ImageReady saves all of the slices on the screen as separate image files in a folder called Images. Also by default, ImageReady names the slices with the document file name, an underscore, then the slice number. If you wish to change the default folder for image, choose File > Output Settings > Saving Files. In the Optimized file section of the Output Settings dialog box, enter the new folder name for your files. If you wish to change the default naming style for slices, choose File > Output Settings > Slices. Use the pop-up menu to change naming options, as shown in Figure 10-6.

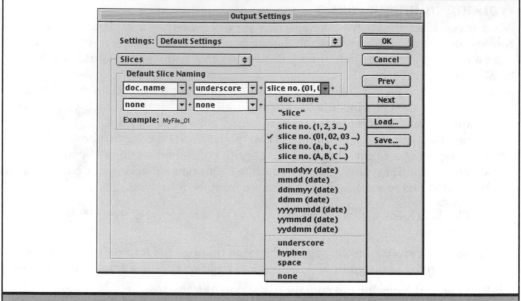

Figure 10-6.   *The Output Settings dialog box with options for slice file names*

Creating Animated GIF Files

Adding animation to a Web page is undoubtedly one of the easiest ways to liven it up and make Web surfers pause for a moment or two to watch the show. Even the simplest animation, such as flashing text or words scrolling across the screen, can add spark to a static page. For instance, in an animated logo we created for one of our Web pages, the words *AD Design* move along a curve, first in one direction and then in the other. In Figure 10-7, you can see how the words gradually change position in ImageReady's Animation palette.

The simplest and most common method of creating Web animation is to use an animated GIF file. Like standard GIF files, animated GIFs are limited to a color palette of 256 or fewer colors, and they can use ImageReady transparent areas.

Using the Animation Palette

Although you can use Photoshop files as the basis for animated GIFs, you need to create the actual animation in ImageReady. ImageReady's Animation palette, shown in Figure 10-8, lets you create, select, rearrange, and even reverse frames. You can specify in the Delay pop-up menu how long each frame is delayed before the animation continues. In the Looping menu, you can set how many times your movie should be

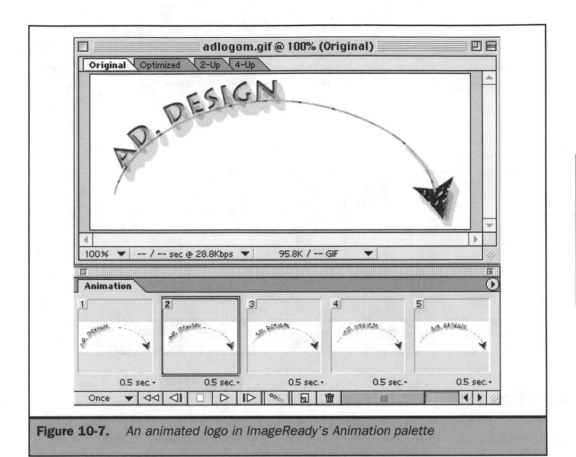

Figure 10-7.   *An animated logo in ImageReady's Animation palette*

repeated. The buttons at the bottom of the screen, which are similar to a VCR's controls, allow you to play, stop, rewind, and fast-forward the animation. To open the Animation palette, select Window > Show Animation.

The palette's pop-up menu allows you to copy and paste frames, reverse the frame sequence, and optimize animation. As you'll see later in this chapter, you can also use the palette menu to turn Photoshop layers into animation palette frames. To quickly create animation, leave the Add Layer to New Frames option selected. This automatically creates a new layer each time you create a new frame in the Animation palette. When you paint in the new layer, the new information appears only in the current new frame.

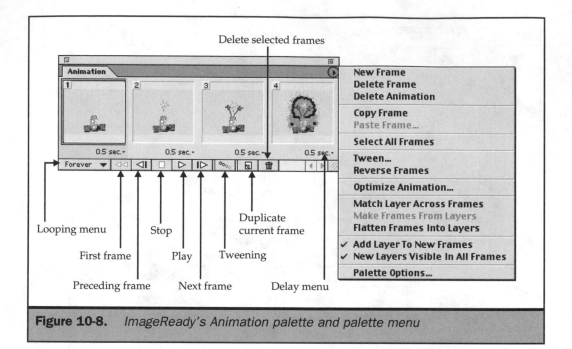

Figure 10-8. *ImageReady's Animation palette and palette menu*

Animating Layers in Frames

Before you begin to use the Animation palette, you need to understand the relationship between the image in the document window and each frame in the palette. In many animation programs, each frame represents a different image, and each image is loaded as you move from frame to frame. In ImageReady, the same image always remains on the screen in the document window; you create animation by displaying and hiding layers.

To understand how layers work with animation, try creating a simple, two-frame animated short:

1. Load an image in ImageReady by choosing File > Open. Notice that the image appears in the Animation palette. If the Animation palette is not open, choose Window > Show Animation.

2. Create a new frame by choosing New Frame from the Animation palette menu or by clicking the New Frame icon in the Animation palette. As soon as you create a new frame, the image on screen is copied into the frame. If the Add Layer to New Frames option is selected in the Animation palette menu (if it isn't selected), a new layer is automatically created in your image. Now when you paint on the screen, you'll be painting on a new layer.

3. Use the Paintbrush or another tool to paint a line in the document window. After you paint the line, it appears in the new frame but not in the first frame. This is because the image information in the first frame is on the first layer.

4. Click on Frame 1. The line you've drawn disappears from the document window.

5. Look at the Layers palette. You'll see that the line has disappeared because the layer is hidden. Each time you create a new frame and a new layer, ImageReady displays the new layer in the new frame but hides the new layer from the previous frames.

This simple technique of showing and hiding layers creates animation. To see the effects, simply click on the Play button in the Animation palette. After you click, you'll see a simple animated effect of your line appearing and disappearing from the screen. Stop the animation by clicking on the Stop button.

A Flower Grows in ImageReady

The best way to fully understand how to create an animated GIF is to jump right in and start animating. The following example leads you step by step through the process of creating a simple animation of a flower growing out of a pot.

1. Create a new file in ImageReady by choosing File > New. In the New dialog box, set the dimensions to be 150 (width) by 250 (height). Set the background to Transparent, and then click on OK.

2. Start by ensuring that you will be painting with Web colors. Click the foreground color swatch in the Toolbox to open the Color Picker. In the Color Picker dialog box, select the Only Web Colors checkbox. Now choose a color for your flower pot. Click on OK to close the Color Picker.

3. Use the Paintbrush tool to paint a flower pot, or use the Rectangle tool to create a shape that looks like a flower pot and fill it with color.

4. If the Add Layer to New Frame option is not selected in the Animation palette, select it. Create a new frame by choosing New Frame in the Animation palette's menu.

5. Once the new layer is automatically created in the Layers palette, pick a new color, and then draw the flower stem.

6. Create a new frame by clicking on the Animation palette's New Frame button.

7. Pick a new color, and then draw a flower petal. Figure 10-9 shows how each layer corresponds to an individual frame. Notice that the base of the flowerpot is in the bottom layer but is visible on the screen, no matter what frame you are on.

8. Continue adding frames (and layers) and drawing your flower.

9. Once you have completed the flower, preview the animation by clicking on the Animation palette's Play button. When the animation runs, you'll see your flower growing on the screen, as ImageReady steps through each frame.

10. After viewing the preview, click on the Animation palette's Stop button to stop the animation.

IMAGE EDITING
FUNDAMENTALS

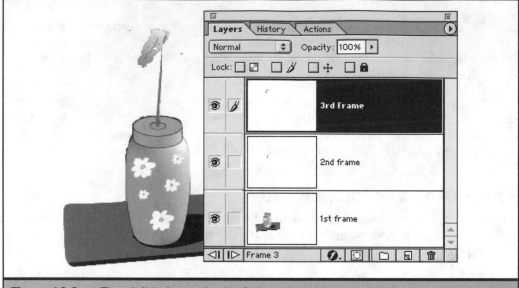

Figure 10-9. *The visible layers in the frame show how the animation progresses*

Before saving the file in GIF format, you may wish to edit a frame, rearrange the frames, or set looping options. These subjects are covered in the next section.

Editing Animation Frames

As you create an animated GIF file, you may wish to make changes and set delays and looping. You can make modifications in the document window and through the Animation palette as follows:

■ To edit a frame, simply click on it; then make editing changes in the document window.

■ To rearrange the sequence of frames, click on a frame and drag it in front of another frame or after another frame in the Animation palette.

■ To set the delay time of an individual frame, click in the Delay pop-up menu under the frame in the Animation palette and choose an interval.

■ To set the delay of all frames, first select all of the frames by choosing Select All Frames in the Animation palette menu. Then choose the frame delay in the Delay pop-up menu.

■ To specify how many times you wish your animation to run on a Web page, choose an interval from the Looping pop-up menu, in the bottom-left corner of the Animation palette. You can choose Once or Forever, or click on Other and specify how many times.

IMAGE EDITING
FUNDAMENTALS

Optimizing Animations

Although you can preview your animation in the Animation palette before saving it in GIF format, you need to save it in GIF format before you can output it to the Web. Your first step is to open the Optimize palette by choosing Window > Show Optimize, and then choose your optimization settings (discussed in Chapter 9). Next, you should take a look at the animation-specific optimization settings that can also help your animation run smoother and faster. Select Optimize Animation from the Animation palette menu to open the Optimize Animation dialog box.

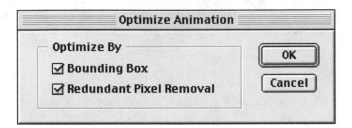

The Bounding Box option crops each frame so that only the changed information is added to the next frame. The Redundant Pixel Removal option converts pixels from previous frames that don't change into transparent pixels. For most animated GIF files, you'll probably want to leave both options selected.

Saving Animation Files

Generally, it's a good idea to save your animation files twice: in Photoshop format (by default, ImageReady saves in Photoshop format) and as a GIF file for outputting to the Web. As you work, choose File > Save to preserve all layer work and effects. After you optimize the file and are ready to preview it in a browser, choose File > Save Optimized As. This saves the file in GIF format.

If you wish to have ImageReady create a file with HTML coding instructions to load your file into a browser, select the Save HTML File option. For instance, the following HTML code is all you need to load your animated GIF file into a Web page:

```
<IMG SRC="myanimation.gif" WIDTH=150 HEIGHT=250>
```

Animation Tricks and Special Effects

Creating animated GIF files is quite simple, but creating frame-by-frame effects can be a bit tedious. Fortunately, ImageReady provides a few shortcuts that can help streamline your efforts.

Using Layer Masks

Layer masks allow you to hide and reveal image areas in layers. Since animation in ImageReady is layer based, you can use all of the layer tricks described in Chapter 17, where layer masks are discussed in detail. For instance, you can create a clipping group and move the group to create animation. You can create a layer mask and create animated effects by changing the transparency of the mask or by simply moving the mask.

Tweening Frames

Tweening automatically creates new frames between two existing frames and fills in the new in-between frames with effects that gradually change. You can use tweening to change the opacity of images gradually in one layer or move an image gradually from one part of the screen to another. You can also use tweening to introduce a layer effect automatically. When you use ImageReady's Tween command, you specify whether you wish to create a motion, layer, or transparency effect, and how many frames you wish to add.

The following example shows you how to create a simple fade-out effect using tweening. In this example, you'll have ImageReady automatically create ten new frames that gradually turn the image from 100 percent transparency to 20 percent transparency.

1. Open the Donut file from this book's CD-ROM, or use any image with a transparent background.

2. Create a new frame by clicking on the New Frame icon in the Animation palette.

3. Duplicate the layer in the Layers palette by dragging the layer over the New Layer icon. Turn off the visibility of the original layer in the second frame. Lower the Opacity setting of the new layer to 20%.

4. Select the first frame in the Animation palette by clicking on it.

5. Open the Tween dialog box by choosing Tween from the Animation palette menu.

```
┌─────────────────────────────────────────────────┐
│                      Tween                        │
├─────────────────────────────────────────────────┤
│                                                   │
│    Layers:  ● All Layers                          │
│             ○ Selected Layer        ┌─────────┐   │
│                                     │   OK    │   │
│  Parameters:  ☑ Position            └─────────┘   │
│               ☑ Opacity             ┌─────────┐   │
│               ☑ Effects             │ Cancel  │   │
│                                     └─────────┘   │
│                                                   │
│  Tween with:  [ Next Frame      ⬍ ]               │
│                                                   │
│  Frames to Add:  ⬍ 5                              │
│                                                   │
└─────────────────────────────────────────────────┘
```

6. Make sure that the Opacity box is checked. In the Tween With pop-up menu, choose Next Frame. This tells ImageReady to tween in between Frame 1 and Frame 2. In the Frames to Add field, enter **10**. Click on OK, Now ten frames are added between Frame 1 and Frame 2, each gradually changing in opacity.

7. Preview the animation by clicking on the Play button in the Animation palette. To stop the animation, click on the Stop button in the Animation palette.

Choosing a Frame Disposal Method

ImageReady's frame disposal option allows you to control whether previous frames appear through transparent areas of the next frame. Normally, you do not want previous images to appear through the next frame's transparent areas; however, you may wish to use this feature to create special masking effects.

To see the frame disposal options, press CONTROL and click on the frame (Windows users should right-click on the frame). A small pop-up menu provides the following choices:

■ Automatic is the default option. ImageReady automatically disposes of the previous frame if the next frame includes transparency animation. This usually provides the desired results. If the next frame does not contain transparency, ImageReady optimizes the animation by disposing of the previous frame.

■ The Do Not Dispose option does just what its name implies. When you choose it, preceding frames may be visible through transparent areas in the current frame, because ImageReady doesn't dispose of previous frames.

■ The Restore to Background option always removes each frame before the next frame is displayed.

The Restore to Background disposal method cannot be adequately previewed in ImageReady. For the best results, view your image in a browser. You can preview the image directly from ImageReady by choosing File > Preview In, or by loading the file directly into your browser.

Photoshop Animation Tricks

Although Photoshop does not allow you to create animated GIF files, you can easily turn Photoshop images into animated GIFs using ImageReady. With some planning, you can create some great animation effects from Photoshop images.

If you load a Photoshop file into ImageReady, you can automatically convert the Photoshop layers into individual animated frames. If you have saved several Photoshop images in a folder, or if you wish to create a slide show effect, you can have ImageReady convert each image into a single animation frame. The following sections explain these techniques.

Turning a Photoshop File into an Animated GIF

ImageReady can automatically turn each layer in a Photoshop file into a frame in a GIF animation. If you wish to create animation using this technique, you must plan your Photoshop images carefully, because each new layer becomes a subsequent animated GIF frame. Here are the steps to take:

1. Create and save the file in Photoshop.
2. Load the file in ImageReady by choosing File > Open. Alternatively, choose File > Jump To > ImageReady.
3. If the Animation palette is not open, choose Window > Show Animation. In the Animation palette menu, choose Make Frames from Layers.

Once the command is executed, the lowest layer becomes Frame 1, and each new layer in the Layers palette becomes a subsequent frame.

As an example, we created a file named Clouds in Photoshop. To build an animation of a moving cloud-like effect, we applied the Clouds filter in multiple layers, each with a different shade of blue.

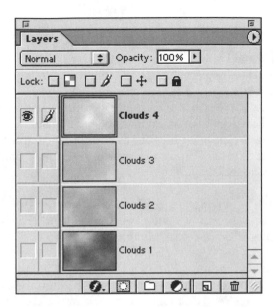

After loading the image into ImageReady, we chose Make Frames from Layers from the Animation palette menu. ImageReady automatically turned each layer into a frame in our animation.

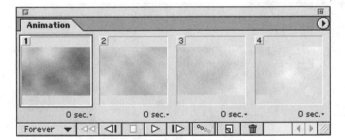

Converting a Folder of Files into an Animated GIF

If you wish to create a slide show effect from Photoshop (or ImageReady) images, place all of the images into one folder on your hard disk. To animate the images, load them into ImageReady by choosing File > Import > Folder as Frames. The files will be loaded into ImageReady animation frames in alphabetical order (by file name).

After you execute the Folder as Frames command, ImageReady's Layers palette will contain each image, with the lowest layer being the first image. Once the images are loaded, you can rearrange them by clicking and dragging on the frames in the Animation palette.

IMAGE EDITING FUNDAMENTALS

Creating Image Maps

Image maps, sometimes called *hotspots*, allow you to place on a page one graphic that has multiple clickable areas. For instance, Figure 10-10 shows a Web graphic with images of CD-ROMs. Instead of creating two different graphics, each with a link to a different page, we created one graphic with two image maps. We couldn't use the Slice tool to create this effect, because this tool creates only rectangular hotspots. ImageReady image maps allow you to create rectangles, circles, and polygons as your image maps. Figure 10-10 shows the image maps around the CD-ROM images, as well as the floating palette we created using ImageReady's Image Map tools.

Note *If you are creating rectangular image maps, consider using slices instead. Slices load faster, and you can optimize different slices with different settings, as described in the "Slicing Web Images" section earlier in this chapter.*

Creating an image map in ImageReady is quite easy. Like most Web effects in ImageReady, image maps are created and managed through the Layers palette. You can either use one of ImageReady's Image Map tools or the content of a layer to make image maps. For images without layers, using the Image Map tools is the easiest approach.

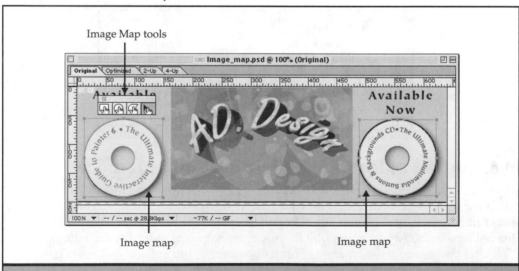

Figure 10-10. *Image maps created with ImageReady's Image Map tools*

Using the Image Map Tools

ImageReady's Toolbar offers three Image Map tools for different shapes and a tool for image selection.

When you select one of these tools, you'll see that its Options bar features the same alignment and distribution options as the Slice Select tool. These options are described in the "Selecting Slices with the Slice Select Tool" section earlier in this chapter.

To use the Circle or Rectangle Image Map tool, click and drag over the area that you wish to designate as a clickable area that will link Web users to another page. As you click and drag, a rectangular image map box surrounds the image. To create a square-shaped image map, hold down the SHIFT key as you drag. To create an image map from its center out, hold down the OPTION (*ALT*) key as you drag.

If you are using the Polygonal Image Map tool, click to start the image map, move the mouse to begin creating the image map shape, and then click again. The Polygonal Image Map tool connects your mouse clicks. Continue moving the mouse and clicking. To complete the image map, double-click or click again on the image map's starting point. To constrain the Polygonal Image Map tool to create 45 angles, press SHIFT as you click to create the image map border.

Here are the steps for creating an image map with an Image Map tool. After you execute these steps, ImageReady creates the HTML necessary to use your image as an image map.

1. Load an image into ImageReady by choosing File > Open. The image must be on a layer or transparent background. If you wish to load a practice image, open the Image_Map file from this book's CD-ROM.

2. Select one of the Image Map tools in ImageReady's Toolbox, click in the image, and create the image map as described at the beginning of this section.

3. If you need to move the image map area, click and drag it with the Image Map Select tool. If you need to resize the image map, click and drag an image map handle with the Image Map Select tool. (You can also change its dimensions in the Image Map palette, as described in the next section.)

You can move an image map in 1-pixel increments by pressing the directional arrow keys on your keyboard.

4. Open the Image Map palette by choosing Show > Image Map. Specify the linking URL in the Image Map palette. You can also enter a name for the image map and an alternate message for users whose browsers do not display graphics. Using the Image Map palette is described in the next section.

5. Optimize the file if necessary. Optimization is discussed in Chapter 9.

6. Save the file by choosing File > Save Optimized. In the Save As pop-up menu, make sure HTML & Image is selected. This saves an HTML code snippet that can be loaded into the HTML of your Web page.

The HTML provides browser instructions for using the linked image map. Here is what the code looks like:

```
<IMG SRC="myimage.gif" WIDTH=397 HEIGHT=600 BORDER=0 USEMAP="#myimage_Map">
<MAP NAME="myimage_Map">
<AREA SHAPE="circle" ALT="" COORDS="164,287,131" HREF="
http://mysite.com/clicklink.htm ">
</MAP>
```

Using the Image Map Palette

In the Image Map palette, you assign a linking URL to your image map. The linking URL is the address of the Web page that users will jump to when they click on the image map area of your Web page. You can also specify image map dimensions, a name, and alternative text in the Image Map palette.

Choose Window > Show Image Map to open the Image Map palette. Figure 10-11 shows an example of how you might enter image map information.

Here is a description of how to use the options in the Image Map palette:

■ In the Name field, you can enter a name for the image map, which ImageReady will use when it generates the HTML code.

■ In the URL field, enter the full path name for the link, such as http://www.myhomepage.com.

■ From the Target pop-up menu, you can choose which frame or window the linked page will appear in. The choices are _blank, _self, _parent, and _top.

■ In the Alt field, you can enter a message for those browsers that do not display graphics.

■ The coordinates in the Dimensions section of the Image Map palette are filled in automatically when you create your image map, but you can edit them in the palette.

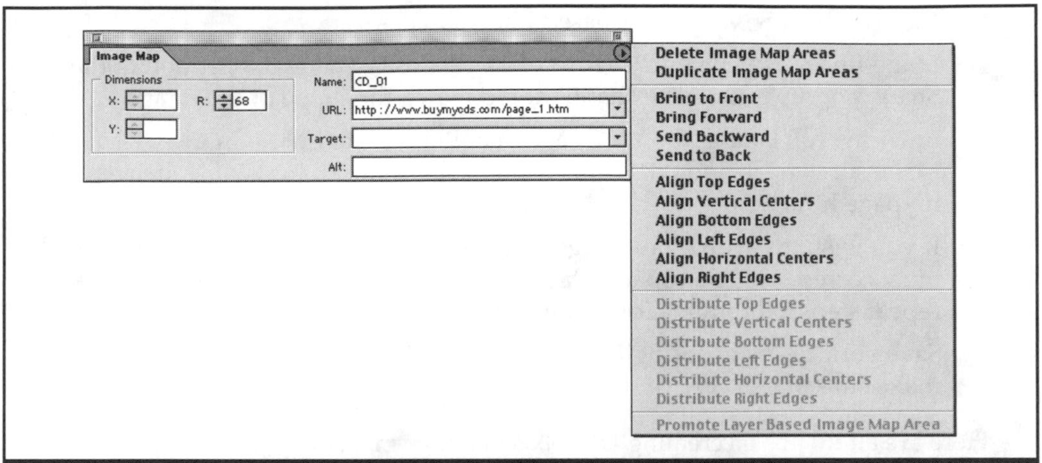

Figure 10-11. *ImageReady's Image Map palette allows you to set a linking URL*

The Image Map palette menu offers a variety of commands for handling image maps. For instance, if you create one image map and need to create an identical map for a different image area, select the first image map with the Image Map Select tool and choose Duplicate Image Map Areas from the Image Map palette menu. If you wish to delete an image map area, you can select the image map and choose Delete Image Map Areas.

| Tip | *You can also delete a selected image map by pressing the DELETE (BACKSPACE) key.* |

The other commands in the palette menu are useful when you have selected more than one image map. The Bring and Send commands change the stacking order of selected image maps. The Align commands move selected image maps so that they align vertically or horizontally at their centers, or along their edges. The Distribute commands allow you to space multiple image maps evenly.

Creating Layer-Based Image Maps

Image maps can also be created from the nontransparent areas of layers. The image must be on a layer or a transparent background. When ImageReady creates the image map, it uses the entire contents of the layer as the map area.

Here's how to create a layer-based image map.

1. Load an appropriate image into ImageReady by choosing File > Open. If you wish to load a practice image, open the Image_Map file, which is divided into several layers, from this book's CD-ROM. If the layer that you wish to use as an image map isn't selected, select it by clicking on it in the Layers palette.

2. Choose Layer > New Layer Based Image Map Area.

3. In the Image Map palette (Figure 10-11), choose a shape description in the Shape pop-up menu. The shape should match the shape of the image.

4. Enter the full URL of the Web page that you wish to link to in the URL field. Make sure you include the http:// prefix, as in http://www.mysite.com/mypage.htm.

5. If you wish to create more image maps in your image, each image map area must correspond to a separate layer. To create image maps in these layers, repeat steps 2 through 4 for each layer.

6. Save your file by choosing File > Save Optimized. In the Save As dialog box, make sure that the HTML file option is selected.

Here are a few tips on creating layer-based image maps:

■ You can use a shape created with of one ImageReady's Shape tools as a layer-based image map, because it is created in a layer. After you create the shape, you can apply a layer style, such as Bevel and Emboss.

■ You can convert a layer-based image map into a tool-based image. To do this, select the image map with the Image Map Select tool, and then choose Promote Layer Based Image Map Area from the Image Map palette menu.

Creating Rollovers

Rollovers are one of the most popular navigational aids used in Web sites. Rollovers allow an image to change when the user moves the mouse over it or clicks on it. To produce the rollover effect, ImageReady creates a text file that includes programming code in a Web-based computer language called JavaScript. The JavaScript instructions tell the browser to swap images based on the position, or the *state*, of the mouse.

Before you create a rollover, you should plan your project. Rollovers are created by swapping graphics in layers or by changing layer styles. You may wish to create the graphics as you create the rollover or copy and paste graphics into layers as you create the rollover.

Using the Rollover Palette

When you create a rollover, you can change images depending on different mouse states. The states are automatically assigned in the Rollover palette shown in Figure 10-12. To open this palette, select Window > Show Rollover.

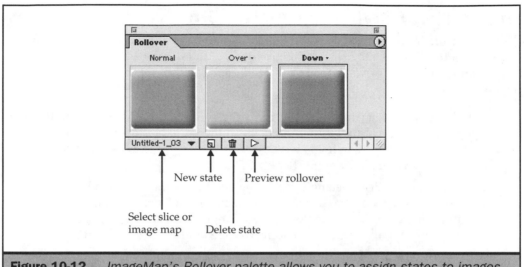

Figure 10-12.   *ImageMap's Rollover palette allows you to assign states to images*

If you click on the assigned state, a pop-up menu of states appears, allowing you to change states. The following states are available:

- **Over**   The mouse rolls over the image. The mouse button is not pressed.
- **Down**   The mouse button is held down over the rollover area.
- **Click**   The mouse button is clicked on the rollover area.
- **Out**   The mouse leaves the rollover area. You won't normally need to use this state, because ImageReady automatically returns the image on screen to its initial state.
- **Up**   The mouse button is released directly over the rollover area. Normally, you would use the Over state instead.
- **Custom**   When you choose this state, a dialog box appears, in which you enter a custom name for the state. To use the state, you must write JavaScript code and insert it into your Web page.
- **None**   While you're developing a rollover sequence, you can assign this state to images that are still being developed. If you assign a rollover to the None state, it appears in the Rollover palette but won't be displayed on a Web page.

Changing Layer Styles to Create a Rollover

In the example in this section, you'll create a rollover by changing layer styles in the Layers palette. To create the slice for the rollover, you'll use the Layer > Layer Based Slice command. When you save the optimized file, you'll save only the slice with the rollover in it.

1. In ImageReady, create a new image that is as large as the size of the button you wish to create. For this example, create an image 200 by 200 pixels. Set the background to Transparent. If you wish to load a button image to use for this example, open the Donut file from this book's CD-ROM.

2. Select the Rounded Rectangle tool in the Toolbox. If the Rounded Rectangle tool is not visible, click on the current Shape tool in the Toolbox, hold down the mouse button, and then choose the Rounded Rectangle tool from the list. Use the Rounded Rectangle tool to create a rounded rectangle in the entire document area.

3. Create a slice of only the image area by choosing Layer > New Layer Based Slice.

4. Pick a color for the shape by choosing Layer > Layer Style > Color Overlay. In the Color Overlay palette, click on the color swatch. When the Color Picker opens, select the Web Safe checkbox, and then click in the Color Picker to choose a color.

5. Add bevel and emboss effects to the button by choosing Layer > Layer Style > Bevel and Emboss.

6. If the Rollover palette is not open, display it by choosing Window > Show Rollover. Notice that the button you created appears in the palette.

7. Create a new state by choosing New State in the Rollover palette menu. A new state appears in the palette; it is automatically assigned the Over state.

8. Change colors by choosing Layer > Layer Style > Color Overlay (change the opacity if desired). Repeat the process of choosing a new color (step 4).

9. Create a new state by clicking on the New State button in the Rollover palette menu. A new state appears in the palette; it is automatically assigned the Down state.

10. Change colors once again by repeating step 4.

11. Preview the rollover effect by choosing Slices > Preview Rollovers and then moving the mouse over the button you created. As you move the mouse, the color of the button changes. Now click the mouse, and you'll see that the color changes once again.

12. Choose Optimization and Transparency settings in the Optimize palette. (The Optimize palette is discussed in Chapter 9.)

13. To generate the HTML and JavaScript code that can be used on a Web page, save your file by choosing File > Save Optimized As. Name your file. Before clicking on Save, choose Selected Slices at the bottom of the Save As dialog box. This instructs ImageReady to save only the slice with the rollover in it.

14. If you wish to control how ImageReady names the rollover images, click on the Settings button. This opens the Output Settings dialog box, where you can change ImageReady's naming system for rollovers. (You can reach the same dialog box by choosing File > Output Settings > Saving Files.)

15. Click on Save in the Save As dialog box.

After you save your rollover, ImageReady generates three different files: one for each rollover state, and one for the HTML containing the instructions to animate the rollover. Your next step would be to copy the text into the HTML used for one of your Web pages.

You can assign navigational links to your rollover by entering a URL for the selected slice in the Slice palette. You'll use this approach in the example in the "Creating a Tabbed Web Page with Slices and Rollovers" section later in this chapter.

Creating Animated Rollovers

If you wish to add action to your rollovers, you can add animation that begins to play when the user clicks on or moves the mouse over the graphic. To create animation in a rollover state, start creating the rollover using the steps described in the previous section. Create a new state in the Rollover palette, and then create your animation in the Animation palette.

If you wish to create a simple example of an animated rollover button, create flashing text as a rollover. To execute this effect, create the first rollover state with text in it. Then create a new state. After you create a new state, create a new frame in the Animation palette, add a new layer, and change colors. Create a few more frames in layers with different colors. When you've completed the animation work, preview the effect in your browser. You'll see the text flash when you hold down the mouse button over the text.

If you make changes to the visibility, position, opacity, blending mode, or layer effects in a layer, you can apply them to all of the states in the current rollover by choosing Match Layer Across States in the Rollover palette menu.

Creating a Tabbed Web Page with Slices and Rollovers

Once you know how to use rollovers and slices, you can create sophisticated navigational effects on your Web pages. For instance, you may wish to create tabs at the top of your Web page, and then create rollovers that go into effect when the mouse moves over the words on the tabs. Using ImageReady, you can also set up links to the pages you want the users to go to when they click on the tab. In the example in this section, you'll create just this type of tabbed Web page, with a simple rollover that changes the color for the tab's text.

> **Note** *We created the Tabs image on the CD-ROM in both ImageReady and Photoshop. We used the Rounded Rectangle tool in ImageReady to create the first tab in a layer. Then we duplicated this several times to create the other tabs. We then filled another layer with the same color as the tabs to create the bottom of the page. You can use this file or create one of your own for this example.*

1. In ImageReady, open the Slice palette and load the Tabs image from this book's CD-ROM, or create your own page with tabs.

2. Select the Slice Select tool in the Toolbox. Change the background default slice to a user slice by choosing Slices > Promote to User-slice. Drag the user slice so that it touches the bottom of the tabs.

3. Select the Slice tool and create a slice over the first tab, as shown in Figure 10-13.

4. Select the Select Slice tool and choose Slices > Duplicate Slices to duplicate the first tab. Drag the duplicate slice over the next tab.

5. Use the Duplicate Slices command to create slices for the other tabs.

> **Note** *You could also create the slices for this example by first creating guides over the areas that you wish to use as slices. To create guides, click and drag from the ruler area. If the rulers aren't on screen, choose View > Show Rulers. To turn the guides into slices, choose Slices > Create Slices from Guides.*

6. Select each slice with the Slice Select tool and enter a URL in the Slice palette. Even if you don't have a Web site, enter a URL in the URL field, such as http://mysite.com/page_1.htm. Continue adding URLs for each of the tabs.

7. Use the Type tool to enter text on the first tab. Choose a color for your text by selecting Layer > Layer Style > Color Overlay.

8. Open the Rollover palette and create a new state for the rollover by choosing New State from the Rollover pop-up menu.

9. Pick a new Web-safe color for your text by changing the color overlay layer style. The quickest way to do this is to click on the Layer Effects button at the bottom of the palette, and then choose Color Overlay.

10. Continue by adding rollover states for the other tabs. Then enter text and create rollovers for each tab.

11. After you've finished entering rollover states, you're ready to preview your work in a browser. Choose File > Preview In and choose your browser in the menu.

12. When the document opens, move your mouse over the tab. The color of the tab text changes as you move the mouse over the text. Also note that the URL appears at the bottom of the browser. This indicates the linked page you would go to if you clicked on the tab.

13. At this point, you can optimize your image. To optimize all slices using the same setting, first link the slices by pressing SHIFT and clicking on each slice. Then choose Slices > Link. Choose optimization settings in the Optimize palette, then save your image by choosing File > Save Optimized.

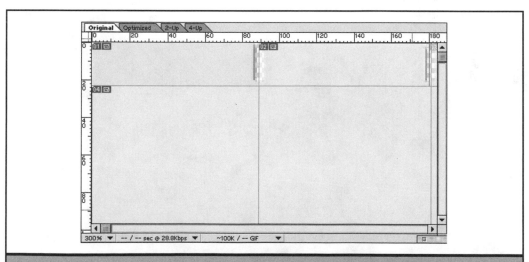

Figure 10-13. *Create a slice over the first tab*

The Complete Reference

Chapter 11

Working with Actions and History States

I n your day-to-day design and production work, you'll undoubtedly discover that some tasks require more perspiration than inspiration. If you're working on a Web or multimedia project, you may find that some days you spend hours just converting images from one file format to another. If you work in publishing, you may discover that you often need to apply the same curve adjustments (Image > Adjust > Curves) to every image you scan. You may also want to be able to easily repeat a complicated technique for creating drop shadows, vignettes, or three-dimensional effects. When these situations arise, you need to turn to Photoshop's and/or ImageReady's Actions palette.

As you'll learn in this chapter, the Actions palette can record many of your mouse clicks and menu choices. You can even save your actions into separate files called droplets, which appear on your computer's desktop. When you need to execute your steps again, all you need to do is play the recorded action or drag the droplet file over your graphics file.

We'll also review the History palette in this chapter. Along with its usefulness for performing multiple undos, the History palette also offers snapshot and history painting features.

Although the Actions and History palettes are separate, unrelated palettes, both are production time-savers. If you know how to use these two palettes, you'll be working at optimum efficiency.

Exploring the Actions Palette

The Actions palette, shown in Figure 11-1, provides numerous features that can help you automate tedious production tasks. Using the Actions palette, you can record selections, tool uses, and color choices, as well as dialog box settings and menu commands. When you record your mouse movements and keystrokes, both Photoshop and ImageReady allow you to assign them a name, which appears in the Actions palette. Each *action* listed in the palette is composed of a series of commands.

After you've recorded an action, you can play it back, applying it to selections or images on your screen or to multiple images in a folder. The palette also allows you to edit different commands in an action, store sets of actions on disk, and apply an action to all the files in a folder.

Note *Photoshop includes several sets of preset actions, which are stored in the Adobe Photoshop Actions folder (in the Presets folder). The sets are named Commands, Frames, Image Effects, Production, Text Effects, and Textures. To load a set, choose Load Actions from the Actions palette menu. After you load a set, click the right arrow next to the set name to see the list of actions in the set.*

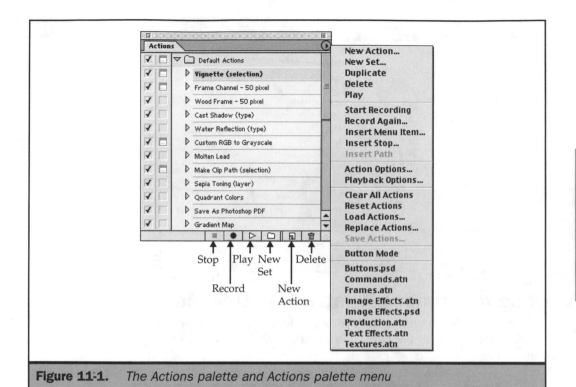

Figure 11-1.   *The Actions palette and Actions palette menu*

Photoshop's Actions palette appears on screen in either List mode or Button mode, which are described in the following sections.

Viewing the Actions Palette in List Mode

In List mode (as shown in Figure 11-1), all of the Actions palette commands are available. You can record new actions, play back and stop actions, create a new set (or folder) for your actions, and delete actions by clicking on buttons at the bottom of the palette. You can also choose commands from the Actions palette menu, which is accessible by clicking on the arrow at the upper-right corner of the palette.

In List mode, you see not only the different actions in the palette, but also the Photoshop commands that will run when the action is played. To see these commands, as shown in the next illustration, click on the triangle just to the left of the action's name.

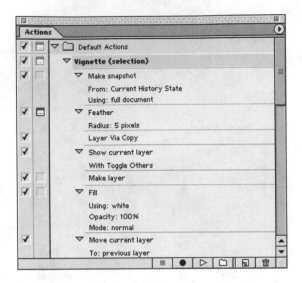

Viewing the Actions Palette in Button Mode

When the Actions palette is in Button mode, shown below, you can use it only to play back actions. To play back an action, you simply click on the corresponding button in the palette.

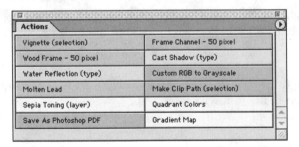

To toggle the palette into Button mode, click on the Button Mode option on the Actions palette menu. After you click, a checkmark appears next to the menu command. To turn off Button mode and return to List mode, click on the Button Mode option once again.

Creating Actions

Any design or production task that you must perform again and again is a candidate for recording as an action. When you create a new action, Photoshop/ImageReady records each step you take, such as making a selection, clicking on a tool, and changing dialog box settings. However, the Actions palette can't record all menu selections and mouse movements. For instance, it can't record painting with the Paintbrush, Airbrush, or the Dodge and Burn tools. But many of the commands that cannot be recorded can be added later.

Recording Actions

Here are the steps for creating a new action, naming it, and recording it:

1. If the Actions palette isn't already displayed, choose Window > Show Actions.

2. In order to create an action in Photoshop, the Actions palette must be in List mode. If the palette isn't in List mode, you won't see the Record and Play buttons at the bottom of the palette. To switch to List mode, open the Actions palette menu by clicking on the arrow in the upper-right corner of the palette. Then click on Button Mode to deselect it.

3. If you wish to store your action in a separate folder in the Actions palette, click on New Set on the Actions palette menu. In the New Set dialog box, give your set a name. The name appears as a folder in the Actions palette. Later, you can save your actions into the folder to help keep the palette better organized.

4. To create a new action, click on the New Action button (the page icon) in the Actions palette, or select New Action from the Actions palette menu.

5. In the New Action dialog box, enter a name for the action.

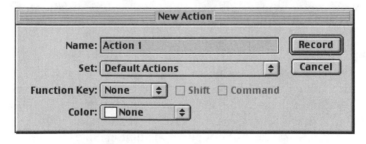

6. If desired, use the pop-up menu to assign the action to the default set (folder) or a set that you created.

7. If you want to assign a keyboard combination, or function key, (such as SHIFT-F1) for running an action, click on the Shift or Command (*Control*) checkbox, and then press a function key (such as F1 or F2).

8. To assign a color to an action, so that it is easily distinguishable in the Actions palette, select a color from the Color pop-up menu.

9. Click on the Record button. When recording starts, the Record icon in the palette turns red.

10. Execute the commands that you want recorded.

Note *When recording actions, most dialog box actions are recorded after you click on OK in the dialog box. Actions won't be recorded if you click on Cancel in a dialog box.*

11. To stop recording, click on the Stop button in the palette or choose Stop Recording from the Actions palette menu.

After recording an action, you should view the list of commands recorded to see if all of the steps you executed were actually recorded. As you record your actions, a list of the steps appears beneath the actions. After you've viewed the steps, you can click on the down arrow that appears next to the actions to hide the steps. When you click, the down arrow changes to a right arrow. To see the list of recorded commands, simply click on the right arrow. To view the actual settings of dialog box commands used when you recorded your actions, click on the right arrow next to the steps in your actions.

Adding Dialog Box Breakpoints

When a dialog box command is recorded, both Photoshop and ImageReady record the dialog box settings as well. In some cases, you will want to change dialog box settings while an action is being played back. For instance, you may record a Save command, but when the action is played, you want to enter a new file name for the file. Using the Actions palette, you can make an action pause so you or another user can change dialog box settings. You can do this for all commands in an action or for individual commands.

Actions that include dialog box commands can be identified by the tiny dialog box icon to the left of the command (visible in Figure 11-1). An empty, embossed square next to your action (an empty dialog box icon) indicates that Photoshop/ImageReady won't pause. If you wish to create a pause at every dialog box in an action, click on the dialog box icon next to the action's name. A red dialog box icon next to the action's name indicates that at least one, but not all, of the dialog boxes in the action is selected. If all of the dialog boxes are selected, the dialog box icon is black.

Inserting Commands and Paths into Recorded Actions

As discussed earlier, the Actions palette cannot record every Photoshop menu command. However, you can insert most menu commands into an action by using the Actions palette's Insert Menu Item command. To insert a menu item after a specific command in an action, click on a command line in the action list of an action. Then, from the

Actions palette menu, choose Insert Menu Item. In the Insert Menu Item dialog box, click on the menu item that you wish to add. The new command is added after the command you originally selected in the Actions palette. You can choose Insert Menu Item while you are recording or after you've finished recording.

You can execute the Insert Menu Item command at the beginning of an action. To do this, select the action, and then click the Actions palette's Insert Menu Item command when you first begin recording the action.

Another task that the Actions palette does not record is the step-by-step creation of a path. However, you can insert a path into an action using the Actions palette's Insert Path command. While recording, the easiest way to use this feature is to choose Insert Path from the Actions palette menu immediately after you create the path. If you wish to insert the path into an existing action, first select the path in the Paths palette, and then choose Insert Path from the Actions palette menu.

Inserting Steps into ImageReady Actions

Like Photoshop, ImageReady does not record every step you make in its Actions palette. For instance, changes made in the Optimize palette aren't recorded.

To add image optimization settings to an action, change the settings in the Optimize palette (displayed by choosing Window > Show Optimize), and then choose Insert Set Optimization Settings from the ImageReady Actions palette menu.

Optimization settings can be automatically recorded into ImageReady droplets. See the "Creating Droplets in ImageReady" section later in this chapter for details.

ImageReady also allows you to designate an "output" folder for images that are processed using actions. After you set the output folder, the image is placed in the folder when the action is completed. To specify the folder, choose Insert Set Output folder from ImageReady's Actions palette menu. This brings up a dialog box that allows you to choose an output location.

To add a layer effect to an action, drag the Layer Effect icon from the Layers palette to the step in the recorded action where you want the effect to appear.

Inserting "Stops" into Actions

The Actions palette's Stop command allows you to add a Stop alert message that appears on the screen. You can also add a Continue button to the Stop alert box. This can be helpful if you want the user to stop to observe the results of an action and continue if the image looks the way it should.

To insert a Stop alert after a command in an action in either Photoshop or ImageReady, click on a command in the Actions palette (if you don't see the command, click on the right arrow next to the action's name), and then choose Insert Stop from the Actions palette menu. You can also choose Insert Stop while recording an action. In the Record Stop dialog box, enter a message in the Message field.

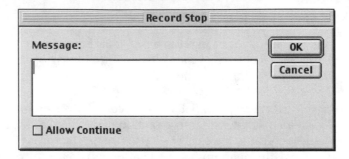

If you wish to allow the user to continue after stopping the action, click on the Allow Continue checkbox. When you include a Continue button, it might make sense to relate your message to the Allow Continue checkbox. For instance, you might add this to the Message field: "If the image looks great, click Continue." When you're finished, click on OK to insert the Stop.

Editing Actions and Re-recording Actions

If you make a mistake when you record your action in Photoshop or ImageReady, you probably won't need to start from scratch and record it again—you may be able to edit the action by rearranging action commands or by adding commands to the action. You can also use the Record Again command to re-record specific choices within a dialog box.

You can edit and re-record actions as follows:

- To change the order of commands in an action, simply click on the command in the Actions palette and drag it to a new position.

- To rename an action or assign it to a different function key after you've recorded it, select the action and then choose Action Options from the Actions palette menu. Alternatively, you can double-click on the name of the action in the palette.

- To add commands after a command in an action, select the command in the Actions palette and click on the Record button (or choose Start Recording from the Actions palette menu). Then execute the command that you wish to add to your action. To stop recording, click on the Stop button (or choose Stop Recording from the Actions palette menu).

- If you want to edit only the options in dialog boxes, select the action and then choose Record Again from the Actions palette menu. Photoshop/ImageReady then plays back the commands. When dialog boxes appear, enter new values in the dialog boxes. If you click on OK, the new values will replace those that were originally entered when you first recorded the action.

■ You may be able to re-record a dialog box setting in an action by double-clicking on the command in the action. This opens the dialog box that was recorded. Change the settings, and then click on OK to stop recording.

■ If you wish to delete an action from the Actions palette, select the action and click on the Trash icon or choose Delete from the Actions palette menu.

■ To delete all actions in Photoshop, choose Clear Actions from the Actions palette menu.

If you wish to create an action similar to another one, you don't need to record it again. Instead, select the action and choose the Duplicate command from the Actions palette menu. Once the duplicate is created, you can edit the action. To integrate one action into another, you can play a previously recorded action when recording a new action.

Playing Actions

Playing actions puts Photoshop/ImageReady on autopilot. When you play back an action, Photoshop/ImageReady plays each command in an action, step by step. If a Stop alert exists, the action stops. If a dialog break point exists, Photoshop/ImageReady allows you to change values in a dialog box.

Playing a Single Action or Parts of an Action

To play back an entire action, select the action and click on the Play button or choose Play from the Actions palette menu. If you are in Button mode (in Photoshop only), you can also simply click on the action's button in the Action palette.

You can also selectively play portions of an action, as follows:

■ If you want to start the action from a specific command within the action, select the appropriate command and click on the Play button (or choose Play from the Actions palette menu.)

■ In Photoshop, to play back only one command, press OPTION (*ALT*) and double-click on the command, or select the command and choose the Play Only command from the Actions palette menu.

■ To skip a command when an action is played, click on the checkmark next to the command in the Actions palette. The checkmark will disappear, indicating that the command will not be executed. To turn the command back on, click next to the command name in the checkmark column. When you turn off a step in an action, the checkmark next to the action name turns red.

Batching an Action to Multiple Files in Photoshop

If you need to apply design or production commands to multiple files, both Photoshop and ImageReady allow you to apply an action to a batch of files. For instance, you may wish to convert many files that will appear in a multimedia production to the same color palette or convert images that will appear on a Web page to a Web-safe palette.

Both Photoshop and ImageReady can apply an action to every file in a folder. When you batch files, you can specify whether you want the edited files to be placed in their original folder or another folder. Photoshop takes a somewhat different approach to batching than ImageReady. In Photoshop, you can execute a batch command from within the program. In ImageReady, you create a droplet, which can be applied to a file or files directly from your computer's desktop. Droplets are discussed in the next section.

Here's how to execute a batch action in Photoshop:

1. Use the Actions palette to record the action that you wish to apply to the files.

2. Move all of the files that you wish to apply the action to into a single folder, or open all of the files in Photoshop.

3. Choose File > Automate > Batch.

4. In the Batch dialog box, shown in Figure 11-2, specify the set and the action that you wish to run in the Play section. (If you just recorded the action, or if it is selected in the Actions palette, it will automatically appear on the Set and Action pop-up menus).

5. If your are batching files that are open on your screen, choose Open Files from the Source pop-up menu. Otherwise, make sure that Folder is selected.

6. Click on the Choose button to select the folder that contains the files to which you wish to apply the action. In the dialog box that appears, click on the source folder, and then click on Select.

7. If you recorded a File > Open command in your action, you will probably want to choose the Override Action "Open" Commands option. The Batch command automatically opens every file in a folder.

8. Click on the Destination pop-up menu to designate where you want the files placed after the action is complete. You can also choose to have the files saved and closed or specify no destination (None). If you choose a folder, Photoshop copies the altered files to a specified folder. This is a good way to prevent your original files from changing. To specify the actual folder in which you wish to save your data, click on the Choose button.

9. If you wish to have Photoshop skip an action's Save commands, choose the Override Action "Save In" Commands option. If you are saving images into a destination folder, this option will prevent Photoshop from saving all of the images in the wrong place.

10. If you don't want the action to stop when an error occurs, set the Errors pop-up menu so that it creates a log in a file specified when you click on the Save As button.

11. If you set the Destination pop-up menu to Folder, the Batch dialog box allows you to change the file names of the altered files. Click on the pop-up menus in the File Naming section. Each pop-up menu concatenates different settings, such as a serial number or date.

12. Click on OK to start the operation.

Note   *If you are recording an action that uses the Save for Web command, be sure to record a Close within the action. If you don't record the Close command, Photoshop creates two copies of the files that are batched.*

IMAGE EDITING
FUNDAMENTALS

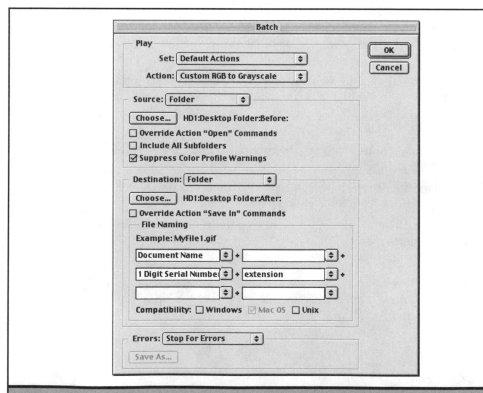

Figure 11-2.   *Specify the set and action to run in the Play section*

You can also import or digitize images in a batch and apply actions to each image. If you wish to import images in a batch, choose Import from the Source pop-up menu in the Batch dialog box. After you select Import, the Choose button changes to a From pop-up menu, which allows you to choose from anti-aliased PICT (Mac Only) or PICT Resource (Mac Only or PDF Image). If you have a plug-in for your scanner installed, its name should appear here as well. Choose the type of image you want from the From menu. When the action runs, an Open dialog box appears, allowing you to load the type of image from disk.

Storing Action Sets

If you create different actions, you can save sets of actions to disk, and then load the sets as you need them. For instance, you may wish to have one set of actions for special effects, another for color-correcting, and another for file conversion.

Saving and loading actions in Photoshop is handled through the Actions palette. Commands for loading, saving, and appending are similar to those in other palettes:

■ To save a set of actions, choose Save Actions from the Actions palette menu. Name the actions in the dialog box that appears. Change destination folders, if desired.

■ To append actions into the Actions palette, choose Load Actions from the palette menu. In the dialog box that appears, select the actions that you want to load and click on OK. The set of actions you load is then appended to those already in the Actions palette.

■ To reset the Actions palette to the original actions, choose Reset Actions from the Actions palette menu.

■ To replace the actions in the palette with a set of actions saved on disk, choose Replace Actions from the Actions palette menu.

■ To remove all actions from the Actions palette, choose Clear Actions from the Actions palette menu.

Note   *You can also delete actions from the Actions palette by choosing Delete Action from the Actions palette menu or dragging the action over the Trash icon. This permanently deletes the action.*

Using Photoshop's Automate Command Actions

Photoshop's Automate command includes a set of plug-in actions. These actions are similar to those found in the Actions palette, except that they are created using a programming language such as C++, rather than from recording steps in Photoshop.

Here is a description of the actions in the Automate submenu:

- **Conditional Mode Change**   Allows you to change different images to one mode. For instance, you could place grayscale and RGB files in a folder and convert all of them to CMYK.
- **Contact Sheet II**   Creates an image of thumbnails of files in a folder.
- **Fit Image**   Resizes images to the values specified in the dialog box without changing the aspect ratio. You need to enter only one value in the dialog box. When Photoshop runs Fit Image, it *resamples* (changes the number of pixels in the image).
- **Multi-Page PDF to PSD**   Converts pages in a PDF file (Adobe Acrobat) to separate Photoshop files.
- **Picture Package**   Creates a page of different size source images. This creates one image similar to a picture package that a photo studio might create, showing a portrait at different image sizes.
- **Web Photo Gallery**   Creates a sophisticated art gallery for Web sites. When you run the command, you can choose to have Photoshop create the art gallery from a folder of images. The resulting Web photo gallery includes a thumbnail page as well as the HTML that allows users to click a thumbnail and navigate to a larger image.

IMAGE EDITING FUNDAMENTALS

Using Droplets

Droplets are small computer files that can run Photoshop and ImageReady actions right from your computer's desktop. Neither Photoshop nor ImageReady need to be opened to run a droplet.

To batch commands in ImageReady, you must save recorded actions into a droplet. After you create the droplet, you can apply the actions within it to one file or all of the files in a folder by simply dragging the droplet file over the folder.

If you would like to try running a droplet, you can experiment with the samples included in the Droplets folder (inside the Samples folder). A good example is the Multi-Save Save droplet in the ImageReady Droplets folder. This droplet saves your file in both GIF and JPEG formats. To try out the droplet, just drag any image over the droplet. When you see a plus sign appear on screen, release the mouse button, and the droplet will execute.

Creating Droplets in Photoshop

To create a droplet in Photoshop, follow these steps:

1. Select the Action in the Actions palette and choose File > Automate > Create Droplet.

2. In the Create Droplet dialog box (which looks like the Batch dialog box shown earlier in the "Batching an Action to Multiple Files in Photoshop" section), the name of your droplet will already be chosen. Specify options in the Play section. For instance, if you recorded the File > Open command, but want the droplet to open files automatically, choose Override Action "Open" Commands. When you drag the droplet over a file or over a folder with files, the file or files will open automatically.

3. Click on Choose to select where to save your file. In the Save dialog box, name your file and click on Save.

4. If you wish to use the droplet to work with multiple files in folder, chose the Folder option in the Destination pop-up menu. Then click on the Choose button and specify the destination folder. You can also choose to change the file name of the batched files in the File Naming section.

5. Click on OK to close the dialog box.

Creating Droplets in ImageReady

To create a droplet in ImageReady, in the Actions palette, select the action that you wish to be included in the droplet. Next, choose Create Droplet from the Actions palette menu. In the dialog box that appears, designate where you wish to save the droplet, and then enter a name for the droplet. You can also create a droplet by dragging the action name from the ImageReady Actions palette folder onto your desktop.

ImageReady allows you to create a droplet directly from the Optimize settings in the Optimize palette. This way, you can quickly create a droplet that can be applied to multiple images that you'll be outputting to the Web. Here are the steps for creating a droplet from the Optimize palette:

1. Open an image in ImageReady.
2. Open the Optimize palette by choosing Window > Show Optimize.

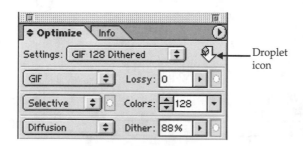

Droplet
icon

3. Choose Optimization settings in the Optimize palette. (Using the Optimize palette is discussed in Chapter 9.)
4. At this point, you can create the droplet by doing one of the following:

- Click on the Droplet icon in the Optimize palette. In the dialog box that appears, choose a location to save the file, and then click on Save.

- Drag the Droplet icon that appears in the Optimize palette onto your desktop. The file will automatically be named for you.

- Choose Create Droplet from the Optimize palette pop-up menu. In the dialog box that appears, choose a location to save the file, and then click on Save.

 You can add the contents of a droplet to an action by dragging the droplet to the action in the Actions palette.

Applying a Droplet

Once you've created a droplet, applying it to a file or multiple files is easy: Simply drag the file or folder icon over the droplet. If ImageReady or Photoshop is not opened, the program will load and the actions in the droplet will execute. On your screen, you'll see a message indicating that the actions are being executed. If you wish to pause the action, click on the Pause button that appears. After you pause the action, you can click on Resume to resume processing.

Editing a Droplet

After you've created a droplet in ImageReady, you can change the action settings for the droplet or its batch preferences. To edit a droplet, choose File > Open to open it directly in ImageReady. If ImageReady isn't opened, you can double-click on the droplet. This opens a Droplet window for the droplet.

IMAGE EDITING
FUNDAMENTALS

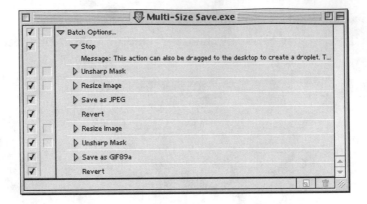

With the Droplet window open, you can modify it as follows:

■ Click and drag on individual actions to change the order of actions.

■ Select or deselect steps in the actions by clicking on the checkmark boxes.

■ Delete action steps by dragging a step to the Trash icon.

■ Add a step to the droplet by dragging the step from the Actions palette into the Droplet window.

■ Reset the batch settings for the droplet (where the file is saved and how the files are named) by double-clicking on the Batch Options line in the Droplet window.

To save the changes made to the action, close it. A dialog box appears, allowing you to save or cancel the changes.

Setting up Batch Preferences for Droplets

Batch preferences for ImageReady droplets can be specified after an action is created or when you are recording actions. If you wish to set batch options before creating a droplet, select the action in the Actions palette, and then choose Batch Options from the Actions palette menu. This opens the Batch Options dialog box, shown in Figure 11-3. If you've already created the droplet, load the droplet by choosing File > Open. After the droplet loads, double-click on the Batch Options line in the Droplet window to open the Batch Options dialog box.

The Batch Options dialog box allows you to specify file-saving choices for the processed files:

■ If you wish to overwrite your original files, saving them with the same name and the same folder, activate the Original checkbox.

■ To save a Web-optimized version of the files, select the Optimized checkbox, and then choose a folder location from the pop-up menu. If you wish to specify a folder on your hard disk, choose the Specific Folder choice. This opens a window that allows you to pick the folder in which you wish to save your files. You can later change the location by clicking on the Choose button.

■ To specify how duplicate file names should be saved, choose from the If Duplicate File Name pop-up menu. This pop-up menu allows you to append a number or letter to duplicate files, as well as to tell ImageReady to warn you if the files are going to be overwritten.

■ To modify the file name extension for a specific type of hardware, specify a choice in the Modify File Name For section.

■ To have the images processed off screen, choose Run In Background. Otherwise, choose Display Images. You can also choose to have the droplet pause in its execution before the file is saved by choosing Pause Before Save. This allows you to cancel the save operation if you don't like the results of the image processing.

IMAGE EDITING
FUNDAMENTALS

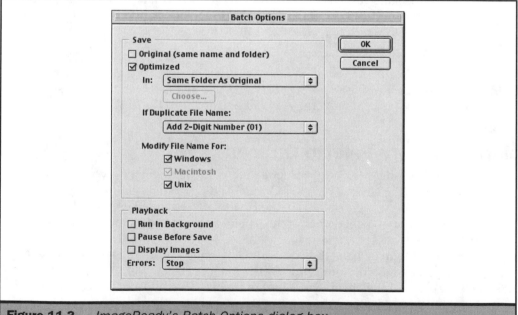

Figure 11-3.   *ImageReady's Batch Options dialog box*

Rewriting Digital History

The History palette is Photoshop's and ImageReady's answer to multiple undos. Just by clicking on a line in the History palette, you can miraculously return to a previous state of your work—even if you didn't save it. Knowing that you have the History palette as a safety net certainly takes some of the stress out of digital creativity. It also means that you can meander off on a digital diversion. If you take a wrong turn, you can always backtrack to a previous fork in the road. If you accidentally destroy a few pixels, you can remove that step from your journey.

As you've discovered from previous chapters of this book, the History palette provides more than just a history of steps that you can easily undo. Using the History palette, you can create snapshots—multiple versions of your image as you work. You can also use the History Brush to paint in previous versions of your work and create special effects at the same time.

If you haven't been using the History palette, open it by choosing Window > Show History. As you work, the palette, shown in Figure 11-4, lists the editing stages of your images, called *states*. If you want to return to a previous state, you simply click on the state, or click and drag the small control icon in the palette (next to the Gradient state in Figure 11-4) to the state you wish to return to. As soon as you click, your image returns to a previous version. If you decide that you undid too much, you can click forward in the History palette to return to a later state.

To quickly return to a previous state in the History palette, press OPTION-COMMAND-Z (ALT-CTRL-Z) or choose Edit > Step Backward. To move to the next state, press SHIFT-COMMAND-Z (SHIFT-CTRL-Z) or choose Edit > Step Forward.

Exploring History Palette Options

Before you begin using the History palette to rewrite digital history, you'll find it helpful to explore the History palette's Options settings, which control how the palette records history. To view the options in the History palette, open its menu by clicking the arrow in the upper-right corner of the palette. In the palette's menu, choose History Options.

The History Options dialog box determines several important aspects of how the History palette records your work. By default, the History palette automatically creates a snapshot of the opening state of your work. The snapshot appears as a tiny thumbnail image at the top of the palette. The snapshot makes it easy to revert to the opening image, without choosing the File > Revert command. To revert to the snapshot, simply click on it in the palette. If you want to conserve some memory, you may wish to deselect the Automatically Create First Snapshot checkbox.

History Options

☑ Automatically Create First Snapshot
☐ Automatically Create New Snapshot When Saving
☐ Allow Non-Linear History
☐ Show New Snapshot Dialog by Default

[OK]
[Cancel]

The Allow Non-Linear History option allows you to specify how you can go backward and forward through states. When this option is off, the History palette keeps a continuous record of how the current image is created. For instance, if you have ten states in the History palette, return to state 5, and then continue editing, Photoshop deletes states 6 through 10. It replaces the old state 6 with the current change you make to your image. If Allow Non-Linear History is selected, states 6 through 10 won't be deleted. This can create a confusing history, but it also allows you more flexibility.

Tip *If you inadvertently return to a previous state in the History palette and delete subsequent states, you can return the deleted states to the History palette by choosing Edit > Undo.*

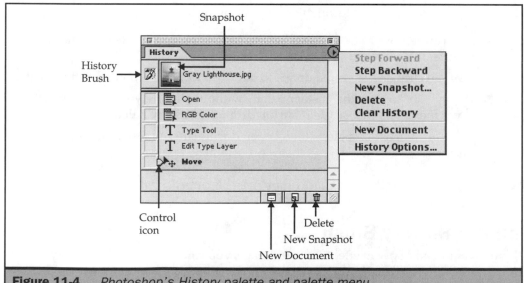

Figure 11-4.   *Photoshop's History palette and palette menu*

IMAGE EDITING
FUNDAMENTALS

To further understand the difference between linear history and non-linear history, turn off the Non-Linear History option and then execute these steps:

1. Create a new document in Photoshop.

2. Paint on screen with the Paintbrush.

3. Convert the image to grayscale by choosing Image > Mode > Grayscale.

4. Return to the RGB version of the image by clicking on the Paintbrush state in the History palette.

5. Paint on the document with the Airbrush tool. As soon as you use the Airbrush tool, the Grayscale state is removed from the palette and replaced with the Airbrush state.

If you try the same steps with the Non-Linear History option selected, the Grayscale state will not be deleted from the palette. You will have a color image on your screen with a Grayscale state in the History palette. This means that the History palette doesn't reflect the image on screen; however, if desired, you could always return to the Grayscale state in the palette.

Clearing History States

Photoshop provides several techniques for clearing history:

- You can remove a state by clicking on it and choosing Delete from the History palette pop-up menu.

- You can click on a state and drag it to the Trash icon at the bottom of the palette.

- If you want to clear the History palette without altering your image (which saves memory), choose Clear History from the History palette pop-up menu.

- To clear the History palette for all open documents, choose Edit > Purge > Histories.

 If you close your document, the History palette is cleared, even if you save the document.

Using the History Brush

If you want to add special effects to your image, you can use one of the History states as a source for the History Brush (a technique described in Chapter 6). As you paint, the state selected in the History palette is painted back on screen. (By default, the History Brush is set to paint back the first snapshot in the palette.) If you're puzzled by the History Brush, think of it as a cloning brush that clones an entire image back on screen. The image it clones is one of the states in the History palette.

To use the History Brush, you first must select it in the Toolbox. If desired, you can change the Opacity and Modes in the History Brush Options bar to create special effects. Next, move the mouse pointer to the History Brush palette and click in the embossed square to the left of the state that you want to paint back into your image. After you click, a History Brush icon (visible in Figure 11-4, shown earlier) appears next to that state in the History palette.

 You can use Photoshop's Magic Eraser to erase to the state set in the History palette by the History Brush. To erase with the Magic Eraser, select the Erase to History checkbox in the Eraser Options bar before using the Eraser tool. You can also press OPTION (ALT) while you click and drag with the Eraser tool.

To experiment with the History Brush, load an image in Photoshop. Then apply the Clouds filter to your image by choosing Filter > Render > Clouds. The Clouds filter completely fills the screen with cloud formations created from the current foreground and background colors. After you apply the Clouds filter, no trace of the original is left. However, using the History Brush you can paint back in the original and add blending effects as you do it. Now click on the state in the History palette just before the Clouds filter state. Paint over your image. As you paint, your image gradually returns to view. When you paint, the History Brush uses the state in the History palette as a type of cloning source.

Try lowering opacity to create a blend between the History Brush state and later states. Then try choosing a blending mode, such as Dissolve or Overlay, to see how the History Brush state can be blended together with other image stages.

 You can fill using the state designated by the History Brush in the History palette. Choose Edit > Fill. From the Using pop-up menu, choose History.

Using Snapshots and Creating a New Document

Just as a snapshot in photography can freeze a moment in time, Photoshop's digital snapshots freeze a moment of digital history. As you work, you can create different snapshot versions and later return to any version you wish.

To create a snapshot, click the New Snapshot icon in the History palette or choose New Snapshot from the palette's menu. After you create a snapshot, it appears in the top section of the History palette. Any time you wish to return to the snapshot version, you simply click on it, as shown in the illustration on the following page.

Snapshots also allow you to delete History states without altering your image. For example, if you create a snapshot and delete the History states leading up to your image, the image remains unchanged.

If you want to experiment, you can also use a snapshot as the source for the History Brush. This allows you to use the History Brush to gradually paint in the snapshot version. To set a snapshot as the source for the History Brush, click in the History Brush column next to the snapshot. After you click, the History Brush appears next to the snapshot in the History palette.

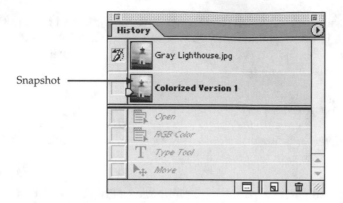

Snapshot

After creating a snapshot, you may want to open the snapshot version into a new document. You can do this by clicking on the snapshot, and then clicking on the New Document icon at the bottom of the palette or choosing New Document from the History palette's pop-up menu.

If you haven't created a snapshot in one of the previous chapters, execute these simple steps to see how it works:

1. Load an image; then use the Type tool to type some text over the image.

2. Try adding a drop shadow by clicking on the Effects pop-up menu in the Layers palette and choosing the Drop Shadow option. In the Layer Style pop-up menu, click on OK to apply the default settings.

3. Create a snapshot by choosing New Snapshot from the History palette pop-up menu. This opens the New Snapshot dialog box, where you can enter a snapshot name in the Name field.

 To rename a snapshot, double-click on the snapshot in the History palette. This opens the Rename Snapshot dialog box, where you can enter a new name for the snapshot.

4. Continue working on your image—add more type or create a transparent gradient over it.

5. Now, assume you want to return to the snapshot version of your image. Simply click on the snapshot version of your file.

6. Try deleting History palette states that you created before making the snapshot. To delete a History state, drag it into the Trash icon at the bottom of the palette. Even though you delete the state, the image on your screen remains unchanged.

7. Once you have a snapshot, you can actually delete the individual History states and save memory. Even if you delete the states leading up to the snapshot, the snapshot remains, and you can always return to the snapshot version.

8. If you wish to continue experimenting without altering your original file, you can place the snapshot version in another document. To create a new document with your snapshot version, click on the New Document icon at the bottom of the History palette, or choose New Document from the History palette menu. Photoshop immediately opens a copy of the document. You can now use the new document and continue editing your image.

You can create a new document from any state in the History palette. Click on the state, and then click on the New Document icon at the bottom of the palette. When the new document is created, it opens with a new History palette.

The Complete Reference

Chapter 12

Using Filters in Photoshop and ImageReady

M any Photoshop and ImageReady filters are designed to do what most digitizing devices *can't* do: enhance an image and disguise its defects. A filter can turn soft, blurred contours into sharp, crisp edges, or it can soften an image that has jagged or harsh edges. Filters can also remove dust and scratches in digitized images, and they can help eliminate color banding (abrupt changes in color values) and noise (randomly colored pixels that can appear in scanned images).

Although many filters are designed to subtly improve scanned images, others create dramatic alterations such as twisting, bending, or spinning an image into motion. Some filters can grab a continuous-tone or painted image and make it appear to be made of three-dimensional blocks or pyramid shapes. Many filters create unusual, eerie, or humorous effects. Digitized images, as well as original images created in Photoshop and ImageReady, can be spherized, zigzagged, or twirled into a digital "soup."

The complex digital effects produced by filters have their roots in photography. Photographic filters are used to filter out light, enhance images, and create special effects. But the photographic filters can't match Photoshop's digital filters in effects or versatility. In Photoshop and ImageReady, filters can be applied again and again, one after another, until just the right effect is achieved for the entire image or within selections in the image. For instance, one filter might be applied to enhance the edges of an image, and another used to give it an embossed effect. The possibilities are endless.

Applying Filters

Each Photoshop/ImageReady filter produces a different effect. Some filters work by analyzing every pixel in an image or selection and transforming it by applying mathematical algorithms to create random or predefined shapes such as tiles, three-dimensional blocks, or pyramids. Many filters achieve their effects by first sampling individual pixels or groups of pixels to define areas that display the greatest difference in color or brightness. Once one of these filters zeroes in on such a transitional area, the filter starts changing color values—sometimes replacing one pixel's color with that of an adjacent pixel, sometimes substituting pixel colors with the average color value of neighboring pixels. The result, depending on the filter, can be a sharpening of the image, a softening of harsh edges, or a complete transformation.

Many filters invite you to be an active participant in determining the outcome of the filter's effects. Before these filters begin their work, a dialog box is presented to you in which you can control the magnitude of the filter's effects and often specify the radius (range) in which changes will occur.

Despite the differences among Photoshop's and ImageReady's numerous filters, the process of applying each one is virtually the same. You start by opening or activating the image you wish to edit. If you wish to apply the filter to a portion of the image only, select that area with one of the selection tools; otherwise, Photoshop/ImageReady will apply the filter to the entire image. If you are working in a layer, Photoshop/ImageReady applies the filter to the colored areas of the layer only; transparent areas are not affected. Photoshop/ImageReady will not apply a filter to more than one layer at a time.

 Some filters can be applied only to RGB files. Changing color modes is discussed in Chapter 13.

If you would like to try out the filters as you work through the discussions in this chapter, use the image files from the Chapter 12 folder of the CD-ROM; or you can use any digitized image.

Choosing a Filter

From the Filter menu, choose one of the filter groups: Artistic, Blur, Brush Strokes, Distort, Noise, Pixelate, Render, Sharpen, Sketch, Stylize, Texture, Video, or Other.

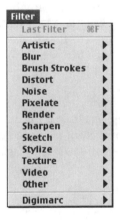

 The Digimarc filters allow you to embed a digital watermark in images for copyright purposes. For more information, visit the Digimarc Web site at www.digimarc.com.

From the submenu that appears, select the filter that you wish to apply. Several of the filters are applied immediately when you select them. For others, you must set dialog box options to control the filter's results.

Many of the filter dialog boxes provide invaluable image previews that allow you to see the filter effect on the image before it is applied. By clicking on the + or – icon, you can enlarge or reduce the image in the preview box by specific ratios. For instance, clicking the + icon to change the image ratio to 200% doubles the image size in the preview box; clicking the – icon to change it to 50% makes it half the size.

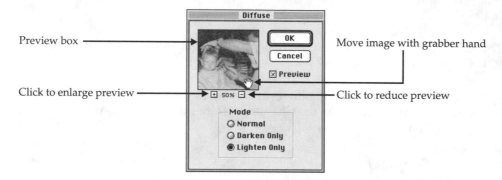

Preview box

Move image with grabber hand

Click to enlarge preview

Click to reduce preview

If the preview box does not show the specific area you wish to view, you can adjust the view by clicking and dragging on the miniature image in the preview box. When you move the mouse over the preview box, a tiny hand icon appears, indicating that you can click and drag to move the image. If you want the preview box to display an image area that is far outside the range of the preview box, you can click outside the dialog box (the mouse pointer changes to a see-through rectangle) on the image area you wish to see in the preview box.

Because many Photoshop filters are sophisticated and require extensive computer processing, they may take some time to execute, particularly in a large image or selection. If you apply a filter and want to stop it before it has finished processing, you can press COMMAND-. (period) (ESC) to cancel.

Applying Filters to Shapes

Filters can be applied to raster images (sometimes called bitmaps). Thus, Photoshop's vector-based shapes must be rasterized before you can apply a filter to them (Layer > Rasterize). If you have a shape text in a layer and you try to apply a filter to it, Photoshop warns you that the layer must be rasterized.

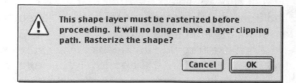

If you click on OK, Photoshop will rasterize the text or shape. Once the text or shape is rasterized, you can no longer edit it with Photoshop's text editing tools or with the Direct Selection tool or Path Component Selection tool.

| Note | *Flattening an image (Layer > Flatten Image) also rasterizes shapes.* |

Reapplying Filters

Sometimes, the effect of a filter on an image will be so subtle that you won't notice it, and you may wish to apply the filter again to enhance the results. To facilitate the process of reapplying filters, Photoshop/ImageReady copies the name of the last filter used from a submenu and installs it at the top of the Filter menu.

To reapply the filter with its previous settings, just select the first menu item in the Filter menu or press COMMAND-F (*CTRL-F*). If the filter requires dialog box settings that you know you want to change from the last time the filter was used, you can press OPTION-COMMAND-F (*ALT-CTRL-F*) to open the dialog box before reapplying the filter.

Fading an Image Back In

After you apply a filter, you may wish to vary the effect or bring part of the image back to its original form. Photoshop's Fade command allows you to alter filter effects by gradually fading out the effects of the filter, using a blending mode. (ImageReady does not have a Fade command.) As you gradually fade out the filter's effects, the previous version of the file begins to appear in the blending mode specified in the Fade dialog box.

In order to use the Fade command, you must first run a filter (or use one of the Image > Adjust commands). After the filter has been applied, the Fade command, which will include the name of the previously used filter, becomes available on the Edit menu. Choose that command to open the Fade dialog box.

To see the effects of the Fade operation, first make sure that the Preview checkbox is selected; then gradually drag the Opacity slider to the left. As you drag, the filter's effects fade from the image. Choosing a blending mode in the Fade dialog box applies the mode to the original image and the filtered image at the specified opacity.

Using the Blur Filters

The five Blur filters are often used to smooth areas where edges are too sharp and contrast is too high. They soften image edges by removing contrast. Blur filters can also be used to blur the background of an image, so that the foreground stands out, or to create a soft shadow effect.

Tips for Applying Filters

As you work with filters, you can also enhance and alter filter effects by trying the following tips:

- Apply filters to one layer at a time. This technique allows you to see the effect gradually on different layers. Remember that you can apply filters only to a layer that is selected and visible. (See Chapters 16 and 17 for details on working with layers.)

- Apply filters to one channel at a time. This technique can also help you apply filters if you do not have a lot of RAM. Some filters do not use your scratch disk while executing, so you must have sufficient RAM to complete the entire filter operation. If you do not, you may still be able to apply the filter to the image one channel at a time. You might find that you can create interesting special effects by applying different filters at different settings to different channels. In Photoshop, try applying a sharpening or blurring filter to the Lightness channel of a Lab image or to the Black channel of a CMYK image to experiment with different sharpening and blurring options. (See Chapter 15 for details on working with channels.)

- For filters that include the Repeat Edge Pixels option, enlarge the canvas area so that the image is in the middle, and then apply the filter. By doing this, you can prevent the filter from laying the colors along the edge of the image. After you apply the filter, crop the image as needed.

- Use the Actions palette to record your work. By recording your steps, you'll always be able to replicate effects and dialog box settings. (See Chapter 11 for details on using the Actions palette and recording actions.)

- Use the History palette to create snapshots as you work. After you create the snapshot, you can experiment with the snapshot version of your image by turning it into a new document. To do this, select the snapshot and click on the New Document icon in the History palette. (See Chapter 11 for information about using the History palette and creating snapshots.)

Applying Blur and Blur More

The Blur filter creates a light blurring effect that can be used to decrease contrast and eliminate noise in color transitions. The Blur More filter blurs about three to four times as much as the Blur filter.

Applying Gaussian Blur

The Gaussian Blur filter allows you to control the blurring effect, creating anything from a slight softening of image edges to a thick haze that blurs the image beyond recognition. This filter is so named because it maps pixel color values according to a Gaussian bell-shaped curve.

In the Gaussian Blur dialog box, you specify a value from 0.1 to 250 in the Radius field to control the range of the blur from transitional areas; the higher the number, the greater the blur. By experimenting with different Radius values, you can often eliminate moiré patterns in scanned images. (A *moiré pattern* is an unwanted mottled effect that sometimes appears during the scanning of printed photographs or when an image is printed at an incorrect screen angle.)

Figure 12-1 shows a photograph of Puck standing on top of New York City's Puck building, scanned from a Pratt Manhattan Art School's course catalog. In the version on the left, notice the moiré pattern over the entire image. The version on the right shows the same image after the Gaussian Blur filter was applied. As you can see, after applying the filter, the pattern is hardly noticeable.

To learn how to use the Gaussian Blur filter to create drop shadows, see Chapter 16. Gaussian Blur is also often used to help create three-dimensional effects, as described later in this chapter in the "Applying Lighting Effects" section.

Applying Motion Blur

The Motion Blur filter creates the illusion of motion. It simulates the effect of photographing a moving object using a timed exposure.

The Motion Blur dialog box allows you to control the direction and strength of the blur. To set the blur direction, type a degree value from –90 to 90 in the Angle box or

A moiré pattern appears over
the original scanned image

Applying Gaussian Blur
diminishes the moiré effect

Figure 12-1. *Before and after applying the Gaussian Blur filter (photo courtesy of Pratt Manhattan and photographer Federico Savini)*

use the mouse to click and drag on the radius line in the circle. To control intensity, enter a pixel value from 1 to 999 in the Distance field.

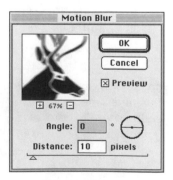

If you zoom in on the pixels after blurring, you will see how the Motion Blur filter works. It copies the image using the number in the Distance field as a guide, offsets (shifts) the duplicate according to the Angle value, and then overlays the copy of the image over the original as it lowers the opacity of the duplicate.

 This illustration shows the results of Motion Blur. To prevent the deer image itself from appearing blurred, we first selected the original image with the Magic Wand and copied it into the Clipboard. Then we chose Filter > Blur > Motion Blur. In the Motion Blur dialog box, we set Distance to 60 pixels and Angle to 45°, to match the deer's jumping angle. Next we pasted the copy of the deer from the Clipboard over the blurred image. Finally, while the copied image was floating, we offset the original about a quarter of an inch away from it.

 If you want to blur different portions of your image, duplicate your image in a layer. Apply the blur to the layer and create a layer mask. In the layer mask, paint with white to gradually unblur and reveal parts of the unblurred underlying layer. To learn more about layer masks, see Chapter 17.

Applying Radial Blur

The Radial Blur filter creates numerous interesting effects. It can spin an image into a circular shape or make it radiate out from its center, creating an explosive effect.

When you activate Radial Blur, a wireframe preview appears in the filter's dialog box, providing a skeletal view of the blur's effect. This is extremely helpful because the Radial Blur filter often takes a long time to execute.

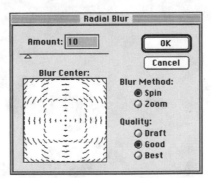

In the Radial Blur dialog box, you can select either Spin or Zoom as the blur method. If you select Spin, the blur is created in concentric circles, often making your image look as if it were spun on a potter's wheel. With Zoom, blurred image lines zoom out from the image's center point.

To control the intensity of the blur, enter a value between 1 and 100 in the Amount field, or drag the Amount slider control until the blur in the preview box shows the effect you desire; the higher the value, the more intense the blur. To change the center of the blur, click and drag on the dot in the center of the Blur Center box.

The Radial Blur dialog box also allows you to specify the quality of the blur. The Best option produces the smoothest blur, but it takes the longest to execute. With the Draft option, Photoshop/ImageReady completes the blur faster, but the results will be grainy. The Good option produces a level of quality between Best and Draft, although for large files, there may be little noticeable difference between Best and Good.

In Figure 12-2, the Radial Blur filter was applied to a pagoda image to produce a tornado-like effect. In the Radial Blur dialog box, we set Amount to 6, chose Spin as the blur method, and selected Best quality.

Applying Smart Blur

The Smart Blur filter allows you to create a variety of blurring effects. You can blur out the folds or wrinkles in an image or change an image so that the overlaid edges are blurred. Using the options in the Smart Blur dialog box, you can also turn a colored image into a black-and-white one, with the image's edges white.

In the Smart Blur dialog box, the Radius slider controls the distance of the blurring effect. The Threshold slider allows you to set how different the pixels must be before the blurring takes effect. If you set the Quality value to High, the filter will take longer

Figure 12-2. *Applying the Radial Blur filter, with the Spin blur method*

to execute, but the image quality will be better. The Mode pop-up menu allows you to choose which part of the image to apply the blurring to. If you choose Normal, blurring affects the entire colored image. If you choose Edge Only (edges are image areas with a great deal of color variation) and raise the Threshold slider, the image edges turn white and the rest of the image turns black. If you choose Overlay Edge, the filter overlays the image edges when applying the blurring effect.

Using the Noise Filters

Noise, composed of randomly colored pixels, is occasionally introduced during the scanning process. The Noise filters blend noise with the surrounding pixels to make it less apparent. You can also use Add Noise to drown an image with so much noise that it is completely transformed into colored pixel patterns. You can use the Add Noise effect to create interesting and unusual textured backgrounds. Noise filters can also be used to add a grainy texture to images. Noise is handy if you are converting 24-bit images to Indexed Color for the Web or multimedia programs. The noise can help smooth transitions in an Indexed Color image.

Applying Add Noise

The Add Noise filter adds noise to an image, blends noise into an image, and helps diffuse color banding that can occur in blends. This filter is sometimes used to help blend images that were created with painting tools into their surroundings or to create interesting patterned backgrounds. When you use it to create background patterns, you should experiment with different file resolutions, because the pattern will change depending on the resolution.

Use the Add Noise dialog box to indicate the amount of noise you wish to add to an image. Enter a value from 1 to 999 in the Amount field; the greater the amount, the greater the noise effect.

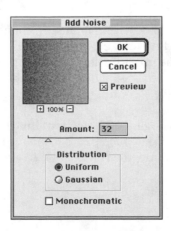

There are two distribution options in the Add Noise dialog box. When you select Uniform, Photoshop/ImageReady generates noise randomly, using the Amount field value to calculate the random values. For instance, if you enter **5** in the Amount field, Photoshop/ImageReady will calculate random color values between –5 and 5 for each pixel's color. With the Gaussian distribution option, the noise is mapped along a bell-shaped curve. This often produces a noisier effect than that of the Uniform setting. The Gaussian option also tends to produce a greater number of light pixels. If you select the Monochromatic checkbox, colors will not be added to the image when noise is created. It is like adding noise to the luminance values of your image.

The following illustration shows a pattern created with the Add Noise filter. This effect was generated by first creating a dark-to-light linear blend horizontally (left to right) on the screen. Then we applied the Add Noise filter once, with the Gaussian option selected and an Amount value of 100.

Applying Despeckle

The Despeckle filter seeks out the areas of greatest color change in an image and blurs everything except transitional edges; thus, detail is not lost. Use this filter when you need to reduce noise or to blur areas that have been pixelated because of oversharpening. The Despeckle filter can sometimes help reduce moiré patterns that can occur after scanned images are printed.

Applying Dust & Scratches

The Dust & Scratches filter hunts down small imperfections in an image or selection and blends them into the surrounding image. Before applying the Dust & Scratches filter, select the area that includes the imperfections you want to eliminate. When you open the filter's dialog box, the selected area will appear in the preview box. In the Dust & Scratches dialog box, click on the + control to zoom in to view the dust and/or scratches you want to eliminate.

In the Dust & Scratches dialog box, Photoshop/ImageReady uses the value entered in the Threshold field to determine which pixels to analyze when cleaning up the image. When you enter a Threshold value, the filter uses it to analyze the difference between the pixel values of the scratches and the pixel values of the surrounding pixels. If you type in **0**, the filter analyzes all of the pixels in an image. By typing in a Threshold value above zero, you begin to restrict the area the filter evaluates. For instance, suppose that you have an image area with a brightness value of 100, and in that image area you have a 1-pixel gray scratch with a brightness value of 150. If you type **49** in the Threshold field, the scratch will disappear. If you type **50** or any number over that, the scratch will not disappear.

Once the filter homes in on a scratch or an imperfection, it uses the Radius value to determine how large an area to clean up. The Radius value controls the range in the scratch or dust area that is cleaned up. If you enter too large a Radius value, your image might begin to look blurry. Try to maintain a balance between the Threshold and Radius so that defects are removed but the sharpness of your image is maintained.

The Dust & Scratches filter, with a little help from the Rubber Stamp tool, was applied to the image shown on the left in Figure 12-3. The result is shown on the right. To try out the Dust & Scratches filter on the original image in this figure, load the Man&Dog file from the Chapter 12 folder from the CD-ROM.

IMAGE EDITING
FUNDAMENTALS

A damaged photo

Applying Dust & Scratches
diminishes the imperfections

Figure 12-3. *Before and after applying the Dust & Scratches filter*

Applying Median

The Median filter reduces noise by blending the brightness of pixels within a selection. It's called the Median filter because it replaces the center pixel in a radius area with the median brightness value of the pixels in that area.

In the Median dialog box, you can enter a Radius value between 1 and 16 pixels. The Radius value is the distance that the filter searches from each pixel to analyze brightness.

Using the Sharpen Filters

The four Sharpen filters clarify images by creating more contrast and are often used to enhance the contours of scanned images. You may want to apply these filters after reducing images (Image > Image Size) or distorting images that have been edited with Edit > Transform commands. The Sharpen filters reduce the blurring that can occur after interpolation.

Be careful not to sharpen too much. If you do, distinct pixels will begin to show through, causing the image to look pixelated.

Applying Sharpen, Sharpen Edges, and Sharpen More

The Sharpen filter sharpens by increasing the contrast between neighboring pixels. The Sharpen Edges filter works like the Sharpen filter, except it sharpens only the edges of an image (smooth areas are unaffected). The Sharpen More filter provides a stronger sharpening effect than the Sharpen filter.

If you need to sharpen small, intricate areas, particularly image highlights, it's better to work with the Sharpen tool in the Toolbox rather than a Sharpen filter, because the tool is more precise.

Applying Unsharp Mask

The Unsharp Mask filter exaggerates the sharpness of an image's edges. It is often helpful to apply this filter after converting an image from RGB to CMYK or after any other Photoshop operation that involves interpolation. Unlike the other Sharpen filters, Unsharp Mask lets you control the amount of sharpening when you apply it.

The Unsharp Mask filter got is name from the unsharp mask traditional photographic masking technique, in which a negative and a blurred positive of an image are combined to make the image stand out.

You can control the intensity of this filter's effect by entering a percentage from 1 to 500 in the Amount field of the Unsharp Mask dialog box; the higher the percentage, the greater the sharpening. Higher-resolution images often require a higher percentage. A percentage of 150 to 200 usually provides good results with high-resolution images.

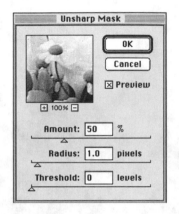

Tip   *Instead of applying an Unsharp Mask filter amount of 150 percent to a high-resolution image, you may get better results by using a percentage of 60 and applying Unsharp Mask twice.*

In the Radius field, you can specify the distance (in pixels) out from transitional edges that you want sharpened; the higher the Radius number, the greater the distance that sharpening will occur beyond image contours. If you enter a low Radius number, the sharpening occurs closer to image edges. Adobe recommends setting the Radius value to between 1 and 2 for high-resolution images. If you use too high a Radius setting, you may find that image contours darken.

In the Threshold field, you can specify a comparison between neighboring pixels for sharpening; the higher you set Threshold, the lower the number of pixels that will be affected. It allows you to prevent sharpening unless contrast between pixels is above the Threshold value. For instance, if the brightness values of neighboring pixels differ by 5, typing in a Threshold value of **4** will cause sharpening to occur. If you enter **5** or larger in the Threshold field, Photoshop/ImageReady will ignore the pixels. Thus, the Threshold value can be used to prevent oversharpening in the entire image or a selected area. If you keep Threshold set at the default level of 0, the filter will change the most pixels possible.

Figure 12-4 shows an image of some flowers with part of the image sharpened. The Unsharp Mask filter was applied three times, with Amount set to 50%, Radius set to 1, and Threshold set to 0. To try out the Unsharp Mask filter on the image shown in Figure 12-4, load the Flower file from the *Photoshop Complete Reference* CD-ROM.

Area sharpened

Figure 12-4. *Applying the Unsharp Mask filter to a portion of an image*

Note *As you work, you may notice that colors in your image change after you apply the Unsharp Mask filter. Adobe recommends converting the image to Lab Color mode and applying the filter to the L channel. Because the L channel is a luminosity channel, not a color channel, the sharpening will not change colors in the image. Also note that you can freely switch between Lab and RGB Color modes without altering color values.*

Using the Render Filters

The Render filters primarily create lighting effects in your images. The filters run from the uncomplicated to the complex. For instance, the Cloud filter simply creates cloudlike effects on your screen. On the other end of the scale, the Lighting Effects filter allows you to point up to 16 different light sources at your image. The Lighting Effects filter can even apply a texture to your image to make it look as if it were a lunar landscape. The 3D Transform filter allows you to take an image, such as a photograph with a three-dimensional effect, and manipulate the perspective in the image.

Note *The Lighting Effects filter and the Lens Flare filter can be applied only to RGB Color images.*

Applying 3D Transform

The 3D Transform filter allows you to manipulate a two-dimensional Photoshop/ImageReady image as if it were created in a 3-D program. The filter works best with slight adjustments to simple images and is most useful for repositioning images composed of shapes such as cubes, spheres, and cylinders. You might use the 3D Transform filter when you need to work with a digitized image that wasn't photographed at the correct angle or that needs to be adjusted so that the perspective of the entire image looks realistic.

In the 3D Transform dialog box, shown in Figure 12-5, choose one of the modeling tools—the Cube, Sphere, or Cylinder tool—depending on the type of image that you want to transform. Then click and drag over the preview of your image in the 3D Transform dialog box. This creates a wireframe skeleton on the screen. Next use the Direct Selection tool (the white arrow) to drag the anchor points of the wireframe over the edges of the image area that you wish to transform. If you wish to move the wireframe, click and drag on the edge of the wireframe with the Direct Selection tool.

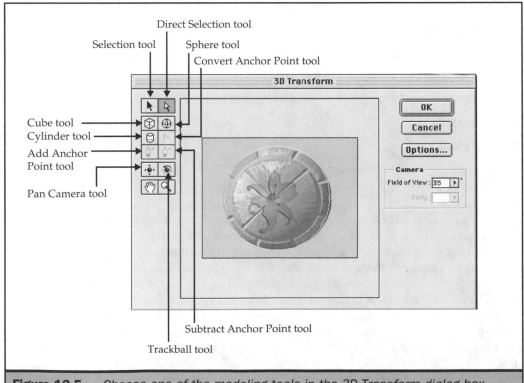

Figure 12-5.   *Choose one of the modeling tools in the 3D Transform dialog box*

IMAGE EDITING FUNDAMENTALS

The Add Anchor Point, Subtract Anchor Point, and Convert Anchor Point tools work with wireframes created with the Cylinder tool. You can use the Add Anchor Point or Subtract Anchor Point tool to increase or decrease the number of anchor points on the wireframe, so that you can outline the image. After you add anchor points, you can use the Direct Selection tool to edit the wireframe. If you need to convert a corner point to a smooth point or convert a smooth point to a corner point, click on the point using the Convert Anchor Point tool, and then drag the mouse.

After you've outlined your image with the wireframe, use the Pan Camera and Trackball tools to manipulate the scene to the desired view. Use the Point of View and Dolly sliders on the right side of the dialog box to fine-tune the scene. To access the sliders, click on the arrows in the Point of View and Dolly fields. As you work with the Pan Camera and Trackball tools and the Point of View and Dolly fields, the dialog box previews the results.

You can activate the tools in the 3D Transform dialog box by pressing keyboard shortcuts. Here are a few:

Tool	Shortcut
Selection tool	V
Direct Selection tool	A
Add Anchor Point tool	+
Delete Anchor Point tool	–
Zoom tool	Z
Hand tool	H
Toggle between the Selection and Direct Selection tool	COMMAND-TAB (*CTRL-TAB*)

Before clicking on OK, click on the Options button to check the Options settings. The Resolution settings control the quality and smoothness. Choosing High Resolution and High Anti-aliasing produces high-quality results, but the filter will take longer to execute. If you want to separate the wireframe selection from its background and have it appear in a layer with a transparent background, deselect Display Background. Click on OK to return to the 3D Transform dialog box, and then click on OK to transform your image.

Figure 12-6 shows a multimedia button before and after the 3D Transform filter was applied. In the image on the right, the button was tilted slightly by clicking and dragging the mouse in the 3D Transform dialog box. To try out the 3D Transform filter on this image, load the Button file from the Chapter 12 folder of this book's CD-ROM.

Caution   *If you experiment with the 3D Transform filter, you'll find that you cannot render color information over all areas that it transforms. If you transform too much, you'll get a white-ribbed cylinder, cube, or sphere in part of your image area.*

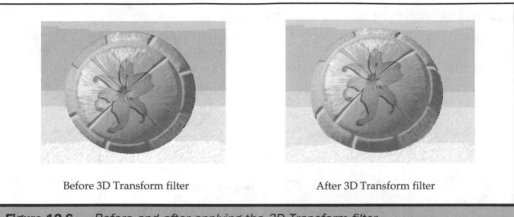

Before 3D Transform filter   After 3D Transform filter

Figure 12-6. *Before and after applying the 3D Transform filter*

Applying Texture Fill

The Texture Fill filter loads a Photoshop grayscale image into an image and repeats it in order to fill a layer or alpha channel. Texture Fill is often used to load a grayscale image into an alpha channel so that it can be used as a texture for the Lighting Effects filter, which is discussed in the next section. You might also apply Texture Fill to load a grayscale image into an alpha channel (in Photoshop, not ImageReady) to use as a layer mask or to create a texture effect in an image. (See Chapters 15 and 17 for more information about alpha channels and layer masks.)

To use Texture Fill to fill an alpha channel, first create a new alpha channel by choosing New Channel from the Channels palette. Then choose Filter > Render > Texture Fill. A dialog box prompts you to load a Photoshop/ImageReady grayscale file. Select the grayscale file that you want to load. After you click on OK, the file is loaded and repeated so that it fills the alpha channel.

Applying Lighting Effects

The Lighting Effects filter allows you to apply different light sources, types, and properties to an image. This helps you add depth to an image and spotlight certain areas, as well as change mood effects. The Lighting Effects filter can also be used to create texture maps from grayscale images. This can add a three-dimensional effect to a flat image by making it appear as if light is bouncing off bumps in the texture.

Note   *The Lighting Effects filter can be applied only to RGB color images.*

Choosing a Style and Creating Lights

In the Lighting Effects dialog box, choose a style in the Style pop-up menu. The default style provides a medium- to full-strength spotlight with a wide focus. Later in this section, you'll learn how to name and save your settings so that they appear in the Style pop-up menu.

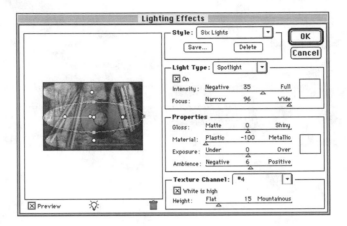

To create new lights, click the light bulb icon (☀) and drag it into the image preview area in the dialog box. To duplicate a light, press OPTION (*ALT*) and drag on the light. If you wish to delete a light, drag the light's circle icon onto the trashcan icon (🗑) in the dialog box. For each new light, you can choose a light type from the Light Type pop-up menu.

Choosing a Light Type

When the On checkbox in the Light Type section of the dialog box is selected, the light is on and you can choose a light type from the Light Type pop-up menu. You can select from the following types of lights:

- **Spotlight** This light type casts the light in a long, elliptical shape. When you choose Spotlight, the preview box shows an ellipse and four boxes. In the preview box, you can move the Spotlight by clicking and dragging on the center circle. You can change the angle and length of the light by dragging the handle on the end of the line to make it larger or smaller. You can change the focus of the light, which determines the amount of light that fills the elliptical area, by dragging on any of the four boxes on the ellipse. Dragging the boxes away from the center will increase the area that is lit.

When altering the Spotlight with the mouse, you can change the size of the ellipse without affecting the angle by pressing SHIFT and dragging. Press COMMAND (CTRL) and drag to change the angle but not the size of the ellipse.

- **Omni**   This light type casts light in all directions, as if the light were above the image. When you choose Omni, the preview box shows a circle and four boxes. To move the light, drag the center circle in the preview box. To give the appearance that the light is closer to the image, drag one of the four boxes closer to the center. Dragging a box farther away makes it appear as though the light is farther away.

- **Directional**   This light type casts light in one straight direction. Directional allows you to change only the direction and angle of the light. To move the light, drag on the center of the circle in the preview box. To change the height, drag the square at the end of the line; the longer the line, the farther away the light will be. Decreasing the size of the line creates a more intense light.

With the Spotlight, Omni, and Directional types, you can drag the Intensity slider in the Light Type section of the dialog box to control the strength of the light. The slider ranges from 100 (brightest) to –100 (pure black). A value of 50 is considered normal intensity. A negative value produces an effect similar to a black light.

The Focus slider in the Light Type section is available only with the Spotlight type. Dragging the slider toward Wide broadens the scope of the light within the ellipse. Dragging the slider toward Narrow produces the effect of a thinner light beam being applied to an image.

If you wish to change the color of the light, click on the rectangular swatch in the Light Type section. This will open the Color Picker dialog box, where you can pick a lighting color. (If the Apple or Windows Color Picker is selected in the General Preferences dialog box, the Apple/Windows Color Picker will appear instead.)

 If a style contains several light types and settings, pressing TAB will move you from one light type and its settings to another.

Adjusting Light Properties

All lights share a set of four properties, which you can adjust in the Properties section of the Lighting Effects dialog box:

- The Gloss property determines how light reflects off an image. Use the slider to vary the surface from Matte to Shiny.

- The Material property controls whether the light or the object the light is shining on has more reflectance. The slider allows you to drag from Plastic to Metallic. Plastic reflects the light's color. Metallic reflects the color of the image on screen.

- The Exposure property lightens or darkens the shining light. You can drag the slider from Under (underexposed) to Over (overexposed).

- The Ambience property can create the effect of blending light from the light source with the room light in an image. Clicking on the rectangular swatch in the Properties section allows you to pick a color for the light. If you drag the Ambience slider to 100 (to the right), the ambient light intensifies (adding the color from the swatch), so that it is not diffused with the light from the Light Type section. Drag the slider to the left, and the Ambient light gradually diminishes.

Using the Texture Channel Option

The Texture Channel option in the Lighting Effects dialog box allows you to use a channel to add texture to an image. When you use the Texture Channel feature, Photoshop/ImageReady bounces light off contours in the image that correspond to the texture. Use this feature to create terrain and embossed effects in your image.

To use this feature, you must first choose a texture in the Texture Channel pop-up menu (the texture can be an alpha channel, one of the RGB channels from your image, or even the currently active layer). Any texture can be copied into or created in an alpha channel to use as a texture. Then you can select the channel from the Texture Channel pop-up menu. In the list of choices, you'll see the RGB channels of your image, as well as any alpha channels you have added. If you are working in a layer, the Texture Channel pop-up menu allows you to select a Transparency choice for your layer. You can use this option to add a black or colored edge to the perimeter of a nontransparent area of your layer.

| Tip | *The Adobe Photoshop CD-ROM includes a folder of textures that can be loaded by the Lighting Effects filter, such as Brick, Carpeting, Caviar, Confetti, Footprints, and Dragon Scales. The textures can be found in the Textures for Lighting Effects folder in the Other Goodies folder.* |

If you wish to create an embossed effect, select the White Is High checkbox in the Texture Channel section of the dialog box. This creates the appearance of light being emitted from the image surface. Turn off this option if you want light to shoot down into the depths of your texture. To create a more bumpy texture, drag the Height slider toward Mountainous. A less bumpy texture will be produced if you drag the slider toward Flat.

Figure 12-7 shows an image before and after using a texture channel created from a flower image. To try out the Lighting Effects filter and Texture Channel option on these images, load the Flower and Artstuff files from the Chapter 12 folder of this book's CD-ROM.

Image used as basis for Texture Fill

Before applying the filter

After applying Lighting Effects
with Texture Channel option

Figure 12-7.   *Before and after applying the Lighting Effects filter with the
Texture Channel option*

Figure 12-8 shows an example of applying the Lighting Effects filter to a new file.
In the new file, we applied the Clouds and Add Noise filters to create a colored background. Next, we created a new channel to which we applied the Texture Fill filter
with the flower image (on the right in Figure 12-7), so that it repeatedly filled the alpha
channel (the steps for doing this are described in the next section). Then we applied the

Figure 12-8.   *Applying the Lighting Effects filter to a new file*

Lighting Effects filter with the Texture Channel option selected. As a result, the items in the alpha channel were applied to the document, creating a textured, embossed effect.

Saving Lighting Styles

The Lighting Effects dialog box also allows you to save your own lighting styles to disk. When you save a style, the settings for all of the lights in the Lighting Effects dialog box are saved, and the style's name appears in the Style pop-up menu. To save the settings as a style, click on the Save button in the Style section of the dialog box. In the dialog box that opens, enter a name for your style, and then click on OK.

If you are using the Texture Channel option, it's important to note that the named style reads the channel's number, not its contents. This means that when you open the image, the texture you need must be loaded in the Channels palette. If you need to make the style appear in another document, you must duplicate the channel into that document. (For information about duplicating a channel, see Chapter 15.)

If you wish to delete a style, select it in the Style pop-up menu and click on the Delete button.

Creating a Lighting Effect with a Texture Fill

The CD-ROM that accompanies Photoshop/ImageReady includes a variety of textures to try out with the Lighting Effects filter. If you don't have a texture map to use, here are step-by-step instructions for converting a color image to grayscale, creating a new channel, loading the grayscale image into the new channel using the Texture Fill filter, and then using the grayscale image as a texture with the Lighting Effects filter. You can use either the Adobe Samples folder images or any other two images.

1. Load the image that you wish to use as a texture. Use the File > Save As command to save it under another name. This ensures that you do not overwrite the original file.

2. To change the image into a grayscale file, choose Image > Mode > Grayscale. An alert box appears, asking whether you wish to discard color information. Click on OK.

3. The file on screen will now be a grayscale image. Choose File > Save, and then close the file.

Note *Make sure to save your file as a Photoshop grayscale file. The filter will not accept images in any other format.*

4. Open the file to which you wish to apply the texture.

5. Open the Channels palette by choosing Window > Show Channels.

6. Click on the Channels palette pop-up arrow. From the list of choices, choose New Channel. If you wish, enter a name in the dialog box to name the filter. Then click on OK. Notice that the new channel (Alpha 1) is selected in the Channels palette. This indicates that it is the target channel—the channel currently being edited.

7. To load the texture image into the new alpha channel, choose Filter > Render > Texture Fill. When the Open dialog box appears, choose the grayscale image (the image from steps 1 through 3). Notice that the pattern filling the screen is created from the grayscale image in the alpha channel.

8. To return to the RGB composite channel and the composite view of your image, click on RGB in the Channels palette.

9. Open the Lighting Effects dialog box by choosing Filter > Render > Lighting Effects.

10. In the Lighting Effects dialog box, load the texture by choosing Alpha1 in the Texture Channel pop-up menu. If you named your channel in step 6, select the channel name.

11. You should see the texture applied to the image on screen. To intensify the effect, move the Height slider to Mountainous. Before clicking on OK to close the dialog box, experiment with different lighting effects.

Creating Beveling Effects with the Lighting Effects Filter

The Lighting Effects filter can be used to quickly create three-dimensional beveling effects with its texture channel. Using the Lighting Effects filter and its Texture Channel option, you can quickly bevel a shape for a special effect, as shown in Figure 12-9.

The following are step-by-step instructions for creating a button shape in a new alpha channel and using the Lighting Effects filter with the Texture Channel option to create a beveled effect.

1. Create a new RGB color file, 2 inches by 2 inches. Set the resolution to 72 ppi.

2. Create a new alpha channel by clicking on the dog-eared icon at the bottom of the Channels palette or by choosing New Channel from the Channels palette pop-up menu. The entire channel should be black. If it isn't, double-click on the channel in the Channels palette and select Color Indicates Masked Area.

3. Set the foreground color to white.

4. Use either the Rectangular or Elliptical Marquee tool to create a marquee selection in the new alpha channel on the screen. Do not deselect the area.

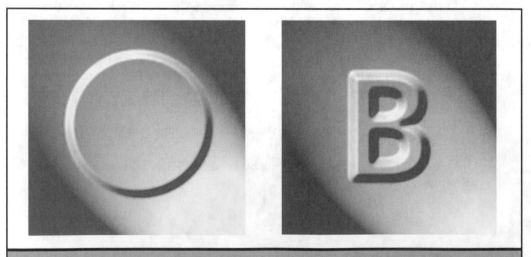

Figure 12-9. *Beveled button and character created using the Lighting Effects filter*

5. Fill the marquee selection with white by pressing OPTION-DELETE (*ALT-DELETE*).

 Instead of using the Marquee tool to create a selection and then filling it to convert it into a shape, you can use Photoshop's Pen tool to create a path and then fill it. You can also import shapes you have created in Adobe Illustrator into Photoshop.

6. Deselect the selection on screen by choosing Select > None or pressing COMMAND-D (*CTRL-D*).

7. To create a soft-edged effect, apply a blur to the image by choosing Filter > Gaussian Blur. Use a setting of 1.5 to 2.0. If you are working with a high-resolution file with a large shape, you will probably need to increase this setting. When working with low-resolution files and small shapes, you will probably need to decrease this setting.

 You can alter the beveling effect by putting a border around the selection (Select > Modify > Border) and then filling and blurring the border.

8. Select the RGB channel in the Channels palette by clicking on it.

9. Open the Lighting Effects dialog box by choosing Filter > Render > Lighting Effects. In the dialog box, set the Texture Channel option to the new alpha channel, Alpha1. Adjust the Height slider, the White Is High checkbox, and the lights and direction to achieve the final effect.

10. When you're satisfied with the effect, click on OK to close the Lighting Effects dialog box.

Applying Clouds

The Clouds filter transforms your image into soft clouds by using random pixel values that fall between the foreground and background colors. Therefore, you need to set the foreground and background colors to the colors you want the clouds to be. If you wish to create a less diffused cloud effect, press SHIFT when you choose the Clouds filter.

You can also use the Clouds filter to create a colored background. Set the foreground and background colors to any bright colors and then apply the filter. Once you've applied the Clouds filter, you might want to try using the Filter > Noise > Add Noise, the Filter > Distort > Glass, the Filter > Distort > Ripple, or the Filter > Distort > Ocean Ripple filter to add more texture to your background.

To try out the Clouds command, create a new 5-by-5-inch RGB color file. Set the foreground color to blue and the background color to white. Apply the Clouds filter by choosing Filter > Render > Clouds.

IMAGE EDITING
FUNDAMENTALS

The Clouds filter can be applied to grayscale images.

Applying Difference Cloud

The Difference Cloud filter inverts your image, blending it into a cloudlike background. The effect is very much like a combination of the Clouds command and the Difference blending mode. When the filter is applied, a cloudlike effect is generated from random pixel values that fall between the values of the foreground and background colors. Next, the filter subtracts the pixel values of the cloud data from the pixel values of your image. If you repeatedly apply the filter, a marbleized version of your image will result.

If you would like to test the effect of the Difference Cloud filter, open any file. Set the foreground color to blue and the background color to yellow, and then choose Filter > Render > Difference Cloud.

Applying Lens Flare

The Lens Flare filter creates an effect similar to that of a bright light shining into the lens of a camera. The Lens Flare dialog box allows you to set the brightness of the light, the center of the light source, and the lens type.

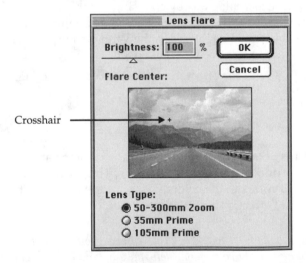

In the Brightness field, type in or use the slider control to enter a value between 10 and 300 percent. Click anywhere on the image icon to choose a center point for the light source. After you click, a crosshair indicates the center point. Before executing the filter, choose one of the Lens Type radio buttons.

Figure 12-10 shows an example of applying the Lens Flare filter to a photograph of a highway. To try out the Lens Flare filter on this image, load the Highway file from the Chapter 12 folder of the CD-ROM.

Using the Pixelate Filters

The Pixelate filters break down your image into pieces to make them look as if they were created from large blocks and squares. Besides making your image more mosaic-like, the Pixelate filters generally flatten them as well.

Applying Color Halftone

The Color Halftone filter makes an image appear to be created from large halftone dots. Photoshop/ImageReady creates this effect by dividing the image into rectangular grids, and then filling each rectangular grid with pixels to simulate the halftone dots. The width and height of the grid are controlled by the Max. Radius field in the Color Halftone dialog box. The dot placement in the image is controlled by the screen angles that you choose in the dialog box.

Figure 12-10.   *Applying the Lens Flare filter*

Applying Crystallize

The Crystallize filter sharpens images by moving similarly colored pixels together into a polygonal grid of pixels. The size of the polygon is controlled by the value you enter in the Cell Size field of the Crystallize dialog box.

Figure 12-11 shows the effect of the Crystallize filter when applied with a cell size of 10 pixels to the flower image shown earlier in Figure 12-4. To try out the Crystallize filter load the Flower file from this book's CD-ROM.

Applying Facet

The Facet filter gives a hand-painted look to an image by grouping and changing sampled pixels into blocks of similarly colored pixels. When this filter is applied, solid and similar colors are emphasized.

Applying Fragment

The Fragment filter creates an unfocused effect by copying an image's pixels four times, averaging them, and then offsetting them. This filter will quickly create an unfocused background over which you can paste objects to make them stand out.

Applying Mezzotint

The Mezzotint filter re-creates your image out of dots, lines, or strokes. In the Mezzotint dialog box, choose the desired effect from the Type pop-up menu. The Fine

Figure 12-11.   *Applying the Crystallize filter*

Dots choice often provides a mezzotint that looks closest to your original. To see the effects of the filter, load any image and then click on each choice in the Type pop-up menu to preview the results.

Applying Mosaic

The Mosaic filter gives your image a mosaic effect. If you are using Photoshop/ ImageReady to create video animation, you can use the Mosaic filter to replicate a technique commonly used in television, which causes an image to appear to gradually break up into pieces and then disappear. Some artists even use the Mosaic filter to make high-resolution images look digitized.

In the Mosaic dialog box, enter a number between 2 and 64 pixels in the Cell Size field or click and drag on the slider. The filter creates the mosaic effect by making all pixels in a cell the same color.

Applying Pointillize

The Pointillize filter breaks up an image into random dots, producing an effect much like that of a pointillist painting. You can control the size of dots in the filtered image by entering a cell value between 3 and 300 in the Pointillize dialog box. When the Pointillize filter is applied, Photoshop/ImageReady uses the current background color as the background.

Using the Distort Filters

The Distort filters are used to create distortions that vary from rippling an image to twirling and twisting it. If you are creating original art with Photoshop/ImageReady's tools, you will find that many of the Distort filters can save you time when you are creating unusual effects.

Applying Diffuse Glow

The Diffuse Glow filter diffuses highlights from images, creating a glowing effect. In the Diffuse Glow dialog box, the Graininess slider adds a sandy type of grain effect. Drag the slider to the right to increase the effect. The Glow Amount slider increases the effect of a glowing light on the image (if the light is the background color). The Clear Amount slider controls how much of your background color appears over the image: the lower the value, the greater the area that the background color covers.

Applying Displace

The Displace filter can bend, shatter, and twist an image. Unfortunately, of all the filters in Photoshop's and ImageReady's varied collection, the Displace filter is probably the most difficult to understand and the hardest to predict. The results seem unpredictable because the filter not only obeys your dialog box directions, but also relies on a *displacement map* to displace your image. You can apply the Displace filter to any Photoshop file, other than a bitmap image.

After you click on OK in the Displace dialog box to accept the settings, an Open dialog box appears, allowing you to select a file to use as the displacement map. After you choose the displacement map file, the Displace filter shifts image pixels according to color values in the displacement map.

Color values in the displacement map are measured on a scale from 0 to 255. Low values (darker colors) produce a displacement down and to the right in the filtered image. Midrange values (near 128) produce little displacement. High values (lighter colors) produce a displacement up and to the left.

In the Displace dialog box, you can enter values that control the degree of horizontal and vertical displacement. By entering a value in the Horizontal Scale field, you specify how much the filter will shift your image left or right according to the color values in the displacement map. The value in the Vertical Scale field specifies the amount the filter will shift your image up or down according to the color values in the displacement map. The highest allowed percentage, 100, displaces your image 128 pixels in areas corresponding to black or white in the displacement map.

There are two choices for handling displacement maps that are not the same size as the area to which you are applying the filter. The Stretch to Fit option transforms the size of the displacement map to match the image. The Tile option uses the displacement map as a repeating pattern.

You can also control the destiny of pixels that would normally be cast off screen by the displacement effect. Under Undefined Areas, the Wrap Around option will wrap the image so that it appears on the opposite side of the screen. The Repeat Edge Pixels option disperses the extra pixels over the edges of the image, which can sometimes create distinct color bands if the color of the extra pixels is different from the rest of the edge.

The Displace filter was applied to the car image shown in the middle of Figure 12-12 using the white-to-black radial blend shown on the left side of that figure as the displacement map. We enlarged the white area (the foreground color) of the blend using the Gradient Editor dialog box. We used a value of 70 for both the Horizontal Scale and Vertical Scale settings in the Displace dialog box. The result is shown on the right side of Figure 12-12. As you can see, the car was bent up and slightly to the left in the areas

Image used as the displacement map

Before applying the filter

After applying Displace

Figure 12-12.   *Before and after applying the Displace filter*

corresponding to the light areas in the displacement map, and it was bent down and to the right in areas corresponding to the dark portions of the displacement map. To try out the Displace filter on the car image in Figure 12-12, load the Car file from the Chapter 12 folder of the CD-ROM.

Producing a Displacement Effect

The best way to get a feel for the Displace filter is to apply the filter using one of Photoshop's or ImageReady's textures and analyze the effects. (The Textures folder can be found in the Goodies folder.)

Before you begin, open the texture called Bumpy Leather to take a look at how the light and dark areas are dispersed in the image. After examining the file, it's a good idea to close it (so that you don't inadvertently apply the Displace filter to it rather than to your image).

1. Open an image to which you wish to apply the filter. You can choose a file such as the Rockies image from the Adobe Samples folder (Goodies > Samples > Rockies).

2. Choose Filter > Distort > Displace.

3. For this exercise, you'll use low displacement values. (Higher values would displace your image so much that you wouldn't be able to decipher the results.) In the Displace dialog box, enter **30** for the Horizontal Scale and **30** for the Vertical Scale.

4. To keep your image from becoming too distorted, select the Tile and Repeat Edge Pixels options, and then click on OK.

5. An Open dialog box appears, in which you will choose a file to use as a displacement map. Open the Bumpy Leather file from the Textures folder (Goodies > Textures > Bumpy Leather).

In a few moments, your image will be displaced according to the Bumpy Leather texture. For most images, you'll probably see an effect of the image shattering into pieces.

 You can also apply the Displace filter to text to create scratchy type effects. Try using some of the filters in the Textures folder as displacement maps.

Analyzing Displacement Maps

Now that you know how to apply the Displace filter, you can begin to analyze how the filter works. Perhaps the most complicated fact about this filter is that its behavior depends on the number of channels in the displacement map. As mentioned earlier in the book, a channel is somewhat similar to a color plate used by a printer. RGB and Lab Color images consist of three channels, a CMYK file has four channels, and a grayscale image has one channel.

In one-channel displacement maps, the Displace filter displaces along the x and y axes. Darker values in the displacement map displace pixels downward according to the Vertical Scale value in the dialog box and to the right according to the Horizontal Scale value. White values are displaced upward according to the Vertical Scale value and to the left according to the Horizontal Scale value.

When the displacement map has more than one channel, the filter displaces according to the first two channels only: horizontally according to the first channel and vertically according to the second channel. In the first channel, darker areas cause displacement to the right and lighter areas cause displacement to the left, according to the dialog box values. In the second channel, dark areas displace the image downward and white areas displace upward, according to the dialog box values. Thus, to predict the outcome of the filter, you not only need to think in different dimensions, but you must also try to figure out how the color range in the displacement maps will affect the image.

If the Displace filter seems confusing to you, try creating your own simple one-channel displacement map and analyze the results. Follow these steps:

1. Create a new grayscale file and set the width and height to about the same size as the image to which you will be applying the filter.

Choose Select > All, then Edit > Copy, and then File > New. The dimensions in the New dialog box will be the same as the document on your screen.

2. Create a radial gradient from black to white in the middle of the screen. To create the gradient, click on the Radial button in the Gradient tool's Options bar, and then click and drag on the screen. Save the circle file in Photoshop's native format. This will be your displacement map.

3. Open the image to which you want to apply the filter. Choose Filter > Distort > Displace.

4. In the Displace dialog box, type **0** in the Horizontal Scale field and **50** in the Vertical Scale field. Choose both the Stretch to Fit and Repeat Edge Pixels options. Click on OK.

5. When the Open dialog box appears, select the file that contains your radial blend. After the filter has finished processing, you will see that the image pixels corresponding to the darkest areas of the displacement map area have moved down. Pixels corresponding to the white displacement areas have moved up.

6. Now undo the changes so that you can analyze the horizontal displacement. Select Edit > Undo. Alternatively, you can choose Filter > Fade and drag the Opacity slider to view how the image has changed.

7. Apply the Displace filter again. This time, type **50** in the Horizontal Scale field and **0** in the Vertical Scale field. Click on OK. Use the same displacement map that you used before. This time, when the filter is applied, the darker areas displace your image to the right; white areas are displaced to the left.

If you wish to experiment more with the Displace filter, you can use a variety of displacement maps included with the Photoshop/ImageReady package. They can be found in the Displacement Maps folder in the Plug-ins folder.

Applying Glass

The Glass filter allows you to distort your image to make it look as though it were seen through glass. The filter creates rippling effects according to a texture.

IMAGE EDITING FUNDAMENTALS

In the Glass dialog box, you can choose from the four preset textures provided with Photoshop/ImageReady: Blocks, Canvas, Frosted, and Tiny Lens. You can also load any Photoshop/ImageReady image as a texture (choose Load Texture from the Texture pop-up menu). The Distortion slider controls how prominent the appearance of the texture will be. The Smoothing slider smoothes the texture. Scaling adjusts the size of the texture. The Invert option reverses the light and dark areas in your image.

Experiment by applying each of the preset textures, and you'll get a good idea of how versatile the filter can be. The Frosted option can often make a scanned image look as if it were painted on the screen.

Applying Ocean Ripple

The Ocean Ripple filter distorts an image to make it look as though it were seen through rippling ocean waves. In the Ocean Ripple dialog box, the Ripple Size and Ripple Magnitude settings allow you to manipulate the ripple effect. Drag the Ripple Size slider to the right to increase the size of the ripples. Drag the Magnitude slider to the right to increase the distortion.

Applying Pinch

The Pinch filter is used to "squeeze" an image inward or outward. Figure 12-13 shows a clock graphic before and after applying the Pinch filter. First, we selected the original image with the Rectangular Marquee tool. We left more space in the marquee selection on the right side of the clock to produce a slight leftward tilt in the Pinch filter effect. Then we applied the Pinch filter using an outward pinch at –100% (100% results in an inward pinch). To try out the Pinch filter, create a clock using the Elliptical Marquee tool, Line tool, and Type tool and then apply the filter to the image.

Applying Polar Coordinates

The Polar Coordinates filter converts an image's coordinates from Rectangular to Polar or from Polar to Rectangular. When you select Rectangular to Polar in the Polar Coordinates dialog box, the filter can take a rectangular object and bend it into a circular shape. When you select the Polar to Rectangular option, the Polar Coordinates filter takes a circular object and stretches it.

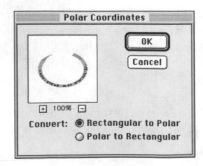

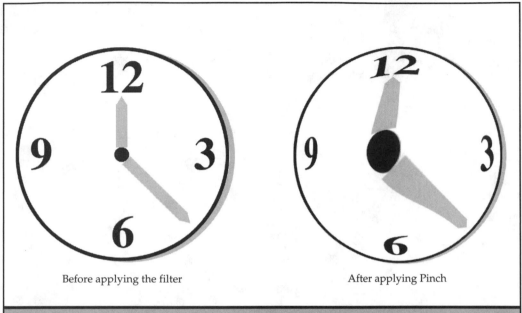

Before applying the filter   After applying Pinch

Figure 12-12.   *Before and after applying the (outward) Pinch filter*

Figure 12-14 shows a pencil graphic before after applying the Polar Coordinates filter to it, using the Rectangular to Polar option. We did not select any areas on the screen before applying the filter. If the pencil had been selected, the filter would have made it look somewhat like a round pie with a wedge cut out of the top. To try out the Polar Coordinates filter, create a pencil using the Rectangular Marquee tool, Lasso tool, Line tool, and Type tool and apply the filter to the image.

The next illustration shows the effects of applying the Polar Coordinates filter with the Polar to Rectangular option to the clock graphic. The snaking line at the bottom was created because a rectangular selection was made around the clock before the filter was applied.

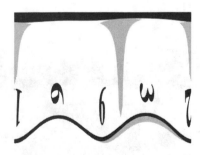

Before applying the filter

After applying Polar Coordinates

Figure 12-14. *Before and after applying the Polar Coordinates filter, with the Rectangular to Polar option*

Applying Ripple

The Ripple filter transforms an image by displacing its pixels to create a ripple effect. The next illustration shows what happened to the pencil graphic after the Ripple filter was applied. To create this effect, we set the Ripple Amount to 100 and the Ripple Frequency to Large in the Ripple dialog box.

Applying Shear

The Shear filter bends an image according to a specified curve. The effect can be used to bend and elongate an object.

To establish the curve in the Shear dialog box, click and drag on the vertical band in the dialog box grid. Each click produces another control point that can be dragged to create the curve. If you need to reset the curve to its starting position, press OPTION (*ALT*) and click on the Reset button. When the filter is applied to an object, it will bend along the curve you have established in the dialog box.

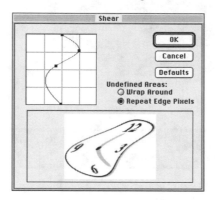

Tip   *If you want to bend a horizontal line, first bend a vertical line by applying the Shear filter to it. Then rotate the bent line so that it is on a horizontal plane.*

Here's the clock graphic, this time with the Shear filter applied.

Applying Spherize

The Spherize filter transforms a selection into a spherical shape. Use it to give text or an object a three-dimensional or bloated effect. In Figure 12-15, the Spherize filter has been applied to a scene from an Italian coast with a grid of lines over it.

Before applying the filter   After applying Spherize

Figure 12-15.   *Before and after applying Spherize filter*

Here's how to create this effect:

1. Load the Italiancoast file from the Chapter 12 folder of the CD-ROM.

2. Create a new layer by selecting Layer > New > Layer. In this layer, you'll create the grid.

3. Choose View > Show Rulers to display the rulers. Set a guide every half inch, horizontally and vertically, by clicking and dragging on guides from the rulers.

4. Select the Line tool in the Toolbox. Set the Opacity to **70%** and the Weight to **4** pixels. Set the foreground color to white, and then click and drag with the Line tool on the guides you created. Make sure View > Snap to Guides is selected.

5. Make the lines thicker, by stroking. Choose Layer > Layer Style > Stroke. In the Layer Style dialog box, set the stroke to **4** pixels. Then click the color swatch and change the color to black. Click on OK.

6. Hide the guides by choosing View > Clear Guides

7. Merge the layers by choosing Layer > Flatten Image.

8. Apply the Spherize command by choosing Filter > Distort > Spherize. In the Spherize dialog box, set the Amount to **100%** and leave the Mode set to Normal.

9. Click on OK to create the spherize effect.

Applying Twirl

The Twirl filter creates swirling pinwheel effects, with the rotation focused toward the center of the object. When you apply it at maximum strength, the Twirl filter makes your image look as if it were whipped in a blender. The next illustration shows the effect of applying the Twirl filter to the clock graphic. In this example, we set the filter effect to 150 degrees.

Applying Wave

The Wave filter helps you create many different undulating effects by providing various wavelength options to distort an image.

In the Wave dialog box, you can select a wave type of Sine (curved), Triangle, or Square. For the settings that control the wave, you can enter values by clicking and dragging on slider controls or by typing numbers into fields. In the Number of Generators field, you can control the number of waves generated, from 1 to 999. The more waves you generate, the more distorted the effect will be, because the peaks and dips of the wavelengths begin to intersect, causing more and more havoc in your image. Creating multiple waves is somewhat analogous to one ocean wave crashing into others; the more waves that crash together, the greater the turbulence.

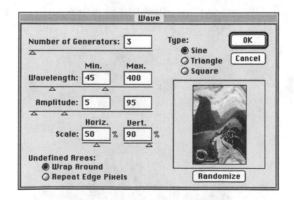

You can specify the distance between wave crests by entering a minimum and maximum Wavelength value. The height of each wave is controlled by the value specified for the minimum and maximum Amplitude values. Wavelength and Amplitude values can range from 1 to 999.9. The Scale percentages determine the degree of the distortions horizontally and vertically, and range from 0% to 100%.

 If you wish to replicate your wave results on other images, do not click the Randomize button, because it creates a random starting point for the Wave effect.

When you apply the Wave filter, an image can sometimes blend and twist off the screen. The Undefined Areas options in the Wave dialog box allow you to control the destiny of these outcast pixels. If you select Wrap Around, images will wrap to the opposite side of the screen. The Repeat Edge Pixels option disperses the extra pixels over the edge of the image, which can sometimes create distinct color bands if the color of the extra pixels is different from the rest of the edge.

 You can also apply the Wave filter to a border selection of an image. When you do this, you convert the straight edges to curved edges.

Figure 12-16 shows an image before and after applying the Wave filter to it to create a tidal wave effect. If you want to try the Wave filter, you can load the Dock file from the Chapter 12 folder of the CD-ROM.

Applying Zigzag

The Zigzag filter can be used to create ripples-in-a-pond and twirling effects. The effect is controlled by the values entered in the Amount and Ridges field and whether you choose the Pond Ripples, Out from Center, or Around Center options in the Zigzag dialog box.

The next illustration demonstrates how the Zigzag filter's Pond Ripples option can be used to create the illusion of pond ripples out of almost anything. In this case, the ripples were created in the flower image, shown earlier in Figure 12-4.

Before applying the filter   After applying Wave

Figure 12-16.   *Before and after applying the Wave filter*

Using the Stylize Filters

The Stylize filters are used to create the look of impressionist paintings and other painterly effects. Many of these effects are so dramatic that you may hardly recognize your original after applying the filter.

Applying Diffuse

The Diffuse filter creates an unfocused effect that breaks up an image as though it were being seen through frosted glass. The Diffuse dialog box has three options for controlling how the effect is created: by shifting pixels at random (Normal option), by replacing light pixels with darker ones (Darken Only option), or by replacing dark pixels with lighter ones (Lighten Only option).

Applying Emboss

The Emboss filter creates a raised effect by outlining the edges in a selection and lowering surrounding color values. This filter is often used for designing raised type or creating a relief effect.

In the Emboss dialog box, the direction of the embossing is controlled by the Angle field. Values can range from –180 to 180 degrees. You can type in the value or click and drag the angle indicator in the circle. Dragging clockwise increases the angle, and dragging counterclockwise decreases the angle.

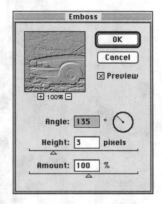

The height of the embossing is controlled by the value in the Height field, which can range from 1 to 10 pixels. To raise or lower the color values in the embossed image, enter a value from 1% to 500% in the Amount field. The lower the percentage, the lower the amount of color; the higher the percentage, the more color is applied to edges.

Figure 12-17 shows the effects of applying the Emboss filter applied to the car image shown earlier. Before applying the filter, we increased the contrast of the image with the Brightness/Contrast command in the Image > Adjust submenu. This emphasized the edges in the image, thereby enhancing the effect of the Emboss filter. In the Emboss dialog box, we set the Angle to 135°, the Height to 10 pixels, and the Amount to 200%.

Applying Extrude

The Extrude filter transforms an image into a series of three-dimensional blocks or pyramids, depending on the option set in the dialog box. Use it to distort images or to create unusual three-dimensional backgrounds.

In the Extrude dialog box, you can set the size of the base of the blocks or pyramids by typing a value from 2 to 255 in the Size field. Enter a value from 1 to 255 in the Depth field to control how far the objects extrude from the screen. Choose the Random radio button if you want the depth of each extruding object to be set to a random value.

If you want brighter parts of the image to protrude more than darker parts, select the Level-Based radio button. This option links the pyramid or block depth to color values. If you choose the Solid Front Faces checkbox, the face of the block is filled with the average color of the object, rather than that of the surrounding image. To ensure that no extruding object extends past the filtered selection, choose the Mask Incomplete Blocks checkbox.

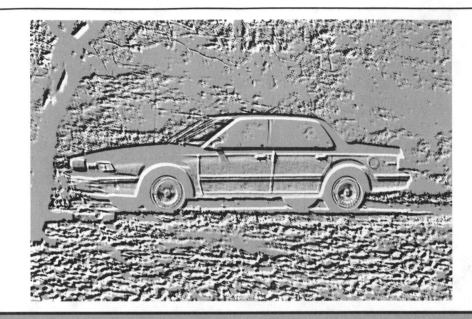

Figure 12-17.   *Applying the Emboss filter*

Figure 12-18 shows the effect when the Extrude filter's Pyramids option is applied to a radial blend from a dark color to a lighter one.

Applying Find Edges

The Find Edges filter searches for image areas that exhibit major color changes and then enhances transitional pixels. It can make an image look as though it were outlined with a pencil.

Figure 12-19 shows the car image after applying the Find Edges filter. Before applying the filter, we increased the contrast of the image with the Brightness/Contrast command in the Image > Adjust submenu. This enhanced the effect of the filter by adding more edges for the filter to outline.

Applying Glowing Edges

The Glowing Edges filter accentuates image edges, similar to the effect produced by the Find Edges filter. Unlike Find Edge, Glowing Edges allows you to control edge width (from 1 to 14 pixels), edge brightness, and smoothness. The filter also fills in dark areas to enhance the glowing effect.

Figure 12-18.   *Applying the Extrude filter's Pyramids option to a Radial gradient*

Figure 12-19.   *Applying the Find Edges filter*

Applying Solarize

The Solarize filter creates the effect of a positive and negative of an image blended together. In photography, you accomplish similar results by adding light during the developing process. See Chapter 19 to learn how to create a solarized effect with the Image > Adjust > Curves command.

Applying Tiles

The Tiles filter divides an image into tiles according to values specified in the Tile dialog box. In the Number of Tiles field, enter the minimum number of tiles you want to appear in each row and column of tiles. In the Maximum Offset field, enter the maximum distance (as a percentage) that you want the tiles offset from their original positions. If you want the area between the tiles filled with color, choose the Background Color or Foreground Color radio buttons in the Fill Empty Area With section. Choosing the Inverse Image radio button causes a reverse color image of your original image to appear through the tile cracks. Choosing the Unaltered Image radio button makes the tiles appear over the original image.

Figure 12-20 shows the effect of applying the Tiles filter with the default settings to the flower image introduced earlier in this chapter.

Figure 12-20. *Applying the Tiles filter*

Applying Trace Contour

The effect of the Trace Contour filter is similar to that of the Find Edges filter, except that Trace Contour draws thinner lines around edges and allows you to specify a tonal level for transition areas.

In the Trace Contour dialog box, you can enter a value between 0 and 255 in the Level field. Darker pixels correspond to lower numbers; lighter pixels to higher numbers. The Upper and Lower options allow you to choose whether you want contours traced above or below the Level value.

Applying Wind

The Wind filter creates a windblown effect by adding small horizontal lines. The Wind dialog box allows you to choose how strong the wind effect is and in what direction you wish the wind to blow.

In the Wind dialog box, select the Wind radio button to create a wind effect. To create a stronger wind effect, choose Blast. If you choose the Stagger option, the wind lines will be offset from one another. In the Directions group, choose From the Left or From the Right to set the wind direction.

Figure 12-21 shows the Wind filter applied to the car image, with the filter's Blast option, then Wind option selected. The Direction was set to From the Left, which is the default direction.

Using the Painterly Effects Filters

The filters in the Artistic, Brush Strokes, Sketch, and Texture submenus are designed to add painting- and sketch-like qualities to your images. Some of the filters can make a scanned photograph look as though it were painted by the hand of a skilled painter. Most of the filters that provide painterly effects are quite easy to use. The dialog box settings are self-explanatory, and the previews provide an excellent rendition of how the final image will appear.

Applying Artistic Filters

The Artistic filters include Colored Pencil, Cutout, Dry Brush, Film Grain, Fresco, Neon Glow, Paint Daubs, Palette Knife, Plastic Wrap, Poster Edges, Rough Pastels, Smudge Stick, Sponge, Underpainting, and Watercolor. The Artistic filters allow you to give your photographs painterly effects.

Figure 12-21.   *Applying the Wind filter, with the Blast option, then Wind option*

Figure 12-22 shows the effect of applying the Cutout filter to a Venice image. If you want to try the Cutout filter, you can load the Building file from the CD-ROM.

Another interesting filter in the Artistic group is the Underpainting filter, which provides a variety of options for changing the texture and lighting in an image. By using Underpainting, you can create three-dimensional textures, giving an image a Brick, Burlap, Sandstone, or Canvas texture. You can even load a Photoshop/ImageReady image and use it as the basis of a texture.

Applying Brush Strokes Filters

The Brush Stroke filters allow you to control the digital brush strokes in an image. The Brush Stroke filters include Accented Edges, Angled Strokes, Crosshatch, Dark Strokes, Ink Outlines, Spatter, Sprayed Strokes, and Sumi-e. Spatter makes your image look as if it were created with spattered paint. Crosshatch not only creates brush strokes, but also

Before applying the filter   After applying Cutout

Figure 12-22.   *Before and after applying the Cutout filter*

blurred lighting effects. Sumi-e can make your image look as if it were created from broad charcoal brush strokes, as seen in Figure 12-23.

Applying Sketch Filters

In general, the Sketch filters attempt to make your images look as though they were sketched by hand. They include Bas Relief, Chalk & Charcoal, Charcoal, Chrome, Conté Crayon, Graphic Pen, Halftone Pattern, Note Paper, Photocopy, Plaster, Reticulation, Stamp, Torn Edges, and Water Paper. Most filters, such as Chalk & Charcoal, Charcoal,

Figure 12-23.   *Applying the Sumi-e filter*

and Graphic Pen, come close to a hand-sketched look. Figure 12-24 shows the effects of applying the Graphic Pen filter.

Some Sketch filters provide unusual effects. For instance, Chrome can make your image look like a silvery mess. Reticulation can make your image look as though it were created from tiny pieces of colored sand or tiny insects.

Applying Texture Filters

Perhaps the most startling effects of all of the Painterly filters are created by the filters in the Texture group. The Texture filters include Craquelure, Grain, Mosaic Tiles, Patchwork, Stained Glass, and Texturizer. Craquelure makes your image look as it if contained small,

Figure 12-24. *Applying the Graphic Pen filter*

three-dimensional cracks—almost like a textured tile with cracks in it. If you want lots of cracks, decrease the crack spacing in the Craquelure dialog box.

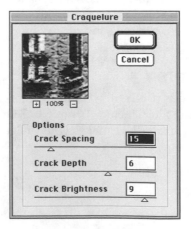

Note   *To see how the Craquelure filter can be used to add texture to a three-dimensional figure created in Fractal Poser, see Chapter 18.*

The Grain filter's Sprinkles option can make your image look as though it were created from colored sprinkles from an ice cream parlor. The Stained Glass filter makes the image look like stained glass. Patchwork creates a patchwork quilt type of effect (which resembles a soft mosaic). The Mosaic Tiles filter, illustrated in Figure 12-25, provides a three-dimensional tile effect that is more interesting than the tiles produced in the Pixelate/Mosaic filter.

Using Video Filters

Photoshop's and ImageReady's Video filters were designed for images that will be input from video or output to videotape.

The NTSC Colors filters reduce the color gamut of the image to acceptable levels for television. The Deinterlace filter smoothes video images by removing odd or even

Figure 12-25.   *Applying the Mosaic Tiles filter*

interlaced lines. This filter is needed when a video frame is captured between an odd and even field and a blurred scan line becomes visible. The Deinterlace dialog box gives you a choice of substituting the line by duplication or interpolation.

 # Using Other Filters

The filters in the Other submenu are a diverse group that don't fit into any other major category. Perhaps the most interesting is the Custom choice, which allows you to create your own filter.

 The DitherBox filter is discussed in Chapter 9. Tile Maker (ImageReady) is covered in Chapter 10.

Creating a Custom Filter

If you would like to try your hand at creating your own filter, select Custom from the Filter > Other submenu. You won't be able to create filters as sophisticated as Photoshop's and ImageReady's filters, but you can design your own sharpening, blurring, and embossing effects.

In the Custom dialog box, you can control the brightness values for all of the pixels that will be filtered. Each pixel evaluated is represented by the text field that is in the center of the matrix of text fields in the dialog box. The value entered in this box is the number by which Photoshop/ImageReady multiplies the current pixel's brightness. You can enter a number between –999 and 999.

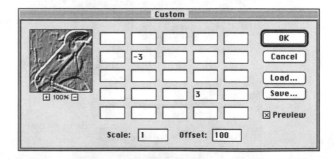

By typing numbers in the surrounding text fields, you can control the brightness of adjacent pixels in relation to the pixel represented in the center box. Photoshop/ImageReady multiplies the brightness value of adjacent pixels by this number. In other words, with the Custom dialog box's default settings, the brightness value of the pixel to the left of the central pixel will be multiplied by –1.

In the Scale field, you can enter a value that will be used to divide the sum of the brightness values. In the Offset field, you can enter a value that you want to have added to the Scale's calculation results.

When the filter is applied, Photoshop/ImageReady recalculates the brightness of each pixel in the image or selected area, summing up the multiplied values used in the dialog box matrix. It then divides this result by the Scale value and adds the Offset value, if there is one.

Here's how you need to adjust the settings to create a filter:

- To create a sharpening filter, you'll need to increase the contrast between neighboring pixels. If you balance a set of negative numbers around the central matrix pixel, you will sharpen your image.

- To create a blur filter, surround the central matrix pixel with positive numbers. The positive numbers reduce the contrast between pixels as the matrix formula passes over the images.

- To create an embossing filter, balance positive and negative values around the central matrix area.

Figure 12-26 shows an image before and after increasing contrast and applying a custom emboss filter. If you want to try applying a custom emboss filter to the horse image, you can load the Horse file from the book's CD-ROM.

You can save and reload your custom filters by using the Save and Load buttons in the Custom dialog box.

Before applying the filter   After applying custom emboss

Figure 12-26.   *Before and after applying a custom emboss filter*

Applying High Pass

The High Pass filter suppresses areas that contain gradual increases in brightness and preserves portions of the image that exhibit the sharpest transitions in color. When you apply this filter, it removes shading and accentuates highlights.

In the High Pass filter dialog box, you can control the size of the transition edge by typing a pixel value from 0.1 to 250 in the Radius field. A large value leaves more of the image's pixels near transitional points. A lower value preserves only the edges of the transition areas. When you apply the filter, it analyzes each pixel from the starting pixel to a specified Radius distance.

Applying Maximum

The Maximum filter expands light areas and diminishes dark areas. When you apply the Maximum filter, the current pixel's brightness value is replaced by the maximum brightness of surrounding pixels. The distance of the surrounding pixels can be specified by entering a value from 1 to 10 in the Radius field in the Maximum dialog box.

The filter can be used in an alpha channel to increase the light area in the channel. (Alpha channels can be used for masking out parts of an image so that they can be edited in isolation, as discussed in Chapter 15.)

Applying Minimum

The Minimum filter has the opposite effect of the Maximum filter. It expands dark areas and diminishes light areas. The Minimum filter can be used in an alpha channel to increase the dark areas. When you apply the Minimum filter, the current pixel's brightness value is replaced with the minimum brightness values of surrounding pixels. You can specify the distance of the surrounding pixels by entering a value from 1 to 10 in the Radius field of the Minimum dialog box.

Applying Offset

The Offset filter moves the filtered image according to values entered in the Offset dialog box. In previous versions of Photoshop/ImageReady, this filter was often used to create shadowed effects. In version 6.0, you can accomplish very much the same result by choosing ImageReady's Edit > Numeric Transform command, and you can use the Layer > Effects > Drop Shadow command to create drop shadows.

In the Offset filter dialog box, specify whether you wish the image to move horizontally and/or vertically. In the Vertical and Horizontal fields, you can enter values between –30,000 and 30,000. Positive values offset right and up; negative values offset left and down. If you wish to have the background of the image filled with the current background color, select the Set to Background radio button.

```
┌─────────────────── Offset ───────────────────┐
│                                               │
│   Horizontal: [0]      pixels right   ( OK )  │
│                                               │
│   Vertical:   [0]      pixels down    (Cancel)│
│                                               │
│   ┌ Undefined Areas ────┐                     │
│   │ ● Set to Background │    ⊠ Preview        │
│   │ ○ Repeat Edge Pixels│                     │
│   │ ○ Wrap Around       │                     │
│   └─────────────────────┘                     │
└───────────────────────────────────────────────┘
```

The Offset filter also includes options for handling pixels that would be offset out of the screen area. The Wrap Around option wraps these pixels so that they appear on the opposite side of the screen. The Repeat Edge Pixels option disperses the extra pixels along the edges of the image.

Chapter 13

Converting Modes for Printing, Multimedia, and the Web

Throughout this book, you have been working primarily in RGB Color mode, which is Photoshop's default image mode. Although RGB Color mode allows you to access the full range of Photoshop image-editing menus and commands, many projects require that you convert images from RGB Color to another mode.

In this chapter, you'll have a chance to explore Photoshop's eight modes: Bitmap, Grayscale, Duotone, Indexed Color, RGB Color, CMYK Color, Lab Color, and Multichannel. You'll learn about the uses for each mode and how to switch between one mode and another.

Why Convert Modes?

The mode you choose for an image depends on your output requirements and design goals. Here are some reasons for switching from one color mode to another:

- To output a file for four-color process printing, you must convert it to CMYK Color mode.

- When you need to work with a palette of 256 (or fewer) colors for multimedia output, you may wish to switch to Indexed Color mode.

- If you choose File > Save to save an RGB file in GIF format for the Web, Photoshop will prompt you to convert the file to Indexed Color mode first.

> **Note** *In most instances, use File > Save for Web to save images for the Web in Photoshop; in ImageReady, choose File > Save Optimized.*

- For other projects, you may need to remove all color from an image. In this case, you can convert from any color mode to Grayscale mode. From Grayscale, you can convert to Bitmap (black-and-white) mode.

- To add color to a grayscale image, you need to convert from Grayscale mode to one of Photoshop's color modes (RGB Color, Indexed Color, CMYK Color, or Lab Color).

Switching modes also allows you to create special printing effects such as duotones and mezzotints. A *duotone* is a grayscale image in which two inks, usually black and another color, are printed over each other. The resulting extra color can add interest and depth to a grayscale image. A *mezzotint* is a bitmap image created from randomly shaped dots.

Since Web graphics are RGB images, ImageReady does not include commands for switching modes. In ImageReady you can reduce the number of colors in an RGB image by "optimizing" it with the Optimize palette. You can also convert a color image to grayscale using one of the options in the Optimize palette. See Chapter 9 for more details.

Converting from RGB Color Mode

RGB Color is Photoshop's native color mode. As discussed in Chapter CD-1, in RGB Color mode, you can create any color by combining different values of red, green, and blue. In Photoshop's RGB Color mode, more than 16.7 million colors are available to you. You can view and edit each of the red, green, and blue color components, called *channels*, individually. Viewing an image's channels can help you better understand the difference between one mode and another.

Using the Channels Palette

In order to see the RGB channels that make up an RGB image, open any RGB Color file in Photoshop. (If you don't have an RGB image, load the Koala image from this book's CD-ROM or an RGB image from Photoshop's Samples folder.) With your file displayed, open the Channels palette by choosing Window > Show Channels.

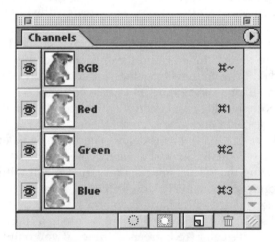

 To ensure that you are viewing colors properly in RGB Color mode, it is extremely important that you calibrate your monitor and then review the settings in the Color Settings dialog box (Edit > Color Settings). For more information, see Chapter 2.

IMAGE EDITING
FUNDAMENTALS

When the Channels palette opens, you'll see the three RGB channels listed. There's also a composite channel, where all of the channels combine to produce one color image. The eye icon (👁) indicates that the components of a particular channel are being viewed. The dark or colored area within the different channel sections means that the channel is selected and its contents will be affected if the image is edited. When a channel is selected, it is often referred to as the *target channel*. The thumbnail image in the channel is a miniature version of the image on your screen. You can change the size of the palette's thumbnail by choosing the Palette Options command in the Channels palette's pop-up menu.

You'll have a better sense of how RGB colors combine to create an image if you take a look at each channel. To do this, click on the name of the channel in the Channels palette. For instance, to view only the Red channel, click on Red in the Channels palette or use the keyboard shortcut COMMAND-1 (*CTRL-1*). In the image on your screen, you will see only the Red channel.

> **Note** *You'll probably see the channel in the Channels pallete as a grayscale image, because Photoshop does not display the individual channels in color unless you change the default Preferences setting for channels. To see the channels in color, select Edit > Preferences > Display & Cursors and select the Color Channels in Color checkbox.*

Take a look at each channel individually. Press COMMAND-2 (*CTRL-2*) to view the Green channel, and then press COMMAND-3 (*CTRL-3*) to view the Blue channel. When you view the Blue channel, notice that the eye icon next to it in the Channels palette is visible, and that the Blue channel section in the Channels palette is selected. This means that the Blue channel is the only channel in view and the only channel that can be edited.

You can view and edit two channels together, independently of the third. While viewing the Blue channel, press and hold SHIFT while you click on Green in the Channels palette. You will see both the Blue and Green channels together on the screen. Now you can begin to see how the colors combine to create the image. If you wish to deactivate and hide a channel, you can SHIFT-click the channel name in the palette. To return to the composite view, click on the RGB composite channel or press COMMAND-~ (*CTRL-~*).

In addition to viewing the RGB channels, you can also edit within them to create special effects. For example, you can click on a channel name so that it will be the only channel that can be viewed and edited and then apply a filter to it. You can also apply paint to each channel separately. If you paint with white in a channel, you will be painting with that channel's color (red, green, or blue); if you paint with black, you add that channel's complementary color to the image.

Switching from RGB to Other Modes

The three RGB channels and the millions of colors that can be produced in RGB images provide you with the proper colors for output to slides and video or for printing to an RGB color printer. However, as you work with Photoshop, your design goals or the output requirements of a project may necessitate switching modes. Table 13-1 lists the modes to which you can convert from RGB Color, with a brief explanation of each one.

Note   *From RGB Color (or any other color mode), you cannot convert directly to Bitmap (black and white) or Duotone; you must convert from RGB Color to Grayscale mode first.*

When you convert from RGB Color to another mode (except Multichannel), Photoshop changes the color data in the image's file. If you save the file after converting and close the file, you will not be able to return to the original color mode unless you are converting between RGB and Lab Color. Thus, before converting from RGB Color to another mode, it's wise to use the File > Save As command to create a second copy of your file. That way, you can always return to your original RGB file, if necessary.

IMAGE EDITING FUNDAMENTALS

Mode	Description
Grayscale	256 shades of gray. From Grayscale, you can switch to Bitmap to work in black and white, or to Duotone.
Indexed Color	256 colors or fewer. Can be used before outputting images to the Web or multimedia programs.
CMYK Color	Used for four-color process printing. Allows you to produce color separations.
Lab Color	Used by Photo CDs and PostScript Level 2 printers. Encompasses both RGB and CMYK color gamuts.
Multichannel	Used to view channels separately (no composite channel is created). Allows you to rearrange the channels in the Channels palette, which may be helpful when printing images with Spot Color channels.

Table 13-1.   *Modes to Which RGB Color Images Can Be Converted*

When you delete a channel from RGB, Lab, or CMYK modes, Photoshop automatically switches to Multichannel mode.

Converting to an 8-Bit Image

You may also want to convert a 48-bit RGB or 64-bit CMYK color image to an 8-bit RGB or CMYK color image.

By default, Photoshop uses 8 bits per color channel (256 color values) for RGB images. Many midrange and high-end scanners can scan using 16 bits per color channel, which provides more precise color information. However, if you load a 16-bit-per-channel image into Photoshop, you cannot use every tool and editing command. For instance, you cannot apply filters to 16-bit-per-channel images. Therefore, you may wish to convert a 16-bit-per-channel image into an 8-bit-per-channel image. To convert a 16-bit-per-pixel image to an 8-bit-per-pixel image, choose Image > Mode > 8 bit/Channel.

Converting to CMYK Color Mode

CMYK Color mode is used for viewing and editing images for output by a commercial printer. CMYK color images are divided into four channels, one for each of the process colors used to create four-color separations: Cyan, Magenta, Yellow, and Black. From the four channels, a prepress house produces the four pieces of film needed by a print shop to create the cyan, magenta, yellow, and black printing plates. When the image is printed, the tiny, colored-ink dots from each plate combine to create countless varieties of color.

If your images are digitized on a high-end scanner, they will probably be saved as CMYK files. These scanners can convert from RGB to CMYK "on the fly," during the process of digitizing the image. When the scanned image is loaded into Photoshop, it will open as a CMYK image in CMYK Color mode. Photo CD "profiles," available from Kodak, can convert Photo CD files directly to CMYK Color mode when the images are opened.

 If you are working with a CMYK color file, it is not advisable to convert it to RGB Color and then back to CMYK Color. When you convert back to RGB Color, you lose color data that will not be restored when you convert it back to CMYK Color.

If you are working with an RGB color file and need to produce four-color separations, you should convert the image from RGB Color mode to CMYK Color mode. Before you convert a file from RGB Color to CMYK Color, bear in mind that CMYK Color files are larger than RGB color files, due to the addition of the fourth channel. Thus, working in RGB Color mode is generally quicker, particularly if your computer is not fast. It's often advisable not to convert a file to CMYK Color until all image editing is complete. If, however, you are color-correcting an image that you will be printing on a printing press, you may want to convert to CMYK Color before you complete a project. This will allow you to edit using the same colors that will be used when the image is printed. When you edit in CMYK Color mode, you'll be able to color-correct and edit the four individual channels.

Understanding the Conversion Process

Although converting an RGB color file to CMYK Color is a simple process, it's vital that you understand the steps Photoshop goes through to complete the conversion. If you don't, you may not be happy with the color quality of the printed image.

The actual conversion process can take a few seconds or even several minutes. When it's done, the RGB colors will be converted to CMYK equivalents, and you will have a larger file because of the fourth channel.

When the conversion begins, Photoshop internally converts from RGB Color to Lab Color, and then to CMYK color. When Photoshop makes the conversion, it analyzes the settings in Color Settings dialog box (Edit > Color Settings). Using the information in this dialog box, Photoshop creates the CMYK Color file.

As explained in Chapter 2, Photoshop selects sRGB as its default RGB color space in the Color Settings dialog box. If you will be converting RGB color images to CMYK color, you should switch to an RGB color space that encompasses more printable colors, such as Adobe RGB. You may wish to switch the Settings pop-up menu in the Color Settings dialog box to U.S. Prepress Defaults (see Chapter 2 for more details).

Previewing with Soft Proofs

Now that you have an understanding of what goes on behind the scenes, you're almost ready to convert your image from RGB Color mode to CMYK Color mode. However, before making the conversion, you might want to make sure that your colors are as accurate as possible.

The best way to begin checking color accuracy before converting from RGB to CMYK is to check the soft proof. A *soft proof* (as opposed to a hard proof) is a screen representation of what the final printed will look like. Photoshop's View menu provides several commands for viewing a soft proof on your screen:

- Choose View > Proof Setup. In the Proof Setup submenu, make sure that CMYK is selected. This allows you to preview your file on your screen (based on the settings in the Color Settings dialog box).

- If you wish to change settings for the CMYK soft proof, choose View > Proof Setup > Custom. In the Proof Setup dialog box, choose a new profile in the Profile pop-up menu.

Note   *The contents of the Intent pop-up menu are discussed in Chapter 2 in the "Choosing Conversion Options" section.*

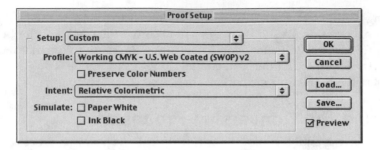

- To Display the proof colors, choose View > Proof Colors. The window now shows RGB/CMYK, indicating that you are viewing the CMYK soft proof.

- If you wish to take a look at the actual Cyan, Magenta, Yellow, and Black channels, choose the channel by choosing View > Proof Setup and then choose Working Cyan, Working Magenta, Working Yellow, or Working Black. A grayscale version of the plate appears. Essentially, this is a preview of how the different channels print on an imagesetter. If you choose Working CMY, you'll see a soft proof of your image without the black plate.

When you print, you can use the Profile setting in the Profile Setup dialog box as your source color space. For more information, see Chapter CD-4.

Viewing Out-of-Gamut Colors

Before converting from RGB Color to CMYK Color, you can have Photoshop check to see if any RGB colors are beyond the CMYK color gamut. (The CMYK color gamut is discussed in Chapter CD-1.)

To see if any of your colors lies beyond the CMYK gamut, choose View > Gamut Warning. In a few moments, Photoshop will turn any out-of-gamut colors in your image to a deep-gray tone.

You can change the opacity or color of the out-of-gamut warning by choosing Edit > Preferences > Transparency & Gamut. In the Preferences dialog box, enter a new opacity or click the swatch labeled Color in the Gamut Warning section to open the Color Picker.

If you wish to select the out-of-gamut colors so that you can edit only within them, choose Select > Color Range. In the Color Range dialog box, choose Out of Gamut from the Select pop-up menu. To ensure that you can see your entire image, leave the Selection Preview pop-up menu set to None. After you click on OK in the Color Range dialog box, only the out-of-gamut colors are selected. (For more information about using the Color Range command, see Chapter 19.)

The easiest way to correct your out-of-gamut colors is to use the Sponge tool. In the Sponge tool's Options bar, set the pop-up menu to Desaturate. Now you can click and drag over the out-of-gamut areas displayed on your screen. As the Sponge tool desaturates, the gray out-of-gamut warning color will gradually disappear. Colors will return to your image, but these colors will be within the CMYK color gamut. As you continue to work, be careful not to desaturate too much, because this can cause your colors to turn gray. You may also wish to use a process color swatch book as a reference guide (as described in Chapter CD-1) in conjunction with the Info palette readouts.

Tip *As you desaturate with the Sponge tool, you might find it helpful to view your image with and without the out-of-gamut gray warning colors. This will make it easier to check your progress as you remove the out-of-gamut colors. To do this, open a duplicate window on screen by choosing View > New View. Turn the Gamut Warning on in one window, and leave the menu command deselected in the other.*

Completing the CMYK Conversion

Once you are satisfied that all out-of-gamut colors have been removed from your RGB color image, you're ready to convert to CMYK Color mode. First, if you haven't already backed up your file, use the Save As command to create another version of your image. Then, to begin the conversion, choose Image > Mode > CMYK Color.

If the file you are converting contains layers, Photoshop allows you to choose whether or not to "flatten" the image before the mode change. If you flatten the image, its file size will be reduced and all of the layers will be merged into the Background. When converting from RGB Color to CMYK Color, it is generally advisable to flatten the image before converting it. This will help ensure that layer-blending mode effects (such as Overlay, Hard Light, and so on) appear as desired. (See Chapter 16 for more information about layers.)

When the conversion is complete, the mode displayed in the title bar changes from RGB to CMYK. After the file has been converted, open the Channels palette and notice that it now displays four channels. If you look at the file size indicator (toward the bottom-left corner of your screen), you'll see that the extra channel has increased the size of the image file. Take a moment to click on each of the channels to see how the image is created from the four process colors—cyan, magenta, yellow, and black.

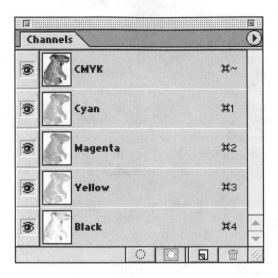

 After converting, it is often advisable to run the Unsharp Mask filter to sharpen the image. See Chapter 12 for more information.

Adding Color to a Black-and-White Image with CMYK Channels

You can use the CMYK Color mode channels to add color to a black-and-white (bitmap) image without affecting the underlying black color. This technique is possible because you can turn off editing in the Black channel while you paint in the CMY channels. Here are the steps:

1. Convert the black-and-white line art to CMYK Color. (If you have a bitmapped image, you need to use the Image > Mode submenu to convert from Bitmap to Grayscale, then from Grayscale to CMYK Color.)

2. Once the image is in CMYK Color mode, deactivate the Black channel so that the black plate will not be affected. To do this, position the pointer over the Black channel in the Channels palette and SHIFT-click.

3. Make the contents of the Black channel visible by clicking in the eye column to the left of the Black channel. Now you can see the Black channel, but any editing changes you make will not affect it.

4. Use Photoshop's painting tools to add color to your image.

5. When you are finished painting, click on CMYK in the Channels palette to reactivate editing in the composite image.

One of the advantages of working in a CMYK Color file is that Photoshop will not allow you to paint with out-of-gamut colors. Also, you can edit in the four individual channels or in any combination of the four channels. This is helpful when you want to color-correct in the individual channels or when you are creating interesting special effects.

After converting to CMYK, you will probably want to save the file so that it can be output for proofing purposes. This often means saving the file in EPS, TIFF, or Scitex CT format before sending it to a service bureau or prepress house. Before you send the file to a service bureau, you may need to import your EPS or TIFF file into a page layout program such as QuarkXPress.

Converting to Indexed Color Mode

Converting a file to Indexed Color mode is a step commonly taken before outputting an image to a multimedia program such as Macromedia Director, Adobe Premiere, or Adobe AfterEffects. You might also first convert a file to Indexed Color mode before converting it to a Web file format such as PNG-8.

Indexed Color mode reduces the number of colors in an image to 256 or fewer colors. Multimedia producers commonly use Indexed Color images to keep file sizes as small as possible, as well as to ensure that their productions can be viewed on computer systems that cannot display more than 256 colors.

Note   *In previous versions of Photoshop, Web designers often converted images to Indexed Color mode before saving the files in GIF format. In Photoshop 6.0. you can reduce the number of colors in an image before saving in a Web file format by choosing File > Save for Web.*

When you convert a file to Indexed Color, Photoshop reduces the channels in the image to one channel and creates a color table that is essentially a palette of colors tied to the document. This table is called a color lookup table (CLUT), and it acts as a type of index for the colors in the image.

You can convert to Indexed Color from RGB Color, Grayscale, or Duotone mode. As mentioned earlier, if you try to save an RGB file in GIF format by using File > Save, Photoshop forces you to change the image to Indexed Color mode first.

Caution   *If your RGB color file contains more than 256 colors, you will lose color information when you convert to Indexed Color. Although you can convert from Indexed Color back to RGB Color, Photoshop will not return the original colors to the file. Thus, you should always keep a backup copy of your original color file before converting.*

If you wish to experiment with converting to Indexed Color mode, you can load any RGB Color file. Make sure that you use the Save As command first to rename the file so that you will later be able to return to the original version.

To convert an RGB Color file to Indexed Color, choose Image > Mode > Indexed Color. In the Indexed Color dialog box, you can choose the desired number of colors, a color palette, and, if you wish, a dithering pattern. Select the Preview checkbox in the dialog box to preview how your image will look after the conversion.

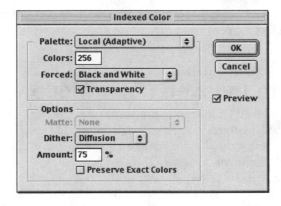

 Once you convert to Indexed Color mode, Photoshop's filters will not be available. You must execute these before converting to Indexed Color.

Choosing Color Palette Options

The Palette pop-up menu provides a variety of color choices for the Indexed Color file:

- The Exact palette uses a table with the same colors that appear in the original RGB color image. This option works only if the image contains 256 or fewer colors. The number of colors in the image is changed according to the resolution setting. No dithering is necessary, because no new colors need to be simulated.

- The System palette uses the Mac or Windows default system palette. If you are working on a multimedia project (not for the Web) that doesn't use scanned images, this option often produces suitable results.

- The Web palette provides 216 Web-safe colors, matching the palette most often used in Web browsers. It uses six different RGB colors to create the 216 colors $(6 \times 6 \times 6 = 216)$.

 In Photoshop 6.0, you may wish to choose File > Save for Web to prepare images for Web viewing. See Chapter 9 for more details.

- The Uniform palette creates a palette from a sample of colors from the color spectrum. You can designate how many colors you wish to have in your image by entering a number in the Color field.

- The Perceptual palette attempts to choose colors to which human vision is most sensitive. You can designate how many colors you wish to have in your image by entering a number in the Color field.

- The Selective palette often produces good results because it combines the concepts used to create the Perceptual table but tries to maintain Web colors and areas of color similarity. You can designate how many colors you wish to have in your image by entering a number in the Color field.

- The Adaptive palette generates a color table from the most commonly used colors in the image being converted. You can specify how many colors you want in the color palette by entering a number in the Color field. For more control, first select an area of the image that includes the colors you wish to retain. Then Photoshop will choose colors based more on the colors in the selection than on all of the colors in the image.

- The Custom choice allows you to create your own custom color table or select a predefined color table. See the "Working with Color Tables" section later in this chapter for details.

- The Previous choice uses the palette from the previous conversion, which is useful when you are converting several images at a time. This choice can be very handy when you use an action to convert many images to the same palette for multimedia productions.

Note that 8-bit color systems can display only one 256-color palette at a time. This means that all buttons and elements on a multimedia page designed for an 8-bit system should be converted to Indexed Color using the same color palette. If you need to convert many files to the same color palette, create an action (see Chapter 11) to batch-process your images. You might also wish to create a "superpalette" by loading several images into one file, and then creating a palette from this file. After the palette is created, apply it to other images that will appear on the page using the Previous palette choice. You might also wish to investigate ImageReady's Master palette option, which is discussed in Chapter 9.

Below the Palette option is the Forced pop-up menu. The choices in the Forced pop-up menu become available when you choose the Exact, Perceptual, Selective, or Adaptive palette:

- The Black and White option adds pure black and pure white to the color table. In previous versions of Photoshop, areas of black and white sometimes turned gray when converting to Indexed Color.

- The Primaries option adds red, green, blue, cyan, magenta, yellow, black, and white to the color table.

IMAGE EDITING FUNDAMENTALS

- The Web option adds Web-safe colors to the color table.

- The Custom option lets you choose colors to add to the color table. After you choose this table, you can click a color; this will open Photoshop's Color Picker.

Setting Transparency and Matte Options

The Transparency option allows you to maintain transparent areas during the conversions. If you don't select this option, transparent areas are converted to white or the color chosen in the Matte pop-up menu. If Transparency is selected and the Matte choice is set to none, image edges may appear jagged.

The Matte pop-up menu allows you to choose a color (or black, white, or gray) that will fill transparent areas. If the Transparency option is not selected, the Matte color fills all transparent and semi-transparent pixels. If you have the Transparency option selected, Photoshop makes all 100% transparent pixels transparent, but uses the matte color for semi-transparent pixels.

Choosing Dither Options

Dithering combines different-colored pixels to give the appearance of colors that are not actually in the image. Choosing a dithering option when you convert to Indexed Color mode may be advisable, because the color table that is created may not contain all of the colors in your image. Dithering is often used when converting images that include gradients. After you choose a Dither option you can enter a Dither percentage. The higher the percentage the greater the dithering effect.

The Dither pop-up menu in the Indexed Color dialog box provides the following options:

- The None option doesn't use dithering. Photoshop picks the closest match it can find in the color table to replace a missing color in the converted image. This usually results in sharp color transitions. This is a good choice if you are creating areas with flat, constant colors; you generally don't want to see dots in flat colors.

- The Pattern option uses a pattern of random dots to simulate a missing color.

- The Diffusion option diffuses the color inaccuracies to surrounding pixels in an image. This is a good choice for scanned photos and images that contain gradients.

- The Noise option reduces seams if you are going to create slices out of the image for placement in a Web page. See Chapter 10 for more information about slicing images for the Web.

| Note | *Applying a Noise filter to an image can also create a dithering pattern. See Chapter 12 for more information.* |

Working with Color Tables

Through the Color Table dialog box, you can choose a predefined color table, as well as edit, save, and load color tables. There are two ways to access the Color Table dialog box:

- If you have already converted to Indexed Color mode, choose Image > Mode > Color Table.

- If you haven't yet converted, choose Image > Mode > Indexed Color, and then select Custom in the Palette pop-up menu.

Viewing the Predefined Color Tables

In the Color Table dialog box, click the Table pop-up menu to see the list of predefined color tables. You can select one to view the colors produced.

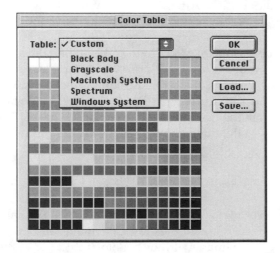

Here's a brief description of these tables:

- The Black Body table transforms the color table based on the colors produced when a black-body radiator is heated. You'll see a range of colors from black to red, as well as orange, yellow, and white. This table can be used for scientific graphic applications or to produce a hot, glowing effect.

- The Grayscale table produces transitional colors through 256 shades from black to white.

- The Macintosh System table is based on the standard Mac color palette.

- The Spectrum table produces the colors in the color spectrum.

- The Windows System table is based on the standard Windows color palette.

IMAGE EDITING
FUNDAMENTALS

When you choose a predefined table or edit a table, the colors of the image on screen will change to those in the color table when it is applied to your image. The colors are applied to the image when you click on OK in the Color Table dialog box.

Editing the Indexed Color Table

If you would like, you can open the color table that is being used by your image and edit the colors. To do this, your image should first be converted to Indexed Color. Once you have an Indexed Color file on screen, select Image > Mode > Color Table. The Color Table dialog box will show the color table for your file.

Changing Colors   In the Color Table dialog box, you can edit any color in the table by clicking on the color. This brings up Photoshop's Color Picker, allowing you to change the colors. Use the dialog box options to pick a color that is not already in the color table, and then click on OK. After Photoshop returns to your document, notice that each pixel that contained the color you clicked in the Color Table dialog box is converted to the new color.

You can also change a range of colors in the table at one time. To change a range of colors, click and drag through a row of colors. When you release the mouse, the Color Picker appears with the message "Select first color." Choose a color and click on OK. The Color Picker reopens with the message "Select last color." When you click on OK, a gradient of colors—from the first color you specified to the last color—appears in the color table. Click on OK in the dialog box to see the effects on your image.

 When the Color Picker opens, you can also click on Custom to choose PANTONE colors.

Colorizing Grayscale Images   You can use the Color Table dialog box to quickly colorize a grayscale image. First load the grayscale image, and then convert it to Indexed Color. Next, choose Image > Mode > Color Table. Select the entire table. When the "Select first color" message appears, choose a starting color, click on OK, and then choose an ending color. After you close the Color Table dialog box, your image will be colorized. This technique can also be handy for changing the colors of GIF images that will be used on the Web.

Adding Transparency to the Color Table   Once an image is converted to Indexed Color (GIF images open in Photoshop as Indexed Colors), you can add transparency to the image by replacing one of the colors with transparency. In the Color Table dialog box, select the eyedropper, and then click on the color that you wish to turn transparent. After you click, the image area containing that color becomes transparent.

Saving and Loading Indexed Color Tables

If you wish to create a custom color table to use with other documents, you can return to the Color Table dialog box and click on the Save button to name the table and save it on disk. When you wish to apply it to a document, click on the Load button to load it.

After the table is loaded, click on OK in the Color Table dialog box to have the colors from the table appear in the document on your screen.

You can load a saved Indexed Color table into the Swatches palette and paint with the colors on it. Mac users can load the table by choosing Load Swatches from the Swatches palette pop-up menu. Mac users can also load a Swatches palette into a color table by clicking on the Load button in the Color Table dialog box. In the Load dialog box, Windows users can click on the Files of type pop-up menu to see the Swatch palette files (.ACO file extension) or Color Table palette files (.ACT file extension).

Converting to and from Grayscale Mode

Grayscale files are 8-bit images that can be composed of up to 256 shades of gray. When a color file is converted to Grayscale mode, all of the color information is removed from the file.

 Although the Image > Mode submenu allows you to convert a grayscale file to a color mode file, you will not be able to return the original colors to a file that has been converted to grayscale. Thus, before converting a color image to grayscale, it's advisable to use the Save As command to create a copy of your color file so that you have a backup.

Photoshop also gives you the ability to add color to a grayscale image. You can convert a Grayscale mode to a color mode, and then colorize it.

Converting from a Color Mode to Grayscale

If you need to convert your digitized color image to grayscale or black and white, you will first need to convert your file to Grayscale mode. From Grayscale, you can convert to a Duotone or Bitmap file, as described later in this chapter.

If you don't have a color file on screen, load one now so that you can convert it to Grayscale mode. Then select Image > Mode > Grayscale. An alert box appears, warning that you will be discarding the color information in the file.

After you click on OK, your file will be converted to a grayscale image, and the Channels palette will display only one channel: Black.

If you have layers in your image, an alert box will ask you if you wish to flatten your image but won't ask you to discard the color information.

When working with a grayscale image, the Color palette displays only one grayscale slider, labeled K (Black). You can change the percentage of gray by clicking and dragging on the slider control. Reducing the percentage lightens the shade of gray, and increasing the percentage makes it darker.

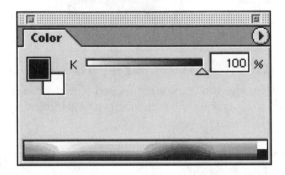

You can make simple tonal adjustments to the converted grayscale image by using the Brightness/Contrast command in the Image > Adjust submenu. (To learn more advanced techniques for making tonal adjustments to grayscale images, see Chapter 19.)

 You can remove the color from an RGB image and create a variety of different grayscale style images using Photoshop 6's Channel Mixer (Image > Adjust > Channel Mixer). The Channel Mixer is discussed in Chapter 19. You can also remove the color from an RGB image by choosing Image > Adjust > Desaturate in Photoshop and ImageReady. Another way to perform this conversion is to choose a grayscale color table in the Save for Web dialog box.

As discussed in Chapter 2, Photoshop uses the dot gain setting in the Color Settings dialog box to compensate for dot gain when it converts to Grayscale mode. If you try changing dot gain settings and converting from RGB to Grayscale; depending on the image, you'll usually see that a dot gain percentage of 30 creates a slightly lighter image than a dot gain percentage of 10. By making the image lighter, Photoshop attempts to ensure that the final printed image is not too dark.

Converting from Grayscale to a Color Mode

While working with an image in Grayscale mode, you cannot add color to it. If you wish to add color to a grayscale image, convert the image to one of the color modes (RGB Color, CMYK Color, Lab Color, or Indexed Color) by selecting that mode from the Image > Mode submenu. After you convert it, you can colorize the image.

Colorizing Grayscale Images

Like the process of creating colorized movies, transforming a grayscale image into color allows the image's shadows, contours, and definition beneath the color to show through. Here are the steps for colorizing a grayscale image:

1. Load a grayscale image. As usual, to ensure that you will be able to return to the original grayscale image, it's always advisable to use the Save As command and rename the file.

2. Open the Colors palette by choosing Window > Show Color.

3. Select Image > Mode and convert your file from Grayscale to RGB Color or CMYK Color.

4. Set the foreground color and choose the Paintbrush tool in the Toolbox.

5. In the Paintbrush Options bar, select a medium-sized, soft-edged brush, set Opacity to 100%, and select Color in the Mode pop-up menu.

6. Use the Paintbrush to add color. Notice the result: The portion you paint changes color, but you can still see the underlying shadows and textures. When you paint using Color mode, Photoshop paints with only the hue and saturation of a color. This allows the underlying brightness values to show through your painting color. If you were painting in Normal mode with Opacity at 100%, the opaque color would completely cover the image.

7. If there are large areas that you wish to color in your image, use the Pen tool or a selection tool to create a selection. Then choose Edit > Fill and set the Mode pop-up menu to Color. After you click on OK, color will be applied to your image, but again, the underlying lightness and darkness levels will show through the color.

You may wish to experiment with the Darken, Lighten, Multiply, Overlay, Soft Light, and Screen painting modes. Lighten and Darken, in particular, can be used to add various color tones to areas that are already colorized. (For a review of Darken, Lighten, Multiply, Overlay, Soft Light, and Screen, flip back to Chapter 5.) Also, you may wish to activate the Blur or Smudge tools to blend colors together. You can use the Sharpen tool to enhance detail by increasing contrast as well.

Using the Colorize Option in the Hue/Saturation Dialog Box

Photoshop also allows you to adjust colors from a variety of dialog boxes that can be accessed from the Image > Adjust submenu. You'll be using these commands extensively when retouching and color-correcting (processes covered in Chapter 19). Only the Hue/Saturation command is discussed here, because it includes an option specifically designed to colorize.

Here are the steps for using the Colorize option in the Hue/Saturation dialog box:

1. Load a grayscale image, select an area in your image that you wish to colorize, and choose Image > Adjust > Hue/Saturation.

2. In the Hue/Saturation dialog box, make sure that the Preview checkbox is selected. The preview lets you see the changes in your image as you colorize. Then select the Colorize checkbox. The selection you made will change to the hue of the foreground color (unless it is black). The Saturation value will be 25 with a lightness of 0.

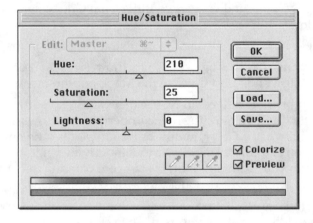

3. Adjusting the Hue slider will change the color of the image. To move through the color spectrum, drag the Hue slider control right or left. Drag it all the way to the left, to 0, and you'll see the color gradually change to red. Drag to the right to 360°, and you'll see the colors return to red.

4. Adjusting the Saturation slider will change the amount of gray in a color. Drag the Saturation slider control to the right to increase the saturation. The more saturation you add, the stronger the colors will be, and the less gray they will contain. Drag the Saturation slider control to the left to decrease saturation.

5. Adjusting the Lightness slider allows you to control how light or dark the color will be. Move the Lightness slider control to the right toward 100 to lighten the color. Then slide it to the left toward 0 to darken it. With Lightness set to 100, the color changes to white; –100 changes it to black. By adjusting the Lightness slider control, you can even add color to pure white and pure black image areas.

6. If you wish to exit the Hue/Saturation dialog box and apply the settings now, click on OK; otherwise, click on Cancel.

If you find it confusing that you returned to red when you dragged the Hue slider to add color, think of the slider as the linear equivalent of a color wheel. When you move along the wheel, you eventually return to the color with which you began. Figure 13-1 shows how the Hue slider values and their corresponding colors would appear if arranged on a color wheel.

After you decide what combination of Hue, Saturation, and Lightness you want to apply to an image area, you can save your settings so that they can be applied to other files. In the Hue/Saturation dialog box, click on the Save button. In the dialog box that appears, enter a name for the settings, and then click on Save to return to the Hue/Saturation dialog box. Then, when you wish to use these color settings again (on another area of the same image or another image), return to the Hue/Saturation dialog box, click on the Load button, and open your saved Hue/Saturation settings file.

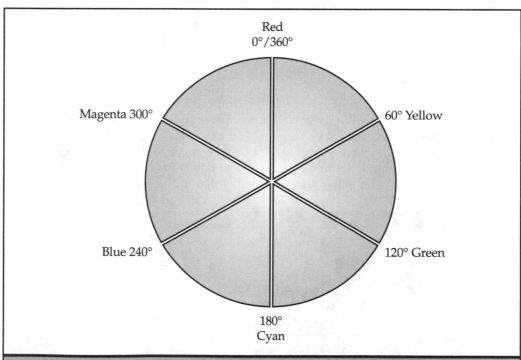

Figure 13-1. *Hue slider values arranged on a color wheel*

After you have finished colorizing, you may want to create special effects by applying any of Photoshop's filters from the Filter menu. See Chapter 12 for more information.

Converting from Grayscale to Duotone

Printing a grayscale image with an extra gray or colored ink can add depth and dimension, making the image look more interesting and dramatic. These enhanced grayscale images are called *duotones*. In Photoshop's Duotone mode, you can create monotones, duotones, tritones, and quadtones—grayscale images to which you add one, two, three, or four colors. This printing technique is usually less expensive than printing four-color images (although printing a quadtone is more expensive than printing four-color images).

Creating a Duotone

To create a monotone, duotone, tritone, or quadtone image, you must start with a grayscale image or convert a color image to a grayscale image. Duotone mode is accessible only for images in Grayscale mode.

Follow these steps to create a duotone from a grayscale image:

1. Load any color file and converting it to Grayscale mode (Image > Mode > RGB Color or CMYK Color).

2. Select Image > Mode > Duotone. In the Duotone Options dialog box, Type is set to Monotone by default (or however you last set it). When the Monotone option is selected, notice that Ink 1 is active. Next to Ink 1 are two squares. The square with the diagonal line represents the Duotone curve—a visual representation of the duotone ink distribution. The second square is the color swatch box. This represents the color that you are applying to your image.

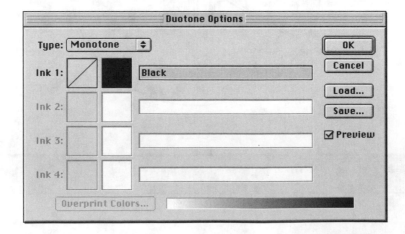

3. To activate another Type option, click on the Type pop-up menu and make your selection. For this example, select the Duotone option. When you choose Duotone

from the Type pop-up menu, Ink 1 and Ink 2 are active, but Ink 3 and Ink 4 are not. This is because duotones are composed of only two colors. The number of inks that appear depends on the option you select in the Type pop-up menu.

> **Note** *When Photoshop prints a duotone, it prints the inks in ascending order. Thus, the darkest ink is usually the first ink, and the lightest ink is the last ink in the Duotone Options dialog box.*

4. For the Duotone option, you need to pick a second ink color. Click on the white color swatch box to the right of Ink 2. The Custom Colors dialog box appears. In the Custom Colors dialog box, you can either pick a custom color or click on the Picker button to access the Color Picker dialog box and then enter CMYK percentages for a process color.

5. To pick a PANTONE Coated color in the Custom Colors dialog box, click on the Book pop-up menu and choose PANTONE Coated if it is not already displayed. To choose a color, type **2645**. Notice that PANTONE 2645 CV becomes the active color. Click on OK to confirm the change and to return to the Duotone Options dialog box.

> **Tip** *If Photoshop does not find the correct color, try quickly retyping the Custom Color number on your numeric keypad.*

6. To see the effects of your changes, make sure that the Preview checkbox is selected in the Duotone Options dialog box. When the Preview option is on, you will see that your image is displayed with black and PANTONE 2645 CV.

> **Note** *If the Short PANTONE Names option in the General Preferences dialog box isn't selected, you'll see PANTONE 2645 CVC when you select that color. Be aware that if you are printing separations from QuarkXPress or PageMaker, you need to use short names.*

Clicking the Overprint Colors button in the Duotone Options dialog box brings up the Overprint Colors dialog box. In this dialog box, you can adjust the screen display of overprint colors (two colors), so that you can visualize how colors will look when ink combinations are output. Click on the color swatch in the Overprint Colors dialog box to adjust the colors. When adjusting the overprint colors, it's best to use a printed sample of the overprint colors as a guide. Also note that the adjustment in the Overprint Colors dialog box affects only the screen display.

Controlling Duotone Ink

After you have selected the second ink color for a duotone, you may want to control ink density in shadow, midtone, and highlight areas. You do this by adjusting that ink's curve. In duotone images, black is usually applied to the shadow areas, and gray or another color is applied to the midtone and highlight areas.

IMAGE EDITING
FUNDAMENTALS

Before and after you make adjustments in the Duotone Curve dialog box, you may want to open the Color palette to see the different shades of Ink 1 and Ink 2.

To change the way an ink is applied to an image, in the Duotone Options dialog box, click on the box with the diagonal line in it for Ink 1 or Ink 2. The Duotone Curve dialog box appears, containing a graph depicting the ink coverage over different image areas.

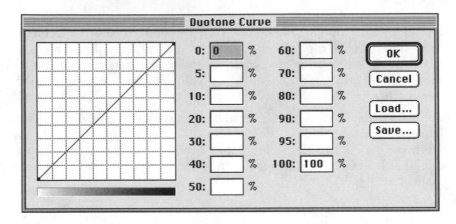

 Consult your printer to determine a total ink coverage for your job. Then set the Info palette's Second Color Readout to display Total Ink so that you can monitor the ink percentages.

In the graph, the X-axis (horizontal axis) represents the tonal range in the original image, from highlights to shadows. The Y-axis (vertical axis) represents the ink density values. The default settings of the graph are always represented by a diagonal line. The diagonal indicates that the printing ink percentage matches the black percentage value of every pixel in the image. This means that if the image contains black values of 100 percent, they will print at 100 percent density (a 100 percent dot of the specified ink color) for the specified ink. A 50 percent midtone pixel will be printed at a 50 percent density (a 50 percent dot of the specified ink).

You can adjust the diagonal line by clicking and dragging on it or by typing percentage values in the entry fields on the right. The numbers entered into the fields set ink density. The 0% field represents highlights (the lightest portions of the image), the 50% field represents the midtones, and the 100% field represents shadows (the darkest portions of the image). Thus, if you enter **80** in the 100% box, it means that an 80 percent dot of the specified ink will be used to print the darkest shadow areas.

Try clicking on the middle of the diagonal line and dragging downward. When you click, a small dot (control point) is added to the curve, and a value is entered into the 50% field. (If you did not click exactly on the middle of the curve, Photoshop enters a value in the field corresponding to the point where you clicked.) The value entered is the percentage of ink density for midtone areas.

Try making some adjustments in the curve by clicking and dragging and by typing percentages into the fields. When you drag the curve upward, you add more of the ink to the image; drag the curve downward, and you use less ink. If you type a percentage into the field, a corresponding control point appears on the curve.

You can save a curve you created in the Duotone Curve dialog box and load it into the Curves dialog box (Image > Adjust > Curves). You can also load a curve that was created in the Curves dialog box into the Duotone Curve dialog box.

When you have finished experimenting with adjustments to the curve, click on OK to return to the Duotone Options dialog box. Click on OK again to see the adjusted curve's effects on your image.

Viewing the Duotone's Readouts in the Info Palette

Once you have examined your duotone image on your screen, you may decide to make adjustments to the curve or to change the color of the inks. Before you do, it's often a good idea to analyze the true colors in your image by viewing the Eyedropper's readouts in the Info palette. Viewing these readouts of ink percentages ensures that you don't rely totally on how the image looks on your monitor.

If the Info palette is not open, select Window > Show Info. If the Info palette readout does not display two inks, click on the Info palette's pop-up menu arrow, which opens the Info Options dialog box. In this dialog box's First Color Readout section, choose Actual Color from the Mode pop-up menu.

For a shortcut to changing the First and/or Second Color Readout settings in the Info Options dialog box, click on the first and/or second Eyedropper in the Info palette.

All duotone colors are displayed in the first readout. The image's actual color values in percentages for both inks appear in the Info palette.

Now move the mouse pointer over different areas of your image. Notice that the Info palette displays the percentage of each duotone ink. This can help you judge the degree

IMAGE EDITING
FUNDAMENTALS

of change if you edit the curve in the Duotone Curve dialog box, as well as give you a sense of how the image will print, regardless of the brightness settings on your monitor.

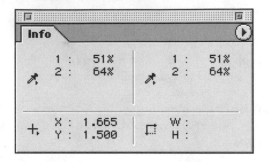

 Use the Color Sampler tool to set sample points in your image before converting to Duotone mode. In Duotone mode, you can then adjust the curves while you view the readouts and preview on your screen.

Reusing Duotone Settings

After you've set duotone curves, ink settings, ink colors, and overprint colors (colors printed on top of each other), you may want to save them for use on other images. To save your settings, reopen the Duotone Options dialog box (select Image > Mode > Duotone) and click on the Save button. In the dialog box, name the file and click on Save.

Once you have saved a settings file, you can load and apply it to other grayscale images that you wish to convert to duotones. To load your settings, click on the Load button in the Duotone Options dialog box and select the file in the Open dialog box.

Using Photoshop's Preset Duotone Curves

If you are hesitant about picking your own colors for creating duotones, you can use Photoshop's preset inks and curves for duotones, tritones, and quadtones. These ink and curve samples are loaded on your hard disk during Photoshop installation. You can find them in the Duotone Presets folder.

To access the sample set, click on the Load button in the Duotone Options dialog box. In the Open dialog box, locate the Duotone folder, in Photoshop 6's in the Presets folder. The Duotone folder contains three folders: Duotones, Quadtones, and Tritones (*Windows users: TRITONE*). Inside each of these folders are other folders for Gray, PANTONE, and Process (CMYK Color) files. Select and open a Gray, PANTONE, or Process file from within its folder. After you open a file, you will be returned to the Duotone Options dialog box. Click on OK to apply the settings to your image.

For example, in the Process Tritones folder, Photoshop has included four different sepia settings for you to use. (A *sepia* is a light reddish-brown tone applied to a photograph to give it an aged effect.) Try creating a sepia, using the grayscale image you converted to a duotone.

1. Open the Duotone Options dialog box by choosing Image > Mode > Duotone.

2. In the Duotone Options dialog box, click on the Load button. In the Open dialog box, locate and open the Duotone Presets folder, and from there select the Tritones folder (*TRITONE*).

3. From the Tritones folder (*TRITONE*), open the Process Tritones folder.

4. In the list of files, notice BMY Sepia 1, BMY Sepia 2, BMY Sepia 3, and BMY Sepia 4. Select and open any one of these Sepia files. Instantly, the settings appear in the Duotone Options dialog box.

5. Click on OK in the Duotones Options dialog box.

After you have previewed the settings, you may want to try another sepia setting; just repeat the above steps to do so.

> **Note** *After you have created a sepia image, you may wish to add to your document other objects or images that contain more colors than the ones in your tritone file. In order to do this, you must convert the tritone file to Indexed Color, RGB Color, Lab Color, or CMYK Color. However, if you convert back to grayscale, your original grayscale image returns, not the curve-adjusted image.*

Converting Duotones to Spot Colors

Although a duotone is a one-channel image, you can convert it to a Multichannel mode image by choosing Image > Mode > Multichannel. Multichannel mode converts the duotone colors to separate spot colors. The spot colors appear as printing plates in the Channels palette.

Once the image is converted to Multichannel mode, you can reorder the position of the colors by clicking and dragging on colors in the Channels palette. You can also create a selection in a channel and remove color from a portion of the channel. See Chapter 15 to learn more about using spot colors in Photoshop.

Printing a Duotone

Before you print your duotone (or tritone or quadtone) image, you need to specify settings for halftone screen angles, printing resolution, and screen frequency. To print your image, choose File > Print. If you wish to print a composite image, click on OK; otherwise, select Separations from the Profile pop-up menu, and then click on OK.

To print a duotone from QuarkXPress or Adobe Illustrator, save the Photoshop file in EPS format. If you are using PANTONE colors or any spot colors in your image, you need to have the same PANTONE names in QuarkXPress as you do in Photoshop. Because QuarkXPress uses short PANTONE names, the Short PANTONE Names option must be selected in Photoshop's General Preferences dialog box (Edit > Preferences > General). If the Short PANTONE Names option was not activated when you chose your PANTONE colors, you must return to the Duotone Options dialog box and choose them again, or you can type in the correct names.

If you will not be outputting your duotone (or tritone or quadtone) files yourself, consult with your prepress house or print shop to ensure that the images will be output properly.

Converting from Grayscale to Bitmap

In order to convert an image to black and white, the image must be converted to Bitmap mode. In Bitmap mode, many of Photoshop's editing options are not available; thus. it is often preferable to edit in Grayscale mode and then convert to Bitmap mode. In this section, you'll learn about the different options available when you convert to Bitmap mode, as well as how to create a mezzotint.

Choosing a Conversion Method

Only Grayscale and Multichannel mode images can be converted to Bitmap mode. When you convert from Grayscale mode to Bitmap mode, a dialog box appears, in which you set the output resolution of the file and the conversion method. After you make your choices, click on OK to apply them to your image. Following are descriptions of the five conversion methods.

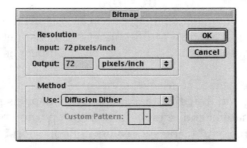

50% Threshold   The 50% Threshold conversion method creates high-contrast, black-and-white images. When the conversion is executed, Photoshop sets the threshold level at 128 pixels. All pixel values in the grayscale image below 128 are converted to black; all pixel values of 128 and above are converted to white.

 To obtain better results, you may wish to choose Image > Adjust > Threshold to better control the image's appearance before converting to Bitmap.

Pattern Dither   Using Pattern Dither conversion, the gray levels are changed into geometric patterns composed of black dots and white dots.

Diffusion Dither   The Diffusion Dither conversion method uses a diffusion process to change a pixel to black and white. This diffuses the error between the original grayscale pixels and the black and white pixels. The result is a grainy effect.

Halftone Screen   The Halftone Screen conversion method makes the image appear as if it were a grayscale image printed using a halftone screen. Halftone Screen is typically used to print images on non-PostScript printers.

When you choose this conversion method, the Halftone Screen dialog box appears. This dialog box includes Frequency, Angle, and Shape options for the halftone pattern. Acceptable values for the screen frequency (often called *line screen*) range from 1.000 to 999.999 for lines per inch and from 0.400 to 400 for lines per centimeter. (Decimal values are acceptable.) Newspapers often use a screen frequency of 85, and magazines use 150. If you do not know the correct screen frequency, check with your print shop. Screen angles from –180 to 180 can be entered. Finally, your shape choices are Round, Diamond, Ellipse, Line, Square, and Cross.

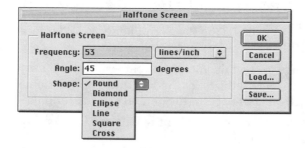

After you adjust the settings in the Halftone Screen dialog box, you can save them by using the Save button. To reuse a saved settings file, click on the Load button in the dialog box.

Custom Pattern   The Custom Pattern conversion method allows you to apply a custom pattern to a bitmapped image. This option will be dimmed unless a custom pattern is defined. To define the pattern, select an area with a selection tool, and then choose Edit > Define Pattern before converting to Bitmap mode. You'll try out this conversion method in the next section, when you create a mezzotint.

Before defining the pattern, you may wish to use the Blur or Blur More command from the Filter > Blur submenu to blur the pattern you will be using in the conversion process, so that the edges of the pattern blend together.

Creating a Mezzotint

A mezzotint is a black-and-white image that appears to consist of randomly shaped dots or shapes. Traditionally, mezzotints were created with halftone screens designed to produce random or unusual dot effects. In Photoshop, creating a mezzotint is fairly easy and can be accomplished in just a few steps.

 You can also use Photoshop's Mezzotint filter to create mezzotints. For more information, see Chapter 12.

Before you can create a mezzotint, you must first define a pattern. After you convert from Grayscale mode to Bitmap mode, you apply the pattern to the bitmapped image to create the mezzotint.

For this exercise, you will load a pattern from the Postscript Patterns folder (found in the Patterns folder within the Presets folder) and use it as the custom pattern when converting a grayscale image to Bitmap mode. In this example, we used the image shown in Figure 13-2, which you can find on this book's CD-ROM.

1. Select File > Open. Open the PostScript Patterns folder located in the Patterns folder (in the Presets folder) and open a pattern file.

2. After you have opened the mezzotint pattern, the EPS Rasterizer dialog box appears, containing settings for the Width, Height, Resolution, and Mode of the pattern. Click on OK to accept the default settings, and the pattern will appear.

3. Choose Select > All to select the entire pattern. Then choose Edit > Define Pattern and close the file.

4. Load the file to which you want to apply the mezzotint. (If the file is not a grayscale image, you'll need to convert it by choosing Image > Mode > Grayscale.)

5. Before you convert your grayscale image to a bitmap image, choose Image > Adjust > Brightness/Contrast. Adjust the settings so that the converted bitmap image will display more contrast. This will produce fewer dots and more solid blacks and whites.

6. Convert the Grayscale mode image to Bitmap mode by choosing Image > Mode > Bitmap.

7. When the Bitmap dialog box appears, select the Custom Pattern option. (It will no longer be dimmed because you defined a pattern in steps 2 and 3.) Enter an Output Resolution (the higher the Output Resolution, the better the image pattern quality). The Input Resolution is the resolution of the original file. Click on OK.

Your image should now appear as a mezzotint. Figure 13-3 shows the horse image after applying the mezzotint effect.

Figure 13-2.   *The horse image before creating the mezzotint*

Figure 13-3.   *A bitmap mezzotint applied to the horse sculpture*

After you have created a mezzotint, you may wish to add color to enhance the image, or create some special effects. To add color to a bitmapped image, you must first convert to Grayscale mode, and then convert to a color mode.

Converting from Bitmap to Grayscale

When you convert from Bitmap mode to Grayscale mode, the Grayscale dialog box appears. Here, you can enter a Size Ratio value from 1 to 16.

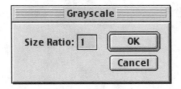

The Size Ratio is the multiple by which you wish to decrease an image's size. For instance, if you enter **2**, the final image will be one-half its original size. Enter **3**, and the image will decrease to one-third its original size.

Using Several Modes to Create a Colored Mezzotint Effect

Here's a design tip that uses a combination of mode changes to create a colored mezzotint effect:

1. Open a color file, select your entire image, and choose Edit > Copy.

2. Create a mezzotint by first defining a pattern, then converting the color image to Grayscale mode, and then converting from Grayscale to Bitmap mode using the Custom Pattern method.

3. After the mezzotint is created, convert from Bitmap to Grayscale, and then to a color mode.

4. After you have converted from Bitmap to a color mode, paste the copied colored image.

5. Use the Lighten mode in the Layers palette to blend the black-and-white mezzotint image with the colored image.

Converting to Lab Color Mode

As discussed in Chapter CD-1, Lab Color is a device-independent color model that helps provide consistent color on various output devices. Also, Lab Color mode is the internal format Photoshop uses while making mode conversions. For instance, when Photoshop converts from RGB Color to CMYK Color, it first converts the RGB colors to Lab Color and then converts from Lab Color to CMYK Color.

Lab Color mode images have three channels: a Lightness (or luminance) channel and two color channels, designated as channel a (green to magenta) and channel b (blue to yellow). Use Lab Color mode if you wish to edit an image's lightness independently of its color values. To do this, click to activate the Lightness channel in the Channels palette. In the Lightness channel, you can edit the Lightness values of an image or even select the entire image and paste it into a new file. The copied image in the new file will be a grayscale version of your original, because you copied and pasted only the Lightness component of the image.

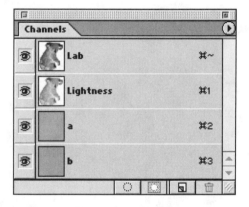

  When working on a multimedia project, try to use as few palettes as possible, because switching palettes can cause flashes on your screen.

Lab Color is also the model used for transferring files between different color systems. For instance, Kodak's Photo CD uses YCC for its images. YCC is Kodak's own version of the Lab Color model; Y is the lightness, or luminance, value, and the two C channels are similar to Photoshop's channels a and b. Thus, when you load a Photo CD image into Photoshop, there should be little or no loss of color data. Because PostScript Level 2 takes advantage of Lab's device-independent color model, Lab Color is the recommended mode for printing to PostScript Level 2 printers.

IMAGE EDITING
FUNDAMENTALS

The
Complete
Reference

Part III

Applying Effects to Your Images

Chapter 14

Creating Paths and Masks with the Pen Tool

When you create objects with Photoshop's Pen tool, it's almost like being in two programs at once: a painting program and a drawing program. Unlike Photoshop's painting tools, which paint directly onto the electronic canvas, the Pen tool can create filled shapes or wireframe *paths* that exist above the underlying pixels. Like the Pen tool in programs like Adobe Illustrator and Macromedia Freehand, Photoshop's Pen tool can create Bézier curves and intricate objects. However, unlike those in drawing programs, Photoshop paths are frequently used for tracing over image areas to create *masks* (which can be turned into selections) to aid in image editing. A mask allows you to protect an area on the screen so that you can edit, paint, or apply a filter within it without affecting surrounding portions of the image.

A path can be a point, a line, or a curve, but usually it's a series of line segments or curve segments connected by their end points. Photoshop paths don't lock down onto the background pixels on screen, and thus they can easily be reshaped, reselected, and moved. They can also be saved and exported to other programs.

Before you can begin to turn paths into artwork and into Photoshop selections, you need to learn some fundamentals. First, you'll learn about the pen and path tools and how they work in conjunction with the Paths palette. Next, you'll discover how to create straight and curved path segments and how to join them together. Then you'll learn how to modify paths and convert them to selections using the path tools and Paths palette.

At the end of the chapter, you'll learn how to create another type of mask, called a *clipping path*. Clipping paths are typically used to silhouette an area and mask out the background image areas so that only the area within the clipping path will appear when the file is placed into another program, such as Illustrator, PageMaker, or QuarkXPress.

Exploring the Pen Tools and the Paths Palette

The most common way of creating a path from scratch is to use Photoshop's Pen or Freeform Pen tool. The pen tools work in conjunction with the Paths palette. The commands accessed through the Paths palette allow paths to be filled, stroked, and turned into selections. Without these commands, the intricate and precise shapes you create with the pen tools would be useless within Photoshop, because most of Photoshop's menu commands and tools have no effect on paths (however, the Edit > Transform commands can be applied to paths).

 Several images in the color insert in this book provide excellent examples of how paths are used by professional Photoshop artists.

The Pen Tools

To access the pen tools in Photoshop (ImageReady does not have a Pen tool), you can press P on your keyboard or click on the Pen tool's Toolbox location with the mouse. If you keep the mouse button pressed, a pop-up menu with Photoshop's pen tools appears. You also can select each of the pen tools one at a time by pressing SHIFT-P.

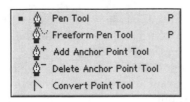

As you can see, there are five pen tools listed in the pop-up menu. Additionally, another pen tool is available from the Freeform Pen tool's Options bar. Here's a brief summary of what each pen tool does:

- **Pen tool**   This is the most precise of all of the pen tools. Use it when you need to create smooth and intricate paths.
- **Freeform Pen tool**   Like a real pen, this tool allows you to create paths as you click and drag to create shapes.
- **Add Anchor Point tool**   This tool is used for adding points to a path that has already been created.
- **Delete Anchor Point tool**   This tool is used for subtracting points from a path.
- **Convert Point tool**   This tool lets you convert a smooth corner of a path into a sharp corner, and vice versa.
- **Magnetic Pen tool**   This tool is available from the Freeform Pen tool's Option bar. It creates a path by automatically tracing over image edges as you click and move the mouse or click and drag.

Next, take a look at the Pen tool's Options bar. If the Options bar isn't on your screen, open it by double-clicking on the Pen tool in the Toolbox.

The two buttons on the left side of the Options bar let you choose whether to create a filled shape or a wireframe path. If you click on the Create New Shape button before drawing with the Pen tool, you create a filled shape in a layer. If you click on the Create New Path button, you create a wireframe path, typically used for masking.

When the Auto Add/Delete checkbox is selected, Photoshop automatically activates the tools for adding or removing points when you move the tool to certain areas. Moving the pen pointer over a path segment activates the Add Anchor Point tool, so that clicking adds another anchor point. If you move the mouse pointer over an anchor point, Photoshop automatically activates the Delete Anchor Point tool.

APPLYING EFFECTS TO YOUR IMAGES

When the Rubber Band checkbox is selected, a path segment trails the Pen tool after an anchor point is created. As you move the Pen tool, the segment is displayed from your last mouse click to the current pen position, as if you were stretching a rubber band. If you don't turn on the Rubber Band option, each path segment appears only after you click the mouse to connect anchor points, rather than as you move the mouse.

When you click on screen with a Pen tool activated, the overlapping shape buttons appear in the Options bar, as do the OK (checkmark) and Cancel (X) buttons. The overlapping shape icons determine how paths will be filled when there are overlapping path segments:

- The Add to Shape Area button adds the new path area to previously drawn shapes or paths.

- The Subtract from Shape Area button removes the overlapping path area from previously drawn paths.

- The Intersect Shape Area button fills only the overlapping areas of paths.

- The Exclude Overlapping Shape Area button excludes the overlapping areas of paths.

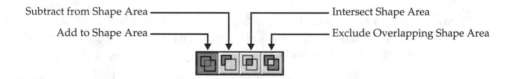

    Clicking on the OK button in the Options bar or pressing ENTER *removes the overlapping drawing icons from the Options bar.*

The Freeform Pen tool's Options bar includes the same Create New Shape and Create New Path buttons, as well as the Auto Add/Delete checkbox. Additionally, it offers the Magnetic checkbox for activating the Magnetic Pen tool and the Curve Fit option. These options are discussed in more detail later in the chapter, in the "Drawing with the Freeform Pen Tool" and "Tracing with the Magnetic Pen Tool" sections.

The Path Selection Tools

Unlike previous versions, Photoshop 6 features two path selection tools, used for editing and selecting paths. To access these tools, you can press A on your keyboard or click on their Toolbox location. If you keep the mouse button pressed, a pop-up menu with both tools appears.

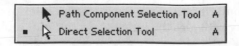

These tools select paths as follows:

- **Direct Selection tool**   This tool selects and deselects segments and points on paths. If you click and drag on a point with the Direct Selection tool, you edit the path.

- **Path Component Selection tool**   This tool selects an entire path. When selecting text converted to paths, the Path Component Selection tool selects an entire letter. Use this tool to select before moving or transforming a path.

The Paths Palette

Once you create a path, it appears in the Paths palette. If you add segments and shapes to the path, they are considered subpaths of the path that appears in the Paths palette. When you create a new path by clicking on the New Path icon in the Paths palette, Photoshop hides all other paths. To view a hidden path, you simply click on its name in the Paths palette.

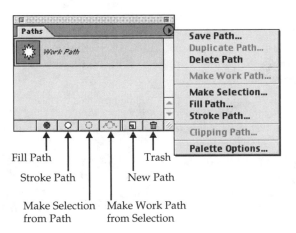

The icons at the bottom of the Paths palette are shortcuts for commands that appear in the palette's pop-up menu. These icons let you quickly fill a path with color, stroke a path with a foreground color, load a path as a selection, make a path from a selection, create a new path, and delete a path.

Click on the Paths palette pop-up menu and choose Palette Options. In the Palette Options dialog box, make sure that the second radio button next to the second starfish ( ) is selected. This allows you to see a small thumbnail of your path in the Paths palette (using a large thumbnail might slow down screen display). If you choose None, the thumbnail preview is turned off. Click on OK to close the dialog box.

Note   *Notice the commands Fill Path and Stroke Path in the Paths palette's pop-up menu. When you wish to fill or stroke a path, you must access these commands from the Paths palette, not from the Edit menu's Fill and Stroke choices. See the "Filling and Stroking Paths and Subpaths" section later in this chapter for more information.*

Creating Paths

There are several ways to create paths in Photoshop:

- The quickest method is to simply start by clicking on the screen with the Pen or Freeform Pen tool. When you create a path this way, Photoshop displays it in the Paths palette and names it Work Path. Later, you can save the path to give it a specific name.

- You can click on the New Path icon in the Paths palette. After you click, Photoshop creates a new path and automatically names it Path 1 in the Paths palette. Subsequent paths are named Path 2, Path 3, Path 4, and so on.

When you create a new path, Photoshop hides all other paths from the screen. To view a hidden path, click on the path's name in the Paths palette.

- You can choose New Path from the Paths palette's menu or press OPTION (ALT) and click on the New Path icon. This opens the New Path dialog box, where you can enter a name for the path. After you click on OK, the name of the path appears in the Paths palette. (If Work Path—a path without a name—is selected in the Paths palette, the New Path command is replaced by the Save Path command.)

If you click on the New Path icon or choose New Path from the Path palette, you still need to click on screen with a Pen tool to create anchor points and segments for the path.

- You can create a path with a shape tool. Before creating the shape, click on the Create New Work Path icon in the Shape tool's Options bar.

If View > Snap to > Grids is activated, the Pen tools only create anchor points on grid lines.

Drawing with the Freeform Pen Tool

All you need to do to create a path with the Freeform Pen tool is to click and drag. When you use the Freeform Pen tool, you draw in much the same manner as you would draw if you had a real pen in your hand. Use the Freeform Pen tool to create a quick outline on screen. Once you create a path, you can always fine-tune it by adjusting it with either the Direct Selection tool or one of the other editing tools discussed later in this chapter.

In this section, you'll see how you can create a simple path with the Freeform Pen tool. Before you start using the Freeform Pen tool, select it in the Toolbox and take a look at its Options bar.

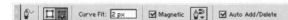

The Curve Fit option in the Options bar controls how many anchor points the Freeform Pen tool creates; the higher the number, the fewer the anchor points, and thus the simpler the curve. In general, simpler curves are easier to edit and produce smooth curves. You can enter a value from 0.5 to 10 in the field. Unless you are creating a very complicated path, leave the Curve Fit field at the default setting of 2 pixels.

The Magnetic checkbox switches the Freeform Pen to the Magnetic Pen tool, which automatically selects image edges. This option is discussed in the next section.

As discussed earlier, the overlapping area icons in the Options bar determine how overlapping paths are filled. If you intend to fill the paths you create at a later time, click on the appropriate icon.

Now try out the Freeform Pen tool.

1. Load an image that includes an object that you want to select. For instance, load the Shells file from the Chapter 14 folder of this book's CD-ROM.

2. Activate the Freeform Pen tool in the Toolbox. Leave the default settings in the Options bar.

3. Move the Freeform Pen tool over the edge of one of the objects in the image (such as a shell) and then click and drag to outline the object. As you click and drag, the Freeform Pen tool creates the path.

4. To stop creating the path, release the mouse button. If you wish to continue the path from where you stopped, click on the last anchor point and continue clicking and dragging. If you wish to finish the path to create a closed path, click and drag to where you started the point. When you return to the path's starting point, a tiny circle appears on screen. Release the mouse button when you see the circle.

Tracing with the Magnetic Pen Tool

Creating complicated paths with the Pen tool takes practice and experience. If you're new to the Pen tool or want to create a path quickly, you may want to try your hand at the Magnetic Pen tool. This tool helps you create intricate paths by automatically snapping to image edges that you trace over.

To activate the Magnetic Pen tool, select the Freeform Pen tool in the Toolbox and click on the Magnetic checkbox in the tool's Options bar. Then click on the Magnetic Pen icon in the Options bar to see the Magnetic Options pop-up menu.

APPLYING EFFECTS TO YOUR IMAGES

The Width option controls image-edge detection. The Magnetic Pen tool uses this value to determine how far from the pen pointer to look for image edges. When the value is set to 10 pixels (the default setting), the Magnetic Pen tool detects image edges up to 10 pixels away. If you are trying to trace over an image that includes twists and turns, you'll probably want to lower the value. Acceptable values are from 1 to 40 pixels.

You can increase the Magnetic Pen width 1 pixel at a time by pressing the close bracket (]) key; to decrease it 1 pixel at a time, press the open bracket ([) key.

The Contrast setting controls how the Magnetic Pen tool reacts to different contrast values along image edges. Enter higher values to have the Magnetic Pen tool recognize edges that contain more contrast. Enter lower percentage values to detect lower contrast. As a general rule, when tracing over images with high-contrast edges, use high Contrast and Width settings. For images with less contrast, use low Contrast and Width values.

The Frequency option controls how fast the Magnetic Pen tool adds anchor points. Higher values drop anchor points faster. You can enter values between 5 and 40.

Note
Stylus users should choose the Stylus Pressure option in the Magnetic Options dialog box. Adding pressure to the stylus increases the pen's width.

The other settings in the Options bar work in the same way as they do for the Freeform Pen tool.

To trace an image with the Magnetic Pen option, start by clicking in the document to establish a magnetic point and then move the Magnetic Pen along the edge of the object. (You don't need to keep the mouse button depressed.) The Magnetic Pen starts creating a path based on the image's edge contrast and the option settings. If the path of the Magnetic Pen jumps off the edge you are tracing, simply click to add a magnetic point, and then continue to move the mouse along the object. There are three ways you can end the path:

- To end the path and close it, double-click.
- To end the path and close it with a straight-line segment, press OPTION (ALT) and double-click.
- To end the path and leave it as an open path, press ENTER or RETURN (ENTER).

Tip
To draw in freehand mode temporarily, press OPTION (ALT) as you click and drag the mouse. To create a straight path segment as your work, press OPTION (ALT) and click.

To create the image shown in Figure 14-1, we used the Magnetic Pen tool, some layer styles, and a filter. We began with the images shown in Figure 14-2. Using the Magnetic Pen tool, we traced around the large shell in the image on the right side of Figure 14-1. As we worked, we found that occasionally we needed to stop and click along the edges of the shell image to ensure that the Magnetic Pen captured the outline

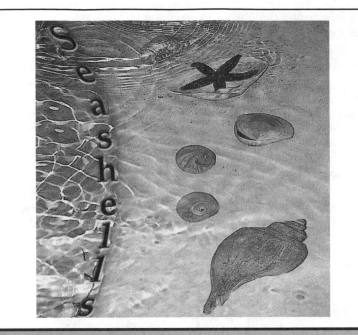

Figure 14-1.   *An image created by adding a larger shell*

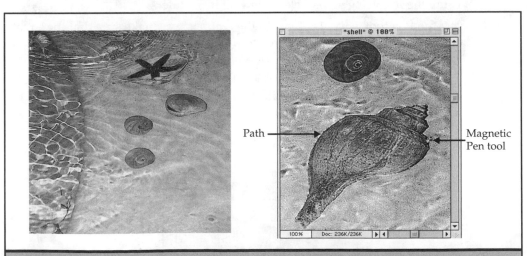

Figure 14-2.   *The images used to create the composition in Figure 14-1*

precisely. Once we created the path, we converted it into a selection by clicking on the Make Selection icon at the bottom of the Paths palette. Then we moved the selection into the image on the left side of Figure 14-2, to add the shell to the picture.

To complete the image, we added type. To add an appearance of depth to the text, we selected Layer > Layer Style > Drop Shadow and Layer > Layer Style > Bevel and Emboss. (See Chapter 18 for details on using layer styles.) Finally, to bend the type, we selected Filter > Distort > Shear. If you want to practice creating a shell composition, load both Shells files from the Chapter 14 folder of this book's CD-ROM.

Drawing Straight Paths

To use the Pen tool to create a straight path, you first click in your document to establish a starting point, move the mouse to another position, and then click again to establish the end point. Each time you click to establish a starting or ending point, you create an *anchor point*.

  If a path already exists on the screen, creating a new path adds the new path to the existing work path. If you wish to create a new path, click on the New Path icon in the Paths palette or choose New Path from the Paths palette menu.

In the following exercise, you'll learn how to create straight paths by connecting anchor points.

1. Select File > New and create a new, 5-by-5-inch RGB file with Contents set to White (it's easier to see paths against a white background). To make it easier to execute the following steps, select View > Show Rulers.

2. Select the Pen tool in the Toolbox. In the Options bar, make sure that the Create New Path button is selected. Leave the Auto Add/Delete option unchecked. If you wish to see the Rubber Band option in action, click on the Rubber Band check box in the Pen Options bar.

3. Move the Pen tool into your document about 2 inches from the top and 1 inch from the left and then click. A small gray or black square—the first anchor point—appears on screen. In the Paths palette, notice that a work path is created. Work Path is the default name that Photoshop assigns to all new paths.

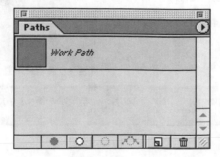

> **Note**   *If* CAPS LOCK *is on or the Other Cursors Precise option is selected in the Preferences Display & Cursors dialog box, the pen pointer changes into a crosshair. The effects of using the Pen tool are the same, whether you work with the pen pointer or the crosshair.*

4. Move the Pen tool to the right about 1.5 inches away from the first anchor point and click. Don't drag the mouse when you click to create an anchor point; otherwise, you will create a curve instead of a line.

5. Notice that you now have a second anchor point, connected to the first anchor point with a straight path segment. The second anchor point is gray or black, and the first one is now hollow. The gray or black anchor point is the one that is currently selected; the hollow anchor point is no longer selected. Also notice that the Work Path thumbnail in the Paths palette updates as you make changes to the path on your screen.

> **Note**   *If you make a mistake while creating your path, press* DELETE *(*BACKSPACE *or* DELETE*) to erase the last path segment. Be careful not to press* DELETE *twice, or you will erase the entire work path. If you press* DELETE *three times, all of the paths on the screen will be erased.*

6. Press and hold down SHIFT while you create a third anchor point anywhere on your screen. By holding down the SHIFT key, you constrain the Pen tool so that path segments are drawn to the nearest 45-degree angle.

The path you have just created is called an *open path.* An open path has two end points: one at the path's beginning and one at its end. If you activated the Rubber Band option, as long as you have an open path and the Pen tool is activated, the Rubber Band will keep stretching from your last anchor point to the Pen tool's current position. Thus, every time you click, you will be extending the open path.

To stop Photoshop from extending an open path every time the Pen tool is clicked, you can save a path or close a path. You can also click again on the Pen tool in the Toolbox, or switch to the Direct Selection tool and deselect. You'll learn how to save, close, and deselect paths later in this chapter.

If you wish to continue experimenting with the Pen tool, move on to the next section, where you will learn how to deactivate the Pen tool in order to move a segment of a path or the entire path.

Adjusting and Duplicating Paths

After you have created a path, you might want to adjust it by moving an anchor point or moving the whole path. Or you may need to duplicate the path so that you can use it elsewhere in the document.

To select (and deselect) anchor points, you use the Direct Selection tool. There are several ways to select an entire path:

- Click on it with the Path Component Selection tool.
- Select additional anchor points by pressing SHIFT as you click on each unselected anchor point.
- Press OPTION (ALT) and click on any segment or anchor point to select the entire path.
- Click and drag over the entire path with the Direct Selection tool pointer.

After you've selected a path, there are several ways that you can copy it:

- Using the Direct Selection tool, press OPTION (ALT) while you click and drag the path to a new location.
- Select a path in the Paths palette and choose Duplicate Path in the Paths palette menu.
- In the Paths palette, click and drag the path over the New Path icon (⬚) at the bottom of the palette. If you press OPTION (ALT) while you drag, the Duplicate Path dialog box opens, allowing you to name the path before copying it.

When you copy a path or create new path segments, Photoshop considers the segments to be subpaths. This distinction will be important when you begin to use the Paths palette pop-up menu commands, which are discussed later in this chapter.

Using the path you created in the previous section (or a new path), experiment with selecting anchor points, moving the path, and copying the path.

1. Select the Direct Selection tool by clicking on it in the Toolbox. If the Direct Selection tool isn't visible, click on the Path Component Selection tool and keep the mouse button pressed. When the Direct Selection tool appears in the pop-up menu, select it.

2. Position the Direct Selection tool over the anchor point that you wish to adjust and click to select it. The selected anchor point turns black.

Note *If you don't see anchor points on your path, click anywhere on the path to display the anchor points. If all of the anchor points on your path are selected, you first need to deselect the path by clicking away from the path. Then click on the path again.*

3. Drag the selected anchor point to a new location. When you click and drag, the path's angle and size are adjusted according to the angle at which you drag the anchor point and how far you move it. Notice that the path moves as if it were floating on another layer above the background pixels. Also notice that the work path in the Paths palette is updated.

4. You can also move anchor points by pressing the directional arrow keys on your keyboard. Press the UP, DOWN, LEFT, and RIGHT ARROW keys a few times. The selected anchor point moves in the direction of the keys you press in 1-pixel increments. If you press and hold down SHIFT while you press one of the directional arrow keys, the selected anchor point moves in 10-pixel increments.

5. Select the entire path on your screen by pressing OPTION (ALT) and clicking on any segment or anchor point of the path. All the anchor points turn black or gray when the path is selected. Then click any segment of the path and drag the path to a new location.

 You can select different path segments by clicking and dragging over them with the Direct Selection tool. You can add to a path selection by pressing SHIFT and clicking anchor points or path segments.

6. To copy the path, press OPTION (ALT) while you click and drag the path with the Direct Selection tool to a new location. You'll see a small, black arrow as you click and drag. A duplicate of the path will appear. After the duplicate appears, release the OPTION (ALT) key and the mouse button. On your screen, you now have two subpaths.

7. Now try joining the two subpaths. Reactivate the Pen tool, click on the end point of one subpath, and then click on the end point of the second subpath. The two subpaths become one path.

8. To deselect the path, activate the Direct Selection tool and then click away from the path. All of the anchor points disappear. Note that the anchor points will reappear when the path is reselected. After you deselect, you can create another subpath if you want to continue to experiment.

9. Delete the path currently on your screen by pressing DELETE once if no anchor points on the path are selected. Press DELETE twice if any anchor point is selected. If you have more than one path on the screen, press DELETE three times.

Now that you understand the basics of drawing and adjusting straight paths, you are ready to learn about working with smooth curves, one of the features for which the Pen tool is best known.

Drawing and Adjusting Curves with the Pen Tool

The Pen tool's ability to draw smooth curves with precision makes it an invaluable aid when you need to create any curved shape or selection. Drawing a curve with the Pen tool does, however, take some getting used to. You can't just draw a curve on screen as you would with the Lasso tool or one of the painting tools. As you'll see in the next exercise, drawing curves that slope in different directions with the Pen tool requires a moving, "seesaw" motion with the mouse.

The curves created with the Pen tool are called Bézier curves, named after the French mathematician Pierre Bézier, who defined the shape of a curve in mathematical terms with four direction points.

As you drag with the Pen tool to create a curve, a *direction line* extends in opposite directions from the anchor point. The size and angle of the direction line determine the length and slope of the curve. The two end points of the direction lines are called *direction points*. By clicking and dragging on either of these points, you can move the direction line—and thus change the size and shape of the curve. Pressing SHIFT constrains direction lines in 45-degree increments. Once the curve has been created and deselected, the direction lines and points disappear.

Another way to adjust the shape of a curve is to click on the curve segment itself with the Direct Selection tool and then click and drag. When you do this, both direction lines will adjust themselves according to how you move the curve. Besides changing the slope of a curve, you can also change its width by moving either one of its anchor points with the Direct Selection tool.

 When creating curves, try to create the fewest possible anchor points and set them as far away from each other as you can. Also, don't create anchor points in the middle of the bulge of paths.

To see how to create and manipulate curves, try the following exercise.

1. If you do not have a document open, create a new, 5-by-5-inch file. Set Resolution to 72 ppi and Contents to White. If you are already in a document that has a path in it, click on the New Path icon at the bottom of the Paths palette. If the rulers and Info palette are not already displayed, select View > Show Rulers and Window > Show Info to turn these features on.

2. Select the Pen tool and move the tip of the tool about 1 inch from the left side of your screen and about 2 inches down from the top. Click to create an anchor point, and then drag down about 1.5 inches to begin creating a curve that faces downward. As you drag, the Pen pointer changes to an arrowhead, indicating that you are specifying a direction for the curve.

3. To create the second anchor point for the curve, move the Pen tool horizontally to the right about 1 inch from the first anchor point. To create a curve, click and drag straight up. Notice that the curve ends at the new anchor point. As you drag, the curve takes shape and a new direction line appears (see Figure 14-4). Release the mouse after dragging up about 1.5 inches.

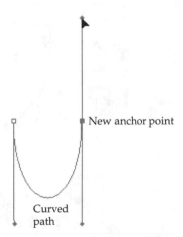

APPLYING EFFECTS
TO YOUR IMAGES

Note   *Don't worry if you are feeling a little overwhelmed by all of the lines, points, and other items on your screen. At this stage, the most important concept to remember is that* the curve slopes in the direction in which you drag the mouse. *The first part of the curve you drew slopes downward (the direction in which you originally dragged the mouse). The second part of the curve slopes upward, the direction in which you dragged in step 3.*

4. To adjust the curve, you need to switch from the Pen tool to the Direct Selection tool. Select the Direct Selection tool, click on the lower-left direction point of the curve, and drag to the right. Now click on the lower-right direction point of the curve and drag to the left. Notice that the curve gets more pointed. If you wish to flatten the curve, drag both bottom direction points in opposite directions.

5. Click and drag on the lower-left, then lower-right direction points to make both direction lines smaller and thus reduce the size of the curve. After you have experimented with changing the direction lines, click and drag on the direction points to return the direction lines to their original length of about 1.5 inches from the anchor point.

6. Select the Pen tool again and click on the last anchor point you created so that you can create another curve segment.

7. To begin creating the next curve, move the Pen tool 1 inch directly to the right of the last anchor point you created. Then click and drag straight down approximately 1.5 inches. Notice the smooth transition between the two continuous curves that you have created. The anchor point between the two curves is called a *smooth point*. When the direction line intersects a smooth anchor point, the curves on either side of the smooth point change whenever the line is adjusted.

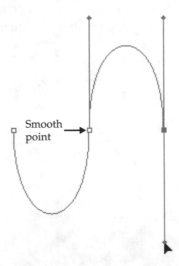

Smooth point →

8. To change the width of your curve, you must activate the Direct Selection tool. Here's a shortcut: With the Pen tool selected, press and hold down the COMMAND (CTRL) key to change the pen pointer (or crosshair) to the Direct Selection tool. Then click on the last anchor point of the curve you just drew and drag to the left about 0.5 inch. Release the mouse button to return to the Pen tool.

9. Continue creating curves, alternating between clicking and dragging up and down. To practice some more, you may want to first press DELETE twice to delete

the path currently on your screen, so that you can start all over again. If you create your first anchor point by dragging up, the first curve will slope upward.

Note *To make the direction lines of a curve segment reappear after a path is deselected, click on that curve segment with the Direct Selection tool.*

10. When you have finished practicing, clear the screen by pressing DELETE twice. If you have more than one subpath on the screen, press DELETE three times.

Drawing Scalloped Curves

You can also draw curves so that they all point in the same direction. These scalloped curves can be used to create curved border effects around images. Scalloped curves cannot be drawn like the continuous curves you just created. When you create scalloped curves, you create a corner point in order to change the direction in which the curve is drawn. As you'll see in the following exercise, the direction lines that stem from corner points do not work in the same way as direction lines that bisect smooth points. A corner point's direction line controls only one side of one curve.

1. To create the first curve, begin by positioning the Pen tool about 0.5 inch from the left side of your document window and about 2 inches from the top. The first curve you create will point upward, so start by clicking and dragging straight up about 1 inch.

2. Move the mouse horizontally to the right about 1.5 inches from the last anchor point. Click and drag straight down about 1 inch.

Tip *You can press SHIFT to constrain the anchor points and press SHIFT again to constrain the direction line.*

3. The next curve you create will point in the same direction as the first curve. To accomplish this, you need to create a corner point between the curves. To create a corner point, press OPTION (ALT) while you click on the anchor point that you created in step 2. Notice that one of the direction lines disappears. Continue to keep OPTION (ALT) pressed while you drag diagonally up to the right about 1 inch from the anchor point, to create a new direction line, and then release OPTION (ALT) and the mouse button.

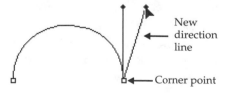

New direction line

Corner point

4. To create the second curve, move the Pen tool directly to the right about 1.5 inches away from the last anchor point. This will be the end point of the curve that you are about to create. Click and drag straight down about 1 inch, and a curve will appear.

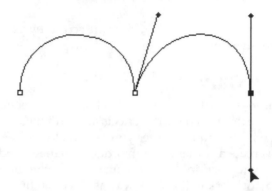

5. To create the third scalloped curve, repeat the technique used in steps 3 and 4. Position the mouse over the last anchor point you created, press OPTION (ALT), and click and drag diagonally upward to create a new direction line. Move the mouse about 1.5 inches to the right of the anchor point, and then click and drag down about 1 inch to create the curve.

6. When you are ready, delete the path currently on your screen by pressing DELETE twice.

Creating a corner point to control the direction of a curve also enables you to create paths in which straight segments are joined to curves, as explained next.

Connecting Curves and Straight Paths

When you are using the Pen tool and working with paths, you'll often need to connect a line to a curve or a curve to a line. Shapes made of both curves and lines are all around you: vases, bottles, paddles, and so on. When you want to trace any of these shapes with the Pen tool or create them from scratch, you'll need to master the Pen tool techniques described in the following exercise.

1. If the Pen tool is not activated, select it. Position the Pen tool about 1 inch from the left side of the screen and about 2 inches from the top. To begin, click and drag straight up about 1 inch.

2. To create the curve, move the mouse 1 inch to the right from the first anchor point, and then click and drag downward about 1 inch.

3. To create the corner point that will allow you to connect this curve to a line, press OPTION (*ALT*) and click on the last anchor point you created. Notice that the bottom direction line disappears. Release the mouse and OPTION (*ALT*).

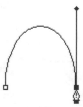

4. To create a line that connects to the curve, move the Pen tool to the right horizontally about 1 inch from the curve's second anchor point and click. Remember, if you want to create a line at an angle of 45 degrees (or increments thereof), you can press and hold down SHIFT while you click. The curve is now connected to a line.

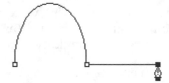

5. Clear your screen by pressing DELETE twice.

6. Now draw a straight path to connect to a curve. Create a line segment about 1 inch long by connecting two anchor points. (If you need to review the steps to create line segments, refer to the earlier section, "Drawing Straight Paths.")

7. Press and hold OPTION (*ALT*) while you click on the last anchor point you created, and then drag diagonally upward to the right about 1 inch. When the direction line appears, release OPTION (*ALT*) and the mouse button.

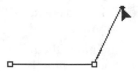

8. Now, to create a curve that connects to the line, move the Pen tool horizontally about 1 inch to the right of the corner point. Then click and drag straight down about 1 inch. If you need to adjust the curve, use the Direct Selection tool.

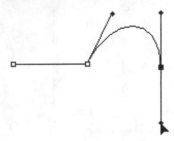

9. When you have finished practicing, clear the screen by pressing DELETE twice. If you have more than one path on your screen, press DELETE three times.

Creating a Closed Path

A *closed path* is a path that ends at its starting point. Once a path is closed, you can move the pen pointer away from it and create other paths. In this next exercise, you will create a closed path in the shape of a triangle by connecting three anchor points.

1. If you do not have a document open, create a new 72 ppi, 5-by-5-inch file RGB file. Set Contents to White. If you are already in a document that has a path in it, click on the New Path icon at the bottom of the Paths palette. If the rulers and Info palette are not already displayed, select View > Show Rulers and Window > Show Info to turn these features on.

2. Activate the Pen tool and move it up toward the upper-middle part of the document. Using the ruler and Info palette as guides, position the Pen tool about 2.5 inches from the left side of the document window and about 0.5 inch down from the top. Click to create the first anchor point of the triangle.

3. To create a second anchor point, move the Pen tool diagonally down and left about 2 inches (in the Info palette, the x-axis is approximately 1.0 and the y-axis is approximately 2.5) and click. This creates a line segment from the first anchor point to the second anchor point.

4. To create a third anchor point, move the Pen tool horizontally to the right of the second anchor point about 3 inches (at the 4-inch mark on the ruler) and click. This creates a line segment from the second anchor point to the third anchor point.

5. To close the path, you must return to the starting point of the triangle. Move the Pen tool to the first anchor point. You will see a small loop at the bottom-right side of the Pen tool, which indicates that you have returned to your starting point.

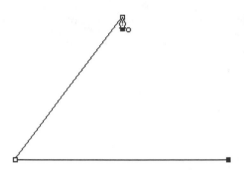

6. Click on the first anchor point, and the path will be closed. When you click the last anchor point, notice that the Info palette displays angle and distance readouts.

Leave the triangle displayed on your screen and proceed to the next section, which explains how adding, subtracting, and editing points on a path can change its shape.

Manipulating Paths

After you've created a path, you can manipulate it in many ways. Using the pen and path selection tools, you can reshape the path. Using the Transform commands on the Edit menu, you can apply transformations to a path. The Path palette provides ways to convert paths to selections, as well as fill and stroke paths.

Adding, Subtracting, and Modifying Points

You've learned how to adjust a path by moving anchor and direction points. Paths can also be reshaped by adding or subtracting anchor points, by converting smooth points to corner points, and vice versa. By combining these techniques with your drawing skills, you will be able to edit the shape of most paths.

To add and subtract points, you use the Add Anchor Point and Delete Anchor Point tools. If the Auto Add/Delete checkbox is selected in the Pen tool's Options bar, you do not need to select either of these tools in the Toolbox. When you move the mouse over a segment, the Add Anchor Point tool appears automatically. When you move the mouse over an anchor point, the Delete Anchor Point tool appears.

Changing Smooth Points to Corner Points

In this next exercise, you will transform the triangular path you created in the previous section into a diamond shape and then back to a triangle. If you do not have the triangle from the previous section on your screen, create one in the middle of your document window now. You'll start creating your diamond by activating the Add Anchor Point tool.

1. To transform the triangle into a diamond, you need to add an anchor point to the base of the triangle. Select the Add Anchor Point tool (or select the Auto Add/Delete checkbox in the Pen tool's Options bar), position the pointer in the middle of the base of the triangle, and click. A new anchor point is added to the path at the point where you clicked.

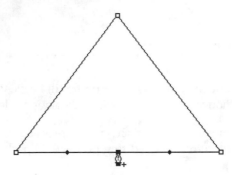

2. To move the new anchor point down to begin creating the diamond shape, you need to switch from the Add Anchor pointer to the Direct Selection tool. Fortunately, Photoshop does this for you automatically. Once the Add Anchor Point tool switches to the Direct Selection tool, click on the new anchor point you created in step 1 and drag it downward about 2 inches, so that the triangle begins to look like a diamond.

3. Notice that the new point is a smooth point. You can turn the round edge into a corner point by using the Convert Point tool in the Toolbox. Select the Convert Point tool, and then click the smooth point. The smooth corner point changes to a sharply angled corner point.

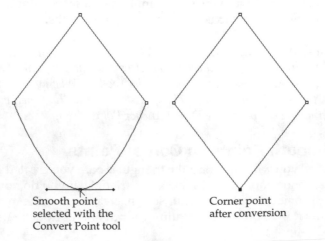

Smooth point
selected with the
Convert Point tool

Corner point
after conversion

4. Now suppose that you've changed your mind and want the diamond switched back into a triangle. To do this, you need to subtract the last anchor point you created. Click on the Delete Anchor Point tool (or select the Auto Add/Delete checkbox in the Pen tool's Options bar) and click on the anchor point you used to create the diamond. The corner point disappears, and the diamond shape immediately snaps back into a triangle.

5. Before proceeding, delete the triangle by pressing DELETE twice.

The ability to convert from smooth points to corner points and corner points to smooth points allows you to edit paths and change their shapes quickly. For example, you can outline a curved object by first connecting straight segments and then generate the necessary curves by changing corner points into smooth points.

Changing Corner Points to Smooth Points

The following exercise demonstrates how you can transform a sharply cornered wedge into a heart shape by changing corner points to smooth points.

1. Using the Pen tool, create and connect four anchor points to create a wedge shape. To make the wedge, start by creating an anchor point in the upper-left corner of your screen. Create the next anchor point at the bottom of your screen, and then create another one in the upper-right corner. Continue creating the closed path so that it looks like the one shown here.

2. Now transform the two top corner points of the wedge to smooth corner points. Start by activating the Convert Point tool in the Pen section of the Tool palette. Position the Corner tool on the top-left corner point, and click and drag downward to the left until a curve is created. Notice that as you drag, the Corner tool changes to an arrowhead pointer because a direction line for the curve is being created.

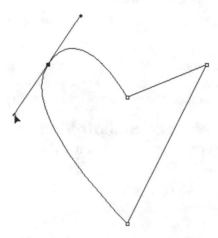

3. To create a curve out of the top-right corner point, click and drag upward to the left on this corner point with the Corner tool. Stop when a curve is created.

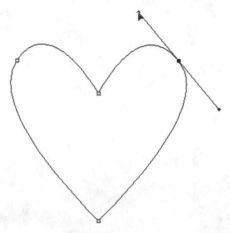

4. If you wish to make adjustments to the curves of the heart, click and drag on the curves' direction points with the Direct Selection tool.

At this point, you may wish to fill, stroke, or save the heart path that you've just created. You'll learn how to perform those tasks in the "Filling and Stroking Paths and Subpaths" and "Saving Paths" sections later in this chapter.

Rotating, Scaling, Skewing, and Distorting Paths

Since most of Photoshop's menu commands have no effect on paths, you may be surprised to find that all of the Edit > Transform commands are activated when a path is selected. Try selecting a path or even an anchor point of a path, and then open the Edit menu. There you'll see the Free Transform Path and Transform Paths commands (if part of the path is selected, the menu commands read Free Transform Points and Transform Points). Click on the Transform Path command, and a whole new world of path manipulation opens up.

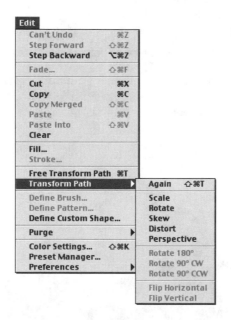

Since the Transform commands are discussed in Chapter 8, we won't repeat instructions here for each Transform submenu command. However, here is a list of procedures you can perform with the Free Transform command. Simply select a path or path segment, and then choose Edit > Free Transform Path (or Free Transform Points). A bounding box with handles will appear around the selected path. To apply the transformation, press RETURN or ENTER (*ENTER*). To cancel a transformation, press COMMAND-. or ESC (*ESC*).

- To move a path, click and drag within the bounding box border.
- To rotate a path, drag outside the bounding box border in an arc-like movement.
- To scale a path, click and drag on a handle. (Hold down the SHIFT key to scale proportionally.) Figure 14-3 shows a path being scaled.

APPLYING EFFECTS TO YOUR IMAGES

■ To skew a path, press SHIFT-COMMAND (*SHIFT-CTRL*) and click and drag on any handle.

■ To distort a path symmetrically, press OPTION (*ALT*) and click and drag.

■ To distort freely, press COMMAND (*CTRL*).

■ To create perspective, press SHIFT-ALT-COMMAND (*SHIFT-ALT-CTRL*) while clicking and dragging.

■ To move the center point on a path before executing the Transform command, click and drag on the center point.

■ To transform a duplicate of a selected path, press OPTION-COMMAND-T (*ALT-CTRL-T*). You can now edit the duplicate without altering the original. (Make sure you select the entire path before executing this command.)

You can duplicate the path or create another path and apply the same transformation to the new path by choosing Edit > Transform Path > Again. To duplicate a path and apply the previous transformation, press SHIFT-OPTION-COMMAND-T (*SHIFT-ALT-CTRL-T*).

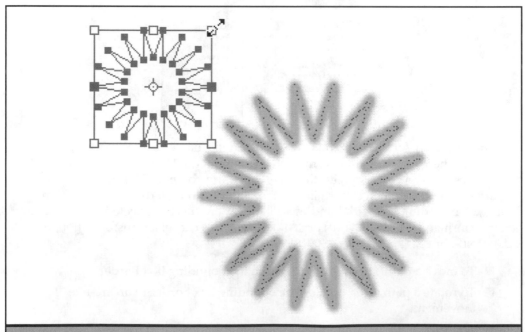

Figure 14-3.   *A path being scaled with the Edit > Free Transform command*

Converting a Path into a Selection

As you work with paths, you'll often need to convert them to selections. Once a selection border is created from the path, you'll be able to use all of the Photoshop commands that affect selections. For instance, you can color-correct the area within the selection or apply a filter to it.

 Before a path can be affected by Photoshop's tools (or many of its menu commands), you must convert the path to a selection.

In the next exercise, you'll learn how to turn a path into a selection and to merge both a path and a selection into one selection.

1. If you don't have a blank document on screen, create a new 72 ppi, 5-by-5-inch file with Contents set to White.

2. Use the Pen tool to create a rectangular path of approximately 2.5 by 2 inches.

3. Use the Elliptical Marquee tool to create a circular selection that overlaps the rectangular path.

4. Open the pop-up menu in the Paths palette and choose Make Selection, or press OPTION (*ALT*) and click on the Make Selection icon (⬚) in the Paths palette. This opens the Make Selection dialog box.

5. In the Make Selection dialog box, you specify the type of selection you want to create from any paths or selections on your screen. The Feather Radius and Anti-aliased options function in the same way as they do with Photoshop's selection tools. The options in the Operation section specify how you want the selection to be created. Select the New Selection radio button. This option creates a selection from the path only. Click on OK, and only the rectangular path is turned into a selection.

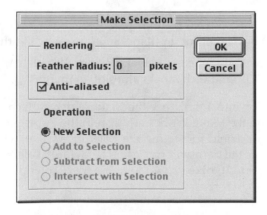

6. Choose Edit > Undo Selection Change to remove the selection.

7. Return to the Make Selection dialog box and select Add to Selection. This option adds the area specified by the path to the current selection on screen. Click on OK, and a selection is created from both the rectangle and circle together.

8. Choose Edit > Undo Selection Change to remove the selection.

9. Open the Make Selection dialog box and select Subtract from Selection. This option removes a path from a selection. Click on OK, and the rectangular area that overlaps the circle will be removed from the circular selection border.

10. Choose Edit > Undo Selection Change to remove the selection.

11. Open the Make Selection dialog box and select Intersect with Selection. This option creates a selection from the area where the path and selection overlap. Click on OK, and the selection is transformed into one selection, including only the overlapping areas of the rectangle and circle.

You can also convert a path into a selection by clicking on the Make Selection icon in the Paths palette or by clicking and dragging the path name over the Make Selection icon. When the Make Selection icon changes color, release the mouse button. Press ENTER on the numeric keypad to create a selection out of a path quickly. When you create a selection this way, the Feather and Anti-aliasing options retain their last settings.

Converting a Selection into a Path

Now that you've seen how Photoshop creates a selection out of a path, let's take a look at how to transform a selection into a path. Occasionally, it's easier to create a path from a selection rather than constructing it from scratch with the Pen tool. For example, you might wish to create a path from these types of selections:

■ An intricate Magic Wand selection that would take too much time to create with the Pen tool

■ A selection you created from nontransparent areas of a layer by COMMAND-clicking (CTRL-clicking) on a layer (other than the Background) in the Layers palette

■ An intricate selection you created by pressing OPTION-COMMAND-1 (*ALT-CTRL-1*) to create a mask from the channel values of an image

To convert a selection into a path, use the Make Work Path command in the Paths palette menu or click on the Make Work Path icon in the Paths palette. The Make Work Path dialog box contains a field for setting the Tolerance value, which determines the number of anchor points the path will include. The default Tolerance value is 2 pixels; you can specify from 0.5 to 10 pixels. If you enter a high Tolerance value, fewer anchor points will be used, and the resulting path will be smoother. With a low Tolerance value, more anchor points are used, resulting in a bumpier path.

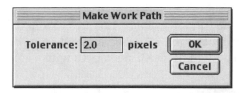

Caution   *If you have a work path on your screen (a path that isn't named or saved) and then create a path from a selection, the new path replaces your original path. Be sure to save your work paths if you want to keep using them (see the "Saving Paths" section later in this chapter).*

The following exercise demonstrates how Photoshop creates anchor points when converting a selection border into a path. You can change any selection into a path, but in this exercise, you'll work with a figure-eight shape, because the path will require numerous anchor points.

1. Clear the screen of all selections by choosing Select > Deselect. Then remove all paths by pressing DELETE three times.

2. Activate the Lasso tool and click and drag to create a figure-eight shape.

3. To turn the figure-eight selection border into a path, select Make Work Path from the pop-up menu in the Paths palette. In the Make Path dialog box, type **1** in the Tolerance field and click on OK. When the path appears, click on it with the Direct Selection tool so you can examine the number of anchor points that were created. Count the number of anchor points.

4. Now try a higher Tolerance setting and observe the results. First, return to a selection on your screen by clicking on the Make Selection icon in the Paths palette. Then reopen the Make Path dialog box. Enter **10** as the Tolerance setting and click on OK. When the path appears, click it with the Direct Selection tool and count the number of anchor points. Observe that the higher Tolerance value results in fewer anchor points.

Caution   *Converting selections to paths sometimes creates paths that are too complicated for printers to print. In this situation, your best bet is to delete some anchor points with the Delete Anchor Point tool or recreate the path using a higher Tolerance setting. Also note that paths created from selections may not look exactly like your original selection.*

APPLYING EFFECTS TO YOUR IMAGES

Keyboard Commands for Editing Paths

There are quite a few keyboard shortcuts for path editing, which you might find helpful. Table 14-1 lists these keyboard shortcuts.

You've now learned the fundamental techniques required for modifying paths with the Paths palette, the pen tools, the path-selection tools, and keyboard shortcuts. In the next section, you'll learn how to fill or stroke a path with a color or pattern.

Filling and Stroking Paths and Subpaths

Photoshop allows you to fill a path with the foreground color or a pattern or from a state in the History palette. You can also fill and stroke a path using many of the same

Function	Shortcut
Select the Direct Selection tool when using any Pen tool	COMMAND (*CTRL*)
Switch between Add Anchor Point and Delete Anchor Point tool when the pointer is over an anchor point	OPTION (*ALT*)
Switch from the Pen tool to the Convert Point tool	OPTION (*ALT*)
Switch from the Direct Selection tool to the Convert Point tool when the pointer is over an anchor point	OPTION-COMMAND (*ALT-CTRL*)
Select another anchor point with the Direct Selection tool activated	SHIFT-click
Select an entire path with the Direct Selection tool activated	OPTION-click (*ALT-click*)
Duplicate a path with the Direct Selection tool activated	OPTION-click and drag (*ALT-click and drag*)
Duplicate a path with the Pen tool activated	OPTION-COMMAND-click and drag (*ALT-CTRL-click and drag*)

Table 14-1.   *Path-Editing Keyboard Shortcuts*

blending modes available for the painting tools and in the Layers palette. When you stroke or fill a path, Photoshop strokes or fills the entire path, including all subpaths (noncontiguous joined segments). When you stroke a path, the stroke width is determined by the current brush size of the stroking tool.

To fill or stroke a path or subpath, use the Fill Path/Subpath or Stroke Path/Subpath command from the Paths palette's pop-up menu. Paths cannot be filled or stroked by Photoshop's Edit > Fill or Edit > Stroke commands.

When you fill or stroke a path, Photoshop fills or strokes underlying pixels *beneath* the path and leaves the path as a separate independent object. This means that you can move the path and execute Fill Path or Stroke Path again, or edit the path, without affecting the filled or stroked images on the screen.

Note   *You cannot fill or stroke a path when a marquee selection is on screen, unless the marquee is over the path.*

Filling a Path Composed of Subpaths

When filling a path, it's important to remember that Photoshop considers all path segments and subpaths on the screen to be one path. Before you fill a path, you should deselect so that no segments are selected. If you select any part of a path, the Fill Path command changes to Fill Subpath in the Paths palette's pop-up menu.

Note   *When you choose the Fill Path command from the Paths palette's pop-up menu, the entire path will be filled, as long as there are no intersecting or overlapping segments. If there are overlapping path segments, the result of the fill depends on which overlapping shape area icon was selected when the path was created.*

To see how Photoshop fills and strokes paths composed of subpaths, you need at least two separate path segments in your document. If you deleted the figure-eight path created in the previous exercise, create another closed path now before beginning the next exercise.

1. Use the Pen tool to create a square subpath to the right of the figure eight (or any other subpath). To ensure that all of the subpaths will be filled, deselect any path that is currently activated or selected. To deselect, activate the Direct Selection tool in the Paths palette and click away from the path segments.

2. To fill all of the paths on your screen, open the Path palette's pop-up menu and select Fill Path, or OPTION (*ALT*) and click on the Fill Path icon ( ) at the bottom of the Paths palette.

Note   *To fill a path in a type or shape layer, you must first rasterize the layer (Layer > Raserize).*

3. In the Fill Path dialog box, set the Use pop-up menu to Foreground Color. (Make sure your foreground color is darker than your background canvas color.) The Use menu also offers options for filling the path with the Background Color, a pattern, the selected state in the History palette, Black, 50% Gray, or White.

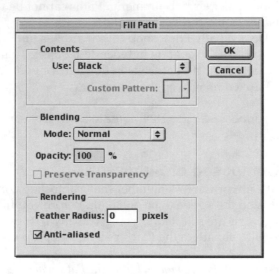

Tip   *If you fill a path with a state from the History palette, you can fill the image area inside the path with a digital image.*

4. Type **50** in the Opacity field and make sure that Mode is set to Normal. The Preserve Transparency checkbox will be available if you are working in a layer that has a transparent background. If you choose Preserve Transparency, transparent areas will not be filled.

5. If you need to soften the edges of your segments, you can set a Feather Radius value from 0 to 250 pixels. Make sure that the Anti-aliased checkbox is checked. These options work the same way here as they do for the selection tools.

6. Click on OK. Both the figure eight and the square subpaths will be filled according to your specifications.

You also can fill a path by clicking on the Fill Path icon in the Paths palette or by clicking and dragging the path name over the Fill Path icon. This will fill your path with the current settings in the Fill Path dialog box.

Stroking a Path

If you don't have the two subpaths on your screen from the previous section, create two subpaths now and then deselect. Now try stroking the path.

1. Change the foreground color to a color that will allow you to see the effects of the stroke.

2. To stroke a path, select Stroke Path from the Path palette's pop-up menu, or press OPTION (*ALT*) and click on the Stroke Path icon (○) at the bottom of the Paths palette.

3. When the Stroke Path dialog box appears, open the Tool pop-up menu. A list of painting and editing tools that use the Brush pop-up menu appears.

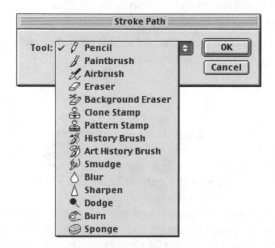

4. Select Airbrush from the Tool pop-up menu and click on OK. The path is stroked using the current brush size and opacity for the Airbrush tool.

To control how the stroke is applied to the path, you may first wish to select the tool with which you will stroke the path and choose the specific settings you want in the Options bar for that tool. Then click on the Stroke Path icon at the bottom of the Paths palette (or click and drag the path name over the Stroke Path icon). Instead of opening the Stroke Path dialog box, Photoshop will automatically stroke with the activated tool in the Toolbox using its brush settings.

You can have one path with multiple strokes. First apply a thick stroke, then a medium stroke in a different color, and finally a smaller stroke in another color.

Filling or Stroking a Subpath

Photoshop allows you to fill or stroke a subpath rather than the whole path. When you click on a path segment or SHIFT-click to activate more than one segment, Photoshop considers that segment to be a subpath.

To see the effects of stroking a subpath, follow these steps:

1. Change the foreground color and make sure that a selection tool is selected in the Toolbox.

2. Choose the subpath that you wish to stroke by clicking on it with the Direct Selection tool. This activates the subpath. You do not need to select every anchor point in the path.

3. Open the pop-up menu in the Paths palette. Notice that the Stroke Path command has changed to Stroke Subpath. Select that command.

4. In the Stroke Subpath dialog box, select a tool and click on OK. Only the subpath you've clicked on is stroked.

Saving Paths

After you've created a path, you may want to save it, especially if you are using the Pen tool to isolate an area of a digitized image. Later, you can convert the path into a selection to use as a mask or create a clipping path out of it, as described later in this chapter. When you save a path, Photoshop saves all path segments as one path, whether they are selected or not. If you edit the path after saving it, or if you add a subpath, the changes to the path will be saved automatically.

It's important to understand that a saved path does not receive an assigned disk file name. Rather, you provide a name for the path that will appear in the Paths palette. The path names that appear in this list are available only in the document in which they were created and saved. If you wish to copy a path from one document into another document, you can use the Edit > Copy and Edit > Paste commands. You can also drag a path name from the Paths palette into another open document or drag the path itself into another open document with the Pen's Direct Selection tool. The path name, as well as the path itself, will be available in the other document.

 Even though a path is saved, it can be deleted by pressing DELETE *when a pen tool or the Direct Selection tool is activated in the Paths palette.*

After you save a path, you can hide it and create more paths. This ability to hide an object is somewhat similar to working in layers. However, unlike with drawing programs or Photoshop's own Layers palette, if you save multiple paths in Photoshop, you cannot view the multiple saved paths simultaneously.

In the next exercise, you'll learn how to save a path, hide a path, and then reload the path. Before you begin, make sure that you have one path displayed on your screen.

1. To save a path, click on the pop-up menu in the Paths palette and select Save Path. (You don't need to select a path before you select the Save Path command, because all of the path segments on the screen are saved automatically.) The Save Path dialog box appears.

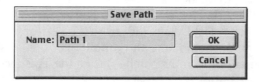

2. In the Save Path dialog box, you can name the path by typing the name in the Name field and clicking on OK. Notice that the name of the path now appears in the Paths palette.

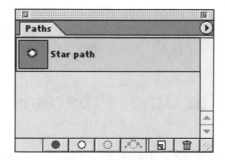

3. Hide the path you've just created, so that you can name and save another path. Click below the name you assigned to the path in the Paths palette. The path on the screen will disappear, but the path name remains in the Paths palette.

4. Create another path. Then choose Save Path from the Paths palette menu. In the Save Path dialog box, Path 2 appears in the Name field. Give the path another name if you wish and click on OK to save the path. The name of the path now appears in the Paths palette.

Note *If you wish to rename the saved path, double-click on the name of the path in the Paths palette. The Rename Path dialog box will appear, allowing you to rename the path.*

5. With two paths now saved, you can view them independently. To return to the first path, click on its name in the Paths palette. This path now appears on screen. To view the second path, click on the name of the second path in the Paths palette. The area around the path name turns gray.

6. Continue to experiment and adjust your saved paths, if you wish. Remember, once a path is saved, you can edit it without resaving.

APPLYING EFFECTS
TO YOUR IMAGES

If you wish to hide all of the paths on your screen quickly so you can create a new path, click directly below the last path name in the Paths palette. Make sure you don't click on an icon. (You may need to enlarge the Paths palette.)

7. Before proceeding to the next section, delete the second path you created. First, activate the path by clicking on the name you assigned to the second path in the Paths palette. Then select Delete Path from the pop-up menu in the Paths palette or click on the path name and drag it over the Trash icon (🗑) in the lower-right corner of the Paths palette. When the Trash icon changes colors, release the mouse button.

You can also save a path by dragging Work Path over the New Path icon at the bottom of the Paths palette or by double-clicking on Work Path in the Paths palette. (Keep in mind that a work path is saved with a document, even if you don't give the path a name.)

 Photoshop paths are saved when you save in TIFF, JPEG, or PICT file formats.

Using Paths with Other Programs

You may want to use your Photoshop paths with other programs or bring a path from Adobe Illustrator into Photoshop. You can export a path from Illustrator to Photoshop or export a Photoshop path to Illustrator. If you wish to create a silhouette mask out of a Photoshop image and place only the masked portion in another application (such as Illustrator or a page layout program), you must create a clipping path.

Exporting a Path from Adobe Illustrator into Photoshop

Since Adobe Illustrator's path capabilities are greater than Photoshop's, you may want to export a path from Illustrator to Photoshop. First, load both programs. Next, open the Illustrator file with the path in it and create a new file in Photoshop (into which you will import the path). In Illustrator, select the path with the selection tool and hold down COMMAND (*CTRL*) while you drag and drop the path from Illustrator into Photoshop.

You can also bring an Illustrator path into Photoshop by copying and pasting. Choose Edit > Copy in Illustrator, activate (or load) Photoshop, and then choose Edit > Paste. A dialog box appears asking whether you wish to Paste as Pixels or Paste as Paths. Select the Paste as Paths option if you want to be able to transform and edit the path. After you paste, all paths are included in the work path. If you want each path to appear as a separate path in the Paths palette, paste each path individually and save each one by choosing Save Path in the Paths palette menu.

Figure 14-4 shows the type of image you can create by exporting a path from Illustrator to Photoshop. Here we used an Illustrator path to create an unusual-shaped frame for a Photoshop image.

Figure 14-4.   *A design created from an Adobe Illustrator path*

We began by creating an oval path in Adobe Illustrator using the Oval Path tool. Then we used Illustrator's Filter > Distort > Punk & Bloat filter to change the shape of the oval path into a flower shape. Next, we selected the path in Illustrator, copied it, and pasted it into Photoshop (using the Paste as Paths option). In Photoshop, the Illustrator path appeared in Photoshop's Paths palette, as shown in Figure 14-5. We used Photoshop's Edit > Transform Path command to scale the path. After we enlarged the path, we moved the path into the desired location.

If you don't have Illustrator and would like to try out this example, here's how:

1. Open the Kids image file from the Chapter 14 folder of this book's CD-ROM. This image includes the path before enlarging. Select the path by pressing OPTION (*ALT*) and clicking on the path with the Direct Selection tool.

2. Choose Edit > Transform Path > Scale. Use the mouse to enlarge the path and position the path over the Kids image.

3. Convert the path into a selection by choosing Make Selection in the Paths palette.

4. Invert the selection by choosing Select > Inverse. This allows you to select the background area, rather than the kids.

Figure 14-5. *A pasted Adobe Illustrator path appears in Photoshop's Paths palette*

5. Use the Eyedropper tool to choose one color from the photograph for Photoshop's background color and one for the foreground color.

6. Activate the Gradient tool to create a gradient that blends from the foreground to the background color.

7. To add depth to the background gradient, apply a texture using Filter > Texture > Mosaic Tiles.

8. To create a beveled look for the path frame, first select the path with the Direct Selection tool. Stroke it with a dark color, using the Pencil tool with a large brush. To stroke the path, choose Stroke Subpath from the Paths palette menu and choose the Pencil tool from the Tool pop-up menu. Next, stroke the path with the Airbrush tool, using a light color. Finally, stroke the path with a small Pencil stroke using a dark color.

9. To make the small flower designs, first choose Duplicate Path from the Paths palette menu. Next, create a new layer by choosing Layer > New Layer. Choose Edit > Transform Path > Scale to decrease the size of the path so that it looks like a flower.

10. With the Pen tool, create a circular path inside the small flower path. Fill the path by first selecting it and then choosing Fill Path from the Paths palette menu.
In the Fill Path dialog box, choose Foreground Color from the Use pop-up menu, set Opacity to 50%, and click on OK. Fill the smaller path with 50 percent of the background color.

11. To add depth, choose Layer > Layer Style > Bevel and Emboss. Add a drop shadow by choosing Layer > Layer Style > Drop Shadow.

12. After you've created one flower design, duplicate it to create the others. First, select it with the Elliptical or Rectangular Marquee tool. To duplicate the design, press OPTION (*ALT*) and click and drag it to a new location with the Move tool.

Exporting a Path to Adobe Illustrator

Exporting a path from Photoshop to Illustrator can be valuable, especially after you've created a path in Photoshop by tracing over a digitized image and want to use it in Illustrator. For instance, you could create an intricate path in Photoshop by tracing over an image with the Pen tool in Photoshop. After you export the path to Illustrator, you could then turn the path into a logo.

To export the path so that you can integrate it into a design in Illustrator, choose File > Export > Paths to Illustrator in Photoshop. Choose the path name from the Paths pop-up menu. Name the file and click on Save.

The exported file can then be loaded directly into Illustrator. To do this in Illustrator, just select File > Open command, locate the file, and open it. To activate and select the path in Illustrator, choose Edit > Select All.

If you don't need to save your path, but you do want to export it into an existing Illustrator file, select the entire path and choose Edit > Copy in Photoshop. Then, in Illustrator, choose Edit > Paste to drop the path into the Illustrator file. To do this, you must have either Illustrator 5.0 or later for the Mac or Illustrator 4.0 or later for Windows.

Using Clipping Paths

One of the most useful features in the Paths palette is the Clipping Path command. A *clipping path* silhouettes an area, masking an image so that only the portion of the image within the clipping path will appear when the Photoshop file is placed in another application.

Figure 14-6 shows a scanned image of autumn leaves. Notice that a path surrounds the leaf at the upper-left corner. Figure 14-7 shows a close-up of the leaf with the path, which was used to create a clipping path. Figure 14-8 shows the results after the leaf image with the clipping path was placed in Adobe Illustrator. Only the leaf with the path was included in the clipping path, so that it could be placed on top of a new background in Illustrator.

Figure 14-6. *Only one leaf in this image is masked by a path*

Figure 14-7. *A close-up of the leaf masked with path*

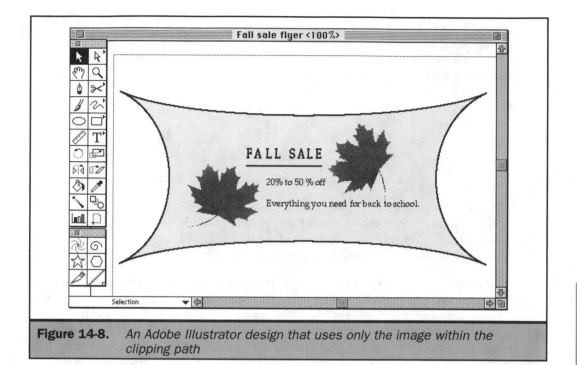

Figure 14-8. *An Adobe Illustrator design that uses only the image within the clipping path*

In Figure 14-8, the leaf image was also duplicated and rotated. Note that the edges of the leaf against the background are hard-edged. If you're going to use clipping paths, it's important to realize that they do not allow feathering. Thus, it can be rather difficult to create soft transitions between the object in your clipping path and its background in an illustration or page layout program.

Creating a Clipping Path

Use the following steps to turn a path into a clipping path.

1. Open a file that contains an image that you wish to silhouette and export to Illustrator or a page layout program. If you would like to create a clipping path similar to the one in Figure 14-8, load the Leaf file from the Chapter 14 folder of this book's CD-ROM.

2. Create a path around the portion of the image that you wish to include in the clipping path. Only one path can be saved as a clipping path.

3. Once you've created the path, choose Save Path from the Paths palette pop-up menu or double-click on Work Path in the Paths palette. In the Save Path dialog box, enter a name for your path.

4. After the path is saved, choose Clipping Path from the pop-up menu in the Paths palette. When the Clipping Path dialog box appears, select the name of

your saved path from the Path pop-up menu. You can leave the Flatness field empty for now. You may need to enter a value if you receive a PostScript "limitcheck" error when printing the clipping path image in another application, as explained after these steps.

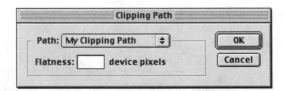

5. To save the path as a clipping path, click on OK. Notice that the name of the path will become outlined in the Paths palette. The image on your screen will not change. You will see the effects of creating a clipping path only when the file containing the clipping path is placed in another program.

If you receive a PostScript limitcheck error when you print the clipping path image from another application, you can try returning to the Clipping Path dialog box and entering a numbIer into the Flatness field. You can adjust the Flatness value to *flatten*, or simplify, paths that may be too complicated to print. A higher Flatness value will reduce the number of straight lines that will be needed to define the curve, thus simplifying the curve. If you flatten the curve too much, however, you will alter the shape of the entire path. Acceptable Flatness values are from 0.2 to 100 pixels. Try entering a value from 1 to 3 in the Flatness field for a low-resolution printer or 8 to 10 for a high-resolution printer.

If you're interested in experimenting with different Flatness values, try printing out simple paths set to different Flatness values on your laser printer. As Flatness gets higher, you'll see circular shapes printed as polygons.

Saving a Clipping Path File

In order to use the clipping path in another program, you must save the Photoshop file in EPS format. (CMYK color images with clipping paths can also be saved in DCS file format.) After you've saved the file in EPS format, it can be imported into another program.

To save your clipping path, choose File > Save As or Save a Copy. When the dialog box appears, name your file, choose Photoshop EPS from the Format (Save As in Windows systems) pop-up menu and click on OK. The EPS Options dialog box appears. You can choose a Preview and Encoding option and other settings as appropriate. For more information about saving in EPS format, see Appendix A.

EPS Options

Preview: Macintosh (8 bits/pixel) [OK]

Encoding: ASCII [Cancel]

☐ Include Halftone Screen
☐ Include Transfer Function
☐ PostScript Color Management
☐ Include Vector Data
☐ Image Interpolation

 If your document contains alpha channels, choose File > Save a Copy so you can save in EPS format without the alpha channels. (For more information about alpha channels, see Chapter 15.)

When the Photoshop document is placed in Illustrator or a page layout program, only the portion of the image within the clipping path appears. If you chose the Windows Preview option, TIFF, in the EPS Options dialog box, you won't see the effects of the clipping path on your screen; however, the document should print properly. If you chose Macintosh as the Preview option, you will be able to view the clipping path transparency in most Mac drawing and page layout programs.

APPLYING EFFECTS
TO YOUR IMAGES

The Complete Reference

Photoshop

Chapter 15

Advanced Masking Techniques, Alpha Channels, and Spot Colors

Before computers came along, the traditional method of isolating parts of an image for color-correcting, image editing, and retouching was to create a mask. A *mask* is a type of stencil, often translucent, that is laid over an image to protect certain areas and allow others to be edited. Cutouts in the mask make selected portions of the image accessible for painting and editing, while the remainder of the image is protected by the stencil. Although the process of creating a mask can be time-consuming, masks do allow precise image editing.

Although you may not realize it, the selections you create with Photoshop's selection tools are masks. When a selection is on your screen, all of the painting and editing you do affects only the area within the blinking selection marquee. Unlike a traditional mask, however, a selection is temporary. When a new selection is created, the previous one disappears. As discussed in Chapter 14, one method of retaining a selection is to create a path with the Pen tool. Unfortunately, the Pen tool can be difficult to master, and it does not create soft-edged masks. To meet the need for maintaining multiple reusable selections that are easy to edit, the designers of Photoshop developed an electronic masking capability that surpasses both the Pen tool and the traditional mask. This electronic capability allows you to save a selection as a mask in an extra channel, called an *alpha channel*, attached to your image.

Once an alpha channel is created, you access it through the Channels palette. The mask in the alpha channel can be loaded on the screen to serve as a selection. Using alpha channels, you can reload and edit complicated selections and easily switch back and forth among selections while working on a document. As you'll see in this chapter, you can even paint on the screen to create an intricate mask that can be used as a selection itself or to create transparency effects.

If the relationship between a mask, an alpha channel, and a selection sounds complicated, don't worry. The examples in this chapter lead you gradually from creating simple masks and working with alpha channels to sophisticated commands that let you superimpose channels and files to create exquisite effects. As you work through the exercises, you'll see a new and powerful facet of Photoshop open up for you. You'll never need to worry about intricate selections disappearing into the digital stratosphere if you inadvertently click on the screen or close your file. Once you learn how to use masks, you'll be able to save, load, and edit any selection easily, no matter how complex.

> **Note** *Because ImageReady includes no Channels palette, use Photoshop rather than ImageReady for intricate masking work.*

Working with Quick Masks

Perhaps the easiest way to understand the relationship between masks and channels is to start by using Photoshop's Quick Mask mode, which creates a temporary mask and a temporary alpha channel. A Quick Mask is similar to a *rubylith*, the red-colored translucent film that is used as an overlay to protect parts of an image in print production.

Like a rubylith, a Quick Mask allows you to view your work through a translucent "overlay." The areas on screen covered by the overlay are protected from image editing; the cutout areas not covered by the overlay are not protected. (If desired, you can change the Quick Mask settings so that the reverse is true.) In Quick Mask mode, the shapes of the cutout areas (the unprotected areas) are easily edited with Photoshop's painting and editing tools. You can even edit the mask with the Edit > Transform commands. When you exit Quick Mask mode, the unprotected areas are transformed into selections (or one selection).

Take a look at the Quick Mask mode icon in Photoshop's Toolbox. The default setting is a shaded square with a clear circle cut out of it. The shaded area represents the translucent mask; the circle cutout is the unprotected area. The Standard mode icon (beside the Quick Mask icon) depicts what you will see when you exit Quick Mask mode: The overlay is gone, but a blinking selection marquee remains on screen.

Clicking on the Quick Mask mode icon puts you in Quick Mask mode. Double-clicking on the icon activates Quick Mask mode and opens the Quick Mask Options dialog box as well.

Creating a Quick Mask

Let's go through the procedure for creating a Quick Mask. Along the way, you'll take a look at the Quick Mask options and the Channels palette. For this example, we used a photograph with a horse and carriage that we wanted to isolate from the rest of the photograph. If you wish to follow along, you can load the Horse and Carriage file (hcarriage) from the Chapter 15 folder of this book's CD-ROM.

Begin by using the Elliptical Marquee tool to create a small elliptical selection around a portion of the horse, as shown in Figure 15-1. Don't deselect.

To select a large area, you may want to SHIFT-click with the Magic Wand before entering Quick Mask mode. Be sure to adjust the Magic Wand Tolerance setting as needed. (To review using the Magic Wand, see Chapter 4.) You can also move a selection with the Move tool.

Double-click on the Quick Mask mode icon to open the Quick Mask Options dialog box. Once the Quick Mask Options dialog box appears, as shown in Figure 15-2, you'll see that a red overlay also appears on screen. If the default settings are active, the red overlay area represents the protected area. The unprotected area (the area not covered by red) is the area you originally selected.

If you can't see the unprotected area on your screen because the Quick Mask Options dialog box opened in front of it, move the dialog box by clicking and dragging in its title bar.

In the Quick Mask Options dialog box, you can designate whether you want the color overlay to indicate the masked (protected) areas or the selected (unprotected) areas. By default, the Masked Areas radio button is selected. The default color setting

APPLYING EFFECTS TO YOUR IMAGES

Selected area

Figure 15-1. *The original horse and carriage image*

for the overlay is red with 50% opacity. With the Masked Areas radio button selected, the specified color and opacity are applied to all areas in the image except those that were selected before you entered Quick Mask mode. When the Selected Areas radio button is selected, the translucent colored overlay appears within your selection, rather than around it. (If this is the case now, click on the Masked Areas radio button.)

You can change the overlay color by clicking on the swatch in the Color section of the Quick Mask Options dialog box. As you might expect by now, this opens Photoshop's Color Picker. If you change the percentage in the Opacity field beside the color swatch, the translucency of the overlay is adjusted accordingly. For now, leave the default settings in the Quick Mask Options dialog box (Color Indicates Masked Areas and the overlay color at 50% opacity) by clicking on OK to continue.

The Quick Mask Mode icon in the Toolbox indicates whether the red overlay covers the selected or unselected areas. If you choose Masked Areas in the Quick Mask Options dialog box, the icon is a gray rectangle with a white circle. If you choose Selected Areas, the icon is a white rectangle with a gray circle. You can switch between the Masked Areas and the Selected Areas options without opening the Quick Mask Options dialog box by pressing OPTION (ALT) and clicking on the Quick Mask icon. The Quick Mask icon will change to reflect the option you have chosen. Switching from one option to another is helpful in determining how your mask is coming along.

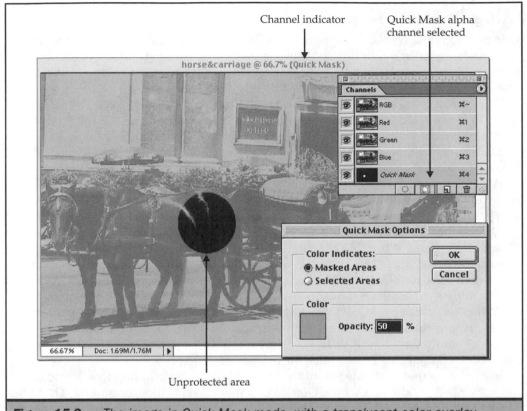

Figure 15-2. *The image in Quick Mask mode, with a translucent color overlay*

You are now in the Quick Mask channel overlay. Before continuing, take a moment to look around and see how your surroundings have changed. First, examine the document's title bar. You should see Quick Mask rather than RGB.

The Channels palette should now be open (if it isn't, open it by choosing Window > Show Channels). In the Channels palette, notice that a new channel called Quick Mask has been added (this is an alpha channel). Next to the Quick Mask channel, the eye icon (👁) means that the channel is visible, and the highlighted area surrounding the words *Quick Mask* indicates the channel is selected and can be edited. The selected channel is often called the *target channel*. Notice that there are eye icons next to each of the RGB channels also, but that none of the RGB channels is a selected area. Thus, even though you can see your image on screen, any editing changes you make now will not affect it; only the mask will be edited.

Painting in Masks

One of the great advantages of using masks is that you can resize and fine-tune them with painting tools. By altering the brush size of the Paintbrush, Airbrush, and Pencil tools and carefully painting in Quick Mask mode, you can create extremely intricate masks (which can later be transformed into selections).

When you paint in a mask, you change the unprotected and protected areas (which changes to the selection marquee on your screen after you exit Quick Mask mode). If the Color palette isn't on your screen, open it. Notice that you can paint only with black, white, or shades of gray. When you paint to edit the mask, these are the only colors you can use. Your Color palette is now restricted to 256 shades of gray.

With the default setting of Color Indicates Masked Areas, when you paint with white in Quick Mask mode, you add to the unprotected area (the selected area). When you paint with black, you subtract from the unprotected area (and add to the protected area). Painting with gray shades creates a type of "partial" selection when you exit Quick Mask mode. When this selection is filled with an opaque color, the result is a translucent color. Table 15-1 summarizes the effects of painting with white, black, or gray when the Color Indicates Masked Areas radio button is selected in the Quick Mask Options dialog box.

When you change the Quick Mask setting to Color Indicates Selected Areas, painting affects the unprotected area rather than the protected area. Table 15-2 summarizes the effects of painting with white, black, or gray when the Color Indicates Selected Areas radio button is selected in the Quick Mask Options dialog box.

Now take a few moments to edit the Quick Mask with a painting tool. If you are not in Quick Mask mode, click on the Quick Mask mode icon before continuing. The Quick Mask Options dialog box should be set to Color Indicates Masked Areas (the default).

Painting Color	Effect in Quick Mask Mode	Effect in Standard Mode
White	Subtracts from colored overlay (protected area); adds to unprotected area	Adds to selection marquee
Black	Adds to colored overlay (protected area); subtracts from unprotected area	Subtracts from selection marquee
Gray	Creates transparency effects	Creates a partially transparent selection

Table 15-1.   *Effects of Painting with Color Indicates Masked Areas in Quick Mask Mode*

Painting Color	Effect in Quick Mask Mode	Effect in Standard Mode
White	Subtracts from colored overlay (unprotected area); subtracts from unprotected area	Subtracts from selection marquee
Black	Adds to colored overlay (unprotected area); adds to unprotected area	Adds to selection marquee
Gray	Adds a partial overlay	Creates a partial selection

Table 15-1.   *Effects of Painting with Color Indicates Masked Areas in Quick Mask Mode* (continued)

To see how painting with white edits the mask and changes the selection, start by setting the foreground color to white. Select any painting tool and pick a medium, soft-edged brush in the Brush pop-up menu. (A soft-edged brush will produce a selection with feathered edges; a hard-edged brush will create a sharper selection.) Make sure Opacity is set to 100% in the tool's Options bar.

Use the painting tool to paint over image (the horse and carriage in our example). As you paint with white, the translucent overlay melts away. As you remove the overlay, you increase the size of the selection that will appear when you exit Quick Mask mode. If you paint too much, you can simply paint with black to paint back in the overlay.

Tip   *You might want to zoom in and use a smaller brush so that you can carefully select the rim and nothing else. If you make a mistake, just paint with black to add to the overlay.*

Before leaving Quick Mask mode, take a moment to view the Quick Mask channel without the composite image displayed. This will give you an idea of exactly what happened in the channel when you painted with white. To turn off the RGB composite display, click on the eye icon to the left of the RGB channel in the Channels palette. The RGB composite image disappears, and you will see the black mask and the white unprotected area. When you painted with white, you subtracted black from the mask. Only when the RGB composite image and mask appear on the screen together is the mask displayed in a translucent color. Restore the RGB image by clicking on the eye icon next to the RGB channel in the Channels palette.

Also take a look at a little-known feature available in Photoshop. Suppose that you need to move the masked area on screen. There's no way you can do this with a painting tool. However, when you are in Quick Mask mode, Photoshop's Edit > Free

APPLYING EFFECTS TO YOUR IMAGES

Transform and Edit > Transform commands are available. Using the Transform commands, you can move, scale, rotate, flip, distort, and add perspective to the Quick Mask. Try resizing your Quick Mask by choosing Edit > Free Transform. Then click and drag on one of the bounding box handles to resize the mask. Press RETURN or ENTER (*ENTER*) to finish the transformation, or press ESC to cancel.

Exiting Quick Mask Mode

To exit Quick Mask mode, click on the Standard mode icon in the Toolbox (or press Q on the keyboard to toggle back and forth between Quick Mask mode and Standard mode). The selection marquee now appears around the area you painted. (If you paint with white in several different areas in the Quick Mask channel, several selection marquees appear on your screen when you exit Quick Mask mode.) In other words, the work you did with the painting tool in Quick Mask mode is now transformed into a selection. Notice that Quick Mask no longer appears in the window's title bar. In addition, if you examine the Channels palette, you'll see that the Quick Mask channel is no longer listed. Thus, your selection remains, but the alpha channel containing the mask has disappeared.

Once you exit Quick Mask mode, you can use the Magic Wand or any other selection tool to add to your selection. To add to your selection, press and hold down the SHIFT key before you use the selection tool to add to the area you want. If you select too much, either undo your selection tool action or press and hold down OPTION (*ALT*) as you trace around the area you want to deselect with the selection tool.

 If you inadvertently deselect, you can reselect the last selection by choosing Select > Reselect. Also, after you create a selection, you can choose Select > Transform Selection and then move it, rotate it, or scale it.

As you fine-tune your selection, move in and out of Quick Mask mode. This will give you a better idea of how your mask is coming along. To fine-tune the horse and carriage selection, for example, you'll probably want to return to Quick Mask mode and use the Paintbrush tool to select and clean up the edges. Be sure to experiment with different brush sizes at different zoom levels. The final selection of the horse and carriage is shown in Figure 15-3.

Now that you have your selection, you can edit it, color-correct the area, or copy and paste the selection to another document. Try using the Brightness/Contrast controls in the Image > Adjust submenu to increase the contrast. As you adjust brightness and contrast, only the selected area changes.

In the example in this chapter, you will use the horse and carriage image later, to create a collage in a new file. If you close the file, you'll lose the selection. The solution is to save the selection. Keep your selection on your screen and proceed to the next section to learn how to do this.

Figure 15-3.   *The selection reflects the area that was painted with white in the Quick Mask channel*

Saving, Loading, and Making New Selections

Any Photoshop selection can be saved, whether or not it was created in Quick Mask mode. When a selection is saved, Photoshop creates a mask from the selection and places it in an alpha channel. After you've saved a selection, you can reload it at a later time.

Saving a Selection

To save a selection that you've created, choose Select > Save Selection. Photoshop opens the Save Selection dialog box.

The Document pop-up menu in the Destination section of the dialog box shows the name of your current document. You can pick any open document or a new document to store your selection.

The Channel pop-up menu is set to New, which will save a selection as a mask in a new alpha channel. By choosing a channel in the Destination Channel pop-up menu, you can alter the mask stored in an existing alpha channel. If you are in a layer (other than the Background), the Channel pop-up menu will also allow you to create a layer mask in a new channel from your selection. (Layer masks are discussed at the end of this chapter and in Chapter 17.) When you select an existing channel in the Channel pop-up menu, the dimmed options in the Operation section of the dialog box become active:

- The New Channel option creates a new mask, completely replacing the mask in the channel chosen in the Channel pop-up menu.

- The Add to Channel option uses the selection on your screen to add to the mask in the channel.

- The Subtract from Channel option works if the selection on your screen overlaps the mask saved in the channel. When this option is selected, the overlapping area is subtracted from the mask in the channel. If the areas do not overlap, the mask in the channel is not affected.

- The Intersect with Channel option also applies if the selection overlaps the mask saved in the channel. When this option is selected, the overlapping area replaces the mask in the channel. If no areas overlap, the mask in the channel disappears.

To see how saving a selection works, you'll continue to work with the selection you created in the previous section (in the Horse and Carriage file, hcarriage on the CD-ROM). You should currently have a selection on your screen.

1. Choose Select > Save Selection. In the Save Selection dialog box, click on OK to create a new channel in your current document.

 Tip *To save a selection to an alpha channel automatically, click on the Save Selection icon ( ) at the bottom of the Channels palette.*

2. Notice that the Channels palette now contains a new channel, named Alpha 1. Click on Alpha 1 to see the alpha channel.

3. Click on the eye icon column next to RGB in the Channels palette. When you select both the mask and RGB eye icon columns, all eye icons become visible. You'll see overlays similar to the Quick Mask overlay.

4. Click on the eye icon next to the RGB channel to turn it off. Without the underlying image, the mask now appears in black and white.

5. Return to your composite image by clicking on RGB. The RGB composite image is displayed, but so is the overlay. To hide the overlay from view, click on the eye icon next to Alpha 1.

You can toggle back and forth between the alpha channel and the RGB composite channel by pressing COMMAND-4 (CTRL-4) *to access alpha channel 4 and* COMMAND-~ (CTRL-~) *to access the RGB composite channel.*

Note that you'll need to save your file in Photoshop format if you are going to save the alpha channel and work with layers.

After you've saved your selection to an alpha channel, you can experiment with the other options in the Save Selection dialog box if you wish. To view the effects of the options in the Save Selection dialog box, the alpha channel should be selected and the colored overlay mask with the cutout area should be displayed on your screen. Create a new selection (using any selection tool), so it slightly overlays the cutout area of the colored overlay on screen. Use any selection tool to create the selection. Then choose Select > Save Selection and make sure that the Document pop-up menu is set to the name of your document and not to New. Choose Alpha 1 in the Channel pop-up menu and then try out each option by clicking on the radio buttons and clicking on OK. After you see the effects on screen, choose Edit > Undo, and then try another option.

After you're finished experimenting with the Save Selection dialog box, change the settings in the Channels palette so you'll be able to see selection marquees on screen. First, turn off Alpha 1 in the Channels palette by clicking on RGB. When the highlighted area disappears from Alpha 1 in the Channels palette, it means that editing work will not affect this channel. Turn off the eye icon next to Alpha 1 in the Channels palette. This removes the overlay from the screen. Now you can take a look at the options in the Load Selection dialog box.

Loading Selections

As you've seen from the previous example, the Save Selection dialog box allows you to save selections. The Load Selection dialog box allows you to load a selection stored in an alpha channel.

To load a selection from an image's channel or alpha channel automatically, COMMAND-*click* (CTRL-*click*) *on the name or number of the channel in the Channels palette.*

To load the selection that you just created, make sure that the selection, stored in Alpha 1, is deselected in the Channels palette (and that the RGB image is selected). Then choose Select > Load Selection. When the Load Selection dialog box appears, notice the Source section settings: the Document pop-up menu shows the name of your current document, and Alpha 1 automatically appears in the Channel pop-up menu. Click on OK to load the selection.

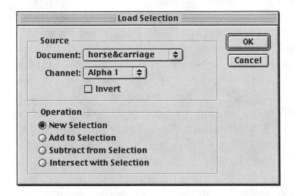

You can load a selection from any open document and choose a channel from any open document. If you are working in a layer, the Channel pop-up menu also provides a Transparency option. This allows you to load the nontransparent areas of the layer as a selection.

 Alpha channels represent a standard method of conveying transparency from one application to another. Many 3-D modeling programs and digital video programs use alpha channels to indicate masked areas. If you create an alpha channel in a 3-D program and load the image with its alpha channel into Photoshop, you will see the mask in the Channels palette. You can then choose Select > Load Selection to load the mask into Photoshop.

The radio buttons in the Operation section allow you to choose how you want the selection stored in the alpha channel to affect the selection on screen:

■ The New Selection option creates a new selection, replacing any previous selection on the screen.

■ The Add to Selection option adds to the selection on screen or creates an additional selection on the screen. A shortcut for adding an alpha channel to a selection in the composite channel (such as RGB or CMYK) is to press COMMAND-SHIFT (*CTRL-SHIFT*) and then click on the channel.

■ The Subtract from Selection option works if the selection in the channel overlaps with the selected area on the screen. When you choose this option, the selection area from the channel is subtracted from the selection on the screen. If the selections do not overlap, the selection on the screen is unchanged. A shortcut for subtracting is to select the channel, press COMMAND-OPTION (*CTRL-ALT*), and then click on the channel.

■ The Intersect with Selection option creates a selection from the overlapping area in the selections if the selection in the channel overlaps the selection on the screen. If no area overlaps, nothing is selected on the screen. A shortcut for intersection is to press COMMAND-OPTION-SHIFT (*CTRL-ALT-SHIFT*) and then click on the channel.

Making Selections from Channels

Here are two quick ways to make a selection from a channel:

■ Drag the channel over the Make Selection icon at the bottom of the Channels palette.

■ Press COMMAND-OPTION (*CTRL-ALT*) and the channel number. For instance, to make a selection from the color information in an RGB file, press COMMAND-OPTION-1, 2, or 3 (*CTRL-ALT-1, 2, or 3*).

You can create a selection from the nontransparent areas of a layer by pressing COMMAND (CTRL) and clicking on the layer in the Layers palette. Then save it into an alpha channel by clicking on the Save Selection icon in the Channels palette.

Creating Selections Based on Color

Another helpful command that allows you to create masks very quickly is Photoshop's Color Range command. Color Range creates a selection based on color. In some respects, the Color Range command is like a combination of the Magic Wand tool and the Select > Similar command in that Color Range selects a color range anywhere in an image. When using Color Range, you can choose to have Photoshop select colors according to preset colors, or you can have it create a selection according to the colors sampled in your image.

To try out the Color Range command, load any image on screen. Then choose Select > Color Range. The rectangular preview area in the middle of the Color Range dialog box displays either the mask or your on-screen image. Clicking on the Image radio button shows your image in the Preview box, as shown in Figure 15-4.

Although you will probably be most interested in monitoring the mask in the Selection preview, choosing the Image radio button is helpful when you zoom into specific image areas. The Image radio button will always show you the entire image or selection, even if you have zoomed into a small area on screen.

Now click on the Selection radio button to see the mask. Notice that the mask is mostly black because the Color Range command has not begun its search for colors. Once you specify what color range you want selected, the selection will be represented by light areas in the mask.

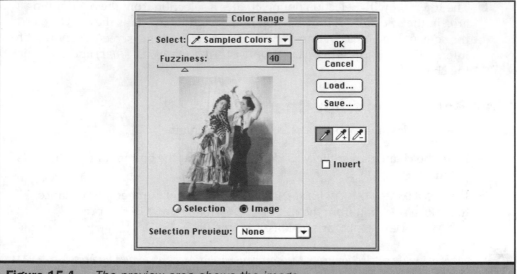

Figure 15-4.   *The preview area shows the image*

> **Tip**   *You can quickly toggle back and forth from the image preview to the mask preview by pressing and holding down CTRL or COMMAND (CTRL).*

To specify which colors you want to select, use the Select pop-up menu, which allows you to pick from preset colors or colors that you sample from your image. The Select pop-up menu also allows you to select according to shadow, midtones, and highlights.

Try a quick test to see how the dialog box can select specific colors for your image. From the Select pop-up menu, choose Reds. Notice that an area of the mask gets lighter. This corresponds to the red areas on screen. It is the area that will be selected when you return to your image. Now try choosing Yellows from the Select menu.

If you wish to soften selection edges, drag the Fuzziness slider to the right. If you drag the slider very far to the right, the selection will be extended. Drag it to the left to reduce the selection.

Next, take a look at how the Selection Preview pop-up menu can help you preview the selection. As you read through a brief explanation of the options in the Selection Preview pop-up menu, try out each one by clicking the menu choice.

■ The Grayscale option previews your image in grayscale. The preview on screen appears as it would if it were in an alpha channel. This mode can be helpful when the Select menu is set to Highlights, Midtones, or Shadows.

- The Black Matte option displays the mask of the selected areas in color. All other areas are black. This mode is especially helpful for seeing a selection that will be created in dark image areas.

- The White Matte option displays the selected areas in color. All other areas are white. This mode is especially helpful when your selection will be created in light image areas.

- The Quick Mask option displays the image using the current settings in the Quick Mask Options dialog box.

Before continuing, set the Selection Preview pop-up menu to None.

To use a color sampled from the image, choose Sampled Colors in the Select pop-up menu. Then you can specify this color range by clicking on the eyedropper icon in the dialog box and then clicking in your image. You can then extend the range by clicking on the eyedropper+ icon or subtract from the range by clicking on the eyedropper– icon.

For example, if you want to select only the flesh tones in the image, select Sampled Colors from the Select pop-up menu. Then move the eyedropper over the flesh tones in the image on the screen, and select another color you wish to use. Click the mouse. Notice that the mask turns lighter in areas corresponding to the color you chose. Now, extend the selection by clicking on the eyedropper+ icon, moving it into your image on screen, and selecting a darker flesh tone or other dark area. After you click, the white area of the mask is extended to include this color range. To see the actual selection in your image, click on OK.

Note   *When the eyedropper is over your image, you can toggle to the eyedropper+ by pressing* SHIFT *or to the eyedropper– by pressing* OPTION (ALT). *Keep in mind also that if you* SHIFT-*click on a document with the Eyedropper tool, you can set color sampler points.*

When the image returns on your screen, you'll see the blinking marquee surrounding the area specified in the mask. At this point, you can either begin to edit the selection in Quick Mask mode or save it to an alpha channel.

Creating a Collage with Masks

The best way to become proficient at using masks and alpha channels is to try your hand at creating a project from a variety of images. In this section, you will create the collage shown in Figure 15-5. For this project, you'll need to load five different image files from this book's CD-ROM: Flowers, Greenery, Sign, Walkway, and Hcarriage. The Horse and Carriage image was shown earlier in the chapter (Figure 15-1). The other images are shown in Figure 15-6.

Figure 15-5. *A collage created with masks from five different images*

1. Load the Flowers file. To create the mask for the flowers, use the Magic Wand to select as many flowers as you can. Remember that to add to your selection, press and hold the SHIFT key as you click with the Magic Wand.

2. With some of the flowers selected, click on the Quick Mask icon in the Toolbox to enter Quick Mask mode. Fine-tune and finish the mask using the Paintbrush and Pencil tools.

3. After you have masked several flowers, load the selection by exiting Quick Mask mode.

4. Load the Greenery file. Copy and paste the flowers into it.

5. In the greenery image, you may wish to scale down the flowers. Use the Edit > Transform > Scale command to do so, and then move the flowers into position using the Move tool. In the Layers palette, lower the opacity of the flower layer so that the flowers don't overpower the greenery in the image.

Figure 15-6.   *The flowers on an arch image, greenery photograph, sign image, and wood walkway image*

6. Load the Sign file. To create the mask for the sign, select it with the Polygonal Lasso tool.

7. After selecting the sign with the Polygonal Lasso tool, click on the Quick Mask icon to enter Quick Mask mode. In Quick Mask mode, use the Paintbrush, Airbrush, or Pencil to clean up the edges of the mask. After perfecting the mask, load the selection, by exiting Quick Mask mode.

8. With the selection on your screen, use the Move tool to drag the sign into the Greenery image. Again, you'll probably need to scale the sign and move it into

position. Then, use the Edit > Transform > Perspective command to apply perspective to the sign to make the scene look realistic.

9. Use the Lasso tool with a low Feather setting (the Feather option is in the Lasso tool Options bar) to create a rough selection of the Walkway image.

10. Once you've created the selection, click on the Quick Mask icon to enter Quick Mask mode. In Quick Mask mode, use the painting tools and selection tools to fine-tune the mask. Exit Quick Mask mode to view the selection.

11. With the selection on your screen, use the Move tool to drag and drop it into the Greenery image. Next, scale and move the walkway and fence image into the appropriate position.

12. Since the fence will not fill the width of the collage in Figure 15-5, you'll need to use the Clone Stamp tool to clone parts of the fence, grass, and sand so that it fills the width of the collage.

13. Apply the Filter > Distort > Twirl filter to the walkway so that it bends toward the entrance way. In the Twirl dialog box, set Angle to 49 degrees. After applying the Twirl filter, you may need to use the Clone Stamp tool again to clone empty areas.

14. To get a better view and more easily edit the mask, double-click on the Quick Mask icon to open the Quick Mask Options dialog box. Switch between Masked Areas and Selected Areas. This changes the overlay so that it covers the area that is not selected, rather than the selected area. Also, you can exit and enter Quick Mask mode to see how the selection/mask is coming along.

15. Since this is a fairly involved mask, you'll probably need to save your selection with your file so that you can continue working on it at another time. To save the selection, choose Select > Save Selection. Then save the file in Photoshop format. When you need to load the selection, choose Select > Load Selection.

16. To finish the collage, you need to load the horse and carriage selection. Choose Select > Load Selection, and then use the Move tool to drag and drop it in the collage image.

17. Use the Edit > Transform > Scale command to scale down the horse and carriage. Then move it into position.

18. To make the greenery more of a golden color, select the fabric from the carriage with the Rectangular Marquee tool and define it as a pattern by choosing Edit > Define Pattern (make sure that the horse and carriage layer is selected in the Layers palette). Before you apply the pattern, make sure the greenery layer is selected. Then choose Edit > Fill. In the Fill dialog box, set the Use option to Pattern, Opacity to 90%, and Mode to Hue. (To learn more about the different modes, turn to Chapter 5.)

When you're finished, your collage should look similar to the one shown in Figure 15-5.

Working with Channels

The Channel palette's pop-up menu offers commands for working with your channels. You can duplicate channels, create new channels, delete channels, and split and merge channels.

Pressing CTRL *and clicking a channel (Windows users should right-click) displays a menu allowing you to delete the channel or duplicate it.*

Duplicating an Alpha Channel

The Duplicate Channel command on the Channels palette pop-up menu allows you to create an exact duplicate of a channel. The Duplicate Channel command can place a duplicate of a channel in an existing file or in a new file.

You can use the Duplicate Channel command to duplicate channels into new files so they can be deleted from their original file, helping to keep file size to a minimum. If you need to load the channel back into the original file, simply use the Duplicate Channel command to copy it back in. The channel can also be loaded as a blinking selection marquee with the Select > Load Selection command.

Some Photoshop users also use the Duplicate Channel command to help create a mask in an alpha channel. To use this technique, first convert your image to Lab Color mode and duplicate the L channel, or duplicate one of the RGB channels (duplicate the one that exhibits the most contrast). After you duplicate the channel, use the mask-editing techniques described in this chapter to fine-tune the mask.

To duplicate an existing channel, click on the channel that you want to duplicate in the Channels palette and then choose Duplicate Channel from the Channels palette pop-up menu. In the Duplicate Channel dialog box, rename the channel, if desired, in the As field. Use the Document pop-up menu to choose the destination file for the channel. If you wish to place the existing channel into a new channel in a new document, choose New from the Document pop-up menu. Name the new file in the Name field, if desired. Selecting the Invert option is similar to choosing Image > Adjust > Invert. It changes light pixels to dark pixels and dark pixels to light, producing a negative of your image.

APPLYING EFFECTS
TO YOUR IMAGES

```
┌─────────────────────────────────────────────────┐
│                 Duplicate Channel                 │
├─────────────────────────────────────────────────┤
│  Duplicate: Alpha 1                  ┌────────┐  │
│         As: │Dupe            │        │   OK   │  │
│                                      └────────┘  │
│    ┌ Destination ──────────────┐    ┌────────┐  │
│    Document: │ New      ▼│          │ Cancel │  │
│                                      └────────┘  │
│        Name: │Untitled-1    │                    │
│             □ Invert                             │
└─────────────────────────────────────────────────┘
```

You can also use the Select > Load Selection command to load a selection from any open file.

You can also use these shortcuts to duplicate channels:

■ To duplicate a channel from one file into another file quickly, click and drag the name or number of the channel from the Channels palette into the other document.

■ You can create a duplicate of a channel in the same file by clicking and dragging the name or number of the alpha channel over the New Channel icon (▣) at the bottom of the Channels palette.

Deleting a Channel

Once you've duplicated a channel into another file or if you're finished working with a channel, you may wish to delete the channel from the document it is in. If you still have a selection stored in an alpha channel from a previous exercise, delete it to keep your file size as small as possible. If you have any other channels that you don't need, you can delete them now.

To delete a channel, select it and choose Delete Channel from the Channels palette's pop-up menu.

As a shortcut, you can click on the channel that you want to delete and then click on the trash icon (🗑) at the bottom of the Channels palette. You can also drag the channel to the trash icon, as follows: Position the mouse pointer over the channel you wish to delete in the Channels palette. The pointer will change to a pointing hand icon. Click and hold down the mouse button and drag the channel toward the trash icon. As you drag, the pointer will change into a grabbing hand icon. Drag the tiny hand icon over the trash icon. When the trash icon changes colors, release the mouse, and the channel will be deleted.

Creating a New Alpha Channel

Photoshop allows you to create a new alpha channel without first creating a selection on your screen. You can then create a mask from scratch using a painting, editing, or selection tool in the new channel. To use the mask as a selection, you can execute the Select > Load Selection command.

In the following sections, you'll create a new channel, and then you'll create a mask to use as a selection.

Creating the Channel

You can create a new channel by choosing the New Channel command from the Channels palette's pop-up menu. As a shortcut, press OPTION (ALT) and click on the New Channel icon in the Channels palette. Both of these methods open the New Channel dialog box. If you just click on the New Channel icon, a new channel is created without the New Channel dialog box appearing.

Follow these steps to create the channel for the mask:

1. Load the Flower file from this book's CD-ROM.

2. To create a new alpha channel, open the Channels palette menu and choose New Channel. A new alpha channel appears in the Channels palette, and the New Channel dialog box opens.

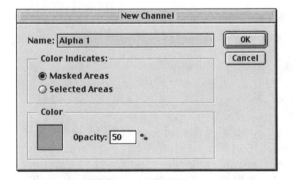

3. Enter a name in the Name field and choose the Selected Areas radio button. This way, when you paint with black, you will be creating a selection; when you paint with white, you will be subtracting from the selection. (Note that this is the opposite of the settings you used when you created the Quick Mask earlier in this chapter.) Leave the color swatch set to red and Opacity set to 50%. Click on OK.

At any time, you can change the options set for an alpha channel by double-clicking on the channel in the Channels palette or by clicking on the channel in the palette and choosing Channel Options from the Channels palette's pop-up menu.

Your screen will now be white because you are in a new, empty channel, and you are viewing only the channel, not the image. Notice that the eye icon appears beside the new channel in the Channels palette, that the channel is selected, and that you can edit it. At this point, none of the other channels can be viewed or edited.

Creating the Mask

Now you are almost ready to create a mask. But you'll want to see the mask in relation to the image on screen.

1. To view the RGB image, click in the eye icon column next to the RGB composite channel. After you click, all of the channels will be visible, but only the new alpha channel will be editable (it's the only one with highlight color surrounding its name in the Channels palette).

2. Use the Paintbrush to paint with black over the red and white flowers. You will be painting with the same type of translucent overlay you worked with in Quick Mask mode. Keep in mind that this setting is opposite the one you used when you created the Quick Mask earlier in this chapter. If you make a mistake, you can erase the overlay by simply clicking and dragging with the Eraser. (This works because the Eraser paints with the background color, white; you could also use the Paintbrush to paint with white.)

Note *See Table 15-2 for a description of the effects of painting in an alpha channel when the Color Indicates Selected Areas radio button is selected in the New Channel (or Quick Mask Options) dialog box.*

3. After you've painted with the colored overlay, take a look at what appears in the new channel. To view the channel as a separate image, turn off the eye icons in the other channels by clicking on the eye icon next to the RGB composite channel. This hides the display of the RGB channels and leaves the alpha channel on your screen. Notice that you painted in black.

4. To load the alpha channel's black area as a selection, first select the RGB composite by clicking on RGB in the Channels palette or pressing COMMAND-~. (CTRL-~), Notice that the alpha channel is no longer the target channel. Then choose Select > Load Selection. In the Load Selection dialog box, choose Invert. This will create a selection out of the background area.

Why Are Masks Stored in Grayscale?

You may wonder why Photoshop (as well as other applications such as CorelPainter) uses grayscale alpha channels to store masks. A gray mask can indicate a change in opacity, which cannot be seen in a selection marquee.

When you create a selection with one of Photoshop's selection tools, it functions as a mask with 100 percent opacity. Thus, if you copy and paste the selection, the selection's pixels completely replace the image area you paste over. However, if you use a mask created by painting with gray in an alpha channel, the gray represents an opacity setting less than 100%. If you paint with gray in a mask and load the mask as a selection (Select > Load Selection), the selection represents a mask with less than 100 percent opacity. If you use the selection created from the gray mask to copy and paste, the image you copy will blend with the image you paste it over—as if you pasted an image with a lower opacity over another.

5. Now that you have a selection, try applying a filter to it. For instance, apply one of Photoshop's Blur filters to blur the background and make the flowers you masked stand out.

Splitting and Merging Channels

A powerful utility offered in the Channels palette allows you to split the channels in a color image into separate files. After you split the channels, you can edit an image's separate channels and then merge them back together.

To split the channels, choose Split Channels from the Channels palette's pop-up menu. The split documents will appear on the screen as grayscale images, and the original document is closed.

Note   *You cannot access the Split Channels option if your image includes layers. If you wish to split the channels of an image that has layers, first flatten it by choosing Layer > Flatten Image. (You might wish to save a copy of the file with its layers before you flatten the image.)*

You can also combine separate channels into a composite image by using the Merge Channels command on the Channel palette's pop-up menu. However, the Photoshop documents that you want to merge must meet the following conditions:

- All of the channels to be merged must be open on your screen.
- All of the images must be grayscale images.
- The channels' width and height in pixels must be equal.

In the Merge Channels dialog box, you can specify the number of channels you want to merge and to what mode (RGB Color, CMYK Color, and so forth). Then click on OK.

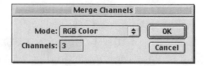

Next, in the Merge RGB Channels dialog box, specify the channels into which you want each open document on the screen loaded. After you click on OK, a new image consisting of the formerly split documents appears in an untitled window.

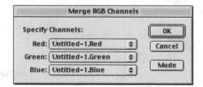

Later in this chapter, in the "Creating a Colored Mezzotint Effect" section, you'll see how splitting and merging channels can be used to create a colored mezzotint effect.

 If you have a DCS file that you can't load, or one that won't print in your desktop publishing program, you may be able to solve the problem by merging the separate files into one CMYK file. After you merge the channels, save the file in one of Photoshop's DCS formats.

Saving a File with Alpha Channels

After you've created an alpha channel, you may wish to save it with your file so the mask can be loaded as a selection at a later time. If you save your file in Photoshop's native format, TIFF, PICT, or TARGA format, all the alpha channels are automatically saved with the file.

If you wish to save a copy of an image in another file format without its alpha channels, choose File > Save As. Click on the As a Copy checkbox in the Save section. Choose a file format from the Format pop-up menu. If the format will not accept alpha channels, the Alpha Channels checkbox will automatically be grayed out.

Creating and Editing an Alpha Channel Mask

Once you've learned the various ways to create and work with alpha channels, you'll often find that each image that you need to mask requires a slightly different approach. For instance, you may be able to start creating a mask by simply clicking and dragging with one of Photoshop's selection tools, and then saving the selection. If your image is well-defined with very light and very dark areas, you may be able to duplicate one of the RGB channels or the L channel of a Lab Color image, and then use the duplicated channel as the basis for a mask that you edit.

We've found that one of the best ways to get started creating masks is to create a selection with Photoshop's Magnetic Lasso (as described in Chapter 4) or create a path with the Magnetic Pen (as described in Chapter 14), and then turn it into a selection. Once the selection is created, we save the selection (Select > Save Selection), which creates a mask in an alpha channel. After the selection is saved, we then edit the mask with the Paintbrush tool, viewing the image through the red overlay. We used this technique to mask the polar bear shown in Figure 15-7. After we masked the polar bear, we placed it in a new background, as shown in Figure 15-8.

Here are the steps we used to create the mask:

1. Load the Bear image from this book's CD-ROM (or another file that you wish to mask).

2. Activate the Magnetic Lasso tool. If the edges of the mask need to be soft, make sure to raise the Feather value field in the Magnetic Lasso tool's Options bar before you create the selection.

Figure 15-7.   *The original image of the polar bear*

Figure 15-8.   *The final image with the masked polar bear placed in a new background*

Remember   *The amount of feathering you use is related to the resolution of your image. If you are working with a 72 ppi image, a feather of 4 pixels creates a larger feather than a 4-pixel feather in a 300 ppi image. For more information about feathering, review Chapter 4.*

3. Outline the image that you want to mask with the Magnetic Lasso tool. Remember to click along the image edge if the Lasso moves off the image. Don't worry if your selection isn't perfect—you will be able to edit the mask later to fine-tune the selection. To close the Magnetic Lasso selection, click where your starting and ending points meet, as shown in Figure 15-9.

Magnetic Lasso tool

Figure 15-9. *Click where your starting and ending points meet to close the selection*

| Tip | *If you forget to set the Feather value before you select your image, you can always add a feather after you create the selection by choosing Select > Feather.* |

4. After you create the selection, save it by choosing Select > Save Selection. If, desired, enter a name for the channel in the Save Selection dialog box (we named our channel Bear). After you click on OK, Photoshop automatically creates an alpha channel with the mask in it. To see the alpha channel you created, open the Channels palette (by choosing Window > Show Channels).

5. To see a full-screen version of the mask, click on Alpha 1 (or Bear, or whatever name you gave the channel) in the Channels palette (see Figure 15-10).

6. To view the mask as a translucent overlay (as seen when you click on the Quick Mask icon), you must have Alpha 1 as the active channel and all the other channels viewable. To activate the Red, Green, and Blue channels, click on the eye icon column next to the RGB channel in the Channels palette. At this point,

you should still have the eye icon displayed for Alpha 1, and Alpha 1 should be the selected channel.

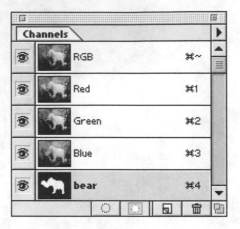

7. If you wish, you can change the color of the translucent overlay. To choose another color, double-click on Alpha 1 in the Channels palette. We changed the overlay color from red to green, because the bucket the bear is holding is red. Otherwise, as we worked, we might have become confused as to what was the mask and what was the bucket.

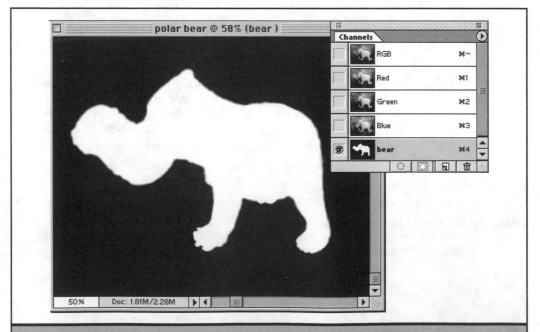

Figure 15-10. *A full-screen version of the mask in the channels palette*

8. To edit the mask, pick a soft-edged brush and paint with black to add to the mask (add to the selection). Paint with white to subtract from the mask (subtract from the selection). Paint with gray to create a translucent mask. (You can also create a translucent mask by setting the foreground color to black and lowering the Opacity setting.)

9. As you edit the mask, switch between the Color Indicates Masked Areas option and the Color Indicates Selected Areas option for the channel settings. By using this technique, you can easily see whether your masking efforts needed adjustments. If part of the background appears in the copied image, you can go back to the original file and continue editing the mask.

 The Color Indicates Masked Areas option displays the color overlay in protected areas. The Color Indicates Selected Areas option displays the color overlay in nonprotected areas.

10. After you've finish editing the mask, load the new selection by choosing Select > Load Selection.

Now you can copy and paste into a new file with a different background. (You can paste your image into any color other than the color in the image.)

Extracting an Image from Its Background

Photoshop's Extract command can save you time when you need to extract an image from its background. Like the Magic Eraser and Background tool, the Extract command erases the background from images in layers. The Extract command requires a little less elbow grease. because there's less clicking and dragging involved. You start by outlining the area that you wish to extract. The outline tells Photoshop where the image edge will be in the mask. You then click on the Extract command's Fill tool to tell Photoshop the area within the outline that you wish to extract. When you finish executing the command, your extracted image sits on a transparent layer.

Tip *If you remove the background from an image, you can use transparency options in Photoshop's Save for Web dialog box or ImageReady's Optimize palettes. (See Chapter 10 for more information.) Furthermore, if you load an image with a transparent background into Adobe Premiere or Adobe AfterEffects, both programs read the transparency as an alpha channel.*

Although the Extract command can serve as a quicker method of masking than using alpha channels, using it can be a bit infuriating—particularly because there is no Undo command available in the Extract dialog box. Nevertheless, for some images, the Extract command can definitely save you time when you need to separate an image area from its background.

Using the Extract Tools

To use the Extract command, choose Image > Extract. The Extract dialog box appears, as shown in Figure 15-11.

The tools in the Extract dialog box work as follows:

■ Use the Edge Highlighter tool to create an outline around the image area you want to protect/isolate (called the Foreground). The size of the highlighter is controlled by the Brush Size setting in the Tool Options section of the dialog box.

■ After you highlight the edge of the image, you can use the Fill tool to fill in the area you outlined with the Edge Highlighter tool. If the area you wish to extract is easily recognizable, make sure that the Force Foreground checkbox is deselected, and then click in the area that you want to extract with the Fill tool.

■ If the edge area is complex or the extract area is primarily one color, click and drag to cover the entire area that you wish to extract with the Edge Highlighter tool, and then select the Force Foreground checkbox. Next, click in the area that you wish to extract with the Extract command's Eyedropper tool.

■ Use the Eraser tool to fine-tune the highlighting area on screen. The size of the Eraser is controlled by the Brush Size slider.

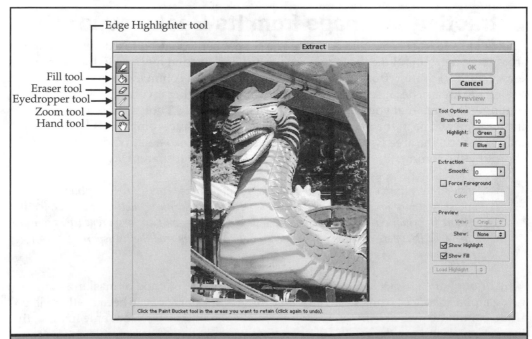

Figure 15-11. *The Extract dialog box, with the selected image*

- Use the Zoom tool to zoom into areas that require intricate work.
- To avoid zooming in and out again and again, use the Hand tool to move around in your image.

 If your image has an alpha channel, you can load it as the basis for the edge highlight by choosing the alpha channel in the Load Highlight pop-up menu at the lower-right side of the dialog box.

Putting an Image on a New Background

We used the Extract command to isolate the dragon from the background area in Figure 15-12. Then we dragged the dragon into the rocky beach scene shown at the left in Figure 15-13, copied some rocks from the photograph at the right, and pasted them below the dragon so that it looked as if the dragon were on top of the rocks. The final collage is shown in Figure 15-14.

Figure 15-12.   *Original image of dragon*

Figure 15-13. *Rocky beach image and the rock image*

Here are the steps for creating the dragon collage:

1. Load the Dragon file from this book's CD-ROM.

2. Choose Image > Extract. Then click on the Edge Highlighter tool and begin clicking and dragging to outline your image.

Figure 15-14.   *The final dragon collage*

3. If the brush size is too large, click on the Brush Size pop-up menu to access the slider. Drag to the left to lower brush size. (You can also raise and lower the brush size by pressing the [or] key.)

4. If you make a mistake, you can use the Eraser tool to erase the unwanted highlight marks. As mentioned earlier, you can control the size of the Eraser by activating the Brush Size slider.

5. Use the Zoom tool and Hand tool to zoom in and move around in your image. If desired, you can change the highlight color by selecting a color from the Highlight pop-up menu in the Tool Options section of the dialog box.

6. After you have used the Edge Highlighter to outline the dragon, make sure that the Force Foreground checkbox in the Extraction section of the dialog box is deselected, select the Fill tool, and click in the image that you want to extract.

7. Click on the Preview button to preview the extract. Compare the extracted image with the original by clicking on the View pop-up menu and choosing Original. You can also click on the Show menu in the Preview section to see the background of the image as colored, black and white, gray, or transparent, or as a mask.

8. If you wish to edit the extract, you can use the Edge Highlighter and Eraser tools. You can also use the Fill tool again. But be aware that clicking on a fill area removes the previous fill.

9. If stray bits of the image appear at various points in the extract, click and drag on the Smooth slider in the Extraction section of the dialog box. Dragging to the right cleans more "artifacts."

10. When you are satisfied with the outlined extract area, extract the image by clicking on OK.

11. After you've masked the dragon you are ready to place it in the beach scene. Open the beach image (the left-hand image in Figure 15-13) and place it next to the dragon image.

12. Select the Move tool. Then click on the dragon and drag it to the beach scene. Move it into position and scale it down as needed. At this point, you may want to use the File > Save As command to save your file (we named our file Dragon Collage).

13. Open the rocks file (the right-hand image in Figure 15-13). Double-click on the Lasso tool. In the Lasso tool's Options bar, set Feather to 10. Then click and drag over a few large rocks in the center of the image. Copy and paste them into the Dragon Collage file. You may need to use the Eraser tool to omit any unnecessary pieces. You may also need to go back to the rock photograph to get more rocks for the dragon.

After you've put the images together, you may wish to add type to the collage to make it into a book cover or brochure. We added some vertical and horizontal type. (See Chapter 3 for details on adding type.) We also applied several Layer > Layer Style commands to the type. (Layer styles are discussed in Chapter 19.)

Creating Effects with Alpha Channels

The following sections provide exercises that will broaden your understanding of alpha channels and put you on the road to creating sophisticated effects with them.

Using Alpha Channels to Create Shadowed Text

Now that you possess the power to save and load selections, creating special effects becomes easier. For instance, by using the alpha channel features covered in this chapter, you can easily create shadowed type, like the text shown below.

Note   *You can often create shadow effects quickly using channels. See Chapter 17 to learn how to create drop shadows using layer styles.*

In this exercise, you'll create two alpha channels: one for the shadow area of the text and the other for the text.

1. Select File > New and create a 5-by-5-inch, RGB color file. Set Contents to White. Open the Channels and Color palettes if they are not already open. Set the foreground to a light color.

2. Use the Type tool's Type Mask option to create some text on screen. For our example, we used an Adobe font called Remedy Double Extras. When the text is on screen, move it into the center of your document window. Fill the text with the foreground color. Keep the text selected.

3. While the text is still selected, choose the Select > Save Selection command to create a mask in an alpha channel (Alpha 1) of the text floating on screen. In the Save Selection dialog box, leave the default settings (the current document and a new channel) and click on OK. Don't deselect the text on screen.

4. Create a duplicate mask in an alpha channel of the text floating on screen. Choose Select > Save Selection and click on OK (use the defaults again). After you have a mask of the floating text in the second alpha channel (Alpha 2), deselect the floating text.

Remember *If you deselect a selection, you can return to the last selection by choosing Select > Reselect.*

5. Click on Alpha 2 in the Channels palette to activate the alpha channel.

6. To offset the text in Alpha 2, choose Filter > Other > Offset. In the Offset dialog box, type in the amount you want to offset the text horizontally and vertically. Type a positive number less than 10 in the Horizontal and Vertical fields to offset the shadow text to the right and down (a negative number offsets to the left and up). Click on the Wrap Around radio button in the Undefined Areas group and click on OK.

Tip *If you want to create a dramatic effect and make the type look as if it is jumping off the page, increase the Offset values in the Offset dialog box.*

7. If you want your shadow to have a soft-shadowed look, apply the Gaussian Blur filter (Filter > Blur > Gaussian Blur) to Alpha 2. In the Gaussian Blur dialog box, type in a number between 1 and 10, depending on how much of a blur you want. If you don't want a soft-shadowed look, skip this step and proceed to step 8.

8. Load the selection from Alpha 1 into Alpha 2 by choosing Select > Load Selection. When the Load Selection dialog box appears, make sure that the Channel pop-up menu is set to Alpha 1, and then click on OK. The selection from Alpha 1 should now appear in Alpha 2.

9. Fill the selection in Alpha 2 with black using the Edit > Fill command. The white area you see in Alpha 2 will create the drop shadow after you load the selection.

Note *If the Selected Areas option is selected in the Channels Options dialog box, choose Masked Areas instead. To open the Channels Options dialog box, double-click on the Alpha 2 channel in the Channels palette.*

10. Click on RGB in the Channels palette to return to the composite image.

11. Choose Select > Load Selection. In the Load Selection dialog box, choose Alpha 2 from the Channel pop-up menu, and then click on OK. After the selection appears, fill it with a dark color. Deselect to see the effects.

At this point, both the text and drop shadow selections are saved in two different alpha channels. This means that you can fill your entire screen with white, reload the selection in Alpha 1 (text), fill it with a color, reload the selection in Alpha 2 (shadow), and then fill it with a different color. You can also fill either selection with a blend or apply a filter.

Even though this exercise applied a drop shadow to text, you can apply the same steps to create a drop shadow for any object. Just make sure that your object is selected before you choose Select > Save Selection (beginning with step 3).

Save your file if you wish, and proceed to the next section to learn how to create three-dimensional effects using alpha channels.

Creating a Three-Dimensional, Raised-Type Effect

You can create striking three-dimensional effects by loading and filling selections from alpha channels. You can even save a sliver of a selection that has just the look you want and reload it to be used as a light source or a shadow.

The exercise in this section demonstrates how to create a raised-type, or embossed, effect by filling one selection as a light source and another selection as a shadow. Before starting, examine Figure 15-15. Notice the raised look of the text, This effect is created primarily from the thin slivers of light and dark along the sides of the letters. The white slivers along the top and left edges create the illusion of a light source, and the dark slivers along the bottom and right edges appear as shadows. Together, they create the depth needed to produce the raised-type effect.

To achieve the raised-type effect, you'll create a separate mask for the light source and another for the shadow. Then you will fill the selections with white and black. You'll also create another mask for the front part of the text, just in case you want to lighten or darken this part.

Figure 15-15.   *A three-dimensional, raised-type effect*

Note *This example provides a look at how to create three-dimensional effects manually. Photoshop's layer styles can automatically create many three-dimensional effects for you. Layer styles are covered in Chapter 18.*

1. Start by opening any file to which you would like to add raised text. If you don't have a suitable image, load the Italian Riviera (Iriviera) file from this book's CD-ROM.

2. Activate the Type tool and select the Type Mask option in the Options bar. Type the text to be added to your image and click on OK in the Options bar. Once the type selection appears on screen, move it to the desired position.

3. While the text is still selected, choose Select > Save Selection. In the Save Selection dialog box, make sure the Document pop-up menu is set to the current file and the Channel pop-up menu is set to New. Name the channel **Front**. This is the channel you will use if you want to change the front part of the text. Click on OK to close the dialog box. Then deselect the text.

4. Duplicate the Front alpha channel by clicking on it and dragging it over the New Channel icon at the bottom of the Channels palette. Double-click on the duplicated alpha channel in the Layers palette to display the Channels Options dialog box. Name the channel **Shadow** and make sure the Masked Areas radio button is selected. Click on OK to close the dialog box. This is the channel you will use to create the shadow for the text.

5. To lay the groundwork for creating the black shadow slivers, apply the Emboss filter (Filter > Stylize > Emboss) to the entire Shadow channel. In the Emboss dialog box, type **135** in the Angle field, **3** in the Height field, and **100** in the Amount field. Click on OK to execute the filter.

6. Duplicate the Shadow alpha channel by clicking on it and dragging it over the New Channel icon at the bottom of the Channels palette. This channel will provide the basis for the light source for the raised text.

7. To rename this duplicated channel, double-click on it in the Channels palette. When the Channel Options dialog box appears, name the alpha channel **Highlight** and click on OK.

Tip *You can copy and rename a channel at the same time by pressing OPTION (ALT) while you drag the channel onto the New Channel icon.*

8. Select Image > Adjust > Invert to reverse the light and dark areas on the screen.

9. If you want the Shadow and Highlight areas to be thicker, apply the Image > Adjust > Equalize command before you proceed to the next steps.

10. Next, you will isolate the white area of the Highlight alpha channel. Choose Image > Adjust > Threshold. In the Threshold dialog box, set the slider control somewhere between 135 and 255 and click on OK. Before continuing, compare your image with Figure 15-15. Remember that white represents the image area that will become a selection for the white area.

| Note | *If you don't apply the Threshold command to the Highlight channel, and then you load the channel and fill it with white, it will tint your entire photograph, not just the type. You might want to try doing this for a different effect.* |

11. To isolate the area that will provide the black shadow for the text, click on the Shadow channel in the Channels palette. Then choose Image > Map > Threshold. In the Threshold dialog box, set the slider control somewhere between 135 and 255 and click on OK. Once again, compare your image with Figure 15-15. The white area on screen represents another selection that will be loaded into your image. This selection area will be filled with black to create the shadow areas.

12. To create the raised-type effect. select the RGB composite channel by clicking on RGB in the Channels palette or by pressing COMMAND-~ (CTRL-~). Revisit steps 10 and 11 if you want the shadow areas to have hard edges. If you want to soften the edges of the shadow and highlight, click on the Shadow and Highlight channels in the Layers palette and choose Filter > Blur > Gaussian Blur.

13. To create the shadow portion of the text, load the Shadow selection. Choose Select > Load Selection, and then select Shadow in the Source Channel pop-up menu. Keep the Document pop-up menu set to Italian Riviera. Click on OK. When the selection appears, fill it with black. Choose Edit > Fill and set the Use pop-up menu to Black, Opacity to 100%, and Mode to Normal. To examine the shadow you just created, hide the selection marquee by choosing View > Hide Edges.

14. To create the light source for the text, choose Select > Load Selection again and select Highlight in the Source Channel pop-up menu. Keep the Document pop-up menu set to Italian Riviera. Click on OK. Fill the selection with white by choosing Edit > Fill. In the Fill dialog box, set the Use pop-up menu to White, the Opacity to 100%, and the Mode to Normal. Deselect to finish.

At this point, you can add more depth to the text by loading the Front channel and either lightening or darkening the selection. You can use the Image > Adjust > Brightness/Contrast command, the Image > Adjust Levels command, or the Image > Adjust > Curves command. If you want to keep your file, use the File > Save As command to save your document under a new name.

This three-dimensional effect can be applied to any object or shape, not just to text. Also, if you would like, you can reload the White Shadow and Black Shadow selections and fill them with other colors using various opacities. Try experimenting to create different effects. Fill the Black Shadow selection with white and the White Shadow selection with black, then try filling the white selection with yellow and Opacity set at 50%.

If you wish to create your own three-dimensional effects, start by analyzing shadow and light sources, and text or object areas. Use the Offset and Emboss filters to help create displacement effects. Use the Image > Adjust > Threshold, Invert, or Levels command to control the brightness levels. Experiment by filling the selections with the different colors.

Using a Luminance Mask

You can create masks out of the brightness or luminance levels of an image. (Perhaps the easiest way to conceptualize the *luminance level* is to imagine a grayscale version of your color image.) Using a luminance mask, you can create blends between one image and another, and even use the mask to brighten or darken an image.

In this example, you'll turn an image from a beach sunset scene to a beach daylight scene by lightening a selection created from the luminance values of the image. To do this, you'll convert the image to Lab Color and copy the lightness channel of the image into an alpha channel and use the channel as a mask.

1. Open the Rockybch file from this book's CD-ROM.

2. Convert the Image to Lab Color mode by choosing Image > Mode > Lab.

3. Select the L (lightness) channel in the Channels palette. Immediately, the image shows a grayscale version of the file. Select the entire file by pressing COMMAND-A (CTRL-A). Then press COMMAND-C (CTRL-C) to copy the image.

4. Click on the New Channel icon in the Channels palette to create a new channel. Then press COMMAND-V (CTRL-V) to paste the image into the alpha channel.

5. Convert the image back to RGB mode by choosing Image > Mode > RGB Color. In the Channels palette, click on RGB to return to the RGB composite.

6. Choose Select > Load Selection to load the mask as a selection.

7. To hide the selection but keep it selected, press COMMAND-H (CTRL-H).

8. To brighten the selection, choose Image > Adjust > Levels. Drag the midtone slider to lighten the image and turn the beach sunset scene into a daylight scene. (For a detailed description of the Levels command, see Chapter 20.)

If you would like, you can take this exercise one step further to create a blend between two images. Choose Select > All. Next, choose File > Open to load another image on screen. Then choose Edit > Paste. The result is that you can see through different areas of the beach image. The blend between the two images conforms to the grayscale levels of the mask. Image areas that are dark are more opaque. Image areas that are light are less opaque.

Creating a Colored Mezzotint Effect

The Split Channels and Merge Channels commands can be used to create an interesting colored mezzotint effect. Here are the basic steps:

1. Load an RGB or CMYK file. (If the image has layers, flatten the image by choosing Layer > Flatten Image; otherwise you will not be able to split the channels.)

2. Select the Split Channels command from the Channel palette's pop-up menu to split the image into separate grayscale files.

3. Create a custom pattern by opening Mezzotint-shape pattern from the Postscript Patterns folder (The path to the file is Presets\Patterns\Postscript Patterns.)

4. To define the pattern, choose Select > All, then Edit > Define Pattern.

5. From the Mode menu, change each file to Bitmap (Image > Mode > Bitmap), and choose the Custom Pattern option from the Use pop-up menu in the Bitmap dialog box.

6. Choose the pattern from the pattern pop-up menu that appears. Click on OK to apply the pattern.

7. Repeat step 5 for each file, and then convert each file back to grayscale.

8. Select the Merge Channels command from the Channel palette's pop-up menu to merge the channels back together. The color image will reappear, but with a black mezzotint pattern overlaying the colors. The final effect will depend on the colors in the original image.

> **Note**   *Photoshop's Mezzotint filter (Filter > Pixelate > Mezzotint) can also create a variety of colored mezzotint effects. See Chapter 12 for more details.*

Using Mathematical Channel Operations

Once you begin to understand how to use channels, you may wish to apply effects to your images using mathematical channel operations. Photoshop's Apply Image and Calculations commands allow you to take the pixel values of one channel and apply a mathematical formula to them using the pixel values of another channel. The formulas are applied when you choose an option in the Apply Image or Calculations dialog box's Blending pop-up menu. The choices in the Blending pop-up menu include many of the blending modes that appear in the Layers palette and Painting tool options bar.

By applying a blending calculation, you can create interesting composite effects. These commands also can be used to color-correct an image by lightening or darkening the pixels in a channel.

> **Note**   *The Layers palette allows you to create many of the same effects provided by the Apply Image and Calculations commands. Most users find layers easier to use and more versatile. For more information about using layers, see Chapters 17 and 18.*

When Photoshop executes the Apply Image or Calculations command, it blends channels together by applying calculations to the corresponding pixel values in each channel. For instance, when Photoshop applies the Difference command, it subtracts corresponding pixel values. This means that the value of the first pixel in the first row in one channel is subtracted from the value of the first pixel in the first row of the second channel. The second pixel's value in the first row of the first channel is subtracted from the second pixel's value in the first row of the second image, and so on.

It is important to understand that pixel values are measured on a scale of 0 to 255, with 0 representing the darkest value and 255 representing white. Therefore, when pixel values increase, the image grows lighter; when pixel values decrease, the image grows darker.

Several of the commands include a scale option that allows you to fine-tune the blending effect.

Here are a few examples of the calculation formulas, which may help you conceptualize the pixel mathematics that occur when you use Apply Image and Calculations:

- **Add** Source Pixels + Target Pixels ÷ Scale + Offset = Result
- **Difference** Source Pixels − Target Pixels = Result
- **Multiply** (Source Pixels) × (Target Pixels) ÷ 255 = Result
- **Screen** 255 − (255 − Source Pixels) × (255 − Target Pixels) ÷ Scale = Result
- **Darken** Compares the channel color values and create colors from the darkest values
- **Lighten** Compares the channel color values and creates colors from the light values

Every Photoshop image is created from a grid of pixels. You might think of an image as being created by painting in the rows and columns of grid boxes on a sheet of graph paper. Each grid box is the equivalent of a pixel, and each pixel in a channel has a color value from 0 to 255.

Blending Channels with the Apply Image Command

The Apply Image command allows you to edit any of the channels of the active document by blending another channel with it. You can blend channels from the same document or a different document. The Apply Image command can be used to create interesting blending effects and to alter the color of selected channels in an image. A requirement is that both images must have the same width and height in pixels.

Note

Although the Apply Image command can be used to create blending effects, many of the same blending effects can be created using layers, layers masks, and blending modes in the Layers palette (Chapters 16 and 17 cover layers). The options in the Layers palette allow for more experimentation and let you easily change and undo settings. Use Apply Image when you wish to make a permanent change to the channel in an image.

To use the Apply Image command, open an image and select Image > Apply Image. You'll see that the Apply Image dialog box has Source and Target choices. You blend a source channel with a target channel. The target channel is a channel in the active document on your screen. The source channel can be a channel from the same image or another image.

```
┌─────────────────────────────────────────────────────┐
│                      Apply Image                      │
├─────────────────────────────────────────────────────┤
│    Source: │ Piano.psd    ▲▼ │      ┌──────────┐      │
│                                    │    OK    │      │
│     Layer: │ Background   ▲▼ │     └──────────┘      │
│                                    ┌──────────┐      │
│   Channel: │ RGB     ▲▼ │  □ Invert │  Cancel  │     │
│                                    └──────────┘      │
│                                    ☑ Preview         │
│    Target:    Piano.psd (RGB)                        │
│  Blending: │ Multiply     ▲▼ │                       │
│   Opacity: │ 100 │ %                                 │
│            □ Preserve Transparency                   │
│            □ Mask...                                 │
└─────────────────────────────────────────────────────┘
```

By default, the Target section in the dialog box is where the Apply Image effect will be applied. The target image is always the current active document on screen. The names of the channel and layer that the blending effect will appear in are shown in parentheses next to the name of the target image. The target channel and the target layer are the currently selected channel and layer for the active document on your screen. The target channel and the target layer are both indicated by a highlight color in the Channels and Layers palettes.

The options in the Apply Image dialog box allow you to specify how the channels will be blended:

■ From the Source pop-up menu, choose the document file that you wish to use as one of the blending files. Only documents that have the same width and height in pixels as the active document on your screen appear in the Source pop-up menu.

■ From the Layer pop-up menu, pick a layer from the source document. If your document does not have any transparent layers, Background appears in the Layer pop-up menu. If your source image has several layers, the Layer pop-up menu allows you to choose Merged. If you choose this option, the Apply Image command applies calculations to the source image as if all its layers were merged into one layer.

■ From the Channel pop-up menu, pick a channel from the source document to use for the blend. If you choose a layer in the Layer pop-up menu (other than the Background), Transparency appears in the Channel pop-up menu. If you use this option, a mask of the channel is used in the blend. In the mask, transparent layer areas are black, and colored areas are white.

■ The Invert checkbox adjacent to the Source group allows you to invert the pixel values of the source pixels. If you click on Invert, black pixels will be read as white, white as black, and pixel values of colors as their complements.

■ From the Blending pop-up menu, select a blending effect. Each choice produces a different effect by telling Photoshop to use a different set of pixel calculations when blending source and target pixels. Several of the choices in the Blending pop-up menu are the same as those in the Mode menu in different palettes and dialog boxes. These perform virtually the same functions when blending channels as they do when painting or compositing layers.

- In the Opacity field, enter the opacity percentage that will be used when channels are blended together. Low opacities will make the source channel more translucent. High opacities make the pixels in the source channel less translucent.

- The Preserve Transparency checkbox becomes accessible only when your target layer is not the background. When the Preserve Transparency checkbox is selected, transparent areas of the target image will not be affected by the Apply Image command.

- The Mask checkbox allows you to designate a channel in an image to use as a mask. The dark areas in the mask hide corresponding areas of the source image, allowing more of the target pixels to show through. Light areas in the mask reveal more source pixels and fewer of the target pixels.

When you experiment with the Apply Image dialog box options, make sure that the Preview checkbox is selected. This way, you can examine the different channel-blending effects without closing the dialog box. After you've examined the effects, you can click on OK to apply the effect to your target document or click on Cancel to cancel the operation.

Editing Channels with the Calculations Command

The Image > Calculations command provides many of the same features as the Apply Image command described in the previous section. Both allow you to create composites between channels by choosing a blending option and changing opacity. Both require that all images used have the same width and height in pixels.

The primary difference between Apply Image and Calculations is that the Calculations command does not produce its effects in a composite channel. The resulting effect can appear in a selection or alpha channel other than an image's composite channel, or in a new channel or a new file with a new channel in it. The result can also be a layer mask.

A layer mask is a mask created in a new channel that allows you to hide or reveal portions of different layers. After you create the mask, you can edit it to reveal more or less of the layer you are in and more or less of the underlying layer. See Chapter 17 for more information about layer masks.

To use the Calculations command, choose Image > Calculations. Unlike the Apply Image dialog box, the Calculations dialog box shown in Figure 15-16 allows you to specify two sources. The channels in the source documents contain the data that Photoshop uses when it applies Calculations.

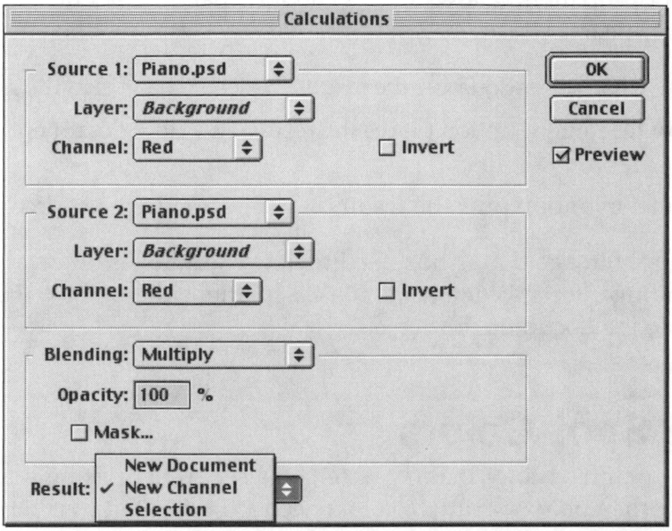

Figure 15-16.   *The Calculations dialog box lets you work with two source documents*

The Source 1 pop-up menu allows you to choose any open document whose pixel dimensions in width and height match the active document's pixel dimensions. In the Layer pop-up menu, you can choose the layer from the Source 1 document that you wish to use when blending. The Channel pop-up menu allows you to choose any channel from the Source 1 document that you wish to use when blending.

The Source 2 pop-up menu works exactly the same as the Source 1 pop-up menu. Only images whose pixel dimensions are the same as the active document's will appear in the pop-up menu. The Layer and Channel pop-up menus refer to layers and channels in the Source 2 document.

For Source 1 and Source 2, an Invert option is available. If you select Invert, the channels' pixels are inverted to create a negative of the image.

The Calculations dialog box includes the same blending options as the Apply Image dialog box. To see the blending choices, click on the Blending pop-up menu. As in the Apply Image dialog box, you can set the opacity for the blend.

If you select the Mask checkbox, the dialog box expands to allow you to choose a source document for the mask, as well as the channel and layer that the mask is in. When a mask is used, dark areas of the mask allow more of the Source 1 document to appear, and light areas allow the Source 2 image to appear.

The Result pop-up menu allows you to choose where the results of the Calculations dialog box will appear:

- The New Channel option puts the results in a new channel in the source document.
- The New Document option places the results in a new document that Photoshop creates for you.
- The Selection option puts the results in a selection in the source document.

As in the Apply Image dialog box, the Preview checkbox is an invaluable aid in predicting blending effects. When using the Calculations dialog box, the preview appears in the active document on screen.

Creating Spot Colors

A *spot color* is a premixed color that is printed on a separate printing plate. Often, spot colors are used when only one or two colors need to be printed over a portion of an image. Spot colors are often used as a fifth color (in addition to CMYK colors) to attract attention to logos or text. Typically, spot colors are first chosen from a PANTONE or TRUMATCH swatchbook as a means of matching and predicting how colors will be printed. As discussed in Chapter CD-1, you can find colors created by PANTONE, TRUMATCH, and other companies in Photoshop's Custom Color palette (choose Custom from Photoshop's Color Picker). When you create colors using Photoshop's spot-color channels, Photoshop opens the Color Picker.

Although spot colors in Photoshop will prove adequate for many digital-imaging projects, designers will find projects requiring spot colors with well-defined images are better handled in drawing programs like Adobe Illustrator and page layout programs such as QuarkXPress and Adobe PageMaker. Photoshop's spot colors will not automatically *knock out* underlying colors. In Photoshop, spot colors overprint the composite image and overprint other spot colors. Despite these drawbacks, creating spot colors in Photoshop is quite easy and logical.

 When one color "knocks out" an underlying color, the underlying color is removed. This prevents one color from overprinting another color, and thus producing a third underlying color. A technique for manually knocking out an underlying color is discussed in the "Editing Overlapping Spot Colors" section later in this chapter.

Using a Channel to Create Spot Colors

The easiest way to get started creating spot colors is to create a selection. Here are steps for creating spot colors using a spot channel:

1. Load an image to which you wish to apply a spot color.
2. Open the Channels palette by choosing Windows > Show Channels.

3. Create a selection on the screen, or load a previously saved selection by choosing Select > Load Selection.

4. In the Channels palette's pop-up menu, choose New Spot Channel. You can also press COMMAND (*CTRL*) while you click on the New Channel icon in the Channels palette. Either action opens the New Spot Channel dialog box.

New Spot Channel

Name: Spot Color 1   [OK]

Ink Characteristics   [Cancel]

Color: ▢   Solidity: 0 %

5. Click on the color swatch to open the Color Picker dialog box. Choose a color in the Color Picker or choose a PANTONE, TRUMATCH, or other custom color by clicking on the Custom button. After you click on the Custom button, click on the color you wish to add to your image in the Book pop-up menu. (You can also type the color's number on the keyboard.) Click on OK to return to the New Spot Channel dialog box.

 If you use a custom color for a spot channel, do not rename the spot-color channel. If you rename the channel, the color may not be interpreted by the other publishing applications.

6. To specify the solidity of the color, enter a value between 0 and 100 in the Solidity field. A value of 100% provides an on-screen simulation of how a printed ink completely covers any inks beneath. A Solidity of 0% can be used to simulate a varnish. Varnishes can be used as a protective or glossy coating. The Solidity value does not affect the printed output.

7. To apply the spot color to your image, click on OK.

8. If you need to change the settings in the New Spot Channel dialog box, double-click on the spot-color channel in the Channels palette or select the channel and choose Channel Options from the Channels palette's pop-up menu.

 To convert an alpha channel to a spot channel, double-click on the channel. In the Channel Options dialog box, select the Spot Channel option. Click on the color swatch to choose a color. After you've chosen a color, select a Solidity percentage.

Adding Spot Colors with Painting Tools

After you've created a spot-color channel, you can edit the color using Photoshop's painting and editing tools. For instance, you can use the Paintbrush tool to paint spot colors in an image. You can click and drag with the Eraser to remove spot colors.

Set the foreground color to black to paint with the spot color. To paint with a lower opacity, paint with a shade of gray. Painting with the Eraser tool or painting with white removes the spot color.

 If you wish to apply a spot color to an entire image to tint the image, create a duotone and apply the color to the duotone plate. Creating duotones is discussed in Chapter 13.

Editing Overlapping Spot Colors

If you are using more than one spot color, you may wish to prevent one spot color from overprinting underlying spot colors. To prevent overprinting of spot colors, you can delete the area in one channel where the spot channels overlap. In order to delete the colors, you select the area in the spot channel that you want printed and delete the underlying area. Essentially, this means you can manually knock out color beneath a spot-color channel. You can use this process when spot colors overlap other spot colors, or when spot colors overlap CMYK colors.

Here are the steps for manually knocking out overlapping color:

1. Select the spot-color channel that you do want to print—the channel from which you will not be deleting overlapping color.

2. Create a selection on the screen from the spot color channel by choosing Select > Load Selection. In the Load Selection dialog box, choose the correct channel in the Channel pop-up menu and click on OK. Alternatively, you can create the selection by pressing COMMAND (CTRL) and clicking on the spot channel in the Channels palette.

3. Before continuing, make sure that the background color is set to White. Then click on the spot-color channel that you want to knock out (in the Channels palette)—the channel from which you want to remove color. Press DELETE (BACKSPACE) to remove it.

After creating the selection in step 2, you can expand or contract it by choosing Select > Modify > Expand or Contract. This affects the area deleted in step 3.

Printing Spot Colors

Although you can create spot colors in RGB Color and Grayscale mode files, spot colors can only be printed from CMYK Color and Multichannel mode files. If you will be exporting an image with a spot color to another program, your Photoshop file must be saved in DCS 2.0 format. CMYK Color, Multichannel, and Grayscale mode files can be saved in DCS 2.0 format.

Since a spot color channel simulates a printing plate, you will need to use Photoshop's Separations option to print separations, which can be printed in CMYK Color or Multichannel mode images. If you need to convert your image to CMYK, choose Image > Mode > CMYK Color. (See Chapter 14 for details about converting from RGB to CMYK color.) To print separations, choose File > Print. In the Profile pop-up menu, choose Separations. When the image is output, the name of each spot color appears when the channel is printed.

When you print, spot colors are overprinted according to their order in the Channels palette. If you wish to move a spot color channel above one of Photoshop's CMYK channels, convert the image to Multichannel mode and click and drag in the Channels palette to move the spot color channel.

If you wish to print your image as a composite (on one page) as a proof, you can merge the spot colors with the image's other channels by choosing Merge Spot Colors from the Channels palette's pop-up menu. This deletes the spot channel from the Channels palette and flattens layers in images. Note that the colors will not look exactly the same as when printed on a printing press, because the colors in the composite will be created from cyan, magenta, yellow, and black.

APPLYING EFFECTS
TO YOUR IMAGES

The
Complete
Reference

Chapter 16

Working with Layers

Layers open up a new world of artistic freedom and design possibilities. When you start using layers, digital art you imagined but never thought feasible lies within your grasp. Layers set you free from many of the restraints imposed by a pixel-based program. They allow you to experiment with an infinite range of design possibilities without needing to spend hours of time selecting, reselecting, or returning to earlier versions of your files.

When you work in a layer, it's as though you're editing an image on a sheet of acetate. Images below the acetate can show through the transparent areas. If you have multiple layers, you can reposition them in any order. If you erase an object on a layer, background images will show through. If you move a layer, all of the objects on the layer move together as a group, independent of other layers.

You manage layers with the Layer menu and the Layers palette, which are available in both Photoshop and ImageReady. Used together, the Layer menu and Layers palette allow you to create new layers, reorder layers, select a target layer to edit in, merge layers, create layer masks, and delete layers.

This chapter starts with a discussion of layer fundamentals, including how to create and delete layers, move objects in layers, change target layers, and rearrange layers. Once you've mastered the technical aspects of creating layers, you'll move onto explore the artistic possibilities opened by the world of layers.

Creating Layers

As you work through this chapter, you'll see that Photoshop provides a variety of different ways to create layers. A common way to create a new layer is by using the Layers palette and its pop-up menu. In the Layers palette, you can press OPTION (ALT) and click on the New Layer icon in the Layers palette, or click on the pop-up menu arrow and choose the New Layer command from the palette's menu. Both techniques open up the New Layer dialog box, in which you can name the layer, assign it a color in the Layers palette, and choose a blending mode before the layer is created. (If you don't press OPTION (ALT), a new layer is created, but the New Layer dialog box doesn't open.)

The Layer menu provides several commands for creating a new layer:

- Layer > New > Layer creates a new layer.
- Layer > New > Fill Layer creates a layer filled with a solid color, gradient, or pattern.
- Layer > New > Layer Via Copy or Layer Via Cut creates a new layer from a selection. If you choose Layer Via Cut, the selection will be cut and pasted into a new layer. If you choose Layer Via Copy, the selection will be copied into the new layer.

- Layer > New > Layer from Background creates a layer from the Background pixels.

In some cases, you don't need to choose to create a new layer, because Photoshop does it for you automatically. A new layer is created when you perform the following actions:

- Drag and drop an image from one file to another.
- Copy and paste an image area over another image area.
- Create type with the Text Layer button selected in the Type tool's Options bar.
- Create a shape with the Create New Shape Layer icon selected in the Shape tool's Option bar.

In the following exercises, you'll learn how to create layers by working with a few simple shapes and some text, as shown in Figure 16-1. Each element will be created in a separate layer, which will allow you to move and edit the shape or text without affecting other layers.

APPLYING EFFECTS
TO YOUR IMAGES

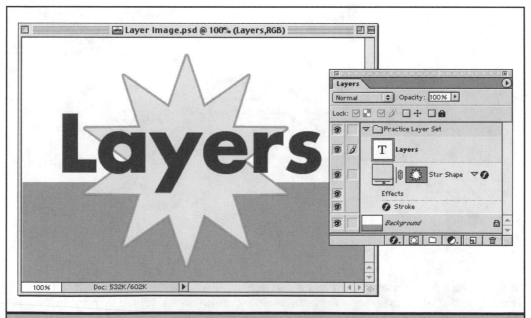

Figure 16-1.   *Two layers and a background were used to create this image*

Exploring the Layers Palette

The Layers palette provides most of the tools you need to create and manage your layers. It shows you what is happening on each of your layers and includes icons and a pop-up menu for working with them.

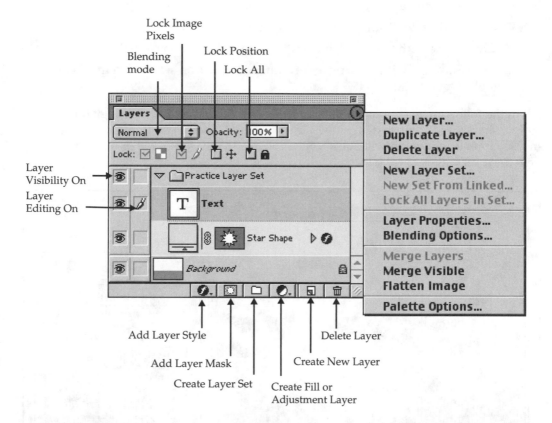

The base layer of any file that is created without a transparent background appears in the Layers palette designated as the Background. Also notice the eye icon (👁) that appears to the left of the layers. This indicates that the layers are visible in your document. The paintbrush icon (✏) and the highlighted or colored area surrounding a layer name in the Layers palette indicate the current target layer, which is the layer you are editing.

ImageReady's Layers palette and Layer menu are almost identical to Photoshop's. When you load a Photoshop file with layers into ImageReady, all Photoshop layers and layer effects are maintained by ImageReady. This means that you can safely move your layer-laden files back and forth between ImageReady and Photoshop.

> **Note**   *ImageReady does not create Background layers or maintain Photoshop background layers. When a Photoshop file with a Background is loaded into ImageReady, the Background is converted into a standard layer. Using ImageReady layers to create animation is covered in Chapter 10.*

Let's begin by seeing how the Layers palette reflects what is happening in a document.

1. If the Layers palette isn't open, choose Window > Show Layers to display it.

2. Select File > New and create a 7-by-5-inch, RGB color file. Set Resolution to 72 ppi and Contents to White.

3. Before adding a layer to your file, create a colored area on the background so that you see how it affects the Layers palette. Start by changing the foreground color to red.

4. Use the Marquee tool to create a rectangle that covers the entire lower portion of your file.

5. Fill the rectangle with the foreground color by selecting Edit > Fill (see Figure 16-1). Then deselect it.

6. To organize your layers in folders in the Layers palette, click on the palette pop-up menu arrow and choose New Layer Set. Photoshop will automatically add the next layers you create to the current layer set. After you execute the command, Photoshop opens the New Layer Set dialog box, in which you can name your new layer set. Layers created before the layer set was created can be dragged into the layer set folder.

In the Layers palette, notice that a red rectangle appears in a miniature thumbnail version of the layer. Before continuing, you might wish to change the size of the thumbnail in the palette. To do this, click on the Layers palette pop-up menu arrow and select Palette Options. The dialog box that appears lets you choose another size for your thumbnails.

Creating a Shape Layer

The Shape tool allows you to add a new layer for a shape when you create it. You'll use this technique to create a new shape layer for the star in our example.

1. Change the foreground color to yellow. When you create the shape, it will automatically be filled with the foreground color.

2. Activate the Shape tool by clicking on its location in the Toolbox. If the Custom Shape tool isn't active, keep the mouse button pressed until the pop-up menu of shapes appears. Then click on the Custom Shape tool.

3. In the Custom Shape pop-up menu in the Options bar, choose one of the star shapes.

4. In the Shape tool's Options bar, select the Create New Shape Layer icon (▮).

5. To create the shape, click and drag diagonally in your document. When you release the mouse, Photoshop creates the new shape layer. In the Layers palette, the layer is represented by the solid color. The shape (called a *clipping path*) is represented by the clipping path icon to the right of the shape layer icon.

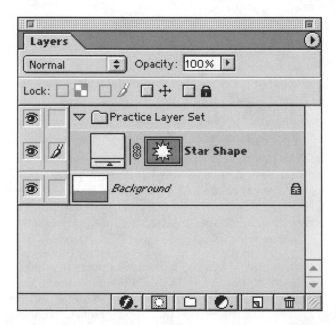

6. Name the new layer by choosing Layer Properties in the Layers palette menu. In the dialog box, type **Star Shape** in the Name field and click on OK. Notice that Star Shape appears in the title bar of your document, indicating that you are working in the Star Shape layer.

⊞ 🖼 **Layers.psd @ 100% (Star Shape,RGB)**

When you have several layers on screen, it's very easy to forget which layer you're working in. Every now and then as you're working, take a quick glance at the title bar.

Now examine the Layers palette. At the top of the palette, below the layer set name, is the Star Shape layer, which indicates that it's the top layer in the document. The layer at the top of the palette is always the top layer in the document; the layer on the bottom is the base layer of your image.

In the Layers palette, the eye icons to the left of the Background and Star Shape layers indicate that both of these layers are visible. The paintbrush icon next to the Star Shape layer means that only the Star Shape layer can be edited. The colored shading in the Star Shape layer section confirms what the document title bar is telling you—that you are working in the Star Shape layer. This is your target layer. As soon as you create a new layer, Photoshop automatically designates it as the target layer.

Adding a Layer Style

To add more definition to the star, you'll apply a Stroke layer style. The Layer Style dialog box offers many different effects that you can add to your layers.

1. Choose Layer > Layer Style > Stroke. The Stroke section of the Layer Style dialog box appears, as shown in Figure 16-2.

2. In the Layer Style dialog box, click and drag on the Size slider to adjust the stroke size to the width you desire. We choose 3 pixels.

3. Click on the color swatch at the bottom of the dialog box to choose a color for the stroke. Then click on OK to close the dialog box.

If you wish to change the color of the star shape, choose Layer > Layer Content Options. This opens the Color Picker dialog box, in which you can choose a new color for your shape. Alternatively, you can choose Layer > Change Content > Solid Color.

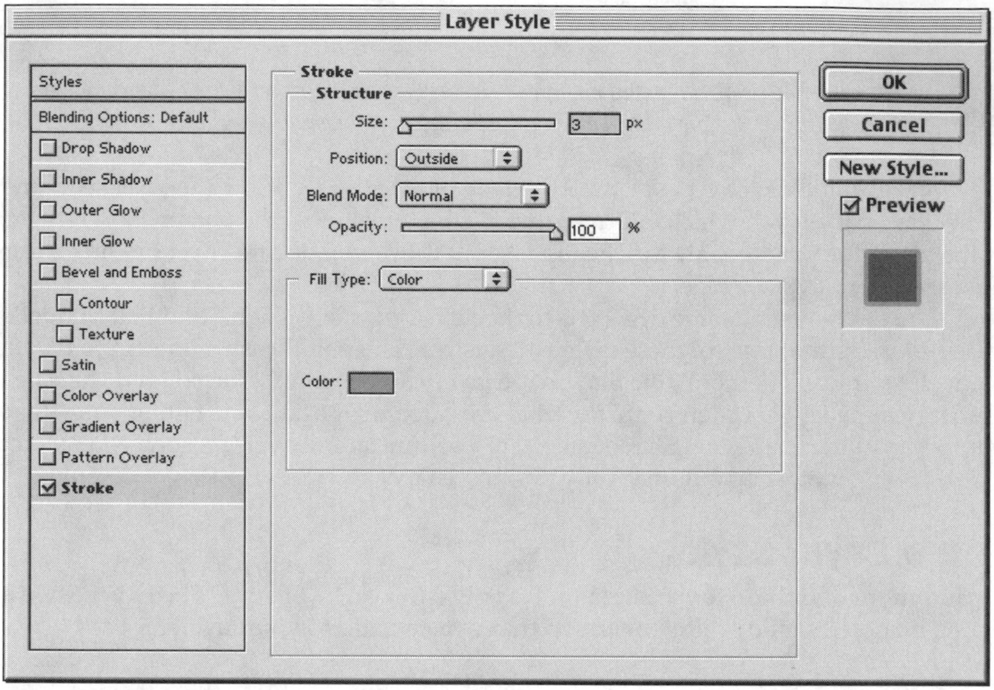

Figure 16-2. *The Stroke section of the Layer Style dialog box*

Notice that the Star Shape layer in Layers palette now has an icon with a script *f*. This indicates that you've added a layer effect to this layer. (See Chapter 17 for more information about using layer styles.)

Now take a look at the memory indicator in the lower-left corner of the screen. In the next section, you'll learn how layers increase file size.

Checking Layer Memory

When working with layers, it's easy for file size to grow quickly. The file size will depend on the amount of information you put in the layer.

As you create layers, you should know how much memory the layers are consuming. You can see this information in Photoshop's memory readout in the lower-left corner of the screen, as long as this indicator is set to show document size. Check this now by clicking on the pop-up menu arrow in the lower-left corner of your document. Select Document Sizes if it isn't already the active choice.

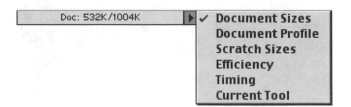

As explained in Chapter 1, the document size number on the left indicates the size of your image without any layers (this is also the size of the file sent to your printer in Photoshop format); the number on the right indicates the file size with all layers included. When a new layer is created, colored areas in the layer add to your file's size. Fortunately, the transparent area of a layer does not add to document memory. Later, you'll learn how to merge layers to reduce file size and flatten layers so that you can return the file to its original size.

If you do not have extra memory or a lot of free space available on your scratch disk, you'll need to work carefully with layers, possibly merging them as you finish working on different image areas. If you need to keep doing this, though, you're taking some of the versatility out of working with Photoshop. If you want to work with many layers, your best bet is to install more RAM and/or purchase the largest hard disk you can afford to use as a scratch disk. Once you're free of memory worries, you'll be able to work comfortably with several layers in your document.

Now that you've been cautioned about the memory consumption of layers, you're ready to add another layer to your practice file.

 Higher image cache settings (Edit > Preferences > Memory & Image Cache) will speed up your layer operations but take up more disk space and RAM. If you are working with large files, you may wish to increase the default setting beyond 4.

Using the Type Tool to Add a New Layer

In this section, you'll create a new layer by entering text with the Type tool. Photoshop automatically creates a new layer for text.

1. Set the foreground color to blue.

2. Select the Type tool in the Toolbox. If the Type tool's Options bar is not open, open it by double-clicking on the Type tool.

 3. In the Type tool's Options bar, select the New Text layer button in the Options bar. Pick a font and set the size to **130**.

4. In your document, type **Layers.** After you've finished typing the word, click on the OK (checkmark) icon in the Options bar. In the Layers palette, you'll see a new layer named Layers.

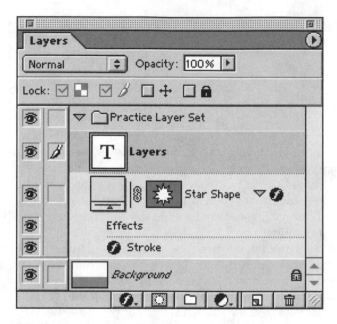

Notice that the text layer is the only layer with the paintbrush icon next to it and the color surrounding its name. Any image editing you do now affects only this layer. Even though you see the Star Shape layer on your screen, you cannot edit it now, because it is not in the current target layer. Photoshop allows you to have only one target layer at a time. Thus, if you wish to move or edit the Star Shape layer, you will need to switch target layers.

Working with Layers

After you've created layers, you can manipulate them in many ways. However, before you can affect a layer, you need to make it the target layer. An easy way to do this is to click on the layer name. You can also use some keyboard combinations to make a layer the current target:

- To move to a higher layer and make it the target layer, press OPTION-] (*ALT-]*).

- To move to the layer beneath the current target and make it the target layer, press OPTION-[(*ALT-[*).

- To move to the base layer and make it the target layer, press SHIFT-OPTION-[(*SHIFT-ALT-[*).

- To move to the top layer and make it the target layer, press SHIFT-OPTION-] (*SHIFT-ALT-]*).

As noted earlier, you can tell which layer is the target layer by the color in the Layers palette and the name in the document's title bar.

Moving Layers

We mentioned earlier that layers are like sheets of acetate overlaying each other. If you move a Photoshop layer, all of the objects in the layer move as one unit, as if they were all on the same acetate sheet. Being able to move layers independently of other layers gives you the freedom to experiment with many design options quickly without worrying about the pixels locking down on the underlying images.

Using the Move Tool's Auto Select Layer Option

In Photoshop, you can move a layer by simply clicking and dragging on it with the Move tool. However, before using the Move tool, you should take a look at the tool's Options bar, because the tool's functionality changes, based on its settings. To open the tool's Options bar, double-click on the Move tool.

The most important choice in the palette is the Auto Select Layer option. When Auto Select Layer is *not* selected, clicking and dragging anywhere in a layer moves the entire layer—even if you click and drag over a transparent area. If Auto Select Layer is chosen, the Move tool ignores transparent areas and moves a layer only if you click over a nontransparent area. If multiple layers exist, the Move tool looks for nontransparent image areas. If you click and drag over a nontransparent image area, you will move the first layer beneath the Move tool with nontransparent image information, even if it isn't the active layer.

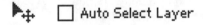 □ Auto Select Layer

For instance, if you've been following the exercises so far, you have text in the active layer. Turn on the Auto Select Layer option in the Move tool's Options bar, then click and drag over any part of the Star Shape layer that is not covered by text. The Move tool activates the Star Shape layer and moves the star, even though the original active layer was the text layer.

 On layers other than the Background, you can create a selection from nontransparent areas by pressing the COMMAND *(*ALT*) key and clicking on a layer name in the Layers palette.*

Moving and Linking Layers

If you wish to move a layer in 1-pixel increments, first activate the Move tool and then press any of the directional arrow keys on the keyboard. Pressing SHIFT while pressing any of the directional arrow keys moves the layer in 10-pixel increments (a 10-pixel increment moves you one frame in a filmstrip file created in Adobe Premiere).

Photoshop also allows you to link layers together so they can be moved as a unit. Layers other than the target layer can be linked to the target layer by clicking on the empty column (link column), which appears to the left of the layer name and to the right of the eye column in the Layers palette. After you click, the link icon (🔗) appears in the column. If you click on the link column of a layer above or below the target layer, Photoshop links that layer with the target layer. Clicking in the link column next to other layers adds those layers to the layers that are already linked.

In the next exercise, you'll practice moving the Star Shape and text layers independently and then linking them so they move together. For this exercise, you should already have the layers set up as shown earlier in Figure 16-1.

1. Try moving the text you've just created by first activating the Move tool, and then clicking and dragging on the text. As you drag the text, the entire layer moves. Move the text to different locations to experiment with image composition.

2. To set the Star Shape layer as your target layer so that you can work with it, click on its name in the Layers palette. The Star Shape layer is selected, and the title bar of your document now includes the layer name.

3. To move the yellow star on the screen, use the Move tool to click and drag on the star, and reposition it so that it is placed near the text.

4. To link the Star Shape and text layers, with Star Shape still the target layer, click on the Layers layer's link column (to the left of the layer name and to the right of the eye icon column) in the Layers palette. A link icon appears next to the text layer in the Layers palette.

5. To move the two linked layers, activate the Move tool, and then click and drag anywhere in the document. Both the Star Shape and Layers layer will move together.

Aligning and Distributing Linked Layers

Once you've linked layers together, you can have Photoshop automatically align a linked layer or several linked layers at the top, bottom, left, right, or middle of the active layer. For instance, you can have Photoshop automatically align the middle of the text with the middle of the star (as shown in Figure 16-1). Of course, you could do this manually using the Move tool, but Photoshop's aligning options will do it for you quickly and precisely.

To align linked layers with the active layer, choose Layer > Align Linked, and then choose one of the commands in the submenu. As you read through the descriptions of the choices, notice how they are visually depicted in the submenu:

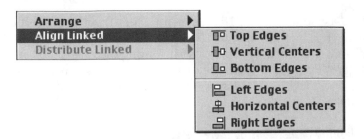

- **Top Edges**   Aligns the top of linked layers to the top of the active layer. If a selection exists in the active layer, the linked layers align to the top of the selection.

- **Vertical Centers**   Moves the linked layers up or down and aligns the pixels to the vertical center of the active layer. If a selection exists in the active layer, the linked layer aligns to the vertical center of the selection.

- **Bottom Edges**   Aligns the bottom edge of the linked layers to the bottom edge of the active layer or to the bottom of a selection border. If a selection exists in the active layer, the linked layer aligns to the bottom of the selection.

- **Left Edges**   Aligns the left edge of the linked layers to the left edge of the active layer. If a selection exists in the active layer, the linked layer aligns flush left to the left edge of the selection.

- **Horizontal Centers**   Moves the linked layers left or right to align to the horizontal center of the active layer or to the horizontal center of a selection.

- **Right Edges**   Aligns the right edge of the linked layers flush right with the right edge of the active layer. If a selection is in the active layer, the linked layer aligns flush right to the right edge of the selection.

Tip   *If you create a selection on screen, you can align a layer or several linked layers to the selection. After you create the selection, the Align Linked option changes to Align to Selection.*

If you find the concepts of vertical and horizontal centers hard to conceptualize, imagine having two layers, each with a different-sized doll against a transparent background. If the dolls were standing, the vertical center of each image would approximately be the navels of the two dolls. If you were to select Layer > Align Linked > Vertical Centers, the doll in the linked layer would move up or down so that its navel would be aligned with the navel of the doll in the active layer. If both dolls were posed in a reclining position and you applied the Horizontal Centers option, the doll in the linked layer would shift left or right to align to the navel of the doll in the active layer.

You can also have Photoshop distribute three or more linked layers to space the layers equidistantly. To distribute linked layers, first link three or more layers and then select Layers > Distribute Layers. The submenu offers Top Edges, Vertical Centers, Bottom Edges, Left Edges, Horizontal Centers, and Right Edges options. Each choice essentially tells Photoshop where to start distributing the layers. For instance, if you choose Top Edges, Photoshop starts the distribution process from the top pixel of each layer. If you choose Horizontal Centers, Photoshop starts from the horizontal center pixel of each layer.

When aligning or distributing layers, Photoshop ignores pixel values that are less than 50 percent opaque. Thus, if your active layer includes a border setting that is less than 50 percent opaque, aligned linked layers will not align to the actual edges of the layer. Instead, alignment will occur where the pixels have an Opacity value greater than 50%.

Before continuing to the next section, try aligning the text and star layer at their horizontal center position by choosing Layer > Align > Horizontal Centers. Then unlink the layers by clicking on the link icon in the link column.

Viewing and Hiding Layers

If you wish to view only the images in one layer without seeing objects in other layers, you can hide the other layers. To hide a layer, click on the layer's eye icon in the Layers palette. This turns the icon off and hides the corresponding layer. Clicking again in the same place (the eye icon column) returns the eye icon to the Layers palette and brings the layer into view. If you click and drag over different eye icons in the column, you will hide all of the corresponding layers. If you click and drag in the eye icon column again, the layers and their corresponding eye icons will return to view.

In the next exercise, you'll delete a portion of the star, as shown in Figure 16-3, and then hide the other layers to see how the Star Shape layer is affected. Before you begin, make sure that you are working with the elements shown in Figure 16-1 and that the Star Shape layer is your target layer.

1. Activate the Rectangular Marquee tool and use it to create a rectangular selection approximately ¼ inch wide in the middle portion of the star.

2. To delete this section of the Star Shape layer, press the DELETE key. Only the yellow area of the star is removed, as shown in Figure 16-3. Neither the text nor the background is affected, because each is in another layer. When you delete, you wipe away the yellow pixels of the star, leaving behind its transparent background. The text and background show through the transparency. You'll be able to see this by hiding both the Background and the text layers.

3. Hide the background by clicking on the Background layer's eye icon. The eye icon disappears from the Layers palette, and the white-and-red background disappears from the screen. The star and text layers remain on screen. You should now see the familiar transparent checkerboard pattern in the star and text layers, indicating that their backgrounds are transparent.

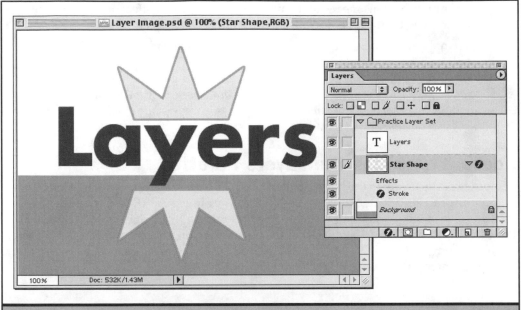

Figure 16-3. *When a portion of the Star Shape layer is deleted, the background shows through the deleted area*

> **Tip** *If you wish to change the checkerboard pattern of a transparent layer, choose Edit > Preferences > Transparency & Gamut.*

4. Hide the text layer by clicking the eye icon next to its layer name in the Layers palette. Now only the Star Shape layer remains visible on your screen. In the middle of the star, you see the checkerboard pattern.

> **Tip** *If you OPTION-click (ALT-click) on the eye icon column, Photoshop hides all visible layers except the layer of the eye icon that you click on. If you OPTION-click (ALT-click) again in the same area of the eye icon column, all layers will be visible.*

5. To return the text and Background layers to the screen, click on the eye icon column to the left of the text layer and to the left of the Background in the Layers palette.

6. To hide the Star Shape layer, click on the eye icon for that layer. The star vanishes. All you see are the text and Background layers. It's important to realize that the Star Shape layer is still your target layer. Notice that the selection color still surrounds the Star Shape name in the Layers palette and Star Shape remains in

your title bar. This means that editing the file now will affect only the Star Shape layer, even though you don't see that layer on your screen.

7. To make the Star Shape layer visible, click on its eye icon column in the Layers palette. The star reappears on screen.

You can copy all visible layers into the Clipboard by selecting an area and then choosing Edit > Copy Merged. You can then paste the visible layers into another file, in which the selection will appear flattened into one layer.

Reordering Layers in the Layers Palette

The order of the layers in the Layers palette governs how the layers overlap. Continuing with your practice document, you can make the star in Figure 16-3 overlap the text, instead of the text overlapping the star. There's no need to cut and paste between layers. All you need to do is reposition the layers' stacking order in the Layers palette, as shown in Figure 16-4.

Try changing the order of these layers in the Layers palette.

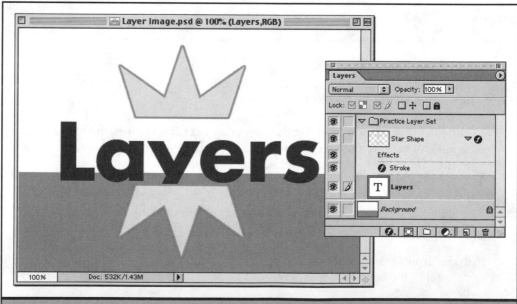

Figure 16-4.   *The Star Shape layer moved above the text layer*

1. Position the mouse pointer over the Star Shape layer name in the Layers palette. The mouse pointer will change to a pointing hand icon (🖑).

2. Click and keep the mouse button pressed; then drag up. As you drag, the pointing hand will change to a grabbing hand icon (🖐), and an outline of the Star Shape layer will move into the Layers palette.

3. Once the Star Shape layer is above the text layer, release the mouse. On your screen, the star now overlaps the text. In the Layers palette, the Star Shape layer is now the top layer. Now return it back to its original position by dragging it below the text layer in the Layers palette.

> **Note**
>
> *The Background layer in the Layers palette cannot be moved unless you change its name. The easiest way to change the name of the Background layer is to double-click on it in the Layers palette. The Make Layer dialog box will appear with Background renamed Layer 0. Click on OK to activate the change. Alternatively, choose Layer > New > Layer from Background.*

Changing Layer Opacity

The Layers palette provides a variety of options that allow you to blend images and create special effects. The easiest way to blend layers is to change the Opacity setting in the Layers palette. When you change opacity, you change it for the entire target layer.

For example, suppose that you would like the red background in Figure 16-2 to show through the star that overlaps it. One way of achieving this is to lower the opacity in the Star Shape layer.

1. Make sure that the Star Shape layer is the target layer (the one selected in the Layers palette), and then click on the small arrow next to the current Opacity value at the top of the Layers palette. When the slider appears, move the slider control beneath the slider to the left. Set the Opacity slider to 50%.

> **Tip**
>
> *If the Move tool, a selection tool, the Hand tool, or the Zoom tool is selected in the Toolbox, you can change the opacity for a layer by typing a number into the Opacity field. Type **1** to set opacity to 10%, **25** to change opacity to 25%, or **0** to set opacity to 100%.*

2. The Info palette keeps track of the opacity of a layer. To see the opacity readout for the Star Shape layer, open the Info palette by choosing Window > Show Info. Then click on one of the eyedropper icons and choose Opacity. Next, click on the eye icon for the Background layer in the Layers palette to hide it (the Opacity readout in the Info palette will not appear for the target layer if the Background is visible). Now, move the mouse pointer over the star and notice that an Op value of 50% is displayed in the Info palette.

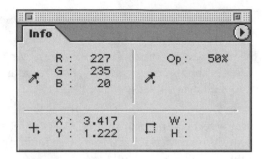

3. Move the mouse pointer over the text and notice that the Op value in the Info palette is 100%. If you wish, experiment by changing the text layer to the target layer and changing its opacity. You won't be able to change opacity in the Background layer unless you rename it. The Opacity slider in the Layers palette and the Op value in the Info palette are active only if you are in a layer with a transparent background or if a floating selection exists on your screen. After you are finished experimenting, make sure that all of the layers are displayed on screen.

Your next step in exploring the Layers palette is to investigate how the blending modes can create special blending effects between layers.

 If you fill a selection on screen or move a selection with the Move tool, you can change the selection's opacity by choosing Edit > Fade. In the Fade dialog box, drag the Opacity slider to the left to lower opacity.

Using Layer Blending Modes

One of the fastest ways to create special effects while blending layers is to use the Layers palette's Mode pop-up menu. In order to access the Mode pop-up menu in the Layers palette, you must be in a layer other than the Background or have a floating selection on the screen.

In the Mode pop-up menu. you'll see a familiar list of choices, starting with Normal and ending with Luminosity. These are the same blending modes described in Chapter 5. They work in much the same way when blending layers as they do when painting with the painting tools. When used with layers, the blending modes affect the appearance of both the target layer and the layer directly beneath it.

Try using Dissolve mode to break up the colors of the images in the Star Shape and text layers in your practice document:

1. Make the Star Shape layer (from Figure 16-2) your target layer. If the Star Shape layer and/or Background layer are hidden, click in the eye icon column to view them.

2. To change blending modes, click on the Mode pop-up menu (initially set to Normal) and choose Dissolve mode. Dissolve mode randomly removes pixels from the target layer, sometimes creating a crayon-like effect. Keep the Opacity value for the Star Shape layer set to 50%.

3. If you wish to enhance the effect, apply the Bevel and Emboss layer style by clicking on the *f* icon at the bottom of the Layers palette and choosing Bevel & Emboss. When the Layer Style dialog box opens, you can experiment with the Bevel and Emboss options or simply click on OK.

Tip *To save space in the Layers palette, you can click on the triangle next to the f icon for a specific layer to close its effects line in the palette.*

4. Set the target layer to the text layer (click on the Layers layer in the Layers palette, and apply the Dissolve mode once again. Set Opacity to 70%. This time, the effect will dissolve pixels from the text and star layers. After you change the mode to Dissolve, adjust Opacity as desired. Your image should look somewhat like Figure 16-5.

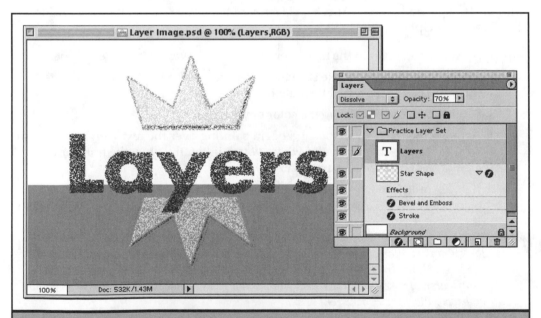

Figure 16-5. *The text and star layers with the Dissolve blending mode applied*

5. If you would like to experiment, try the Lighten, Darken, and Difference blending modes.

To quickly experiment with different blending modes, press SHIFT-+ *(plus) to step forward through the blending modes one at a time; press* SHIFT- – *(minus) to step backward through the blending modes.*

You'll have a chance to practice using different modes for special effects in the "Using Layers to Create Special Effects" section later in this chapter.

Preserving Transparency and Rendering a Type Layer

The Preserve Transparency option at the top of the Layers palette locks in the transparent area of a layer so that it cannot be edited. This feature can be helpful when you are filling selections in layers or when you are painting in layers.

In the next exercise, you'll try out the Preserve Transparency option with the text layer in your practice document (Figure 16-4). For this example, you want to change the colors of the text in the text layer, but you don't want to paint over the text inadvertently. If you wish to paint or fill a type layer, the layer must be rendered onto the background pixels. (After text is rendered, the type cannot be edited using the Type tool's Options bar.)

1. Set the target layer to the text layer and choose Layer > Rasterize > Type.

2. In the Layers palette, make sure that the Lock Transparency icon is selected (next to Lock at the top of the palette).

3. Set the foreground color to the color of your choice.

4. Activate the Paintbrush tool and begin painting over the text with broad brush strokes. Notice that no matter where you paint on the type, the transparency area of the layer remains transparent.

5. If you would like to experiment a bit more, use the Gradient tool to create a blend over the text. You'll see that only the letters will be affected by the blend.

The Eraser tool produces slightly different effects, depending on whether or not the Lock Transparency option in the Layers palette is selected. If Lock Transparency is not selected, the transparent background shows through the area you erased. If Lock Transparency is selected, the Eraser applies the background color. Both options do not, however, affect the transparent areas.

Using the Transform Commands with Layers

The Transform commands in the Edit menu allow you to embellish and tweak selections and images in layers. As discussed in Chapter 8, the Transform commands allow you to scale, rotate, skew, distort, and add perspective to selections and layers. If you want to execute several transformations with the mouse, your best bet is to choose Edit > Free Transform.

If you apply a transformation to a linked layer, the transformation affects all nontransparent elements of the linked layers. Figure 16-6 shows an example of the Perspective transformation applied to the linked text and Star Shape layers in the practice document used in this chapter. (Remember that you must first render your text in order to apply the Perspective or Distort transformation commands.)

Here are a few tips that may come in handy when you are transforming layers:

■ If the Move tool is activated, you can transform layers by clicking and dragging with the Move tool on the image in the layer and then fine-tuning the transformation by changing the settings in the Move tool's Options bar. To complete the transformation, click on the OK button (checkmark) in the Move tool's Options bar.

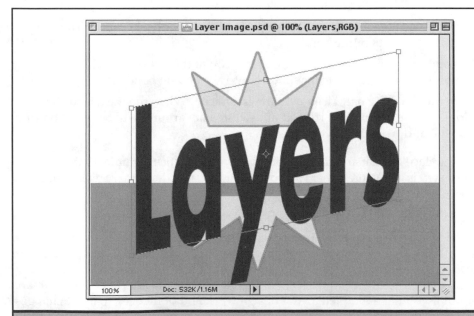

Figure 16-6.   *The Perspective transformation applied to the text layer*

- You can duplicate a layer while transforming it with the Free Transform command by pressing COMMAND-OPTION-T (*CTRL-ALT-T*). If you wish to duplicate while using one of the other Transform commands, press OPTION (*ALT*) while selecting the command.

- You can repeat a transformation with a layer other than the one you originally transformed by choosing Edit > Transform > Again.

- You can change the center point of the transformation by clicking and dragging on the center point icon before beginning the transformation. This is most useful when rotating.

The Transform commands also transform selections, paths, and the mask in Quick Mask mode. See Chapter 15 for details about using Quick Mask mode.

Deleting Layers

To remove a layer from your image, you must first set it to be the target layer. Once you have set the target layer, you can remove the layer by choosing Layer > Delete Layer, choosing Delete Layer from the Layers palette pop-up menu, or dragging a layer to the trash icon (🗑) in the Layers palette.

Here's how to delete the Background layer from your practice file:

1. In the Layers palette, position the mouse pointer over Background. The icon will change to a pointing hand.

2. Click and drag the layer toward the trash icon at the bottom of the Layers palette. As you drag, the icon will turn into a grabbing hand icon.

3. Move the grabbing hand icon over the trash icon. When the trash icon changes colors, release the mouse. The red-and-white background will be removed from your file and from the Layers palette.

Before you place the star and text remaining in your practice document into another file, your next step is to compress them into one layer by using the Merge Layers command.

Merging and Flattening Layers

The Merge Visible command on the Layer menu (also found in the Layers palette menu) compresses all visible layers into one layer. If you have a Background layer, the layers are merged into it. If you don't have a Background layer or if the background isn't visible, the layers are merged into the target layer. Hidden layers are not affected. This command can be helpful if you have completed your design work and don't need to make changes in specific layers. By merging layers, you can also keep your file size low.

You can merge a layer with its underlying layer by choosing Layer > Merge Down. You can also merge all visible layers into a new layer. After you create the layer, press and hold down OPTION (ALT) while you choose Layer > Merge Visible.

Try merging the layers in your practice document by choosing Merge Visible from the Layers palette pop-up menu.

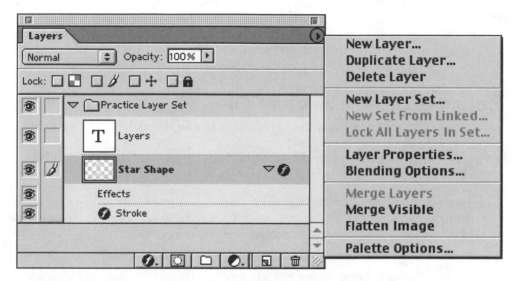

After the layers are merged, the file size is reduced. Notice that transparency of the elements is still intact, even though there is only one layer in the Layers palette.

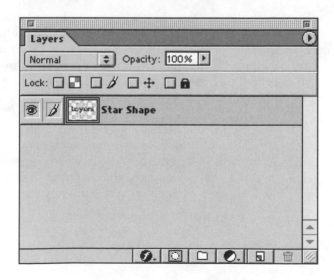

Another command that compresses visible layers and reduces file size is Flatten Layers. It's important to understand the difference between flattening and merging layers. Unlike merging layers, flattening layers removes all hidden layers from the file. The flattened file has no transparent background. This means that it can be saved in a variety of different file formats, not just Photoshop's.

You can use the History Brush to create fade effects between merged layers. After you've merged layers, set the History Brush state in the History palette to the step at which you created the layer that you eventually merged. When you paint with the History Brush, you'll be painting in the pre-merged version. See Chapters 6 and 11 for more information about the History palette and the History Brush.

Duplicating a Layer in Another File

The Duplicate Layer command in the Layer menu and Layers palette pop-up menu copies a layer from one file to another.

Now that you have deleted the Background and merged the Star Shape and text layers in your practice file, you can place the merged layers into another file.

1. Open any file that you wish to use as a new background file. If you don't have an image to use as a background, open a file from this book's CD. After the file is loaded, activate your practice image by clicking on it.

2. Choose Duplicate Layer from the Layers palette pop-up menu.

3. In the Duplicate Layer dialog box, click on the Document pop-up menu and choose the file that you want to place the layer into. Optionally, you can name the layer in the As field. Then click on OK.

The Star Shape layer is duplicated into the background file, and the elements are placed in the center of the background. In your new background file, notice that the elements in the Star Shape layer from your practice file retain their names and transparency. If your background file is smaller than the elements in the duplicated layer, Photoshop will not clip the elements in the layer. This means that the portion of the layer that is not visible still exists.

You can copy a layer from one file to another by dragging the layer name from the Layers palette into an open file's document window. In addition, you can drag individual or linked layers from one file into another. However, if you copy linked layers from one document to another, drag and drop the layer from the document window with the Move tool, not from the Layers palette. If you drag from the Layers palette, only one layer will be copied.

Preserving Layers When Saving a File

If you wish to save your file with all its layers, select File > Save As to save the file in Photoshop format. If your document already has a name, enter a new name for your file so that you don't replace the original version. When an image is flattened using File > Save As, only the visible layers appear in the flattened file.

If you wish to flatten layers when you save your image, choose File > Save As and deselect the Layers option in the Save As dialog box. If desired, you can then click on the Format pop-up menu and choose a file format other than Photoshop's native file format. (More information about using different file formats is included in Appendix A.)

Using Layers to Create Special Effects

Now that you have learned the fundamentals of using layers, you're probably eager to use them to create special effects. In the following sections, you'll learn how to use layers to create drop shadows, place images into text, and blend images.

Creating Drop Shadows in Layers

Creating a drop shadow in a layer gives you complete control over where the shadow appears and how much of a three-dimensional effect you create. In the exercise in this section, you will create a drop shadow by duplicating a layer and then applying the Gaussian Blur filter to the duplicate layer. The blurred layer will create the shadow effect. Figure 16-7 shows the image you will create by applying a drop shadow to a digitized maple leaf over a background of clouds.

Before you begin producing the drop shadow, you will use the Clouds filter to create a background for your final image. If you prefer, you can skip steps 1 through 3 by loading a digitized background image.

1. Create a new 5-by-5-inch RGB color file. Set Contents to White. If the Layers palette is not already on your screen, open it by choosing Window > Show Layers.

2. Set the foreground color to light blue and the background color to white. These are the colors that the Clouds filter will use.

3. Apply the Clouds filter by choosing Filter > Render > Clouds. Your file now looks like soft clouds against a blue sky.

Figure 16-7.   *Leaf image with a drop shadow created from layers*

Tip   *To add to the clouds effect, keep reapplying the filter by pressing* COMMAND-F *(CTRL-F). To diminish the clouds effect, keep pressing* SHIFT-COMMAND-F *(SHIFT-CTRL-F) to fade out the filter gradually.*

4. Open the leaf image from the Chapter 16 folder on this book's CD-ROM. (If you prefer, you can use another image silhouetted in a layer with a transparent background). The image should be smaller than the background file on your screen and have the same resolution.

Tip   *Before creating a drop shadow, you may wish to silhouette the image using the Pen tool, the Color Range command, and/or the selection tools. By using a silhouetted image as the image to which you apply the drop shadow, you will make the shadow look more realistic.*

5. Use the Move tool to click and drag the leaf file into your background image. As you drag the image out of the original file, the pointer changes to a tiny grabbing hand. When the grabbing hand icon enters your file with the background image, a black frame will surround the file. After you see the black frame, you can release the mouse. This will create a new layer over the background, with the leaf in the new layer. Notice that the Layers palette now shows the Background and Layer 1 layers. The target layer is the layer you just created. Use the Move tool to position the image in the center of the file.

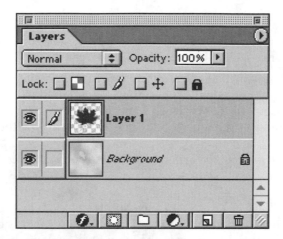

6. To duplicate the layer for the drop shadow, position the mouse pointer over Layer 1. The mouse pointer will change to a pointing hand. Click and drag the layer toward the New Layer icon at the bottom of the Layers palette. As you drag, the pointer changes to a tiny, grabbing hand. Drag the grabbing hand icon over the New Layer icon. When the New Layer icon changes colors, release the mouse. A copy of the leaf layer is automatically created.

7. To change the name of the layer, choose Layer > Layer Properties. This opens the Layer Options dialog box. Type **Drop Shadow** in the Name field and click on OK. At this point, you should be viewing all of the layers (all eye icons are displayed in the Layers palette) and your target layer should be the Drop Shadow layer (this is the layer that is selected in the Layers palette and whose name appears in the title bar of the current document).

Remember

Although you can view multiple layers at once, you can edit only one layer at a time.

8. With the Drop Shadow layer as the target layer, use the Move tool to move the image in this layer so that it is slightly offset from the image in Layer 1. Offset it in any direction.

9. After you've moved the image in the Drop Shadow layer, your next step is to darken it to create the shadow effect. It will be easier to do this if the drop shadow layer is the only layer visible on screen. To hide the other layers, click on the eye icons for both Layer 1 and the Background layer. The remaining eye icon next to the Drop Shadow layer indicates that you are viewing only this layer.

10. Set the foreground color to the color you want the drop shadow to be. Choose either a very dark green or black, depending on the desired effect. Choose Edit > Fill. In the Fill dialog box, set the Use pop-up menu to Foreground Color, set the Mode pop-up menu to Normal, and set Opacity to between 80 and 100%,

depending on the desired effect. Make sure the Preserve Transparency option is selected so that the Fill command fills only the image on screen, not the transparent area. Then click on OK to fill the leaf.

11. To create the soft drop shadow effect, apply the Gaussian Blur filter to the Drop Shadow layer by choosing Filter > Blur > Gaussian Blur. In the Gaussian Blur dialog box, use a number between 3 and 10 in the Radius field. The higher the number, the greater the blur effect. Click on OK to apply the filter.

Remember   *If the Lock Transparency icon is selected in the Layers palette, the Gaussian Blur will have no effect.*

12. To view the image in Layer 1 and see the effects, click on the eye icon next to Layer 1. Notice that the image in the Drop Shadow layer is on top of the image in Layer 1. To place the image in the Drop Shadow layer below the image in Layer 1, click on Drop Shadow in the Layers palette and drag it over Layer 1.

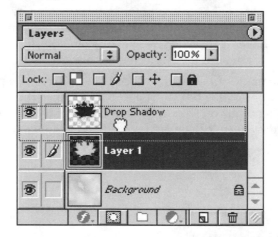

13. If you would like to move the shadow, make sure that the Drop Shadow layer is your target layer. Then use the Move tool to move the shadow. When you are satisfied with the position of the shadow, click on the eye icon column for the Background in the Layers palette to see the entire image.

14. At this point, if you wish to reposition the image and the drop shadow together, you will need to link the layers so that you can move them as a single unit. To link the layers, with Drop Shadow as the target layer, move the mouse into the blank area to the right of the eye icons and to the left of Layer 1 in the Layers palette and click. The chain (link) icon appears next to the Drop Shadow layer to indicate that the two layers are linked. With the Move tool activated, you can now

move both the top layer and the Drop Shadow layer together. When you're finished, unlink the layers by clicking on the link icon in the Layers palette.

15. Choose File > Save and save your file as **Shadow** in the Photoshop file format to retain its layers.

16. Create a duplicate of this file with its layer (to use in the next exercise) by choosing File > Save As. Name this version **Shadow2** and make sure the format is set to Photoshop.

 Chapter 18 provides further details about creating drop shadows with Photoshop's Layer Style commands.

Duplicating an Image with Its Drop Shadow

After you've completed all the steps in the previous exercise, you may want to create yet another image with a drop shadow. The easiest way to do this is to merge the leaf and its shadow together and then duplicate the merged layer.

1. To hide the Background layer, click on its eye icon in the Layers palette.

2. To merge the image and its shadow, choose Merge Visible or Merge Linked from the Layers palette pop-up menu. In the Layers palette, notice that the two layers (Layer 1 and Drop Shadow) are merged into the target layer.

3. After the layers have been merged, click the Background eye icon column to make it visible again.

4. To duplicate the merged layers, click on Drop Shadow in the Layers palette and drag it over the New Layer icon. A new layer named Drop Shadow copy appears in the Layers palette and becomes the target layer. The Drop Shadow layer with the original leaf image and drop shadow is directly below the Drop Shadow copy layer (the new layer that was just created).

5. To see the two images with their drop shadows, use the Move tool to drag the image and its shadow in the Drop Shadow copy layer in any direction. As you drag, you'll see the original leaf image in the Drop Shadow layer.

6. You may also want to move the original leaf image in the Drop Shadow layer. To do so, set the Drop Shadow layer to the target layer and then move the original leaf image with the Move tool.

At this point, feel free to embellish the image. You may want to use some of the Image menu commands to scale, rotate, lighten, or color it. Figure 16-8 shows two leaves with scaled and rotated drop shadows.

After you've saved your work, close your file. Then proceed to the next section to learn how the Layers palette can help you blend images together.

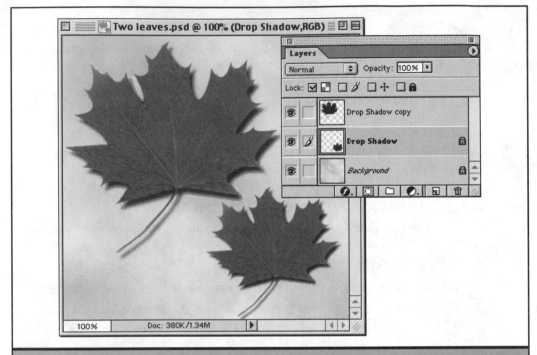

Figure 16-8.   *The leaf image after the Drop Shadow layer was copied, scaled, and rotated*

Using the Layers Palette to Blend Multiple Images

Earlier in the chapter, you saw how Dissolve mode can be used to create an unusual speckled blend between layers. By trying out the modes with images, rather than with the simple shapes you used earlier, you will gain a better understanding of the power of the Layers palette's Mode pop-up menu.

Open two files with images that you want to blend and place them side by side or so that they overlap. For this exercise, you can use the sky file and the bottles file in the Adobe Samples folder. If you overlap the images, put the image you wish to use as the overlying (target) layer (the bottles file) over the image you want for your background (underlying) layer (the sky file). Next, activate the Move tool and drag the file you want to place in the target layer over the background, underlying layer. Photoshop creates a new layer.

 If you drag an image into another file, Photoshop will not clip any image areas that extend beyond the work canvas. However, if you choose Select > All, only the area within the canvas border is selected. (Changing the canvas size is discussed in Chapter 8.)

As discussed earlier in this chapter, the modes in the Layers palette work much the same way as when a painting tool is activated. (To review the blending modes, see Chapter 5.) The difference is that Photoshop applies the blending modes based on the pixels in the target layer and the underlying layer, rather than the foreground color and the color you are painting over.

Now try switching from one mode to another. Here's a brief review of how some of the more powerful modes in the Layers palette work:

- To create a composite where darker pixels in the target layer replace corresponding lighter pixels in the underlying layer and darker areas from the underlying layer replace lighter pixels in the target layer, choose Darken.

- To create a composite where lighter pixels in the target layer replace corresponding darker pixels in the underlying layer and lighter pixels from the underlying layer replace darker pixels in the target layer, choose Lighten.

- To blend the Hue and Saturation values of the target with the underlying layer, choose Color. The Luminosity value of the underlying image will not be affected, thus preserving the underlying layer's brightness levels.

Note   *To prove to yourself that the brightness values of the image don't change when Color mode is chosen, select Image > Histogram. You can then view the histogram of your underlying layer with the target layer hidden. View the histogram again (in Color mode) with both layers visible. You'll see that the histogram doesn't change.*

- To create a darker composite from the pixel values of both the target and underlying layers, choose Multiply. This can produce a result similar to overlaying colored magic markers.

- To create a lighter composite from both the pixel values of the target and underlying layers, choose Screen. This often creates the effect of bleaching out colors from an image.

- To create a random effect from the pixels in both the target and underlying layers, choose Dissolve and use the Opacity slider to adjust the results. As you lower the opacity, the top layer gradually dissolves, revealing more of the underlying layer.

- To create a blend using the texture of your target layer, choose Luminosity. Photoshop creates a blend with the brightness values of the target layer and the hue and saturation of the underlying layer.

- To subtract the color values of one layer from another layer, choose Difference. Difference can darken an image and change a color to its complement in areas underlying or overlying white regions in another layer.

APPLYING EFFECTS
TO YOUR IMAGES

■ To lighten or screen where light areas overlap and darken where dark areas overlap, and still preserve the highlights and shadows of the underlying layer, choose Overlay.

Figure 16-9 shows two images used for a blended composite: a backyard scene that was placed in a layer over a waterfall background image.

After the new layer for the backyard scene was created, we selected the Darken blending mode in the Layers palette. When we applied Darken mode, Photoshop compared the pixel values in the target layer to the pixel values in the underlying layer. It then replaced lighter pixels with corresponding darker pixels. Thus, the lighter areas of the waterfall in Figure 16-8 were replaced by the darker trees and fence from the backyard scene. To make more of the underlying image visible, we lowered the Opacity setting in the Layers palette to 50%. The resulting composite is shown in Figure 16-10.

Figure 16-9.   *The underlying layer (left) and the target layer (right) before being blended together*

Figure 16-10.   *The final picture, enhanced by the darken blending mode and a lower Opacity setting*

The Complete Reference

Chapter 17

Advanced Layer Techniques

Throughout this book, you've seen how layers provide almost limitless power to edit and blend images together. This chapter further illustrates the versatility of layers.

As you work through this chapter, you'll explore how to use Photoshop 6's new *shape* layers, which allow you to create vector-based shapes in layers. You'll also learn how to blend together images from different layers pixel by pixel.

Another topic covered in this chapter is how to create a *layer mask*. With a layer mask, you can paint in a mask to hide a portion of one layer as you reveal portions of the layer or layers beneath it. Layer masks, combined with layer blending modes, present you with even more ways to blend images together.

Later in the chapter, you'll learn how Photoshop's adjustment layers can provide you with the power to edit and correct images with layers. After creating an adjustment layer, you can even fine-tune the adjustment layer effect with the stroke of a Photoshop brush.

Working with Shape Layers

Photoshop 6 and ImageReady 3 allow you to create shapes that appear on your screen as separate objects in layers. Unlike painted image areas, shape objects (often referred to as *vector objects*) can be freely moved, resized, and recolored. Using Photoshop's layer style options, you can stroke, fill, bevel, and add drop shadows to shapes. You can even use a shape as a mask that hides or reveals areas of underlying layers.

Photoshop allows you to edit shapes with its Direct Selection tool and other path editing tools. You can create more than one shape in a layer and control how intersecting shapes are created. Photoshop also allows you to create shapes with its pen tools, as well as with its shape tools.

Note *In general, Photoshop is a more powerful shape creator than ImageReady. ImageReady only allows you to edit shapes using Edit > Transform commands. ImageReady does not provide a Pen tool, a Polygon tool, or a Custom Shape tool, which are available in Photoshop.*

When it comes time to output your file, shapes can be printed as high-quality images on PostScript printers. The quality of the printed shape is based on the output resolution of the printer, not Photoshop's file resolution. Since shapes use vector data (a mathematical description of the shape), shape edges are sharp and shape curves are smooth. Shapes can also be imported into programs such as Adobe Illustrator and Macromedia Freehand.

Using the Shape Tools

Photoshop's shape tools allow you to create a variety of preset shapes in layers. Select a shape tool from the Toolbox (the Rectangle tool appears in the Toolbox location by default).

When a shape tool is selected, you can change the shape's drawing options by opening its pop-up menu in the Options bar. The Options bar allows you to create shapes as vector objects in layers, as paths, or as filled painted areas on screen.

This chapter focuses on creating vector shapes in layers. When you're creating vector shapes, the Create New Shape Layer icon (▣) should be selected in the Shape's Options bar. For complete instructions for creating shapes and overlapping shapes, see the "Creating Shapes" section later in this chapter.

To open the pop-up menu for any shape, click on the shape in the Options bar and then click on the pop-up menu arrow. When creating a shape, click and drag on screen. When you're finished, click on the OK (☑) button in the Options bar.

*When choosing weight (line width) and radius options for shapes, the default measurement unit is pixels. Some entry fields use inches. If you wish to change default measurement units, enter the number and then enter **px** for pixels, **in** for inches, or **cm** for centimeters.*

The Rectangle, Rounded Rectangle, and Ellipse Tools

The Rectangle, Rounded Rectangle, and Ellipse tools create the shapes implied by their names. Their pop-up menus offer similar options.

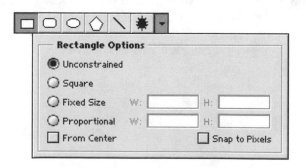

To create a rectangle, oval, or rounded rectangle freely, choose the Unconstrained option. If you choose Proportional, enter a ratio in the adjacent width (W) and height (H) fields. For instance, when creating a rectangle, entering 1 for both the width and height creates a square; entering 1 for the width and 2 for the height creates a rectangle twice as high as it is long. If you choose Fixed Size, you can specify the size of the shape you wish to create. For instance, when creating a rectangle, entering 1 in for Width and 1 in for Height creates a rectangle that's 1-by-1 inch.

When you choose the Rounded Rectangle tool, the Options bar displays a Radius field, which allows you to control how round the rounded rectangle will be. Higher Radius values create rounder rectangles.

The Line Tool

The Line tool creates lines with or without arrowheads. You can constrain the Line tool to creating straight lines or lines at 45-degree angles by pressing SHIFT as you click and drag.

The Line tool's pop-up menu has options for controlling line thickness, as well as arrowhead size and concavity (curvature). The line thickness is based on the setting in the Weight field in the Line tool's Options bar.

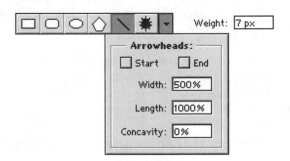

For example, the illustration shown next was created with the Line tool. In the Line tool's pop-up menu, Start and End were selected for Arrowheads, the Width was set to 500%, Length was set to 1000%, and Concavity was set to 25%. In this case, 500% indicates that arrowhead width is five times greater than the line's width, and the arrowhead length is twice as long as the arrowhead width.

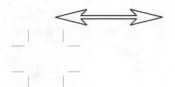

The Polygon Tool

The Polygon tool creates shapes with multiple sides. The Sides field in the Polygon tool's Options bar allows you to specify the number of sides for the polygon.

The Polygon tool's pop-up menu includes options for the radius, as well as for smooth corners, indented sides, and smooth indents. You can enter a value in the Radius field to set the size of the polygon; the larger the radius, the larger the polygon. If you don't set a radius, you can control the size of the polygon with the mouse. If you choose to create a polygon with smooth corners and smooth indents, the polygon is created with curves, rather than with sharp edges.

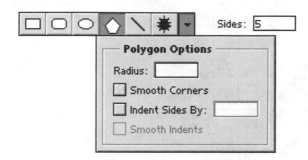

For example, the shape shown next was created with the Polygon tool, with Sides set to 20. In the tool's pop-up menu, Smooth Corners and Smooth Indents were selected, and Indents Sides By was set to 25%.

The Custom Shape Tool

The Custom Shape tool creates preset shapes—anything from simple arrows to bare feet. Select the Custom Shape tool in the Toolbox or in the Options bar, and then choose a shape from the Shape pop-up menu (Figure 17-1). The Shape pop-up menu also features its own submenu, which allows you to load and save shapes on disks.

Here, you see the Shape pop-up menu choices after loading the custom shapes file from the disk (in the Custom Shapes folder in the Presets folder), as well as the custom shape we created for Chapter 3.

To customize the shape further, you can set the options in the Custom Shape tool's Options pop-up menu.

APPLYING EFFECTS
TO YOUR IMAGES

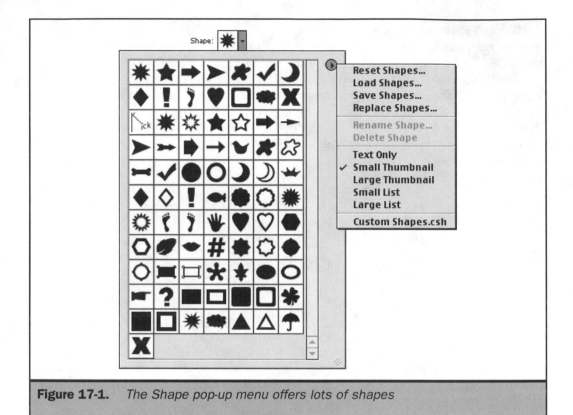

Figure 17-1. *The Shape pop-up menu offers lots of shapes*

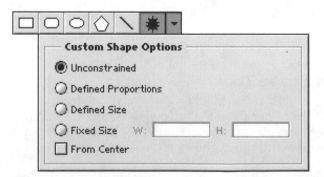

Overlapping Shapes

When you create one shape over another, you can have Photoshop create a new shape out of the overlapping shape or cut a transparent hole in the overlapping areas. The resulting shape is based on which overlapping shape icon is selected in the shape tool's Option bar. Each overlapping shape icon provides a visual representation of the result of adding the shapes together. To create overlapping shapes, simply click on the appropriate icon before creating another shape in a shape layer. (Remember to click on the OK (checkmark) icon when you've finished creating your shapes.)

Add to Shape

Subtract from Shape

Intersect Shape Area

Exclude Overlapping Areas

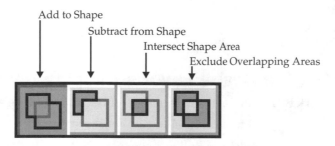

The following illustration shows the results of overlapping a custom shape with a shape created with the Line tool. Before adding the line, the Subtract from Shape icon was selected.

Creating Shapes

To create a shape in Photoshop, you can use a shape tool or a pen tool. As explained in the previous section, the shape tools provide predefined geometric shapes such as polygons, lines, and rectangles. If you wish to create a shape by tracing over an image, or you want to draw a shape with intricate curves, use the Pen or Freeform Pen tool. When you create a shape with a shape tool or pen tool, Photoshop automatically places the shape into a new shape layer.

Shapes are automatically filled using the current foreground color. Before you create a shape, set the foreground color.

If you wish to create a freeform shape using a pen tool, select the Pen or Freeform Pen tool. Next, click on the Create New Work Path icon in the tool's Options bar (⊟). Using the Pen tool, click on the screen, move the mouse, and click and drag again to create the shape. With the Freeform Pen tool, click and drag on screen to draw the shape. (See Chapter 14 for an in-depth discussion of using the pen tools.)

To create a shape in a layer with a shape tool, select the tool you want to use in the Toolbox. In the shape tool's Options bar, select the Create New Shape Layer icon. Change options in the tool's Options bar if desired. Then click and drag on the screen to create the shape.

APPLYING EFFECTS TO YOUR IMAGES

To add more shapes to the existing shape layer (Photoshop only), click and drag on your screen to create more shapes. (You can switch shape tools before adding shapes to a shape layer.) If you are creating overlapping shapes, choose an overlapping shape option in the shape tool's Options bar.

At this point, you can also change attributes of the shape's clipping path or the shape's fill layer, as described in the next section. When you are finished creating the shape, click on the checkmark icon in the Options bar.

Working with a Shape Layer's Clipping Path and Fill Layer

As you work with shapes, it's important to understand that the shape layer is composed of two parts:

- The geometric shape, called a *clipping path*
- The layer itself, called a *fill layer*

In the Layers palette, the clipping path and the fill layer are represented by two distinct icons, as shown in Figure 17-2. The clipping path appears in the right side of the Layers palette. The fill layer is represented by the rectangular icon to the left of the clipping path.

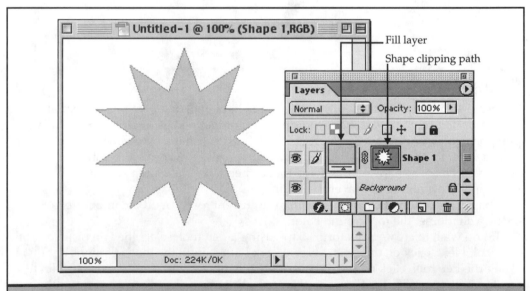

Figure 17-2.   *The Layers palette with a shape's fill layer and clipping path*

Note *The link icon in the Layers palette indicates that the shape and its background fill layer are locked together. You can unlink the two areas by clicking on the link icon. This is handy when the fill layer is a digitized image masked out by the shape, rather than a solid color or gradient.*

If you double-click on the fill layer icon in the Layers palette (instead of the clipping path icon), Photoshop opens the Color Picker, where you can change the fill color for the layer. To change the opacity of the fill layer, click and drag the Opacity slider in the Layers palette.

Double-clicking on the clipping path icon in the Layer palette opens the Layer Style dialog box, where you can change the opacity of the fill within the shape (not the shape layer). Using the Layer Style dialog box, you can also apply layer blending effects or add a stroke, bevel or drop shadow to the clipping path (the shape).

Note *If you drag the fill layer icon into the trash, the entire shape layer is deleted. However, if you drag the clipping path icon into the path, only the geometric shape residing in the layer is deleted. After the clipping path is deleted, the layer appears as a solid color on your screen.*

Editing a Shape's Clipping Path
Once you've created a shape, you can edit its clipping path as follows:

- Use the Edit > Transform commands, as described in Chapters 8 and 16.

- Freely transform the shape by clicking and dragging on the shape with the Move tool.

- Change the shape's path by clicking and dragging on any anchor point with the Direct Selection tool (described in Chapter 14).

- To further edit the path, use the Add Anchor Point, Delete Anchor Point, or Convert Point tool (also described in Chapter 14).

Filling Shapes with Colors, Gradients, and Patterns
If you wish to change the fill attributes of a shape layer, you can use the Layer > Change Layer Content commands, as follows:

- To change the color of a shape layer, choose Layer > Change Layer Content > Solid Color and select a color in the Color Picker. (You can also change the color of a shape by choosing Layer > Layer Style > Color Overlay. In the Layer Style dialog box, click on the small color swatch and choose a color in the Color Picker.)

APPLYING EFFECTS
TO YOUR IMAGES

- To make a gradient with a shape layer, select Layer > Change Layer Content > Gradient. In the Gradient Fill dialog box, click on the Gradient pop-up menu and choose a gradient.

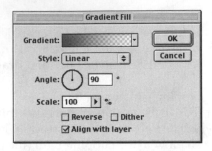

- To apply a pattern to a with a shape layer, choose Layer > Change Layer Content > Pattern Fill and choose a pattern from the Pattern Fill dialog box.

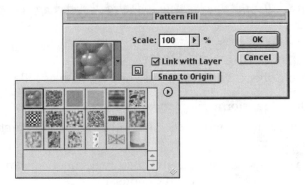

- To stroke, add a bevel, or change the fill opacity of the shape, choose Layer > Layer Style > Blending Options (or double-click on the clipping path icon in the Layers palette) to open the Layer Style dialog box. To change the opacity of the interior of the shape, click and drag on the Fill Opacity slider. To add a drop shadow, stroke, or other effect, select the appropriate style in the dialog box.

  The Blending Options section of the Layer Style dialog box is discussed in more detail in the "Blending Images" section in this chapter.

Creating a Mask from a Shape Layer

One of the most intriguing uses of shapes is as mask for digital images. Figure 17-3 shows a Photoshop custom shape of a bare foot used to mask out the background digitized image.

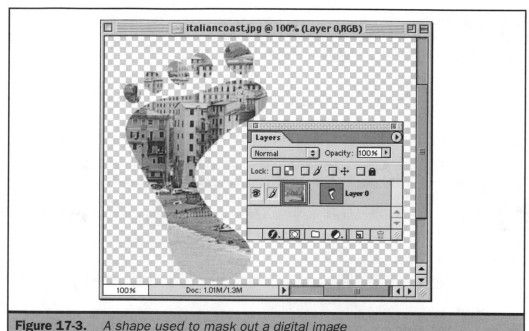

Figure 17-3.   *A shape used to mask out a digital image*

Here are the steps for creating this effect:

1. Load an image to be used as the background image. You can also use the Venice image, which you can find in the Chapter 17 folder of this book's CD-ROM.

2. To create the masking effect, the background image must be in a layer. If the image does not have a layer, choose Layer > New > Layer from Background (or double-click on Background in the Layers palette). In the New layer dialog box, enter a name for you layer or leave it named Layer 0.

3. Select a shape tool or the Pen tool (with the Create New Shape option selected in the Pen tool's Options bar). Select the Add to Shape icon in the Options bar. (If the Add to Shape icon—the default setting—was not previously selected in the Options bar, the shape will cut a hole in the image, instead of appearing in the shape.). In this example, we selected the Custom Shape tool and choose the barefoot shape from the Shapes pop-up menu—but don't create the shape yet.

4. To mask out the image and show it through the shape that you will create, choose Layer > Add Clipping Path > Reveal All.

If you wish your shape to cut a transparent hole out of the background image, choose Layer > Clipping Path > Hide All or select the Exclude Overlapping Areas icon in the Options bar and choose Layer > Clipping Path > Reveal All.

5. Click and drag with the shape tool or the Pen tool to create a shape in a new shape layer. In the Layers palette, notice that the shape and the image are in the same layer.

6. To complete the shape, click on the checkmark icon in the tool's Options bar.

The image on your screen will be masked by the shape. At this point, you can stroke or apply other effects to the shape layer by choosing Layer > Layer Style > Blending Options.

 To learn how to create similar masking with layers, see the "Masking Images Using Clipping Groups" section later in this chapter.

If you wish to move the shape independently of the image, click on the link icon to separate the image and its clipping path. Then click and drag the image on the screen.

Blending Images

The Blending Options section of the Layer Style dialog box, shown in Figure 17-4, includes options for controlling how your images are blended together. To open this dialog box, click on a layer name in the Layers palette and choose Layer > Layer Style > Blending Options. Alternatively, you can click on the *f* icon in the Layers palette and choose Blending Options.

The Layer Style dialog box will show a preview of the effects you are setting if the Preview checkbox is selected.

Blending with the Layer Blending Sliders

Photoshop's layer blending sliders, in the Advanced Blending section of the Layer Style dialog box, allow you to control exactly which elements from a target layer and underlying layers will appear in a composite image. The sliders (called *composite controls* in early versions of Photoshop) are shown next.

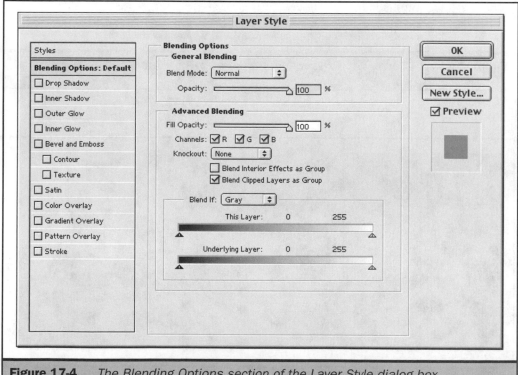

For example, the layer blending sliders were used to create the composite shown in Figure 17-5. Figure 17-6 shows the contents of each of the layers used in the composite: a textured background (created by applying the Zigzag and Add Noise filters to a linear gradient) and an image of a boat. Adjusting the sliders allowed the lightest pixels from the boat layer to be eliminated so that the textured background could show through.

Figure 17-4.   *The Blending Options section of the Layer Style dialog box*

Figure 17-5. *A composite image created with the layer blending sliders*

Figure 17-6. *The layers used in the composite*

To experiment with the sliders, you'll need images in layers that you want to blend. If you wish to try creating the composite shown in Figure 17-5, you can use the following steps to re-create the created the textured image for the underlying layer (the background, on the left in Figure 17-6) and create a layer with the image to blend with the underlying layer (the boat, on the right in Figure 17-6).

1. Select File > New and create a 3.5-by-4-inch file. Set Contents to White.

2. Choose a dark foreground and a light background color to be the starting and ending colors for the linear blend.

3. To transform the image into a rippled pond, apply the Zigzag filter (Filter > Distort > Zigzag). Choose the Pond Ripple radio button and set Amount to 87 and Ridges to 20.

4. Apply the Add Noise (Filter > Noise > Add Noise). Set Distribution to Uniform and Amount to 20. Click on the Monochromatic option to prevent more colors from being added. (Apply the filter two or three times if you want to add more speckling.)

5. Open a file that you wish to blend with the textured background. If you wish to re-create the image, open the Sailboat image from the Chapter 17 folder of this book's CD-ROM.

6. Select the entire file, or select an area of it that you wish to paste into the background file.

7. Choose Edit > Copy, and then close the file.

8. Activate the textured background image. Choose Edit > Paste. Open the Layers palette if it is not already open. Note that the new layer you've created is the target layer—the layer that is selected in the Layers palette.

9. Choose Layer Options from the Layers palette's pop-up menu or double-click on the top layer to open the Layer Style dialog box.

Now that you have two layers set up for blending, you can see the layer blending sliders at work.

Controlling the Blend

The Layer blending sliders allow you to control how the pixels in an overlying layer and an underlying layer blend together. You can pick which pixels in the underlying layers will be replaced by the pixels in the target layer.

The slider labeled This Layer controls exactly which pixels to include in and exclude from the target layer. The slider labeled Underlying Layer controls the pixels for the layer beneath the target layer. For both sliders, the black slider control affects dark areas and the white slider control affects light areas. The range of both sliders is from 0 (black) to 255 (white).

When you drag This Layer's black slider control to the right, darker pixels of the target layer are not included in the composite image. When you drag This Layer's white slider control to the left, lighter pixels of the target layer are not included in the composite image. All pixel values designated in the range between the target layer's slider controls appear in the composite image.

Remember *Before you begin adjusting the sliders, make sure the Preview checkbox is selected in the Layer Style dialog box so that you can preview the results.*

To see how the sliders work, try dragging This Layer's black slider control to the right. This will remove the darker pixels from your target layer. Drag the white slider control to the left, and you remove the lighter pixels in the target layer from the composite. The results will be more obvious if you drag the black slider control back to 0 before moving the white slider control.

Before you begin experimenting with the Underlying Layer slider, reset the This Layer slider to its original settings. This will make it easier for you to see the effect of adjusting the Underlying Layer slider controls. To quickly reset all options, press OPTION (*ALT*) to change the Cancel button to a Reset button and then click on Reset to reset the settings and remain in the dialog box.

Try clicking and dragging the Underlying Layer's black slider control to the right. As you drag, you add dark pixels from the underlying layer and remove any pixels from the target layer that would have appeared over this area. Move the black slider control back to 0 and move the white slider control to the left. Notice that as you drag, you are adding light pixels from the underlying layer to the composite and removing pixels that from the target layer.

Splitting the Slider Controls

To create a smoother composite effect, you can split each individual slider control into two parts. To split a slider control, press OPTION (*ALT*), and then click and drag on one of the edges of the control. For each slider control that is split, you will see two values showing the range between the split controls. The pixels in the range defined by the split slider control will be only partially colored. This can help smooth the blend between the target layer and underlying pixels.

Applying Other Layer Blending Options

The remaining options in the Blending Options section of the Layer Style dialog box provide you with more controls for refining a composite image.

The Blend If pop-up menu above the layer blending sliders allows you to control the blend based on the color values of individual color channels. When viewing an RGB image, the Gray option in the Blend If pop-up menu indicates that the sliders affect the luminance or brightness values of the pixels in all channels. In an RGB color image, Blend If lets you work separately in the red, green, or blue channel of the image.

Thus, if Red were chosen in the Blend If pop-up menu, you could control the range of red values (from 0 to 255) for both the target and underlying layers.

You'll also find the familiar Blend Mode pop-up menu and Opacity slider in the Blending Options section of the Layer Style dialog box. By entering an Opacity value of less than 100%, you can make your target layer more translucent. The Blend Mode pop-up menu offers the same modes that are available in the Layers palette. These modes work almost exactly as they do when you use the Layers palette to blend layers together (as described in the preceding chapter), but with one major difference: the effect applies only to the pixel values specified by the layer blending sliders.

Experiment with the modes and opacities in the Layer Style dialog box until you achieve the effects you desire. Once you are satisfied with the preview of your image, click on OK to apply the changes.

Now that you've explored the Layer Style dialog box's powerful blending options, you probably feel that you've exhausted all of Photoshop's blending features. However, there are still more powerful Layers palette options to investigate that allow you to create effects that seamlessly blend images together. Save your file if you wish. Then close it and proceed to the next section to learn about how one image in a layer can mask out another image in another layer.

You can use context-sensitive menus to activate a layer. With the Move tool selected, press CTRL *and click in an image (Windows users should right-click). If the Move tool is not selected, press* COMMAND-CTRL *and click (Windows users should press* CTRL *and right-click).*

Masking Images Using Clipping Groups

When you are working with layers in either Photoshop or ImageReady, you can create a special layer group in which the bottom layer controls the shape, transparency, and mode of the other images in the layers above it. This type of layer group is called a *clipping group*.

In the next examples, you'll see how clipping groups can be used to place one image into the shape of another image. One image is used as the shape; the other is the background image that is placed into the shape. The image that is used for the shape creates a mask. This technique is often used to place textures or other images into text.

Creating a Clipping Group

In the example in this section, you will place an image into a shape, as shown in Figure 17-7. To achieve the effect, you will need two images: One image will be used for the shape of the final image, and the other will be placed into the shape. In the figure, a sailboat was used as the image that was placed into the leaf shape.

Figure 17-7. *A clipping group was used to make the sailboat from one layer appear within the leaf image in another layer*

To create the silhouetted leaf shown in Figure 17-7, we used the Pen tool to outline a digitized leaf and added the drop shadow (using the techniques described in Chapter 16). When both images were placed in a clipping group, the leaf masked the sailboat image, making it appear as if the sailboat were in the leaf.

Try out the following steps to create the same effect with two images. If you wish to re-create the example shown in Figure 17-7, use the Sailboat and Leaf image files from the Chapter 17 folder on this book's CD-ROM.

1. Open the image that you wish to place into the shape. If you wish to have the leaf image clip the boat image, load the Boat file from the CD-ROM. Open the Layers palette if it isn't already open.

2. Load the Leaf file from the CD-ROM (or create the image you want to use as the shape). If you use the Leaf file from the Chapter 17 folder, click in the white area of the file with the Magic Eraser tool to create a transparent background.

Tip *If you wish, you can also use a shape layer as the layer that clips an image.*

3. Place the two images side by side or so that the shape image (the silhouetted image) overlaps the destination image. Activate the Move tool and then click and drag the shape image into the destination file. The pointer will change to a grabbing hand. Position the hand in the middle of the destination image, and

then release the mouse. A new layer will be created in the destination image, with the shape image in a layer.

4. Rename the layer by double-clicking on the name of the new layer in the Layers palette. Name the layer **My Shape**.

5. If you wish, use the Edit > Transform Path> Scale or Edit > Free Transform Path command to enlarge the image in the shape layer. This will make more of the image show in the shape.

6. Before you can use a clipping group to place an image into the shape on screen, you must place the My Shape layer underneath the bottom layer in the Layers palette. (Unfortunately, Photoshop won't let you do this if your base layer is named Background. So, first rename the Background layer by double-clicking on it and then clicking on OK in the Make Layer dialog box. It becomes Layer 0.)

7. Move the My Shape layer below Layer 0 (or below the bottom layer in your Layers palette).

Note *When you load a Photoshop file into ImageReady, it converts Photoshop's Background into a normal layer.*

8. Move the mouse pointer to the dividing line in the Layers palette that separates My Shape and Layer 0. Press and hold down OPTION (*ALT*). When the mouse pointer changes to the grouping icon (⁺◉) click the mouse button to create a clipping group.

After you click, the image on your screen changes so that the layer above the shape is seen within the shape. Notice the L-shaped arrow in the Layers palette in the top layer. This indicates that its appearance is being controlled by the previous layer. Notice also that the layer being clipped is indented in the Layers palette.

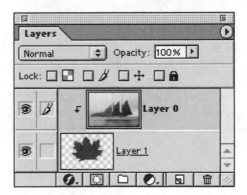

APPLYING EFFECTS
TO YOUR IMAGES

Tip
To create a clipping group, you can also choose Group with Previous from the Layer menu or press COMMAND-G (CTRL-G). To ungroup, press COMMAND-SHIFT-G (CTRL-SHIFT-G). To remove a layer from a clipping group, you can choose Layer > Ungroup or OPTION-click (ALT-click) on the dotted line that divides the clipping group members in the Layers palette.

As you've just seen, creating a clipping group changes the shape of all visible layers above the base layer in the group to the shape of the base layer. In this exercise, you've created a clipping group by OPTION-clicking (*ALT-clicking*) between layers in the Layers palette.

At this point, you can reposition the image in the shape or reposition the shape itself. If you wish, you can move either of the layers independently of the other or link them so that they move together. Here are some of the other changes you might make:

- Use the Edit > Transform Path > Scale command to resize the image that is in the shape.

- If you rescale the image, sharpen it with a sharpening filter, if necessary.

- Lighten or darken the image in the shape with the Image > Adjust > Brightness/Contrast command.

- Experiment with various opacity settings and modes in the Layers palette.

- Apply layer styles by choosing Layer > Layer Style > Blending Options.

When you are satisfied with the image's appearance, you may wish to flatten the layers in the image to conserve memory.

Once you create a clipping group, you can paint, add gradients, and so on to the target layer. As you work, the clipping group is still maintained. Clipping groups are often used with adjustment layers to color-correct silhouetted images. (Adjustment layers are discussed later in this chapter.)

Tip
You can clip more than one layer by OPTION-clicking (ALT-clicking) again on the dividing line between the next layer above the clipping group. You can also create more than one clipping group in the Layers palette.

If you wish to save your layers with your file, use the Photoshop format; otherwise, use the File > Save a Copy command to flatten the layers when you save. After saving your work, close the file and proceed to the next section.

Creating a Knockout

Photoshop 6 allows you to create knockout effects through layers. Essentially, a knockout creates a transparency cutout through layers. The knockout can cut through to the bottom layer, or it can stop at a specific layer. Figure 17-8 shows text knocked out down to the shape layer (a hand shape with a gradient fill).

To create the image in Figure 17-8, we used two clipping groups: one to create a mask for the cloud layer and the other to mask out the text layer. The gradient seen within the text does not come from the text layer. Instead, a knockout was used to cut through the layers down to the shape layer. Thus, the gradient shades seen in the text are produced from the gradient fill in the shape layer.

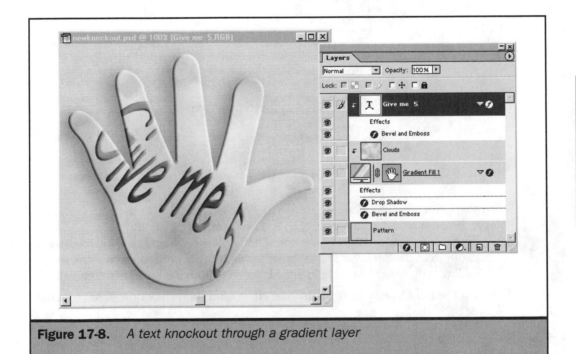

Figure 17-8. *A text knockout through a gradient layer*

To create a knockout effect through layers or clipping groups:

1. Create a shape or text in a layer above another layer.

2. Choose Layer > Layer Style > Blending Options.

3. In the Advanced Blending section of the Layer Style dialog box, drag the Fill Opacity slider to approximately 50% and then choose either Deep or Shallow in the Knockout pop-up menu.

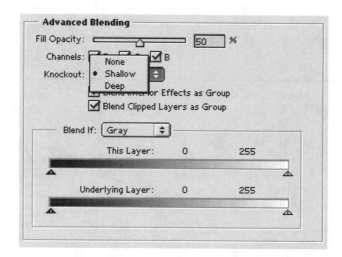

4. In most cases, Deep creates a transparency knockout through to the Background layer. If you have a clipping group, Deep knocks out to the clipping group. Choose Shallow to knock out within a layer set. (The Shallow choice allows you to create a knockout from the top layer in a layer set through to the bottom layer in the set. This allows you to see a layer below the layer set within the knockout area.)

5. Adjust the Fill Opacity to fine-tune the effect, and then click on OK to close the Layer Style dialog box.

Note *If you are creating a knockout through a layer set and wish to see the layer below the layer set, adjust the Fill Opacity slider to 0%.*

Creating a Mask by Pasting into a Selection

Photoshop's Edit > Paste Into command allows you to paste an image into a selection. For example, you can use Paste Into to place an image into text, as shown in the following illustration. When Paste Into is executed, the effect is similar to creating a clipping group. However Paste Into creates a new layer and converts the selection into a layer mask for the pasted image (layer masks are described in next section "Using Layer Masks to Blend Images Together.")

Here are the steps for pasting an image into text:

1. Open the Venice image from the Chapter 17 folder on this book's CD-ROM (or use another image of a city or landscape). If the Layers palette isn't open, open it now.

2. Choose Select > All, and then choose Edit > Copy to copy the image to the Clipboard. Then close the file.

3. Create a new file. When you choose File > New, you'll see that the settings in the New dialog box reflect the dimensions of the image stored in the Clipboard. In the New dialog box, make sure that the radio button in the Contents group is set to Transparent. Click on OK to create the new file.

4. Activate the Type tool and click in the middle of the image. Type **VENICE** (or some other word or phrase).

5. In the Type tool's Options bar, set the style and size for the type. A heavy typeface allows more of the image to appear through each letter. For this example, we used Helvetica Black in a Bold style at 70 points. Click on OK in the Options bar to have Photoshop place the text on screen. If necessary, use the Move tool to reposition the text in the middle of the screen.

6. Use the Edit > Transform > Scale command to enlarge the type to the size of your document. This will allow more of the image to show through the letters. But be careful—if you scale too much, your text may appear fuzzy at the edges.

7. Turn the text into a selection by pressing COMMAND (*CTRL*) and clicking on the text layer in the Layers palette.

8. With the text selection on your screen, choose Edit > Paste Into. Your image now appears in each letter of the text.

As soon as you paste, a new layer appears in the Layers palette. Alongside the layer thumbnail in the palette is another thumbnail, indicating that a layer mask has been created. The layer mask creates a mask out of the text selection so that the image shows through the white area of the mask. If you wish to experiment, click on the layer mask thumbnail and try painting with different shades of gray. Using this technique you can reveal more of the image through the layer or hide different parts of the type. After you have finished, click on the text layer's thumbnail to reactivate the layer.

If you wish to reposition the image in the text, use the Move tool and click and drag your text. If you wish, you can also use the Edit > Transform > Scale command to resize the image that is in the text. If you rescale the image, sharpen it with a sharpening filter, if necessary. Don't click on the layer mask thumbnail in the Layers palette or you'll affect the layer mask and not the layer. If you've already clicked on the layer mask thumbnail, click on the layer thumbnail or layer name to turn editing back on.

If you wish to move the text and image together, click between the layer mask thumbnail and the layer thumbnail. A chain icon will appear. You can then drag the text and image as a group.

You can also click on the bottom layer and either paste in more images or add a gradient.

When you are satisfied with your image's appearance, save it with both layers by saving the file in Photoshop format. Then close the file and proceed to the next section.

Using Layer Masks to Blend Images Together

Photoshop's and ImageReady's Layer Mask options combine the power of layers with the power of masks. Layer masks can be used to create seamless composites between layers. One of the chief advantages to using a layer mask is that it allows you to use a painting tool to edit a mask between two layers. As you gradually paint areas in the mask, you reveal or hide image areas from different layers. This allows images from the underlying layer or layers to appear through the areas you mask in the target layer. The result can be a beautiful mix between layers or an ethereal effect in which images in one layer gradually fade into another.

When using a layer mask, you paint with shades of gray (including black and white). This is exactly like editing an alpha channel, as described in Chapter 15. By using different shades of gray or different opacities of black and white, you can control how transparent the target layer becomes and thus how much of the underlying layer or layers appears through it.

When you create a layer mask, you can make it hide the entire layer or reveal the entire layer. If you have a selection on screen, you can choose to create the mask hiding the selection or revealing the selection.

When you use a layer mask, your image changes according to how you edit the layer mask. It is important to understand, however, that you are not actually editing your layer—you are editing a mask and viewing your layers through the mask. For this reason, working with a layer mask provides you with the ability to undo any previous changes you have made. Once you're satisfied with the on-screen effect of the layer mask, you can decide whether you want to apply the effects to the layer.

If this sounds like an elaborate procedure, don't worry. You'll soon see that using and applying a layer mask can be quite simple. The following sections lead you step by step through the process of creating a layer mask in Photoshop and using the mask to blend one layer into another.

Creating a Layer Mask

Figure 17-9 shows the results of a layer mask used to blend images gradually. The images used in the blend are shown in Figure 17-10.

Figure 17-9.   *Two layers blended together using a layer mask*

Figure 17-10. *The background layer and koala bear used to create the image*

Note *Although you can create and edit layer masks in ImageReady, we use Photoshop in this example because you can view and edit the mask in Photoshop's Channels palette. ImageReady does not have a Channels palette.*

In the next exercise, you'll drag and drop one file into another—which will automatically create a new layer. Then you'll add a layer mask and edit the mask. If you don't have two images that you want to blend together, use the Koala and Sydney files from the Chapter 17 folder on this book's CD-ROM.

Before you begin, make sure that Photoshop's Layers and Channels palettes are both open as separate palettes on screen. If these palettes are in a palette group, separate them by clicking on the Layers or Channels palette's tab and dragging it away from the palette group.

1. Open the Sydney file from this book's CD-ROM (or load another image that you wish to use as your base layer). Then open the Koala file (or the image that you want to apply the layer mask to).

2. Activate the Move tool and drag the koala image over the opera house image. Photoshop creates a new layer for the koala image. (Notice that the Layers palette shows a Background layer and a Layer 1.)

3. Before you create a layer mask, make sure the target layer is Layer 1 (the koala). To create the layer mask, choose Layer > Add Layer Mask > Reveal All.

Tip *You can also create a layer mask by clicking on the New Layer Mask icon at the bottom of the Layers palette (▣).*

Notice that the title bar now includes the name of your file, the name of your layer, and the words "Layer 1 Mask."

SYDNEY.JPG @ 100% (Layer 1,Layer Mask)

In the Channels palette, you will see that a new channel called Layer 1 Mask appears. (If you don't see these words, you'll probably need to enlarge the size of the palette.) Notice that the Layer 1 Mask in the Channels palette is selected. This means that any changes you make on the screen will now affect only the mask, not your image.

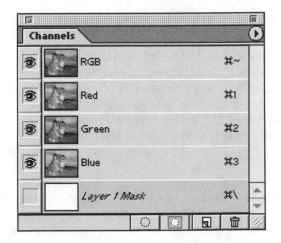

Viewing and Controlling the Layer Mask

In the Layers palette, the mask (at this point, a white rectangle, because there is nothing in the mask) appears directly to the left of the layer name. Notice that the paintbrush icon that used to be in the Layers palette has been replaced by the layer mask selected icon. This icon tells you that any editing you do now affects the layer mask, not the layer.

You can click in the Layers palette to turn editing in the layer mask off or on. To turn off editing in the layer mask, click on the layer's name or its thumbnail (the rectangle with a miniature of your image). After you click, the paintbrush returns, indicating that any editing you do affects the layer, not the layer mask. You'll also notice that the black border disappears from the layer mask thumbnail and appears around the layer thumbnail.

To turn the layer mask back on, click on the layer mask thumbnail. After you click, the paintbrush disappears and the layer mask selected icon reappears. The black border now returns to the layer mask thumbnail.

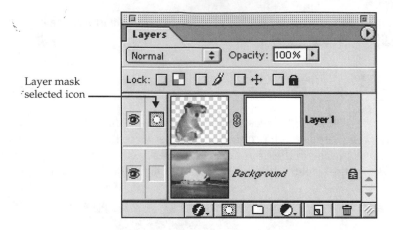

Layer mask selected icon —

Between the layer thumbnail and the mask thumbnail is a chain icon. The chain means that the layer and its mask are linked. If you move the layer, the mask moves with it; if you move the mask, the layer moves with it. If you wish to unlink the layer from its mask, simply click on the chain icon. To link the layer to its mask, click in the space between the layer thumbnail and the layer mask thumbnail. The link icon appears.

Next, you'll have a chance to edit the layer mask by painting over it with the Paintbrush tool.

If you wish to view or edit the layer mask as it appears in its channel, OPTION-click (ALT-click) on the layer mask thumbnail. To return the layers to view, OPTION-click (ALT-click) again. If you wish to view or edit the mask in Quick Mask mode, press SHIFT-OPTION (SHIFT-ALT) and click on the layer mask thumbnail.

Editing the Layer Mask

Before continuing, make sure that the layer mask selected icon appears next to the eye icon in the Layers palette. If it doesn't, select the mask by clicking on the layer mask thumbnail (to the right of the layer thumbnail, on the left side of the layer name).

As you complete the following steps, you won't actually be changing pixels in the target layer, even though it appears that they are changing. When the layer mask thumbnail is selected, Photoshop shows you how your image appears through the layer mask that you are editing.

If you have not yet created a layer mask, place an image on a layer on your screen above the background or another layer. Then choose Layer > Add Layer Mask > Reveal All.

Next, open the Color palette. Notice that your palette of painting colors has changed. In the Color palette, the color slider now indicates a range from black to white. When you edit the layer mask, you can paint only in black, white, or shades of gray. If you paint with black or darker colors, you will hide areas in the target layer (because you are adding to the mask); paint with white or lighter colors, and you reveal areas in the target layer (because you are subtracting from the mask). If you paint with gray, you create a blend between the two layers.

Set the foreground color to black. Try using the Paintbrush tool with a soft-edged brush to paint over the image in the target layer. Make sure the Mode pop-up menu in the Paintbrush tool's Options bar is set to Normal and Opacity is set to 100%. As you paint, the areas you paint over turn transparent. Painting with black hides target layer image areas and reveals underlying layer image areas.

Remember   *When the layer mask thumbnail is selected, all painting and editing affects only the layer mask.*

Change the foreground color to white. Try painting with white over the areas you just painted. Notice that the portions of the image that you've wiped away gradually return, as shown in Figure 17-11. Painting with white in the layer mask reveals the target layer and hides the underlying layer. To vary the effect, try changing to different shades of gray in the Color palette, and keep painting or change the opacity in the Options bar. As you paint, you'll see a blend between the target layer and the underlying layer. Painting with 50 percent gray blends equal parts of the target layer and the underlying layer. Painting with darker shades of gray reveals more of the underlying layer. Painting with lighter shades of gray reveals more of the target layer.

Figure 17-11.   *Using the Paintbrush to edit the layer mask gradually removes portions of the koala*

APPLYING EFFECTS TO YOUR IMAGES

Next, try editing the layer mask by creating a gradient. Select the Gradient tool in the Toolbox and choose a linear gradient. In the Options bar, set Mode to Normal, Opacity to 100%, and the Gradient pop-up menu to Foreground and Background. Before you use the Gradient tool, set the foreground color to white and the background color to black. Position the mouse pointer about 1 inch from the left of the screen and then click and drag to the right of the screen. The target layer gradually appears on screen.

If you wish to experiment further with layer masks, try adding text to the mask by typing the text directly into the mask. Press OPTION (*ALT*) while you click on the layer mask thumbnail. This allows you to edit the grayscale mask directly on the screen. Set the foreground color to white, and type text using a large point size. After you've typed the text, press OPTION (*ALT*) and click to remove the full-screen version of your mask. You'll now be able to see parts of the target layer through the type in the mask.

Creating Special Effects with Filters and Layer Masks

Once you understand the concept that the effects of a layer mask are based on the shape and transparency of the mask, it's quite easy to create special effects using filters and layer masks. For example, the image in Figure 17-12 was created with the building in one layer and clouds in another. Then we created the layer mask from a gradient and edited it with the Mosaic Tiles and Emboss filters. By applying the filters to the layer masks, we created a textured effect, blending the building and the clouds.

Figure 17-12. *Mosaic Tiles and Emboss filters applied to a layer mask*

Here are the steps for creating the effect:

1. Load the Castle file from the Chapter 17 folder of this book's CD-ROM.

2. Create a new layer for the clouds portion of the image. Set the foreground color to blue and the background color to white. Now apply the Clouds filter by choosing Filter > Render > Clouds.

3. Click on the building layer in the Layers palette. Then add a layer mask to the image by choosing Layer > Add Layer Mask > Reveal All.

Remember *If your image is on the layer called Background, you can't add a layer mask to it. You first need to double-click on it and rename it.*

4. Press OPTION (*ALT*) and click on the layer mask in the Layers palette to place the mask on your screen.

5. Apply a gradient, and then apply the Mosaic Tiles filter (Filter > Texture > Mosaic Tiles) to the mask (or use another texture filter).

6. To increase the depth of the texture, apply the Filter > Stylize > Emboss filter.

7. Press OPTION (*ALT*) and click on the layer mask again to return the RGB image to the screen. You'll now see your images through the mosaic and emboss in the mask.

At this point, you may want to make some color corrections to the RGB image so that you can better see the image and the effect. (See Chapter 19 for details on color correcting.)

If you wish to edit the layer mask in the mask channel, open the Channels palette. Click on the eye icon column to the left of the mask channel. The red overlay (discussed in Chapter 15) appears. You can now use the painting tools to edit the mask by adding to and subtracting from the overlay. When you're finished editing, click on the eye icon column in the Channels palette again to make the overlay disappear.

Applying or Removing a Layer Mask

Once you've completed editing the mask, you can decide whether to apply the layer mask, save your image with the mask, or discard the mask. Applying the layer mask removes the mask from the Layers palette and applies the visual effects to the actual pixels in the target layer.

To begin, select the layer mask thumbnail in the Layers palette and choose Layer > Remove Layer Mask or click on the trash icon in the Layers palette. (You can also drag the layer mask thumbnail into the trash.) An alert box appears, asking it you want to apply the mask to layer before removing it.

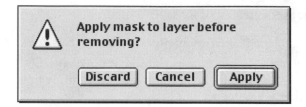

You have three choices:

- If you choose Apply, the layer mask will be applied to your image.
- If you choose Discard, the layer mask will not be applied to your image.
- If you choose Cancel, the Remove Layer Mask command will be ignored.

To apply the layer mask, choose Apply. The target layer on your screen will be updated to reflect the changes you've made to the layer mask.

After you've applied the layer mask, the layer mask thumbnail disappears from the Layers palette. Any image editing you do now in the target layer affects only that layer.

Creating a Selection from a Layer Mask

To create a selection in the target layer from your layer mask, press CTRL (Windows users should right-click) and then click on the layer mask thumbnail. A pop-up menu appears allowing you to choose whether to create a new selection, add to one on screen, subtract one, or create an intersection between the layer mask and a selection on the screen.

You can also use keyboard commands:

- If you wish to make a selection out of the layer mask, press COMMAND (*CTRL*) and click on the layer mask thumbnail icon.
- To add a selection made from the layer mask to an existing selection in the target layer, press SHIFT-COMMAND (*SHIFT-CTRL*) and click on the layer mask thumbnail.
- To subtract the layer mask from a selection in the target layer, press COMMAND-OPTION (*CTRL-ALT*).
- If you wish to create a selection from the intersection of a selection in the target layer and the layer mask, press COMMAND-OPTION-SHIFT (*CTRL-ALT-SHIFT*) and click on the layer mask thumbnail in the Layers palette.

Layer Mask Tips and Tricks

If you would like to experiment more with layer masks, try dragging another image into your file and creating a layer mask for it. After the new layer appears on screen, create a selection and then create the mask out of the selection by choosing Layer >

Add Layer Mask > Reveal Selection or Hide Selection. After the mask is created, edit it with the Paintbrush or Airbrush tool.

Here are a few shortcuts for creating and using layer masks and converting layer masks to selections:

- Click on the New Layer Mask icon at the bottom of the Layers palette to create a layer mask that reveals the entire target layer. Paint with black or a shade of gray to reveal the underlying layer (as well as all underlying visible layers). Paint with white to hide the underlying layer.

- OPTION-click (*ALT-click*) on the New Layer Mask icon to create a layer mask that hides the entire target layer (revealing the underlying layer). Paint with white or a light shade of gray to reveal the hidden parts of the target layer.

- If you have a selection on the screen, clicking on the New Layer Mask icon reveals the target layer in the selection; in all other areas, you'll see the underlying layer. OPTION-clicking (ALT-clicking) on the New Layer Mask icon hides the target layer in the selected area but shows the underlying layer in the selected area.

- In Photoshop's Channels palette, you can duplicate a layer mask by clicking and dragging its thumbnail over the New Layer Mask icon.

- You can load a selection created from a layer mask by using the Channel pop-up menu in the Load Selection dialog box (Select > Load Selection).

- To turn off the visual effects of the layer mask temporarily, press SHIFT and click on the layer mask thumbnail icon in the Layers palette. SHIFT-click again to see the mask effects. You can also use the Layer > Disable Layer Mask and Layer > Enable Layer Mask commands to turn the mask off and on.

- To see and edit a full-screen version of the layer mask, OPTION-click (*ALT-click*) on the layer mask thumbnail in the Layers palette. Repeat the procedure to return your image to the screen.

- You can drag and drop a layer linked to a layer mask from one file to another.

When you're finished experimenting with layer masks, use the File > Save a Copy command to flatten the image to conserve memory and rename the file, or use the Save As command to save the file with its layers under a new name.

Using Adjustment Layers

Using Photoshop's adjustment layers, you can color-correct and make tonal adjustments to your images through a mask. If you don't like the effects or you need to change them, you can undo them or adjust them without changing the actual pixels in your image. Using adjustment layers can save time when you need to make tonal and color corrections to images. Adjustment layers are extremely valuable; fortunately, they're also very easy to create.

You cannot create adjustment layers in ImageReady. However, the effects of the adjustment layer are maintained when you "jump" to or from ImageReady.

Using adjustment layers, you can apply Photoshop's color-correction commands—Curves, Levels, Brightness/Contrast, Color Balance, Hue/Saturation, Selective Color, Channel Mixer, and Color Range—through a mask. (Curves, Levels, Color Balance, Hue/Saturation, Channel Mixer, and Color Range are discussed in detail in Chapter 19.) You can also create adjustment layers for effects that remap the pixels of layers: Invert, Threshold, and Posterize. When using any of the adjustment layer options, you see the effects on your screen, through the adjustment layer. If you remove the adjustment layer, your image returns to its original state.

As you work, you can create one adjustment layer over another. For instance, you might create one adjustment layer that uses the Curves command to adjust an image's tonal effects. On top of that adjustment layer, you might create another adjustment layer that changes an image's color balance. On top of that adjustment layer, you could create another one to change the hue and saturation of an image. After you print a proof, you could return to make changes to any adjustment layer.

Tip *Changes to an adjustment layer affect all of the layers beneath it. If you wish to make an adjustment layer affect specific layers, create a clipping group out of the adjustment layer and the layers you want in the clipping group. As discussed earlier in this chapter, to create a clipping group, OPTION-click (ALT-click) on the line separating the two layers in the Layers palette.*

Creating and Editing Adjustment Layers

Before creating an adjustment layer, open an image that you wish to edit or correct. If you wish to edit or color correct a selection, make a selection on your screen.

To create an adjustment layer, choose Layer > New Adjustment Layer. In the Adjustment Layer submenu, choose the type of adjustment layer that you wish to create. Alternatively, you can create a new adjustment layer by clicking on the New Fill Adjustment Layer icon in the Layers palette.

After the New Layer dialog box opens, enter a name for the adjustment layer in the Name field. Change the mode or opacity if desired. Then click on OK.

The next dialog box that opens allows you to edit the image. The dialog box is the same one you would see if you had simply chosen Image > Adjust > Levels, Image > Adjust > Curves, and so on. After you make adjustments in the dialog box, click on OK. The adjustment layer is added to the Layers palette. In the palette, the name of the adjustment appears.

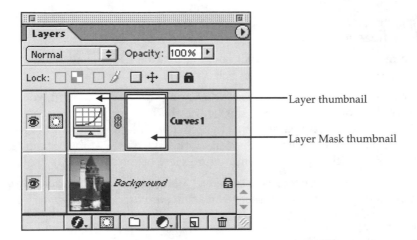

Layer thumbnail

Layer Mask thumbnail

Tip	*You can create an adjustment layer and not change any of the tonal or color commands in the dialog box. Just click on OK to create a "dummy" adjustment. You can then use this layer to apply a blending mode to affect the layers below it. Multiply, Screen, Soft Light, Hard Light, Color Dodge, Color Burn, Difference, and Exclusion can alter your image. Change the Opacity setting in the Layers palette to fine-tune the effect.*

If you want to reopen the adjustment layer to make further editing changes, double-click on the layer thumbnail icon the Layers palette.

If you want to hide the effects of the adjustment layer in your image, simply click on the adjustment layer's eye icon in the Layers palette. To view the effects of the adjustment layer, click in the eye icon column again.

Editing Adjustment Layer Masks

You can fine-tune the effects of an adjustment layer mask by painting in the mask layer with a painting tool. Painting in an adjustment layer edits the adjustment layer's mask, just as painting in a layer mask edits the layer mask. When you paint, only black, white, and shades of gray are available. If you paint with black, you remove the adjustment layer's effect. To reveal the full effect of the layer, paint with white. Painting with a shade of gray partially reveals or partially hides the effect.

To try out the effects of editing a layer adjustment mask, follow these steps:

1. Open the Leaf file from the Chapter 17 folder in this book's CD-ROM.

2. Create a new adjustment mask by choosing Layer > New > Adjustment Layer. In the Adjustment Layer submenu, choose Hue/Saturation.

3. In the New Layer dialog box, click on OK. This opens the Hue/Saturation dialog box.

4. In the Hue/Saturation dialog box, click on Colorize. Adjust the Hue slider to change hues and click on OK.

5. Open the Color palette. Note that only a grayscale slider is available because you are painting in a mask layer. Select a dark shade of gray.

6. Activate the Paintbrush or Airbrush tool and paint. As you paint, you gradually remove the Colorize effect. The darker the shade of gray, the more you paint away the effect. If you paint with a lighter shade of gray, you paint more of the Colorize effect into the image. As you work, take a look at the adjustment layer thumbnail, which shows you a miniature view of the mask you are editing.

7. Paint the Colorize effect back on screen. Change your painting color to white, and paint the same area you painted over in step 5.

If you want to experiment more, try painting with different modes and creating gradients in the adjustment layer.

Adjustment Layer Mask Tips and Tricks

Here are a few tips about editing and using the masks in adjustment layers:

■ You can temporarily turn off the effects of an adjustment layer mask by pressing SHIFT and clicking on the adjustment layer thumbnail in the Layers palette. SHIFT-click again to return the adjustment layer effects to your image.

■ You can create a selection out of the adjustment layer mask, and you can add, subtract, or intersect this selection with selections on screen. To access the selection options, CTRL-click on the adjustment layer thumbnail (Windows users should right-click on the adjustment layer).

■ You can open the adjustment layer mask and edit the mask in its channel by OPTION-clicking (*ALT-clicking*) on the adjustment layer thumbnail in the Layers palette. Repeat the procedure to return to your image.

■ You can drag an adjustment layer from one file to another in order to apply the same effect to different files. Just click on the adjustment layer in the Layers palette and drag it into the other file.

■ You can use the mask created in an adjustment layer in the Apply Image (Image > Apply Image) and Calculations (Image > Calculations) dialog boxes. Masks from adjustment layers can also be accessed from the Channels pop-up menu in the Load Selection dialog box (Select > Load Selection).

■ If you applied an adjustment layer to a selection, you can move the adjustment layer area by clicking and dragging on it with the Move tool.

You can create one adjustment layer on top of another. You also can create clipping groups from adjustment layers and layers.

Merging and Removing Adjustment Layers

If you're happy with the changes you made to your image with the adjustment layer, you can make the adjustments permanent by merging layers. If you would like to remove the adjustment layer, you can delete it. The procedures for merging and removing adjustment layers are the same as they are for regular layers (as explained in Chapter 16).

To merge a layer with the layer below, choose Layer > Merge Down or choose Merge Down from the Layers palette's pop-up menu. To merge the adjustment layer with all visible layers, choose Layer > Merge Visible or choose Merge Visible from the Layers palette's pop-up menu.

If you want to discard an adjustment layer, click on it and choose Layer > Delete Layer or click on the trash icon in the Layers palette. Alternatively, you can drag the adjustment layer into the trash.

APPLYING EFFECTS
TO YOUR IMAGES

Chapter 18

Still More Special Effects

Throughout this book, you've experimented with a variety of special effects: drop shadows, mezzotints, filter effects, glowing text, images that appear through text, beveled buttons, and posterized and colorized images. This chapter takes you on a tour of special effects that you can quickly create using various Photoshop and ImageReady commands and techniques. You will see how layers, layer styles, channels, blending modes, and filters can be combined to create striking textures and three-dimensional lighting effects that can be applied to both images and text.

This chapter also provides an overview of software that can help spice up your print, Web, and multimedia work. Programs like Corel Painter and Curious Labs' Poser can be used in conjunction with Photoshop to create precisely the effects you desire. The information presented here is intended to inspire you to combine all of the features of Photoshop and try out other digital-imaging software.

Creating Special Effects with Layer Styles

Undoubtedly, the fastest way to generate eye-catching special effects is to use Photoshop's or ImageReady's Layer Style commands. Using the styles available in the Layer Style dialog box, you can quickly create drop shadow, glows emboss, and bevel effects. The Layer Style dialog box even includes a Pillow Emboss style, which we used to create the image shown below. And, as you'll learn in the "Using ImageReady's Layer Styles to Create Web Buttons" section later in this chapter, if you want to create Web or multimedia buttons quickly, your first stop should be the Layer Style dialog box.

Although some third-party special-effects filters provide more startling results than Photoshop's layer styles, you'll generally find that Photoshop's are easy to apply, edit, and reapply. Another time-saving feature of Photoshop's layer styles is that you can easily copy and paste the settings of one style into another layer in the current document or another document. Once you paste the layer style, it is applied to any object in the pasted layer or any new object created in the layer.

Applying layer styles is quite easy. You don't need to blur, emboss, duplicate, and offset layers step by step. All you need to do is create a shape, text, or an image in a layer, and then choose an effect from the Layer > Style submenu or from the

Layer Style dialog box. When you make a selection from the Layer > Style submenu, Photoshop opens the Layer Style dialog box and previews the effect on screen (if the Preview checkbox is selected).

The basis of most effects are highlights and shadows applied using Photoshop's layer-blending modes. If you wish to alter or tweak an effect, you can change blending modes, opacity, and lighting colors. Some commands allow you to change lighting angles and blur options as well.

Using the Layer Style Dialog Box

Once you understand how to use the Layer Style dialog box, the possibilities for creating effects are endless. Here are the basic steps:

1. Create an object with a transparent background. You can also create text and shapes on layers and apply layer styles to them.

2. Choose Layer > Layer Style > Blending Options to open the Blending Options section of the Layer Style dialog box, as shown in Figure 18-1. Alternatively, if you know the style that you wish to create, choose Layer > Style and choose the style from the Layer Style submenu. You can also choose a style or blending options by clicking on the *f* icon at the bottom of the Layers palette.

3. In the Styles list on the left side of the Layer Style dialog box, click on the name of the style that you wish to apply. For instance, click on Bevel and Emboss. (If you click on only the checkbox, you won't see the options for that style, so make sure that you click on the name of the style.) After you select a style, the dialog box displays options for that style. Figure 18-2 shows the options for the Bevel and Emboss style.

4. Use the settings in the dialog box to edit the style as desired. The preview box shows the effect you are creating. For example, if you wish to change the contour of the bevel, click on the Contour pop-up menu and choose a style, as shown here.

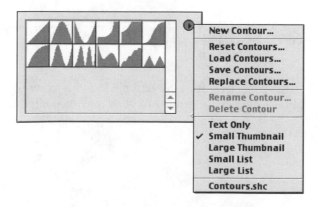

APPLYING EFFECTS TO YOUR IMAGES

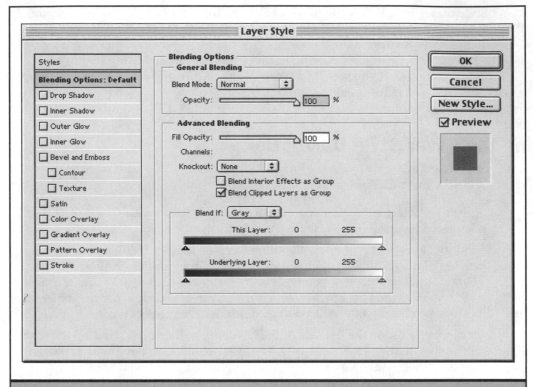

Figure 18-1. The Blending Options section of the Layer Style dialog box

5. If you wish to apply more layer styles, click on another style name in the Styles list and then edit the settings for that style in the corresponding section of the Layer Style dialog box.

In the Layer Style dialog box, you can press the up arrow or down arrow key on the keyboard to increase or decrease percentage, degree, or pixel values after clicking in a field.

6. If you wish to save the style for later use, click on the New Style button. In the New Style dialog box, name your style and then click on OK.

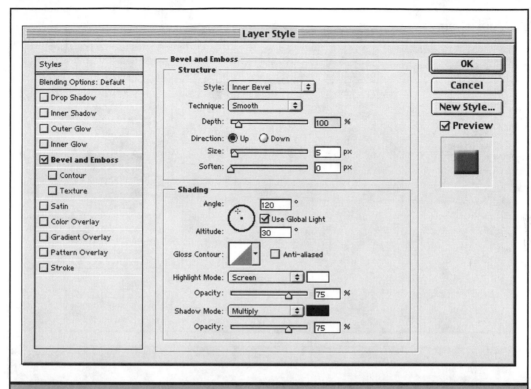

Figure 18-2. *The Bevel and Emboss section of the Layer Style dialog box*

If you wish to return to the settings for a layer style you've applied, simply double-click on the *f* icon for that style in the Layers palette. If you want to reload a previously saved style, choose Layer > Style > Blending Options. In the Layer Style dialog box, click on the word *Styles* (in the upper-left corner). This changes the dialog box to show all saved styles, as shown in Figure 18-3. To use a style, click on it. You can also load more Photoshop predefined styles from disk by choosing a set from the bottom of the Style submenu shown in Figure 18-3. Notice that Photoshop 6 includes button styles, text effects, and texture styles.

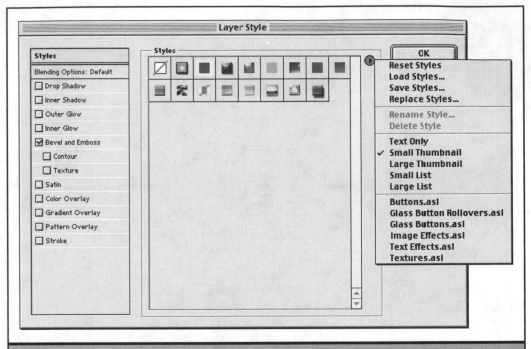

Figure 18-3. *The Styles section and Styles submenu of the Layer Style dialog box*

Creating a Drop Shadow and Bevel Effect

To obtain the most eye-catching results from layer styles, you'll often find that two layer styles are better than one. We used this technique to create the arrows in Figure 18-4. To create the arrow, we used the Line tool's Arrows option. (See Chapter 17 for details about using the Line tool.) To add the speckled effect to the arrows, we applied Photoshop's Glass filter (Filter > Distort > Glass) with the Tiny Lens texture.

The following steps show how to apply both a drop shadow and an inner bevel to text or to an image.

1. Use the Type tool to create text on the screen, or create a new file with a transparent background. In the transparent layer, create a shape or use the Line tool to create an arrow.

Using the Line tool, you can create a painted line on a transparent background by creating a layer, and then clicking the Create Filled Region icon in the Line tool's Options bar.

Figure 18-4.   *Drop Shadow and Inner Bevel layer styles*

2. To create a drop shadow, choose Layer > Layer Style > Drop Shadow. The Layer Style dialog box opens with the options for the Drop Shadow style chosen and the Preview checkbox selected, as shown in Figure 18-5.

3. In the Layer Style dialog box, you can edit the Drop Shadow effect by changing the blending mode, opacity, and angle of the shadow (the Use Global Light checkbox is described after these steps). The Distance option controls how far the shadow is from the image. The Intensity option controls the darkness of the shadow color. To change the color of the shadow, click on the black swatch next to the layer-blending mode. This opens the Color Picker, where you can pick a color for the shadow.

Tip   *You can also drag the shadow on screen with the mouse to change the distance and lighting angle settings.*

4. To add a bevel to the image, click on the name Bevel and Emboss in the Styles list on the right side of the dialog box. In the Bevel and Emboss section of the Layer Style dialog box, click on the Inner Bevel option in the Style pop-up menu (if it isn't already selected).

5. Adjust the Angle and Blur options to fine-tune the effect, and then click on OK.

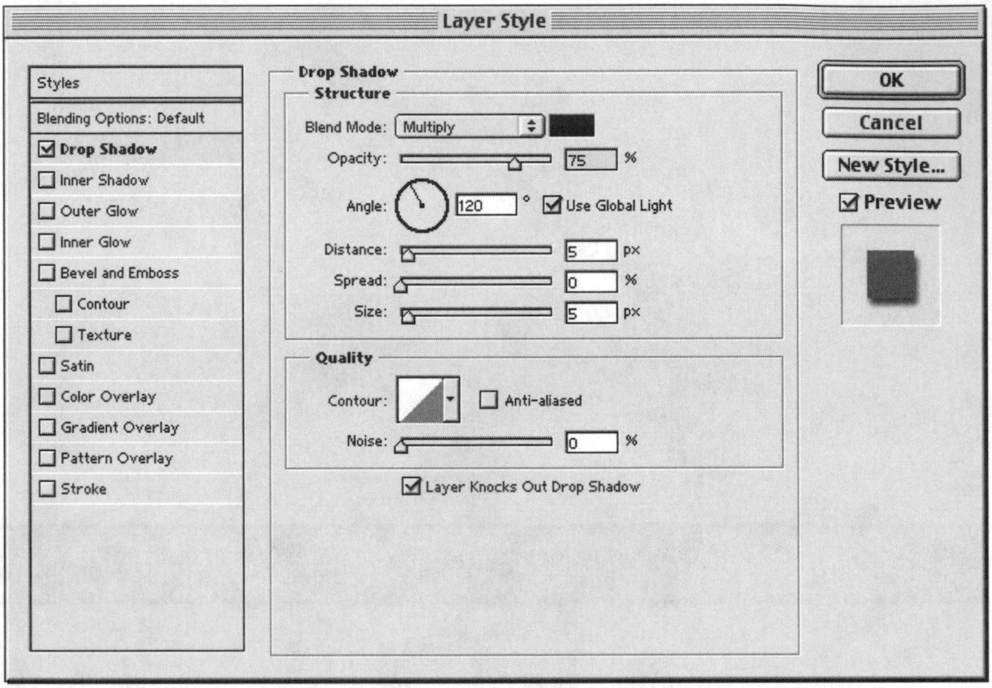

Figure 18-5. *The Drop Shadow section of the Layer Style dialog box*

The Drop Shadow, Inner Shadow, and Bevel and Emboss layer styles allow you to set a lighting angle. If you wish to apply a global angle to each command, select the Use Global Angle checkbox in the dialog box. To set a new global angle, choose Layer > Layer Style > Global Light. In the Set Global Angle dialog box, specify a global angle and/or altitude (by using the slider or entering a value in the fields). If the Preview checkbox is selected, you'll see a live preview of how the angle change affects the image on your screen.

Creating Recessed Type

Creating a woodcut or recessed effect is quite easy using layer styles. To create the effect shown here, we applied the Inner Shadow style, and then the Outer Bevel style from the Layer Style dialog box.

After creating the text using the Type tool, we opened the Inner Shadow section of the Layer Style dialog box (Layer > Layer Style > Inner Shadow) and accepted the default settings, as shown in Figure 18-6. Next, we selected Bevel and Emboss in the Layer Style dialog box and choose Outer Bevel from the Style pop-up menu.

For the layer styles, the default settings are a good way to start, but you can adjust any of the settings to fine-tune the effect. For example, if you wish to change the color of the shadow, click on the black swatch in the Bevel and Emboss section and change colors when the Color Picker opens. Then return to the Inner Shadow section and change the shadow color there as well.

Using ImageReady's Layer Styles to Create Web Buttons

Using ImageReady's layer styles, you can create attractive Web buttons. We used layer styles and filters in ImageReady to create the Web button shown here.

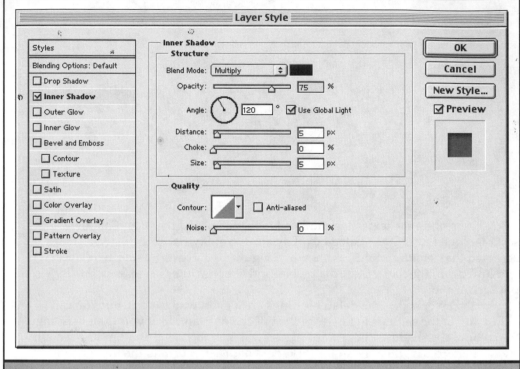

Figure 18-6. *The Inner Shadow section of the Layer Style dialog box*

Here are the steps for creating the button:

1. Create a new file in ImageReady by choosing File > New. Make the file just a little larger than the button that you wish to create. (Remember that there are 72 pixels in an inch.)

2. To create the rounded-rectangular button background, select ImageReady's Rounded Rectangle tool. (Click on the Rectangle tool and keep the mouse button pressed until you see the Rounded Rectangle tool.) Then click and drag to draw the background rectangle.

3. To fill the shape with color, choose Layer > Layer Style > Color Overlay. To pick a Web-safe color, click on the down arrow next to the color swatch in the Color Overlay palette and select Other from the pop-up menu. When the Color Picker opens, use the sliders to pick a color. Make sure that the Only Web Color checkbox is selected.

4. Add bevel and emboss effects to the shape by choosing Layer > Layer Style > Bevel and Emboss. If desired, change the settings to enhance the effects.

5. Choose a Web-safe color for the oval by clicking on the foreground color in the Toolbox and choosing a color from the Color Picker.

6. To create the oval, switch from the Rounded Rectangle tool to the Ellipse tool in the ImageReady Toolbox. (The tools share the same Toolbox location.) Click and drag to draw the oval. Then use the Move tool to position the oval over the rectangle.

7. Choose a Web-safe color for the arrow by clicking on the foreground color in the Toolbox and choosing a color in the Color Picker dialog box.

8. To create the arrow, double-click on the Line tool. In the Line tool's Options bar, make sure the create new layer icon is selected.

9. Set the Weight option to approximately 10, select the Arrows: End checkbox and click on the Shape button to edit the shape. Use the screen icons as guides for width, length, and concavity. Then click and drag to draw the arrow. Position the arrow over the oval and rectangle using the Move tool.

10. Add a bevel to the arrow by choosing Layer > Layer Style > Bevel and Emboss once again.

11. If you wish to add texture to any of the shapes, try applying the Texturizer Filter (Filter > Texture > Texturizer). We applied the Canvas filter to both the rectangle and the oval. Alternatively, you can try applying the Pattern Overlay choice in the Layer Style dialog box.

12. Once you're satisfied with your button, you can optimize the image and save it as a GIF file (File > Save Optimized As). For more information about optimizing and converting images to GIF format, see Chapter 9.

At this point, you can copy your button to a Web server and use HTML to create a link from your button's page to another page. To learn how to create a link to your button or to create a rollover effect with it, see Chapter 10.

Copying, Converting, and Removing Layer Styles

If you need to repeat a style, you can copy and paste the layer style settings without copying and pasting the actual image. To copy a layer style, select the layer and choose Layer > Style > Copy Layer Style. To paste the layer style into a layer, choose Layer > Layer Style > Paste Layer Style. To copy the style into multiple layers, first link the layers, and then choose Layer > Layer Style > Paste Style to Linked. (See Chapter 16 for details on linking layers.) If any previous layer styles existed, the pasted layer styles replace them.

APPLYING EFFECTS
TO YOUR IMAGES

To convert a layer style to standard Photoshop layers, select the layer containing the style and then choose Layer > Layer Style > Create Layers. Photoshop breaks the layer style into multiple layers, where you can see how the style was created. You can then further edit the images in these layers to create more effects.

To remove all layer styles from a layer, choose Layer > Layer Style > Clear Layer Style.

Creating Special Effects Manually in Photoshop

In this section, you will see how you can create beveled effects, different backgrounds, and other interesting effects the old-fashioned way—by manually creating multiple layers, applying filters, and using other Photoshop features. As you work through the following examples, don't be afraid to experiment on your own. If you want to keep track of your experiments, record an action. Later, you can play back the action and edit it to perfect your effects. (See Chapter 11 for details on using actions.)

Creating Embossed Type

To create the embossed effect shown in Figure 18-7, we used three different versions of the type in three different layers. We used the Type Mask tool and floated the text, and then created a layer from the floating text. This process maintained the textured background within the borders of the text.

Here are the steps for creating the embossed type effect:

1. Start by creating a background. You can either use a digitized image or create your own background using the Clouds filter (Filter > Render > Clouds) or the Texturizer filter (Filter > Texture > Texturizer).

2. Once you have a background image, create some type using the Type tool with the Type Mask button selected in the Options bar. Then position the text as desired.

3. Send the type selection into a new layer by choosing Layer > New > Layer Via Copy. After the layer is created, choose Layer > Layer Options and rename the layer **Type**. Again, adjust the placement of the text as necessary.

4. Duplicate the Type layer two times by dragging the layer name (Type) in the Layers palette over the New Layer icon twice.

 Instead of duplicating the layer twice, you could duplicate it once and use the Emboss filter on the new layer to create a highlight and a shadow effect.

5. Rename the two layers by double-clicking on them in the Layers palette. Name one **Highlight** and the other **Shadow**.

6. Move the Type layer in the Layers palette so that it is above the Highlight and Shadow layers. Then use the Move tool to move the Highlight layer diagonally up and to the left.

7. Fill the nontransparent areas of the Highlight layer with white. Choose Edit > Fill. In the Fill dialog box, set the Fill pop-up menu to White, Opacity to 100%, and Mode to Normal. Make sure that the Preserve Transparency checkbox is selected.

8. Using the Move tool, drag the Shadow layer diagonally down and to the right. Then, to fill it with black, choose Edit > Fill and set the Fill pop-up menu to Black, Opacity to 100%, and Mode to Normal. Once again, make sure that the Preserve Transparency checkbox is selected.

9. Using Figure 18-7 as a guide, adjust the different layers to achieve the desired effect.

10. If you want to soften the bevel effect, apply the Gaussian Blur filter (Filter > Blur > Gaussian Blur) to the Highlight and Shadow layers. You can also reduce the opacity of the layers. In addition, you may want to use either the Levels or Curves command on the Type layer to change the midtones, highlights, or shadows.

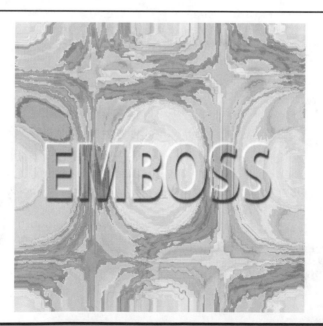

Figure 18-7. *An embossed type effect*

Creating Soft Beveled Text

The following steps create a soft beveled effect, as shown in the following illustration. (Some of the techniques used in this example are similar to those used to create text in this book's color portfolio insert.)

1. Create your own background using the Clouds filter (Filter > Render > Clouds) or the Texturizer filter (Filter > Texture > Texturizer).

2. Set the foreground color to black and the background color to white.

3. Use the Type tool to add some type. Then create a selection out of the type by using a keyboard shortcut: press COMMAND (*CTRL*) and click on the text layer in the Layers palette. Save the selection to an alpha channel by choosing Select > Save Selection.

4. Deselect the selection on screen and reduce the opacity of the black type by clicking and dragging the Opacity slider in the Layers palette. Set the level to around 20%.

5. Create a new layer and fill the layer with 100% black.

6. Load the selection from the alpha channel into the black layer you just created by choosing Select > Load Selection. In the Load Selection dialog box, choose the correct channel in the Channel pop-up menu. Fill the selection with 100% white. Deselect the type.

7. Make sure that the Preserve Transparency checkbox is not selected in the Layers palette. Apply a Gaussian Blur filter (Filter > Blur > Gaussian Blur) to the type. For a low-resolution image, set the blur to 1.5. For a high-resolution image, set the blur to about 2.5.

8. Load the text selection from the alpha channel (Select > Load Selection). In the Load Selection dialog box, choose the correct channel in the Channel pop-up menu. Then use the Marquee tool to offset the selection slightly down and to the right.

9. Invert the selection by choosing Select > Inverse. Subtract the inverted selection from the blurred type by pressing DELETE (*BACKSPACE*), and then deselect.

10. On screen, the type should already look soft. Apply the Emboss filter to enhance the effect (Filter > Stylize > Emboss). In the Emboss dialog box, we set a low angle and low height. Experiment to get the best effect.

11. You can vary the effect by applying a different layer blending mode, such as Soft Light. (See Chapter 16 for information about layer blending modes.) Also. try painting with the Airbrush using the Soft Light or Hard Light blending mode. You may also wish to adjust the placement of the text with the Move tool.

Creating Flying Type

Converting a text selection into a path allows you to distort the type. After the text is distorted, you can apply filters to create a blurred, flying effect.

1. Create a background using the Clouds or Texture filter.

2. Add type using the Type tool. To convert the type to a path so you can distort it, choose Layer > Type > Create Work Path.

3. Activate the Direct Selection tool. Click and drag on anchor points to distort the type. You may wish to add anchor points (using the Add Anchor Point tool), and then drag them to enhance the distortion.

Note   *You can also select path points and distort the path using Edit > Transform.*

4. After you've distorted the type, select the entire path by clicking and dragging over it with the Direct Selection tool. Then change the path back into a selection by choosing Make Selection from the Paths palette menu or clicking on the Selection button in the Paths palette. If you choose the Make Selection command, leave the Feather Radius option set to 0 pixels.

5. Save the selection to a channel by choosing Select > Save Selection and then deselect.

APPLYING EFFECTS TO YOUR IMAGES

6. To erase the path, use the Direct Selection tool to click and drag over all of the letters and press DELETE (*BACKSPACE*.).

7. Create a new layer by clicking on the New Layer icon in the Layers palette, and then reload the text selection by choosing Select > Load Selection. In the Load Selection dialog box, choose the correct channel in the Channel pop-up menu.

8. Fill the type in the new layer with a color, and then deselect.

9. Apply the following filters (varying the effects creates different distortions):

   ■ Filter > Blur > Gaussian Blur

   ■ Filter > Blur > Motion (set the angle to about 20 degrees)

   ■ Filter > Stylize > Wind (set the direction to From the Left)

10. Create a new layer to hold another version of the text (to make the image more legible). Choose Select > Load Selection and choose the correct channel from the Channel pop-up menu. Then fill the selection with same color you chose in step 5.

Note *If you haven't created more selections, you can reselect the previous selection by choosing Select > Reselect.*

11. Choose Soft Light as the blending mode in the Layers palette. The combination of the blurred layer with the Soft Light unblurred layer allows you to see the flying effect and read your text.

Creating a Glass Effect

The effect shown in Figure 18-8 was creating using a quick and simple way to simulate glass. The glass effect consists of slightly blurred, embossed text, combined with two layer blending modes: Hard Light and Difference.

1. Create a background texture. We used the Clouds filter with the foreground color set to blue and the background set to white. Then we applied the Filter > Distort > Zigzag command to create the pond-ripple effect.

2. Use the Type tool to create white type. Then render the type by choosing Layer > Rasterize > Type.

3. Apply the Gaussian Blur filter (Filter > Blur > Gaussian Blur) at a low setting. Then apply the Emboss filter (Filter > Stylize > Emboss).

4. In the Layers palette, set the blending mode to Hard Light.

5. Duplicate the type layer by dragging it over the New Layer icon in the Layers palette.

6. Set the blending mode to Multiply. Then use the Move tool to offset the layer so you can fine-tune the three-dimensional effect.

Figure 18-8.   *A glass effect created with layers*

7. If you wish to enhance the effect, lower the opacity in the Layers palette, create an adjustment layer, and then use the Hue/Saturation option to adjust the colors. (See Chapter 17 for details on creating adjustment layers.)

Creating Screened Type

In Figure 18-9, we combined some type with an image of a sailboat using layers. Using the Soft Light blending mode allowed the shimmering light of the background to show through the image.

Here's how to duplicate the screened-type effect:

1. Open an image that includes reflective light. (You can use the Sailboat image file from the Chapter 18 folder of this book's CD-ROM.)

2. Create a new layer and fill it with white. If the Lock Transparency icon is selected in the Layers palette, turn it off. Then set the layer Opacity value to 14%.

3. Set the foreground color to black.

4. Activate the Type tool and add some type. We typed **sailing** and selected the vertical orientation button in the Type tool's Options bar.

5. Set the layer blending mode to Soft Light in the Layers palette.

Creating Quick Image Blends with Selections

You can create interesting effects by making a selection from one channel of an image. After you make the selection, simply copy and paste it into another. (See Chapter 15 for more information about using channels.)

Figure 18-9. *A screened-type effect*

You can use keyboard shortcuts to select a channel in an RGB, Lab, or grayscale file:

■ To select the Red channel in an RGB file, the Lightness channel in a Lab file, or a grayscale file channel, press COMMAND-OPTION-1 (*CTRL-ALT-1*)

■ To select the Green channel in an RGB file, press COMMAND-OPTION-2 (*CTRL-ALT-2*)

■ To select the Blue channel in an RGB file, press COMMAND-OPTION-3 (*CTRL-ALT-3*).

Here's how to create an interesting blend using this selection technique:

1. Open a file and convert it to Lab Color mode by selecting Image > Mode > Lab.

2. Press COMMAND-OPTION-1 (*CTRL-ALT-1*) to select the Lightness channel.

3. Choose Edit > Copy. (If your image contains layers, choose Edit > Copy Merged to copy all visible layers.)

4. Close the image, and don't save the changes.

5. Open another file and choose Edit > Paste.

The final image shows a blend between the two images. The first image will display different opacities, depending on the lightness values in the original image.

Creating Textured Backgrounds

If you wish to create textured backgrounds, Photoshop's Filters menu and Layers palette will help get you started. For example, here's how to create a crumpled fabric effect:

1. Open a new file. Pick a color for the foreground and another for the background.

2. Apply the Difference Clouds filter (Filter > Render > Difference Clouds).

Note *The color on screen will be the color of your fabric. If you want to change the color, use an adjustment layer. (See Chapter 17 for details on creating adjustment layers.)*

3. Duplicate the layer you are on by dragging it over the New Layer icon in the Layers palette.

4. Apply the Chrome filter (Filter > Sketch > Chrome) to the duplicated layer. Drag the Detail and Smoothness slider to adjust the effect.

5. Set the blending mode in the Layers palette to Hard Light.

You can also use adjustment layers, layer masks, different blending modes, and different layer opacities to create the background effect you want.

Creating an Ice Texture

Here's how to create a background texture that looks like glacial ice:

1. Open a new file. Set the foreground color to a dark yellow and the background color to white.

2. Apply the Difference Clouds filter (Filter > Render > Difference Clouds).

3. In order to get an attractive ice color, create an adjustment layer and choose the Color Balance option. In the Color Balance dialog box, move the Cyan/Red slider to the left so that you reduce the cyan in the layer. When you are satisfied with the color, click on OK.

4. Duplicate the background layer by dragging it over the New Layers icon in the Layers palette.

5. Apply the Bass Relief filter (Filter > Sketch > Bass Relief) to the duplicated layer.

6. Set the blending mode in the Layers palette to Soft Light to blend the two layers together to create the ice effect.

Liquifying Images

Photoshop 6's Liquify command may be just what you need to stir up an image. Liquify allows you to click and drag to create distortions that make your images look as if they've been melted or turned into goo. As you work, you can *freeze* image areas, preventing them from being distorted anymore, and you can *thaw* frozen image areas, so that you can distort them again.

Tip *Use the Edit > Fade command to fade out distortions.*

To use the Liquify command, select the image area that you wish to Liquify (or don't make a selection if you wish to Liquify an entire image) and choose Image > Liquify. Figure 18-10 shows the Liquify dialog box with an image of a building being distorted. (If you wish to use the building image with the Liquify command, load it from the Chapter 18 folder of this book's CD-ROM.)

Using the Liquify Tools

To take advantage of the Liquify dialog box fully, you should become familiar with the painting tools along the left side of the dialog box. Click and drag in your image to try out each tool as you read its description. You'll see the distortions previewed in the dialog box. To change your image with the distorted effect, click on OK; otherwise, click on Cancel.

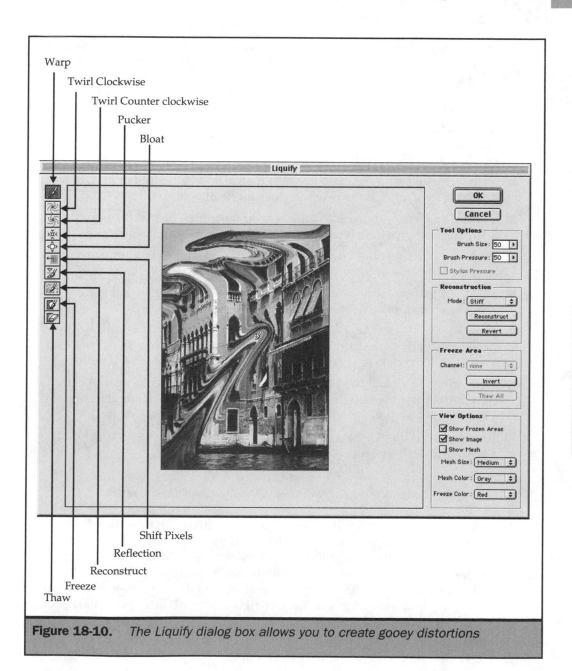

Warp

Twirl Clockwise

Twirl Counter clockwise

Pucker

Bloat

Shift Pixels

Reflection

Reconstruct

Freeze

Thaw

Figure 18-10. *The Liquify dialog box allows you to create gooey distortions*

- **Warp** Liquification is created with the Warp Tool. The size and pressure of the brush are controlled by the Tool Options settings in the upper-right side of the dialog box. You can change brush sizes by clicking in the slider, entering a number, or pressing the UP ARROW and DOWN ARROW keys on your keyboard after clicking in the Size field. The Brush Pressure value controls how fast or slow changes are made. Start with a low pressure setting so that distortions are not made too quickly. When you click and drag with this tool, it moves the pixels in the same direction as you drag.

- **Twirl Clockwise** When you keep the mouse button pressed or click and drag with this tool, it twirls the pixels in a clockwise direction.

- **Twirl Counterclockwise** When you keep the mouse button pressed or click and drag with this tool, it twirls pixels in a counterclockwise direction.

- **Pucker** When you hold down the mouse or click and drag with this tool, it sucks pixels toward the center of the brush stroke.

- **Bloat** When you hold down the mouse or click and drag with this tool, it pushes pixels away from the center of the brush stroke.

- **Shift Pixels** When you click and drag with this tool, it pushes pixels perpendicularly to the brush stroke. It shifts pixels to the left by default. Hold down the OPTION (ALT) key as you drag to shift pixels to the right.

- **Reflection** This tool copies pixels back into the brush stroke area. As you drag, pixels are reflected perpendicularly to the brush stroke on the left side. Press OPTION (ALT) to reflect in the opposite side of the brush stroke.

- **Reconstruct** Use this tool to undo distortion effects. The tool may only partially undo the effect.

Note *As you work, you can press COMMAND-Z (CTRL-Z) to undo the last stroke.*

- **Freeze** After you've liquified an image area, you can limit further distortions by clicking and dragging over liquified areas with this tool. The amount of freezing is controlled by the Brush Pressure setting, with 100% fully freezing the area. (If you drag over an area with Brush Pressure set to less than 100%, you can make the area fully frozen by clicking and dragging more than once.) The View Options settings in the lower-right corner of the Liquify dialog box allow you to view and choose colors for frozen areas. Areas that are not 100% frozen appear in a tint of the freeze color.

- **Thaw** When you click and drag over a frozen area with this tool, it unfreezes that area. The amount of thawing is controlled by the Brush Pressure setting, with 100% fully thawing the area. (If you drag over a frozen area with Brush Pressure set to less than 100%, you can make the area fully thawed by clicking and dragging more than once.)

Choosing Reconstruction Options

The Reconstruction section of the Liquify dialog box includes a Mode pop-up menu, which contains options that allow you to push distortions from frozen areas into unfrozen areas. Other Mode menu options copy distortions based on the starting point of the area that you are reconstructing. To use these options, first freeze image areas that have been liquified, then choose an option from the Mode pop-up menu and then click and drag with the Reconstruct tool.

The Mode pop-up menu includes the following options:

- The Revert option reverts back to the original as you paint with the Reconstruct tool.

- The Rigid option keeps right angles between frozen and nonfrozen areas. Nonfrozen areas can be reconstructed close to their original state using this option.

- The Stiff option, when used between frozen and nonfrozen areas, spreads unfrozen areas to frozen areas.

- The Smooth option smoothly spreads distortions in frozen areas into unfrozen areas.

- The Loose option produces an effect similar to Smooth, but creates less distortion between frozen and unfrozen areas.

- The Displace option changes the displacement of unfrozen areas to match the starting point of the reconstruction.

- The Amplitwist option changes the displacement of unfrozen areas to match displacement, rotation, and scaling of the starting point of the reconstruction.

- The Affine option changes the displacement of unfrozen areas to match all liquification (displacement, rotation, scaling, and skewing) of the starting point of the reconstruction.

Beneath the Mode pop-up menu are Reconstruct and Revert buttons. To reconstruct all nonfrozen areas, click on the Reconstruct button. If you wish to revert the whole image to its original state, click on the Revert button.

Choosing Freeze Area Options

The Channel pop-up menu in the Freeze Area section of the Liquify dialog box lets you use an alpha channel to specify a frozen area. Just click on the Channel menu and choose the alpha channel that you wish to use.

To thaw all frozen areas, click on the Thaw All button in the Freeze Area section. If you wish to freeze all unfrozen areas and thaw all frozen areas, click on the Invert button.

Using Photoshop with Other Programs

If you're interested in adding more special effects to your Photoshop project, you might wish to investigate other graphics programs, such as Adobe Illustrator. The image shown in Figure 18-11 was created using both Adobe Illustrator and Photoshop. If you're interested in creating Web animation with Photoshop files, check out Adobe LiveMotion and Macromedia Flash. If you wish to integrate Photoshop files into digital-video productions, Adobe Premiere and Adobe AfterEffects are two excellent choices.

The following sections provide brief descriptions of three popular graphics programs: Curious Labs' Poser, Corel Bryce, and Corel Painter. These are just a few of the many useful programs that you can use in conjunction with Photoshop.

Figure 18-11. *Am image created with Illustrator and Photoshop*

Modeling Human Forms with Poser

If you've ever tried drawing a three-dimensional human figure on the computer, you'll appreciate Curious Labs' Poser (Curious Labs recently purchased the program from MetaCreations). Using Poser, you can quickly create three-dimensional human forms and pose them. You can import the human forms into Photoshop, or you can use a Photoshop texture to wrap around a Poser figure.

When you first load Poser, you're greeted by a fully modeled human figure. Using the Poser pop-up menus, you can choose poses from different libraries, such as Action Sets, Comic Sets, and Sporting Sets. Figure 18-12 shows an example of the Ideal Male Adult in the Alien Abduction pose from Poser's Body Sets library.

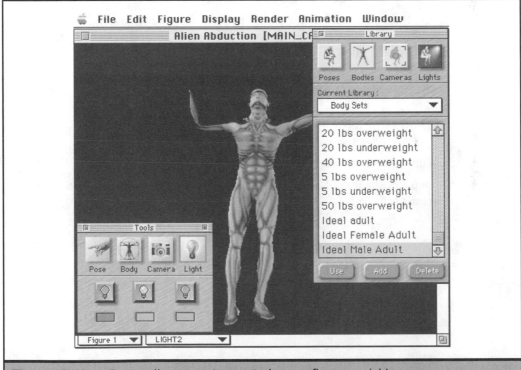

Figure 18-12.   *Poser allows you to create human figures quickly*

Using the program's Move tool, you can spin the object in three-dimensional space. When you turn the character around, its back is fully modeled. Before you render the model into a three-dimensional image, you can choose a muscle texture or apply a texture created in another program.

Figure 18-13 shows an example of a Poser model with Photoshop's Craquelure texture applied to the model. After the model was rendered in Poser, it was saved and loaded into Photoshop, where we applied the Clouds filter to the background. The procedure is so quick and simple, we've provided the steps.

1. Create a texture in Photoshop. We created a new blank file and applied two filters: Clouds (Filter > Render > Clouds) and Craquelure (Filter > Texture > Craquelure).

2. Save the file in PICT format on a Mac or in BMP format on a Windows system.

3. Open Poser. Choose a model, lighting, and pose.

4. Apply the Photoshop file as a texture or bump map by choosing Render > Surface Material. In the pop-up menus for Bump Map and Texture, you can load PICT or BMP files.

5. Save the file in Poser in PICT or BMP format. When the file is saved, Poser automatically creates an alpha channel that masks the human figure from its background.

6. Open the Poser image in Photoshop.

7. Load the selection in the alpha channel (which was created by Poser) by choosing Select > Load Selection.

8. Apply the Clouds filter. The filter is applied to the selection surrounding the human figure.

Figure 18-13.   *Photoshop's Craquelure texture applied to Poser image*

Creating 3-D Terrains in Corel Bryce

If you wish to create striking three-dimensional landscapes or supernatural extraterrestrial terrains quickly, your best bet is to turn to Corel Bryce. Figure 18-14 shows an image being created in the main document window of Bryce.

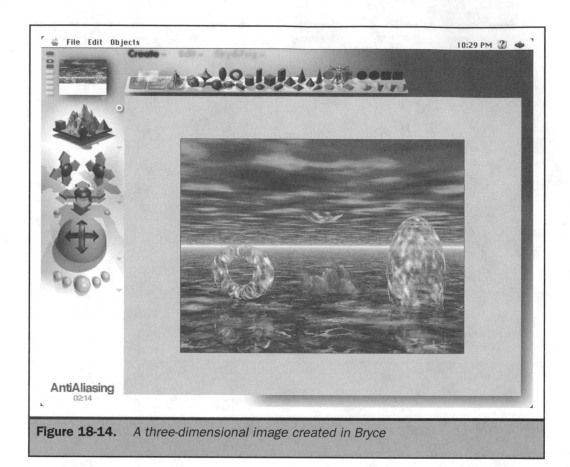

Figure 18-14. *A three-dimensional image created in Bryce*

Using Bryce is quite easy. You can start by simply clicking on terrain, sphere, and cube objects in the Create palette. You can move and resize the terrain or any other shapes. To add atmosphere, you can click on sky and fog presets. To add material to your models, you can create bump maps of muddy stones, grass, or icy snow. The effects and possibilities of this program are enormous. You can even take a grayscale image from Photoshop, save it in PICT format (Mac and Windows versions), and turn the Photoshop image into a terrain.

Painting with Corel Painter

If you find that Photoshop doesn't provide all of the painting tools you need, you should investigate Corel Painter, one of the most powerful and versatile painting programs available both for Macintosh and Windows systems. If you create layers in Painter, the blending mode can be read by Photoshop.

Painter allows you to paint with charcoal, pastel, oil, watercolor brush, and many other effects. There's even a brush called the Image Hose, which allows you to paint with digital images. When you paint, numerous palettes and pop-up menus allow you to control brush size and bristle effects. Painter also lets you turn your paintings into digital movies.

The following image was created with Painter. To create the image, we scanned a photograph of pears, then used Painter's Tracing Paper option and different brushes (Ink and Watercolor) to trace the image.

The Complete Reference

Chapter 19

Retouching and Color Correction

A Photoshop image frequently undergoes numerous transformations before it is finally output to a printed page, a videotape, a transparency, or the Web. No matter what the project, two latter-stage steps, retouching and color correction, are essential to ensuring that the final design matches the artist's vision.

Retouching is the process you engage in when you're digitally removing little bits of litter and debris from the beach, for example. Retouching can involve smoothing a few wrinkles or clearing up a pair of bloodshot eyes on a tired face. Even picnic food can be made to look more inviting; with the cloning options provided by Photoshop's Clone Stamp, you can toss more shrimp on the barbecue and add more strawberries to the shortcake. You can also use retouching to create collages that are more believable and more interesting.

Color correction involves changing an image's hue, saturation, shadows, midtones, and/or highlights so that the final output has maximum visual appeal. Color correction is often required to compensate for loss of color quality as a result of digitization. The process of translating your Photoshop image to the printed page often makes color correction a necessity as well. For instance, paper stock, resolution, and impurity of printers' inks may force you to adjust your Photoshop image's colors to produce a suitable printed version.

Color correction is important in making sure that an image's colors conform to those of the original and may in fact produce an improvement over the original. A photo of a beach resort taken on a damp, cloudy day will show the beach and water looking brown, the sky gray, the models pale, and the picnic food soggy and uninviting. Photoshop's color-correction tools can turn the sky and water magnificent shades of blue, make the models tan, and turn the sand pearly white. When reality must take a back seat to your message or design goals, you can summon the magic of retouching.

Retouching and color correction generally go hand in hand. To get you started with the fundamentals of these operations, this chapter begins with a discussion of how to improve the tonal qualities of a grayscale image. After you learn how to correct a grayscale image, you'll see how to retouch faded, damaged old photographs, like the before shown in Figure 19-1 and the after shown in Figure 19-2. Next, you'll apply retouching techniques to eliminate wrinkles and blemishes in faces and to improve color in different scenes. The chapter concludes with the steps you'll take when color-correcting your images.

Since retouching and color correction both require the use of many of the tools and techniques discussed throughout this book, you might wish to review previous chapters. For color correction, you should be familiar with the basics of color theory (covered in Chapter CD-1). For advanced work, you will need to know how to select areas using the Pen tool (Chapter 14) or isolate an area in Quick Mask mode to save selections to channels so they can be reloaded later (Chapter 15).

For retouching your images, you will need to know how to use the Eyedropper, Clone Stamp, Pencil, Paintbrush, Airbrush, Smudge, Blur/Sharpen, and Dodge/ Burn/Sponge tools (Chapters 5 and 6). You may also need to know how to use the Dust & Scratches filter (Chapter 12).

Figure 19-1.   *Digitized version of an old, damaged photograph before retouching (left) and after (right)*

Figure 19-2.   *A second digitized photograph before retouching (left) and after (right)*

Retouching and color correction both call for some artistic skill—as well as some practice. The more experience you gain with Photoshop's color-correcting commands and retouching tools, the better your skills will be. You'll also be able to save yourself and your clients a substantial amount of money if you can correct images and retouch them on your desktop computer. The color examples you'll see in this chapter are from professional work created in Photoshop that in previous years would have required high-end computer workstations or dot etchers who would edit the individual halftone dots by hand on the film separation.

Before You Begin...

This chapter doesn't just introduce you to new Photoshop commands; it also shows you how to obtain the best-quality results from your work. With these goals in mind, we must again emphasize the importance of preparatory *calibration*. If your monitor is not calibrated, your output image may ultimately look quite different in print from the one you see on screen in Photoshop.

Remember *Before you begin retouching or color-correcting your images, make sure that you've taken the calibration precautions detailed in Chapter 2.*

Analyzing the Image

When you start with the best possible original and digitized image, you'll have less retouching and color correction to do. If the original image is underexposed, overexposed, damaged, or defective in any way, the digitized version will reflect this. Thus, before digitizing, always try to obtain high-quality originals, since corrections are easier if problems are small. Of course, correcting a bad image may not be impossible, but it could involve completely re-creating parts or even most of the original image. You'll have to decide whether it's worth the time to perform major surgery.

After your image is digitized, look carefully for imperfections. Many digitized images may seem near perfect when viewed on screen at actual size, but flaws may become apparent when the images are magnified or printed. To analyze an image properly, zoom in to different areas and carefully check for noise or *posterization*, which is a lack of sufficient tonal levels, and for whether the image is sharp and crisp or blurry and out of focus. Keep in mind that if an image looks flawed on screen, it may be best to redigitize it with better equipment or at a higher resolution before you begin your fine-tuning.

Remember *Your onscreen images are most authentic when viewed at 100 percent. When you view them at a different percentage, you may see "flaws" that are actually produced by the screen.*

Adele, one of this book's authors, once worked on a project that involved correcting faded and scratched grayscale images for a Reader's Digest book. She digitized the images on a midrange scanner (Agfa Arcus) rather than on a low-end scanner. Images that had been test-scanned on a less sophisticated scanner often exhibited noise and black blotches in shadow areas. The blotches were caused by posterization. The images were eventually rescanned on the Agfa Arcus to ensure that no problems arose during the printing or tonal-correction process.

Note   *For more information on digitizing your images, review Chapter 7.*

Once you have the best possible digitized image, you should preserve a backup copy of the image in its first digitized form. This is extremely important, because you may find that some of your attempts at retouching and color correction don't have the desired effect. If you accidentally remove some crucial detail or alter a color that must be preserved, an expedient way to reverse your change is to sample a section of the original image and clone it over the flawed section in your working file. To make a backup of your original file, select File > Save As. In the As a Copy dialog box, click on the Save A Copy option in the Save section.

Try to make a habit of saving different snapshots in the History palette (discussed in Chapter 11). That way you'll always be able to return to a previous version. Another very powerful aid is adjustment layers (discussed in Chapter 17), which let you preview color and tonal corrections without changing the actual pixels in your images.

Tip   *As you work with the color correction commands, you can use the Fade command to gradually lower the opacity of your most recent effect. After using one of the commands in the Image > Adjust submenu, choose Edit > Fade.*

When you have digitized your image and made a backup copy, avoid the temptation to dive right in and start making changes. Take a few moments to identify your objectives. Decide carefully how you want to improve your image. Obviously, your goal is to make the final electronic image look as good as—or better than—the original; nevertheless, it should still look natural and believable.

Whether you are working on a color or grayscale image, start the correction process by taking readings of the image using the Info palette and the Eyedropper and Color Sampler tools. The Info palette assists you in reading gray and color values. When you move the eyedropper or click the Color Sampler over various areas in the image, the Info palette reads out the exact color or gray values of the underlying pixels. Once you grow accustomed to reading them, you'll learn to rely on the Eyedropper readouts (rather than on your monitor) as a true guide to an image's tones and colors.

APPLYING EFFECTS
TO YOUR IMAGES

| Note | *Before you begin using the Eyedropper and Color Sampler tools to gauge grayscale and color adjustments, it's a good idea to set their sample size to a 3-by-3 pixel sample rather than a Point sample, which evaluates only 1 pixel at a time. This way, one errant pixel won't unduly influence the Info palette readout. To reset the sample size, double-click on the Eyedropper in the Toolbox and choose 3-by-3 Average from the Sample Size pop-up menu in the Eyedropper Options bar. (This also changes the Sample Size in the Color Sampler tool.)* |

Correcting a Grayscale Image

Before you start correcting a grayscale image, it's important to ensure that your settings are correct in the Photoshop Color Settings submenu. To view the grayscale settings, choose File > Color Settings > Grayscale Setup. If you are correcting a grayscale image that will appear on the Web or in a slide or multimedia production, choose the RGB option. When you choose RGB, Photoshop does not compensate on screen for dot gain.

If you are working on an image that will be printed, choose Black Ink in the Grayscale Settings dialog box. When you choose Black Ink, Photoshop adjusts the screen to compensate for dot gain that occurs when printing (it does not change the actual data saved in the file or how the file is output). The dot gain settings used are those specified in the Color Settings dialog box (Edit > Color Settings); these settings are discussed in Chapter 2.

If you wish to learn how to correct the tones of a grayscale image, open any grayscale image, or load one of the Chapter 19 grayscale files from the book CD.

When you make tonal corrections, you increase detail in the shadows, midtones, and highlights of an image. Figure 19-3 shows a digitized photograph that we'll use here to demonstrate the techniques involved in correcting a grayscale image. The photograph, taken in the late 1800s, is of Medora von Hoffman de Mores, a French nobleman who came to the Dakotas to raise cattle. The problems in the photograph are numerous: details are faded, the image is too dark, and dirt and dust spots are sprinkled throughout. Ken Chaya, art editor of the Reader's Digest book *Discovering America's Past*, asked your author, Adele, to retouch the photograph of Medora. The right-hand image in Figure 19-3 shows the same photograph after the gray tones were corrected and the image was retouched.

Read on to learn exactly how Adele retouched this image. If you'd like to try your hand at retouching, load the image from the Chapter 19 folder on this book's CD.

Using the Eyedropper and Info Palette to Take Readings

Once you have a grayscale image on screen and the Eyedropper tool is activated, open the Info palette and move the eyedropper over different parts of your image. Notice that the *K* (black) value in the Info palette displays the percentage of black in the area touched by the eyedropper. Your next step is to take readings of the darkest and

Figure 19-3. *The old, damaged photograph before (left) and after (right) tonal adjustments and retouching*

lightest points in your image. It's important to do this, because areas with less than 5 percent black tones will often print as white. Dot gain in printing may cause areas with over 95 percent black tones to look blotchy. If you are outputting to newsprint, dot gain increases, so try to keep the darkest shadow areas around 80 percent black; as a general rule use 85 percent for uncoated paper and 95 percent for coated paper. Depending upon the image, use either 0 or 4 percent as your whitest white.

In Figure 19-4, the darkest shadow area reads 99% K (black). Soon you'll see how these dark areas were diminished.

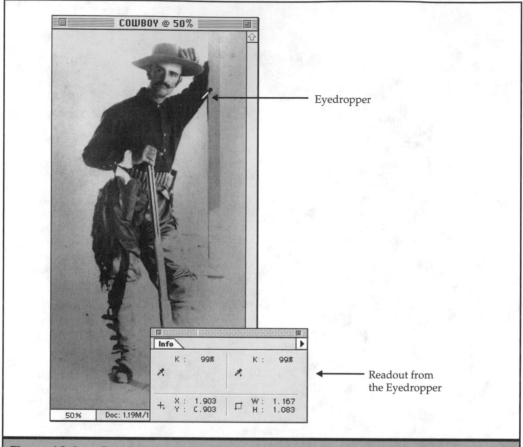

Eyedropper

Readout from
the Eyedropper

Figure 19-4. Reading the darkest areas of the image with the Eyedropper tool

Note *The paper, screen frequency, and printing press used all affect the quality of the final output. Consult your print shop if you have questions.*

Once you know the values of your darkest and lightest points, take a reading of the midtones. If the midtone areas are too light or too dark, you'll probably want to adjust these levels during the tonal correction process.

Remember *You can also use the Color Sampler tool to take up to four readings, which are displayed in the Info palette. After you click, Photoshop leaves a sample icon at the point where you clicked. You can then move the sample by clicking and dragging it with the Color Sampler tool. To remove a sample icon from the screen, press OPTION (ALT) and click on the sample location.*

Since it's impossible to take a reading of every pixel of your image by using the Info palette and the Eyedropper, it's often valuable to view a histogram of the image, as described next.

Using a Histogram to View the Grayscale Tonal Range

When you open a grayscale image on screen, every pixel in the image can have a gray value between 0 (black) and 255 (white). Darker pixels have lower gray values; lighter pixels have higher values. A *histogram* plots the disbursement of the gray tones in an image and gives you a visual sense of an image's tonal range. To display a histogram of your image, select Image > Histogram. If part of your image is selected, the histogram charts only the selected area.

The Histogram dialog box graphs the number of pixels in relation to the tonal range of all possible gray values in an image. The x-axis represents the possible gray values from 0 to 255. The y-axis represents the number of pixels for each tone/color. Beneath the x-axis is a gradient bar showing the actual gray levels from black to white. Dark image areas are graphed on the left of the graph, midtones in the middle, and light areas on the right. The height of each vertical line represents the number of pixels for each tone on the x-axis; the higher the line, the more pixels at that gray level are in the image.

If the histogram is weighted predominantly toward the right, your image is probably too light. This is often called a *high-key* image. If it is weighted toward the left, it's probably too dark. These are called *low-key* images. A histogram that bulges in the middle is stuffed with too many midtone values and thus may lack contrast. In general, a well-balanced image will show pixels spread over the entire tonal range, with most in the midtone area. This is often called a *normal-key* image.

The Histogram dialog box also displays the following precise statistics for your image:

- The Mean value represents the average brightness.
- The Std Dev (Standard Deviation) value represents the variance of the brightness values in the image.
- The Median value represents the middle brightness value in the image.
- The Pixels value is the total number of pixels in the image or selection.

When you move the mouse within the graph, the pointer becomes a crosshair. When you move the crosshair over the histogram, the Level, Count, and Percentile values will change, as follows:

- The Level represents the level of grays at the crosshair location on the graph: 0 is the darkest level (black) and 255 is the lightest level (white).
- The Count represents the number of pixels at the crosshair location on the graph.
- The Percentile is a percentage based on the crosshair's position on the x-axis.

The Cache Level value represents the cache value Photoshop is using when the histogram is displayed. This value changes if the Use Cache for Histograms option is selected in the Image Cache section of the Preferences dialog box (Edit > Preferences > Image Cache). When this option is chosen in the Preferences dialog box, the histogram is created from a sampling of pixels from the image, rather than from all pixels. This results in a faster display.

Move the crosshair from left to right over the histogram, and as you do, the Level and Pixels values will display brightness values and a pixel count. Next, click and drag in the middle of the histogram. A colored or black bar appears above the area over which you drag, and the Level readout displays the gray-level range.

As you make adjustments to your image, you should return periodically to the histogram to get a sense of how your changes are affecting the tonal range.

The histogram's crosshair readout in Figure 19-5 shows that at level 255, the pixel count is 0. Thus, there are no white pixels in the cowboy image and no need to reduce the highlights in the image. Figure 19-6 shows the histogram after very dark values were eliminated to ensure better printing of shadow areas. Notice that the histogram's crosshair readout indicates that at level 0 (black), the pixel count is 0.

When you think you are well acquainted with the tonal distribution in your image, you are ready to make tonal adjustments.

If you wish to view a histogram when a spot color channel or alpha channel is selected in the Channels palette, press OPTION (ALT) as you select Image > Histogram.

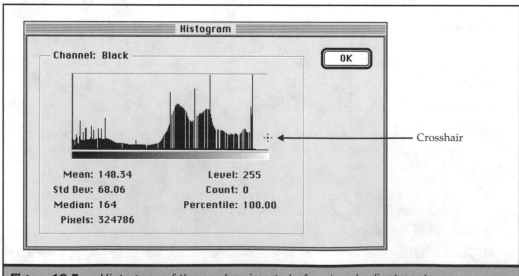

Figure 19-5. *Histogram of the cowboy image before tonal adjustments*

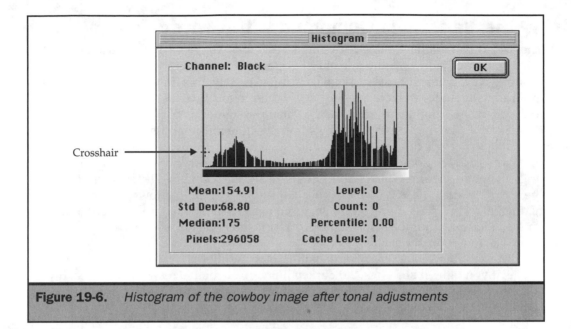

Crosshair

Figure 19-6. *Histogram of the cowboy image after tonal adjustments*

Fine-Tuning Grayscale Images

What do you do if the shadows in your image are over 95 percent black, the highlights under 5 percent black, and the midtones either too dark or too light? When you make tonal adjustments, you often must increase the brightness or contrast. Sometimes you need to expand the tonal range of an image—the range from the lightest point in the image to the darkest point.

To change the darkest, lightest, and midtone areas in an image, you can use the Variations, Levels, and/or Curves commands in the Image > Adjust submenu. (You won't use the Image menu's Brightness/Contrast command, because it has no controls for adjusting shadows, highlights, and midtones.) The command you choose for adjusting these elements in your image will often depend upon the image itself and on how comfortable you are with the available tools. Sometimes you may need to use the Adjust command more than once to complete the operation. It's a good idea to practice using these commands before you attempt to correct images in a real project.

The next sections explain how to use the Variations, Levels, and Curves commands, as well as the Dodge and Burn tools to improve tonal range by adjusting highlights, midtones, and shadows for grayscale images. All these procedures can also be used for correcting color images, as discussed in the section "Color Correction Procedures for Printed Documents," later in this chapter.

Using the Variations Command with Grayscale Images

The Variations command provides a simple and quick way to visually adjust highlights, midtones, and shadows, using miniature image previews—undoubtedly the most intuitive way to adjust tones in an image. Unfortunately, this method does not provide exact adjustment for the color or grayscale values in image areas. Though you can make an image's highlights, midtones, or shadows lighter or darker by clicking on the thumbnail images, you cannot specify a precise value for lightness or darkness as you can using the Levels or Curves commands.

Open the Variations dialog box by selecting Image > Adjust > Variations. The original image, before adjustments, is displayed in the thumbnail labeled Original at the top of the dialog box. You make your adjustments to the shadows, midtones, and highlights by selecting the appropriate thumbnail. To make image areas lighter or darker, click on a thumbnail labeled Lighter or Darker; the effects are then displayed in the Current Pick thumbnail.

Generally, if you darken shadows and lighten highlights, you add contrast to your image. If you lighten shadows and darken highlights, you decrease the contrast. If you want to revert to the original image, press and hold OPTION (*ALT*) while you click on the Original thumbnail, or click on the Reset button.

Note   *If the Variations command does not appear in the submenu after you select Image > Adjust, it may mean that the Variations plug-in module has been removed from Photoshop's Plug Ins/Filters folder.*

The Fine/Coarse slider allows you to specify the level of change in brightness that will occur when you click on a Shadows, Midtones, or Highlights thumbnail. When you drag the slider control to the right toward Coarse, the difference between lighter and darker grows larger. When you drag the slider control to the left toward Fine, the difference decreases. Each increment on the slider is double the previous incremental change.

The Show Clipping option, shown in Figure 19-7, turns grayscale image areas in one of the variation boxes to white if making them lighter or pushes, or boosts, the area to pure white. (In color images, the Show Clipping option turns image areas a neon color if image area change to black or white.)

To try out the Variations command, move to the Shadows column and click on the Lighter thumbnail. This tells Photoshop to make the darkest parts of the image lighter. Notice how the thumbnails change to reveal the Current Pick. Try another variation: move to the Highlights column and click on the Darker thumbnail; this will darken the lightest parts of the image. If you wish, try adjusting the Fine/Coarse slider and then examine the effects on various thumbnails.

Note   *Unfortunately, when the Variations dialog box is open, you can't move the eyedropper over your image to gauge the degree of change as you can when the Levels and Curves dialog boxes are used. Also note that if you don't see changes in your image, you probably have the Fine/Coarse slider set too fine.*

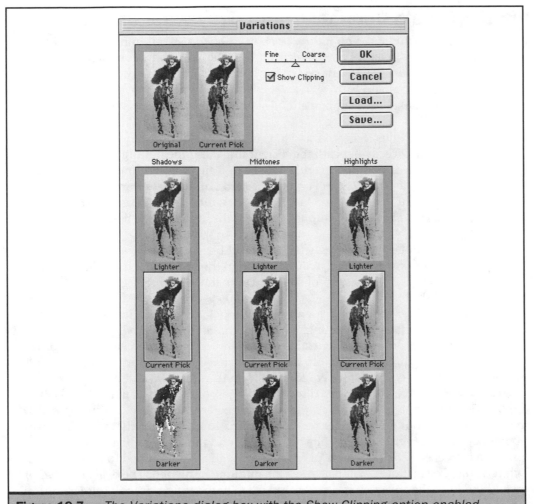

Figure 19-7. *The Variations dialog box with the Show Clipping option enabled*

Be sure to cancel the adjustments you have made before exiting the dialog box if you don't want to change your image. To cancel your changes, click on Cancel or press OPTION (*ALT*) while you click on the Original thumbnail.

 You can use the Levels command in an adjustment Layer. See Chapter 17 for an in-depth discussion of adjustment layers.

Using the Levels Command with Grayscale Images

With the Levels command, you reduce or increase shadows, midtones, and highlights by dragging sliders. It allows more precision than the Variations command does because specific values can be entered in the Levels dialog box. Another advantage to using the Levels command is that it allows Eyedropper and Info palette readings to be taken while you make tonal adjustments. The Info palette displays these readings as "before" and "after" settings.

Select Image > Adjust > Levels, and a histogram of your image will appear in the Levels dialog box. Directly beneath the histogram, along the bottom axis, is the Input Levels slider, which allows you to add contrast by adjusting shadows, midtones, and highlights. The white slider control on the right side of the histogram primarily adjusts the image's highlight values. When you move the white slider control, corresponding values—0 (black) to 255 (white)—appear in the right Input Levels field at the top of the dialog box.

The black slider control on the left of the Input Levels slider primarily adjusts shadow values. Its corresponding values appear in the left Input Levels field at the top of the dialog box. The values for shadows, like those for highlights, range from 0 (black) to 255 (white).

The middle slider control represents the midtones, or gamma, in the image or selection. The default gamma setting, which appears in the middle Input Levels field, is 1.00. Moving the middle slider control to the left raises the gamma value and primarily makes midtones lighter; moving it to the right primarily makes midtones darker. When the gamma is set at 1, it's always equidistant from the shadows and highlights.

When you change values for shadows, midtones, or highlights in the Levels dialog box, Photoshop remaps, or shuffles, the image's pixels accordingly. For instance, if you reset the white Input Levels slider control from 255 to 230, values that were 230 are remapped to 255; highlights are thus brightened, and the total number of highlight pixels is increased. The rest of the pixels in the image are reassigned to reflect the new white value. For instance, you'll also see the midtone lightened. The exact number of pixels and how they are remapped is based upon how far you drag the slider control, so be aware that lightening the highlights can cause a rippling effect that partially lightens midtones and shadows.

When the Preview checkbox in the Levels dialog box is selected, the image or selection changes according to the values in the Input Levels fields.

The Output Levels slider at the bottom of the dialog box reduces contrast by subtracting white or black from an image. Move the black slider control to the right and you will subtract shadow areas from your image, thereby lightening it. Move the white slider control to the left and you will subtract highlight areas, thus darkening your image. When the image is lightened or darkened, Photoshop remaps the pixels according to the new Output Levels values.

For instance, if you drag the white Output Levels control to the left, resetting it from 255 to 200, you remap the image so that 200 is the lightest value. Any pixels with a value of 255 are changed to have a value of 200, and all values are remapped accordingly to make the image darker. The same is true if you move the black control. If the black control is moved from 0 to 50, 50 becomes the darkest value in the image. Pixels that were 0 would now have a value of 50.

At this point, you may be somewhat confused about the difference between the Input Levels and Output Levels sliders. When you drag the left Output Levels slider control to the right, the values increase and the image lightens. But the values also increase when you drag the left Input Levels slider control to the right—yet the image darkens.

Here's and example that may help you understand the distinction between the two: Assume you change the left (black) Input Levels value to 40. This tells Photoshop to take all the shadow values between 40 and a lesser value and change them to 0 (black). Thus, darker pixels are added and the image grows darker. The difference between the lightest and darkest pixels is increased; thus the contrast is increased. On the other hand, if you move the left (black) Output Levels slider control to the right to 40, you are telling Photoshop to take all pixels with values of 0 to 39 and shift them to be 40 and more. Thus, darker pixels are subtracted and the image brightens, but the contrast is reduced. Also, remember that the Input Levels slider focuses on highlights, midtones, and shadows; the Output Levels slider adjusts the entire tonal range.

If the shadows in your image are too dark, try dragging the left Output Levels slider control to the right. Figure 19-8 illustrates how this was done to decrease the black areas in the cowboy image. After the blacks were decreased—with the Levels dialog box still open—the mouse pointer (which turns into an eyedropper if CAPS LOCK is not depressed) was placed over the image to measure the degree of change. Notice that the Info palette in Figure 19-8 shows the before and after readouts: as you can see, dark areas of 99% were changed to 97%. To avoid any lightening of midtones and highlights, the shadow areas were not reduced any further in the Levels dialog box. Instead, the Curves dialog box was used for fine-tuning the shadows, as you'll see in the next section.

> **Tip** *If the white areas in your image are too light, try dragging the right (white) Output Levels control to the left.*

If you've moved the sliders too much in your experimentation, and you're unhappy with the results, you can reset the image by holding OPTION (*ALT*) while you click on the Reset button in the Levels dialog box. (When you press OPTION (*ALT*), the Cancel button changes into a Reset button.)

> **Tip** *If you achieve levels settings that you think you will use frequently, you can keep them handy by clicking on the Save and Load buttons. You can even work on a low-resolution image, save the settings, and apply them to high-resolution files.*

You might have noticed the three eyedropper icons and the Auto button in the Levels dialog box. The white and black eyedroppers can be used to expand an image's tonal range automatically, which can become compressed during the digitization

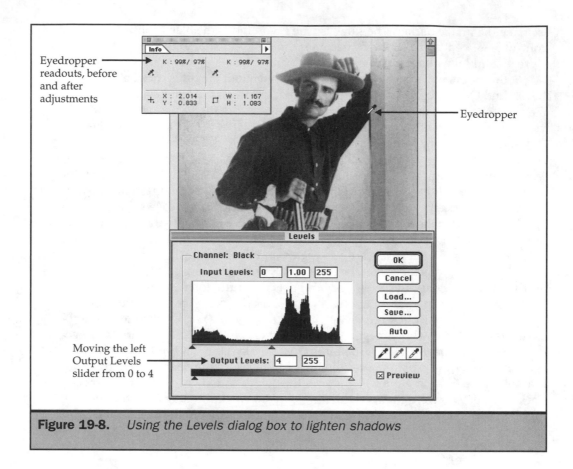

Eyedropper readouts, before and after adjustments

Eyedropper

Moving the left Output Levels slider from 0 to 4

Figure 19-8. *Using the Levels dialog box to lighten shadows*

process. The eyedroppers and the Auto button function similarly to the Auto Levels command in the Image > Adjust submenu. These will be discussed later in this chapter in the "Setting White, Black, and Neutral Points" section.

While using the Levels, Curves, and Hue/Saturation commands, you set color sample points by pressing SHIFT *and clicking in your image. To move a sample point, press* SHIFT *while you click and drag. To delete a sample point, press* SHIFT-OPTION (SHIFT-ALT) *and click on a sample point.*

Next, you will investigate Photoshop's most powerful and precise tool for adjusting colors and tones: the Curves dialog box.

Using the Curves Command with Grayscale Images

The Curves dialog box is probably the most versatile and powerful of Photoshop's tone- and color-correcting utilities. It allows the adjustment of any point on an image's tonal curve. By clicking on your image when the dialog box is open, you can also find where that portion of your image is plotted on the curve. When the cowboy image was corrected, the Curves dialog box was used to pinpoint all shadow areas that were set above 95%.

Remember | *The Curves command can be used in an adjustment layer.*

Select Image > Adjust > Curves. In the Curves dialog box, you'll see a graph displaying a diagonal line. The x-axis on this graph represents an image's Input values; these are the brightness values in the image when the dialog box opens. The y-axis represents the Output values, which will be the new values after the curve is changed. Perhaps it's easiest to think of Input values as the "before" values and Output values as the "after" values. When the dialog box first opens, all Input values equal all Output values, since no values have yet been changed. This produces a diagonal line, because at each point on the graph, the x- and y-axis values are the same. The range of both Input and Output values is from 0% (white) to 100% (black).

To see a readout of the points on the diagonal line, move the mouse pointer over the graph. The pointer will change to a crosshair. Move the crosshair anywhere on the diagonal line, and you will see that both the Input and Output values are displayed at the bottom of the Curves dialog box. Notice that both values are the same. If the dialog box hasn't been changed from its default settings, the gradient bar (under the graph) depicting the gray values of the x-axis starts with white at the left and gradually blends to black. If the gradient bar on your screen starts with black at the left and blends to white, click on either one of the arrows in the middle of the bar, or click on the bar itself, to reset the curve to the default settings.

When white is the starting point on the x-axis, the lower-left corner of the graph— with coordinates of 0%, 0%—plots the lightest possible part of an image. The upper-right corner—100%, 100%—represents the darkest possible area in an image. The slope of the line represents the tonal range, with its bottom depicting the image's shadows and its top the image's highlights. The middle of the slope represents the midtones. The coordinates between the midtones and the highlights are called the *quarter (1/4) tones*. The coordinates between the midtones and the shadows are called the *three-quarter (3/4) tones*.

Since the curve allows you to change an image's tonal range, highlights are adjusted by clicking and dragging on the bottom part of the diagonal line in the graph, shadows by clicking and dragging on the top part of the diagonal line, and midtones by clicking and dragging in the middle of the diagonal line.

If you click on the arrows in the gradient bar to reverse the black and white endpoints, the tone curve is also reversed, causing shadows to be represented at the bottom left of the graph and highlights at the top right. This also causes Input and Output levels to be displayed in brightness values from 0 (black) to 255 (white). You may prefer to work using percentage values, since the percentages of black correspond to the percentage values of halftone dots that make up a printed grayscale image.

The curve icon and the pencil icon at the bottom left of the dialog box tell you what mode you are in. When the curve icon is active (the background of the icon is black), you are in *Curve mode*; in this mode you adjust the diagonal line by setting *control points* on it and then dragging the points to move the line until it becomes a curve (you can also enter values in the Input and Output fields). When the pencil icon is active, you are in *Arbitrary mode*; in this mode the pencil is used to draw new lines in the graph. Arbitrary mode is used primarily for creating special effects. The Preview checkbox allows you to preview changes made by the curve in the image behind the dialog box. If the Preview checkbox isn't selected, click on it now.

The Curves dialog box is unique because it can pinpoint any area of an image along the curve's tonal range. When you position the mouse pointer over part of an image and click, a circle appears on the curve, displaying exactly where that image area is plotted. All image areas corresponding to that point on the curve are edited by adjusting the point where the circle appears.

To see this powerful feature in action, move the mouse pointer outside the Curves dialog box and click anywhere in your image. Notice that the mouse pointer turns into the eyedropper cursor and the circle appears on the curve, representing the pixel's exact tonal location. (Note that when working with a CMYK image, this feature works only when viewing the curves of the individual color channels, not the CMYK composite.) Now click on any dark or shadow area of your image. The circle appears near the top of the curve. Examine the Input and Output values; they should reflect high numbers (75% to 100%). Now click on any highlight or bright area. The circle moves toward the bottom of the curve, and Input and Output values decrease to 25% or less. Click on the gray or midtone areas of your image. Now the circle is in the middle of the curve, and the Input and Output values are near 50%.

Note   *You can enlarge the Curves dialog box by clicking on the dialog box's Zoom box. This can make it easier to create intricate adjustments. Also note that* OPTION-*clicking (*ALT-*clicking) in the grid area of the Curve dialog box displays a finer grid.*

To help you better understand how to use the curve to adjust shadows, midtones, and highlights, assume you want to lighten the darkest areas of your image and darken the lightest areas. First you must determine where the darkest parts of your image lie on the curve. To do this, move the pointer to the darkest part of your image—the pointer will change to an eyedropper. Now click and hold down the mouse button. Immediately, you'll see a circle appear on the curve, as in Figure 19-9. Notice the values in the Input and Output fields at the lower-left corner of the dialog box. This is the percentage of black for the area you've clicked on. Now release the mouse button.

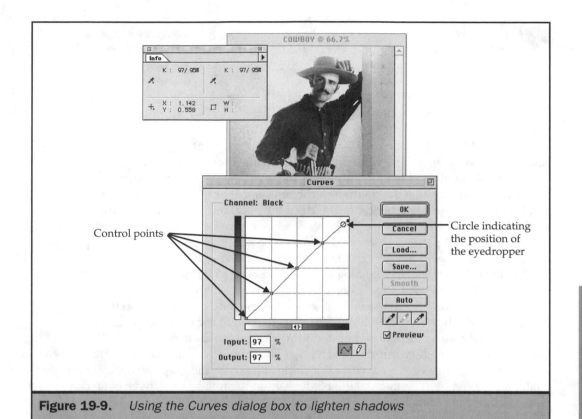

Figure 19-9. *Using the Curves dialog box to lighten shadows*

To decrease the percentage of black, click and drag down on the area where the circle appeared As you drag, try to keep the Input percentage as close as possible to its original percentage, but make the Output percentage lower—your image will become lighter. Dragging the curve this way tells Photoshop to take the darkest pixels and remap them to make them lighter, which lightens the shadow areas. However, because you are clicking and dragging a curve, and not just one individual point, other Input values besides the one represented by the control point now have new values. You can see this by examining the middle point of the curve; it's now lower. When you clicked and dragged on the shadow area of the curve, some of the midtone values came along for the ride. If you truly want to isolate the shadow area and keep other Input values from changing, you'll need to click on the graph to establish control points, which serve as anchors on the curve. We'll look at them next.

Before proceeding, note that the Input and Output fields became activated as you dragged the curve. To fine-tune your adjustments, you can enter values into the Input and Output fields. For instance, you could set the input value to 98% and the Output value to 90% by typing in values rather than by clicking and dragging the mouse. This would remap pixels that were originally 98 percent gray to 90 percent gray.

Once you select the Input or Output field, you can increase or decrease a value by pressing the UP *or* DOWN ARROW *on your keyboard. This works in most Photoshop dialog boxes and palettes.*

Suppose you wish to darken the highlights in your image, but you don't want the change to affect the midtones. Click on the brightest area of your image to see where it is plotted on the curve. To prevent areas other than the highlights from changing, set a control point by clicking on the curve—to set a control point in the midtone area, click about halfway along the curve. A small dot appears, indicating that a control point exists. Create another control point where the brightest part of the image is plotted on the curve. Now position the pointer on the bottom of the diagonal, and click and drag up. Notice how the curve bends as you drag the new control point while the other control points serve as anchors. To prevent swaying in the middle of the curve, you can add more control points. If you need to eliminate a control point, click on the point and drag it out of the grid box, or COMMAND-click (*CTRL-click*) on a point.

In Figure 19-9 the Curves dialog box is being used to lighten just the darkest shadows of the cowboy image. Look carefully and you'll see control points applied at each quadrant along the diagonal line, as well as one additional point in the shadow area. This point has been dragged downward to lighten the darkest shadows. As you can see in the figure, the mouse pointer, which turned into an eyedropper, has been placed over the image to sample the change. The mouse was clicked to locate the adjusted image area on the curve, and a circle appears in the graph to indicate the area that was clicked on. The Info palette confirms that the image areas have been changed to the desired percentage: 95%.

Figure 19-10 illustrates how various points on the curve can be selected at one time. We selected multiple points by pressing SHIFT and then clicking on the curve—the selected control points turn black. When one is dragged, the selected points move in unison, as if they are locked together. In the figure, several points in the shadow area of the curve were selected and then dragged to lighten those areas.

Here are a few tips and shortcuts for using curves:

■ To select control points, press SHIFT as you click on the curve.

■ To deselect control points, press SHIFT and click on selected control points.

■ Use the UP, DOWN, LEFT, and RIGHT ARROW keys to move selected points. To move in increments of 10, press SHIFT as you press the keyboard arrow keys.

To gain more of a feel for using the curves, try a few more tonal adjustments. You can reset the curve by pressing OPTION (*ALT*) and clicking on the Reset button. After you adjust the curve, always examine the Info palette to see the before and after percentages. For example, suppose you've already adjusted an image's highlights and shadows, yet

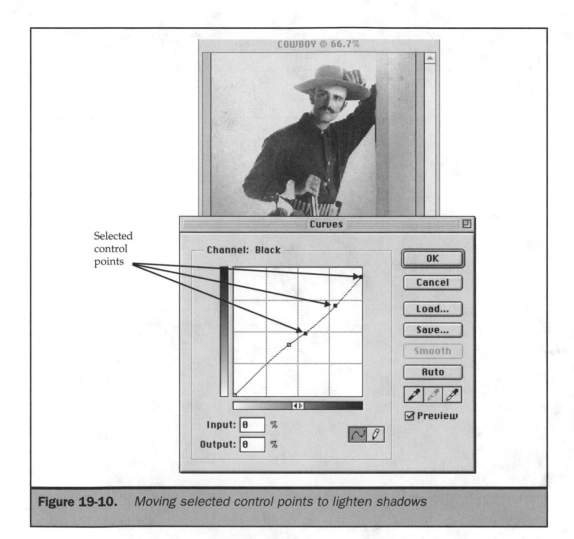

Selected control points

Figure 19-10. *Moving selected control points to lighten shadows*

APPLYING EFFECTS
TO YOUR IMAGES

the image is too dark. To lighten an image overall, set a control point in the middle of the curve and drag the curve downward. If your image is too light, you can darken it by dragging in the opposite direction.

Reset the slope to the default settings again so that you can create a curve that will be used to bring out the contrast, particularly in the highlight and shadow areas of images that are flat. This type of curve is called an *S curve*. To create it, drag the top part of the slope up to darken shadows, and then drag the bottom of the slope down to lighten highlights. This creates the S-shaped curve shown in Figure 19-11. (This same curve will increase or decrease the contrast in a CMYK image.)

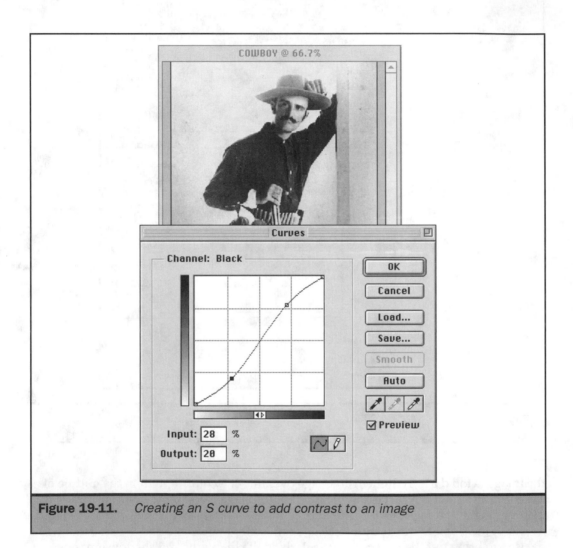

Figure 19-11. *Creating an S curve to add contrast to an image*

With the S curve created, move the mouse pointer over your image and examine the Info palette. Notice the readout that shows the before and after brightness values.

The curve set in these examples uses percentages. Your dialog box settings may range from 0 to 255 instead of 0 to 100%. If you are not using percentages, you can reverse the shape of the curves by clicking on the horizontal gray bar just below the curve.

You can simulate a duotone effect using adjustment layers and the Curves command. First load a grayscale image on screen. Convert the image to RGB or CMYK by using the Image > Mode command. Next, create an adjustment layer and set the type to Curves. In the Curves dialog box, choose a color channel, and then click and drag the curve to add color to the image. To alter the effect, change modes and/or opacity in the Layers palette.

If you'd like, continue experimenting with the Curves dialog box, making adjustments to the highlights, midtones, and shadows in your image. If you find a setting for the curve that you will need later, be sure to save it by clicking on the Save button. A curve can be reloaded by clicking on the Load button.

Saved curves can be used as duotone curves, and vice versa. Duotones are covered in Chapter 13.

Using the Curves Arbitrary Mode to Create Special Effects

In both grayscale and color images, you can create special effects by clicking on the Curves dialog box's pencil icon to switch to Arbitrary mode and then dragging it over the graph to create either lines or curves. One effect you can create is to *posterize* (reduce the gray levels of) your image. Reset the curve to the default settings and use the pencil to create some small lines cutting through the diagonal line, as shown in Figure 19-12. The more lines you create and the longer they are, the greater the posterizing effect will be.

To invert your image to create a negative, click on the upper-left corner of the graph; then press and hold the SHIFT key while you click on the lower-right corner of the graph. This produces a diagonal line from the upper-left corner to the lower-right corner, making all black areas white and all white areas black, as shown in Figure 19-13. Creating this slope produces the same effect as executing the Invert command, which is described in Chapter 8.

APPLYING EFFECTS
TO YOUR IMAGES

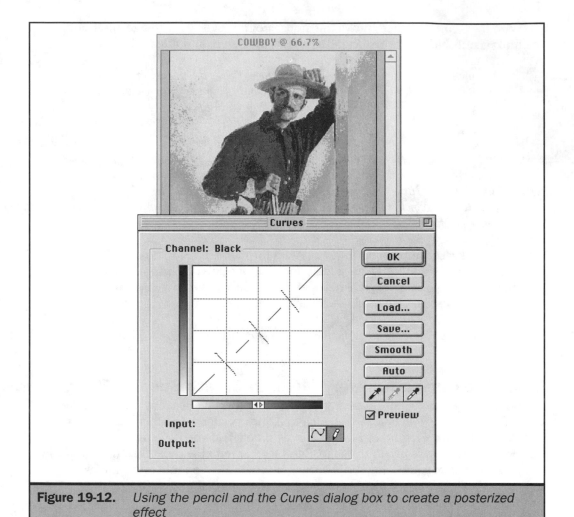

Figure 19-12. *Using the pencil and the Curves dialog box to create a posterized effect*

To create a *solarized* effect, which turns part of your image into a negative, use the pencil to change your graph to look like the one in Figure 19-14. To create this graph quickly, click on the upper-left corner of the graph, and then SHIFT-click in the center of the graph. SHIFT-click again on the upper-right corner. The resulting image looks the same as if you had applied the Solarize filter from the Filter > Stylize submenu.

You can create many other unusual color special effects by using the pencil icon to adjust the graph in the Curves dialog box. For instance, you can use the pencil to create a few individual lines and then join them by clicking on the Smooth button.

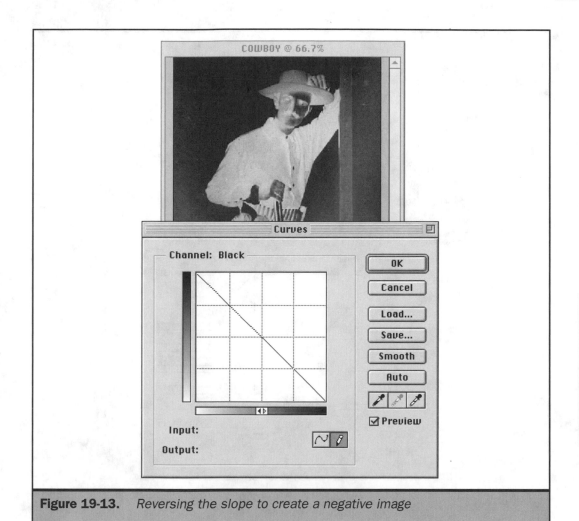

Figure 19-13.   *Reversing the slope to create a negative image*

Using the Dodge and Burn Tools to Darken and Lighten Areas

If the areas in your image that need lightening or darkening are small, and they don't need much tonal adjustment, you might wish to use the Dodge and/or Burn tools for the task. As discussed in Chapter 6, the Dodge and Burn tools are used to lighten and darken, respectively, portions of an image. In Figure 19-15, the Burn tool was used to add tone to the pistol in the cowboy's holster. Here the Exposure value was raised to 25% to add more contrast to the lighter midtones.

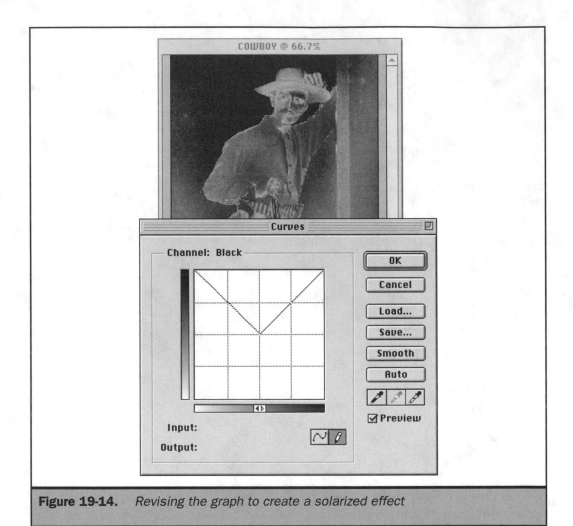

Figure 19-14. *Revising the graph to create a solarized effect*

 After painting a stroke with the Dodge or Burn tool, you can lower the opacity of the last stroke in the Fade dialog box. (Select Edit > Fade.)

 If you need to correct an image that doesn't have any tone in certain areas, you may want to use the Clone Stamp tool to clone tone from other areas.

Once you are happy with the shadows, midtones, and highlights of your image, you're ready to perform any retouching that might be necessary to clean up the image or make it better than the original.

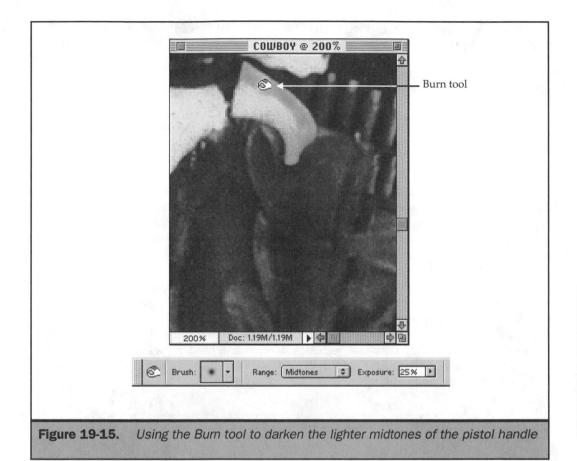

Burn tool

Figure 19-15.   *Using the Burn tool to darken the lighter midtones of the pistol handle*

Retouching Old Photographs

Old photographs often present significant challenges in retouching. The pictures are often marred by spots and scratches, as well as being torn and faded. For badly damaged photographs, be prepared to apply some painting and drawing skills to re-create entire sections in your digitized image. It's often best to begin with the elements that will be easiest to fix and then proceed to the more difficult ones. Once you have analyzed your image and decided how to proceed, you are ready to begin retouching.

A good place to start is to look for any dust, dirt, scratches, or spots that appear in your image as a result of the digitizing process or due to a flawed original. Spots and scratches can usually be eliminated by using the Clone Stamp's cloning option to clone background areas over the particles. If you do need to correct spots and scratches, experiment with different opacities and brushes until you achieve a soft and natural effect. Another method of removing dirt, dust, and scratches from an image is to use the Dust & Scratches filter. See Chapter 12 for more details.

As you work, it's often helpful to have two windows open, both containing the same image but set to different magnifications. This way you can zoom into a specific area, yet view the results of your work simultaneously at actual size. To open a duplicate window on screen, choose View > New View. Also, don't forget that when you zoom in, you can use the Toolbox's Pencil tool with the smallest, hard-edged brush to edit your image one pixel at a time.

In the cowboy image, the dirt spots in the original photograph and the dust spots introduced by the scanner were cloned away with the Clone Stamp tool. After the spots were removed, the hat was the next item to be retouched, since it was the simplest part of the project. A sample from another part of the hat was duplicated over the faded area. The retouching continued from the hat down to the leg and foot—the most difficult area to correct.

Follow along with the techniques used to retouch the cowboy image and try them on one of the Chapter 19 grayscale images on this book's CD. To restore the cowboy's left arm, the Eyedropper, Airbrush, Paintbrush, and Clone Stamp tools were all put to use. First the Eyedropper was activated to change the foreground color to match the gray tone of the arm. Then the Airbrush tool was selected and used to paint a light outline to serve as a boundary that would not be painted over. The boundary line helped Adele visualize the missing limb while she worked to re-create it.

The area where the limb was re-created was painted using the Clone Stamp and the Paintbrush, with a medium-sized, soft-edged brush. Although a mask could have been used to isolate the arm, it wasn't necessary. If the area beyond the boundary line had been painted over, it could have been easily corrected by changing the foreground color to the correct color and painting with that color.

Remember *If you want to be cautious, or if an area is particularly intricate, you should create a mask and then work in the unprotected (selected) area bordered by the mask (see Chapter 14).*

The Airbrush tool was also used to restore detail and tone to the shotgun. The edges of the shotgun's handle were restored with a small, hard-edged brush with Pressure set at 50%.

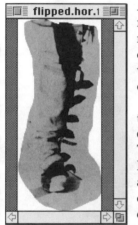

After the simpler retouching tasks were completed, all that remained was to restore the lower part of the left leg. This was more difficult to repair because it required that more details be created, and several steps were involved. First, the Airbrush tool was used to sketch the left leg, as shown in Figure 19-16. Again, the outline served as a boundary line to visualize the missing limb.

Once the left leg was sketched, the Lasso was used to select the lower right leg. This selection was duplicated by pressing COMMAND-OPTION (*CTRL-ALT*) and dragging on the selection. The selection was flipped using the Edit > Transform > Flip Horizontal command, and then the leg was cut and pasted into a new file. (Remember that when you copy or cut an image and create a new file, the new file settings will be the same size as the cut or copied image.) Then the flipped image and the original one were placed side by side so that the flipped leg could be cloned into the original file. In Figure 19-17, the crosshair indicates the sampled area, and the Clone Stamp pointer shows the target area where the cloning is being applied.

Before using the Clone Stamp, Adele saved the file so she could revert to the last saved version if necessary. When working in Photoshop, Adele often creates snapshots in the History palette, so she can later paint in a snapshot version of the file with the History brush, if needed.

After all the retouching was finished, the Unsharp Mask filter was applied to the image to sharpen it and bring out details. Chapter 12 describes how to use Photoshop's sharpening filters.

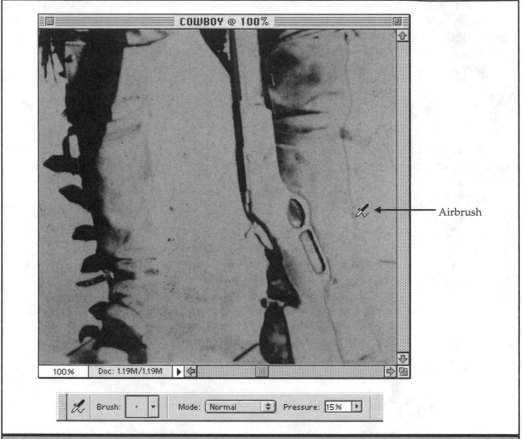

Airbrush

Figure 19-16.   *Using the Airbrush to create an outline for the missing parts of the leg and foot*

Removing Wrinkles or Freckles from Faces

Another common retouching task—particularly for advertising projects—involves eliminating facial wrinkles and otherwise improving images of people. Using the Clone stamp and the Smudge and Airbrush tools, you can easily remove wrinkles and blemishes.

In the following example, the original image (at left) shows wrinkles surrounding the person's eye; notice that the retouched image (at right) is much improved.

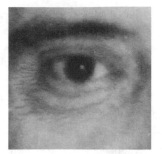

Before retouching

After retouching

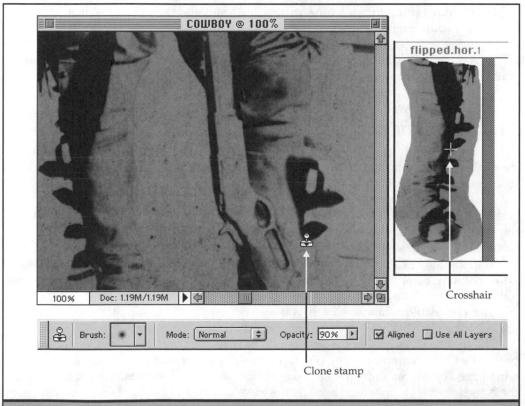

Crosshair

Clone stamp

Figure 19-17. *Retouching the lower-left leg by cloning the flipped lower-right leg*

The trick to removing wrinkles, or any other facial blemish, is to apply a vibrant skin color over that area of the image. Dark skin crevices can easily be blended into lighter flesh tones with the help of the Smudge and Rubber Stamp tools.

If you want to try removing wrinkles, load the Eye file from the book CD.

1. Use the Zoom tool to magnify the target area.

2. Use the Eyedropper to change the foreground color to the desired skin color.

3. Use the Smudge, Clone Stamp, and Airbrush tools to blend skin tones together in the magnified area. For a gentler, softer effect, use a small-to-medium, soft-edged brush with Opacity in the Options bar set from 2% to 90%.

4. In our example, the smaller wrinkles were blended into the face using the Smudge tool. To remove the more pronounced lines, use the Rubber Stamp's cloning option to clone the surrounding tones and then use the Airbrush tool to produce a more subtle blend.

Another trick when removing wrinkles is to select the area with the Lasso tool, feather the selection as needed, and then choose Image > Adjust > Curves to match the surrounding tones.

Retouching Landscapes

Retouching not only restores old photographs and makes people look younger and more glamorous; it is also used to transform landscapes so that they are more attractive than their real-life originals.

For example, the art director of Reader's Digest General Books, Dave Trooper, wanted the scene for the cover of a proposed book, *Back Roads of America*, to look better than reality. The original image was a near-perfect photograph of a lovely New England scene. Figure 19-18 shows the image before retouching.

Marring the beauty of the original image were the telephone poles and overhead wires running through the town. For the cover design, Dave wanted to put a map next to the photograph and to remove the road sign for Junction 14. The stop-light warning sign, barely visible behind the trees, was also deemed a detraction that needed to be erased. Figure 19-19 shows the final retouched image.

The Junction 14 sign was the first item to be retouched, as shown on the following page. The Clone Stamp's cloning option was used to remove it, with a medium, hard-edged brush rather than a soft-edged brush. A soft-edged brush would have made the cloned area look unnatural because the leaves on the trees were sharp and crisp, not soft and faded. To maintain a natural look, a variety of different leaves from several tree areas were sampled and cloned over the sign. During the cloning process, the Opacity in the Clone Stamp Options bar was set to varying values between 65% to 85% to blend the leaves into the trees.

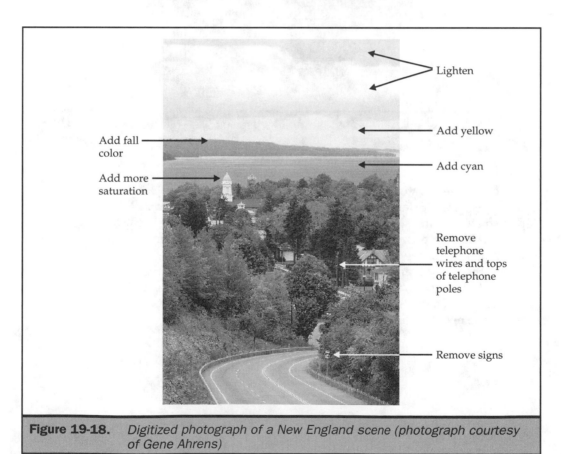

Figure 19-18.   *Digitized photograph of a New England scene (photograph courtesy of Gene Ahrens)*

Figure 19-19. *Proposed book cover after retouching and color correction*

To eliminate the sto light warning sign, part of the road was cloned over the sign and the trees were extended into the road. The Clone Stamp's cloning feature and the Airbrush were both used to retouch the area. Some of the railing area was re-created with the Airbrush because the cloning tool couldn't create a perfect match between the old railing and the new railing.

Then the Clone Stamp's cloning option was used again, this time to remove the unwanted wires (shown in the following illustration). For a more natural effect, both a hard-edged and a medium soft-edged brush were used. Opacity was set to about 75% to blend the new leaves with the old leaves.

Try using the Clone Stamp tool on the snowy scene in Figure 19-20. The Snowy day image is in the Chapter 19 folder of this book's CD.

Figure 19-20.   *Removing unwanted wires from snowy scene*

The following section provides an overview of how to undertake a color correction project, and we will continue using the book cover project as an example. If you have a grayscale image on screen, close it now, because you will be using a color file for the remainder of this chapter. If you wish to create another version of your file, select the File > Save As command. Otherwise, close the file without saving it.

Fine-Tuning Color Images

Many of the issues involved in grayscale tonal correction also arise when you're correcting color. As with grayscale images, it may not be possible to transform an inferior color original or a poorly scanned color image into a perfect picture. Exposure and lighting defects found in many grayscale images are also the most common problems in color images. However, correcting color is much more complicated than correcting grays, because every pixel has the potential of being any one of millions of possible colors, rather than just 256 levels of gray.

The number of colors in an image brings up an important display issue: If your image contains many more colors than your monitor can display, color-correcting that image will be difficult. With a video card that displays only 256 colors, you won't be able to judge the colors of continuous-tone images accurately by their appearance on screen. If you are serious about color correction, you will want to invest in a 24-bit video card, which can display more than 16 million colors.

Even if your system is calibrated and you are working in 24-bit color, you must still be wary of how colors look on your screen. As discussed in Chapter CD-1, differences between onscreen and printed colors are to be expected. The best way to judge colors is by using the Eyedropper tool and the Info palette. For instance, if an apple on the screen looks rich, juicy, and crisp, but the Info palette reading lacks a high magenta percentage, this tells you that your monitor is not displaying the correct colors. For bright red, you should see CMYK values of approximately 20 percent cyan, 100 percent magenta, 80 percent yellow, and 5 percent black—or RGB values of red 161, green 0, and blue 49.

If you are working on color images that will be printed, it's crucial that CMYK colors are displayed in the Info palette. This readout will display exclamation points alongside the CMYK values of any colors that fall outside the CMYK printing gamut.

 You can preview out-of-gamut colors by using the View > Gamut Warning command. (See Chapter 13 for more information.)

To see the Eyedropper tool and Info palette in action, load an RGB or CMYK file (if you don't already have a color image on screen). You can load a file from the Chapter 19 folder on the book CD.

If the Info palette is not displayed, open it now. If you do not see the RGB and CMYK percentages, click on the Info palette's pop-up menu. In the Info Options dialog box, make sure that the Mode pop-up menus for First Color and Second Color Readouts are set to RGB and CMYK.

You might wonder why you should keep the RGB values displayed in the Info palette if you are working on a CMYK color file. As discussed in Chapter CD-1, when you *add* cyan, magenta, or yellow to an image, you *subtract* its complement (red, green, or blue). When you *subtract* cyan, magenta, or yellow, you *add* the color's complement. With both color readouts showing in the Info palette, you'll be able to judge how much of a color or its complement is added or subtracted.

Take a look at the relationship between RGB and CMYK colors in your image. Move the mouse pointer over your image, and notice that any color showing a high RGB value displays a low percentage of its CMYK complement and vice versa. For instance, a color with a high red value displays a low cyan percentage, and a color with a high cyan percentage displays a low red value. The relationship between RGB and CMYK colors is clearly depicted in a color wheel. Before you start making color adjustments, you may wish to consult a color wheel and keep it handy. On a color wheel, each color resides between the two colors that create it. For instance, green is created by adding cyan and yellow. On the opposite side of each color is its complement; for example, opposite green on the color wheel is magenta.

Basic Tips

As you work on color-correction projects, here are a few suggestions to keep in mind:

- **Fashion** Work carefully with white and black fabric because it's difficult to maintain detail and definition in very dark and very light image areas. Be careful not to oversharpen, or fabric will not look real. Too high a percentage of yellow can make white look dull. Low cyan values will keep reds vibrant; low yellow values will keep blues vibrant. You might wish to obtain fabric samples so you can compare real colors and materials with screen colors.

- **People** Strands of hair should be as sharply defined as possible. Teeth should be white rather than dull and yellow, though pure white teeth will look unreal. Consult your print shop concerning the effects of dot gain on flesh tones.

- **Food** It's often impossible to make all the food in a shot look delicious. For example, brilliant red tomatoes may look delicious, but meat too red will appear raw. Analyze or ask your client what should be the center of attention in the image. Foods that have bland, unrecognizable colors, such as cereals and soup, can be difficult to correct.

- **Outdoors**   Strengthen greens, blues, and reds with the Sponge tool. Use black to make greens darker, rather than magenta, which will lower saturation. Examine the grays in an image to make sure they are gray and aren't exhibiting color casts. When creating sky, the relationship between cyan and magenta will determine the shade of sky you are creating. For instance, by adding more and more magenta, you can go from bright blue to dark blue.

- **Snow Scenes**   Snow should not be pure white because detail will be lost. Concentrate on adding detail to the highlights. Avoid losing detail in darker areas when enhancing whites.

RGB or CMYK?

A question that many Photoshop users wrestle with is whether to work in an RGB color or a CMYK color file. In making your decision, consider the following guidelines.

If you are outputting to slides, video, or the Web, make your color corrections in RGB because slides and video monitors use RGB colors rather than CMYK. If you are creating images for an onscreen presentation or the Web, you may be using only 256 RGB colors rather than thousands or millions of RGB colors. If this is the case, you may want to set your monitor to 256 colors instead of thousands or millions so that you can work in the number of colors you'll actually be using. This will help you ensure that your corrections are accurate. Most new computers display thousands or millions of colors.

For output to a commercial printing press, you may want to fine-tune your colors in CMYK mode; this way you will be working with the same colors that your print shop uses for your job. It is also helpful to color-correct in CMYK when you are adjusting blacks in your image. If need be, you can change only the blacks in a CMYK file by making adjustments to the black channel (with RGB colors, no black channel is available).

Since CMYK files are always larger than their RGB counterparts, you may wish to adjust your colors in RGB mode and then output your image to either slide or chrome. You can give a prepress house the slide or chrome to be scanned and converted to CMYK.

If you are correcting an image that was digitized on a high-end scanner, chances are that the image was saved as a CMYK color file. If you scanned the image yourself on a low-end or midrange flatbed or slide scanner, the file will probably be digitized in RGB rather than CMYK. Digital and video cameras digitize images in RGB rather than CMYK color.

If you wish to work in CMYK mode, you can do so by converting your RGB color image to CMYK color, but do not convert without first verifying the settings in the Color Settings dialog box. (As discussed in Chapter 2, most Photoshop users who are outputting for print should change Photoshop's Default RGB Color space from sRGB to Adobe RGB.) Before converting an image to CMYK, review Chapters 2 and 13. It's important to understand that if you convert to CMYK with improper calibration settings, you may be forced to return to your original RGB file. Once you have reset the calibration options to the correct settings, you'll need to reconvert to CMYK and start your corrections again from scratch.

If your system cannot handle large, high-resolution CMYK color files, another alternative is to work on a low-resolution color file and save your dialog box settings. Then use the Load button in the Levels, Curves, Hue/Saturation, and Variations dialog boxes to apply the settings to the high-resolution version and make final color adjustments as needed. Alternatively, you can create adjustment layers in the low-resolution files and drag them from the Layers palette into the high-resolution files. Then make the final adjustments in the high-resolution files.

Color Correction Procedures for Web-Based Documents

Everyone who has a Web site wants to attract visitors and keep them coming back. Unfortunately, color correction for the Web can be quite problematic, and here are the two biggest complications:

- Color varies from one type of monitor to the next. Colors also look different on Macintosh screens than they do on PC screens. (A pop-up menu in Photoshop's Save for Web dialog box lets you preview images as they appear on Macs and on Windows computers. Click on the small circled-arrow symbol at the upper-right corner of the dialog box to access this pop-up menu.)

- Many users can view only 256 colors on their systems and must view images dithered by their Web browsers (the Save for Web dialog box pop-up menu previews browser dither). For more information about finessing images for the Web, see Chapter 9.

Thus, an image that looks perfect on your computer system may look quite different when viewed on the Web.

Understanding the Web Color Settings

The best way to tackle the problem of viewers using different monitors and computer systems to display your Web images is to set up Photoshop's RGB color settings properly, as discussed in Chapter 2. After you decide whether you will be outputting images for the Web, you should choose Edit > Color Settings. In the Color Settings dialog box, choose the Web graphics default in the Settings pop-up menu.

If you are working with a team of Web designers, have all members of the team change their computer's color settings to the Web Graphics Defaults

Mastering the Web Palette

Undoubtedly, the most annoying aspect of color-correcting images for the Web is coping with the color restrictions required by the Web-safe palette. As discussed in Chapter 9, when working with images that will be output to the Web, you can save in

JPEG, PNG, or GIF formats. JPEG and PNG 24 allow you to compress your file size without reducing the number of colors in the images. However, many Web users still own computers that display only 256 colors at a time. If you decide that you need to reduce the number of colors in your image and save to a Web-safe palette, image quality is often sacrificed. Your best bet is to use Photoshop's Save for Web and/or ImageReady's Optimize palette to preview the results. If you choose the Web palette option, you'll generally achieve the best results by choosing Diffusion dither and specifying a high dither percentage. If you are not satisfied with the results, you might attempt a different approach: try stylizing the image or use Photoshop filters to create a painterly effect.

For instance, assume you wish to create a button out of a scanned image. Instead of simply converting the image to a Web-safe palette, try applying one of Photoshop's Pixelate filters. For instance, both Mezzotint and Facet can produce interesting stylized versions of your images. Since both filters actually reduce the number of colors in an image, converting to a Web palette after running the filter often leaves the stylized effect intact.

If you'd like to experiment with this technique, try the following exercise:

1. Load the Fruit file from the Chapter 19 folder of this book's CD.

2. Run the Mezzotint filter by choosing Filter > Pixelate > Mezzotint. Choose the Medium Dots option.

3. In Photoshop, choose File > Save for Web. (If you are using ImageReady, click on the Optimized tab). Click on the 2-Up Setting tab so that you can see the original and the optimized version. Choose Web as the palette and Diffusion as the Dither choice. Notice that the Web version and the original version look nearly identical.

Ensuring Best Results on the Web

Whether or not you reduce the number of colors in your images before outputting them to the Web, your steps for correcting images will generally be the same.

Here's list of procedures that should produce good results for most images.

■ Work with RGB images, using the Web Graphics Defaults setting (described in Chapter 2).

■ To lighten or darken images, or raise or lower RGB color channels, choose Image > Adjust > Levels in either Photoshop or ImageReady. Though it's a bit more difficult, you can also use Photoshop's Curves command. (Levels and curves are discussed in "Using the Levels Command with Grayscale Images" and "Using the Curves Command with Grayscale Images" sections earlier in this chapter.)

■ To change color values, choose Image > Adjust > Hue/Saturation in Photoshop or ImageReady. (Photoshop's Hue/Saturation command is more sophisticated than ImageReady's.) We've found that Photoshop's Color Balance command is also quite useful for changing colors of Web images. (Hue/Saturation and Color Balance are covered in the "Using the Hue/Saturation Command" and "Using the Color Balance Command" sections of this chapter.)

■ Optimize the image for the Web: choose File > Save for Web in Photoshop. In ImageReady, the document window always displays tabs set up for viewing optimized versions of your image. To change optimization settings in ImageReady, use the Optimize palette.

Color Correction Procedures for Printed Documents

When you are ready to color-correct an image for print, your first step should be to adjust the overall tonal range of the image; you can then make corrections to specific areas.

The New England scene in the Reader's Digest book cover (see Figures 19-18 and 19-19) will be used here to demonstrate the steps involved in color correction. If you wish, you can follow along, using the Fruit file or the Flamingo file found on the book CD.

The New England image was scanned by a prepress house on a high-end drum scanner to obtain the best digitization. In the scanning process, the image was converted to a CMYK file and saved in TIFF format. Since the file was larger than 30MB, it was saved on a removable hard disk cartridge so it could be delivered to the client.

After examining a Matchprint (a proof made from film separations) from the original scan, it was decided that the clouds should be lightened so that the book title would stand out as much as possible. The decision to color-correct was made not because the original image or scan was flawed, but because the design of the book cover required it. The art director also decided to enhance the color of the foliage in the town. Additionally, he felt that the colors of the water and church dome were a little light and that the saturation should be increased. Finally, he wanted a more autumn-like look to the hills across the bay.

Before color correction, the colors in the Matchprint were compared to those on the CMYK color file on the monitor. After the two were analyzed, slight calibration changes were made in the CMYK Setup dialog box.

Taking Readings with the Eyedropper and Info Palette

The next step in color-correcting the New England image was to analyze the problem areas as well as the good areas. To evaluate colors in an image, take readings using the Eyedropper and Info palette. Taking readings is an important step in making a more dramatic and colorful image. If you wish to practice taking readings of a CMYK file, you can use the Flamingo file found on the book CD.

Once you know the RGB values or CMYK percentages of the image areas, you can evaluate the colors that need to be added or taken out, and in what percentage. In the photograph for the proposed book cover, readings were taken of the clouds, water, hills across the bay, church dome, and foliage. The Eyedropper readings of some of the foliage showed a predominance of cyan, with little yellow and little magenta. These would obviously need to be boosted to improve the impression of autumn colors.

Readings of the Flamingo image showed that magenta needed to be reduced throughout the image. The only area where we didn't want the magenta lowered was the flamingos—we wanted to increase the magenta in the flamingos. Also, the green needed to be increased overall, except for the flamingos. Therefore, we isolated the flamingos using the Lasso tool and saved the selection so that we could work in the flamingo area separate from the background area. When we needed to color-correct the flamingo, we would load the selection from the alpha channel. When we needed to work everywhere except on the flamingo, we loaded the flamingo selection and then inverted it by choosing Select > Inverse.

Using a Histogram to View the Tonal Range

After analyzing the areas that needed enhancement, the next step was to view the image's histogram. As explained earlier in the "Using a Histogram to View the Grayscale Tonal Range" section, a histogram is useful for examining the tonal range of an image—from its brightest to its darkest points. In a color image, a histogram provides not only a visual impression of the brightness values of the entire image, but of the separate channels as well. Before color correction, the histogram of the New England image revealed that the tonal range was fairly broad, with few shadow pixels.

To view a histogram of an RGB image, you can load the Car file from the Chapter 12 folder of book CD. To work with a CMYK image, use the Flamingo file.

With the image file open on screen, choose Image > Histogram. Click to open the Channel pop-up menu:

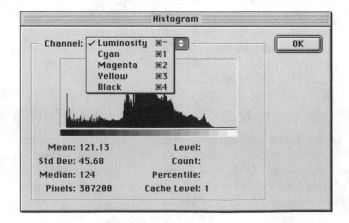

If you are viewing a CMYK image, the Channel pop-up menu allows you to view brightness (Luminosity) values of the CMYK composite and the color values of the individual Cyan, Magenta, Yellow, and Black channels. For an RGB image, you'll see a Luminosity channel for the composite brightness values and one for each of the Red, Green, and Blue channels.

If you are working with the Car file, click on the Channel pop-up menu in the Histogram dialog box and take a moment to view each channel to see the color values. You'll see that the Red channel contains many light pixels, the Blue channel contains many dark pixels, and the Green channel contains both light and dark pixels but not many pixels in the midtones. Choose Image > Adjust > Levels to view how the colors disperse in the shadows, midtones, and highlight areas. You can also use this dialog box to adjust the colors. To adjust the colors separately, click on the Channel pop-up menu and choose a channel.

If you are using the Flamingo file, you'll see that the image has most of the cyan, magenta, and yellow pixels in the midtone area, and the black pixels are evenly distributed between the midtone and highlight areas.

Setting White, Black, and Neutral Points

During scanning, an image's tonal range can be compressed, particularly by low-end scanners that cannot reproduce as broad a range of colors as high-end scanners. The histogram often reveals this compression: images with compressed tonal ranges often lack shadow and highlight areas. One technique for expanding the tonal range of an image is to set a white (highlight) point and a black (shadow) point. By setting a white and black point, you specify areas in your image that you wish to have as its lightest and darkest points. The eyedropper icons in the Curves and Levels dialog boxes, described earlier in the "Using the Levels Command with Grayscale Images" and "Using the Curves Command with Grayscale Images" sections of this chapter, allow you to set these points—as well as a gray point to help eliminate color casts from an image.

The tasks of eliminating color casts and of setting white and black points are often handled during the digitization process. If your image was scanned on a high-end scanner and converted to CMYK (as the New England image was), you will probably not need to set a white, black, or gray point. On the other hand, when you work with RGB-digitized images, or images converted from RGB to CMYK color, you should be aware of how setting these points can be helpful.

In Photoshop you can set the white and black points automatically, manually, or by setting levels in the Color Picker. Before you work through the following descriptions of these methods, load any color image on screen.

Setting the White and Black Points Automatically

The easiest way to set the white and black points is to have Photoshop do it automatically—with the default settings, the lightest areas in an image are remapped to white and the darkest areas to black. This often expands the tonal range, providing more contrast in images that are flat and dull.

With your color image on screen, open the Levels dialog box (choose Image > Adjust > Levels). If you like, use the Car file on the book CD. To have Photoshop set the white and black points automatically, click on the Auto button. Immediately, you will see a change in your image, which is reflected in the histogram—you'll often see that the balance between shadows, midtones, and highlights is improved.

To ensure that Photoshop does not use only one tone when it sets the white and black points, a preset *clipping* percentage range is built in when Photoshop adjusts the image. This can prevent very light or very dark areas from overly influencing the tonal change when Photoshop sets the white and black points.

This clipping range can be changed in the Auto Range Options dialog box. To open this dialog box, press OPTION (*ALT*) and click on the Options button. Notice that when you press OPTION (*ALT*), the Auto button changes to the Options button.

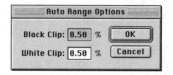

Acceptable values for the Black Clip and White Clip fields are from 0% to 9.99%. The value entered is the percentage that Photoshop will ignore when it automatically sets the white and black points. For instance, if you enter 9% in the Black Clip field, Photoshop ignores the darkest 9 percent of your image when it redistributes pixel values after you click on the Auto button.

If you are unhappy with the results of Photoshop's automatic setting of the white and black points, you can return your image to its original settings. First, press and hold down OPTION (*ALT*), and the Cancel button will change to a Reset button. Click on Reset to return your image to its original settings and try the manual method of setting white and black points.

Note   *The tonal range of an image can also be expanded by executing the Auto Levels command in the Image > Adjust submenu. This command produces the same effect as the Auto button in the Levels dialog box and uses the clipping percentage set in the Auto Range Options dialog box.*

Setting the White and Black Points Manually with the Eyedroppers and Color Picker

If you are color-correcting an RGB image that you will convert to CMYK, or if you are correcting a CMYK color image, you may wish to gain more control when you set the white and black points to ensure that you don't lose detail in highlight and shadow areas. From the Levels and Curves dialog boxes, you can use the eyedroppers to access the Color Picker to set color levels for the white and black points. If you choose this method, you'll first want to take color readings with the eyedroppers to locate the lightest and darkest parts of your image. Don't click on the eyedroppers in the dialog box yet—here are the steps to follow:

Note *When setting white and black points with the Eyedropper, it's best to have the Eyedropper tool set to the 3-by-3 Average choice in the Eyedropper's Sample Size pop-up menu in the tool's Options bar.*

1. Move the mouse pointer (which will change to an eyedropper) over the lightest areas of your image, and examine the Info palette readouts as you go. Very light areas display high values of each RGB component. Generally, when evaluating an image to set the white point, you should search for highlight areas with detail, not pure white areas.

2. Locate the darkest part of your image and move the eyedropper over it. Dark image areas display low values of each RGB component. When searching for the black point, look for shadow areas that are not pure black.

3. Now that you've found the lightest and darkest points, you're ready to set a white and a black level. To set a value for the white level, double-click on the white eyedropper in the Levels dialog box. The Color Picker dialog box opens; notice the words "Select white target color" at the top.

4. Let's assume you want to ensure that the lightest areas of your image are not pure white, that is, not created from the absence of ink on paper. For standard images that are neither to light or dark, Adobe recommends that a Cyan value of 5, with Magenta and Yellow both to 3 and Black (K) set to 0 should provide good results. Click on OK to close the Color Picker.

5. Move the eyedropper tool over the lightest portion of your image that you identified earlier and click the mouse. Photoshop automatically adjusts the tonal range in the entire image using your new white point—any pixels lighter than the white point you set become pure white.

6. The procedure for setting a target value for the black point is virtually identical to that for setting the white point, except you use the black eyedropper. Double-click on the black eyedropper. The Color Picker dialog box opens, and you'll see the words "Select black target color" at the top.

7. Recommended values from Adobe are 65% C, 53% M, 51% Y, 95% K. (These values should produce good results if you are converting an RGB image to CMYK with Photoshop's default color settings.). Click on OK to close the Color Picker.

<table>
<tr><td>**Note**</td><td>*When you are setting the white and black points of a grayscale image, you may wish to set the white point at 5% in the K field (leaving the CMY fields blank) and the black point at 95% K (again, leave the CMY fields blank).*</td></tr>
</table>

8. Move the eyedropper pointer over the darkest portion of your image that you identified earlier, and click the mouse. The tonal range is adjusted proportionally to your new black point—all pixel values that were darker than this value are now set to black.

If the results of setting the black and white points are not satisfactory, try setting different points in the image or slightly adjusting the white and black point levels in the Color Picker. Also, remember that not all images will improve when setting the white and black points and that different images printed on different types of paper may require different black and white points.

After setting the white and black points, you may wish to fine-tune the tonal balance in your image by lightening or darkening it. If so, you can use the Output Levels slider in the Levels dialog box to reduce the white and dark values of your image. As described earlier in the "Using the Levels Command with Grayscale Images" section of this chapter, drag the right Output Levels slider control to the left to reduce the brightness in image highlights, and drag the left Output Levels slider control to the right to lighten shadow areas. You may also want to enhance the midtones, and you can do this by clicking on the middle (gamma) Input Levels slider control. Dragging left lightens midtones, and dragging right darkens them.

When you're satisfied with the tonal adjustments in your image, click on OK. Your next step is to eliminate any color casts that may exist.

Adjusting for Color Casts by Defining a Neutral Tone

Color casts can be the result of several factors. Photographs taken in fluorescent light often produce pink color casts. Outdoor images taken with indoor film might display a blue color cast. Indoor scenes shot with daylight film may yield a yellow color cast. Color casts can also be introduced inadvertently during the digitizing process.

Both the Curves and Levels dialog boxes include a gray eyedropper icon that can be used to reduce color casts and adjust color balance. Here are the steps:

1. Click on the gray eyedropper in the dialog box and move it over your image to the most neutral, or gray, area. You can also use the Color Sampler tool and click on a neutral gray area of your image.

2. Double-click on the gray eyedropper in the Levels dialog box to open the Color Picker dialog box, in which you enter the values that you wish to set for neutral gray (equal red, green, and blue values produce gray).

3. Click on the neutral gray area in your image. Photoshop shifts the hue and saturation values to match neutral gray and continues to shift hue and saturation values to eliminate color casts.

Creating Masks to Isolate Areas for Color Correction

After you have adjusted the basic tonal range in your image and eliminated any unwanted color casts, you can begin fine-tuning any problem areas. To color-correct specific areas of an image, you must first select them. As discussed in Chapters 14 and 15, it is often helpful to create masks of these areas in alpha channels or using the Pen tool, since you will likely need to select them again and again. (There are various ways to create and edit a mask in an alpha channel. For more information, see Chapter 15).

If you wish, you can use one of the Pen tools to create a selection. First, create a path and then click on the Make Selection icon in the Paths palette. For more information about paths, see Chapter 14.

In the New England image, five different masks were created in alpha channels: one for the church dome, one for the water, one for the hills across the bay, and two for different parts of the sky. These masks were created so that they could be reloaded in case more changes were needed. Because alpha channels increase file size, only one mask was included in the New England file at any given time. The masks that weren't being used were exported into a new file by means of the Select > Save Selection command. Masks of the foliage were created when needed using the Lasso tool (the Magnetic Lasso tool could also have been used) and the Quick Mask mode. The Select > Color Range command could also have been used. These masks weren't saved; they could easily be re-created, and they didn't need to be as precise as the others.

Using the Image > Adjust Commands for Color Correction

Once all of the preparation work has been accomplished, you are ready to begin selective color correction. The same Image > Adjust commands you used to correct grayscale images are also available for correcting color images, except that more options are available. For instance, the Variations command allows saturation to be added and subtracted. The Curves and Levels dialog boxes allow you to work with the individual RGB or CMYK channels.

During color correction of the New England image, a selection was generally loaded before a dialog box was opened. As mentioned earlier, Adele had previously duplicated channels into separate files to work more efficiently. When she needed to load the mask selection, she opened the file containing the alpha channels with the masks. Then she chose Select > Load Selection to copy the selection into the New England image file. She loaded the dome selection by choosing Select > Load Selection, and used the Variations command to correct the color on the dome.

Using the Variations Command with Color Images

Often it's a good idea to begin correcting specific selections with the Variations command, because it's the easiest and most intuitive color-correction tool to use. As described in the "Fine-Tuning Grayscale Images" section of this chapter, the Variations dialog box features thumbnails that preview how your image will be changed.

If you'd like to experiment with the Variations command, start by selecting an area of your color image or load a saved selection. Choose Image > Adjust > Variations. When you are working with a color image, the Variations dialog box also allows you to adjust the saturation of a color, in addition to shadows, midtones, and highlights. Strong, full colors are saturated; pale colors are undersaturated; and neutral tones, such as black, white, and gray, contain no saturation. In most instances, fully colored, saturated images are preferable, but too much saturation can also make an image look unreal, gaudy, or blotchy, which can also cause printing problems.

In the New England image, the Variations command was used to add a touch of yellow to the midtones of the church dome. Figure 19-21 shows the church dome selected; in the Variations dialog box, the Midtones radio button was chosen. After the midtones were enhanced, the Saturation radio button was selected, and the More Saturation thumbnail was clicked on to boost saturation. The changes transformed the dome from looking flat to looking full-bodied. The Sponge tool with its Saturation option could also have been used. If you oversaturate, you can use the Sponge tool's Desaturate option.

Back to the Flamingo image: use the Variations command to add a touch of magenta to the midtones and highlights of the flamingos. This makes the flamingos look more vibrant, as they often do in postcards.

If you like how the Variations command works, you might wish to investigate Vivid Details Test Strip, a color-correction plug-in for Photoshop.

Using the Color Balance Command

The next step in correcting the New England image was to add fall colors to the foliage in the town using the Color Balance command. This command allows you to mix colors together to improve the color balance in an image. If you have a sense of color theory, you will find the Color Balance dialog box to be very intuitive.

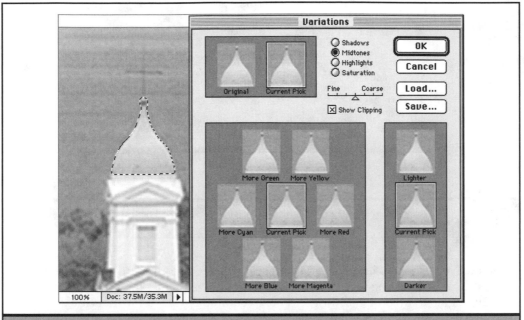

Figure 19-21.   *Using the Variations dialog box to adjust saturation in the dome of the church*

Remember   *The Color Balance command can be used in an adjustment layer.*

Before the Color Balance dialog box (seen in Figure 19-22) was opened, we took color readings of various selections of the foliage (we also wrote these down) using the Eyedropper and Info palette. During the correcting process, the Lasso tool and the Quick Mask mode were used to isolate the background trees that would be corrected.

To open the Color Balance dialog box, choose Image > Adjust > Color Balance. In the dialog box you will see radio buttons for selecting Shadows, Midtones, and Highlights, and three color sliders. The slider triangles turn black, gray, or white, depending upon whether the Shadows, Midtones, or Highlights radio button is selected.

The first slider ranges from Cyan (on the left) to Red (on the right). The second slider ranges from Magenta to Green, and the third ranges from Yellow to Blue. If you move a slider control to the right, you add that slider's RGB color to your image. Move the slider control to the left, and you add that slider's complement (a CMY color) to your image. By clicking and dragging the slider controls, you can move through the range of each RGB color and into the color range of its CMYK complement. RGB values go from 0 to 100, and CMYK colors are measured in negative numbers from 0 to −100.

Keeping the Preserve Luminosity checkbox selected helps ensure that brightness values don't change while you adjust color balance.

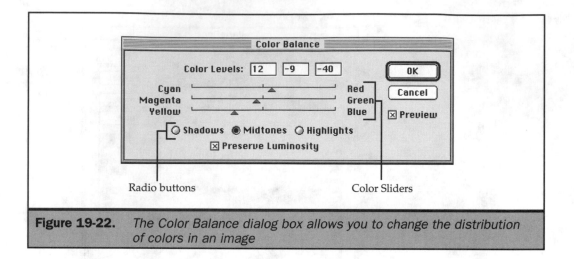

Figure 19-22. *The Color Balance dialog box allows you to change the distribution of colors in an image*

In the New England image, the various selections of trees were made to look more autumn-like by adjusting the Color Balance sliders and selecting the Shadows, Midtones, and Highlights radio buttons. Most selections required adding more magenta and yellow and decreasing cyan. As the colors were changed, the Eyedropper tool and Info palette were used to compare the old CMYK values to the new settings to ensure that the selections were the correct color.

After the foliage was corrected, the hills selection was loaded to receive the same color correction. Red, magenta, and yellow were added to the shadows, midtones, and highlights. In addition to providing fall color, the change also enhanced the detail in the hills.

Practicing Color Enhancement

In the Fruit image, try creating different selections and enhancing the color with the Color Balance command. As you work, leave the Preserve Luminosity option selected.

1. Create a selection around one or two red grapes. In the Color Balance dialog box, select the midtones options, and then click on the Magenta/Green slider and add more magenta. As you drag the slider, you'll see the color for the grape turn into a richer red.

2. Select one or two blueberries and click on the Cyan/Red slider. As you drag the slider toward Cyan, the blue becomes darker. Drag it toward the Red color, and the blue gradually turns redder.

3. Select one or two grapes and click on the Green/Magenta slider. Drag the slider to add more green. As you drag, the grapes become a richer, more attractive color.

Using the Levels Command with Color Images

The next step in color-correcting the New England image was to add cyan to the water. To do this, the Image > Adjust > Levels command was used, because it allows more precise control than the Variations command. The Levels dialog box, like the Curves dialog box, gives you access to individual color channels for color correction.

To add more cyan to the water, the Cyan channel was selected from the Channel pop-up menu in the Levels dialog box. The right Output Levels slider control was dragged to the left to 236, as shown in Figure 19-23. This took the lightest cyan value over 236 and remapped it to 236, making the cyan level darker; all values over 236 were remapped accordingly. (If the left slider control had been dragged instead to the right, cyan would have been subtracted and red, cyan's complement, would have been added.) Notice that the Info palette in Figure 19-23 shows that when cyan was increased, the level of red in the Info palette decreased.

Here's how to color-correct a CMYK and RGB file using the Levels dialog box. To color correct an RGB file, first load an RGB file that contains red.

1. Select a red area in your image.

2. Open the Levels dialog box and select Red in the Channel pop-up menu.

3. Click and drag on the left Output Levels slider control. Notice that as you drag to the right, red is added. If you drag the right Output Levels slider to the left, cyan is added. For each RGB and CMYK channel, the sliders move from one color to its complement. The left Input Levels slider control is always a CMYK color, and the right Input Levels slider control is always an RGB color.

APPLYING EFFECTS
TO YOUR IMAGES

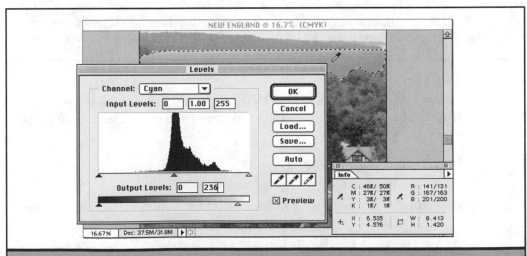

Figure 19-23.   *Using the Levels dialog box to increase cyan in the water*

To color-correct a CMYK file:

1. Load a CMYK file that contains cyan.

2. Select a cyan area.

3. Open the Levels dialog box and switch channels in the Channel pop-up menu to Cyan.

4. To reduce cyan in your image, click and drag on the right Input Levels slider control.

Using the Curves Command with Color Images

The next step taken in the New England image was using Image > Adjust > Curves to lighten the clouds in the sky. As discussed earlier in the "Using the Curves Command with Grayscale Images" section of this chapter, the Curves dialog box allows a specific area to be corrected precisely by pinpointing the area on the curve, and so it was the best tool to use to correct the clouds. Before the correction process began, the cloud selections were loaded as needed with the Load Selection command.

Like the Levels dialog box, the Curves dialog box allows you to make corrections to individual color channels. When color correction is being performed on CMYK images, Photoshop will not plot image points on the curve if you are working in the Composite channel. If a CMYK channel is selected from the Channel pop-up menu, dragging diagonally upwards on the curve adds the channel's color (when the gradient bar is set for light at the left to dark at the right); dragging diagonally downward subtracts the color, adding its complement.

If you click on the gradient bar so that it changes to dark at the left to light at the right, the directions for dragging the curve are reversed. When the gradient bar is set for light to dark, the Input and Output Levels are measured in CMYK percentages; otherwise, Input and Output are displayed in brightness values from 0 to 255. When

Practice Using Levels

In the Flamingo file, we will use the Levels dialog box to increase the green everywhere except the flamingos. To follow along, first load the Flamingo file from the book CD. Then follow these steps:

1. Create a selection out of the flamingos.

2. Invert the selection by choosing Select > Inverse.

3. Open the Levels dialog box by choosing Image > Adjust > Levels.

4. In the Levels dialog box, set the Channel pop-up menu to Magenta. To increase green and reduce magenta in the image, drag the left Output Levels slider to the right. Next, move both the right and midtone Input Levels sliders to the left.

5. Click on OK to apply the changes to the image.

you are working with an RGB color file and if a channel is chosen in the Channel pop-up menu (and the gradient bar is set for light to dark), dragging downward on the curve will add the channel's color; dragging up will add the channel's complement.

Since the easiest way to lighten the dark clouds in the New England image was to remove black from the selection, the Black channel was chosen in the Curves dialog box. Next, the Eyedropper was used to click on the middle of the dark area in the cloud selection. A circle appeared on the curve, showing the precise point that represented the cloud's color. To lighten the image, the part of the curve where the circle appeared was dragged downward and to the right. This lightened all areas in the same tonal range within the selection.

Remember   *You can SHIFT-click in your image to set Color Sampler points.*

After the blacks were reduced in the cloud area, the Cyan channel was selected so that cyan could be reduced in the darkest parts of the light clouds. To reduce cyan and add a bit of red, the part of the curve representing only the darkest part of the cloud was dragged downward. The Info palette in Figure 19-24 shows the change in cyan (from 14% to 8%) and red (from 224 to 237) after the eyedropper was clicked to resample the corrected area. When cyan was reduced, its complement, red, was added automatically. During the correction process, several points were selected by SHIFT-clicking on the different points. After the points were selected, they could be dragged together as a group.

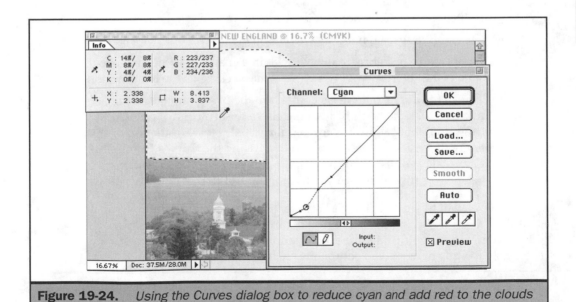

Figure 19-24.   *Using the Curves dialog box to reduce cyan and add red to the clouds*

If you SHIFT-click in the Channels palette to select more than one channel at a time, the selected grouping of channels will appear in the Channel pop-up menu in both the Curves and Levels dialog boxes.

To complete the correction of the clouds, a sensation of sun and warmth was added by adjusting the Yellow channel's curve upwards.

After each of the preceding corrections, the Eyedropper was used to sample areas that were changed. By keeping an eye on the Info palette, it was possible to gauge the amount of each change. Once all color correction was complete, the Unsharp Mask filter was applied to sharpen the image. (For more information on the Unsharp Mask filter, see Chapter 12.) The image was then saved on a cartridge and delivered to Reader's Digest General Books, and from there to the prepress house that had scanned the image. Using the retouched and color-corrected image file, the prepress house produced a Matchprint, which was used as a proof before printing the image.

Use the Curves command for individual channels to help eliminate color casts.

Practice Using Curves

If you wish to experiment with the Curves command using an RGB image, load an RGB file.

1. In the Curves dialog box, set the Channel to Red.

2. Click and drag diagonally downward on the curve to add the red to the image.

3. If you wish to experiment further with this image, reset the image to its original state by holding down OPTION (*ALT*) while clicking on the Reset button.

4. To use the curve to increase contrast in the overall image, set the channel to RGB, click on the middle of the curve to set a control point, and then drag up on it at about the three-quarter point toward the top of the curve to create an S shape, as shown in the "Using the Curves Command with Grayscale Images" section earlier in this chapter. More contrast is created because you've increased the highlights and darkened the shadows.

If you wish to work with a CMYK file, try experimenting in the Cyan channel of the image. Dragging the curve downward subtracts cyan, adding cyan's complement; dragging upward adds cyan. As with an RGB image, creating an S curve for this image in the composite channel adds contrast.

Using the Hue/Saturation Command

The Hue/Saturation command was not used to color-correct any part of the New England image; however, this dialog box can be very helpful when you wish to focus on changing the hue, saturation, or lightness values of specific colors in an image. Photoshop's Hue/Saturation dialog box features a preview option, which allows you to preview exactly how a color is being changed. In the dialog box, two color bars represent colors as they appear in the color wheel. (See Chapter CD-1 for a discussion of using the color wheel, as well as definitions of hue and saturation.) The upper slider represents colors before changes have been made, and the lower bar will show you how the change affects the hues on the color wheel.

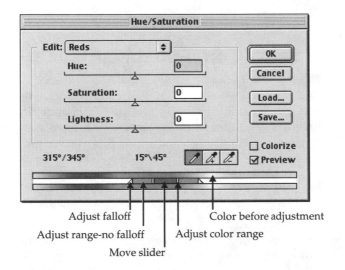

Adjust falloff
Adjust range-no falloff
Move slider
Color before adjustment
Adjust color range

Your first step is to decide exactly what colors you wish to correct in your image. You can correct the reds, yellows, greens, cyans, blues, or magentas. Each of these choices is available in the Edit pop-up menu. If you wish to edit all of the colors, choose Master in the Edit pop-up menu.

To try out the Hue/Saturation dialog box, load an image on screen. Open the Hue/Saturation dialog box by choosing Image > Adjust > Hue/Saturation. Assume that you wish to correct the red areas of an image. Choose Reds from the Edit pop-up menu. Notice that as soon as you pick a color, the eyedroppers on screen become activated, and you can use them to click on a red area on screen to set the specific area that you wish to correct. Try clicking on a red area on screen with the eyedropper (or pick another color depending upon your image). Notice that the color bars at the bottom of the dialog box register the color area in the image that will be corrected. If you want to expand the area, select the Eyedropper+ icon; if you wish to reduce the area, click on the Eyedropper– icon. Then click in your image.

While using the Eyedropper tool, you can activate the Eyedropper+ tool by pressing SHIFT or the Eyedropper– tool by pressing OPTION (ALT).

To make hue adjustments, simply drag on the Hue slider. Dragging to the right simulates a clockwise rotation around the color wheel; dragging to the left simulates a counter-clockwise rotation around the color wheel. As you click and drag, notice how the hues in your image change.

Now locate the red area on the first color bar at the bottom of the dialog box. This bar represents the colors before adjustments are made. Note the color below it should be the color that you see on screen. The bottom slider is showing you the change in the image. To boost the saturation (purity of color), click and drag to the right on the Saturation slider. Dragging to the left lowers saturation. To increase lightness, click and drag to the right on the Lightness slider. To decrease lightness, click and drag to the left.

Using the Hue/Saturation Adjustment Slider

As you drag the sliders, you'll notice that the range of the change is restricted by the gray adjustment slider that appears between the two color bars. The adjustment slider controls the range of change and the falloff (how quickly change occurs). The middle (dark area) of the adjustment slider is the actual range of colors affected by the adjustments. The lighter areas to the left and right of the darker part represent the falloff. The percentage change allowable appears above the slider.

Here are the four ways to adjust the slider:

■ To choose a different color area to adjust, click and drag the middle of the gray slider.

■ To adjust the width of the range of color correction, click and drag the either vertical white bar to the left or the right.

■ To adjust the range for color correction, but not the falloff, click and drag the lighter area of the bar.

■ To adjust the falloff, but not the range of color correction, click and drag one of the white triangles.

 The Hue/Saturation command is available when you create an adjustment layer.

If you select the Colorize checkbox option in the Hue/Saturation dialog box, the colors in the image change to one color (the currently selected foreground color, if it isn't black or white). In this case, adjusting the slider controls lets you tint the image with the color controlled by the Hue slider. (To review image colorization using the Hue/Saturation dialog box, turn to Chapter 11.)

 If you wish to colorize a Grayscale mode image, change the image's mode to RGB or CMYK color.

Replacing Colors with the Replace Color Command

Another helpful color-correcting option that works hand-in-hand with the Hue, Saturation, and Lightness sliders is the Replace Color command. You might think of this command as being a type of search-and-replace feature for color. The command creates a mask around a specified color and then allows you to change the hue, saturation, and lightness of the areas within the mask.

To try out the Replace Color command, load any color image. After the image is loaded, choose Image > Adjust > Replace Color.

To view your image in the Replace Color dialog box, click on the Image radio button. (Clicking on the Selection radio button displays the mask that Photoshop creates in the image.)

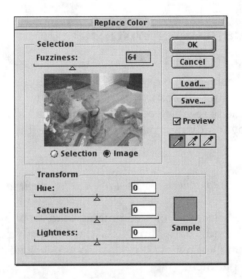

APPLYING EFFECTS TO YOUR IMAGES

To start creating the mask, you must choose a color in your image that you want masked. Start by clicking on the first eyedropper in the dialog box. Move the eyedropper cursor over a color in the image you wish to replace and click in the image. To see how Photoshop creates the mask based on the color, click on the Selection radio button in the Replace Color dialog box. The white area in the Preview box is the area within the mask.

You can expand or contract the mask by clicking and dragging on the Fuzziness slider or by entering a value between 0 and 250 into the Fuzziness field. The Fuzziness slider extends the edges of the color range within the mask.

If you wish to add colors, click on the Eyedropper+ or Eyedropper– icon, and then click on the mask in the dialog box or in the image. Try extending the range of the mask by clicking on the Eyedropper+ and then clicking on another color in your image. After you click, the color will be added to the mask.

You can temporarily switch between the mask and the image in the Preview area of the dialog box by pressing CTRL, regardless of whether the Selection or Image radio button is selected.

Once the mask shows the desired area of your image, use the Hue and Saturation sliders to correct or alter the colors. Notice that the sample color swatch previews the colors you create.

If you wish to use your settings again so that they can be reloaded at a later time, click on the Save button so that you can name your settings and save them to disk. The Load button will allow you to load the settings when you need them again.

If you're happy with the changes you made, click on OK to close the dialog box; otherwise, click on Cancel.

Changing Ink Percentages with the Selective Color Command

Once you begin to color correct RGB or CMYK files, you may wish to fine-tune the color in your images by using Photoshop's Selective Color command, which allows you to add or subtract the percentage of inks used in colors. For instance, you could make an apple redder by removing a percentage of cyan—red's complement—and/or adding magenta.

 The Selective Color command can be used in an adjustment layer.

Before trying out the Selective Color command, load an image on screen. To use the Selective Color command, choose Image > Adjust Selective Color. In the Selective Color dialog box, click on the Preview checkbox so you will be able to see the changes in your image as you experiment.

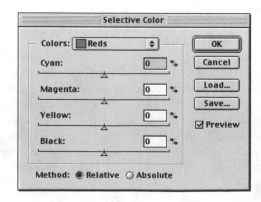

Using Total Ink Percentages

When using the Selective Color command, you might wish to set the Eyedropper so it displays total ink percentages. To do this:

1. Click on the Info palette's pop-up menu and choose Palette Options.

2. In the Info Options dialog box, set First or Second Color Readout to Total Ink.

3. After you make changes in the Selective Colors dialog box, move the eyedropper over your image to view the total percentages for all CMYK inks. You can also SHIFT-click in your image to set Color Sampler points and view the ink percentages of the points.

Next, choose a color from the Colors pop-up menu. This is the color in your image that you wish to change. (You can also change whites, grays, and blacks.)

The percentage of ink added or subtracted is calculated differently, depending on whether you select the Relative or Absolute radio button. Relative applies the percentage based upon the percentage of the original ink. Absolute just adds the percentage to the original ink percentage. For instance, assume you are adding color to a pixel that is 50 percent cyan. If you add 5 percent cyan in Relative mode, Photoshop will compute 5 percent of 50 percent ($.05 \times .5$), which produces a 2.5 percent increase. Thus, the cyan ink setting will be changed to 52.5%. If you add 5 percent of cyan in Absolute mode, Photoshop simply adds 5 percent to the 50 percent, which results in a 55% cyan setting.

Try clicking on the Absolute radio button, and then watching how your image changes when you drag the sliders to adjust the colors. When you're done experimenting, click on Cancel or OK to reject or accept the ink changes. If you'd like, you can also use the Save and Load buttons to save and load settings for use on other images.

APPLYING EFFECTS
TO YOUR IMAGES

Plug-Ins

A variety of third-party vendors have created plug-ins that can speed up and simplify the task of color-correcting your images. For example, Vivid Details' Test Strip uses an intuitive interface similar to Photoshop's Variation commands. However, Test Strip provides full-screen previews and zooming controls and allows changes in 1-percent increments. It even allows you to save a Test Strip view to create a Test Proof.

PrePress Technologies' Spectre plug-ins set up a color-correction table that can quickly be applied to images.

Monaco Systems' MonacoCOLOR features batch processing. This allows many images to be corrected automatically while the computer is unattended. MonacoCOLOR also features scanner calibration options and provides many image-correction features that can be run with one keystroke.

Working with the Channel Mixer

As you make your color corrections, you may find that correcting poorly digitized images is quite a task. Photoshop's Channel Mixer is a high-end prepress utility that allows you to edit an image's channels by adding or subtracting color to the color channels in an image. The Channel Mixer also provides a quick means of creating tinted and grayscale image effects. You can even use it to edit an image's channels to use as a mask. To use the Channel Mixer, load an image on screen. Then choose Image > Adjust > Channel Mixer to open the Channel Mixer dialog box, shown here.

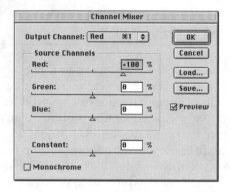

Make sure the Preview checkbox is selected so you can preview the adjustments you make to your image.

Start by choosing the channel that you wish to edit. To experiment, choose an Output channel to change in your image, such as Red if you are using an RGB color image.

1. Click and drag on a Source channel. As you click and drag, you add color to the Output channel.

2. With the Channel Mixer dialog box open, move the eyedropper over the colors (or SHIFT-click to set Color Sampler points in your image) to view the color changes in the Info palette. You'll see that the color in the Output Channel is boosted when you click on one of the Source channel sliders.

3. If you wish to darken or lighten the Output channel, click and drag on the Constant slider or enter a value into the Constant field. Dragging left or entering negative values darkens the image; dragging right lightens the image. Technically, the Constant slider adds a black channel with different opacities over the Output channel if you drag left; when you drag right, a white channel with varying opacity is added to the channel.

4. To create a grayscale image out of the channels, click on Monochrome and then adjust the sliders to produce the effect you desire.

Basic Training with the Channel Mixer

If you start using the channel mixer with an RGB or CMYK image, you may find it somewhat difficult to predict exactly what is happening when the colors in your image change. If so, try the following example, which shows you step by step how colors can change when channel values are added or subtracted in a simple RGB image. Before you begin, create a new 5-by-5 RGB color file with a white background. Next, open up the Channels palette by choosing Window > Show Channels.

1. To understand the Channel Mixer, it's helpful to change the Color Channels so that they display their thumbnails in color. To do this, choose Edit > Preferences > Display & Cursors. In the Preferences dialog box, select the Color Channels in Color option.

   Notice that each color channel in the Channels palette is filled with color. This tells you that the white background you see on screen is created from Red 255, Green 255, and pure Blue 255.

2. Create three different overlapping shapes on screen: make one shape red, one green, one blue. Use the Rectangular Marquee tool to create a rectangular selection on screen, and fill the selection with pure red. Use the Elliptical Marquee tool to create a circle on screen, and fill the selection with green. Use the Polygon Lasso tool to create a triangle, and fill the triangle with blue. (To fill, choose Edit > Fill—or press OPTION-DELETE (*ALT-BACKSPACE*) to fill with the foreground color.)

3. Open the Channel Mixer dialog box by choosing Image > Adjust > Channel Mixer.

4. Set the Output Channel to Red. This means that the changes you make in the Channel Mixer will edit the Red channel in your image.

5. In the Source Channels section, remove red from the Red channel by clicking on the Red slider and dragging it to the left until the Red slider readout is 0. Notice that the red square on screen changes to black. Why? You've removed all red from the Red channel. Thus, in the square image area on screen, there is no red, no green, and no blue. Red 0, Green 0, and Blue 0 produce black. To confirm this, look at the Red channel in the Channels palette. The channel is completely black because there is no color in the channel.

   Now take a look at the background of your image. Notice that it changed from white to cyan. The color change occurred because the background of your image is now composed entirely of blue and green. If you create a color in an image from Blue 255 and Green 255, you create cyan.

6. Now click and drag the Green slider in the Source channels to the right, to the 100% point. The green circle on your screen now changes to yellow, and the background changes to white. This may seem a bit confusing: Why does green

change to yellow when you output green to the red channel? Here's the explanation: First, take a look at the Channels palette. Notice that you can see the shape of the circle in both the Red and Green channels. The circle is yellow in the composite RGB image because it is composed of green from the Green channel and 100% red (which you added with the Channel Mixer). If you create a color with Red 255 and Green 255, you create yellow. The background changed to white because you added 100% color to the Red channel. This means that the background area of the screen is composed of Red 255, Green 255, and Blue 255—which makes white.

7. Change the Output Channel to blue, and drag the Green Source slider to 100%. The circle area on screen changes to white. It changes because you added 100% green to the Blue channel. This means that the circle area on screen is now composed of 100% red, 100% blue, and 100% green. In other words, the white area is created from Red 255, Blue 255, and Green 255.

The foregoing exercise should help you get started with the Color Mixer. At this point, feel free to change the Output Channel and Source percentages to analyze other changes in the image.

Note
You can easily re-create this exercise to analyze how the Color Mixer affects CMYK images. Start with a CMYK color file and make sure that the Channels palette displays the channels in color. Then create four different shapes, each filled with a different CMYK color. (Fill the shapes with 100% cyan, 100% magenta, 100% yellow, and 100% black.) Set one of the CMY channels as the Output channel, and then drag one of the Source channels to the right. Note how the colors change in the Channels palette, and then observe the change on screen.

Using Adjustment Layers

As you fine-tune your work, Photoshop gives you the power to return to your image and change settings again and again through adjustment layers. As discussed in Chapter 17, adjustment layers allow you to view your image corrections through a mask. You can edit the mask without affecting the underlying pixels, which means you can experiment with image corrections, or print proofs, or try them out on the Web and then go back to make further adjustments until the image is as perfect as you can make it. If you need to change a previous adjustment, you can make the change through the adjustment layer. You can choose from among 11 adjustments: Levels, Curves, Color Balance, Brightness/Contrast, Hue/Saturation, Selective Color, Channel Mixer, Gradient Map, Invert, Threshold, and Posterize.

Here's a brief review of the steps involved in creating an adjustment layer:

1. Choose File > Open to open any digitized image (either a scanned image, an image captured from a digital camera or camcorder, or a stock image. If you wish, you can use one of the images supplied to you on this book's CD).

2. To correct a selected area, create a selection on screen using one of the Selection tools. If you want to correct the entire file, don't select an area.

3. Choose Layer > New Adjustment Layer.

4. In the New Adjustment layer submenu, choose the type of adjustment you wish to make. Alternatively, you can click on the create new adjustment layer icon at the bottom of the Layers palette. In the pop-up menu that appears, choose a command. Try using either the Levels or Hue/Saturation command.

Tip   *You can have multiple Adjustment layers to create the effect you want.*

5. When the New Layer dialog box opens, enter a name for the layer.

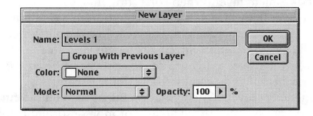

6. Click on the Color pop-up menu to give the adjustment layer in the Layers palette a color (as shown next).

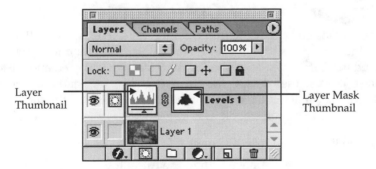

7. At the bottom of the dialog box, click on the Mode and Opacity pop-up menus, and choose settings. The settings you choose will affect the adjustment layer and the image you are working on.

8. Click on OK in the New Layer dialog box to open the Adjustment dialog box.

9. In the Adjustment dialog box, change the settings to correct your image. Click on OK to see the effect of the adjustment.

10. Once you've created a new adjustment layer, you can see the adjustment layer in the Layers palette. (Choose Window > Show Layers, to display the Layers palette.) Notice that in the Layers palette, the adjustment layer consists of a

APPLYING EFFECTS
TO YOUR IMAGES

Layer thumbnail and a Layer mask thumbnail (to the left of the Adjustment Layer name, as shown in the previous illustration). If you created a selection, the selection will appear in the Layer mask thumbnail. You can add or subtract to the selection in the Layer mask thumbnail using one of the painting tools to paint with either black or white.

11. If you created a selection on screen and need to move the area where the adjustment is applied, simply click and drag this area with the Move tool.

12. If you need to return and make further adjustments, simply double-click on the Layer thumbnail. When the dialog box opens, edit the adjustment layer by changing the dialog box settings. Then click on OK.

When using adjustment layers, remember that you can use one adjustment layer on top of another adjustment layer. When correcting images, it's often best to start with an adjustment layer that corrects the tones in your images (lightness, darkness, and contrast). Then create another adjustment layer to correct color balance, and then correct adjustment layers to fine-tune specific colors in your image. It's also important to remember that you can use clipping groups to apply specific adjustments to specific layers. Finally, remember that you can use the Paintbrush and Airbrush tools to edit the mask in the adjustment layer. When you edit the mask, you can fine-tune the effects of the adjustment layer to specific image areas. For more information about editing the mask in adjustment layers, review Chapter 16.

Collaging and Color Correcting

To create the Vamos collage in Figure 19-25, we used five images (all shown in Figure 19-27: the barn doors, the Eiffel tower, a heart, cabanas, and the brick wall). We color-corrected the Eiffel tower and cabanas images and then copied and pasted them into the barn image. We also used the Overlay mode to collage the heart onto the barn door.

To re-create the Vamos collage, follow these steps and load the files from the Chapter 19 folder of this book's book CD:

1. Load the Barn image from the book CD.

2. Load the Eiffel tower image. When the Eiffel tower image is on screen, lighten the image—we used the Levels dialog box to do so. To open the Levels dialog box, choose Image > Adjust > Levels and in the dialog box, move the highlight (upper-right) and midtone (upper-middle) sliders to the left. To add contrast, move the shadow (upper-left) slider to the left. Click on OK to adjust your image.

3. To add the Eiffel tower image to the barn image, choose Select > Select All and then Edit > Copy. Then close the Eiffel tower image.

4. Activate the Barn image, and then use the Rectangular Marquee tool to select the open area of the barn door. With the selection on screen, choose Edit > Paste

Figure 19-25. *Collage created from various images*

Into. Notice that the Eiffel tower image is pasted into the selected area. To scale the image down, use Edit > Transform > Scale.

5. Load the Cabana file image. With the Cabana image on screen, lighten the image. We used the Levels dialog box as we did in step 2.

6. Choose Select > Select All and Edit > Copy to copy the Cabana file. Then close the file.

7. Before you add the Cabana file to the Vamos collage, you need to increase the canvas size by choosing Image > Canvas Size. In the Canvas Size dialog box, set the Height field to 4.4 inches and move the Anchor box from the middle to the top middle. Click on OK to increase the canvas size.

8. With the canvas enlarged, choose Edit > Paste. When the cabana file appears, use the Move tool to move it to the bottom of the document. For the Cabana file to appear behind the barn door, click on the cabana layer in the Layers palette and drag it below the barn door layer.

9. Load the Heart image. Choose Select > Select All and Edit > Copy to copy the Heart file. Then close the file.

Figure 19-26. *Images used in collage*

10. Activate the Barn image, and then choose Edit > Paste. Move the heart image over a section of the barn door and scale it using the Edit > Transform > Scale command so that it fits perfectly over the section of the door. For a more interesting effect, click on the heart layer in the Layers palette and set the mode to Overlay.

11. Duplicate the heart layer three times and move the duplicates in the different sections of the barn door. To duplicate the heart image, click on the heart layer and drag it over the Create New Layer icon. To move the heart image, use the Move tool.

12. Before you can add the brick image to the collage, you need to increase the canvas size. To do so, choose Image > Canvas Size, and in the Canvas Size dialog box, set the Height field to 5.6 inches and move the Anchor box from the middle to the lower middle. Click on OK to increase the canvas size.

13. Now load the Brick file. With the Brick file on screen, choose Select > Select All and Edit > Copy to copy the Brick file. Then close the file.

14. Activate the collage file, and then choose Edit > Paste. Use the Move tool to move the brick layer to the top of the collage.

15. If you want to add a line between the brick and barn images, click on the Line tool in the Toolbox (for a shortcut, press U on your keyboard until the Line tool is selected). Change the foreground color in the Toolbox to the color you want the line to be. For a medium size line, type **7** in the Weight field. Then click and drag from one side of the document to the other side.

16. To add text to your document, click on the Type tool. Set the font and font size—we used the font Hoefler Text with a font size of 24 points. After we had the text on screen, we rotated it using the Edit > Transform > Rotate command.

The Complete Reference

Photoshop 6

Part IV

Appendixes

The Complete Reference

Photoshop 6

Appendix A

Importing and Exporting Files

Y ou may often find yourself using Photoshop as one part of a team of graphics applications. This appendix covers file formats and the techniques you can use for exporting files created in Photoshop to other programs and importing files created in other programs into Photoshop.

Using the Save As Command

When you need to save a new file in a new format, you can select File > Save or File > Save As. If you've already saved the file, you must select File > Save As to switch formats. The Save As dialog box, shown in Figure A-1, allows you to choose whether to save an ICC color profile with the file and to choose a specific format from the Format pop-up menu.

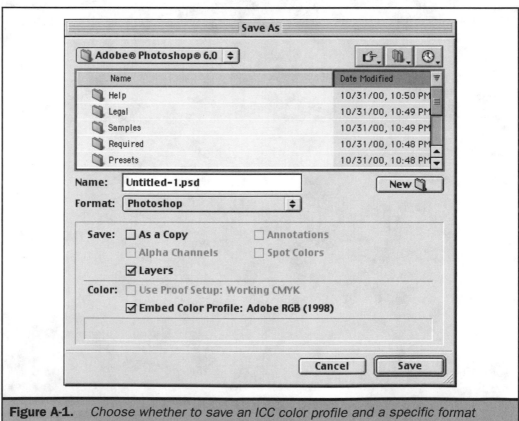

Figure A-1. *Choose whether to save an ICC color profile and a specific format in the Save As dialog box*

For example, when you're saving an RGB image, the Format pop-up menu looks like this:

✓ **Photoshop**
Photoshop 2.0
BMP
CompuServe GIF
Photoshop EPS
JPEG
PCX
Photoshop PDF
PICT File
PICT Resource
Pixar
PNG
Raw
Scitex CT
Targa
TIFF
Photoshop DCS 1.0
Photoshop DCS 2.0

The Save As command allows you to flatten layers of an image. It also allows you to save an image without its alpha channels. If a file format does not support alpha channels, the Alpha Channels checkbox is automatically deselected and grayed out in the Save As dialog.

After you choose a new file format and click on the Save button, Photoshop may display a File Format dialog box, in which you can specify your conversion preferences.

Note   *You can save a copy of your image and still remain in the original document by choosing File > Save As. Then enter a new name for your document and click on the As a Copy checkbox before clicking on Save.*

Working with EPS Files

The EPS (encapsulated PostScript) format is widely accepted by graphics and page-layout programs in Mac and PC environments. The format was originally created as an output format for printing graphical images. If you need to output your files to programs such as QuarkXPress, Adobe Illustrator, or Adobe PageMaker, you can use the EPS format. If you are producing your file to be output by a service bureau, you may need to convert your file to EPS format.

The DCS 1.0 version of the EPS dialog box allows you to save color separations for CMYK and multichannel files. The DCS 2.0 format is used for exporting Photoshop CMYK images that include spot color channels. If you are working in a Bitmap mode file, the EPS format also allows you to save white areas of your image as transparent areas.

APPENDIXES

*Platemaker is a Photoshop plug-in that allows you to export DCS files that include channels for spot colors, varnishes, foil stamping, and embossing plates. For more information, visit **www.alap.com/**.*

Saving a File in EPS, DCS 1.0, or DCS 2.0 Format

To save a file in Photoshop EPS, DCS 1.0, or DCS 2.0 format, choose Save As from the File menu. If you are using File > Save As, rename the file so that you don't overwrite the original version. In the Format pop-up menu, choose Photoshop EPS, Photoshop DCS 1.0, or Photoshop DCS 2.0. (Windows users will see the filename extension change to .eps.) To continue the conversion process, click on the Save (*OK*) button.

Photoshop opens the EPS Options dialog box (if you are saving in Photoshop EPS format):

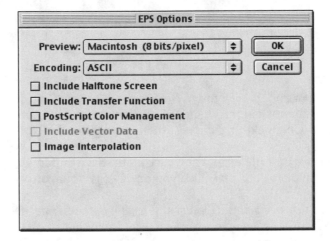

Many programs, Adobe Illustrator included, let you preview the EPS file. If you choose the 1 bit/pixel option in the Preview pop-up menu, the preview will appear in black and white. The 8 bits/pixel choice allows 256 colors or shades of gray. Mac users can create previews for the PC by choosing either the TIFF (1 bit/pixel) or TIFF (8 bits/pixel) option. Mac users can also choose Macintosh (JPEG) to save the preview using the JPEG compression format.

The Encoding pop-up menu options allow you to specify whether the EPS file will be saved as a binary file, an ASCII file, or a compressed JPEG file. JPEG removes image data from your file, which can produce a loss in quality. The binary and ASCII formats do not remove data from your file, but a binary file is more compact than an ASCII file. Photoshop provides both formats because some applications cannot read the binary format.

In general, you will want to avoid using the Include Halftone Screen and Include Transfer Function checkbox options; both of these options may override the settings of an imagesetter or a page-layout program. Check with your service bureau before you turn on these options. Here is what they do:

- **Include Halftone Screen**   Sends the halftone screen angles and screen frequency settings that are entered into the Halftone Screens dialog box (accessed by clicking on the Screens button in the Page Setup dialog box). Enabling this option may override an imagesetter's or other application's halftone screen settings.

- **Include Transfer Function**   Sends transfer-functions information to the EPS file. The Transfer Functions dialog box (accessed by clicking on the Transfer button in the Page Setup dialog box) allows you to specify dot gain settings to compensate for miscalibrated imagesetters. A well-run service bureau keeps its imagesetters properly calibrated; thus, any Transfer Functions settings you make can adversely affect the quality of the final color separations.

If you have a PostScript printer and want to have it convert your file to the printer's color space, choose PostScript Color Management. (Select this option only if you haven't already converted the file in Photoshop.) To avoid inconsistent color, particularly in page layout programs, don't choose this option if you will be importing the image into a file in a program that uses color profiles. For CMYK images, this option is supported only by PostScript Level 3 printers. If you need to use Postscript Color Management on a Postscript 2 printer, convert the file to Lab Color mode before saving.

If your file includes shapes or text, and you wish to preserve the vector data for high quality output in other programs, select the Include Vector Data checkbox.

If you are saving a file in Photoshop DCS 1.0 format, you can create separate EPS files for use with programs that utilize Quark's Desktop Color Separation (DCS) format. When you choose one of the Multiple File choices in the pop-up menu, Photoshop creates a file for each CMYK component. A fifth file, called a *master file*, contains a preview of the composite image. If you want a color preview file, choose the 72-pixels/inch color option; for a grayscale preview, choose the 72-pixels/inch grayscale option. If you choose one of the No Composite options, you cannot print a composite from the file. (Keep in mind that all five DCS files must be in the same folder if you wish to reload the composite file.)

As mentioned earlier, Photoshop DCS 2.0 is used to save any file that includes spot color channels. Like the DCS 1.0 Format dialog box, the DCS 2.0 Format dialog box allows you to save your separated file either as multiple files or as a single file with grayscale or colored previews.

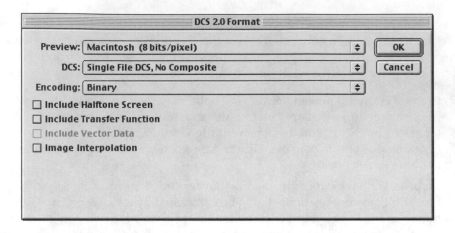

 If you wish to export a clipping path, the Photoshop file should be saved in EPS format. (For more information about clipping paths, see Chapter 14.)

Opening an EPS File

Photoshop's EPS format is designed to read EPS files created by different graphics applications. To open an EPS file created in another application, follow these steps:

1. Choose File > Open. If you don't see the file, click on the Show All Files checkbox.

2. Select the file you wish to open. Notice that the file format name is displayed in the File Open dialog box. Click on OK.

3. If the file was exported by as an EPS file by Adobe Illustrator, Adobe Dimensions, or a similar program, the Rasterize Generic EPS Format dialog box appears to help you in converting from a drawing or vector program to Photoshop's pixel-based or raster format. In the dialog box, you can change the image's Width, Height, Resolution, and Mode. You also choose whether to use anti-aliasing. If you want Photoshop to soften the edges of the imported file, click on the Anti-aliased checkbox.

4. Turning on the Constrain Proportions option ensures that the Width and Height settings will remain at the same ratio in the converted file. When Constrain Proportions is enabled, a change in either the Width or Height measurement forces a proportional change in the other dimension.

5. When you're ready to load the file, click on OK. In a few moments, the file opens into Photoshop.

Although the EPS file is now open in Photoshop, it has not been converted to Photoshop's native format. If you intend to edit the file and save and reload it, it's best to convert (save) the file to Photoshop format. Otherwise, you will be met by the Rasterize Generic EPS Format dialog box each time you load the file.

6. To save the file in Photoshop format, choose either Save or Save As from the File menu. Before continuing to save the file in another format, Mac users should rename the file to prevent overwriting the previous file on the disk. (On the PC, when you change file formats, Photoshop changes the filename extension of the file to .psd; thus, the original file is not overwritten. It's a good idea to rename the file anyway, however, to avoid confusion between versions.) To switch to Photoshop format, choose Photoshop from the list in the Format pop-up menu. Click on Save to execute the conversion.

 On the Mac, if the Append File Extension setting is set to Always in the General Preferences dialog box (Edit > Preferences > Saving Files), Photoshop will always add a three-letter file extension to each file you save.

Placing an EPS File into a Photoshop Document

At times you may want to place an Adobe Illustrator document into a file that is already open in Photoshop. If you want the image to be anti-aliased, select the Anti-alias PostScript checkbox in the General Preferences dialog box. You can access this dialog box by choosing File > Preferences > General.

Here are the steps for placing an EPS file into a Photoshop file:

1. Open the Photoshop file into which you intend to place the Illustrator file.

2. Choose File > Place.

3. From the list of files that appears, select the file that you wish to place and click on Place.

4. The EPS file appears within a bounding box in a layer. If you wish to move the imported image, position the mouse pointer on the border box. (The selection pointer should be the arrow pointer.) Click and drag the image to the desired location. If you don't see an image on screen, no preview may have been saved with the file, but you can still complete the steps in this section. After you press ENTER, you should see the image on screen.

   ■ If you wish to resize the image and change the width-to-height (aspect) ratio, click and drag on one of the image corners. If you wish to change the

APPENDIXES

image size but maintain the aspect ratio, press SHIFT while you click and drag the mouse. If you wish to rotate the image, click and drag outside of its borders in the direction that you wish to rotate.

■ To skew the placed EPS file, press COMMAND (*CTRL*) while you click and drag on a handle.

5. Once you are satisfied with the size and placement of the imported image, press ENTER. (Mac users can also press RETURN.)

CompuServe GIF

CompuServe GIF is a common format used to output images to the Web. (Chapter 9 covers Photoshop and ImageReady commands for saving images for the Web.) Because CompuServe GIF allows only 256 or fewer colors, CMYK and Lab color images must be converted to Indexed Color before being saved in this format. However, if you attempt to save an RGB file in CompuServe GIF, the Indexed Color dialog box appears, in which you can convert the image immediately before saving it in CompuServe GIF format.

When you save your file in CompuServe GIF, a dialog box appears, allowing you to choose whether to save your image in Normal or Interlaced Row format. If you choose interlaced, the image gradually comes into focus when viewed on the Web.

Remember	*When you export to GIF format, alpha channels mask your image. This can cause the final image to be cropped according to the mask.*

PNG Format

PNG (usually pronounced "ping") is a new file format specifically designed to compress images that will be output to the Web. Many Web experts predict that PNG will eventually replace GIF as the preferred Web file format. Unlike GIF files, PNG files can support more than 256 colors. Web browsers that support PNG include Internet Explorer 4.0 and higher. Netscape Navigator 2.0 and higher support PNG with a plug-in.

Images saved in PNG format maintain all color and all alpha channels, which allows you to blend image edges with Web page backgrounds. PNG images are compressed using a lossless filtering process. When you save in PNG format, a dialog box appears allowing you to choose a compression algorithm and whether you want the image to gradually come into focus when viewed on the Web—if you do, choose the Adam 7 interlacing method. The dialog box also allows you to choose Filter options. For indexed and bitmap (black and white) images, choose None. If your image includes blends or patterns that are horizontal, choose Sub; if the image has vertical patterns, choose Up. The Paeth choice (named after programmer and author A.W Paeth) attempts to apply surrounding colors during compression to image areas where noise occurs. If you don't know which filter to use, choose Adaptive, which applies the best filter for your specific image.

Working with TIFF Files

TIFF format is frequently used for both Mac and PC graphics files. TIFF, which stands for Tagged Image File Format, was introduced by the Aldus Corporation (which was bought out by Adobe) as a format for saving scanned images. Although the format is used by most page layout programs, it is not accepted by all drawing programs.

TIFF files can be loaded directly into Photoshop. When you save a TIFF file in Photoshop, the TIFF Options dialog box appears.

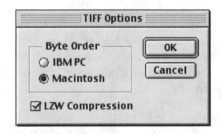

Here you can specify whether the document is for Macintosh or IBM PC-compatible computers. Just choose the appropriate radio button under Byte Order.2

Note   *If you have created alpha channels in your Photoshop file, the Alpha Channels checkbox is automatically selected when you choose the TIFF file format in the Save As dialog box. If you don't want alpha channels to be saved, deselect the Alpha Channels checkbox when you save the file.*

One valuable advantage of exporting files in TIFF format is that TIFF files can be compressed. In the TIFF Options dialog box is a checkbox you can select to enable LZW (Lempel-Ziv-Welch) Compression. LZW is a lossless compression format; the file is compressed without removing image data from it. Most page layout programs can read compressed TIFF files.

Note   *If you choose Enable Advanced TIFF Save Options in the Edit > Preferences > Saving Files dialog box, the TIFF Options dialog box allows you to choose from these file formats: ZIP, JPEG, and LZW. ZIP is a common compression format that provides lossless compression. The JPEG file format allows you to reduce file size by reducing image quality. The TIFF Options dialog box also allows you to click on a checkbox to save image transparency.*

Working with PICT Files

PICT is one of the most common data file formats available on the Macintosh. Most multimedia programs, such as Macromedia Director, can import PICT files, and most 3-D programs can import PICT files. Most Macintosh graphics applications can save files in this format. Some PC programs, including CorelDRAW and Corel Painter, also accept the format. Both PICT and PICT2 (colored PICT) images can be loaded directly into Photoshop.

When you are saving files in PICT format, the PICT File Options dialog box appears (Figure A-2), which allows you to designate the Resolution (pixel depth) of the image. Which dialog box you see depends upon whether you are saving a grayscale or color file.

- If you are saving a grayscale file, specify 2 bits/pixel for 4 colors, 4 bits/pixel for 16 colors, and 8 bits/pixel for 256 colors.

- The choices for color images are 16 bits/pixel or 32 bits/pixel. If you are exporting a 24-bit color image, choose the 32 bits/pixel option. This 32-bit option appears because the Macintosh includes an extra 8-bit channel (an alpha channel). If you are not using 24-bit color in Photoshop, choose the 16-bits/pixel option; this keeps file sizes smaller.

When QuickTime is installed, the Compression section allows you to reduce file size with JPEG compression. (See the section "Using JPEG Format for File Compression" later in this appendix.)

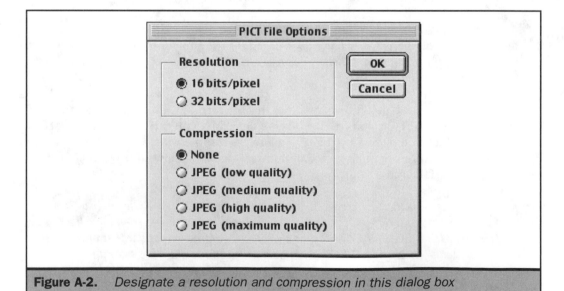

Figure A-2.   *Designate a resolution and compression in this dialog box*

Note *You cannot save CMYK Color images, Lab Color images, or images with more than one alpha channel in PICT format.*

Using the Anti-Aliased PICT Command to Import PICT Images

Although PICT images load directly into Photoshop when you select File > Open, Mac users may prefer to select File > Import to import PICT images. With the Import command, you can select the Anti-Aliased PICT option; this activates a plug-in that offers options similar to those in the Rasterize Generic EPS Format dialog box. (For more information, see "Opening an EPS File" earlier in this appendix.)

The Anti-Aliased PICT dialog box lets you change width and height proportionally and choose to open the document as a grayscale or RGB color file. When you execute the Acquire command and import the PICT file, Photoshop uses anti-aliasing to soften image edges.

Using BMP Format

BMP (Windows Bitmap) format is commonly used by many Windows graphics programs. Most multimedia programs require you to save images in BMP format before you can import them. When you export an image, you can choose to export the image for Windows or OS/2. You can also choose to export your image as a 1-, 4-, 8-, or 24-bit image; 4 and 8-bit images can use RLE (Run-Length Encoding) compression. This is a lossless compression format and thus doesn't result in degradation of image quality.

Note *CMYK files cannot be converted to BMP format.*

Using JPEG Format for File Compression

The JPEG file format is commonly used to compress files before outputting them to the Web. Web designers often use JPEG format to save scanned images to the Web—images for which color gradations are important. JPEG (Joint Photographic Experts Group) is a *lossy* standard, which means information is removed from the file during the compression process. Usually, the absence of the subtracted information is not noticed if the image is compressed using a high-quality setting. When the file is reopened, the lost information is not returned to the file. If you've opened any of Photoshop's tutorial files, you may have already worked with JPEG files. JPEG files can be opened directly into Photoshop.

When saving a file in JPEG format, choose File > Save As and choose JPEG from the Format pop-up menu. The JPEG Options dialog box appears (Figure A-3), allowing you to choose a Quality option and to include paths in the image. To obtain the best fidelity, select BaseLine Optimized.

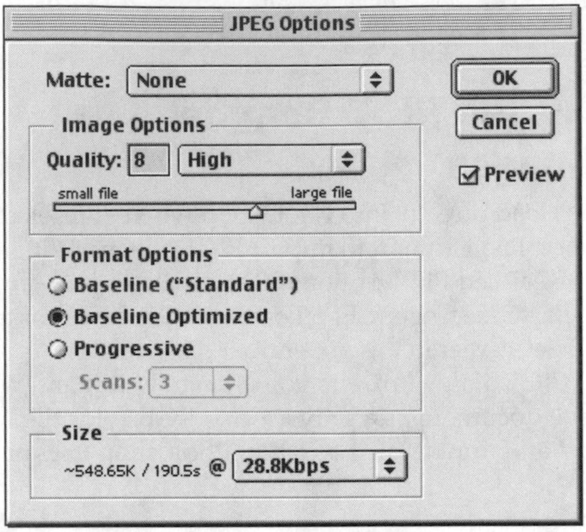

Figure A-3. *Choose a quality option and include paths in the image in this dialog*

If you are outputting your image to the Web and want to have it gradually come into focus on screen as it is downloaded from the Web, choose Progressive. When you choose this feature, you can also specify how many "scans" are made as the image is downloaded.

> **Note** *Not all browsers support the Progressive option.*

Here are some of the JPEG options provided:

- **Matte** This option fills transparent areas with the matte color.
- **Quality** Higher quality produces better color fidelity and sharper images. However, higher quality images mean larger file sizes.
- **Preview** This option previews the JPEG settings.
- **Size** When Preview is selected, this option previews the file size and estimates download time of the image after you choose the modem speed.

Scitex CT Files

Scitex workstations are used at many prepress houses for image editing and color correction. Files created by Scitex workstations using the Scitex CT (continuous tone) format can be loaded directly into Photoshop.

Only grayscale, RGB color, and CMYK color Photoshop files can be saved in the Scitex CT format. Also, you can't save a file with alpha channels in Scitex CT format. If you have a Scitex system, you need special utilities created by Scitex to complete the transfer process.

PDF Files

PDF (Portable Document Format) is a file format created by Adobe Systems. If you save your file in Photoshop PDF format, users can view it with Adobe's Acrobat Reader software (provided on the Adobe Photoshop CD-ROM), even though they may not own Photoshop. Using Adobe Acrobat software (not the Acrobat Reader), users can embed navigation and hypertext features in PDF files. PDF files can also be embedded into Web HTML documents.

If you wish to load a PDF file into Photoshop 6, simply choose File > Open and load the file. If you wish to save a file in Photoshop PDF format, choose Photoshop PDF from the Format menu. In the PDF Options dialog box (Figure A-4), specify the options desired for your file.

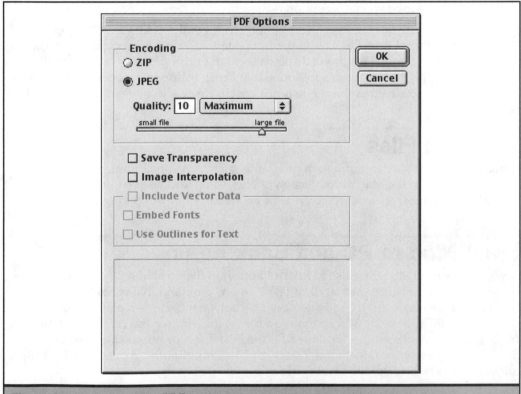

Figure A-4.   *Specify the PDF options you want*

APPENDIXES

The following options are available in the Photoshop PDF dialog box:

■ **Encoding** This option allows you to compress the file. ZIP is a lossless compression format. If you choose the JPEG option, you can reduce the file size by reducing image quality. Click and drag the slider to the left to the lower the file size and reduce image quality.

■ **Save Transparency** This option preserves transparency when the file is opened in other computer applications. Note that Photoshop and ImageReady always read transparency, whether this option is checked or not.

■ **Image Interpolation** This option anti-aliases low-resolution images.

■ **Include Vector Data** If your image includes shapes and type layers, this option preserves the vector information, allowing you to print high-quality text and graphics dependent upon the output resolution, rather than file resolution. When this option is selected, you can choose these options:

   ■ **Embed fonts** Choose this option to ensure that fonts are displayed properly on systems that do not have installed fonts that are used in the image. File size is increased when this option is chosen.

   ■ **Use Outlines for Text** This option creates outlines for fonts. This option results in lower file sizes in the embedded fonts. Adobe recommends using this option if fonts aren't displayed or don't print properly or if you will be opening the file in an application that doesn't support embedded fonts. Note that text saved in this mode is not searchable or selectable in Acrobat Reader.

Filmstrip Files

Filmstrip files are used in animation programs, such as Adobe Premier. Filmstrip files can be loaded into the Macintosh version of Photoshop and resaved using Filmstrip format. You cannot, however, convert a file created in Photoshop into a Filmstrip file.

From Mac to PC and Back Again

If you are using a Mac and wish to load a Photoshop file created on the PC, or vice versa, you need only use the standard File > Open command. No special conversion procedures are necessary to load and save files between these two platforms.

To use a PC file on the Mac or to save a file on the Mac for use on the PC, you need to save the file on a medium formatted for the PC (a disk or removable hard drive). Several utility programs, including DataViz's MacLinkPlus and Apple's PC Exchange, allow PC files to be displayed on the Mac.

Format	Extension
CompuServe GIF	.gif
Encapsulated PostScript	.eps
Illustrator > ASCII EPS	.ai
JPEG (compressed)	.jpg
PC Paintbrush	.pcx
Photoshop standard	.psd
Pixar	.pxr
Raw	.raw
Scitex CT	.sct
Targa	.tga
TIFF	.tif
Windows bitmap	.bmp

Tip *If you're a Mac user, you can instruct Photoshop to add PC file extensions to your filenames by default. Choose Edit > Preferences > Saving Files. In the Append File Extension pop-up menu, choose Always.*

Here is a list of PC-compatible filename extensions for different palettes and settings:

Palette or Setting	Extension
Arbitrary	.amp
Brushes palette	.abr
Color table	.act
Colors palette	.aco
Curves	.crv
Custom filters	.acf
Displacement maps	.psd
Duotone options	.ado
Halftone screens	.ahs
Hue > Saturation	.hss

Palette or Setting	Extension
Levels	.alv
Printing inks	.api
Separation setup	.asp
Separation table	.ast
Transfer functions	.atf
Variations	.psv

Saving PC Files on Mac Disks

Many service bureaus accept data on Iomega cartridges. If you use Photoshop for Windows and need to load and save files on Mac-formatted disks, you might wish to purchase DataViz MacOpener 2000 (**www.dataviz.com**). MacOpener mounts Mac-formatted Zip and Jaz cartridges onto the PC's desktop as if they were formatted PC disks.

Appendix B

Calibration and Output

No matter how exquisite your Photoshop images, all of your design and image-editing work may be in vain if the final printed (or other) output does not match the onscreen image. To get sharp and vibrant printed images, you need to have a clear understanding of how they are produced and how system calibration affects output quality.

This appendix focuses on two subjects: the printing process and system calibration. Most Photoshop users do not need to have a thorough knowledge of the printing and calibration processes because the prepress house or print shop can take care of these complicated issues. On the other hand, even if you don't output your own proofs and film separations, and even if you don't have to set screen frequency in the Halftone Screens dialog box, understanding the prepress concepts covered here will make for a smoother and more efficient production process. With that goal in mind, this appendix provides an overview of the printing process and explains how proofs can be used to predict color accuracy. It concludes with step-by-step instructions for printing separations.

Once you grasp the printing process, you'll understand how output resolution, screen frequency, paper stock, and halftones affect the output quality of your images.

The Role of Halftones in Image Output

When an image is prepared prior to printing on a printing press, it is called a *halftone*; each halftone consists of many small dots. The size and shape of these dots, and the angle at which they are printed, create the visual illusion of continuous grays or continuous colors. In traditional printing, halftones are created by placing a glass or mylar screen containing a grid of dots between an image and the film or negative paper on which the image is printed. This photomechanical process re-creates the image as a pattern of dots. Dark areas have large dots, and light areas have small dots.

In color publishing, cyan, magenta, yellow, and black screens are used in the traditional halftone process. The print quality depends on how close together the dots are—the finer the dots, the better the quality. The final result also depends upon the screen angles at which the halftones were created. Specific angles must be used to provide clear and consistent color. The traditional screen angles are 105 degrees for cyan, 75 degrees for magenta, 90 degrees for yellow, and 45 degrees for black. When screen angles are not correct, a mottled and undesirable pattern, called a *moiré*, may appear.

Commercial printers use the halftone screens to create plates for each of the four process colors. In the printing process, paper is printed with patterns of different-sized cyan, magenta, yellow, and black dots to create the illusion of countless colors. Take a magnifying glass and look closely at a printed color image, and you'll see the pattern of dots in various colors and sizes.

Digital Halftones

As in traditional printing, digital images that are output to a printer or imagesetter are also separated into halftone dots. The output device creates the halftone dots by turning groups of smaller dots, often referred to as *pixels*, on or off.

If the output device is an imagesetter, it can output to film as well as paper. An imagesetter producing output at a resolution of 2450 dots per inch (dpi) creates more than 6 million dots per square inch. At 300 dpi, a standard laser printer creates images with 90,000 dots per square inch. The more dots an image has, the better its resolution and the higher its printed quality.

It's important to remember that these pixels are *not* the halftone dots. In the printing process, the pixels are organized into a system of cells, and it is within these cells that the halftone dots are created. For instance, the dots from a 1,200 dpi imagesetter might be divided into 100 cells per inch. By turning the pixels off or on inside each cell, the printer or imagesetter creates one halftone dot.

The number of halftone dots per inch is called the *screen frequency*, *screen ruling*, or *line screen* and is measured in lines per inch (lpi). A high screen frequency, such as 150 lpi, packs the dots very closely together, producing sharper images and distinct colors. When the screen frequency is low, the halftone dots are spread out and produce coarser images with less-refined colors.

For the highest-quality reproduction of digital images, image file resolution generally should be 1.5 to 2 times the screen frequency (as measured in lines per inch). Also, remember that quality often depends on the paper stock used. (To review the relationship between image resolution and screen frequency, see Chapter 7.)

Calculating Gray Levels

The number of pixels that the imagesetter turns off or on to create a halftone determines the maximum number of gray levels that can be printed in an image. The number of gray levels determines the quality of continuous-tone images and whether a gradient blend prints properly. If you print at a screen frequency of 150 and a resolution of 2,450 dpi, you produce output with the maximum number of grays possible (256). Most continuous-tone images require at least 150 shades of gray for acceptable printed results.

Tip *If you need to eliminate banding due to insufficient gray levels in a blend, try applying the Add Noise filter to each channel containing color in your CMYK color image. (Filters are explained in Chapter 12.) Selecting the Dither checkbox in the Gradient Options palette can also eliminate banding.*

To ensure the image quality you desire, you can calculate the number of gray levels (including white) that will be printed using this formula:

Number of Grays = (Output Resolution ÷ Screen Frequency)^2 + 1

On an output device printing at 1,200 dpi and with a screen frequency of 100, each cell is a 12×12 matrix of pixels (1,200 ÷ 100 = 12). The pixels in each cell produce one halftone dot. In this 12×12 cell, the different combinations of pixels being turned on or off produce 145 levels of gray, including white (12^2 = 144 + white = 145).

Figure B-1 illustrates how a halftone is created from pixels and how the number of pixels in the cell determines the number of gray levels. In a 5×5 cell, 26 combinations of gray (5^2 + white) are possible. White is created when no pixels are turned on, 50 percent black is created when half the pixels are turned on, and 100 percent black is created when every pixel is turned on.

Conversely, if you know your output resolution and the number of grays desired, you can compute the required screen frequency with the following formula:

Screen Frequency = Output Resolution ÷ Number of Grays

If more grays are desired, the screen frequency can be reduced. For instance, if the screen frequency drops to 80 lpi and the resolution remains at 1,200 dpi, the halftone cell size is increased to a 15-pixel square (1,200 ÷ 80 = 15), which produces 226 grays (15^2 + 1). This can create a dilemma: the greater the number of grays, the lower the screen frequency; the greater the screen frequency, the sharper the image, yet the

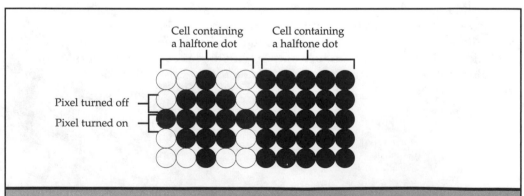

Figure B-1. *Pixels turned on and off create halftone dots and determine gray levels*

fewer the gray levels. The simple solution to this predicament is to print at the highest resolution with the highest screen frequency, ensuring sharp images, crisp colors, and 256 shades of gray.

Unfortunately, printing at the highest possible resolution and screen frequency may not always be possible because of two factors: paper stock and printing presses. Not all printing presses can handle high screen-frequency output, and not all paper is suitable for high screen-frequency printing. For instance, when you print at a high screen frequency on newspaper stock, it absorbs the dots, causing too much ink to spread and producing a muddy output. Thus, paper stock is often the determining factor in deciding what screen frequency to use. Newspapers are usually printed at 85 lpi. American magazines printed on coated stock often use a screen frequency of 133 or 150 lpi; European magazines often use a higher screen frequency. A glossy magazine or art book may be printed at 200 lpi.

Resolution, screen frequency, and paper stock are all issues that should be discussed with your print shop, prepress house, or service bureau. You should also decide whether you want your output on paper or film. Although film is more expensive than paper, it provides sharper output, which is especially important at screen frequencies over 100 lpi. This is the reason color separations are output to film.

If you are producing color separations, the imagesetter will produce four different film separations. The four pieces of film will not be in color, but rather four grayscale versions of the cyan, magenta, yellow, and black components of your image. The print shop will use the four pieces of film (for each of the four process colors) to create plates for use on a printing press.

Printing Proofs of Your Images

Before you go to press with a Photoshop project, you should view a printed sample, or *proof*, of your image. The proof will help you judge the anticipated quality of the final printing job. Proofs can warn you that colors will not print correctly or that moirés may appear, and they will tell you the degree of dot gain to be expected. (*Dot gain* is the expansion or contraction of halftone dots, usually due to ink spreading on paper.)

If you are printing a grayscale image, you may feel that your 300 or 600 dpi laser printer output is sufficient as a proof. If you are creating color images, there are a variety of choices available for color proofs: digital proofs, off-press proofs, and press proofs.

Note   *No matter how good your proofs look, various problems can occur on press that affect the quality of your images. It's a good idea to check a printed proof prior to the printing the entire job if you're working on a job that's particularly important.*

Digital Proofs

A *digital proof* is output directly from the digital data in your Photoshop file. Most digital proofs are created by printing to a thermal-wax printer, color laser printer, or dye-sublimation printer. Digital proofs can also be output on a high-end inkjet printer, such as the Scitex IRIS, or on other high-end printers, such as the Kodak Approval Color Proofer. Digital proofs are often very helpful as the design process proceeds.

Because digital proofs are not created from an imagesetter's film, color output may not be highly accurate, although high-end printers from Kodak, Scitex, and 3M can come close to matching film output. Commercial printers generally will not accept a digital proof as a *contract proof* that they will contractually agree to match.

 If a service bureau will be creating a digital proof of your image, you may be asked to save your file in EPS format.

Off-Press Proofs

Off-press proofs are created from the imagesetter's film, which will eventually be sent to the print shop. Thus, an off-press proof is considered more reliable than a digital proof as an indicator of how the image will print. The two major types of off-press proofs are *overlay proofs* and *laminated proofs.*

The overlay proof is made up of four different images exposed on acetate sheets that are overlaid. An overlay proof is generally considered not as accurate as a laminated proof, where each colored layer is developed and laminated to a base material. Apart from providing a reliable indication of color, laminated proofs can be very helpful in predicting whether moirés will appear in your final output. Dupont's Chromalin and 3M's Matchprint are two well-known laminated systems. When analyzing a Matchprint, be aware that it can make colors look more intense than actual colors produced by inks on a printing press. This is often because the proofs don't represent ink seepage into certain paper stocks.

Press Proofs

A press proof is considered the most accurate proof because it is made from the actual plates the printer will use, and it is printed on the stock that has been chosen for the job. Thus, the press proof will be a good indicator of dot gain, and it will also provide an accurate assessment of final color.

Bear in mind that press proofs are often printed on sheet-fed presses, which may be slower than the press used for the actual print job. The cost of creating printing plates and inking the press make the press proof the most expensive proofing process. For this reason, most clients have traditionally opted for off-press proofs. However, press proofs are becoming more popular in direct-to-press print jobs, where no film is used. Most direct-to-press print jobs are used for short-run printing.

Many artists do not need their images printed on printing presses, yet desire high-quality fine art prints of their work. To satisfy this demand, several digital printmaking studios have pioneered outputting digital images using long-lasting inks and printmaking papers. Most of these printmakers create high-quality prints by outputting images on a Scitex IRIS printer. Using the IRIS, these service bureaus can output images to a variety of substrates such as canvas, rice paper, linen, and silk. Three companies that provide these services are Cone Editions in East Topsham, Vermont; Digital Pond in San Francisco; and Nash Editions in Manhattan Beach, California.

Why You Should Calibrate Your System

You will want to proof your images as often as possible during a project—the earlier you catch problems with color and design, the easier and cheaper it is to fix them. Another way to help avoid problems in attaining color accuracy is to *calibrate* your monitor and system properly. Calibration helps ensure that the image you see on screen portrays your final output as accurately as possible. Calibration is necessary because monitors, scanners, printers, and printing presses vary in the way they render color.

 Jobs that are sent to different printers may require different calibration settings. You may need to change the options in the RGB, CMYK, or Grayscale Setup dialog boxes. (See Chapter 2 for more details.)

Monitor Calibration and Color Setup

Calibration is discussed in several places in this book. (In Chapter 2 of the text, you'll find instructions for running the Adobe Gamma utility and choosing an RGB color space.) Although the setup may seem confusing to some users, we placed the instructions in the second chapter of this book to emphasize the importance of calibrating your system as soon as possible, particularly before you start using Photoshop for color image work. Ideally, you've been working through the exercises in this book with Photoshop's color options properly set.

If you have neglected to investigate Photoshop's color settings options, you may be working with onscreen colors that are tainted by color casts. Images may appear lighter or darker on screen than they will print. Also, don't forget that the settings in the Color Settings dialog box (Edit > Color Settings) are used when Photoshop converts from RGB color to CMYK color.

If you have not run the Adobe Gamma utility or selected appropriate options in the Color Settings dialog box, turn to Chapter 2 of the text and follow the instructions provided there. Once your monitor is calibrated and you've chosen the proper color space for your system, you can fine-tune it further using a printed proof as a guide.

APPENDIXES

Using Photoshop Color Management when Printing Proofs

Once you've calibrated your system and chosen color settings, you can use Photoshop 6's color management features to help provide accurate color output. For instance, using Photoshop's color setting you can print to your studio printer using proofing profiles to simulate printing to different high-end output devices.

Printing using color management requires two major steps before printing—designating the image's current color profile (or current proof profile), and then designating the output or printer color space.

Here are the steps:

1. Choose File > Print.

2. In the Print dialog box, choose the Source space (your image's color space) or the proofing space. The proof profile is the current proof profile (View > Proof Setup > Working CMYK or View > Proof Setup > Custom). The list of proof profiles includes choices such as US Web Coated, US Web Uncoated, US Sheetfed Coated, US Sheetfed Uncoated, 3M Matchprint Euroscale, and Kodak SWOP Proofer-CMYK.

3. In the Print Space section of the dialog box, choose your printer's profile.

Note   *If you don't have a profile of your printer or if you are printing an RGB EPS file, Adobe recommends choosing PostScript color management as the Print Space profile. When you choose PostScript color management, the printer manages color. If you are proofing a CMYK image on a PostScript Level 2 printer, Adobe recommends choosing the Lab Color profile.*

4. Under intent, choose an option. These options are explained in Photoshop's Color Settings dialog box (Edit > Color Settings). Here is a summary of the choices:

   - **Perceptual**   Maintains color relationships among the colors, even if the colors fall out of gamut. In general, it produces attractive color.

   - **Saturation**   Maintains the saturation relationship among the colors. Colors will be highly saturated, but not necessarily accurate. This is generally a good choice if you are printing color charts and graphs.

   - **Relative Colorimetric**   The default choice for color conversions. It provides the best conversion option when the source colors are not out of the destination gamut. As Photoshop converts from RGB to Lab, then from Lab to CMYK, this choice attempts to map color coordinates from one color space to the other. During the process, it also remaps the white points from the source to the destination color space.

■ **Absolute Colorimetric**   Generally not recommended for color conversion. This method attempts an exact match between destination and source Lab coordinates.

5. Click on OK.

Color profiles on the Mac are stored in the System/Colorsync Profiles Folder. In Windows 2000 they are located at WinNT/System/Spool/Drivers/Color, in Windows NT at WinNT/System/Spool/Drivers/Color, and in Windows 98 at Windows/System/Color.

Trapping in Photoshop

When calibration is completed and you are ready to produce your output, your next consideration is whether you'll need to correct for registration problems that might occur during the printing process. Photoshop's Image > Trap command can help.

The Image > Trap command is available only with CMYK color images.

As paper passes through a printing press, misalignment or movement of the printing plates may cause thin white gaps or color halos to appear around adjoining areas of colors. *Trapping* fixes these discrepancies by slightly overlapping the colored areas so that the gaps won't appear during on-press printing.

When Photoshop traps, it spreads lighter colors under darker ones. Pure cyan and pure magenta, however, spread equally under each other.

Remember   *Before you begin to adjust trap settings, bear in mind that trapping is primarily needed when solid tints adjoin. Since most Photoshop images are continuous-tone images with gradual color transitions, trapping is usually unnecessary.*

After consulting with your print shop on the width of the trap adjustment, select Image > Trap. In the Trap dialog box, select a measurement unit from the pop-up menu, and in the Width field enter the width for the trap.

Here's an example of how trapping works: Suppose you entered a value of 2 pixels for the trap width. When a portion of an image with a high percentage of yellow adjoined a dark color, the yellow (because it is the lighter color) would spread out by 2 pixels. Thus, if a gap existed between the two plates that was 2 points or less, the yellow ink would fill the gap.

If you wish to see the Trap command in action, create a CMYK file with a swatch of a dark color overlapping a swatch of yellow. Execute the Trap command. Then use the Channels palette to view only the yellow channel. To see the difference—before and after applying the trap—use the Edit > Undo command.

 Discuss trapping issues with your prepress house before outputting your image to film. They may use a specific software package for trapping, so make sure to find out early about any special requirements they may have.

Photoshop's Page Setup and Printing Options

Now that you have an understanding of the printing and calibration processes, you'll probably want to explore all of the options available in Photoshop's Page Setup and Print dialog boxes. The Page Setup dialog box provides numerous output features, several of which fall into the realm of the prepress house or service bureau. If you are not printing to a color printer or imagesetter, you may never need to access these options; nonetheless, getting familiar with them will help complete your knowledge of the printing process.

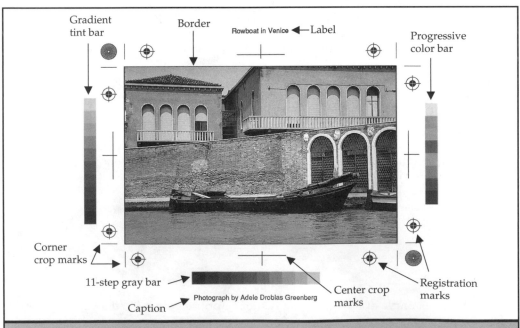

Figure B-2.   *You can print calibration bars, labels, a caption, a border, and registration and crop marks for your image in the Page Setup dialog box*

When Photoshop prints, it outputs all visible layers. (If you wish to print only a specific layer, see Chapter 16 to learn how to hide layers.)

The Page Setup Dialog Box

The Page Setup dialog box allows you to specify whether labels, registration marks, and crop marks will be printed on a page. As you'll see in this section, this dialog box also contains prepress options that govern screen frequency and halftone angles.

Figure B-2 shows a composite output of an image with a label, crop marks, registration marks, calibration bars, a caption, and a 1-pixel-wide border around the image.

To access the Page Setup dialog box, choose File > Page Setup. Mac users will choose a printer using the Chooser in the Apple menu; the Chooser cannot be accessed while the Page Setup dialog box is displayed. (Mac users may also need to choose Photoshop 6 in the pop-up menu at the upper left of the dialog box.) Windows users will choose a printer from the Page Setup dialog box, shown here.

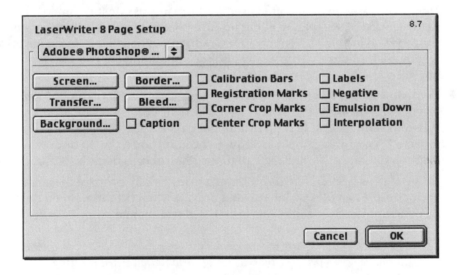

 In Photoshop 6, you can also access the Page Setup dialog box by choosing File > Print Options and clicking on the Show More Options button. You can use the Print Options dialog box to center your image on a page, reduce the image on the page, or print a selected area.

APPENDIXES

Here are the options in the Page Setup dialog box:

- **Calibration Bars** This option prints an 11-step gray bar, a progressive CMYK color bar, and a CMY gradient tint bar (if the image is a CMYK color image) on each page. The calibration bars are used to match a proof to the screen image; you can see how closely screen grays or colors match the printed output. The gray bar on the page prints from 0 to 100 percent gray in 10-percent increments.

- **Registration Marks** Registration marks are used to align pieces of film for printing color separations or duotones. Turn on Registration Marks when you want these marks printed around the edges of the image.

- **Corner Crop Marks** Crop marks indicate where paper should be trimmed. Turn on Corner Crop Marks to print these marks at the edges of your image.

- **Center Crop Marks** Select Center Crop Marks to place crop marks around the center of your image.

- **Labels** Select Labels to print the document name and channel name on the page with the image.

- **Negative** Negatives are often used for film output. Most commercial printers in the United States require a film negative to create plates, although other countries create plates from positives, rather than negatives. Ask your printer whether a film positive or negative is required. If you are printing to paper, do not select the Negative option.

- **Emulsion Down** Both film and photographic papers have a photosensitive layer called *emulsion*. When examining film, the emulsion side is the dull side. When the emulsion side is up in a film negative, type will be readable and not reversed. Your print shop may require the emulsion to be up or down. Usually, printing on paper is Emulsion Up; this is Photoshop's default setting.

- **Interpolation** Some PostScript Level 2 printers can improve the appearance of low-resolution files by interpolating pixels when printing. If you do not have a PostScript Level 2 printer, this option will not change output quality.

 In Photoshop, it's faster to use the Image > Transform > Rotate Canvas command to rotate an image before printing than to change orientation when printing.

The Page Setup dialog box also includes buttons that open additional dialog boxes with more printing options. These buttons are described next.

Printing with a Border

Click on the Border button if you wish to have a black border printed around your image. In the Border dialog box, you can select a unit of measurement and a width for the border.

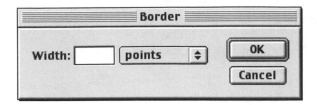

Printing with a Caption

Select the Caption checkbox if you wish to print the information entered in the Caption field of the File Info dialog box. To access the File Info dialog box, choose File > File Info. If the caption information does not appear in the dialog box, choose Caption from the Section pop-up menu.

Printing with a Background Color

If you are outputting to slides, you may wish to have a colored background printed to fill in the area surrounding the image. When you click on the Background button, the Color Picker appears. Choose the color that you wish to have as your background and click on OK.

Transfer Functions

As mentioned earlier, when an image is output to film, dot gain can occur due to miscalibration of the imagesetter. The Transfer functions are used to compensate for this. Photoshop's Transfer functions can also be used to create a custom dot-gain curve if you are using ICC profiles specified in the CMYK Setup dialog box.

To open the Transfer Functions dialog box, click on the Transfer button.

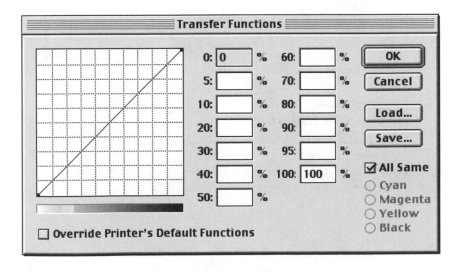

Enter compensating values in fields that correspond to the dot-gain percentages in the image. For instance, if dot gain is higher than it should be, subtract the desired dot value from the dot gain caused by the miscalibration and enter the value in the appropriate field.

If you check the Override Printer's Default Functions option in the Transfer Functions dialog box and you export an EPS file with Include Transfer Function selected in the EPS Format dialog box, the transfer information is used in the exported file.

Here's an example: Assume that an imagesetter is printing halftone dots at 60 percent, when they really should be printed at 50 percent. The difference between the two figures is 10 percent. Subtract 10 percent from 50 percent and you get 40 percent. Thus, you enter **40** in the 50% field of the Transfer Functions dialog box.

Don't change any of the settings in the Transfer Functions dialog box without first consulting your service bureau.

Setting Halftone Screens

The Screen button opens a Halftone Screens dialog box, in which you can specify elements such as screen frequency, screen angle, and halftone dot shape.

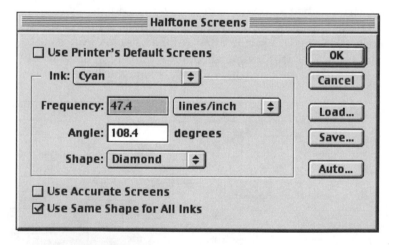

Before changing the default settings in the Halftone Screens dialog box, consult with your service bureau or print shop.

- **Use Printer's Default Screens** If you select this option, any dialog box settings are overridden, and output will be based upon halftone screen settings built into the printer. When this checkbox is selected, most of the options in the Halftone Screens dialog box are disabled.

- **Ink** If you are working with a CMYK color image, click on this pop-up menu to select the channel. Enter the screen frequency and angle for each channel. If you are printing color separations, the angle for each screen must be set properly to prevent the appearance of moiré patterns. To access these options, deselect the Use Printer's Default Screens checkbox.

- **Auto** If you wish to have Photoshop calculate the screen angles, click on the Auto button. In the Auto Screens dialog box, enter the printer resolution and screen frequency. Click on OK to have Photoshop calculate the best screen angle for all four halftone screens.

- **Shape** This pop-up menu in the Halftone Screens dialog box offers a list of custom halftone shapes that you can select to create various printing effects. If you want all four inks to have the same halftone shape, select the Use Same Shape for All Inks checkbox.

- **Use Accurate Screens** If you are sending output to a PostScript Level 2 printer or an Emerald controller, Adobe recommends that you turn on this option.

- **Load and Save buttons** Use these buttons to store and use your halftone screens settings. If you wish to change the default settings, press OPTION (*ALT*), and the Load and Save buttons will change to Default buttons. To create new default settings, click on the ->Default button; to return to the original default settings, click on <-Default.

Producing a Bleed

The Bleed button in the Page Setup dialog box allows you to print crop marks inside your image. These crop marks provide the printer with a guide for trimming so that the image can extend (or bleed) to the edge of the page.

 Even if you enter a value for a bleed, crop marks will not appear unless you select the Corner and/or Center Crop Marks options.

After you click on the Bleed button, a dialog box appears, in which you can enter a value up to 3.18 mm (.125 inches). This is the distance from the edge of your image that will be trimmed away.

APPENDIXES

The Print Dialog Box

After you have selected all the desired options in the Page Setup dialog box, your next step in printing an image is to open the Print dialog box (Figure B-3) by choosing File > Print. Most of the options in the Print dialog box will be familiar to Mac and Windows users, except for the options at the bottom of the dialog box. These options vary depending on the image mode (RGB, CMYK, and so on).

The following options are important to understand when printing Photoshop images:

- **Encoding**   Binary is Photoshop's default encoding format for outputting files. However, some networks and spoolers will not process binary data. If this is the case for your spooler or network, select ASCII. Bear in mind that an ASCII file is approximately twice as large as a binary file, so transferring data to the printer will take longer. The JPEG encoding options should be used only with PostScript Level 2 output devices. JPEG encoding compresses output files, which means data is downloaded faster. When outputting with JPEG encoding, Photoshop utilizes the highest quality compression. Nevertheless, since JPEG is a lossy compression format, output quality may be reduced.

- **Source Space**   This section allows you to specify the document's source color space or its proofing color space. Using this option is discussed in the "Using Photoshop Color Management when Printing Proofs" section earlier in this chapter.

- **Print Space**   Choose your printer's profile in this section. Using this option is discussed in the "Using Photoshop Color Management when Printing Proofs" section.

- **Print Space**   If you wish to print separations, choose Separations from the Print Space's Profile pop-up menu. Printing separations is described in the next section. The Separations option is available only when you are working with a CMYK color or duotone image.

Note   *In previous versions of Photoshop, the Print dialog box allowed you to specify a selection to print. To print only a selected area, choose File > Print Options. In the Print Options dialog box, choose Print Selected Area.*

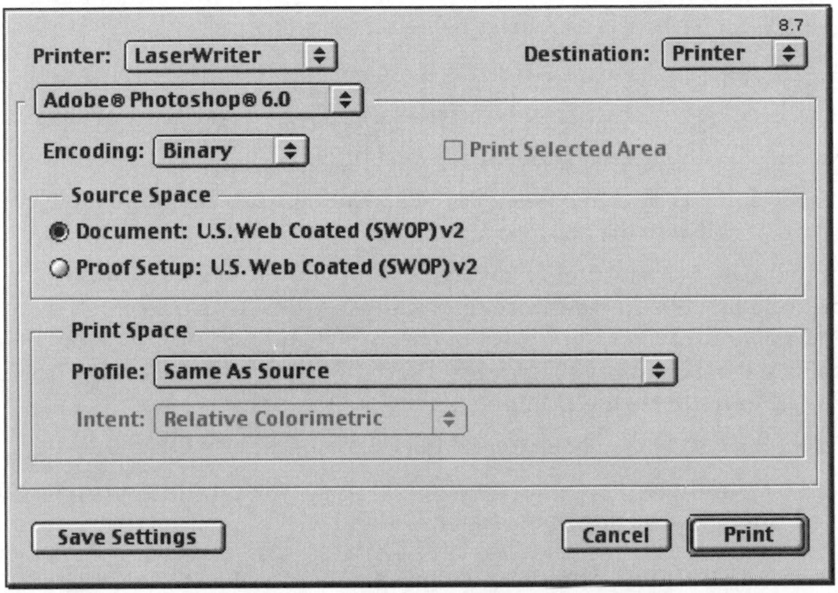

Figure B-3. *The Print dialog box*

Printing Separations

This section leads you step by step through the process of printing a CMYK separation. Even if you're producing output to a 300 dpi laser printer, you may find it educational to see the separation process in action.

To print separations, you will need a CMYK color image or an RGB color image converted to CMYK color. When converting, Photoshop uses the settings in the RGB Setup and CMYK Setup dialog boxes. Before you convert an image from RGB color to CMYK color, make sure these settings are correct. Also, always use the File > Save As command and rename your file before converting, so you'll have a copy of your original image. After converting to CMYK color, apply the Unsharp Mask filter to sharpen your image. (For a complete discussion of converting from RGB color to CMYK color, see Chapter 13.)

Suppose you want to print your CMYK color image with registration marks, the image's file name, and crop marks. Follow these steps:

1. Choose File > Page Setup.

2. In the Page Setup dialog box, select the Registration Marks, Labels, and Crop Marks checkboxes. Click on the Screen button.

3. In the Halftone Screens dialog box, click on the Auto button to have Photoshop automatically set the halftone screen angle.

4. In the Auto Screens dialog box, enter your printer's resolution. If you are printing to a 300-dpi laser printer, type **300**. Enter **53** as the screen frequency, and make sure lines/inch is set in the corresponding pop-up menu. If you are using a PostScript Level 2 printer, select the Use Accurate Screens option. Click on OK to return to the Halftone Screens dialog box.

5. Select the Use Same Shape for All Inks option. Click on OK.

6. In the Print dialog box, select Separations from the Profile pop-up menu in the Print Space section and click on OK.

When the separations print, four images will be output, one for each of the CMYK colors.

The Future of Printing

The printing and prepress industries are constantly seeking ways to improve color reproduction and speed up turnaround time. The past few years have brought new developments that could change how Photoshop users work with images that must be output to printing presses. Two of the most important developments are direct-to-plate digital printing and stochastic screening.

Direct-to-Plate Digital Printing

Direct-to-plate printing is a process in which images are printed directly from digital files; no filmed negatives are needed. Theoretically, the process is similar to printing directly to a standard laser printer. Direct-to-plate printing has proven most effective in small print runs because quality color output can be produced quickly and at a low cost.

Stochastic Screening

In traditional four-color printing, the overlaying of different-sized CMYK halftone dots creates the illusion of countless colors. *Stochastic screening* (sometimes known as *FM,* or *frequently modulated* screening) creates colors by producing similar-sized dots that are smaller than halftone dots. The precise distribution of the dots creates the illusion of continuous-tone color. In many respects, the process is similar to dithering (the way Photoshop creates the illusion of many colors in an image that is composed of 256 or fewer colors).

Proponents of stochastic screening contend that the process produces finer detail and can reproduce colors better than traditional color printing. Those who have already begun using stochastic screening say that they can scan images at lower resolutions than those needed for traditional color printing.

In general, stochastic screening produces a grainier look in areas with light tones, but as improvements are made in stochastic screening technology, many predict that a majority of commercial printers will adopt the system by the end of the decade.

A Final Note

This appendix has shown how Photoshop allows you to enter into a technical realm once open to prepress professionals only. Undoubtedly, many Photoshop users would rather not worry about calculating gray levels, compensating for dot gain, and choosing between GCR and UCR. Although these prepress tasks can be avoided to some degree, you'll find that the more you work with Photoshop, the less daunting they will become. If you establish good relations with prepress houses and commercial printers, you'll have an easier time overcoming problems and getting your questions answered.

Appendix C

On the CD-ROM

The CD that comes with *Photoshop 6: The Complete Reference* contains several folders with images from the exercises in the book's chapters, tryout versions of software from Adobe and Alien Skin, and bonus content not included in the print version of the book.

Getting Started

The CD-ROM is optimized to run under Windows 95/98/NT/2000 using the Adobe Acrobat Reader version 4.0, included on the disc. The first time you access the CD, the End User License Agreement (EULA) will automatically pop-up on your screen, and after you agree to the terms listed in the EULA, you will not see the EULA again.

Once you have accepted the terms of the EULA, you can use Windows Explorer to access any of the components on the CD.

For Windows 3.1 Users

You must use Acrobat Reader version 3.0, which is included on the CD. Use File Manager to see the contents of the CD, and double-click on any of the folders to access the contents.

For Macintosh Users

You must be running under Mac OS version 7.1.2 or higher.

What's On the CD

When you view the CD contents in Windows Explorer, File Manager, or on your Macintosh desktop, you'll see the following folders:

- Adobe Product Tryouts, including Photoshop 6.0
- Adobe Acrobat 4.0
- Alien Skin product tryouts
- The bonus online chapter on color theory
- Exercise images

You can simply double-click any of these folders to get at the contents within.

To Use the Exercise Images

The images from the book's exercises are provided for you here so that you can follow along and create the effects and results described in the book's chapters. The images are organized according to the chapter in which they appear; double-click on any of the folders to get at a specific chapter's images.

To Install Acrobat Reader 4.0

To install Acrobat Reader 4.0:

1. Double-click on the My Computer icon on your Desktop.

2. When the My Computer window opens, double-click on the icon for your CD drive. You should see a list of the contents of the CD.

3. Double-click on the folder named install. Within this folder, double-click on the subfolder called Win 95-98-2000.

4. In this folder, you will see a file named rs405eng or rs405eng.exe. Double-click on this file to start the installation program.

To Use the Adobe Product Tryouts

To use any of the Adobe Tryout Versions, double-click first on the Adobe Products folder and then on an individual product folder. Chose either the folder of Macintosh Tryouts or Windows Tryouts. In each product folder, you'll see an application file and also a folder of PDF files. Double-click on the application file to launch the tryout version of the product. The PDF documents included give you an overview of the product and provide feature highlights, product uses, and other interesting product details.

In the Adobe Product Tryouts folder, you'll find trial versions of

- Adobe Photoshop 6.0
- Adobe After Effects
- Adobe Dimensions
- Adobe GoLive
- Adobe Illustrator 9.0
- Adobe inDesign 1.5
- Adobe LiveMotion
- Adobe PageMaker Plus 6.5
- Adobe Premiere 5.0
- Adobe Streamline 5.0

To Use the Alien Skin Product Tryouts

In the Alien Skin Product Tryouts folder, you'll find the following products.

Eye Candy 4000 Product Tryouts   Eye Candy 4000 is Alien Skin's collection of 23 timesaving filters that will fortify any user's creativity. Eye Candy combines practical effects like shadows, bevels, and glows with stunning effects like Chrome, Fire, Smoke, and Wood. In the demo version of Eye Candy 4000 on this CD, 3 of the 23 filters are fully functional: Glass, Marble, and Shadowlab. You will be able to preview, apply, and save effects on your work using these three filters. The other 20 filters allow you to preview, but not apply or save, their effects. Double-click on the Eye Candy folder to install these filters.

Xenofex Product Tryouts   Xenofex is a collection of 16 inspirational special effects from Alien Skin that will energize any graphics project. Realistic natural phenomena and sophisticated distortions are easy to create with the product's simple, intuitive interface, and a fully resizable and zoomable preview window is included to allow you to see the effect on any part of your image with a single click. Xenofex also includes more than 160 presets to help you begin creating complex special effects in seconds.

In the demo version included on this CD, 2 of the 16 filters are fully functional: Crumple and Stain. You will be able to preview, apply, and save effects on your work using these two filters. The other 13 filters allow you to preview, but not apply or save, their effects. Double-click on the Xenofex folder to install these filters.

To View the Bonus Content on Color Theory

The bonus chapter is in PDF format and once you have installed Adobe Acrobat Reader, you simply double-click on the PDF file icon to bring up the file. On the right side of your screen, you'll see the text itself, while on the left side of your screen you'll see an outline of this material shown by a list of "bookmarks." Click on any topic in the bookmark column, and you will instantly go to that topic. In most instances, a small plus sign (+) also appears next to the topics. If you click on the plus sign, the main headings under the topic will appear. If you click on the plus sign next to a main heading, the subheadings will appear. You can click on any heading or subheading to go to the page where that topic begins.

If you prefer a graphical representation of opening pages rather than bookmarks, you can click on the tab labeled "Thumbnails," and small images of the pages will replace the bookmarks. You can hide the bookmarks/thumbnails feature and make more room for viewing pages by clicking on the Show/Hide Navigation Pane button on the toolbar directly above the Thumbnails tab.

Use Acrobat Reader to View and Find Topics in the Bonus Content

The Adobe Acrobat Reader included on the CD allows you to view and use pages in a number of ways. Feel free to experiment, explore, and adapt the Acrobat Reader to whatever style works best for you. Adobe has provided an extensive Help file that you can access by clicking Help on the Acrobat menu bar when the Adobe Acrobat Reader software is open on your desktop.

Viewing Individual Pages of the PDF

When the full-page image is sized to fit the window on your computer screen, the text may be too small to read comfortably. If so, you can magnify the text to a size that works well for you. To do so, click the magnifying glass on the tool bar at the top of the screen. Your pointer will change from a hand to a magnifying glass. Place the magnifying glass pointer over the text and click to increase the size of the page. Repeated clicks will further magnify the image incrementally.

A faster way to magnify the image is to place the magnifying glass at the upper corner of the desired text, press and hold down the mouse button, and then drag the pointer across the area. A dotted line will appear around the area as you drag the magnifying glass. When you have outlined all of the desired area, let go of the mouse button. The view will instantly zoom in on the area you outlined.

To return the text to its original size, select one of the three document buttons on the toolbar that runs across the top of the screen. The first button makes the image appear to be the actual size of a book page (100% view). The middle button resizes the image to fit completely in the window. The third button resizes the image to fit the full width of the window; you will need to scroll down to see the whole page.

Using the Find Tool

Acrobat Reader has a Find tool that you can use with this document. The Find tool is represented by a pair of binoculars on the toolbar. You can use this tool to search the document for every occurrence of a word. However, Find can look at only one document at a time, and it is relatively slow because it must look at every word on every page.

More detailed information about performing searches, setting search preferences, and refining searches can be found in the Adobe Acrobat Reader Help file on the Help menu that you'll see when you have Adobe Acrobat open on your computer.

If you have Problems with the CD

If you have followed the instruction above and the program will not work, you may have a defective drive or a defective CD. Be sure the CD is inserted properly in the drive. (Test the drive with other CDs, to see if they run.)

If you need help, call Hudson Software at (800) 217-0059 for technical support.

APPENDIXES

Index

INTERNATIONAL CONTACT INFORMATION

AUSTRALIA
McGraw-Hill Book Company Australia Pty. Ltd.
TEL +61-2-9417-9899
FAX +61-2-9417-5687
http://www.mcgraw-hill.com.au
books-it_sydney@mcgraw-hill.com

CANADA
McGraw-Hill Ryerson Ltd.
TEL +905-430-5000
FAX +905-430-5020
http://www.mcgrawhill.ca

**GREECE, MIDDLE EAST,
NORTHERN AFRICA**
McGraw-Hill Hellas
TEL +30-1-656-0990-3-4
FAX +30-1-654-5525

MEXICO (Also serving Latin America)
McGraw-Hill Interamericana Editores S.A. de C.V.
TEL +525-117-1583
FAX +525-117-1589
http://www.mcgraw-hill.com.mx
fernando_castellanos@mcgraw-hill.com

SINGAPORE (Serving Asia)
McGraw-Hill Book Company
TEL +65-863-1580
FAX +65-862-3354
http://www.mcgraw-hill.com.sg
mghasia@mcgraw-hill.com

SOUTH AFRICA
McGraw-Hill South Africa
TEL +27-11-622-7512
FAX +27-11-622-9045
robyn_swanepoel@mcgraw-hill.com

**UNITED KINGDOM & EUROPE
(Excluding Southern Europe)**
McGraw-Hill Education Europe
TEL +44-1-628-502500
FAX +44-1-628-770224
http://www.mcgraw-hill.co.uk
computing_neurope@mcgraw-hill.com

ALL OTHER INQUIRIES Contact:
Osborne/McGraw-Hill
TEL +1-510-549-6600
FAX +1-510-883-7600
http://www.osborne.com
omg_international@mcgraw-hill.com

WARNING: BEFORE OPENING THE DISC PACKAGE, CAREFULLY READ THE TERMS AND CONDITIONS OF THE FOLLOWING COPYRIGHT STATEMENT AND LIMITED CD-ROM WARRANTY.

Copyright Statement

This software is protected by both United States copyright law and international copyright treaty provision. Except as noted in the contents of the CD-ROM, you must treat this software just like a book. However, you may copy it into a computer to be used and you may make archival copies of the software for the sole purpose of backing up the software and protecting your investment from loss. By saying, "just like a book," The McGraw-Hill Companies, Inc. ("Osborne/McGraw-Hill") means, for example, that this software may be used by any number of people and may be freely moved from one computer location to another, so long as there is no possibility of its being used at one location or on one computer while it is being used at another. Just as a book cannot be read by two different people in two different places at the same time, neither can the software be used by two different people in two different places at the same time.

Limited Warranty

Osborne/McGraw-Hill warrants the physical compact disc enclosed herein to be free of defects in materials and workmanship for a period of sixty days from the purchase date. If you live in the U.S. and the CD included in your book has defects in materials or workmanship, please call McGraw-Hill at 1-800-217-0059, 9 A.M. to 5 P.M., Monday through Friday, Eastern Standard Time, and McGraw-Hill will replace the defective disc. If you live outside the U.S., please contact your local McGraw-Hill office. You can find contact information for most offices on the International Contact Information page immediately following the index of this book, or send an e-mail to omg_international@mcgraw-hill.com.

The entire and exclusive liability and remedy for breach of this Limited Warranty shall be limited to replacement of the defective disc, and shall not include or extend to any claim for or right to cover any other damages, including but not limited to, loss of profit, data, or use of the software, or special incidental, or consequential damages or other similar claims, even if Osborne/McGraw-Hill has been specifically advised of the possibility of such damages. In no event will Osborne/McGraw-Hill's liability for any damages to you or any other person ever exceed the lower of the suggested list price or actual price paid for the license to use the software, regardless of any form of the claim.

OSBORNE/McGRAW-HILL SPECIFICALLY DISCLAIMS ALL OTHER WARRANTIES, EXPRESS OR IMPLIED, INCLUDING BUT NOT LIMITED TO, ANY IMPLIED WARRANTY OF MERCHANTABILITY OR FITNESS FOR A PARTICULAR PURPOSE. Specifically, Osborne/McGraw-Hill makes no representation or warranty that the software is fit for any particular purpose, and any implied warranty of merchantability is limited to the sixty-day duration of the Limited Warranty covering the physical disc only (and not the software), and is otherwise expressly and specifically disclaimed.

This limited warranty gives you specific legal rights; you may have others which may vary from state to state. Some states do not allow the exclusion of incidental or consequential damages, or the limitation on how long an implied warranty lasts, so some of the above may not apply to you.

This agreement constitutes the entire agreement between the parties relating to use of the Product. The terms of any purchase order shall have no effect on the terms of this Agreement. Failure of Osborne/McGraw-Hill to insist at any time on strict compliance with this Agreement shall not constitute a waiver of any rights under this Agreement. This Agreement shall be construed and governed in accordance with the laws of New York. If any provision of this Agreement is held to be contrary to law, that provision will be enforced to the maximum extent permissible, and the remaining provisions will remain in force and effect.

NO TECHNICAL SUPPORT IS PROVIDED WITH THIS CD-ROM.